MICROSOFT® BASIC
Programming the IBM PC
Second Edition

■ Brooks/Cole Series in Computer Science

Program Design with Pseudocode, Third Edition
T. W. Bailey and Kris Lundgaard

BASIC: An Introduction to Computer Programming, Third Edition
Robert J. Bent and George C. Sethares

BASIC: An Introduction to Computer Programming with the Apple, Second Edition
Robert J. Bent and George C. Sethares

Business BASIC, Third Edition
Robert J. Bent and George C. Sethares

BASIC Programming with the IBM PC
Peter Mears

Absolutely BASIC Computing
Peter Mears

An Introduction to Personal Computing: BASIC Programming on the TRS-80
Robert R. Hare

Learning BASIC Programming: A Systematic Approach
Howard Dachslager, Masato Hayashi, Richard Zucker

Beginning Structured COBOL, Second Edition
Keith Carver

Structured COBOL Programming and Data Processing Methods
Thomas R. McCalla

Problem Solving and Structured Programming with Pascal
Ali Behforooz and Martin O. Holoien

Pascal Programming
Irvine Forkner

Pascal for the Eighties
Samuel Grier

FORTRAN 77 PDQ, 2nd Edition
Thomas A. Boyle

Problem Solving and Structured Programming with FORTRAN 77
Martin O. Holoien and Ali Behforooz

Introduction to ADA: A Top-Down Approach for Programmers
Phillip Caverly and Philip Goldstein

Introduction to DECSYSTEM-20 Assembly Programming
Stephen A. Longo

LOGO: Principles, Programming and Projects
George Lukas and Joan Lukas

MICROSOFT BASIC
Programming the IBM PC
Second Edition

Robert J. Bent
George C. Sethares

Bridgewater State College

Brooks/Cole Publishing Company
Pacific Grove, California

Brooks/Cole Publishing Company
A Division of Wadsworth, Inc.

© 1985, 1989 by Wadsworth, Inc., Belmont, California 94002.
All rights reserved.
No part of this book may be reproduced, stored in a retrieval system, or transcribed,
in any form or by any means—electronic, mechanical, photocopying, recording,
or otherwise—without the prior written permission of the publisher,
Brooks/Cole Publishing Company, Pacific Grove, California 93950,
a division of Wadsworth, Inc.

Printed in the United States of America

10 9 8 7 6 5 4 3 2 1

Library of Congress Cataloging in Publication Data

Bent, Robert J. [date]
    Microsoft BASIC: programming the IBM-PC / Robert J. Bent & George
  C. Sethares. —2nd ed.
        p.   cm.
    Includes index.
    ISBN 0-534-10116-X
    1. IBM Personal Computer—Programming. 2. BASIC (Computer program
language) I. Sethares, George C., [date]. II. Title.
QA76.8.I2594B46 1989
005.265—dc19   88-25888
                                                                      CIP

Microsoft is a registered trademark of Microsoft Corp.
IBM PC is a registered trademark of International Business Machines Corp.

Sponsoring Editor: *Michael J. Sugarman*
Editorial Assistant: *Mary Ann Zuzow*
Production Editor: *Linda Loba*
Manuscript Editor: *Brenda Griffing*
Permissions Editor: *Carline Haga*
Interior and Cover Design: *Roy Neuhaus*
Cover Illustration: *Roy Neuhaus*
Art Coordinator: *Lisa Torri*
Interior Illustration: *John Foster, Vantage Art*
Photo Researcher/Editor: *Sue C. Howard*
Typesetting: *Bi-Comp, Inc.*
Printing and Binding: *Malloy Lithographing, Inc.*

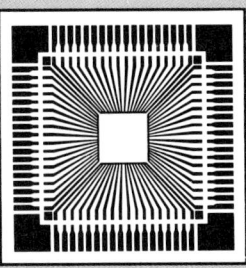

Preface

This book is intended to serve as an introduction to computer programming in the environment of an IBM Personal Computer (PC) system. The programming language used is Microsoft® BASIC, an extended version of BASIC implemented on the IBM PC and many other microcomputer systems. No prior experience with computers or computer programming languages is assumed. Included are descriptions of the computer equipment you will encounter and procedures for using this equipment.

Most of the material is semitutorial and intended to be studied with a PC close at hand. For beginning programmers, hands-on experience with a real computer is the most effective way to learn about computers. The programming language Microsoft® BASIC is described in detail and illustrated in numerous examples drawn from a wide range of applications areas, including business, sports, economics, personal finance, the natural and social sciences, and mathematics. A working knowledge of elementary algebra is the only mathematics needed to understand most of the material and to complete the assignments successfully. The examples and problems involving more advanced topics in mathematics, such as the trigonometric functions, may be omitted with no loss in continuity.

■ Organization and Coverage

We wrote this book with two principal goals in mind. First, we felt it important to present the elements of Microsoft® BASIC so that meaningful computer programs could be written at the earliest possible time. We adhere to the notion that one learns by doing. But the development of programming habits, both good and bad, will begin with the first programs written. For this reason, fundamental principles of program design are considered at the outset. Specifically, Chapter 2 describes the top-down approach to problem solving, illustrates the importance of input/output specification, modularization, and stepwise refinement, and points out some of the benefits to be gained by adhering to these problem solving principles.

Our second goal was to write a book that would serve as a general introduction to programming, not just to a programming language. Toward this end we have included examples that illustrate several major application areas of computer programming and that also describe important programming techniques that can be used effectively in many diverse programming situations. But a complete introduction to programming requires more than a description of application areas and programming techniques. Equally important is a consideration of the entire programming process that takes us from a problem statement to the finished product: a well-documented computer program that correctly carries out the task described in the problem statement. The approach we have taken toward achieving this objective is to use consistently the problem-solving methods introduced in Chapter 2, to introduce new programming principles as they can be appreciated in the context of the applications being considered, and to illustrate and reinforce these programming principles in the worked-out examples.

A few remarks are appropriate concerning the order in which we have introduced the elements of Microsoft® BASIC. The INPUT statement (Chapter 5) is introduced early, before the READ and DATA statements, to emphasize the interactive nature of BASIC. In Chapter 6, the WHILE statement and a limited form of the IF statement are used to introduce program loops. Chapter 7 expands upon the description of the PRINT statement given in Chapter 3 and introduces the PRINT USING statement. These output statements are introduced early so that well-formatted output can be illustrated in the examples and can be produced while carrying out all subsequent programming exercises. The general form of the IF statement and its use as a selection statement are described in Chapter 8. The BASIC statements described in Chapters 3–8 were selected because they allow meaningful structured programs to be written. Section 8.10 describes how structured algorithms can be coded as structured BASIC programs. Chapters 9, 11, and 12 (FOR loops, READ/DATA statements, and subroutines) complete what is sometimes called Elementary BASIC. Selecting an order in which to present the remaining BASIC statements was not so easy. So that a person using this book will not be tied down to the order we have chosen, the introductory material for the remaining BASIC statements is presented in a way that allows these statements to be taken up in any order after Chapter 12.

■ Special Microsoft® BASIC Features

Screen displays. Chapter 10 illustrates the PC's capability for color displays (Section 10.3) as well as its extended character set (Section 10.4).

Graphics. Chapter 19 presents a tutorial on computer graphics. Descriptions of the PC's medium- and high-resolution graphics are given. Examples include a kaleidoscope program and a video-game illustration.

A complete chapter on data files. Both sequential access files (Section 17.1) and random access files (Section 17.6) are described, together with programming techniques used in file processing. A separate section on file maintenance is included.

■ Features New to this Edition

Several new features have been included in this revision. Following are brief descriptions of the more significant changes.

An Expanded Introductory Chapter on Problem Solving

Fundamental problem-solving principles, including the top-down development of algorithms, are discussed in Chapter 2. Greater emphasis is placed on input/output specification, modularization, and stepwise refinement. Chapter 2 also explains the sense in which computer programs and algorithms are equivalent and illustrates the steps leading to the discovery of algorithms.

Improved Examples and Programming Exercises

Worked-out examples and programming exercises that illustrate application areas not covered in the previous edition have been added. Several examples and exercises, some of which were redundant, have been deleted. Also, many new programming exercises that are suitable for one- or two-week programming projects have been added to the problem sets.

A Separate Introductory Chapter on Loops

The IF and GOTO statements are used in Section 6.1 to introduce the concept of a program loop. The use of IF as a selection statement is taken up separately in Chapter 8. The WHILE and WEND statements are described in Section 6.2 and are used to code all loops in subsequent examples until FOR loops are taken up in Chapter 9.

A New Section on Menu-Driven Programs

The concept of a menu-driven program is described early (Chapter 8) and illustrated in several examples in the subsequent chapters. Writing BASIC code for menu-driven programs by using IF statements or the ON GOTO statement is described in Section 8.4. The use of subroutines and the ON GOSUB statement in menu-driven programs is taken up in Section 12.3. New programming exercises that call for menu-driven programs have been added to many of the problem sets beginning with Chapter 8.

An Expanded and Earlier Chapter on Subroutines

The topic of subroutines is taken up much earlier in this edition. Subroutines are described in Chapter 12, just after the READ and DATA statements, and their application is illustrated in many of the subsequent chapters.

A New Section on Table Processing

Section 15.3 illustrates the application of the array data structure to programming tasks that involve tables. The problem of deciding whether or not to use arrays to store tabular data is discussed and illustrated in the worked-out examples. New programming exercises that involve table processing have been included in the problem sets.

Increased Emphasis on the Application of String Variables

Many new string processing examples and programming exercises have been added. String arrays, which in the previous edition were introduced in a separate chapter after the numerical arrays, are now taken up with numerical arrays in a single chapter. The string conversion functions CHR$, ASC, STR$, and VAL are described earlier, with all other string and string-related functions, and their applications have been expanded to several new topics, including the conversion of lowercase letters to uppercase.

■ Acknowledgments

While preparing this revision, we were fortunate to have the comments of many users of the first edition. Their thoughtful criticisms and suggestions were carefully considered and, in many instances, incorporated as changes in the book. We are grateful for this assistance.

We wish to take this opportunity to acknowledge the helpful comments of our reviewers: Professor Celine Dorner, Pacific Lutheran University, Washington; Professor Walter Feldt, University of Wisconsin; and Professor Jimmy Woods, North Georgia College. We feel that their many thoughtful suggestions have led to a greatly improved book.

A very special thanks goes to Patricia Shea, our typist, proofreader, debugger, and general assistant. Her twelve years of cheerful cooperation are greatly appreciated. Finally, we are happy to acknowledge the fine cooperation of the staff at Brooks/Cole Publishing Company.

Robert J. Bent
George C. Sethares

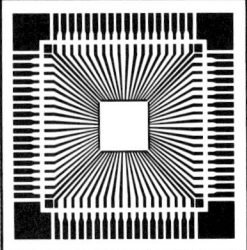

Contents

Chapter 1 IBM Personal Computer Systems 1

    1.1   Computer Hardware 4
    1.2   Computer Software 5
    1.3   Review True-or-False Quiz 8

Chapter 2 Problem Solving: Top-Down Approach 9

    2.1   Algorithms 9
    2.2   Variables 14
    2.3   Problems 17
    2.4   Review True-or-False Quiz 19

Chapter 3 A First Look at Microsoft® BASIC 21

    3.1   Numerical Constants and Variables 22
    3.2   String Constants and Variables 23
    3.3   Arithmetic Operations and Expressions 24
    3.4   Problems 26
    3.5   The LET Statement: Assigning Values to Variables 27
    3.6   The PRINT Statement 29
    3.7   The REM Statement: Remarks as Part of a Program 30
    3.8   Multiple Statements in a Programming Line 32
    3.9   Problems 33
    3.10 Review True-or-False Quiz 35

Chapter 4 First Session at the Keyboard 37

    4.1   The PC Keyboard 37
    4.2   Entering a Programming Line 38
    4.3   Spacing and the Length of a Programming Line 39
    4.4   The System Commands LIST and RUN—The Function Keys F1 and F2 40

- 4.5 Making Corrections 41
- 4.6 Error Messages 42
- 4.7 Immediate and Deferred Execution Modes 43
- 4.8 Directing Output to the Printer 45
- 4.9 On Writing Your First Program 45
- 4.10 Problems 47
- 4.11 Review True-or-False Quiz 50

Chapter 5 Interacting with the Computer 51

- 5.1 The INPUT Statement 51
- 5.2 Problems 55
- 5.3 Review True-or-False Quiz 57

Chapter 6 A First Look at Loops 59

- 6.1 Coding Loops with the IF and GOTO Statements 59
- 6.2 WHILE Loops 66
- 6.3 Problems 70
- 6.4 Review True-or-False Quiz 73

Chapter 7 More on the PRINT Statement 75

- 7.1 Displaying More Values on a Line 75
- 7.2 Suppressing the RETURN 78
- 7.3 Problems 78
- 7.4 The TAB and SPC Functions 80
- 7.5 Problems 83
- 7.6 The PRINT USING Statement 84
- 7.7 Problems 89
- 7.8 Review True-or-False Quiz 91

Chapter 8 The Computer as a Decision Maker 93

- 8.1 IF as a Selection Statement 93
- 8.2 Logical Expressions 97
- 8.3 Problems 100
- 8.4 Menu-Driven Programs 102
- 8.5 Problems 106
- 8.6 Flowcharts and Flowcharting 107
- 8.7 Problems 113
- 8.8 Summing with the WHILE Statement 114
- 8.9 Problems 118
- 8.10 Structured Programming 119
- 8.11 Problems 125
- 8.12 Review True-or-False Quiz 129

Chapter 9 Loops Made Easier 131

- 9.1 FOR Loops 131
- 9.2 Problems 136

9.3 Nested Loops 138
9.4 Problems 141
9.5 Review True-or-False Quiz 143

Chapter 10 More on Screen Displays 145

10.1 The Cursor Moving Statement: LOCATE 145
10.2 Problems 151
10.3 The COLOR Statement 152
10.4 The IBM PC Display Characters 156
10.5 Problems 160
10.6 Review True-or-False Quiz 162

Chapter 11 Data as Part of a Program 165

11.1 The READ and DATA Statements 165
11.2 Problems 171
11.3 The RESTORE Statement 174
11.4 Problems 181
11.5 Review True-or-False Quiz 183

Chapter 12 Subroutines 185

12.1 The GOSUB and RETURN Statements 185
12.2 Problems 192
12.3 The ON GOSUB Statement 194
12.4 Problems 199
12.5 Review True-or-False Quiz 201

Chapter 13 Numerical Functions 203

13.1 Built-in Numerical Functions 203
13.2 Problems 215
13.3 User-Defined Functions: The DEF FN Statement 219
13.4 Problems 222
13.5 Review True-or-False Quiz 224

Chapter 14 More on Processing String Data 227

14.1 String and String-Related Functions 227
14.2 Combining Strings (Concatenation) 232
14.3 The Search Function INSTR 233
14.4 Problems 234
14.5 The BASIC Character Set 237
14.6 Problems 239
14.7 BASIC Conversion Functions 240
14.8 User-Defined Functions Involving String Data 244
14.9 Problems 245
14.10 Review True-or-False Quiz 247

Chapter 15 Arrays 249
- 15.1 One-Dimensional Arrays 249
- 15.2 The DIM Statement (Declaring Arrays) 256
- 15.3 Table Processing 258
- 15.4 Problems 263
- 15.5 Higher-Dimensional Arrays 268
- 15.6 Problems 274
- 15.7 Review True-or-False Quiz 278

Chapter 16 Sorting 279
- 16.1 The Bubble Sort 279
- 16.2 The Shellsort and Binary Search Algorithms 284
- 16.3 Problems 286
- 16.4 Review True-or-False Quiz 289

Chapter 17 Data Files 291
- 17.1 Sequential Access Files 292
- 17.2 Detecting the End of a Sequential File 297
- 17.3 Problems 298
- 17.4 Maintaining Sequential Files 301
- 17.5 Problems 307
- 17.6 Random Access Files 310
- 17.7 Problems 323
- 17.8 Review True-or-False Quiz 324

Chapter 18 Random Numbers and Their Application 325
- 18.1 The RND Function 325
- 18.2 Repeating a Random Process 329
- 18.3 Problems 331
- 18.4 Random Integers 333
- 18.5 Simulation 334
- 18.6 Problems 336
- 18.7 A Statistical Application 338
- 18.8 Monte Carlo 339
- 18.9 Problems 341
- 18.10 Review True-or-False Quiz 342

Chapter 19 Graphics 345
- 19.1 Medium-Resolution Graphics: Getting Started 346
- 19.2 Drawing Lines and Rectangles: The LINE Statement 352
- 19.3 Problems 362
- 19.4 Drawing Circles and Ellipses: The CIRCLE Statement 363
- 19.5 Coloring Areas of the Screen: The PAINT Statement 373
- 19.6 Problems 377
- 19.7 Moving Objects: The GET and PUT Statements 378
- 19.8 Simulated Motion 383

19.9	Problems 391	
19.10	High-Resolution Graphics 393	
19.11	Problems 396	
19.12	Review True-or-False Quiz 397	

Appendix A	**Getting Microsoft® BASIC Up and Running 399**	
Appendix B	**The Disk Operating System (DOS) 401**	
Appendix C	**A Typical Session with Disk or Advanced BASIC 405**	
Appendix D	**Microsoft® BASIC Reserved Words 411**	
Appendix E	**Editing Features 413**	
Appendix F	**IBM PC Numeric Codes 417**	
Appendix G	**Microsoft® BASIC Statements 421**	
Appendix H	**Microsoft® BASIC Commands 425**	
Appendix I	**BASIC Functions 427**	
Appendix J	**Answers to Selected Problems 429**	

Index 446

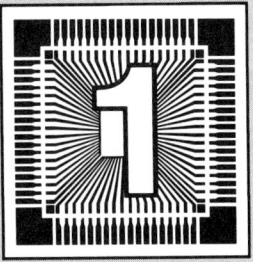

IBM Personal Computer Systems

Any electronic device that can receive, store, process, and transmit data (information)—and can also receive and store the instructions to process these data—is called a **computer.** Figure 1.1 shows an IBM personal computer (PC) with its cover removed. The *system board* shown in the figure contains many miniaturized electronic and magnetic devices together with the circuitry interconnecting them. The system board is the computer component that can receive, store, process, and transmit data.

A **computer system** is any group of interrelated components that includes a computer as one of its principal elements. Figure 1.2 shows a complete IBM personal computer system that includes an IBM computer with two disk storage units, a detachable keyboard, a video display screen, and a printer for producing printed documents.

A computer system has the ability to store large quantities of data, to process these data at very fast rates, and to present the results of this processing in ways that are meaningful to the task at hand. If the task is to prepare a payroll, for example, employee data will be transmitted to the computer, the computer will process these data to calculate relevant wage statistics, and the results will be presented in printed form, possibly including paychecks. This payroll example illustrates the three principal tasks involved in every computer application: data must be presented to the computer **(INPUT),** data must be processed **(PROCESS),** and results must be presented in a useful way **(OUTPUT);** (see Figure 1.3).

Today, computer applications are so numerous and widespread that it is not always easy to distinguish between tasks we should assign to computers and tasks we should do ourselves. Certainly, tasks requiring large numbers of numerical calculations are best delegated to computers. Computers carry out thousands of calculations per second without error; we perform but a few per minute—even with a calculator in hand—and must exercise the greatest care and concentration to avoid errors. The very first computers were built precisely for such tasks (see Figure 1.4).

Applications of the computer, however, are no longer restricted to numerical tasks. Modern computers are useful tools in many application areas that have nothing to do with arithmetic. Word processing and communications systems, for example, allow for easy storage, retrieval, editing, and transmission of most types of correspondence (see Figure 1.5).

In our rapidly changing technological society, an understanding of computers and how they are used is becoming more and more essential. But the purpose of this chapter is not to convince you that a computer can "do" many things nor even to indicate the computer applications you will be able to carry out after completing this book. Rather, the objectives of this chapter are to introduce you to the types of computing equipment you may encounter, to describe what a computer program is, and to introduce certain terminology that is helpful when talking about computers.

2 Chapter 1 IBM Personal Computer Systems

Figure 1.1 IBM Personal Computer with cover removed. (*Courtesy of IBM Corporation.*)

Figure 1.2 An IBM Personal Computer system. (*Courtesy of Roy Neuhaus.*)

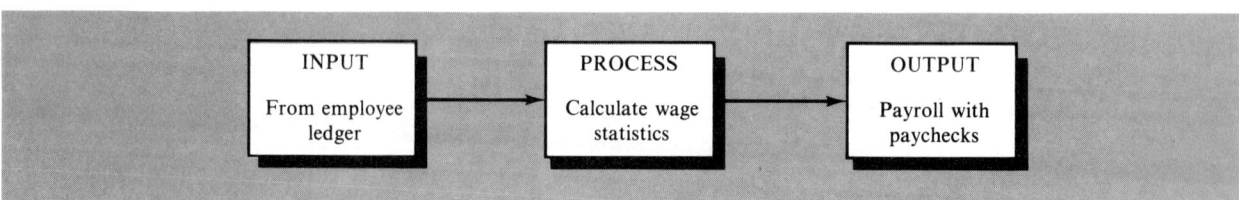

Figure 1.3 An INPUT-PROCESS-OUTPUT diagram.

Figure 1.4 Presentation of the first UNIVAC I (first-generation UNIVersal Automatic Computer) to the Smithsonian Institution, where portions of it are now on display. Designed by John W. Mauchly and J. Presper Eckert, Jr., and built under their direction by Remington Rand Corporation, the UNIVAC I was the first commercially available electronic computer and the first computer to be used for business data processing. Unlike its predecessors, which were built for specific scientific applications, the UNIVAC I was a general-purpose computer. Early applications included the tabulation of U.S. census data—the first UNIVAC I was delivered to the U.S. Bureau of the Census in 1951—and the analysis of election returns during the 1952 presidential election. The early projection of Dwight D. Eisenhower as the winner over Adlai E. Stevenson was an impressive feat that greatly increased public awareness of computers. Courtesy of Sperry Corporation.

Figure 1.5 Data terminals are rapidly replacing the typewriter as the standard office tool. With modern word processing systems, letters, memos, reports, and even entire books can be typed at terminal keyboards for transmission to a computer, which automatically stores the information on high-speed disk storage devices. The information can later be used in many ways. It can be displayed for reading on a video screen, modified by typing changes at the keyboard, formatted for output by typing special editing marks, and transmitted to an output device to obtain printed copy. If the word processing system is part of a communications system, the information can also be transmitted to other locations. Courtesy of Texas Instruments.

1.1 Computer Hardware

Central to every computer system is an electronic computer whose principal function is to process data. The computer component that does this is called the **central processing unit (CPU)**. The IBM's CPU is called a **microprocessor** because of its microminiaturized circuitry. The CPU contains an **arithmetic and logic unit (ALU),** consisting of circuitry that performs all the arithmetic and logical operations the computer was designed to carry out. The PC's ALU is an *integrated circuit* about the size of a fingernail and is housed in a special protective container located on the system board.* Computers such as the PC, whose CPUs are microprocessors, are called **microcomputers.**

In addition to the CPU, every computer has a **memory unit** that can store data for processing. This memory unit consists of thousands of memory locations, each with its own address. The term **random access memory (RAM)** is used when referring to a computer's memory. This term indicates that data can be obtained from or transmitted to any memory storage unit directly if its address is specified. The PC's RAM consists of ICs placed on the system board. It is *volatile* memory—that is, when you turn the power off, everything stored in RAM is lost. [The term **read only memory (ROM)** refers to computer memory that can be accessed but not changed. ROM is not volatile.]

Fortunately, you don't have to understand how a computer stores and processes data to make it work for you. The circuitry in a computer is not unlike that in an ordinary pocket calculator, and all who have used calculators know that no knowledge of their circuitry is needed to use them.

Data must be transmitted to the computer (*input*), and results of the processing must be returned (*output*). Devices that transfer data to and from a computer are called **input** and **output (I/O) devices.** As you learn computer programming on the PC, you are likely to encounter the following I/O devices, which serve as the principal means of communication between you and the PC:

Keyboard and **video display screen** (Figure 1.2): You transmit information to the computer simply by typing it at the keyboard and the computer transmits the results back to you by displaying them on the video screen.

Printers: A printer, such as shown in Figure 1.2, serves only as an output device. Figure 1.6 shows a **line printer** capable of printing an entire line of output simultaneously. A single line printer can be used as the output device for many PCs.

Most modern computer systems are equipped with memory storage devices other than the main memory unit. They are called **external** (or **secondary**) **storage devices** because, unlike the memory unit, they are not part of the computer. The following external storage devices are used with personal computers:

Cassette tape units: Information is stored on magnetic tapes (cassettes) as sequences of magnetized "spots" by using an ordinary cassette tape recorder. Data are "read" from a tape sequentially until the desired data are found. For this reason, tape units are called **sequential access devices.**

Disk storage units: Information is stored on rotating **diskettes** that resemble phonograph records. The diskettes have no grooves, however; the data are stored as sequences of magnetized spots appearing on concentric circles. Disk units are called **random access devices.** As with RAM, the term **random access** indicates that the data stored on any part of a disk can be accessed directly without having to read through the

---

* An integrated circuit (IC) is an electronic circuit that has been etched into a small, thin wafer of a glasslike substance such as silicon. A single IC less than a square inch in area can contain several thousand distinct but interconnected electronic components such as transistors and diodes.

Figure 1.6 Dataproducts' B-series band printer. (*Courtesy of Dataproducts Corporation.*)

entire disk to find the desired data. Figure 1.7 shows a $5\frac{1}{4}$-inch diskette being inserted into an IBM PC disk unit.

Video display units, printers, tape units, disk units, and all other mechanical and electrical devices other than the computer itself are referred to as **computer peripherals.** The computer and all peripherals constitute the **hardware** of the computer system. Figure 1.8 illustrates the flow of information between a computer and its peripherals.

■ 1.2 Computer Software

The physical components, or hardware, of a computer system are inanimate objects. They cannot prepare a payroll or perform any other task, however simple, without human assistance. This assistance is given in the form of instructions to the computer. A sequence of such instructions is called a **computer program,** and a person who composes these instructions is called a **programmer.**

Figure 1.7 Diskette being inserted into an IBM PC disk unit. (*Courtesy of Judy Blamer.*)

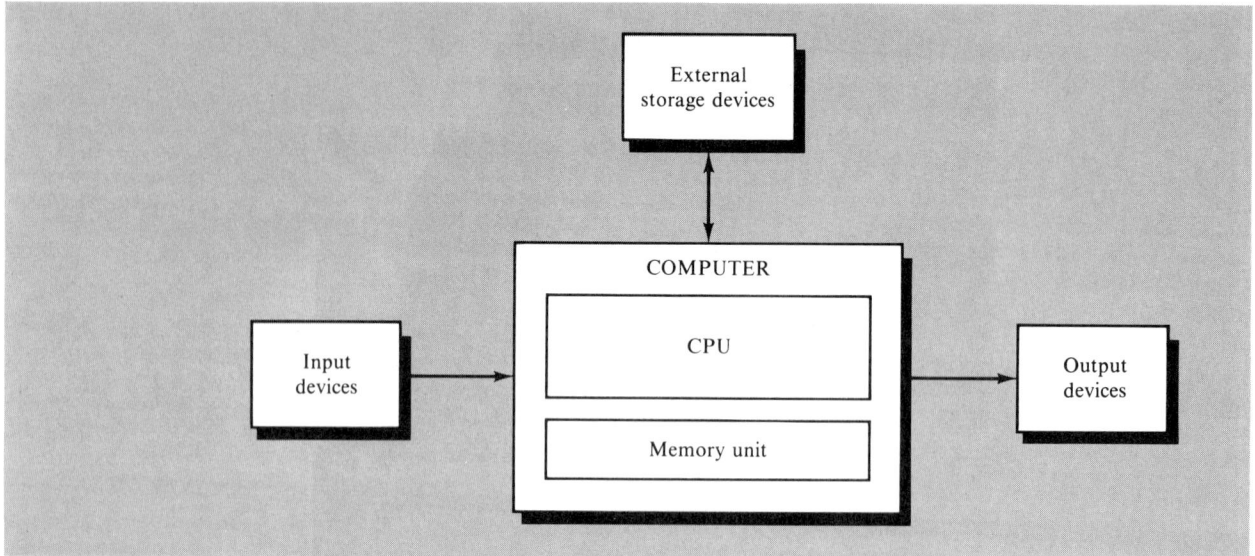

Figure 1.8 Flow of information through a computer system.

The precise form that instructions to a computer must take depends on the computer system being used. **BASIC** (Beginner's All-purpose Symbolic Instruction Code) is a carefully constructed English-like language used for writing computer programs.* **Microsoft® BASIC** is an extended version of BASIC used with many computers, including IBM personal computers. Instructions in the BASIC language are designed to be understood by people as well as by the computer. Even the uninitiated will understand the meaning of this simple BASIC program:

```
1 LET A=3
2 LET B=A+5
3 PRINT B
4 END
```

A computer is an electronic device and understands an instruction such as LET A = 3 in a very special way. An electronic device can distinguish between two electrical or magnetic states. Consider, for instance, an ordinary on/off switch for a light fixture. When the switch is in the "on" position, current is allowed to flow and the light bulb glows. If we denote the "on" position by the number 1 and the "off" position by the number 0, we can say that the instruction 1 causes the bulb to glow and the instruction 0 causes it not to glow. In like manner, we can envision a machine with two switches whose positions are denoted by the four codes 00, 01, 10, and 11 such that each of these four codes causes a different event to occur. It is this ability to distinguish between two distinct states that has led to the development of modern computers. Indeed, modern computers are still based on this principle. For example, each memory location in the PC's RAM can store a sequence of 0s and 1s, and one or more such sequences can be used to represent either data (in coded form) or instructions to the PC's processing unit. These instructions are called the computer's *machine language*. Although the PC's hardware understands only these machine instructions, you will not be required to write programs in machine language. Your personal computer comes with a **translator,** which automatically translates your BASIC instructions into equivalent machine language instructions that are then executed by the computer. There are two essentially different types of BASIC translators, called **interpreters** and **compilers.** An *interpreter* translates a BASIC instruction into machine code each time it is to be carried out; a *compiler* translates an entire program into machine code only once. For

---

* BASIC was developed at Dartmouth College under the direction of John G. Kemeny and Thomas E. Kurtz.

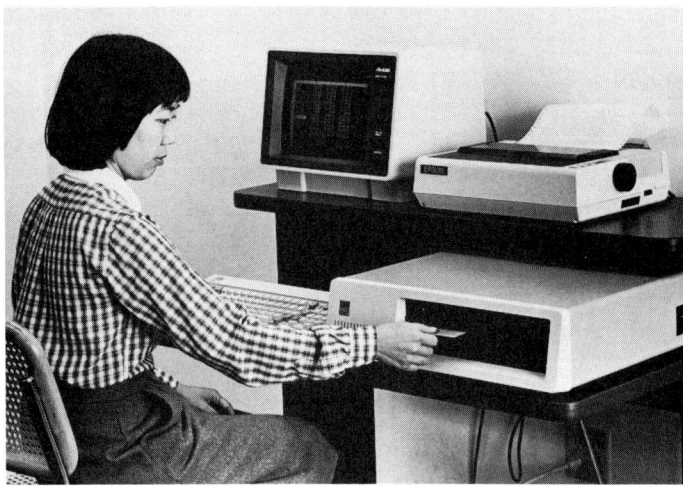

Figure 1.9 IBM PC system in an office setting. (*Courtesy of Frank Keillor.*)

this reason, a BASIC program will execute much more rapidly on computers that use compilers than on computers that use interpreters. The difference can be significant! Most microcomputers, including IBM personal computers, use BASIC interpreters. Compilers are available, but they must be purchased separately.

BASIC interpreters and compilers are themselves computer programs. They are called **systems programs** because they are an integral part of the computer system itself. The BASIC programs in this book, as well as the programs you will write, are called **applications programs.** They are not an integral part of the computer system, so they are not called systems programs. All computer programs, both systems programs and applications programs, are called **computer software.**

In addition to the BASIC interpreter, your system contains other systems programs. The most important of these are programs that allow you to use a disk unit as an external storage device. These include programs to store information on diskettes, to retrieve any information previously stored on a diskette, and to perform several other useful tasks involving disk units. Together, all systems programs designed to carry out disk operations are called the **disk operating system (DOS).**

The emergence of computer science as a new discipline has been accompanied by a proliferation of new words and expressions. Although they are useful for talking about computers, they are for the most part absolutely unnecessary if your objective is to

Figure 1.10 IBM PC system in an educational setting. (*Courtesy of Frank Keillor.*)

learn a computer language such as BASIC to help you solve problems. In our discussion of computer hardware and software, we have introduced only fundamental concepts and basic terminology. Even so, if this is your first exposure to computers, you may feel lost in this terminology. Don't be disheartened: much of the new vocabulary has already been introduced. You will become more familiar with it and recognize its usefulness as you study the material in the subsequent chapters. You will also find it helpful to reread this chapter after you have written a few computer programs.

■ 1.3 Review True-or-False Quiz

1. Any electronic device that can process data is called a computer.   T F
2. Input/output devices, external storage devices, and the central processing unit are called computer peripherals.   T F
3. A computer whose central processing unit is a microprocessor is called a microcomputer.   T F
4. The terms *microprocessor* and *integrated circuit* are used synonymously.   T F
5. An automobile that uses a microprocessor to control the gas and air mixture is correctly referred to as a computer system.   T F
6. Whatever information is stored in the PC's RAM is lost when the power to the PC is cut off.   T F
7. There is a significant difference between memory units called RAM and memory units called ROM.   T F
8. The terms *compiler* and *interpreter* are used synonymously.   T F
9. A BASIC program written to solve a particular problem is called a systems program.   T F
10. A computer system must contain at least one printer.   T F
11. Disk storage units are called *random access devices* because information stored on a diskette is accessed by randomly searching portions of the diskette until the desired data are found.   T F
12. The PC's disk operating system (DOS) is a computer system.   T F

Problem Solving: Top-Down Approach

A computer program consists of a sequence of instructions to the computer. These instructions describe a step-by-step process for carrying out a specified task. Such a process is called an **algorithm.** Algorithms have been with us since antiquity: the familiar division algorithm was known and used in ancient Greece; the activities of bookkeepers have always been guided by algorithms (an algorithm to determine a tax assessment, an algorithm to calculate a depletion allowance, and so on); even the instructions for assembling a child's new toy are often given in algorithmic form.

Since a computer program describes an algorithm, the process of writing computer programs can be equated to the process of discovering algorithms. For this reason, an understanding of what is, and what is not, an algorithm is indispensable to a programmer.

In Section 2.1, we define the term *algorithm* and illustrate, with simple examples, the method of designing algorithms called the *top-down approach to problem solving.* In Section 2.2, we define the term *variable,* an essential concept in programming, and illustrate the use of variables in writing algorithms.

■ 2.1 Algorithms

An algorithm is a prescribed set of well-defined rules and processes for carrying out a specified task in a finite number of steps. Here is an algorithm giving instructions for completing a financial transaction at a drive-in teller port:

    a. Press the call button.
    b. Remove the carrier from the tray.
    c. Place your transaction inside the carrier.
    d. Replace the carrier.
    e. When the carrier returns, remove the transaction.
    f. Replace the carrier.

To see that these six steps describe an algorithm, we must verify that each step is well defined and that the process stops in a finite number of steps. For example, Step (a) requires that there be only one call button, Step (b) requires that there be but one tray containing a single carrier, and Step (e) requires that the carrier return automatically after being placed in the tray as specified in Step (d). Having verified that each step is well defined, and noting that the process stops after a transaction has been completed, we can be fairly confident that the six steps do indeed describe an algorithm for the specified task.

The drive-in teller example illustrates the following three properties of an algorithm:

1. Each step must be well defined—that is, unambiguous.
2. The process must halt in a finite number of steps.
3. The process must do what is claimed.

The examples in this section are intended to help you understand what an algorithm is and to allow you to gain some practice with the process of designing algorithms. In keeping with current terminology, we will refer to this process as the **problem-solving process.** In each example, we begin with a description of the task to be performed (the **problem statement**), illustrate the essential steps in the problem-solving process, and end with an algorithm for the specified task.

EXAMPLE 1 Let's find an algorithm to produce a report showing the name, annual salary, and year-end bonus for each salaried employee in a firm. Employees are to receive 2% of their annual salary or $400, whichever is larger.

To produce a bonus report, we will need to know the names and salaries of the employees. (These data are called the *input*.) To keep things as simple as possible, we'll assume that all names and annual salaries are contained in an employee ledger and are obtained simply by reading the ledger.

Since our algorithm is to produce a year-end bonus report (called the *output*), we must decide upon a format for this report. A quick reading of the problem statement suggests a report such as the following:

Year-end bonuses (1989)

Name	Salary	Bonus
Susan Andrade	27,000	540
Lester Barkley	16,500	400
.	.	.
.	.	.
.	.	.

To help us design a detailed algorithm to produce our bonus report, we'll begin with the following short algorithm that simply identifies what tasks must be performed:

a. Write the title and column headings for the bonus sheet.
b. Read the ledger to determine and fill in the name, salary, and bonus for each employee.

To carry out Step (a), a payroll clerk would simply copy the information from the output format already specified. To carry out Step (b), a clerk might proceed as follows:

b1. Open the employee ledger.
b2. Read the next employee's name and salary.
b3. Determine the employee's bonus.
b4. Write the employee's name, salary, and bonus on the bonus sheet.
b5. If all bonuses have not been determined, return to Step (b2).
b6. Close the ledger.

It is not difficult to see that Steps (b1) to (b6) constitute an algorithm for Step (b). Each step is well defined, and because a business can employ only a finite number of people, the algorithm will terminate in a finite number of steps. Moreover, if this algorithm is followed—without error—all employee bonuses will be determined as specified.

Although the algorithm does what was asked, the process could be made more specific by including more detail in Step (b3). Recalling the method specified for calculating bonus amounts, we can substitute the following for Step (b3):

b3.1. Multiply the salary by 0.02 to obtain a tentative bonus.
b3.2. If the tentative bonus is less than $400, set the bonus to $400; otherwise make the bonus equal to the tentative bonus.

Making this change, or *refinement,* we obtain the following more detailed algorithm for Step (b):

b1. Open the employee ledger.
b2. Read the next employee's name and salary.
b3.1. Multiply the salary by 0.02 to obtain a tentative bonus.
b3.2. If the tentative bonus is less than $400, set the bonus to $400; otherwise make the bonus equal to the tentative bonus.
b4. Write the employee's name, salary, and bonus on the bonus sheet.
b5. If all bonuses have not been determined, return to Step (b2).
b6. Close the ledger.

Our final detailed algorithm consists of eight steps—Step (a) followed by this seven-step algorithm for carrying out Step (b).

■ **REMARK** In this example, we started with a problem statement describing the task to be carried out (produce a year-end bonus report) and ended with an algorithm describing how to accomplish this task. The steps you take while designing an algorithm are called a **problem analysis.** For simple problems, a description of the input and output may lead directly to a final algorithm. For more complicated problems, a thorough analysis of alternative approaches to a solution may be required. In any case, the term *problem analysis* refers to the process of designing a suitable algorithm.

The method used to design an algorithm for Example 1 illustrates three important principles of problem solving:

1. Begin by describing the input (information needed to carry out the specified task) and the output (the results that must be obtained). In the example, we described the input as salary information to be read from the employee ledger and the output as a table showing the names, salaries, and bonus amounts for the employees. An essential first step in the problem-solving process is to read and understand the problem statement. It is unlikely that a correct algorithm will be found if the task to be performed is not understood exactly. *Giving a clear and precise description of the input and output is an effective way to acquire an understanding of a problem statement.*

2. Identify individual subtasks that must be performed while carrying out the specified task. In Example 1 we identified the following two subtasks:

a. Write the title and column headings for the bonus sheet.
b. Read the ledger to determine and fill in the name, salary, and bonus for each employee.

If a complicated task can be broken down into simpler, more manageable subtasks, the job of writing an algorithm can often be simplified significantly: you simply describe the order in which the subtasks are to be carried out. This was especially easy to do in Example 1—simply carry out Subtask (a) followed by Subtask (b). The process of breaking down a task into simpler subtasks is called **problem segmentation** or **modularization**—the subtasks are sometimes called **modules.** As in Example 1, the details of how to carry out these modules can be worked out after an algorithm has been found.

3. If more details are needed in an algorithm, include the additional details separately for each step. In Example 1 we started with a two-step algorithm:

  a. Write the title and column headings for the bonus sheet.
  b. Read the ledger to determine and fill in the name, salary, and bonus for each employee.

Next, we included more detail in Step (b) by breaking it down into these six steps:

  b1. Open the employee ledger.
  b2. Read the next employee's name and salary.
  b3. Determine the employee's bonus.
  b4. Write the employee's name, salary, and bonus on the bonus sheet.
  b5. If all bonuses have not been determined, return to Step (b2).
  b6. Close the ledger.

Finally, we included more detail in the algorithm by rewriting Step (b3) as follows:

  b3.1. Multiply the salary by 0.02 to obtain a tentative bonus.
  b3.2. If the tentative bonus is less than $400, set the bonus to $400; otherwise make the bonus equal to the tentative bonus.

The important thing to notice is that we introduced details into the algorithm by refining the steps separately—that is, by breaking down the individual steps one at a time—and not by combining steps or otherwise changing the algorithm. This method of designing a detailed algorithm is called the **method of stepwise refinement.** You begin with a simple algorithm that contains few details but that you know is correct. If necessary, you refine one or more of the steps to obtain a more detailed algorithm. If even more detail is needed, you refine one or more of the steps in the derived algorithm. By repeating this process of stepwise refinement, you can obtain an algorithm with whatever detail is needed. Moreover, however complicated the final algorithm, you can be sure that it is correct simply by knowing that you started with a correct algorithm and that each step was refined correctly.

The approach to problem solving used in Example 1 is called the **top-down approach** to problem solving or the **top-down design** of algorithms. The expression *top-down* comes from using the methods of modularization and stepwise refinement. You start at the top (the problem statement), break that task down into simpler tasks, then break those tasks into even simpler ones, and continue the process, all the while knowing how the tasks at each level of refinement combine, until the tasks at the lowest (final) level contain whatever detail is desired. The advantages to be gained by adhering to the three problem-solving principles of the top-down approach will become more evident as you work through the examples and problems in this book. The following example should help you better understand these three principles and their application.

EXAMPLE 2

A wholesale firm keeps a list of the items it sells in a card file. For each item, there is a single card containing a descriptive item name, the number of units in stock (this can be zero), the number of the warehouse in which the item is stored, and certain other information that will not concern us. Our task is to prepare a list of out-of-stock items for each warehouse.

PROBLEM ANALYSIS

The problem statement says that a separate list of out-of-stock items is needed for each warehouse. Thus, we will need to know the warehouse numbers. Let's assume we are told there are three warehouses numbered 127, 227, and 327. With this information, we can include these numbers as input rather than reading through the entire card file to determine them. We can now specify the input and output for our algorithm:

  Input: Warehouse numbers 127, 227, and 327.
  Card file: one card for each item.

Output: Three reports formatted as follows:

WAREHOUSE 127
(Out-of-stock items)

Hammers—Model 2960
Hammers—Model 3375
Saws—Model 1233
.
.
.

WAREHOUSE 227
(Out-of-stock items)
.
.
.

WAREHOUSE 327
(Out-of-stock items)
.
.
.

Having given a precise description of the input and output, we should determine what subtask or subtasks must be performed. The problem statement specifies that three reports are to be produced, one for each warehouse. If we arrange things so that reports are produced one at a time (this is the common practice when using computers), we can use the same procedure for each report. Specifically, for each warehouse number W, we will carry out the following subtask (named R for report):

Subtask R. Prepare the report for warehouse W.

Of course, we will need to include details describing how to carry out this subtask. But even without these details, we can write a simple algorithm that obviously is correct:

THE ALGORITHM

    a. Assign 127 to W.
    b. Carry out Subtask R.
    c. Assign 227 to W.
    d. Carry out Subtask R.
    e. Assign 327 to W.
    f. Carry out Subtask R.

Notice that Subtask R specifies that a report is to be prepared. As in Example 1, we can break this subtask down into two subordinate subtasks R1 and R2 as follows:

R1. Write the report header for warehouse W.
R2. Read through the card file to complete the report.

At this point, we should recognize that Step R1 requires no additional details—the output specification shows how the report header should be formatted. We should, however, include more details in Step R2. In the following algorithm for Subtask R, Steps R2.1 to R2.4 show one way to carry out Step R2:

    R1. Write the report header for warehouse W.
    R2.1. Turn to the first card.
    R2.2. Read the warehouse number (call it N) and the units-on-hand figure (call it U).

R2.3. If N = W and U = 0, read the item name and write it on the report.
R2.4. If there is another card, turn to it and continue with Step R2.2.

Our final algorithm for the given problem statement consists of two parts: the original six-step algorithm [Steps (a)–(f)] that tells us when (but not how) to carry out Subtask R and the five-step algorithm (Steps R1, R2.1–R2.4) that shows us how Subtask R can be accomplished.

■ REMARK

Let's review the problem analysis carried out in this example:

Input/output specification. Our attempt to give a precise description of the input and output led us to include the warehouse numbers 127, 227, and 327 as input. As a consequence, the final algorithm is simpler than what would have been obtained had we begun by reading the entire card file just to determine the warehouse numbers.

Modularization. Our attempt to identify subtasks led us to conclude that there was but one major subtask, namely,

Subtask R. Prepare the report for warehouse W.

By using this subtask, it was easy to write an algorithm [Steps (a)–(f)] that lacked only the details needed to carry out Subtask R.

Stepwise refinement. Our next job was to show how to carry out Subtask R. We began by breaking it down into these two subordinate subtasks:

R1. Write the report header for warehouse W.
R2. Read through the card file to complete the report.

Notice that this two-step refinement of Subtask R represents an application of the principle of modularization applied to Subtask R. At this point we recognize that only Step R2 was lacking in details. We supplied these details by writing a short four-step algorithm (Steps R2.1–R2.4) for Step R2.

□

■ 2.2 Variables

Algorithms can often be stated clearly if symbols are used to denote certain values. Symbols are especially helpful when used to denote values that may change during the process of performing the steps in an algorithm. The symbols W, N, and U used in Example 2 illustrate this practice.

A value that can change during a process is called a **variable.** A symbol used to denote such a variable is the *name* of the variable. Thus W, N, and U in Example 2 are names of variables. It is common practice, however, to refer to the *symbol* as being the variable itself, rather than just its name. For instance, Step (a) of the algorithm for Example 2 says to assign 127 to W. Certainly this is less confusing than saying "assign 127 to the variable whose name is W."

The following two examples further illustrate the use of variables in algorithms.

EXAMPLE 3

PROBLEM ANALYSIS

Let's find an algorithm to determine the largest number in a list of numbers.

Input: A list of numbers.

Output: The largest number in the list.

One way to determine the largest number in a list of numbers is to read the numbers one at a time, remembering only the largest of those already read. To help us give a precise description of this process, let's use two symbols:

LGST to denote the largest of the numbers already read
NUM to denote the number currently being read

The following algorithm can now be written:

a. Read the first number and denote it by LGST.
b. Read the next number and denote it by NUM.
c. If NUM is larger than LGST, assign NUM to LGST.
d. If all numbers have not been read, go to Step (b).
e. Write the value of LGST and stop.

To verify this algorithm for the list of numbers

4, 5, 3, 6, 6, 2, 1, 8, 7, 3

we simply proceed step by step through the algorithm, always keeping track of the latest values of LGST and NUM. An orderly way to do this is to complete an assignment table, as follows:

Algorithm step	LGST	NUM	Output
a	4		
b		5	
c	5		
b		3	
b		6	
c	6		
b		6	
b		2	
b		1	
b		8	
c	8		
b		7	
b		3	
e			8

REMARK 1 If the numbers were written on a sheet of paper, you could look them over and select the largest. This process is heuristic, however, and does not constitute an algorithm.* To see that this is so, imagine many hundreds of numbers written on a large sheet of paper. In that case, attempting to select the largest simply by looking over the numbers could easily result in an error. What we need is an orderly process that will ensure that the largest number is selected. Examining numbers one at a time, as in this algorithm, is such an orderly process.

---

* A **heuristic process** is one involving exploratory methods. Solutions to problems are discovered by a continual evaluation of the progress made toward the final result. For instance, suppose you come upon an old map indicating that a treasure is buried in the Black Hills. You may be able to work out a plan that you know will lead to the location shown on the map. *That's an algorithm*. However, suppose you can find no such plan. Determined to find the location, or to verify that the map is a fake, you decide on a first step in your search, with no idea of what the next step will be. *That's exploratory*. Carrying out this first step may suggest a second step, or it may lead you nowhere, in which case you would try something else. Continuing in this manner, you may eventually find the location, or you may determine that the map is a fake. But it is also possible that the search will end only when you quit. Whatever the outcome, the process is heuristic. Someone else using this process will undoubtedly carry out entirely different steps and perhaps reach a different conclusion.

16 Chapter 2 Problem Solving: Top-Down Approach

■ REMARK 2   The task of finding the largest number in a list of numbers occurs as a subtask in many programming problems. When confronted with such a problem, you can use Steps (a)–(d) of the given algorithm to carry out the subtask. Should you need to find the smallest number, rather than the largest, simply change the word larger in Step (c) to smaller.

EXAMPLE 4   Find an algorithm to prepare a depreciation schedule for a delivery van that costs $18,000, has a salvage value of $2,000, and has a useful life of 5 years. Use the straight-line method.

[The straight-line method assumes that the value of the van will decrease by one-fifth of $16,000 (cost − salvage value) during each of the 5 years.]

PROBLEM ANALYSIS   For each year, let's agree to write one line showing the year, the depreciation allowance for that year, the cumulative depreciation (sum of yearly depreciations to that point), and the book value (cost − cumulative depreciation) at the end of the year. We can now describe the input and output.

Input: The purchased item (van), its cost ($18,000), salvage value ($2,000), and useful life (5 years).

Output: A report formatted as follows:

Depreciation schedule—van

| Cost: $18,000 | | Salvage: $2,000 | |
| Life: 5 years | | Method: Straight-line | |
Year	Depreciation allowance	Cumulative depreciation	Book value
1989	$3,200	$3,200	$14,800
1990	3,200	6,400	11,600
.	.	.	.
.	.	.	.
.	.	.	.

It is not difficult to write an algorithm to produce this report if we leave out the details.

THE ALGORITHM
a. Look up the current year, item name, cost, salvage value, and useful life.
b. Write the report and column headers.
c. Determine and write the table values.

Steps (a) and (b) require no additional details—they are explained in the input/output description. To carry out Step (c) by hand, you might proceed as follows:

1. Determine the depreciation allowance for 1 year.
2. Subtract the depreciation allowance from the book value (initially the cost).
3. Add the depreciation amount to the cumulative depreciation (initially zero).
4. Write one line showing the year, the depreciation allowance for that year, the cumulative depreciation, and the book value at the end of the year.
5. Return to Step (2) until the schedule is complete.

To allow us to write a concise, detailed algorithm describing how to carry out Step (c), let's choose variable names to denote the various values of interest.

ITEM = name of purchased item
  BV = book value (the initial book value is the cost)
  SV = salvage value
   Y = useful life in years
   D = depreciation allowance for 1 year [D = (BV − SV)/Y]
   C = cumulative depreciation (initially zero)
  CY = current year

In the following detailed algorithm, Steps (c1) to (c7) tell how to accomplish Step (c). [Note that Step (a) has been changed only by the use of variable names in place of descriptive names.]

    a. Look up (input) values for CY, ITEM, BV, SV, and Y.
    b. Write the report and column headers.
    c1. Start with C = 0.
    c2. Calculate D = (BV − SV)/Y.
    c3. Subtract D from BV.
    c4. Add D to C.
    c5. Write one line showing CY, D, C, and BV.
    c6. Add 1 to CY.
    c7. Return to Step (c3) until the schedule is complete.

For the input specified in the problem statement and with 1989 as the current year, this algorithm leads to the following depreciation schedule:

Depreciation schedule—van

Cost: $18,000   Salvage: $2,000
Life: 5 years   Method: Straight-line

Year	Depreciation allowance	Cumulative depreciation	Book value
1989	$3,200	$ 3,200	$14,800
1990	3,200	6,400	11,600
1991	3,200	9,600	8,400
1992	3,200	12,800	5,200
1993	3,200	16,000	2,000

REMARK   It is not often that a problem statement exactly describes the task to be carried out. Problem statements are written in a natural language, such as English, and thus are subject to the ambiguities inherent in natural languages. Moreover, they are written by people, which means that they are subject to human oversight and error. Since an algorithm describes a precise, unambiguous process for carrying out a task, the task to be performed must be clearly understood. If it appears ambiguous, the ambiguities must be resolved. If it appears that one thing is being asked but another is actually desired, the difference must be resolved. For instance, the problem statement in the present example asks for only a very limited algorithm (a book value of $18,000, a salvage value of $2,000, and a useful life of 5 years) when what is really desired is the more general algorithm that has a wider application.

2.3 Problems

Problems 1–4 refer to the following algorithm for completing an invoice:

    a. Let AMOUNT = 0.
    b. Read QUANTITY and PRICE of an item.
    c. Add the product QUANTITY × PRICE to AMOUNT.
    d. If there is another item, go to Step (b); otherwise, continue with Step (e).
    e. If AMOUNT is not greater than $500, go to Step (h); otherwise, continue with Step (f).
    f. Evaluate the product 0.05 × AMOUNT.
    g. Subtract this product from AMOUNT.
    h. Record the value AMOUNT and stop.

1. What interpretation could be given to the product appearing in Step (f)? 5% discount
2. What purpose would you say is served by Step (e)? decide if discount is applicable
3. If the values (10, $3), (50, $8), and (25, $12) are read by Step (b), what value will be recorded by Step (h)? 693.5
4. If the values (100, $2) and (50, $1) are read by Step (b), what value will be recorded by Step (h)? 250.00

Problems 5–8 refer to the following algorithm, which is intended for use by a payroll clerk as a preliminary step in the preparation of a payroll:

   a. Read the next time card.
   b. Let H = number of hours worked.
   c. If H is not greater than 32, assign 0 to G and B and go to Step (f); otherwise, continue with the next step.
   d. Evaluate 6 × (H − 32) and assign this value to both G and B.
   e. Let H = 32.
   f. Evaluate 4 × H and add this value to G.
   g. Write the values G and B on the time card.
   h. If there is another time card, go to Step (a); otherwise, stop.

5. If the numbers of hours shown on the first four time cards are 20, 32, 40, and 45, respectively, what amounts will be written on these cards?
6. What is the base hourly rate for each employee?
7. What is the overtime rate?
8. Explain Step (c).

In Problems 9–12, what will be printed when each algorithm is carried out?

9. a. Let SUM = 0 and N = 1.
   b. Add N to SUM.
   c. Increase N by 1.
   d. If N ≤ 6, return to Step (b).
   e. Print the value SUM and stop.

10. a. Let PROD = 1 and N = 1.
    b. Print the values N and PROD on one line.
    c. Increase N by 1.
    d. Multiply PROD by N.
    e. If N ≤ 5, return to Step (b).
    f. Print the values of N and PROD on one line.
    g. Stop.

11. a. Let A = 1, B = 1, and F = 2.
    b. If F > 50, print the value F and stop.
    c. Assign the values of B and F to A and B, respectively.
    d. Evaluate A + B and assign this value to F.
    e. Return to Step (b).

12. a. Let NUM = 56, SUM = 1, and D = 2.
    b. If D is a factor of NUM, add D to SUM and print D.
    c. Increase D by 1.
    d. If D ≤ NUM/2, return to Step (b).
    e. Print the value SUM and stop.

Explain why the step-by-step processes given in Problems 13 and 14 do not describe algorithms.

13. a. Let N = 0.   b. Increase N by 10.
    c. Divide N by 2.   d. If N < 10, go to Step (b).   e. Stop.

14. a. Let NUM = 25.
   b. Print the value of NUM.
   c. Add 2 or 3 to NUM.
   d. If NUM < 35, go to Step (b).
   e. Stop.

In Problems 15–21, write an algorithm to carry out each task specified.

15. A retail store's monthly sales report shows, for each item, the cost, the sale price, and the number sold. Prepare a three-column report with the column headings ITEM, GROSS SALES, and INCOME.

16. Each of several 3 × 5 cards contains an employee's name, Social Security number, job classification, and date hired. Prepare a report showing the names, job classifications, and complete years of service for employees who have been with the company for more than 10 years.

17. A summary sheet of an investor's stock portfolio shows, for each stock, the corporation name, the number of shares owned, the current price, and the earnings as reported for the most recent year. Prepare a six-column report with the column headings CORP. NAME, NO. OF SHARES, PRICE, EARNINGS, EQUITY, and PRICE/EARNINGS. Use this formula:

$$\text{Equity} = \text{number of shares} \times \text{price}$$

18. Each of several cards contains a single number. Determine the sum and the average of all the numbers. (Use a variable N to count how many cards are read and a variable SUM to keep track of the sum of numbers already read.)

19. Each of several cards contains a single number. On each card, write the letter G if the number is greater than the average of all the numbers; otherwise, write the letter L. (You must read through the cards twice: once to find the average and again to determine whether to write the letter G or the letter L on the cards.)

20. A local supermarket has installed a check validation machine. To use this service, a customer must have an identification card containing a magnetic strip and a four-digit code. Instructions showing how to insert the identification card into a special magnetic-strip reader appear on the front panel. To validate a check, a customer must present the identification card to the machine, enter the four-digit code, enter the amount of the check, and place the check, blank side toward the customer, in a clearly labeled punch unit. To begin this process, the CLEAR key must be pressed, and, after each of the two entries has been made, the ENTER key must be pressed. Prepare an algorithm giving instructions for validating a check.

21. Write an algorithm describing the steps to be taken to cast a ballot in a national election. Assume that a person using this algorithm is a registered voter and has just entered the building in which voting is to take place. While in the voting booth, the voter should simply be instructed to vote. No instructions concerning the actual filling out of a ballot are to be given.

■ 2.4 Review True-or-False Quiz

1. The terms *algorithm* and *process* are synonymous.	T F
2. A computer program should describe an algorithm.	T F
3. Every algorithm can be translated into a computer program.	T F
4. The expression *heuristic process* refers to an algorithm.	T F
5. It is always easier to verify the correctness of an algorithm that describes a specific task than the correctness of a more general algorithm.	T F
6. The term *variable* refers to a value that can change during a process.	T F

7. The expressions *input/output specification, modularization,* and *stepwise refinement* refer to principles of problem solving.   T   F
8. A *problem analysis* is the process of discovering a correct algorithm.   T   F
9. The *method of stepwise refinement* is a method of problem solving in which successive steps in an algorithm are combined to produce an algorithm that is easier to read.   T   F
10. *Top-down design* involves the process of *stepwise refinement.*   T   F

3 A First Look at Microsoft® BASIC

We must communicate with a computer before it will perform any service for us. The medium for this communication is the computer program—for our purposes, a sequence of statements (instructions to the computer) in the English-like language BASIC. In this chapter we discuss some topics vital to understanding how a BASIC computer program must be written. These include the following: names of numerical and character string variables allowed in BASIC; how to write numerical expressions in a form suitable for computer evaluation; and how the REM, LET, PRINT, and END statements are used in BASIC programs. In the next chapter we explain how you get a completed program into the computer and cause it to be carried out, or executed.

Here is a BASIC program whose purpose is described in its first line:

```
100 REM PROGRAM TO AVERAGE THREE NUMBERS
110 REM    X, Y, AND Z DENOTE THE NUMBERS.
120 REM    AV DENOTES THE AVERAGE.
130 LET X=43
140 LET Y=27
150 LET Z=23
160 LET AV=(X+Y+Z)/3
170 PRINT "AVERAGE IS";AV
180 END
```

If a computer carries out the instructions in this program, it will produce the following output:

```
AVERAGE IS 31
```

The lines in this program are labeled with *line numbers* that determine the order in which the instructions are carried out by the computer. (Note that the digit zero is denoted by 0 to distinguish it from the letter O.) The program uses four words, called **keywords,** from the BASIC language: REM, to include remarks or comments as part of the program; LET, to associate certain numerical values with certain symbols (for example, line 130 associates 43 with the symbol X); PRINT, to display the results; and END, to terminate the program.

Unlike a natural language such as English, a programming language must not allow ambiguities. The computer must do precisely what it is instructed to do. For this reason, great care must be taken to write BASIC statements precisely according to the **BASIC syntax** (BASIC rules of grammar). The following sections describe how the keywords REM, LET, PRINT, and END can be used to form admissible BASIC programs. A complete treatment of these topics is not intended at this time; our immediate goal is to provide you with the minimal information you need to understand and write some BASIC programs.

3.1 Numerical Constants and Variables

Three types of numerical constants are allowed in BASIC:

Type	Examples
Integer	726 29234 −726 +423 −16023 0
Decimal	726. −133.50 +10.001 −99234. 0.201
Floating-point (exponential)	27.3E4 2.6E−3 1E3 −13.6E01 +2.345E−02

Almost all of your numerical work in BASIC will deal with the first two types, *integer* and *decimal*. Integers are numbers with no decimal point, and decimals are numbers in which a decimal point appears. The use of commas and dollar signs in numbers is not allowed; using 29,234 to represent 29234 will result in an error.

The third type, the *exponential* constant, may be new to you. The E in 27.3E4 stands for exponent. Its meaning is *times 10 to the power*. Thus 27.3E4 means 27.3 times 10 to the power 4 or, in more mathematical symbols, 27.3×10^4. Hence,

$$27.3E4 = 27.3 \times 10^4 = 27.3 \times 10000 = 273000$$

Similarly,

$$2.6E-3 = 2.6 \times 10^{-3} = 2.6 \times .001 = .0026$$

Note that you could obtain the final result 273000 of 27.3E4 by moving the decimal point in 27.3 *four* places to the *right,* and the result .0026 of 2.6E−3 by moving the decimal point in 2.6 *three* places to the *left*. The general form for a floating-point constant, together with its meaning, is

$$nEm = n \times 10^m$$

where *n* can be any integer or decimal, but *m* must be an integer (no decimal point). The values of the other floating-point numbers shown in the table above are:

$$1E3 = 1000$$
$$-13.6E01 = -136$$
$$2.345E-02 = .02345$$

Although in some programming languages you must be careful to represent numbers as integer, decimal, or floating-point constants, in BASIC you are free to use any form desired. For example, the following BASIC statements are equivalent; each assigns the value 230 to the variable A:

```
LET A=230
LET A=230.00
LET A=2.3E2
```

To form names for numerical variables Microsoft® BASIC allows sequences of characters consisting of letters, digits, and the period. The first character must be a letter. In choosing variable names, you must observe two restrictions:

1. Microsoft® BASIC uses certain words (such as LET, PRINT, and REM) for special purposes. These are called **reserved words** and cannot be used as variable names. A complete list of the Microsoft® BASIC reserved words is given in Appendix D.

2. Although variable names may be of any length, Microsoft® recognizes only the first 40 characters in each name. Thus two names that differ only after the fortieth character refer to the same variable. (This is seldom a problem.)

Admissible variable names	Inadmissible variable names	
X	3RD	(begins with a digit)
SUM	S-200	(contains a dash)
LAST.NAME	LAST NAME	(contains a space)
COUNT3	COLOR	(COLOR is a reserved word)
DEPT.17	.PCT	(begins with a period)

The variables just described are called **single-precision real variables** or, more simply, **real variables.** They can be used to store numerical constants (real numbers) with six- or seven-digit accuracy. In addition to the *real variables,* Microsoft® BASIC provides **integer variables** and **double-precision variables.**

Integer variables can be used in applications that involve only the integers from −32768 to 32767. Integer variable names differ from real variable names in one way only: their last character must be the percent symbol (%). Integer values for such variables are obtained by rounding to the nearest integer, if necessary. Thus, the statement

```
LET A%=15.625
```

associates the integer 16 with A%. Integer variables use half the memory space required for real variables.

Double-precision variables can be helpful in applications that require greater accuracy than is provided by real variables. With double-precision variables, results with 16-digit accuracy can be obtained. Double-precision variable names differ from real variable names in one way only: their last character must be the pound symbol (#).

■ 3.2 String Constants and Variables

A **string constant** is a sequence, or **string,** of BASIC characters enclosed in quotation marks. The following are string constants:

```
"Income"          "NANCY JONES"
"X="              "567"
"19 April 1775"   "*****"
"SUM "            "   DISCOUNT"
```

The *value* of a string constant is the sequence of all BASIC characters, including blanks, appearing between the quotes. Thus the value of the string constant "NANCY JONES" is the 11-character string NANCY JONES, and the value of "SUM " is the 4-character string consisting of SUM followed by a blank character. A string may contain up to 255 characters.

Variables whose values are strings are called **string variables.** Their names differ from numerical variable names in one way only: their last character must be a dollar sign ($). Thus B$, NAMES$, A45$, and S.S.N.$ are admissible names of string variables but NAME$ is not—NAME is a reserved word.

3.3 Arithmetic Operations and Expressions

BASIC uses the following symbols to denote the usual arithmetic operations:

BASIC symbol	Operation	Priority
^	Exponentiation	1
−	Negation	2
*	Multiplication	3
/	Division	3
+	Addition	4
−	Subtraction	4

Any meaningful combination of BASIC constants, variable names, and operation symbols is called a BASIC **expression.** In a BASIC expression the order in which the operations are performed is determined first by the indicated priority and then, within the same priority class, from left to right.

EXAMPLE 1 In the following expressions the circled numbers indicate the order in which the operations will be performed by the computer.

$$\begin{array}{c} \text{①} \quad \text{②} \\ \textbf{a.} \ 5 \ - \ 4 \ + \ 3 \ = \\ 1 \ \ + \ 3 \ = \\ 4 \end{array}$$

Since + and − have the same priority, they are performed from left to right. Note that performing the + first gives the different value −2.

$$\begin{array}{c} \text{③} \quad \text{①} \quad \text{②} \\ \textbf{b.} \ 2 \ + \ 6 \ / \ 4 \ * \ 3 \ = \\ 2 \ + \ 1.5 \ * \ 3 \ = \\ 2 \ + \ \ \ 4.5 \ \ = \\ 6.5 \end{array}$$

Since / and * have the same priority, they are performed from left to right. Note that performing the * first gives the different value 2.5.

$$\begin{array}{c} \text{③} \quad \text{①} \quad \text{④} \quad \text{②} \\ \textbf{c.} \ 5 \ * \ 2 \ \widehat{\ } \ 2 \ + \ 3 \ \widehat{\ } \ 2 \end{array}$$

Performing these operations one at a time, we obtain:

$$5 * 2 \wedge 2 + 3 \wedge 2 =$$
$$5 * \quad 4 \quad + 3 \wedge 2 =$$
$$5 * \quad 4 \quad + \quad 9 \quad =$$
$$20 \quad \quad + \quad 9 \quad =$$
$$29$$

$$\begin{array}{c} \text{②} \quad \text{①} \\ \textbf{d.} \ - \ 5 \ \wedge \ 2 \ = \\ -25 \end{array}$$

Since exponentiation (^) has the highest priority, it is performed first. Thus this expression, the negative of the square of 5, results in the value −25. Note that performing the − first gives the different value 25.

Parentheses may be used in BASIC expressions just as in ordinary algebra. They are used to override the usual order in which operations are performed. If you need the negation of the sum of A and B, for example, you can use the expression −(A + B). Parentheses may also be used to clarify the meaning of numerical expressions. For example, 5/2∗3 and (5/2)∗3 have the same meaning in BASIC, but the second form is less likely to be misinterpreted.

EXAMPLE 2   In this table, A = 3, B = −2, and C = 4:

BASIC expression	Value of expression
A/(2∗B)	−0.75
A/2∗B	−3
−(A+C)	−7
−A+C	1
(B+C)/(C−A)	2
B+C/C−A	−4
(B+C)^(−2)	0.25
(−B)^C	16
−B^C	−16
B^C	16

Roots of numbers may be indicated in BASIC by using the exponentiation operator ^. Recall from algebra that

$$\sqrt{9} = 9^{1/2} = 3$$

In BASIC, we write this as

9 ^ (1/2)   or   9 ^ 0.5

EXAMPLE 3   In this table, M = 4 and N = 5:

Algebraic expression	Equivalent BASIC expression	Value
$\sqrt{M}$	M^(1/2)	2
$\sqrt{M+N}$	(M+N)^0.5	3
$\sqrt[3]{2M}$	(2∗M)^(1/3)	2
$\sqrt[3]{7+MN}$	(7+M∗N)^(1/3)	3
$6\sqrt{5+M-N}$	6∗(5+M−N)^0.5	12

CAUTION   BASIC systems are not designed to take roots of negative numbers. For example, the cube root of −8 is −2, but the BASIC expression (−8)^(1/3) will not give this value. BASIC expressions such as A^B will result in an error if A is negative and B is not an integer.

Microsoft® BASIC also provides two additional operations to perform **integer division;** the first finds the *integer quotient* and the second the *integer remainder* when one integer is divided by another.

BASIC symbol	Illustration	Meaning
\	a\b	Find quotient when a is divided by b.
MOD	a MOD b	Find remainder when a is divided by b.

Note: If either a or b is not an integer, it is rounded to the nearest integer before the operation is performed.

In elementary school, before learning about decimals, you probably would have divided 11 by 4 as follows:

$$\begin{array}{r} 2 \text{ quotient} \\ 4\overline{)11} \\ \underline{8} \\ 3 \text{ remainder} \end{array}$$

This is precisely the division accomplished by \ and MOD. Thus 11\4 = 2 and 11 MOD 4 = 3. You could use 200\17 to determine the number of 17-cent adapters that could be purchased for 2 dollars and 200 MOD 17 to determine the change in cents.

EXAMPLE 4 In this table, A = 7, B = 2, C = 8.61, and D = 3.4:

BASIC expression	Value	
A \ B	3	
A MOD B	1	
B \ A	0	
B MOD A	2	
C \ D	3	(C and D are first rounded.)
C MOD D	0	

Table 3.1 gives the order of precedence for all arithmetic operations used by Microsoft® BASIC in evaluating numerical expressions.

Table 3.1 Priority of arithmetic operations

BASIC symbol	Operation	Priority
^	Exponentiation	1
−	Negation	2
* /	Multiplication, division	3
\	Integer quotient	4
MOD	Integer remainder	5
+ −	Addition, subtraction	6

EXAMPLE 5 In this table, M = 5, N = 8.9, and P = 3.2:

BASIC expression	Value of expression
M+N \ P	8
(M+N) \ P	4
P+N MOD M	7.2
2*M MOD P+1	2
21 \ M MOD P/2	0

■ 3.4 Problems

1. *Evaluate the following.*

   a. 2+3*5 **b.** 5*7−2 **c.** −4+2
   d. −(4+2) **e.** −3*5 **f.** −3^2
   g. 1+2^3*2 **h.** 6/2*3 **i.** 1/2/2
   j. −2*3/2*3 **k.** 2^2^3 **l.** −3*(4+0.1)
   m. −2^2*3 **n.** 1.23E7 **o.** 75E−5

p. 9^1/2	q. 9^0.5	r. (2+(3*4-5))^0.5
s. 3*4 MOD 5	t. 8\3 MOD 2	u. 2^3\2+1

2. For $A = 2$, $B = 3$, and $X = 2$, evaluate each of the following.

   a. A+B/X
   b. (A+B)/2*X
   c. B/A/X
   d. B/(A*X)
   e. A+X^3
   f. (A+B)^X
   g. B^A/X
   h. B+A/B-A
   i. A^B+X
   j. B^(X/A)
   k. -A^B
   l. (-A)^B
   m. (B*X+1) MOD A
   n. A^B\B
   o. B*X MOD A*X

3. Some of the following are not admissible BASIC expressions. Explain why.

   a. (Y+Z)X
   b. X2*36
   c. A*(2.1-7B)
   d. SUM*SUM
   e. KEY*7
   f. -(A+2B)
   g. 2X^2
   h. X2^2
   i. X-2^2
   j. A12+B3
   k. -9^0.5
   l. A2-(-A2)

4. Write BASIC expressions for these arithmetic expressions.

   a. $0.06P$
   b. $5x + 5y$
   c. $a^2 + b^2$
   d. $\dfrac{6}{5a}$
   e. $\dfrac{a}{b} + \dfrac{c}{d}$
   f. $\dfrac{a + b}{c + d}$
   g. $ax^2 + bx + c$
   h. $\sqrt{b^2 - 4ac}$
   i. $(x^2 + 4xy)/(x + 2y)$

5. Write equivalent BASIC expressions without using parentheses.

   a. ((X+1)+Y)
   b. (A+B)*(A-B)
   c. A*(A*(A+B)+1)
   d. (A*B)/C
   e. A/(B*C)
   f. X*(X*(X(X+D)+C)+B)+A
   g. P^(Q*R)
   h. 1/(A*B*C*D)

■ 3.5 The LET Statement: Assigning Values to Variables

In Section 3.3 you learned how to write arithmetic expressions in a form acceptable to the computer. Now we will show you how to instruct the computer to evaluate such expressions.

A BASIC statement preceded by a line number (unsigned integer) is called a BASIC **programming line**.* For example,

```
100 LET A=2+5
```

has **line number** 100 and contains the BASIC **statement** LET A = 2 + 5. This line will cause the computer to evaluate the sum 2 + 5 and then assign this value to the variable A.

A BASIC **program** is a collection of BASIC programming lines. The BASIC statements contained in these lines are executed by the computer in the order determined by increasing line numbers, unless one of the statements overrides this order. In this book we'll often use the expression *BASIC statement* to refer to a BASIC statement with its line number. This practice conforms to current programming terminology.

The general form of our first BASIC statement, the LET statement, is

ln LET **v** = **e**

or, more simply,

ln v = **e**   (LET is optional.)

where **ln** stands for line number, **v** denotes a variable name, and **e** denotes a BASIC expression that may simply be a constant. This statement directs the computer to

---

* Microsoft® BASIC allows more than one BASIC statement in a programming line (see Section 3.8).

evaluate the expression **e** and then assign this value to the variable **v**. Only numerical values may be assigned to numerical variables and only strings to string variables.

Examples 6 and 7 contain BASIC programs ready to be typed at the keyboard and executed. (The next chapter will show you how to do this.) The columns to the right of each program show how the values of variables are changed during program execution.

EXAMPLE 6   Assignment of numerical values:

	After execution of each statement	
The program	Value of P	Value of Q
100 LET P=12	12	0
110 LET Q=P/2+1	12	7
120 LET P=Q/2+1	4.5	7
130 LET Q=P/2+1	4.5	3.25
140 END	4.5	3.25

■ **REMARK 1**   Note that a zero value is shown for Q following execution of line 100. Microsoft® BASIC assigns a value of zero to all numerical variables at the time of program execution. This *initial* value is retained by each variable until the variable is reassigned a value by the program. Line 100 assigns only the value of 12 to P. Thus, at this point, Q still retains its initial value of zero.

■ **REMARK 2**   The practice of increasing line numbers by increments other than 1 is a good one (10 is very popular). This practice allows you to insert in their proper places additional statements that have been forgotten or are needed to modify a program.

■ **REMARK 3**   The END statement causes program execution to terminate. Later, you may need to include more than one END in a program. In Microsoft® BASIC, this is allowed.

■ **REMARK 4**   The END statement in this example is optional—program execution will automatically halt whenever the PC runs out of statements to execute. It is common practice, however, to write BASIC programs so that the last statement carried out is an END statement. The END statement in this example serves this purpose.

■ **REMARK 5**   Newly written programs seldom do what they were meant to do. The programmer must find and correct all errors. (The errors are called **bugs,** and making the corrections is referred to as **debugging** the program.) A useful debugging technique is to pretend that you are the computer and prepare a table of successive values of program variables as in this example. Such a table is called a **trace of the program** or, more simply, a **trace**.

EXAMPLE 7   Assignment of string values:

	After execution of each statement		
The program	Value of A$	Value of B$	Value of C$
200 LET A$="AND"	AND		
210 LET B$="SO"	AND	SO	
220 LET C$=B$	AND	SO	SO
230 LET B$=A$	AND	AND	SO
240 LET A$=C$	SO	AND	SO
250 END	SO	AND	SO

■ **REMARK 1**   Strings appearing in LET statements *must* be quoted. Note, however, that it is the *string* and not the *quoted string* that is assigned to the variable.

■ **REMARK 2**   Although no values are shown for B$ and C$ following execution of line 200, Microsoft® BASIC assigns an initial **empty string** (written "") to each string variable.

The BASIC statement

```
40 LET N=N+1
```

does not mean that N is equal to N + 1 (since that is impossible). It means that the expression N + 1 is *evaluated* and this value is *assigned* to the variable N. For example, the effect of the two programming lines

```
30 LET N=5
40 LET N=N+1
```

is that the value 6 is assigned to N. Similarly, the statement

```
70 LET S=S+Y
```

evaluates S + Y and then assigns this new value to S. Thus line 40 increases the value of N by 1 and line 70 increases the value of S by Y.

EXAMPLE 8 In this table, S = 3, Y = −2, H = −4, Z = 6, and M = 10:

BASIC statement	After execution
35 LET S=S+Y	S has the value 1.
90 LET H=H+2*Z	H has the value 8.
40 LET M=2*M−Z	M has the value 14.

■ 3.6 The PRINT Statement

Every computer language must be designed so that the results can be made available in a usable form. The Microsoft® BASIC statements PRINT and LPRINT meet this requirement: PRINT is used to direct output to the PC's display screen, and LPRINT is used to direct the output to a printer. The examples in this section illustrate the PRINT statement. LPRINT is described in Section 4.8.

The simplest form of the PRINT statement is

ln PRINT **e**

where **ln** denotes a line number and **e** denotes any string or numerical expression. When executed, this statement displays the value of the expression **e** and then causes a RETURN to be executed—that is, the screen cursor is positioned at the beginning of the next display line for subsequent output. Here are four admissible PRINT statements.

```
200 PRINT "THIS IS A MESSAGE."
210 PRINT 3-8*7
220 PRINT X
230 PRINT A$
```

If X has the value 723.45 and A$ has the string value END OF MESSAGE, lines 200 to 230 will produce the following output:

```
THIS IS A MESSAGE.
-53
 723.45
END OF MESSAGE
```

Note that the PC displays 723.45 with a leading blank as shown. This is the sign position, which is left blank when positive numbers are displayed.

As illustrated in the next example, BASIC allows you to display the values of more than one expression on a single line.

EXAMPLE 9 Displaying labels for output values.

```
100 REM ** AUTOMOBILE SALES TAX PROGRAM **
110 REM
120 PRINT "TAXATION DEPARTMENT"
130 LET PRICE=7295
140 PRINT "PRICE: ";PRICE
150 PRINT "SALES TAX: "; .05*PRICE
160 END
```

When this program is executed, it will produce the following output:

```
TAXATION DEPARTMENT
PRICE: 7295
SALES TAX: 364.75
```

Both line 140 and line 150 display a numerical value preceded by a label identifying what this value represents. Separating two expressions in a PRINT statement by a semicolon as in lines 140 and 150 causes the two values to be displayed next to each other—the blank space preceding each number in the output is the sign position mentioned previously.*

REMARK In this program, string constants are included in PRINT statements to display a heading (TAXATION DEPARTMENT) and two labels (PRICE: and SALES TAX:) identifying the numerical output values. You can also use string *variables* for this purpose. For instance, if you add the line

```
125 LET P$="PRICE: "
```

to the program and change line 140 to

```
140 PRINT P$;PRICE
```

the program will produce exactly the same output as before.

3.7 The REM Statement: Remarks as Part of a Program

In the program shown at the outset of this chapter, certain comments are included (lines 100 to 120) to indicate the program's purpose and to identify what values the variables X, Y, Z, and AV represent. The BASIC statement that allows you to insert such comments is the REM (REMark) statement. The general form is

ln REM comment

or

ln ' comment   (The apostrophe can replace the keyword REM.)

where **comment** denotes any comment or remark you may wish to include. REM statements cause nothing to happen when a program is executed by a computer. Their sole purpose is to allow you to include documentation as part of your programs. The following example further illustrates the use of REM statements.

EXAMPLE 10 Typical uses of REM statements.

```
100 REM PROGRAM TO DETERMINE THE RATE OF RETURN
110 REM GIVEN THE CURRENT PRICE AND EARNINGS
120 REM
```

---

* The forms of the PRINT statement described in this section are adequate for many programming tasks. Chapter 7 presents a more detailed description of how Microsoft® BASIC allows you to format your output values.

```
130 REM     P DENOTES THE CURRENT PRICE OF A SECURITY.
140 REM     E DENOTES THE RECENT ANNUAL EARNINGS.
150 REM     R DENOTES THE RATE OF RETURN.
160 REM
170 LET P=80.00
180 LET E=6.00
190 REM
200 REM CALCULATE THE RATE OF RETURN AND
210 REM PRINT SUMMARY RESULTS.
220 LET R=100*E/P
230 PRINT "PRICE: ";P
240 PRINT "EARNINGS: ";E
250 PRINT "RATE OF RETURN: ";R
260 END
```

If this program is executed, the output will be as follows:

```
PRICE: 80
EARNINGS: 6
RATE OF RETURN: 7.5
```

In the program, REM statements are used for four different purposes: to give a brief description of the program (lines 100 and 110); to separate one section of the program from another (lines 120, 160, and 190); to describe the values represented by the variables used (lines 130, 140, and 150); and to describe the action of certain groups of programming lines (lines 200 and 210). Using REM statements in this manner is an excellent programming practice. Your programs will be easier to read and understand, easier to modify later (should that be required), and easier to debug.

The comments in REM statements and the quoted messages in PRINT statements are intended for two different audiences. REM statements give information to people who actually read the program, whereas the messages in PRINT statements give information to users of the program. The needs of these two audiences are very different. For instance, a *reader* of your program may want to understand how the program carries out its task, but the *user* would be interested only in the results. To illustrate, consider the following statement:

```
200 REM --- CALCULATE THE GROSS PAY G ---
```

This informs the reader that the gross pay is denoted by G and that the programming lines that follow this statement will calculate this value. A user of the program, however, has no need for this information. To assist the user, you would include a statement such as

```
500 PRINT "GROSS PAY $";G
```

so that the output value G is labeled in a meaningful way. You would not use

```
500 PRINT "G=$";G
```

The user neither cares nor needs to know that G is used to denote the gross pay. Messages in PRINT statements should never presume that a user has read the program and is familiar with the variable names.

Good programming practice dictates that you include clarifying REM statements for someone reading your program, as well as messages in PRINT statements that are useful to the program user. For example, the following two programs calculate and display exactly the same value (278.16), but Program A gives no information to the reader concerning the purpose of the program nor to the user as to what the output value 278.16 represents. Program B, on the other hand, gives useful information to both the reader and the user.

Program A
```
10 LET X=38
20 LET Y=7.32
30 LET Z=X*Y
40 PRINT Z
50 END
```
Output: 278.16

Program B
```
10 REM PROGRAM TO COMPUTE GROSS PAY
20 REM    H DENOTES HOURS WORKED.
30 REM    R DENOTES HOURLY RATE.
40 LET H=38
50 LET R=7.32
60 REM CALCULATE THE GROSS PAY G.
70 LET G=H*R
80 PRINT "GROSS PAY";G
90 END
```
Output: GROSS PAY 278.16

As explained in the next section, the comments in Program B can be written as follows:

```
10 REM PROGRAM TO COMPUTE GROSS PAY
20 REM
30 LET H=38                  'Hours worked
40 LET R=7.32                'Hourly rate
50 LET G=H*R                 'Gross pay
60 PRINT "GROSS PAY";G
70 END
```

Output: GROSS PAY 278.16

■ 3.8 Multiple Statements in a Programming Line

To this point, each line of a BASIC program has contained only one BASIC statement. Microsoft® BASIC, however, allows you to include many statements in a single programming line—you simply separate the statements with colons. For example,

```
10 LET A=5 : LET B=7 : PRINT A+B
```

is an admissible Microsoft® BASIC programming line that assigns 5 to A and 7 to B before displaying their sum. The general form of a multiple-statement programming line is

ln *statement* {: *statement*}

where **ln** denotes a line number and *statement* denotes a BASIC statement without a line number.* The statements are executed from left to right unless one of them overrides this order. The number of statements allowed in a programming line is limited only by the 255 maximum number of characters per line.

If a multiple-statement line contains a REM statement, anything that follows the keyword REM is part of the remark. Thus the following two lines are admissible but not equivalent:

```
10 REM PRINT THE RESULT : PRINT X
10 PRINT X : REM PRINT THE RESULT
```

The first is simply a remark and will cause no action during program execution. The second will display the value of X.

Be cautious when using multiple-statement lines. Overusing them tends to clutter a program and obscure its meaning. Their appropriate uses will be illustrated as we go along. The following program shows how REM statements in this context can clarify the action of the program.

---

* The notation {*item*} means that *item* may be repeated one or more times or omitted entirely. (In this instance, *item* refers to : *statement*.)

EXAMPLE 11

Multiple-statement lines:

```
10 LET N=130         'Number sold
20 LET C=300         'Cost of each item
30 LET S=1.2*C       'Selling price of item
40 LET G=N*S         'Gross sales
50 LET P=G-N*C       'Profit
60 PRINT "SALES";G
70 PRINT "PROFIT";P
80 END
```

■ REMARK Lines 10–50 use REM statements as the last statement in a multiple-statement line. When these remarks are indicated by the apostrophe, rather than the keyword REM, the colon need not be used to separate them from the previous statement. Thus

```
10 LET N=130         'Number sold
```

and

```
10 LET N=130 : REM Number sold
```

are equivalent. Most programmers use the first form, and also take great care to align the comments as was done in this example.

■ 3.9 Problems

1. *Write LET statements to perform the indicated tasks.*

   a. Assign the value 7 to M.
   b. Increase the value assigned to B by 7.
   c. Double the value assigned to H.
   d. Assign the value of the expression $(A - B)/2$ to C2.
   e. Assign the tenth power of $1 + R$ to A.
   f. Decrease the value assigned to X by twice the value assigned to Y.
   g. Assign the string COST to C$.
   h. Replace the value of A$ by the string DOE,JANE.
   i. Store the contents of P$ in Q$.
   j. Assign the string ***** to S$.

2. *Which of these are inadmissible LET statements? Explain. (Be sure to check the table of reserved words.)*

   a. `10 LET X=(A+B)C`
   b. `15 LET M=A1-A2`
   c. `20 LET A+B=S`
   d. `25 LET DEPT#5=17`
   e. `30 LET A3=A*A*A`
   f. `35 LET 5M=2+7*X`
   g. `40 LET X=1.23E5`
   h. `45 LET Y%=X+0.5`
   i. `50 LET Z=4E2.5`
   j. `55 LET AREA=LENGTH*WIDTH`
   k. `60 LET SUM=SUM+NEXT`
   l. `65 LET DIFF=FIRST-SECOND`
   m. `70 LET A$=SAMMY`
   n. `75 LET NAME$="JANE DOE"`
   o. `80 LET P$=Y$`
   p. `85 LET "DEPT#7"=D$`
   q. `90 LET M="MONTHLY RENT"`
   r. `95 LET D$="A+B+5"`

3. *Which of these are inadmissible PRINT statements? Explain. (Be sure to check the table of reserved words.)*

   a. `10 PRINT SO-AND-SO`
   b. `15 PRINT SO.AND.SO`
   c. `20 PRINT "5+13=";5+13`
   d. `25 PRINT SPACE$;X`
   e. `30 PRINT "RATE-OF-RETURN"`
   f. `35 PRINT SEVEN$;7`
   g. `40 PRINT WIDTH`
   h. `45 PRINT "FINAL RESULT";AVERAGE`

4. *Show the output of each program.*

   a.
   ```
   100 LET A=5
   110 LET B=A+2
   ```

   b.
   ```
   10 LET P=100
   20 LET R=8
   ```

```
                    120 LET C=A+B                    30 LET I=R/100
                    130 PRINT "RESULT";C             40 LET A=P+I*P
                    140 END                          50 PRINT "AMOUNT=";A
                                                     60 END

              c.  500 LET X=0                   d. 10 LET A=2
                  510 LET X=X-1                    20 LET B=6
                  520 LET Y=X^2+3*X                30 LET A=2*A
                  530 PRINT "RESULT";Y             40 LET B=B/2
                  540 END                          50 LET C=(A^2+B^2)^(1/2)
                                                   60 PRINT "RESULT";C
                                                   70 END

              e.  10 LET L=10      'Length     f. 10 LET L$="LIST PRICE"
                  20 LET W=5       'Width         20 LET D$="DISCOUNT"
                  30 LET H=4       'Height        30 LET S$="SELLING PRICE"
                  40 LET V=L*W*H   'Volume        40 LET L=45
                  50 PRINT "VOLUME";V              50 LET D=(10/100)*L
                  60 LET L=W : H=W                 60 LET S=L-D
                  70 PRINT "VOLUME";V              70 PRINT L$;L
                  80 END                           80 PRINT D$;D
                                                   90 PRINT S$;S
                                                   99 END

              g. 10 PRINT "BOBBY LOVES"       h. 10 LET A%=7 : B%=5
                 20 LET M$="MARY. "              20 LET B%=A%/B%
                 30 LET B$="BARB. "              30 LET M=A%+B%
                 40 LET B$=M$                    40 PRINT M\5
                 50 LET M$=B$                    50 PRINT M MOD 3+1
                 60 PRINT M$                     60 END
                 70 END
```

5. *Complete the tables of values as in Examples 4 and 5.*

a.
```
10 LET A=1 : B=2 : C=1
20 LET C=C+B
30 LET A=B^2
40 LET B=C-B+A
50 LET C=C-1 : B=A*B
60 LET A=A/C : C=B/A+1
70 END
```

A	B	C

b.
```
10 LET N=1 : PRINT N
20 LET N=N*(N+1) : PRINT N
30 LET N=N*(N+1) : PRINT N
40 LET N=N*(N+1) : PRINT N
50 END
```

N	Output

c.
```
100 LET X=0
110 LET Y=X+7
120 LET Z=Y+X^2
130 PRINT Z
140 LET X=Z
150 LET Y=X*Y*Z
160 PRINT Y
170 END
```

X	Y	Z	Output

6. *Prepare tables showing the successive values of all variables and the output.*

```
a. 10 LET S=0 : A=25
   20 LET S=S+A : PRINT S
   30 LET S=S+A : PRINT S
   40 LET S=S/2 : PRINT S
   50 END
```

```
b. 100 LET X=1.5
   110 LET Y=3/(2*X+2)
   120 PRINT Y
   130 LET X=-X
   140 PRINT X
   150 PRINT Y
   160 END
```

```
c. 10 LET N=130       'COUNT
   20 LET C=3.00      'COST
   30 LET S=1.2*C     'PRICE
   40 LET G=N*S : PRINT "SALES";G
   50 LET P=G-N*C : PRINT "PROFIT";P
   60 END
```

```
d. 100 PRINT "NTH POWERS OF 10"
   110 LET A=10 : P=10
   120 PRINT "FOR N=1";P
   130 LET P=A*P
   140 PRINT "FOR N=2";P
   150 LET P=A*P
   160 PRINT "FOR N=3";P
   170 LET P=A*P
   180 PRINT "FOR N=4";P
   190 REM "END OF TABLE"
   200 END
```

■ 3.10 Review True-or-False Quiz

1. Parentheses may be used only to override the usual order in which numerical operations are performed by the computer.   T F
2. A BASIC program is a collection of BASIC programming lines.   T F
3. (A + B)^0.5 and (A + B)^1/2 have the same meaning.   T F
4. 2/3 is a numerical constant in BASIC.   T F
5. 1.0E1 = 10.   T F
6. If A = 3, the statement 43 LET 1+A^2=B1 assigns the value 10 to the variable B1.   T F
7. 150 LET A3=A3*A3 is a valid BASIC statement.   T F
8. 300 LET M="1984" is a valid BASIC statement.   T F
9. 350 LET X=X+1 is a valid BASIC statement but will result in an error because there is no number X for which X = X + 1.   T F
10. 400 PRINT HARRY is a valid BASIC statement, but it will not display the name HARRY.   T F
11. 500 PRINT A+B : 510 PRINT A*B is a valid programming line.   T F
12. 600 INT=A+B : PRINT INT is a valid programming line.   T F
13. REM statements can be used to display messages during program execution.   T F
14. Comments appearing in REM statements must be enclosed in quotation marks.   T F
15. The programming line 250 LET A=5 : B=A assigns the same value to both A and B.   T F
16. NUM# is an admissible variable name.   T F

4 First Session at the Keyboard

In Chapter 3 we presented examples of BASIC programs ready to be typed at the PC keyboard. Before beginning to type a program, you must have Microsoft® BASIC up and running. Three versions of BASIC are available on the PC—*cassette, disk,* and *advanced.* All of the material in this book except Chapter 17 and parts of Chapter 19 can be performed in any of the three versions.

Getting BASIC up and running is not difficult. The steps you must take to activate a particular version are described in Appendix A. The purpose of this chapter is to show how BASIC programs are entered at the PC keyboard and also to guide you in your first encounter with the computer. In what follows, we assume that BASIC is operational. As described in Appendix A, this means that the screen displays the **BASIC prompt Ok** followed on the next line by a blinking underscore character _ called the **cursor.**

To get the most out of this chapter, you are urged to read through the material quickly to get a general idea of what is involved, and then to read it again, this time being sure to try the examples on your computer.

■ 4.1 The PC Keyboard

The keys on the PC keyboard are organized into three general areas. To get started, you will need only the middle portion, labeled *typewriter keyboard* in Figure 4.1. This area contains keys for the 26 letters of the English alphabet, the digits 0 through 9, and certain other familiar characters, such as $ # , . ; : = ( ) - /. In addition, there are the space bar, two shift keys ⇧ which allow the typing of uppercase letters or the top character on the keys that type two characters, and several other keys whose functions are explained as the need arises. At the outset, you should learn how to use the following four special keys.

This is the **Enter key.** After typing a programming line, you must press this key to *enter* the line as part of the program. This key is also used to enter other information you type. (See Section 4.2.)

This key is an ON/OFF switch: press it once to type all uppercase letters; press it again to return to lowercase. This key affects only the letter keys; you must still use the shift key to obtain the top characters on those keys that type two characters. Experiment!

When typing a BASIC program, you can use any combination of upper- and lowercase letters. Keywords and variable names typed in lowercase letters, however, will be converted to uppercase letters by BASIC; remarks and string constants will be left as typed.

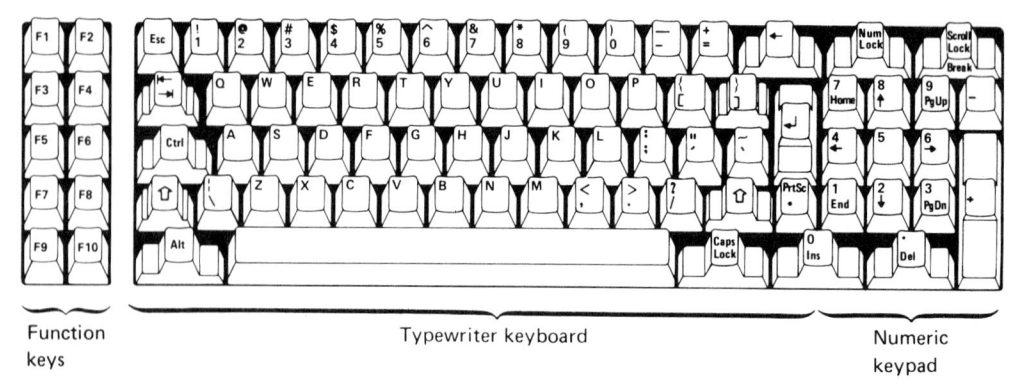

Figure 4.1 The IBM PC keyboard.

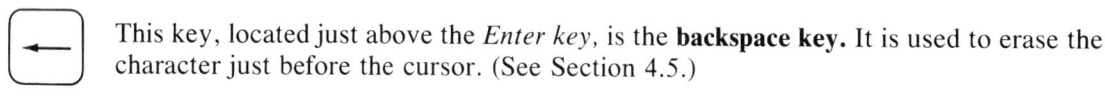

This key, located just above the *Enter key,* is the **backspace key.** It is used to erase the character just before the cursor. (See Section 4.5.)

PrtSc stands for **Print Screen.** It is used to obtain a printed copy of whatever appears on the screen. Since PrtSc is at the top of the key, you must press it while holding down the shift key. (See Section 4.8.)

All keys on the PC keyboard are **typematic;** that is, they repeat as long as you hold them down. You should find this keyboard feature to be very helpful.

■ 4.2 Entering a Programming Line

Here is a program ready to be entered at the keyboard:

```
100 REM      First session at the
110 REM      IBM Personal Computer
120 REM Find sum and product.
130 let a=5
140 let b=8
150 let sum=a+b
160 let product=a*b
170 end
```

Before you begin typing this program, type

NEW ⏎

NEW is the first of several commands referred to as **system commands.** A system command has no line number and is not part of a BASIC program. It is an instruction to the computer to do a specific task at the time the command is issued. The NEW command clears the part of the PC's random access memory (RAM) in which BASIC programs are stored. It is carried out as soon as you press the Enter key. Now type the first line of the program and enter the line by pressing ⏎. Your screen should display

```
NEW
Ok
100 REM      First session at the
_
```

The BASIC prompt Ok tells you that the PC is ready for you to make another entry. The underscore character _ denotes the cursor. When a line being typed begins with a number (100, in this case), pressing the Enter key causes the line to be entered (stored in the computer's memory); it is not executed. You then continue typing.

```
110 REM      IBM Personal Computer
120 REM Find sum and product.
130 let a=5
140 let b=8
150 let sum=a+b
160 let product=a*b
170 end
```

Remember you must press ⏎ to enter each line. If you make a typing error, simply press ⏎ and retype the entire line, including the line number.

Since this program contains no PRINT statement, there will be no output if it is executed. To rectify this situation, you could add PRINT lines by typing the following:

```
155 Print "Sum is";sum
165 Print "Product is";product
```

BASIC allows you to enter these lines out of their natural numerical order; the program will still be executed according to the sequence of line numbers from smallest to largest. Thus if you omit a line in typing a program, you can insert it at any time before execution simply by typing it and pressing ⏎.

The PC's video screen is limited to 25 horizontal display lines.* As you undoubtedly have discovered, making an entry on the twenty-fourth line causes it and all lines above it to be moved up, with the top line being scrolled off the screen. (In Microsoft® BASIC, the twenty-fifth line is not scrolled up.) Scrolling a line off the screen in no way affects what has already been stored in memory. Indeed, you can even clear your entire program from the screen without affecting the program. To do this, type

```
CLS ⏎
```

The command CLS clears the first 24 lines and moves the cursor to the upper left corner of the screen. Your program, although not visible, remains intact.

■ 4.3 Spacing and the Length of a Programming Line

Spaces may be used to improve the appearance and readability of BASIC programs. During program execution, the only significant spaces are those that appear in quoted strings and those that separate BASIC keywords from other items in a programming line. All other spaces are ignored; thus, the three programming lines

```
130 LET S=P+Q
130 LET      S = P + Q
130      LET S=P+Q
```

are equivalent BASIC statements.

Good programming practice dictates that this freedom of spacing be used to advantage; a program listing should be easy to read. Here are two helpful rules.

1. Insert at least one space before and after each BASIC keyword such as LET, PRINT, REM, and END. Thus, write

   ```
   130 LET S=P+Q
   ```

   but not

   ```
   130LETS=P+Q
   ```

---

* The twenty-fifth line displays information concerning the use of the function keys F1–F10 on the left side of the PC keyboard. These keys are discussed in Section 4.4.

2. (This rule must be observed.) Do not insert spaces within BASIC keywords, variables, line numbers, or constants. Thus, write

```
250 LET S=X1 + 24.75
```

but not

```
2 50 L E T S= X 1 + 24. 75
```

Each display line on the PC's video screen has a maximum capacity of 80 characters. Should you need to enter a programming line that exceeds this 80-character maximum, just keep typing and the PC will automatically continue onto the next display line. In all, a programming line can contain up to 255 characters counting ⏎. This means that a programming line can occupy three complete display lines (240 characters) plus part of a fourth line. Here is an admissible programming line:

```
500 LET FIRST=25 : SECOND=5*FIRST :
    PRINT "Starting value is"; FIRST :
    PRINT "Next value is"; SECOND
```

After typing the colon at the end of the first and second lines, simply hold down the space bar until the cursor moves to the desired position on the next line. Do not press the Enter key to move to the second and third lines; that will terminate the statement.

■ 4.4 The System Commands LIST and RUN—The Function Keys F1 and F2

The command LIST is used to display some or all of the programming lines you have entered.

Command	Effect
LIST	Entire program is listed.
LIST ln	Only line ln is listed.
LIST ln$_1$ – ln$_2$	Lines ln$_1$ through ln$_2$ are listed.

We illustrate the LIST command for the program entered in Section 4.2. Although the symbol is not shown, the Enter key must be pressed after each LIST command.

```
LIST                                  (You type this.)
100 REM     First session at the      (Displayed by the PC.)
110 REM     IBM Personal Computer
120 REM Find sum and product.
130 LET A=5
140 LET B=8
150 LET SUM=A+B
155 PRINT "Sum is";SUM
160 LET PRODUCT=A*B
165 PRINT "Product is";PRODUCT
170 END
Ok
List 155                              (You type this.)
155 PRINT "Sum is";SUM                (Displayed by the PC.)
Ok
List 130-150                          (You type this.)
130 LET A=5                           (Displayed by the PC.)
140 LET B=8
150 LET SUM=A+B
Ok
—
```

Note that lines 155 and 165 have been inserted in their proper places even though they were actually typed after line 170. Note also that keywords and variable names are displayed in uppercase letters, but remarks and string constants are left as typed. The command LIST, like all system commands, can be entered in lower- or uppercase letters.

When you are reasonably certain you've typed the program correctly, you can cause it to be executed (run) by typing RUN ⏎. The command RUN causes the program statements to be executed according to the sequence of their line numbers. We illustrate for the program just entered.

```
RUN               (You type this.)
Sum is 13         (Displayed by the PC.)
Product is 40
Ok
—
```

At this point, you can save the program for later use by using the SAVE command. Appendix C describes how to do this.

The bottom line (line 25) of the display screen lists 10 of the commands available while BASIC is operational. These commands are associated, in order, with the 10 **function keys** F1, F2, . . ., F10 at the left of the PC keyboard (Figure 4.1). Pressing a function key is equivalent to typing what is shown for that key in line 25. For instance, 1LIST means that pressing F1 is equivalent to typing LIST, and 2RUN← means that pressing F2 is equivalent to typing RUN ⏎. Thus, to list your program press F1 and ⏎; to run your program, simply press F2.

As you learn more about BASIC, you will find some, or all, of the other function keys useful. Appendix E.9 shows how the commands associated with the function keys can be changed, should that be desired.

■ 4.5 Making Corrections

During a session at the keyboard you will most likely make occasional typing errors. As mentioned previously, you can change any line in a program simply by retyping the entire line, including its line number. To erase a line, type its line number and then press ⏎. (In all subsequent examples, we will show the BASIC prompt Ok and cursor only if doing so helps to clarify what is being illustrated.)

EXAMPLE 1   **Changing and deleting program lines:**

```
30 LET Z=5        (You type this.)
40 PRINT X
50 LET Z-7=X
60 PRINT X
70 END
40                (Delete line 40.)
50 LET X=Z-7      (Correct line 50.)
LIST

30 LET Z=5        (Displayed by the PC.)
50 LET X=Z-7
60 PRINT X
70 END
```

BASIC also allows you to make corrections as you are typing a line—that is, before you press ⏎. This editing feature requires the use of the backspace key ⟵ positioned just above the Enter key ⏎. (A similar key ⬅ to the right of the Enter key serves a different purpose, as explained in Appendix E.) Suppose, while typing the line

   55 PRINT M

you notice that you have typed

   55 PTIN

42   Chapter 4   First Session at the Keyboard

At this point you can press the backspace key three times. This moves the cursor back three spaces, erasing characters as it moves:

    55 P_

Then type the correct character R and continue as usual. Appendix E describes other editing features that you will find helpful in correcting your BASIC programs.

■ 4.6 Error Messages

You may not always be fortunate enough to detect *syntax errors* (violations of BASIC rules of grammar) before attempting to run your program. Should you issue the RUN command for such an incorrect program, the PC will display an error message indicating the line number at which the error occurs, followed by the Ok prompt and then the program line as entered. The next example illustrates how error messages can help you to correct a program.

EXAMPLE 2   **Finding and correcting syntax errors:**

```
10 LET X=7                       (You type this.)
20 LET X+9=Z
30 PRINT 'ANSWER IS';Z
40 END
RUN
Syntax error in 20              (Displayed by the PC.)
Ok
20 LET X+9=Z
20 LET Z=X+9                    (You type this.)
RUN
Syntax error in 30              (Displayed by the PC.)
Ok
30 PRINT 'ANSWER IS';Z
30 PRINT "ANSWER IS";Z          (You type this.)
RUN
ANSWER IS 16                    (Displayed by the PC.)
Ok
```

As illustrated in the following example, error messages are sometimes displayed even though a program contains no syntax errors.

EXAMPLE 3   **Here is a syntactically correct program with an error.**

The following program is designed to compute the ratio

$$\frac{\text{Cost} + \text{markup}}{\text{Cost} - \text{markup}}$$

```
10 REM C DENOTES THE COST.
20 LET C=100
30 REM M DENOTES THE MARKUP.
40 LET M=100
50 LET R=(C+M)/(C-M)
60 PRINT "RATIO =";R
70 END
RUN
Division by zero

RATIO = 1.701412E38
Ok
```

Each line in the program is an admissible BASIC statement; hence the program is syntactically correct. When run, the computer assigns 100 to C (line 20), assigns 100 to M (line 40), and then attempts to evaluate the expression in line 50. The error message tells you that the computer does not "know" how to divide by zero. Under these circumstances, BASIC assigns the value 1.701412E38 (known as *machine infinity*) to R and allows the program to continue. The error message should warn you that the output is not correct. Programming errors that cause error messages during program execution are called **run-time errors.**

Unfortunately, error messages are not always displayed when incorrect programs are run. Here is a program with an error that the computer will not detect.

```
10 REM COMPUTE THE AVERAGE OF X AND Y.
20 REM THIS PROGRAM IS SYNTACTICALLY CORRECT
30 REM BUT PRODUCES INCORRECT RESULTS.
40 LET X=10
50 LET Y=5
60 LET AV=X+Y/2
70 PRINT "AVERAGE IS";AV
80 END
RUN

AVERAGE IS 12.5
```

The computer does precisely what you instruct it to do; it does not do what you meant it to do. The programming error in line 60 is an error in the *logic* of the program. It is not a syntax or run-time error. Such programming errors can be very difficult to find.

■ 4.7 Immediate and Deferred Execution Modes

You will recall that we have been typing each NEW, CLS, LIST, and RUN command without a line number, whereas each REM, PRINT, END, and LET statement has been preceded by a line number. In Microsoft® BASIC, each line whose first character is a digit (0–9) is entered as a programming line and is not executed until a RUN command has been issued. This is called **deferred execution mode**—execution of the statement (or statements) contained in the line is deferred until later. If a keyboard entry does not begin with a line number (that is, if the first character is not a digit), the PC will understand the entry as a command to be carried out immediately. This is called **immediate execution mode.***

Each BASIC statement and command described to this point can be issued in either deferred or immediate mode. Here is an illustration showing LET, PRINT, and LIST.

Display screen	Explanation
PRINT 2+3*5 17 Ok	The PRINT statement is executed as soon as the enter key is pressed.
LET A=24 Ok	The PC reserves memory space for the variable A and assigns the value 24 to A.
PRINT A+25 49 Ok	The PRINT statement is executed as soon as the enter key is pressed. Note that A has retained the value 24.
B=A+2 Ok	The PC reserves memory space for the variable B and assigns the value 26 to B. (Recall that the key word LET is optional.)
200 LIST	The LIST command is entered as line 200 of the BASIC program being typed. It will not be carried out until the program is executed.

* The terms *direct* and *indirect mode* are sometimes used for *immediate* and *deferred mode*, respectively.

Immediate execution mode can often be used effectively while you are debugging a program. After a program has been run, the PC retains the final values of all variables. Thus if your program produces incorrect results, you can use PRINT statements to examine these final values. This information may be just what you need to locate the error. We illustrate with a short program that contains a single error.

EXAMPLE 4 **Immediate mode and debugging.**

```
100 REM INCREASE SALARY BY 4.5 PERCENT.
110 REM
120 LET OLDSAL=24500            'Old salary
130 LET RAISE=4.5*OLDSAL        '4.5% raise
140 LET NEWSAL=OLDSAL+RAISE     'New salary
150 REM
160 PRINT "OLD SALARY: ";OLDSAL
170 PRINT "NEW SALARY: ";NEWSAL
180 END
RUN
OLD SALARY: 24500
NEW SALARY: 134750
Ok
```

Clearly this program has a bug—the new salary amount is much too large. Let's examine the final values of the variables:

```
PRINT OLDSAL
 24500
Ok
PRINT RAISE
 110250
Ok
```

At this point we can see that OLDSAL is correct (assigned in line 120) but RAISE (assigned in line 130) is not. Thus the error must be in line 130. You would now type

```
130 LET RAISE=.045*OLDSAL
```

and run the program again to get the correct result.

If you enter an inadmissible immediate mode instruction, the PC will usually display:

```
Syntax error
Ok
```

Nothing you type gently at the keyboard can harm the PC. If at any time the PC behaves in a way you don't understand, you can try to retrieve the Ok prompt by using the **Break key** (top right key): hold down the key labeled Ctrl (to the left of A) and press the Break key. This is called the **Control-Break** (or **Ctrl-Break**) **command.** In most cases the PC will respond by displaying the Ok prompt. If nothing works, simply turn off the PC and start over. No harm will have been done and, at worst, you will have to retype your program.

Since most BASIC statements and commands can be used in exactly the same way (with and without line numbers), you may wonder why some are called *statements* and others *commands*. By tradition, the term *command* (or *system command*) refers to an instruction to the computer that operates principally on programs. For example, LIST produces a program listing, RUN causes a program to be executed, and NEW clears a program from the computer's memory. If we deviate from this tradition, it is simply because computer terminology is not always exact. It is constantly changing to keep up with advances in computer technology.

■ 4.8 Directing Output to the Printer

Thus far in your work at the PC, every character typed by you at the keyboard, or generated as the result of some action by the computer, has appeared only on the display screen. Often, though, you will want a printed copy of your program or its output. For this your PC must be equipped with a printer, connected by cable to an adapter at the rear of the computer.

To obtain a printed copy of your program, first make sure the printer is turned on, and then type the command LLIST rather than LIST. After the program is printed, the BASIC prompt Ok will be displayed on the screen.

To have output from your program transmitted to the printer rather than displayed on the screen, use the LPRINT statement in place of the PRINT statement and run your program as usual. For example, the statement

```
50 LPRINT "THIS GOES TO THE PRINTER"
```

will print THIS GOES TO THE PRINTER on the printer but will not display it on the screen. To print and display the string BOTH PLACES, you can use the two statements

```
180 PRINT "BOTH PLACES"
190 LPRINT "BOTH PLACES"
```

As mentioned in Section 4.1, you can use the **PrtSc key** to obtain a printed copy of whatever appears on the display screen. You simply press the PrtSc key while holding down the shift key. Your printed copy will contain every character displayed on the screen, and in the same format. If you don't want the information that appears on the bottom screen line (line 25) to be printed, you must erase it before issuing the PrtSc command. To do this, type

```
KEY OFF ⏎
```

To get the bottom line back, type

```
KEY ON ⏎
```

If you have version 2.1 or later of the IBM disk operating system, you can use the Ctrl key with the PrtSc key to instruct the computer to direct all output to the printer and screen simultaneously. To do this, press the PrtSc key while holding down the Ctrl key. This command acts as an on/off switch and is in effect until issued a second time.

■ 4.9 On Writing Your First Program

You are now ready to write your first program. Since a computer program is an algorithm (that is, a set of instructions to the computer to carry out a specified task), the principles of algorithm design described in Chapter 2 are also principles of program design. They will help you design algorithms that are both correct and easily translated into BASIC programs. Following is a brief summary of these principles:

1. *Input/output specification.* Begin by describing the input (information needed to carry out the specified task) and the output (the results to be obtained and the form in which they should appear). Giving a clear and precise description of the input and output is an effective way to acquire an understanding of a problem statement. This principle of program design should be observed even for the relatively simple problems you will first encounter. The experience you gain while identifying and describing the input and output for simple problems will help you when you are confronted with problems that are not so simple.

2. *Modularization.* Identify individual subtasks that must be performed while carrying out the specified task. As illustrated in Chapter 2, the job of writing an algorithm (or program) is often simplified if the given task is broken down into simpler, more manageable subtasks. The importance of this principle of program design will become increasingly more evident as you learn more of the BASIC language and are confronted with more substantial programming problems.

3. Stepwise refinement. As illustrated in Chapter 2, you begin with a simple algorithm that contains few details but is known to be correct. (This initial algorithm can be a one-step algorithm describing the task to be carried out.) If necessary, you refine (break down) one or more of the steps to obtain a more detailed algorithm. If even more detail is needed, refine one or more steps in the derived algorithm. This process of stepwise refinement is repeated until you obtain an algorithm with whatever detail you need. The significance of this approach is that you can be sure that the final detailed algorithm is correct just by knowing that you started with a correct algorithm and that each step was refined correctly. As with modularization, the value of this principle of program design will become increasingly more evident as you progress in your study of programming.

The development of programming habits, both good and bad, begins with your first program. The following five-step approach to programming is presented to help you get started. It is not a complete description of the programming process but is adequate for many programming tasks, including those you will first encounter. Example 5 illustrates the application of this five-step process. At the end of this chapter you will be asked to write some programs. To learn good programming habits from the start, you should follow this five-step approach to programming.

1. *Be sure you thoroughly understand what is being asked in the problem statement.* A good way to do this is to identify the following items:

   Input: Data to be presented to the computer for processing.

   Output: The results called for in the problem statement. This may involve identifying what the output values are and in what form they are to be displayed.

2. *Identify what, if any, mathematical equations will be needed.* For example, to find the total cost C, including the 5% sales tax, of a television set listed at L dollars, you could use the equation

   $C = L + 0.05 \times L$

3. *Devise a step-by-step process (algorithm) that, if carried out, will result in a correct solution.* For simple programming tasks, this step usually is not difficult. For example, to find the total cost of the television set referred to above, you could use the following algorithm:

   a. Assign a value to L.
   b. Calculate $C = L + 0.05 \times L$.
   c. Print the result C and stop.

4. *Write the program statements to carry out the algorithm you have described.* This is called *coding the program*. Be sure to include adequate and meaningful REM statements.

5. *Debug the program.* This means running it to test for syntax errors and also to convince yourself that the program produces correct results.

EXAMPLE 5   Write a program to calculate the simple interest and the amount due for a loan of P dollars, at an annual interest rate R, for a time of T years. Use the program to find the interest and amount due when P = $600, R = 0.1575, and T = 2.

A quick reading of this problem statement shows that the input and output values are as follows:

Input: P, R, and T.

Output: Simple interest and the amount due.

We should all recognize the familiar formulas that govern this situation:

Simple interest: $I = P \times R \times T$

Amount due: $A = P + I$

Knowing these formulas, we can write the following algorithm:

    a. Assign values to P, R, and T.
    b. Calculate the interest I and the amount due A.
    c. Display the results (I and A) and stop.

THE PROGRAM
```
100 REM SIMPLE INTEREST PROGRAM
110 REM   P DENOTES AMOUNT OF LOAN.
120 REM   R DENOTES ANNUAL INTEREST RATE.
130 REM   T DENOTES TERM OF LOAN IN YEARS.
140 REM
150 REM ASSIGN VALUES TO P, R, AND T.
160 LET P=600
170 LET R=.1575
180 LET T=2
190 REM
200 REM CALCULATE THE INTEREST I AND AMOUNT DUE A.
210 LET I=P*R*T
220 LET A=P+I
230 REM
240 REM PRINT THE RESULTS.
250 PRINT "INTEREST: "; I
260 PRINT "AMOUNT DUE: "; A
270 END
RUN

INTEREST: 189
AMOUNT DUE: 789
```

REMARK 1   To find the interest and amount due for other loans, simply change the given values at lines 160, 170, and 180. To test the program, try values for P, R, and T for which you know the results. For instance, P = 100, R = 0.06, and T = 1 should yield

```
INTEREST: 6
AMOUNT DUE: 106
```

Another good test would be P = 1, R = 0, and T = 1, which should yield

```
INTEREST: 0
AMOUNT DUE: 1
```

In Chapter 5 you will see how different values can be assigned to P, R, and T without having to retype programming lines.

REMARK 2   Notice that the REM statements in lines 150, 200, and 240 correspond to the three steps in the algorithm written for this example. Not only does this emphasize how the coding process follows from the algorithm, but it also suggests that each step in an algorithm should contain enough detail so that it can be coded easily. Writing your algorithms according to this principle and using the individual steps as REM statements are excellent programming practices.

■ 4.10 Problems

In problems 1–4, assume that the lines shown are typed immediately after the command NEW has been carried out. What will be displayed if the LIST command is entered? The RUN command?

1. 100 LET A=14
   110 LET B=20
   120 LET S=A+B
   130 PRINT "SUM IS S"
   140 END
   110 LET B=30
   130 PRINT "SUM IS";S

2. 100 LET X=5
   110 LET X=10
   120 LET Y=20
   130 PRINT "X+Y"=S
   110
   125 LET S=X+Y
   130 PRINT "X+Y=";S
   140 END
   150 RUN
   150

3. 100 PRINT "DISCOUNT CALCULATION"
   100 REM DISCOUNT PROGRAM
   100
   110 LET P=120
   120 LET D=0.1*P
   130 LET P=P-D
   140 PRINT "DISCOUNT";D
   150 PRINT "COST";C
   130 LET C=P-D
   160 END

4. 100 LET L$=AVERAGE
   110 LET A=5
   120 LET B=7
   130 LET M=A+B/2
   140 PRINT L$;M
   150 END
   110 LET A=9
   130 LET M=(A+B)/2
   100 LET L$="AVERAGE"

In Problems 5–10, the programs contain one or more bugs—either syntax errors (violations in the BASIC rules of grammar) or programming errors (errors in the logic of a program). Find each bug and tell which type of error it is. Then correct the programs, and show the output that will be generated if the corrected programs are run.

5. 10 REM PROGRAM TO COMPUTE
   20 REM SIX PERCENT OF $23,000
   30 LET D=23,000
   40 LET R=6
   50 LET R*D=A
   60 PRINT "ANSWER IS";A
   70 END

6. 10 REM PROGRAM TO AVERAGE
   20 REM TWO NUMBERS
   30 LET N1=24
   40 LET N2=15
   50 LET A=N1+N2/2
   60 PRINT AVERAGE IS;A
   70 END

7. 10 REM SALES TAX PROGRAM
   20 REM T=TAX RATE : T=5
   30 REM P=PRICE : P=120
   40 LET S=P+(T/100)*P
   50 PRINT "TOTAL COST: ";S
   60 END

8. 10 REM PROGRAM TO FIND SOLUTION X
   20 REM TO THE FOLLOWING EQUATION:
   30 REM   35X+220=0
   40 LET A=35
   50 LET B=220
   60 LET A*X+B=0
   70 PRINT "SOLUTION IS";X
   80 END

9. 100 REM PROGRAM TO SWAP THE VALUES OF A$ AND B$
   110 LET A$="STOCK"
   120 LET B$="BOND"
   130 PRINT "A$=";A$
   140 PRINT "B$=";B$
   150 REM INTERCHANGE A$ AND B$.
   160 LET A$=B$
   170 LET B$=A$

```
        180 PRINT "A$=";A$
        190 PRINT "B$=";B$
        200 END
```

10.
```
        100 REM "PROGRAM TO COMPUTE THE EXCISE TAX ON TWO CARS"
        110 REM "VALUED AT V DOLLARS, IF THE RATE IS $66 PER $1000."
        120 LET V=4500
        130 LET R=66/1000
        140 LET T=V*R
        150 PRINT TAX ON FIRST CAR IS T
        160 LET V=5700
        170 PRINT TAX ON SECOND CAR IS T
        180 END
```

Write a BASIC program for each of the tasks listed below. Be sure to follow the guidelines suggested in Section 4.9. Use PRINT statements to label all output values, and be sure to include adequate comments.

11. Compute the selling price S for an article whose list price is L if the rate of discount is D percent.
12. Compute the original price if an article is now selling at S dollars after a discount of D percent.
13. Compute the state gasoline tax in dollars paid by a driver who travels M miles per year if the car averages G miles per gallon and the tax is T cents per gallon.
14. Find the commission C on sales of S dollars if the rate of commission is R percent.
15. Find the principal P that, if invested at a rate of interest R for time T years, yields the simple interest I. (Recall that $I = P \times R \times T$.)
16. Compute the weekly salary, both gross G and net N, for a person who works H hours a week for D dollars an hour (no overtime). Deductions are S percent for state taxes and F percent for federal taxes.
17. Compute the batting average A of a baseball player who has S singles, D doubles, T triples, and H home runs in B times at bat. (A = number of hits/B.)
18. Compute the slugging percentage P of the baseball player who is described in Problem 17 (P = total bases/B.)
19. Find the total cost C of four tires if the list price of each is L dollars, the federal excise tax is E dollars per tire, and the sales tax is S percent.
20. Compute the total cost C of a table listed at L dollars selling at a discount of D percent if the sales tax is S percent.
21. Convert degrees Celsius to degrees Fahrenheit [$F = (9/5)C + 32$]. Run the program for several values of C, including $C = 0$ and $C = 100$.
22. Convert degrees Fahrenheit to degrees Celsius. Run the program for several values of F, including $F = 0$, $F = 32$, and $F = 212$.
23. Convert pounds L to grams G (1 oz = 28.3495 g).
24. Convert grams G to pounds L.
25. Convert yards Y to meters M. Run for several values of Y, including 1760 (1 in. = 2.54 cm).
26. Convert meters M to yards Y. Run for several values of M, including 1 and 1000.
27. Compute the area of a triangle of base B and height H.
28. Compute both the circumference and the area of a circle given the radius. Use $\pi = 3.14159$.
29. Solve the equation $AX + B = 0$. Run the program for several values of A and B, including the case $A = 0$.
30. Find the total taxes T on the McCormick property assessed at D dollars if the rate is R dollars per 1,000. If the community uses X percent of all taxes for schools, find how much of the McCormick tax is spent for schools.
31. The market value of a home is M dollars, the assessment rate is A percent of the market value, and the tax rate is R dollars per 1,000. Compute the property tax.
32. Compute the volume and surface area of a rectangular solid.

33. Compute the area of a triangle whose sides are a, b, and c. (Heron's formula for such a triangle is $A = \sqrt{s(s-a)(s-b)(s-c)}$, where $s = (a + b + c)/2$.)
34. A tin can is H inches high and the radius of its circular base is R inches. Calculate the volume and surface area. (Volume = area of base × height. Curved surface area = circumference of base × height.)
35. The equation

$$A = P \times \left(1 + \frac{R}{C}\right)^{N \times C}$$

is an alternative form of the compound interest formula that gives the amount A in an account after N years on an investment of P dollars at an annual interest rate of R percent if the interest is compounded C times per year. Use this form in a program to help you determine the better investment: $1,000 for one year at 8% compounded semiannually or $1,000 for one year at 7.75% compounded daily. (Note that, for the rate 8%, R must be 8/100 or 0.08 and not 8.)

■ 4.11 Review True-or-False Quiz

1. System commands are carried out as soon as they are entered. T F
2. The command NEW is used to clear the part of the PC's random access memory (RAM) in which BASIC programs are stored. T F
3. `10 CLS` is an admissible programming line. T F
4. The PrtSc command is used to obtain a printed copy of the entire screen, including line 25. T F
5. If you forget the line number while typing a BASIC statement, the PC will respond by displaying an error message. T F
6. To correct an error committed while typing a program, you must retype the entire line. T F
7. A line may be deleted from a program simply by typing its line number and then pressing the Enter key. T F
8. Programming lines exceeding 80 characters cannot be used in Microsoft® BASIC programs. T F
9. A program containing no syntax errors can cause error messages to be displayed. T F
10. PRINT and LPRINT statements must not be used in the same program. T F
11. The program statement `20 PRINT "13(2 + 3) = 500"` contains a syntax error. T F
12. The statements

    ```
    10 LET A=5000
    20 LET R=12.5
    30 PRINT R*A
    ```

    will display 12.5% of 5,000. T F
13. The input values required in a program should be identified before an algorithm has been written, whereas it is best to identify the required output values after the algorithm has been described. T F
14. Each step in an algorithm for a computer program should correspond to a single program statement. T F
15. A good programming practice is to choose REM statements to correspond to the individual steps of an algorithm. T F
16. Coding a BASIC program involves determining the programming lines to carry out a known algorithm. T F

5 Interacting with the Computer

Most computer programs are written to process input data that will be different each time a program is run. The LET statement (Chapter 3) is not intended as a means for presenting such data to the computer. As we have mentioned, the use of LET statements to assign input values to variables requires that you retype these statements each time you run the program for different input data. If a program is to process 100 different input values, you would have to type 100 LET statements. Not only is this inconvenient, but it means that only those who know how to write correct LET statements can use the program. This violates an important rule of programming: the users of a program should not be required to have any knowledge of programming.

The BASIC language includes several statements intended specifically for data input. In this chapter we discuss the INPUT statement, which allows you to type values for variables during program execution. Thus, by using INPUT statements to obtain data from the keyboard, you will be able to run your programs for different input data without having to change programming lines in any way. In a sense, the INPUT statement allows you to *interact* with the computer while a program is running—the computer displays a message (PRINT statement) concerning the value or values to be typed, you type the input value or values, and then the computer processes the input data and displays the results. As you progress in your study of BASIC, you will learn other ways to effect meaningful "dialogues" between the user and the computer.

■ 5.1 The INPUT Statement

The INPUT statement is best illustrated by example. (The general forms for the INPUT statement are shown at the end of this section.)

EXAMPLE 1 Here is a program to display the square of any number typed at the keyboard.

```
10 PRINT "TYPE A NUMBER."
20 INPUT NUM
30 LET SQUARE=NUM^2
40 PRINT "SQUARE IS";SQUARE
50 END
```

When line 20 is executed, a question mark (BASIC's *input prompt*) will be displayed. Nothing further will take place until you type a BASIC constant and enter it by pressing ↵. The value of the constant will be assigned to NUM, and only then will program execution continue. Let's run this program:

```
RUN                     (You type RUN ⏎.)

TYPE A NUMBER.          (Displayed by the PC.)
? 13                    (You type 13 ⏎.)
SQUARE IS 169           (Displayed by the PC.)
Ok
```

■ **REMARK** The PC begins displaying the output of a program beginning on the line following the RUN command. We include a blank line for readability. If you want the PC to skip this line, you can insert

```
5 PRINT
```

in the program. This statement will produce no output, but it will cause a RETURN to be executed. If you include

```
5 PRINT : PRINT
```

☐

two blank lines will appear after the word RUN.

More than one value may be assigned by an INPUT statement. The program statement

```
90 INPUT X,Y,Z
```

causes a question mark to be displayed, and three numerical constants, separated by commas, should be typed. If you type 5,3,24 after this question mark and then press ⏎, the value 5 will be assigned to X, 3 to Y, and 24 to Z. If you do not type exactly three values, the PC will display the message

```
?Redo from start
```

You must then reenter all three values.

EXAMPLE 2 Here is a program to compute the cost C of renting a car for D days and driving it M miles. The rental rate is $12 per day and 11¢ per mile.

```
10 PRINT "ENTER NUMBER OF DAYS AND NUMBER"
20 PRINT "OF MILES, SEPARATED BY A COMMA."
30 INPUT D,M
40 LET C=12*D+0.11*M
50 PRINT
60 PRINT "TOTAL COST: ";C
70 END
RUN

ENTER NUMBER OF DAYS AND NUMBER
OF MILES, SEPARATED BY A COMMA.
?
```

At this point simply follow the instructions and type two numbers separated by a comma. Let's complete this run as follows.

```
? 3,253              (You type underlined characters.)

TOTAL COST: 63.83
Ok
```

■ **REMARK** Lines 10 and 20 display a message telling the user how to respond when the input prompt ? is encountered. Without this explanation, a user would have no way of knowing what to type. It is a cardinal rule of programming never to confront the person using the program with an unexplained input prompt.

☐

Although lines 10 and 20 in the previous example instruct the user how to respond to the input prompt, there is the possibility that the inexperienced user will not follow instructions exactly. For example, the user might type

    253, 3

This will cause 253 to be assigned to D and 3 to M, and incorrect results will follow. You can prevent the user from making such errors by requiring only one response to each input prompt. Replacing lines 10, 20, and 30 by

```
10 PRINT "NUMBER OF DAYS"
15 INPUT D
20 PRINT "NUMBER OF MILES"
30 INPUT M
```

is one way to do this. Let's run this revised program:

```
RUN

NUMBER OF DAYS
? 3                    (You type underlined character.)
NUMBER OF MILES
? 253                  (You type underlined characters.)

TOTAL COST: 63.83
```

EXAMPLE 3   **This example shows that the INPUT statement can be used to input string values for string variables.**

```
10 PRINT "ENTER A NAME."
20 INPUT N$
30 PRINT "ENTER THE DATE."
40 INPUT D$
50 PRINT
60 PRINT N$
70 PRINT "INITIATION DATE: ";D$
80 END
RUN

ENTER A NAME.
? STEVE MARTIN         (You type underlined characters.)
ENTER THE DATE.
? MAY 1989

STEVE MARTIN
INITIATION DATE: MAY 1989
```

Note that the two input strings STEVE MARTIN and MAY 1989 were typed without quotation marks. Unlike strings in PRINT and LET statements (which must always be quoted), strings typed in response to INPUT statements must be quoted only in two situations:

1. When significant blanks begin or terminate the input string. If such a string is not enclosed in quotation marks, the leading and trailing blanks are ignored.
2. When a comma is included in the input string. BASIC uses the comma as a delimiter (separator) of input values. If we had typed

    MARTIN, STEVE

in response to the statement INPUT N$, the PC would display the message

    ?Redo from start

since there are two input values but only one variable N$ in the INPUT statement. However, typing

    "MARTIN, STEVE"

instructs the PC that all characters between the quotes, including the comma and the blank, constitute the string being input.

It is always correct to quote input strings, even when quotes are not required.

The readability of your output can often be improved by having an input value appear on the same line as the message identifying this value. In Microsoft® BASIC this can be accomplished in two ways:

1. If you end a PRINT statement with a semicolon, the RETURN normally occurring after execution of the PRINT statement is suppressed. Thus if you type 358 in response to the programming lines

```
200 PRINT "WEEKLY INCOME";
210 INPUT WI
```

your screen will display

```
WEEKLY INCOME? 358
```

2. You can include the message identifying what is to be input as part of the INPUT statement. Simply place the quoted string after the keyword INPUT and separate it from any variables whose values are to be input with a semicolon or comma. If you type 358 in response to the statement

```
200 INPUT "WEEKLY INCOME";WI
```

your screen will display

```
WEEKLY INCOME? 358
```

If you use a comma instead of the semicolon, the question mark will not be displayed. Thus, if you type 358 in response to the statement

```
200 INPUT "WEEKLY INCOME: $",WI
```

your screen will display

```
WEEKLY INCOME: $358
```

EXAMPLE 4

Determine the yearly income and savings of a person whose weekly income and average monthly expenses are given.

Two values must be specified (weekly income and monthly expenses), and two values must be determined (yearly income and savings). Let's agree to use the following variable names:

Input: WI = weekly income
           ME = monthly expenses

Output: YI = yearly income (note that YI = 52 × WI)
           YS = yearly savings (note that YS = YI − 12 × ME)

An algorithm for solving this problem can now be written:

   a. Assign values to WI and ME.
   b. Determine yearly income and savings.
   c. Display the results.

Before this algorithm can be coded, you must decide how to assign values to WI and ME. Available are the LET and INPUT statements. Since we may use this program for different weekly incomes and monthly expenses, the decision is easy: use an INPUT statement.

THE PROGRAM

```
100 REM PROGRAM TO FIND YEARLY INCOME AND SAVINGS
110 REM GIVEN THE WEEKLY INCOME AND MONTHLY EXPENSES
120 REM
130 INPUT "WEEKLY INCOME";WI
140 INPUT "MONTHLY EXPENSES";ME
150 REM
160 REM COMPUTE YEARLY INCOME AND SAVINGS.
```

```
170 LET YI = 52*WI
180 LET YS = YI-12*ME
190 PRINT "YEARLY INCOME: ";YI
200 PRINT "YEARLY SAVINGS: ";YS
210 END
RUN

WEEKLY INCOME? 350          (You type underlined characters.)
MONTHLY EXPENSES? 1300
YEARLY INCOME: 18200
YEARLY SAVINGS: 2600
```

The preceding examples illustrate the general forms of the INPUT statement:

INPUT **input list**
INPUT quoted string; **input list**
INPUT quoted string, **input list**

where **input list** denotes a list of variable names separated by commas. (Most often just one variable name will be included.) When executed, the first form displays the input prompt (?), the second displays the included string followed by a question mark, and the third displays only the included string. In each case, you must respond by typing a value for each variable in the input list. The values you type must be separated by commas, and their types (numerical or string) must agree with the types of the input variables.

5.2 Problems

Complete the following partial program so that it will perform the tasks specified in Problems 1–15. Be sure that messages displayed by line numbers 100 and 130 are appropriate to the problem being solved. Do not refer to the variable names X and A in these messages.

```
100 PRINT "         "
110 INPUT X
120 LET A=
130 PRINT "         ";A
140 END
```

1. Determine how much $100 earning 6% interest compounded annually will be worth in X years (value after X years is $100(1 + 0.06)^X$).
2. Determine the commission earned by a salesperson who sells a $625 television set if the rate of commission is X percent.
3. Determine the total cost of an article whose selling price is X dollars if the sales tax is 4.5%.
4. Determine the weekly salary of a part-time employee working X hours at $4.47 per hour (no overtime).
5. Determine the cost per driving mile for a car that averages 19.2 miles per gallon if gasoline costs X cents per gallon.
6. Determine the average of the four grades for a student who has received grades of 73, 91, 62, and X on four exams.
7. Determine the equivalent hourly salary, assuming a 40-hour week, for a worker whose annual salary is X dollars.
8. Determine the amount of sales for a salesperson whose commission is X dollars if the rate of commission is 14%.
9. For a single taxpayer whose taxable income X is more than $17,850, the federal tax due is $2,677.50 plus 28% of the amount by which X exceeds $17,850. Determine the tax due for such a taxpayer.
10. Determine the amount that must be invested at X percent simple interest to yield $1,000 at the end of 1 year.

56 Chapter 5 Interacting with the Computer

11. Convert dollars to yen (1 dollar = 133.84 yen).
12. Convert yen to dollars.
13. Convert dollars to deutsch marks (1 dollar = 1.8045 deutsch marks).
14. Convert deutsch marks to dollars.
15. Convert deutsch marks to yen.
16. Convert yen to deutsch marks.
17. Determine the area of a circle given its diameter.
18. Determine the diameter of a circle given its area.
19. Convert inches to centimeters (1 in. = 2.54 cm).
20. Convert centimeters to inches.
21. Convert degrees to radians (1 degree = $\pi/180$ radians; use π = 3.14159).
22. Convert radians to degrees.
23. Determine the distance A to the horizon as viewed over a smooth ocean from a vantage point X feet above sea level. (Consider the right triangle in the following diagram.)

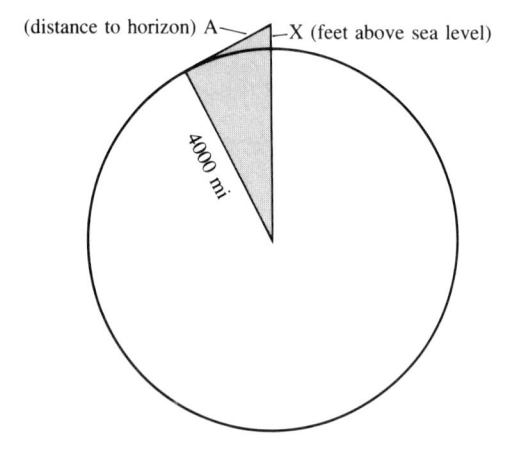

Write a program to perform each task specified in Problems 24–32. Be sure to label results and let users know what values are to be entered.

24. For any three numbers A, B, and C, determine the three sums A + B, A + C, and B + C, and find the average of these sums.
25. For any three numbers P, Q, and R, determine the mean M, the differences P − M, Q − M, and R − M, and the sum of these differences.
26. Semester grades are based on three 1-hour tests and a 2-hour final examination. The 1-hour tests are weighted equally, and the final counts as two 1-hour tests. (All exams are graded from 0 to 100.) Determine the semester average for a student whose grades are G1, G2, G3, and F (F for final).
27. Janet and Jim are bricklayers. In 1 hour Janet can lay J1 bricks and Jim can lay J2. Determine how long it will take both of them to complete a job if the number of bricks required is known.
28. A baseball player is to be paid P dollars the first year of a 3-year contract. Find the total dollar value of the contract over 3 years if the contract calls for an increase of I percent the second year and J percent the third year.
29. Determine the yearly gross pay, net pay, combined tax deductions, and retirement deductions for a person whose monthly salary is given. The combined tax rate is R percent, and 6% of the gross salary is withheld for retirement.
30. A manufacturer produces three items that sell for $550, $620, and $1,750. A profit of 10% is realized on items selling below $1,000, and 15% is realized on all other items. Determine the profit before and after taxes for a particular year, given the quantity of each item sold. The current tax rate on profits is R percent.

31. The monthly payment M on a loan of L dollars at the annual rate R for T years is given by

$$M = \frac{L \times R/12}{1 - (1 + R/12)^{-12 \times T}}$$

The Hendersons apply for a $65,000 mortgage for 25 years at an annual rate of 12.5%. Determine their monthly payment and the total amount repaid to the bank during the lifetime of their mortgage. (R must be .125, not 12.5.)

32. Determine driving expense statistics for Charlene's parents, who are visiting her at college. They note that at the outset of the trip, the odometer reads M1 miles and the tank is full. Just before returning they fill the tank with G1 gallons of gasoline at a cost of C1 dollars. After they arrive home the tank is filled again, this time taking G2 gallons at a cost of C2 dollars. The odometer now reads M2 miles. The output should be as follows:

```
GALLONS OF GASOLINE  _____
COST OF GASOLINE  _____
NUMBER OF MILES DRIVEN  _____
COST PER DRIVING MILE  _____
MILES PER GALLON OF GASOLINE  _____
```

Try your program using 12,347 and 12,903 for odometer readings, and 13.4 gallons at $12.75 and 12.7 gallons at $11.20 as the two purchases. These values are to be typed during program execution.

■ 5.3 Review True-or-False Quiz

1. The PRINT and INPUT statements provide the means for two-way communication between a user and a running program.   T F
2. Using a PRINT statement immediately following an INPUT statement is an effective method of identifying what values should be typed at the keyboard.   T F
3. BASIC allows you to type 3/4 in response to the statement INPUT X.   T F
4. BASIC allows you to type 3/4 in response to the statement INPUT X$.   T F
5. It is never correct to type THORPE,JIM in response to an INPUT statement.   T F
6. The statement INPUT B,A$ is admissible.   T F
7. The statement INPUT A;B;C is admissible.   T F
8. The statement INPUT "COST";C contains a syntax error.   T F
9. Quotation marks must always be used when a string is included in a LET statement or a PRINT statement or is typed in response to an INPUT statement.   T F

6 A First Look at Loops

All programs presented up to this point have executed sequentially according to the order of the line numbers. In this chapter we show how you can override this normal sequential order. Specifically, we show how you can direct the computer to execute sections of a program repeatedly (this is called **looping**) and thus cause it to perform many hundreds of calculations with only a few programming lines. In addition we describe a form of the PRINT statement that is sometimes useful for generating reports in tabular form. (A complete description of the PRINT statement is given in Chapter 7.)

Microsoft® BASIC provides four statements that are used exclusively for coding loops. In Section 6.2, we describe the WHILE and WEND statements and illustrate how they are used to code loops. This method of coding loops is adequate for all programming applications. An alternative method, which in many special situations is more convenient, uses the FOR and NEXT statements. To keep this introductory chapter on loops as simple as possible, the construction of loops with FOR and NEXT statements is taken up later (in Chapter 9).

We begin this chapter by introducing two BASIC statements (IF and GOTO) that will help us explain the precise action caused by the WHILE and WEND statements. Although the IF and GOTO statements provide a simple way to code loops (as shown in Section 6.1), they are intended for other uses as explained in Chapter 8. In Microsoft® BASIC, it is the common practice to code loops by using WHILE and WEND, or FOR and NEXT statements.

The BASIC statements IF, GOTO, WHILE, and WEND introduced in this chapter are called **control statements** because they control the order in which the statements in a program are executed.

■ 6.1 Coding Loops with the IF and GOTO Statements

If you need to calculate 6% of several different amounts, you can use these programming lines:

```
100 INPUT "AMOUNT";A
110 PRINT "6% OF AMOUNT IS";0.06*A
120 PRINT
130 GOTO 100
```

The statement GOTO 100 in line 130 transfers program control back to line 100. Thus, these four BASIC statements will be executed repeatedly. We illustrate for the input values 43, 100, and 89:

```
RUN

AMOUNT? 43
6% OF AMOUNT IS 2.58

AMOUNT? 100
6% of AMOUNT IS 6

AMOUNT? 89
6% of AMOUNT IS 5.34

AMOUNT?
```

If you need 6% of other amounts, simply type them one at a time. Notice, however, that the four programming lines do not provide a means for stopping execution. You must stop it manually. To do so, use Ctrl-Break: press down the Break key (top rightmost key) while holding down the Ctrl key (left side of keyboard). Program execution will terminate and the PC will display

```
Break in ln
Ok
```

where **ln** denotes the line number of the last statement that was executed. Thus a completion of this run would be displayed as follows:

```
AMOUNT?           (You type Ctrl-Break.)
Break in 100
Ok
```

The use of GOTO statements to execute BASIC statements repeatedly can transform the computer into a very fast and useful calculator. The following is another example of using the computer as a calculator. [The values N*(N+1)/2 in this example are called IRS values because they are used in certain tax calculations.]

```
100 LET N=10
110 PRINT "NUMBER";N
120 PRINT "IRS VALUE";N*(N+1)/2
130 PRINT
140 LET N=N+1
150 GOTO 110
RUN

NUMBER 10
IRS VALUE 55

NUMBER 11
IRS VALUE 66

NUMBER 12
IRS VALUE 78

NUMBER 13
IRS VALUE 91

NUMBER 14
^C                (You type Ctrl-Break.)

BREAK in 110
Ok
```

Unlike the loop in the previous example, this loop contains no INPUT statement to slow it down, so the results may be scrolled off the display screen before you can read them. In such situations, you can use **Ctrl-NumLock:** press the **NumLock** key (just to the left of the Break key) while holding down the Ctrl key. This will stop program execution temporarily, giving you all the time you need to read what is on the screen.

To continue execution, press a key—almost any key will do. To stop the program and get back the Ok prompt, use Ctrl-Break—if Ctrl-NumLock is in effect, you must first press a key.

As you write longer and longer programs, you will find Ctrl-NumLock and Ctrl-Break helpful in other situations. While listing a program, for example, you can use Ctrl-NumLock to stop the listing to give you time to read what is on the screen. To continue the listing, you would press a key.

Commands such as Ctrl-Break and Ctrl-NumLock are programmers' tools; they are not intended for people who use programs. Unless you are using the computer as a calculator, your programs should always halt automatically when the intended tasks have been carried out. This means that you should not code loops using only the GOTO statement. In the following examples, we describe a limited form of the IF statement that can be used to cause an exit from a loop when its task has been completed.

EXAMPLE 1   **Here is a program to display the IRS values N*(N+1)/2 for N = 6, 12, 18, and 24.**

```
110 LET N=6
120     PRINT "NUMBER: ";N
130     PRINT "IRS VALUE: ";N*(N+1)/2
140     PRINT
150     LET N=N+6
160 IF N<=24 THEN 120
170 END
RUN

NUMBER: 6
IRS VALUE: 21

NUMBER: 12
IRS VALUE: 78

NUMBER: 18
IRS VALUE: 171

NUMBER: 24
IRS VALUE: 300
```

The expression N<=24 in line 160 is how you write $N \leq 24$ in BASIC. This IF statement transfers control back to line 120 if the condition $N \leq 24$ is true. If the condition is false, the sequential execution of the program statements is not interrupted and control passes to the line immediately following the IF statement—line 170 in this program. Thus, the action of the program is as follows:

Line 110 assigns the initial value 6 to N, lines 120–140 display this number and its IRS value followed by a blank line, and line 150 increases N by 6 to give 12. Since 12 is less than 24, the condition $N \leq 24$ is true and the IF statement transfers control back to line 120. This looping continues until the condition $N \leq 24$ is false. This happens when line 150 increases N from 24 to 30. Control then passes out of the loop to line 170, which in this program stops execution.

■ **REMARK 1**   This program provides for no interaction between the user and the computer. It simply displays the specified output and halts when it has finished. The user doesn't have to stop execution manually.

■ **REMARK 2**   The IF statement in this program sets up a loop in which statements in lines 120–150 are executed repeatedly. Indenting these statements as shown in the program listing improves the readability of the program. The practice of indenting program statements is not new to us. In several of the examples considered thus far, REM statements describing the meanings of variable names used in a program were indented. Other situations in which indentations should be used to improve the readability of your programs will be mentioned as they arise.

EXAMPLE 2   Here is a program to determine the sum S of any number of input values.

```
100 PRINT "TYPE NUMBERS TO BE ADDED, ONE PER LINE."
110 PRINT "TYPE 0 WHEN ALL NUMBERS HAVE BEEN TYPED."
120 LET S=0
130 INPUT X
140 IF X=0 THEN 180
150     LET S=S+X
160     INPUT X
170 GOTO 140
180 PRINT "THE SUM IS";S
190 END
RUN

TYPE NUMBERS TO BE ADDED, ONE PER LINE.
TYPE 0 WHEN ALL NUMBERS HAVE BEEN TYPED.
? 25
? 30
? -10
? 15.75
? 0
THE SUM IS 60.75
```

Lines 100 and 110 instruct the user, and line 120 starts with a sum S of 0. (It is a good programming practice to include line 120 even though the PC automatically assigns the initial value 0 to S. By including this statement, your program will be easier to understand because it shows explicitly that S starts out as 0.)

Line 130 displays the first ? and we type 25 for X. Since the condition X = 0 in the IF statement is false, program execution continues with line 150, which adds 25, the value of X, to S. Line 160 displays another ? and we type the next number. The GOTO statement in line 170 then transfers control back to line 140 and the condition X = 0 is tested again. This looping continues until we type 0 for X. When this happens, the IF statement transfers control out of the loop to line 180 and the final sum is displayed.

■ **REMARK**   You may have noticed that we used two INPUT statements when one would have sufficed. For instance, you could replace lines 130–170 by

```
130     INPUT X
140     IF X=0 THEN 180
150     LET S=S+X
160 GOTO 130
```

Both forms are correct. The first, however, conforms to an important programming principle: *When coding a loop, the statement that causes an exit from the loop should start the loop or end it.* Experience has shown that programs written according to this principle are easier to read and considerably easier to modify, should that be required.

□

In Example 2 we used the statement

```
140 IF X=0 THEN 180
```

to transfer control to line 180 if the condition X = 0 is true. This condition is called a **relational expression**—it is true if the equals symbol correctly describes the *relationship* between X and 0. In Example 1, we used the relational expression N <= 24 to test if the symbol <= correctly describes the relationship between N and 24. The symbols BASIC allows in relational expressions are as follows:

BASIC symbol	Arithmetic symbol	Meaning
=	=	Equal
<	<	Less than
>	>	Greater than
<>	≠	Not equal to
<=	≤	Less than or equal to
>=	≥	Greater than or equal to

Here are some correctly written IF statements:

BASIC statement	Meaning
100 IF X>50 THEN 240	Transfer control to line 240 if X is greater than 50.
200 IF A<>B THEN 120	Transfer control to line 120 if A and B are not equal.
300 IF 2*N+1>=75 THEN 150	Transfer control to line 150 if the value of 2*N+1 is greater than or equal to 75.
400 IF T$="YES" THEN 700	Transfer control to line 700 if the string value of T$ is YES.

The condition in each IF statement used in this chapter is a single relational expression. In Chapter 8 we explain how you can use keywords such as AND and OR (and others) to write conditions that involve two or more comparisons. For instance, the statement

```
300 IF C$="Y" OR C$="y" THEN 200
```

transfers program control to line 200 if C$ has either the value Y or the value y.

Notice that strings appearing in relational expressions must be enclosed in quotation marks. It would not be correct to write

```
400 IF T$=YES THEN 700
```

A good use of string comparisons involves testing a user's response to input prompts. For instance, a program containing the lines

```
290 INPUT "Are you done (Y or N)";C$
300 IF C$="N" OR C$="n" THEN 200
310 END
```

will transfer control back to line 200 if the user types N or n in response to the input prompt. If the user types anything else, control will pass to the line that follows the IF statement, which in this case is an END statement. String comparisons involving the relational symbols <, <=, >, and >= are discussed in Chapter 14.

Programming tasks often involve generating reports in tabular form. These reports usually consist of one or more columns of data, each with a descriptive column heading. In the next example, we use a loop containing a PRINT statement of the form

PRINT expression1,expression2,expression3

to display the values in a three-column salary report. It is the commas in this PRINT statement that cause the values of the expressions to line up in columns. We also use PRINT statements of the same form to display the column headings. A more detailed description of the use of commas in PRINT statements is given in Chapter 7.

EXAMPLE 3

Prepare a report showing the weekly and annual salaries for persons working 40 hours a week if their hourly rates are $4.50, $4.60, $4.70, . . . , $5.50.

PROBLEM ANALYSIS

The weekly pay W for a person who is working H hours a week at R dollars an hour is W = H × R dollars; the annual salary A for this person is A = 52 × W dollars. The hourly rates R = 4.50, 4.60, 4.70, and so on, should not be input. Since successive R values differ by the same amount (0.10), you can start with R = 4.50 and simply keep adding 0.10 to R (LET R = R + 0.10) to get the other values.

THE ALGORITHM

  a. Display column headings.
  b. Let H = 40 and R = 4.50.
  c. Evaluate W = H × R and then A = 52 × W.
  d. Display R, W, and A on one line.
  e. Add 0.10 to R and go to Step (c) if R ≤ 5.50.
  f. Stop.

64 Chapter 6 A First Look at Loops

THE PROGRAM

```
100 REM SALARY REPORT PROGRAM
110 REM   H DENOTES HOURS WORKED.
120 REM   R DENOTES HOURLY RATE.
130 REM   W DENOTES EQUIVALENT WEEKLY SALARY.
140 REM   A DENOTES EQUIVALENT ANNUAL SALARY.
150 PRINT "HOURLY RATE","WEEKLY SALARY","ANNUAL SALARY"
160 PRINT "-----------","-------------","-------------"
170 LET H=40
180 LET R=4.50
190     LET W=H*R
200     LET A=52*W
210     PRINT R,W,A
220     LET R=R+0.10
230 IF R<5.51 THEN 190
240 END
RUN

HOURLY RATE   WEEKLY SALARY  ANNUAL SALARY
-----------   -------------  -------------
4.5           180.           9360.
4.6           184.           9568.
4.7           188.           9776.
4.8           192.           9984.
4.9           196.           10192.
5.            200.           10400.
5.1           204.           10608.
5.2           208.           10816.
5.3           212.           11024.
5.4           216.           11232.
5.5           220.           11440.
```

■ **REMARK 1** Lines 190–230 constitute the loop used to display the table values. Since the column headings must be displayed first, and only once, the statements that do this (lines 150 and 160) must be executed before the loop is entered.

■ **REMARK 2** Note that in line 230 we use the IF condition $R < 5.51$ rather than $R <= 5.50$. Your computer will store integers exactly but in most cases will store only close approximations of numbers with fractional parts—just as you might use 0.66666 or 0.66667 for 2/3. The number 0.10 is one of the numbers your computer does not store exactly. Thus, if you start with $R = 4.50$ and repeatedly add 0.10 to R, you may get an approximation such as 5.500001 or 5.499998 instead of 5.50. By using the condition $R < 5.51$ we ensure that the last output line will be displayed. To see for yourself that R will not attain the exact value 5.50, type and run these lines (you'll need to halt execution manually):

```
10 LET R=4.50
20 PRINT R
30 LET R=R+0.10
40 IF R<>5.50 THEN 20
```

In light of Remark 2, we state an important rule of programming:

Never test numbers for equality unless they are known to be integers.

We conclude this section with an example illustrating the following programming practices that we have been stressing:

1. To discover a correct algorithm for a given problem statement, carry out a complete problem analysis and record it in writing. The first step should be to determine precisely what is being asked. Determining the input and output values is a good way to begin.

2. Use PRINT statements (or INPUT statements containing string prompts) to tell the user what values are to be input during program execution. Also use PRINT statements to label all output values. The precise form of these statements is usually determined during the coding process—that is, after the algorithm has been described.

3. Use comments to make your program more readable and to clarify what is being done at every point.

EXAMPLE 4

A man lives in a large house with many rooms. He wants to paint the walls and ceiling of each room, but before buying paint he naturally needs to know how much paint is necessary. On the average, each window and door covers 20 square feet. According to the label, each quart of paint covers 110 square feet. Write a program that will allow the man to enter the dimensions of each room and the number of doors and windows in each room and then determine how many quarts of wall paint and how many quarts of ceiling paint he needs for that room.

PROBLEM ANALYSIS

Although this problem statement is somewhat lengthy, it should not be difficult to identify the input and output:

Input: Name of each room.
Length, width, and height of each room.
Number of doors and windows in each room.

Output: Quarts of wall paint and quarts of ceiling paint needed for each room.

To determine how many quarts of wall paint are needed for a particular room, we must determine the wall area (in square feet) to be covered and divide this value by 110, since 1 quart of paint covers 110 square feet. Similarly, the amount of ceiling paint is obtained by dividing the ceiling area by 110.

Before attempting to write an algorithm for carrying out this task, let's choose variable names for the values of interest. This will allow us to write a concise algorithm by using variable names rather than verbal descriptions for these values.

ROOM$ = name of the room in question
L, W, H = length, width, and height of ROOM$ (in feet)
DW = total number of doors and windows in ROOM$
AW = area of all walls in ROOM$ including door and window space
[AW = 2 × (L + W) × H]
ADW = area of the DW doors and windows (ADW = 20 × DW)
AC = area of a ceiling (AC = L × W)
QWP = quarts of wall paint needed [QWP = (AW − ADW)/110]
QCP = quarts of ceiling paint needed (QCP = AC/110)

Using these variable names, we can write the following five-step process (note that the order in which the steps are to be taken is just how you might carry out this task with tape measure, pencil, and paper):

   a. Enter values for ROOM$, L, W, H, and DW.
   b. Determine the areas AW, ADW, and AC.
   c. Determine the number of quarts of paint needed (QWP and QCP).
   d. Display the values of QWP and QCP.
   e. Go to Step (a) and repeat the process for the next room.

There is a difficulty with this five-step process. It does not describe how the process will end—thus, we don't have an algorithm. Noting that the first item to be input for any room is the room name ROOM$, we will instruct the user to type END for the room name after all results have been obtained. The following algorithm incorporates this change. Note that only Step (a) of our five-step process was changed.

THE ALGORITHM

   a1. Enter a value for ROOM$.
   a2. If ROOM$ is END, stop.
   a3. Enter values for L, W, H, and DW.
   b. Determine the areas AW, ADW, and AC.
   c. Determine the number of quarts of paint needed (QWP and QCP).
   d. Display the values of QWP and QCP.
   e. Go to Step (a1) and repeat the process for the next room.

THE PROGRAM

```
100 PRINT "PAINT CALCULATION PROGRAM"
110 PRINT
120 PRINT "WHEN DONE, TYPE END FOR ROOM NAME."
```

```
130 PRINT
140 INPUT "ROOM NAME";ROOM$
150 IF ROOM$="END" THEN 400
160     INPUT "LENGTH";L
170     INPUT "WIDTH";W
180     INPUT "HEIGHT";H
190     INPUT "TOTAL NUMBER OF WINDOWS AND DOORS";DW
200     REM
210     REM ------ CALCULATE AREAS ------
220     REM
230     LET AW=2*(L+W)*H          'AREA OF WALLS
240     LET ADW=20*DW             'AREA OF DOORS AND WINDOWS
250     LET AC=L*W                'AREA OF CEILING
260     REM
270     REM ------ QUARTS OF WALL AND CEILING PAINT ------
280     REM
290     LET QWP=(AW-ADW)/110      'QUARTS OF WALL PAINT
300     LET QCP=AC/110            'QUARTS OF CEILING PAINT
310     REM
320     REM ------ DISPLAY RESULTS FOR ROOM ROOM$ ------
330     REM
340     PRINT "QUARTS OF WALL PAINT";QWP
350     PRINT "QUARTS OF CEILING PAINT";QCP
360     PRINT
370     REM ------ GET NEXT ROOM NAME OR END ------
380     INPUT "ROOM NAME";ROOM$
390 GOTO 150
400 END
RUN

PAINT CALCULATION PROGRAM

WHEN DONE, TYPE END FOR ROOM NAME.

ROOM NAME? KITCHEN
LENGTH? 13
WIDTH? 13
HEIGHT? 9
TOTAL NUMBER OF WINDOWS AND DOORS? 5
QUARTS OF WALL PAINT 3.345455
QUARTS OF CEILING PAINT 1.536364

ROOM NAME? FRONT BEDROOM
LENGTH? 12
WIDTH? 9
HEIGHT? 9
TOTAL NUMBER OF WINDOWS AND DOORS? 4
QUARTS OF WALL PAINT 2.709091
QUARTS OF CEILING PAINT .9818182

ROOM NAME? END
```

■ 6.2 WHILE Loops

The WHILE statement is used only for writing loops. The general form of a loop coded with the WHILE statement is as follows:

WHILE *condition*
_____   (Statements to be repeated)
_____
_____
_____
WEND

The statements between the WHILE and WEND statements are executed repeatedly as long as the *condition* (a relational expression) is true—that is, *while* the condition is true. Loops coded with WHILE statements are called WHILE loops.

EXAMPLE 5

Here is a WHILE loop to display the numbers 1, 3, 5, 7, and 9.

```
100 LET N=1
110 WHILE N<=9
120    PRINT N
130    LET N=N+2
140 WEND
150 END
RUN

1
3
5
7
9
```

The WHILE loop (lines 110–140) instructs the computer to execute lines 120 and 130 repeatedly while the condition $N <= 9$ is true. Thus the action of this program is as follows:

Line 100 assigns the initial value 1 to N, and line 110 tests the condition $N <= 9$. Since $1 <= 9$ is true, execution continues with line 120, which displays the value 1 of N. Line 130 then increases N to 3, and the WEND statement instructs the computer to test the WHILE condition again. This looping continues until line 130 increases N from 9 to 11. When this happens, the WHILE condition $N <= 9$ is false so that program control passes to the line immediately following the WEND statement, which in this program halts program execution.

We could have coded the loop in Example 5 in the following equivalent way:

```
100 LET N=1
110 IF N>9 THEN 150
120    PRINT N
130    LET N=N+2
140 GOTO 110
150 END
```

The only differences are that we used an IF statement instead of the WHILE statement and a GOTO instead of a WEND. There are two good reasons for writing WHILE loops; both concern program readability:

1. The WHILE statement is used only to code loops, whereas the IF statement has many uses, as explained in Chapter 8. Thus, when you see a WHILE statement you know that it starts a loop. When you see an IF statement, it may start a loop, it may end a loop, or it may have nothing to do with looping.

2. The condition in a WHILE statement is *always* the condition needed to *continue* looping. In Example 5 this condition is $N <= 9$. This is not so with the IF statement. For instance, the IF/GOTO form of the loop uses the IF condition $N > 9$—that is, the condition needed to *stop* looping. The following equivalent form of the loop, however, uses the condition $N <= 9$.

```
100 LET N=1
110    PRINT N
120    LET N=N+2
130 IF N<=9 THEN 110
```

EXAMPLE 6

In this example, we show how the loops in Examples 1–4 of Section 6.1 can be coded as WHILE loops.

a. Changes for the program in Example 1:

```
115 WHILE N<=24
160 WEND
```

b. Changes for the program in Example 2:

```
140 WHILE X<>0
170 WEND
```

c. Changes for the program in Example 3:

```
185 WHILE R<5.51
230 WEND
```

d. Changes for the program in Example 4:

```
150 WHILE ROOM$<>"END"
390 WEND
```

We conclude this section with two examples further illustrating the application of WHILE and WEND statements. Example 7 involves compound interest calculations and also shows that an entire WHILE loop can be included in a single programming line. Example 8 shows that WHILE loops can be **nested**—that is, the statements being repeated in one WHILE loop can contain another WHILE loop.

EXAMPLE 7

A local bank pays interest at the annual rate of R percent compounded monthly. Let's write a program to show how a single deposit of A dollars grows until it doubles in value.

PROBLEM ANALYSIS

Input: R = annual percentage rate
A = amount of the single deposit

Output: A table showing the account balance, month by month, until the balance is at least twice the initial deposit. (A two-column table with the column headings MONTH and BALANCE is appropriate.)

It is not difficult to write an algorithm for the specified task if we leave out the details:

a. Input values for A and R.
b. Display the column headings MONTH and BALANCE.
c. Calculate and display the table values.

Steps (a) and (b) are not new to us. To carry out Step (c), we must decide how to carry out the required compound interest calculations. First, notice that the problem statement specifies that the annual rate R is a percentage. This means that we must use R/100 instead of R in any calculations. Since interest is compounded monthly, the interest rate for one month is (R/100)/12 or R/1200. Thus, if the balance at the beginning of a month is A, the balance at the end of the month will be A+(R/1200)*A or A*(1+R/1200).

Having determined how the balance will increase for a single month, it is not difficult to code Step (c). In the following program segment for Step (c) we use two additional variables:

TARGET = double the amount of the initial deposit
    M = month number (initially 0)

```
LET TARGET=2*A
LET M=0
WHILE A<=TARGET
   LET M=M+1                'Move on one month.
   LET A=A*(1+R/1200)       'Balance at end of month.
   PRINT M,A                'Display one line of table.
WEND
```

Writing code to complete the program is routine and is left as an exercise.

REMARK 1 Notice that by using WHILE instead of IF to code the loop, we were able to write down the BASIC code without referencing line numbers. Writing program segments without line numbers is an excellent programming practice. The result will almost always be a program whose action is reasonably easy to follow.

■ REMARK 2 The WHILE loop written for Step (c) of the algorithm can be written on a single programming line as follows:

```
WHILE A<=TARGET : M=M+1 : A=A*(1+R/1200) : PRINT M,A : WEND
```

The effect is the same. This one-line form, however, executes more quickly (though the difference will not be noticed) and uses less of the PC's memory (line numbers require space). Unless speed and memory space are important considerations, you should use the form that improves the readability of your program.

■ REMARK 3 Notice that the expression 1+R/1200 is evaluated on each pass through the WHILE loop. It isn't necessary to do this. Simply include the statement

```
LET FACTOR = 1+R/1200
```

□ before the WHILE statement and change 1+R/1200 in the WHILE loop to FACTOR.

EXAMPLE 8 **Nested WHILE loops. This program allows the user to obtain many sums during a single program run.**

```
100 PRINT "This program is used to add lists of numbers."
110 PRINT
120 INPUT "Do you have a list to add (Y or N)";C$
130 WHILE C$="Y"
140    PRINT "Enter numbers, one per line."
150    PRINT "Type 0 when list is in."
160    LET SUM=0                          'Start with zero sum.
170    INPUT X                            'First number in list.
180    WHILE X<>0
190       LET SUM=SUM+X
200       INPUT X                         'Next number in list.
210    WEND                               'WEND for WHILE X
220    PRINT "Sum is";SUM
230    PRINT
240    INPUT "Is there another list (Y or N)";C$
250 WEND                                  'WEND for WHILE C$
260 END
RUN

This program is used to add lists of numbers.

Do you have a list to add (Y or N)? Y
Enter numbers, one per line.
Type 0 when list is in.
? 23
? 39
? 0
Sum is 62

Is there another list (Y or N)? Y
Enter numbers, one per line.
Type 0 when list is in.
? -15
? 25
? -30
? 0
Sum is-20

Is there another list (Y or N)? N
```

The inside WHILE loop consists of lines 180–210. This loop is used to determine the sum of all input values up to the input value zero. The outside WHILE loop consists of lines 130–250. This outer WHILE loop is included to allow the user to determine many sums during a single program run. By typing Y in response to the INPUT statement at line 120 or 240, the user instructs the computer to repeat this outer WHILE loop.

Here are a few key points concerning the use of the WHILE and WEND statements.

1. A program must contain the same number of WHILE statements as WEND statements.
2. If the program segment to be repeated in a WHILE loop contains any part of a second WHILE loop, then it must contain the entire second WHILE loop.
3. The PC detects errors in WHILE loop constructions only during program execution. If a WHILE without a correctly matched WEND is encountered, the PC displays the message

    ```
    WHILE without WEND in ln
    ```

    where **ln** is the line number of the WHILE statement. Similarly, WEND without a correctly matched WHILE produces the message

    ```
    WEND without WHILE in ln
    ```

■ 6.3 Problems

1. *Show the output of each program.*

    a.
    ```
    10 LET S=0
    20 LET N=1
    30 WHILE N<25
    40     LET S=S+N
    50     PRINT N,S
    60     LET N=2*N
    70 WEND
    80 PRINT N
    90 END
    ```

    b.
    ```
    10 LET K=1 : P=1
    20 WHILE P<1000
    30     PRINT K,P
    40     LET K=K+1 : P=K*P
    50 WEND
    60 END
    ```

    c.
    ```
    10 LET NUM=100
    20 LET COUNT=0
    30 WHILE NUM>0
    40     LET NUM=NUM\2
    50     LET COUNT=COUNT+1
    60     PRINT COUNT,NUM
    70 WEND
    80 END
    ```

    d.
    ```
    10 LET A=1
    20 LET B=0
    30 LET FIB=A+B
    40 WHILE FIB<10
    50     PRINT FIB
    60     LET A=B
    70     LET B=FIB
    80     LET FIB=A+B
    90 WEND
    99 END
    ```

    e.
    ```
    100 LET A$="A"
    110 LET B$="B"
    120 LET C$="C"
    130 LET T$=""
    140 WHILE T$<>"A"
    150     PRINT A$,B$,C$
    160     LET T$=A$
    170     LET A$=B$
    180     LET B$=T$
    190     PRINT A$,B$,C$
    200     LET T$=C$
    210     LET C$=A$
    220     LET A$=T$
    230 WEND
    240 END
    ```

    f.
    ```
    10 LET X=10
    20 WHILE X>0
    30     PRINT X
    40     WHILE X>4
    50         LET X=X-1
    60     WEND
    70     LET X=X-2
    80 WEND
    90 PRINT X
    99 END
    ```

2. If A=1, B=2, and C=3, which of the following relational expressions are true?

   a. A+B<=C
   b. A+B=C
   c. 3<>C
   d. A*B*C>=6
   e. A/C=.333
   f. 3-(C/B)=3-C/B

3. Explain what is wrong with each statement. The problem may be a syntax error, or the statement may serve no useful purpose.

   a. `10 IF A<B THEN 10`
   b. `20 IF X<X-B THEN 21`
   c. `30 IF M-N<27, THEN 150`
   d. `40 WHILE A$=OK`
   e. `50 WHILE "NOT DONE"`
   f. `60 WHILE M<5 THEN 200`

4. Correct each WHILE loop in the following programs:

   a.
   ```
   10 REM PROGRAM TO DISPLAY THE ODD
   20 REM WHOLE NUMBERS THROUGH 15
   30 WHILE N<=15
   40     LET N=1
   50     PRINT N
   60     LET N=N+2
   70 WEND
   80 END
   ```

   b.
   ```
   100 REM PROGRAM TO DO MULTIPLICATION
   110 PRINT "FOLLOWING EACH ? TYPE TWO NUMBERS."
   120 PRINT "MAKE THEM EQUAL TO STOP."
   130 INPUT A,B
   140 WHILE A=B
   150     LET P=A*B
   160     PRINT "PRODUCT IS";P
   170 WEND
   180 END
   ```

   c.
   ```
   10 REM PROGRAM TO DISPLAY 8 PERCENT
   20 REM OF THE AMOUNTS 100,101,102,...,110
   30 LET A=100
   40 WHILE A<=110
   50     PRINT "AMOUNT","8% OF AMOUNT"
   60     LET A=A+1
   70     PRINT A,.08*A
   80 WEND
   90 END
   ```

Write a program to display each table described in Problems 5–20. Begin each program with a PRINT statement describing the table. If a table has more than one column, display column headings.

5. The first column contains the number of dollars (1, 2, 3, . . . , 10), and the second column gives the corresponding number of yen (1 dollar = 133.84 yen).

6. The first column contains the temperature in degrees Celsius from −10 to 30 in increments of 2, and the second column gives the corresponding temperature in degrees Fahrenheit [F = (9/5)C + 32].

7. The first column gives the amount of sales ($500, $1,000, $1,500, . . . , $5,000), and the second gives the commission at a rate of R percent.

8. The first column contains the principal (50, 100, 150, . . . , 500), and the second column gives the corresponding simple interest for 6 months at an annual interest rate of R percent.

9. The first column contains the annual interest rate (7.0%, 7.25%, 7.5%, . . . , 9.0%), and the second column gives the simple interest on a principal of $1,000 for 9 months.

10. The first column gives the list price of an article ($25, $50, $75, ..., $300), the second gives the amount of discount at 25%, and the third gives the corresponding selling price.
11. Ucall Taxi charges 45 cents for a ride plus 13 cents for each tenth of a mile. The first column gives the number of miles (0.1, 0.2, 0.3, ..., 2.0), and the second gives the total charges.
12. The first column contains the number of years ($n = 1, 2, 3, ..., 15$); the second shows the amount to which an initial deposit of A dollars has grown after n years. The interest rate is R percent compounded annually. [The value of A dollars after 1 year is $(1 + R/100) \times A$.]
13. Produce a two-column table showing how a single deposit of A dollars grows until it doubles in value. The annual interest rate is R percent compounded monthly. (See text Example 7.)
14. Interest is earned at the annual rate R percent, compounded quarterly. Produce a table showing how a single deposit of A dollars will grow, quarter by quarter, until it doubles in value. R and A are to be input.
15. A one-column table (list) containing the terms of the arithmetic progression $a, a + d, a + 2d, a + 3d, ..., a + 10d$. Values for a and d are to be assigned by the user.
16. A one-column table (list) of the terms of the geometric progression $a, ar, ar^2, ar^3, ..., ar^{10}$. Values for a and r are to be assigned by the user.
17. The first column contains the radius of a circle in inches (1, 2, 3, ..., 15), and the second and third columns give the circumference and area of the circle.
18. The first column shows the radius in inches (1.0, 1.1, 1.2, ..., 2.5) of the circular bottom of a tin can; the second gives the volume of the can if its height is H inches. (H must be input.)
19. The first column contains the number of miles (1, 2, 3, ..., 15); the second column gives the corresponding number of kilometers (1 mi = 1.6093 km).
20. You require an accurate sketch of the graph of

$$y = \sqrt{1.09}x^3 - \sqrt[3]{8.51}x^2 + (1.314/1.426)x - 0.8$$

on the interval $1 \leq x \leq 3$. To make this task easier, produce a table of the y values where the x's are in increments of 0.1.

In Problems 21–28, write a program for each task specified.

21. A young man agrees to begin working for a company at the very modest salary of a penny per week, with the stipulation that his salary will double each week. What is his weekly salary at the end of 6 months and how much has he earned?
22. Find the total amount credited to an account after 4 years if $25 is deposited each month at an annual interest rate of 5.5% compounded monthly.
23. Mary deposits $25 in a bank at the annual interest rate of 6% compounded monthly. After how many months will her account first exceed $27.50?
24. A list of numbers is to be typed at the keyboard. After each number is typed, the program should cause two values to be displayed: a count of how many numbers have been typed and the average of all numbers entered to that time. The program should halt when the user types 0.
25. A person wishes to determine the dollar amount of any collection of U.S. coins simply by specifying how many of each type of coin are included. Your program should assist the user in this task and should halt only when the user so specifies.
26. Two numbers X and Y are to be typed. If the sum of X and Y is greater than 42, the computer should display the message SUM IS GREATER THAN 42. If the sum is not greater than 42, increase X by 10, decrease Y by 3, display these new X and Y values, and again check to see if the sum is greater than 42. This process should be repeated until the message SUM IS GREATER THAN 42 is displayed. When this happens, the user should be able to type two new values for X and Y or end the program.
27. Division of one positive integer A by another positive integer B is often presented in elementary school as repeated subtraction. Write a program to input two positive integers A and B, and determine the quotient Q and the remainder R by this method.
28. Input a positive number N and determine the smallest positive integer P whose cube is greater than N.

6.4 Review True-or-False Quiz

1. If the condition in an IF statement is false, the normal sequential execution of the program is interrupted. T F
2. String constants appearing in relational expressions must be quoted. T F
3. If the statements

    ```
    149 PRINT "FIRST", "SECOND", "THIRD"
    150 PRINT A, B, C
    ```

    appear in a loop, all A, B, and C values will be displayed in columns with the headings FIRST, SECOND, and THIRD. T F
4. If the statement

    ```
    50 PRINT X, Y
    ```

    appears in a loop, the column of X values and the column of Y values will be aligned according to decimal points. T F
5. The WHILE statement is used only to code loops. T F
6. The condition in a WHILE statement is always the condition that must be true for looping to continue. T F
7. A program must contain exactly the same number of WHILE statements as WEND statements. T F
8. The statement

    ```
    50 IF X$<>NO THEN 90
    ```

    will transfer control to line 90 if X$ has the value YES. T F
9. A computer can store every number between 0 and 1 exactly, but it must use approximations for some numbers larger than 1. T F
10. The following program will display the integers 1 through 10 and no other numbers:

    ```
    10 LET N=0
    20 WHILE N<>1
    30    LET N=N+.1
    40    PRINT 10*N
    50 WEND
    60 END
    ```
    T F

7 More on the PRINT Statement

U p to now we have been working with very limited forms of the PRINT statement. As a consequence, we have had little control over the format of the output generated by a program. In this chapter we'll show how you can display many string and numerical values on a line (Sections 7.1 and 7.2) and how the spacing functions TAB and SPC can be used to specify precise positions along a line for these values (Section 7.4). In Section 7.6, we describe the PRINT USING statement, an extended form of the PRINT statement that provides a convenient way to specify an exact format for all output values.

All of the material in this chapter can be used whether the output from your programs is directed to the display screen or to a printer. For printer output, simply use LPRINT and LPRINT USING.

■ 7.1 Displaying More Values on a Line

When you first enter Microsoft® BASIC, the PC is set to display (or print) a maximum of 80 characters per line. This maximum of 80 can be changed by using the WIDTH statement in either immediate or deferred execution mode. The statement

    WIDTH 40

clears the screen and changes the screen width to 40 somewhat larger characters. The statement

    WIDTH 80

clears the screen and changes the screen width back to 80 (40 and 80 are the only screen widths allowed).

To use the WIDTH statement for a printer, you can use the statement

    WIDTH **device, n**

where **device** denotes the name associated with the printer (most likely "LPT1:"), and **n** denotes an integer from 0 to 255. Thus, if your printer allows 132-character lines, you can use

    WIDTH "LPT1:",132

To change back to 80, you would use

    WIDTH "LPT1:",80

In our discussion of the PRINT (and LPRINT) statements, we will assume that the line width is 80 and that the *character positions* are numbered 1 through 80. We will also continue to use the expression *display line* when referring to a line of output, whether displayed on the screen or printed by the printer.

When programming in BASIC, we consider a line to be divided into units called **print zones** or **tab fields**. On the IBM PC, the zones are as follows:

Zone 1	Zone 2	Zone 3	Zone 4	Zone 5	Zone 6
1–14	15–28	29–42	43–56	57–70	71–80

The statement PRINT A,B,C,D,E will display the values of the five variables, one per zone. BASIC interprets *commas* in PRINT statements as instructions to *move to the beginning of the next print zone*. Thus, the two commas in the statement

```
PRINT,,A
```

instruct the computer to skip *two* print zones and display the value of A in zone 3.

EXAMPLE 1   Displaying numerical values.

```
100 LET A=20
110 LET B=-3
120 LET C=0.123
130 PRINT ,,A,B,C
140 END
RUN
```

Zone 1	Zone 2	Zone 3	Zone 4	Zone 5	Zone 6
		20	-3	.123	

When a numerical value is displayed, the first position in its zone is reserved for the sign of the number. However, if the number is positive or zero, the sign is omitted and the first position is left blank. Note also that C is assigned a value with the statement LET C = 0.123, but that the leading zero is not displayed.

You can include more than five variables separated by commas in a PRINT statement. If you do this, you will obtain either five or six values on the first line, and the remaining values will be displayed on subsequent lines, five or six to the line. Whether you get five values or six on a line will depend on the particular values being displayed, and also on the version of Microsoft® BASIC being used. In any case, at most one number will be displayed in each zone.

Commas can be used in PRINT statements to separate string as well as numerical expressions. Strings are displayed beginning in the *first* position of a zone.

EXAMPLE 2   Displaying string values.

```
100 PRINT "FIRST COLUMN","THE SECOND COLUMN","THIRD COLUMN"
110 PRINT "FIRST NUMBERS","SECOND NUMBERS","THIRD NUMBERS"
120 END
RUN
```

Zone 1	Zone 2	Zone 3	Zone 4
FIRST COLUMN	THE SECOND COLUMN		THIRD COLUMN
FIRST NUMBERS	SECOND NUMBERS		THIRD NUMBERS

The string THE SECOND COLUMN displayed by line 100 uses all 14 positions in zone 2 and 3 positions from zone 3. This means that the next string must start in zone 4. The string SECOND NUMBERS displayed by line 110 uses all 14 positions in zone 2. Whenever the 14th position of a zone is used, the next zone is skipped.

■ **REMARK**   If the string variables A$, B$, and C$ have the values FIRST COLUMN, THE SECOND COLUMN, and THIRD COLUMN respectively, the statement

```
100 PRINT A$,B$,C$
```

produces the same output as line 100 in the program.

Many values can be displayed on a single line if we use *semicolons* instead of commas to delimit (separate) the variables in a PRINT statement. If this is done, zones will be ignored and the output values will be displayed right next to each other. It is important to note, however, that whenever a *numerical* value is displayed by Microsoft® BASIC, part of the display is a blank space following the last digit of the number. This means that one space will always separate numbers, with a possible second space if a number is not negative (the sign position). As many numbers will be displayed on a line as will fit. If line 130 of Example 1 is changed to

```
130 PRINT A;B;C;A;B;C
```

the output will be

```
 20 -3  .123  20 -3  .123
```

If *string constants* or *string variables* are separated by semicolons in a PRINT statement, the output will be merged. For example, if A$ = "TO", B$ = "GET", and C$ = "HER!!!", the two statements

```
100 PRINT A$;B$;C$
```

and

```
100 PRINT "TO";"GET";"HER!!!"
```

will both produce the same output

```
TOGETHER!!!
```

If spaces are desired, they must be included as part of a string. Or, you can write

```
100 PRINT A$;" ";B$;" ";C$
```

A PRINT statement, whether it uses semicolons or commas as delimiters, may contain any combination of constants, variables, and expressions. In the next example, we use a single PRINT statement to display the values of two string expressions ("PERCENT OF" and "IS") and three numerical expressions (R, A, and A*R/100).

EXAMPLE 3   **Here is a program further illustrating the use of semicolons in PRINT statements.**

```
10 INPUT "ENTER A NUMBER. ",A
20 LET R=5
30 WHILE R<9
40   PRINT R;"PERCENT OF";A;"IS";A*R/100
50   LET R=R+1
60 WEND
70 END
RUN

ENTER A NUMBER. 500
 5 PERCENT OF 500 IS 25
 6 PERCENT OF 500 IS 30
 7 PERCENT OF 500 IS 35
 8 PERCENT OF 500 IS 40
```

■ 7.2 Suppressing the RETURN

It often happens that a program contains a loop in which a new output value is determined each time the loop is executed. If the PRINT statement is of the form

```
PRINT T
```

successive values of T will be displayed on separate lines. However, if you terminate this print line with a comma or a semicolon, more than one value will be displayed on each line: five or six if a comma is used, and as many as will fit on the line if a semicolon is used.

EXAMPLE 4 Displaying many values per line.

```
100 LET N=1
110 WHILE N<15
120     LET T=2*N-1
130     PRINT T;
140     LET N=N+1
150 WEND
160 PRINT
170 PRINT "THAT'S ALL FOLKS!"
180 END
RUN

 1  3  5  7  9  11  13  15  17  19  21  23  25  27
THAT'S ALL FOLKS!
```

■ **REMARK** When the last number (27) is displayed by line 130, the semicolon prevents the cursor from being positioned at the beginning of the next line. The PRINT statement in line 160 causes a RETURN; that is, it causes subsequent output to appear on a new line.

EXAMPLE 5 Here is a program to display a row of N dashes.

```
10 INPUT "HOW MANY DASHES";N
20 LET K=0
30 WHILE K<N
40     PRINT "-";
50     LET K=K+1
60 WEND
70 PRINT
80 END
RUN

HOW MANY DASHES? 19
-------------------
```

■ **REMARK** The Microsoft® BASIC language includes a function called STRING$ that allows you to replace lines 20 through 70 with the single statement

```
20 PRINT STRING$(N,"-")
```

The value of the expression STRING$(N,"-") is a string consisting of N dashes. If N is 0, the string consists of zero dashes; that is, it is the *empty string*. A complete description of the STRING$ function is given in Section 10.4. Other BASIC functions that you will find helpful are described in Chapter 14.

■ 7.3 Problems

1. Show the exact output (line by line and space by space) of each program.

   a. ` 100 PRINT "BASEBALL'S HALL OF FAME"`
   ` 110 PRINT "COOPERSTOWN, NY ";`

```
   120 PRINT "13326"
   130 END
```

b.
```
   10 PRINT "PASCA";
   20 PRINT "GOULA RIVER"
   30 PRINT "BAYOU";
   40 PRINT " COUNTRY, U.S.A."
   50 END
```

c.
```
   10 LET X=5
   20 LET Y=X+3
   30 PRINT X;"TIMES";Y;"=";X*Y
   40 END
```

d.
```
   10 PRINT "HAPPY"
   20 PRINT, "HAPPY"
   30 PRINT,, "HOLIDAY"
```

e.
```
   10 LET N=0
   20 WHILE N<38
   30    PRINT N,
   40    LET N=N+5
   50 WEND
   60 PRINT "FINI"
   70 END
```

f.
```
   10 LET X=5
   20 WHILE X<=15
   30    PRINT "IF A=";
   40    PRINT X;
   50    PRINT "A+2=";
   60    PRINT X+2,
   70    LET X=X+5
   80    PRINT
   90 WEND
   99 END
```

2. Assuming that X = 1 and Y = 2, write PRINT statements to produce the following output. No numbers are to appear in the PRINT statements.

   a. 1 / 2 = .5   b. X + Y = 3   c. X − 2 = −1
   d. SCORE: 2 TO 1   e. DEPT. NO. 5   f. BLDG 4.25

3. The following programs fail to do what is claimed. Correct them.

a.
```
   10 REM A PROGRAM TO DISPLAY
   20 REM    TEA FOR TWO
   30 PRINT "TEA";"FOR";"TWO"
   40 END
```

b.
```
   10 REM A PROGRAM TO DISPLAY
   20 REM    Sleeping Bear Dunes
   30 PRINT "Sleeping";
   40 PRINT "Bear";
   50 PRINT "Dunes"
   60 END
```

c.
```
   10 REM A PROGRAM TO DISPLAY
   20 REM    7A7A7A
   30 LET X=1
   40 WHILE X<=3
   50    PRINT 7;"A"
   60    LET X=X+1
   70 WEND
   80 END
```

d.
```
   100 REM A PROGRAM TO DISPLAY
   110 REM    1  2  3
   120 REM    4  5  6
   130 LET X=1
   140 WHILE X<=3
   150    PRINT X;
   160    LET X=X+1
   170 WEND
   180 WHILE X<=6
   190    PRINT X;
   200    LET X=X+1
   210 WEND
   220 END
```

Write a program to perform each task specified in Problems 4–13.

4. Fifteen years ago the population of Easton was 3,571; it is currently 7,827. Find the average increase in population per year. The output should be

   ```
   FIFTEEN YEARS POPULATION INCREASE IS _____.
   THIS REPRESENTS AN AVERAGE INCREASE OF _____ PER YEAR.
   ```

5. An item has a list price of L dollars but is on sale at a discount of D percent. Find the selling price. The output should be

```
LIST PRICE $ _____
DISCOUNT OF _____ PERCENT IS $ _____
SELLING PRICE $ _____
```

6. The wholesale price of a car is W dollars and the markup is P percent. Determine the retail price. The output should be

```
WHOLESALE PRICE IS _____ DOLLARS.
MARKUP IS _____ PERCENT.
RETAIL PRICE IS _____ DOLLARS.
```

7. A manufacturer produces an item at a cost of C dollars per unit and sells each unit for S dollars. In addition to the cost of C dollars per unit, a fixed yearly cost of F dollars must be absorbed in the manufacture of the item. The number of units that must be sold in 1 year to break even (breakeven volume) is given by the formula

$$\text{Breakeven volume} = \frac{F}{S - C} \text{ units}$$

Your program is to process several sets of input values C, S, and F and end when the user types 0 as the cost per unit amount. The output for each set of input values should be

```
COST PER UNIT? _____
FIXED COST PER YEAR? _____
PRICE PER UNIT? _____
_____ UNITS MUST BE SOLD TO BREAK EVEN.
THIS REPRESENTS _____ DOLLARS IN SALES.
```

8. Display a row containing M dashes followed by the string THE END. M is to be input.
9. Display THE END beginning in column position N. N is to be input. (Use the statement PRINT " "; to display a space.)
10. Display a square array of asterisks with M rows and M columns. M is to be input.
11. Display a square array of # symbols with N rows and N columns. The display is to begin in column position P. N and P are to be input.
12. Display a square array of asterisks with 12 rows and 12 columns. The design is to be centered on the screen.
13. Display a rectangular array of + signs with R rows and C columns. The design is to be centered on the screen. R and C are to input.

■ 7.4 The TAB and SPC Functions

By using the semicolon in PRINT statements, you can specify exact positions for your output values. However, as you probably found while writing the programs for the preceding problem set, this process can be cumbersome. To alleviate this difficulty, Microsoft® BASIC provides the spacing functions TAB and SPC. Both of these functions are used with PRINT and LPRINT statements. TAB(n) specifies that the next output value is to commence in column position n, and SPC(n) specifies that n spaces are to be skipped before displaying the next item.

EXAMPLE 6   Here is an illustration of the TAB and SPC functions.

```
10 PRINT "12345678901234567890"
20 PRINT
30 PRINT TAB(7); "WET"
40 PRINT TAB(6); "PAINT"
50 PRINT
60 PRINT "BEWARE!"; SPC(4); "ATTACK DOG"
```

```
70 END
RUN

12345678901234567890
        WET
        PAINT

BEWARE!    ATTACK DOG
```

■ REMARK   Note the use of semicolons in the PRINT statements. Remember that a comma specifies that subsequent output is to commence at the beginning of the next print zone.

Several TAB and SPC functions may be included in a single PRINT statement. For example, the lines

```
410 PRINT "12345678901234567890"
420 PRINT TAB(8);"ONE";SPC(4);"TWO"
```

will produce the output

```
12345678901234567890
        ONE    TWO
```

Note that SPC(4) says to skip four spaces; it does not say to move ahead four spaces. Similarly, if N = 3 and A = 1.234 the statements

```
600 PRINT "123456789012345678901234567890"
610 PRINT A;SPC(N);10*A;SPC(N);100*A
```

will produce the output

```
123456789012345678901234567890
 1.234     12.34     123.4
```

with exactly five spaces separating the three output values. The first of the five spaces is produced because a numerical value has just been displayed, the next three are caused by SPC(N) with N = 3, and the last is due to the suppressed plus sign of the next value.

We now give the general form of the TAB and SPC functions. In what follows, WIDTH denotes the current width (usually 80) of an output line.

TAB(**n**)   **n** denotes a numerical expression whose value is rounded, if necessary, to obtain an integer N. The effective tab position is determined as follows.

1. If 1 ≤ N ≤ WIDTH, the tab position is N.
2. If N ≤ 0, the tab position is 1.
3. If N > WIDTH, the tab position is N MOD WIDTH.

(Note that the effective tab position is always from 1 to WIDTH.)

An attempt to tab to a position to the left of the current cursor position will result in a display on the following line. For example, the statement

```
140 PRINT TAB(30);"A";TAB(10);"B"
```

will cause B to be displayed in position 10 of the line following A.

If TAB(**n**) is the last item in a PRINT statement, BASIC assumes a terminating semicolon so that subsequent output can be displayed on the same line.

SPC(**n**)   **n** denotes a numerical expression whose value is rounded, if necessary, to obtain an integer N. The number of spaces to be skipped is determined as follows.

1. If 0 < N < WIDTH, N spaces are skipped.
2. If N ≤ 0, no spaces are skipped.
3. If N ≥ WIDTH, N MOD WIDTH spaces are skipped.

(Note that you can skip at most WIDTH − 1 positions.)

Chapter 7 More on the PRINT Statement

If there are insufficient spaces on the current line, the SPC function can cause a display on the next line. For example, if WIDTH = 80, the statement

```
180 PRINT TAB(30);"A";SPC(60);"B"
```

will display A in position 30, and then skip 60 spaces—the 50 that follow A and the first 10 of the next line. Thus, B is displayed in position 11 of the line following A.

If SPC(**n**) is the last item in a PRINT statement, BASIC assumes a terminating semicolon so that subsequent output can be displayed on the same line.

The following three examples further illustrate the TAB and SPC functions.

EXAMPLE 7 Here is an illustration of the TAB function:

```
10 PRINT "12345678901234567890"
20 PRINT "--------------------"
30 LET K=1
40 WHILE K<6
50    PRINT TAB(K);-3*K
60    LET K=K+1
70 WEND
80 END
RUN

12345678901234567890
--------------------
-3
 -6
  -9
   -12
    -15
```

Each time line 50 is executed, TAB(K) causes the value of −3∗K to be displayed beginning in column position K as shown.

EXAMPLE 8 Here is an illustration of the SPC function:

```
10 PRINT "12345678"
20 PRINT "--------"
30 LET K=0
40 WHILE K<6
50    PRINT "N";SPC(K);"N";SPC(5-K);"N"
60    LET K=K+1
70 WEND
80 END
RUN

12345678
--------
NN    N
N N   N
N  N  N
N   N N
N    NN
N     NN
```

EXAMPLE 9 Here we see TAB and SPC in one PRINT statement:

```
100 PRINT "12345678901234567890"
110 PRINT
120 LET T=8 : S=5
```

```
130 WHILE T<=10
140     PRINT TAB(T);"*";SPC(S);"*"
150     LET T=T+1 : S=S-2
160 WEND
170 PRINT TAB(11);"*"
180 END
RUN

12345678901234567890
          *       *
           *     *
            *   *
             * *
              *
```

Each time line 140 is executed,

   TAB(T);"*"

causes an asterisk to be displayed in column position T, and

   SPC(S);"*"

causes a second asterisk to be displayed after skipping S positions.

■ REMARK   This program can be simplified by replacing SPC(S) in line 140 by TAB(22 − T) and deleting the variable S entirely. The simplified program will produce exactly the same output.

■ 7.5 Problems

1. Show the exact output of each program.

a.
```
10 PRINT TAB(5);"SALES";TAB(15);"COMMISSION"
20 PRINT TAB(5);"-----";TAB(15);"----------"
30 LET SALES=2000
40 WHILE SALES<=5000
50     LET COMM=0.10*SALES
60     PRINT TAB(5);SALES;TAB(17);COMM
70     LET SALES=SALES+500
80 WEND
90 END
```

b.
```
10 LET B$="BASIC"
20 LET N=1
30 WHILE N<=3
40     PRINT B$;SPC(N)
50     LET N=N+1
60 WEND
70 PRINT B$
80 END
```

c.
```
10 PRINT "1234567890"
20 LET I=0
30 WHILE I<=4
40     PRINT TAB(2*I+1);-I
50     LET I=I+1
60 WEND
70 PRINT "THAT'S ENOUGH";
80 END
```

d.
```
10 PRINT "7777777"
20 LET N=1 : S=6
30 WHILE S>=1
40     PRINT TAB(S);N+S
50     LET N=N+1 : S=S-1
60 WEND
70 END
```

```
e. 10 PRINT "1234567890"        f. 10 LET X=0
   20 LET X=1                      20 PRINT TAB(5);"X";SPC(10);"X^2"
   30 WHILE X<5                    30 WHILE X<4
   40   PRINT SPC(2*X);"*"         40   PRINT
   50   LET X=X+1                  50   LET X=X+1
   60 WEND                         60   PRINT TAB(4);X;SPC(9);X^2;
   70 END                          70 WEND
                                   80 END
```

2. Write a single PRINT statement for each task. (Use the TAB and SPC functions.)

   a. Display the letter B in position 6 and the digit 3 in position 10.
   b. Display the values of X, 2X, 3X, and 4X on one line about equally spaced.
   c. Display your name centered on an 80-character line.
   d. Display seven zeros equally spaced along an 80-character line. The first zero is to be in position 2 and the last in position 80.
   e. Display seven zeros as in part (d) except that the first zero is to be in position 1 and the last in position 79.

Write a program to perform each task specified in Problems 3–8. (Use the TAB and SPC functions.)

3. Display your name on one line, street and number on the next line, and city or town and state on the third line. Your name should be centered on a line and successive lines should be indented.
4. Display a row of 15 A's beginning in position 21 and a row of 13 B's centered under the A's.
5. Display a rectangular array of asterisks with five rows and eight columns, centered on the screen.
6. Display a square array of # symbols with M rows and M columns, centered on the screen. M is to be input.
7. Display the numbers 1, 10, 100, 1000, 10000, 100000, and 1000000 in a column that lines up on the right.
8. Display the numbers .33333, 3.3333, 33.333, 333.33, and 3333.3 in a column so that the decimal points line up.

■ 7.6 The PRINT USING Statement

Consider the following simple program with output.

```
100 REM PRINT COLUMN HEADINGS
110 PRINT TAB(5);"N";TAB(14);"1/N^2"
120 PRINT
130 REM PRINT TABLE VALUES.
140 LET N=1
150 WHILE N<=10
160   PRINT TAB(4);N;TAB(13);1/N^2
170   LET N=N+1
180 WEND
190 END
RUN

        N       1/N^2

        1       1
        2       .25
        3       .1111111
        4       .0625
        5       .04
        6       2.777778E-02
        7       2.040816E-02
        8       .015625
        9       1.234568E-02
       10       .01
```

Even though the TAB function is used to control the output format, the second column appears rather cluttered. The PRINT USING statement provides a simple way to rectify this situation. It not only includes the variables and expressions whose values are to be displayed, but also specifies the exact format to be used for these output values. The following example illustrates the two forms of the PRINT USING statement.

EXAMPLE 10 Each of parts (a) and (b) contains a program segment to produce the output:
ASSETS INCREASED BY 23.5 PERCENT.

a. `100 LET F$="ASSETS INCREASED BY ##.# PERCENT."`
`110 LET A=23.487`
`120 PRINT USING F$;A`

The PRINT USING statement displays the value of A in the form specified by the contents of a string variable (F$ in this example). The specification ##.# included in F$ says to display the value of A by using two positions to the left and one to the right of the decimal point. The value 23.487 of A is rounded to fit the specification ##.#.

b. `110 LET A=23.487`
`120 PRINT USING "ASSETS INCREASED BY ##.# PERCENT.";A`

This PRINT USING statement, which is equivalent to the one shown in part (a), does not require a separate statement to assign the form of the output to a string variable. The output format is simply enclosed in quotation marks and placed immediately after the keywords PRINT USING.

Both forms of the PRINT USING statement shown in Example 10 are included in the general form

PRINT USING **s;expressions**

where **s** denotes a string variable (F$ in Example 10.a), or a string constant (as in Example 10.b); and **expressions** denotes a list of numerical or string expressions separated by commas or semicolons. (The commas and semicolons serve *only* to separate the output expressions. They have no effect on the form of the output. That is determined completely by the contents of **s**.)

The string value of **s** is called the **output format**. It consists of strings and other format specifications that determine the exact form of the output. In Example 10, the output format consists of the specification ##.# and the two strings ASSETS INCREASED BY and PERCENT. Each pound symbol in ##.# specifies a position for a possible digit. Any strings included in an output format are displayed exactly as they appear, including any blanks.

The next two examples further illustrate the use of strings and pound symbols as format specifications.

EXAMPLE 11 If X = 453, the program segment

`100 LET A$="12345678901234567890"`
`110 LET M$="ITEM NUMBER #####"`
`120 PRINT A$`
`130 PRINT USING M$;X`

will cause the display

`12345678901234567890`
`ITEM NUMBER    453`

Lines 100 and 120 are included for reference only. The format specification ##### in the string M$ is used to specify how 453 is to appear in the output. Since 453 uses only three of the possible five positions, it is displayed *right justified;* that is, it appears in the rightmost three positions reserved by the specification. (Notice that only one space precedes ##### in the format string M$, whereas three spaces precede 453 in the output.)

EXAMPLE 12

If A = 42.237 and B = 25, the program segment

```
200 LET A$="12345678901234567890"
210 LET H$="####.## ####.##"
220 PRINT A$
230 PRINT USING H$;A,B
```

will cause the display

```
12345678901234567890
   42.24   25.00
```

This example illustrates two points: numbers are rounded (not truncated) to fit a format specification (42.237 is rounded to 42.24), and all positions specified to the right of the decimal point will be displayed (25, the value of B, is displayed as 25.00).

■ **REMARK** If the value of B is 12345, the output will be

```
12345678901234567890
   42.24 %12345.00
```

The % symbol tells you that the specification ####.## is inadequate for the output value 12345. Note that BASIC does, however, display the correct value of B.

Microsoft® BASIC allows two other formatting characters that can be used with pound symbols and periods in numerical format specifications:

1. Place $$ just to the left of a numerical format specification. The numerical output value will be displayed with a single $ just before the leftmost digit. If A = 495.37, the program segment

```
200 LET F$="EQUITY IS $$###.##"
210 PRINT USING F$;A
```

will cause the display

```
EQUITY IS $495.37
```

If A = 7.45, the display will be

```
EQUITY IS   $7.45
```

2. Place a single comma anywhere to the left of the decimal point in a numerical format specification. The output value will be displayed with a comma to the left of every third digit as required—for instance, 2,253,000.1234 instead of 2253000.1234. If A = 2756.13825, the two lines

```
300 LET F$="EQUITY IS $$#,###.##"
310 PRINT USING F$;A
```

will cause the display

```
EQUITY IS $2,756.14
```

If F$="EQUITY IS $$####,.##", the output will be exactly the same.

The preceding examples show how the pound symbol, period, dollar sign, and comma are used to specify exact forms for *numerical* output values. You can also specify exact forms for *string* output values. Each string format specification consists of one of three formatting characters:

    !   to specify that only the first character of the string is to be displayed.
    &   to specify that the entire string is to be displayed.
\n spaces\   to specify that the first 2+n characters of the string are to be displayed. Thus, two characters and an additional character for each space between the backslashes will be displayed: 2 characters for no spaces, 3 characters for 1 space, and so on. If you specify more positions than

needed, the output string is displayed *left justified* with trailing blanks. If you specify too few positions, the output string is truncated on the right.

EXAMPLE 13 Here is a program illustrating string format specifications.

```
100 LET S$="AMOUNT DUE"
110 LET D=35.91
120 LET A$="! ##.##"
130 LET B$="& ##.##"
140 LET C$="\    \ ##.##"
150 LET D$="\            \ ##.##"
160 LET Z$="12345678901234567890"
170 PRINT Z$
180 PRINT USING A$;S$;D
190 PRINT USING B$;S$;D
200 PRINT USING C$;S$;D
210 PRINT USING D$;S$;D
220 END
RUN

12345678901234567890
A 35.91
AMOUNT DUE 35.91
AMOUNT 35.91
AMOUNT DUE      35.91
```

Each of lines 180 through 210 contains the two output variables S$ (AMOUNT DUE) and D (35.91). The output format A$ in line 180 specifies that only the first character A of S$ be displayed, while B$ in line 190 displays the entire string.

Since specification C$ in line 200 does not provide sufficient positions for S$ (it provides only 2 + 4 = 6 positions), the string AMOUNT DUE is truncated on the right to fit the specification. Thus only the first six characters, AMOUNT, are displayed.

D$ in line 210 provides 2 + 12 = 14 positions for the 10-character string S$. Thus, the string AMOUNT DUE is displayed left justified; that is, it appears in the leftmost 10 positions reserved by the format specifications.

REMARK Note that *numerical* output values are displayed *right* justified (see Example 11), whereas *string* output values are displayed *left* justified.

The PRINT USING statement is especially useful when you have to produce reports in which the columns must line up on the decimal points. The next two examples illustrate this use of the PRINT USING statement.

EXAMPLE 14 Here is an improved version of the program shown at the beginning of the section.

```
100 REM ASSIGN OUTPUT FORMATS.
110 LET A$="      N          1/N^2"
120 LET B$="     ##          #.####"
130 REM PRINT COLUMN HEADINGS.
140 PRINT A$
150 PRINT
160 REM PRINT TABLE VALUES
170 LET N=1
180 WHILE N<=10
190    PRINT USING B$;N;1/N^2
200    LET N=N+1
210 WEND
220 END
RUN

      N          1/N^2

      1          1.0000
      2          0.2500
```

88 Chapter 7 More on the PRINT Statement

```
                    3          0.1111
                    4          0.0625
                    5          0.0400
                    6          0.0278
                    7          0.0204
                    8          0.0156
                    9          0.0123
                   10          0.0100
```

Notice that the second column in the output now lines up according to the decimal points and that the exponential forms of numbers are not printed. The format specification #.#### in B$ controls this.

■ **REMARK** Note that each number in the second column, other than the first, is displayed with 0 just before the decimal point. If we had used the format specification .#### the leading zeros would not be displayed, but then the first value 1.0000 would appear as %1.0000.

□

EXAMPLE 15 Here is a program to produce property tax tables.

```
100 REM ***************** PROPERTY TAX PROGRAM *********************
110 REM
120 REM THIS PROGRAM PRODUCES PROPERTY TAX TABLES
130 REM BASED ON THE FOLLOWING INPUT VALUES:
140 REM
150 REM       P    PROPERTY IS ASSESSED AT P PERCENT OF MARKET VALUE.
160 REM     L,H    LOWEST AND HIGHEST MARKET VALUES FOR TAX TABLE.
170 REM            (SHOWN FROM LOWEST TO HIGHEST IN INCREMENTS OF $100.)
180 REM       R    TAX RATE IN DOLLARS PER THOUSAND.
190 REM
200 REM ***************** DATA ENTRY SECTION ***********************
210 REM
220 INPUT "ASSESSMENT PERCENT";P
230 INPUT "LOWEST AND HIGHEST MARKET VALUES";L,H
240 INPUT "TAX RATE PER THOUSAND";R
250 REM
260 REM ***** DISPLAY COLUMN HEADINGS AND ASSIGN FORMAT STRING F$ ****
270 PRINT
280 PRINT "   MARKET     ASSESSED     TOTAL    SEMIANNUAL    MONTHLY"
290 PRINT "   VALUE       VALUE        TAX        BILL        BILL"
300 LET F$=" ######.##    ######.##   ####.##    ####.##     ###.##"
310 PRINT
320 REM ************ CALCULATE AND DISPLAY TABLE VALUES *************
330 REM
340 LET MV=L                                    'Lowest market value.
350 WHILE MV<=H
360    LET ASV=(P/100)*MV                       'Assessed value.
370    LET TAX=ASV*R/1000                       'Tax for one year.
380    PRINT USING F$;MV,ASV,TAX,TAX/2,TAX/12   'Display one line.
390    LET MV=MV+100                            'Next market value.
400 WEND
410 END
RUN

ASSESSMENT PERCENT? 87
LOWEST AND HIGHEST MARKET VALUES? 12500,13400
TAX RATE PER THOUSAND? 56.45

     MARKET      ASSESSED     TOTAL    SEMIANNUAL    MONTHLY
     VALUE        VALUE        TAX        BILL        BILL

    12500.00    10875.00     613.89     306.95       51.16
    12600.00    10962.00     618.80     309.40       51.57
    12700.00    11049.00     623.72     311.86       51.98
    12800.00    11136.00     628.63     314.31       52.39
    12900.00    11223.00     633.54     316.77       52.79
```

```
13000.00    11310.00    638.45    319.22    53.20
13100.00    11397.00    643.36    321.68    53.61
13200.00    11484.00    648.27    324.14    54.02
13300.00    11571.00    653.18    326.59    54.43
13400.00    11658.00    658.09    329.05    54.84
```

Here are two points concerning the use of PRINT USING statements that have not been mentioned, but that you may find helpful.

1. Placing a semicolon or comma at the end of a PRINT USING statement has the same effect as placing a *semicolon* at the end of a PRINT statement. Thus, the loop

```
200 LET N=1
210 WHILE N<=3
220    PRINT USING "Column#    ";N;
230    LET N=N+1
240 WEND
250 PRINT
```

will produce the output

```
Column1   Column2   Column3
```

If the final semicolon in line 220 is changed to a comma, the output will remain as shown. (In PRINT USING statements, commas do *not* specify that subsequent output is to begin in the next print zone.)

2. If an output format contains *fewer* format specifications than output values, the *output format* is repeated. Thus,

```
PRINT USING "#";1;2;3;4;5
```

will produce the output

```
12345
```

If separating spaces are desired, you can use `` #'' or ``# '' instead of ``#''.

Here is a simple way to code the loop shown in point (1).

```
PRINT USING "Column#    ";1;2;3
```

This single statement produces exactly the same output as lines 200–250.

7.7 Problems

1. Show the exact output for each program.

   a.
   ```
   10 LET N=9
   20 WHILE N>1
   30    PRINT USING "##.##";N
   40    LET N=N/2
   50 WEND
   60 END
   ```

   b.
   ```
   10 LET B$="BOAT"
   20 PRINT USING "RIVER\   \";B$
   30 PRINT USING "          \   \SWAIN";B$
   40 END
   ```

c.
```
10 REM STOCK FRACTION VALUES
20 LET F$="   #/#=##.# CENTS"
30 LET D=8
40 LET N=1
50 WHILE N<=7
60    LET V=N/D*100
70    PRINT USING F$;N,D,V
80    LET N=N+2
90 WEND
99 END
```

d.
```
10 LET Y$="TIME## A= #.##"
20 LET J=1
30 WHILE J<=3
40    LET A=0.004*J
50    PRINT USING Y$;J;A
60    LET J=J+1
70 WEND
80 END
```

e.
```
10 LET A=23.60
20 LET W$="1234567890"
30 LET X$="   ##.##"
40 PRINT W$
50 PRINT USING X$;A
60 PRINT TAB(3);A
70 END
```

f.
```
10 LET A$="EYELIDS"
20 LET B$="POPULAR"
30 LET C$="\  \"
40 PRINT USING C$;B$;
50 PRINT USING C$;A$
60 END
```

g.
```
10 LET A$="BOBBY"
20 LET B$="JUDITH"
30 LET C$="\    \ LOVES \    \"
40 LET D$="\    \ LOVES \    \"
50 PRINT USING C$;A$,B$
60 PRINT USING D$;B$,A$
70 END
```

h.
```
10 LET F$="\  \-\   \ ##    "
20 LET T$="TAXATION"
30 LET R$="RATE"
40 LET R=15
50 WHILE R<=35
60    PRINT USING F$;T$,R$,R;
70    LET R=R+10
80 WEND
90 END
```

Write a program to perform each task specified in Problems 2–7.

3. Display the numbers 1, 10, 100, 1000, 10000, 100000, and 1000000 in a column that lines up on the right.
4. Display the numbers .33333, 3.3333, 33.333, 333.33, and 3333.3 in a column so that the decimal points line up.
5. An employer is considering giving all employees a flat across-the-board raise R in addition to a percentage increase P. P and R are to be input. A three-column report with the column headings PRESENT SALARY, AMOUNT OF RAISE, and NEW SALARY is to be displayed. The first column is to list the possible salaries from $10,000 to $15,000 in increments of $500. Columns must line up on the decimal points.
6. Produce a six-column tax table showing 5%, 6%, 7%, 8%, 9%, and 10% for the amounts $100 to $300 in increments of $25. The table should have a centered title, and each column should be labeled appropriately. Columns must line up on the decimal points.
7. Produce a table showing 1%, 2%, 3%, . . . , 8% of the values from 10¢ to $2 in increments of 10¢. Your table should have nine columns, each with a column heading, and all columns are to line up on the decimal points.
8. Agaze Motors offers a new-car buyer a 4-year loan at an annual rate of R percent after a 25% down payment. Write a program to determine the monthly payment if the cost of the car is input. Part of the monthly payment is for interest and part is used to reduce the principal. Interest is charged only on the unpaid principal. The program should produce a table with four columns showing the month number, the interest for the month, the amount by which the principal is reduced, and the loan balance after the payment is made. Columns must line up on the decimal point. Conclude the table with one line indicating the total amount of interest paid during the four years. (See Problem 31 of Section 5.2 for the monthly payment formula.)

7.8 Review True-or-False Quiz

1. A semicolon in a PRINT statement always causes a separation of at least one space between the items being displayed.   T F
2. If you want to suppress the RETURN following execution of a PRINT statement, you must end the PRINT statement with a semicolon.   T F
3. The statement WIDTH 40 will change both the screen and printer line widths to 40 characters.   T F
4. The statement PRINT,X,,Y is an admissible Microsoft® BASIC statement.   T F
5. The statements

   ```
   10 PRINT STRING$(5,"*");
   20 PRINT STRING$(5,"-")
   ```

   will display 5 asterisks followed by 5 dashes, all on one line.   T F
6. The line

   ```
   20 PRINT : PRINT TAB(20);"X"
   ```

   will display the letter X in column position 21.   T F
7. The two program statements

   ```
   50 PRINT
   51 PRINT "1";TAB(5);"5"
   ```

   will cause the digits 1 and 5 to be displayed in column positions 1 and 5, respectively.   T F
8. The statement

   ```
   60 PRINT "GOOD";TAB(6);"GRIEF"
   ```

   will always cause the same output as the statement

   ```
   60 PRINT "GOOD GRIEF"
   ```
   T F
9. The statement

   ```
   60 PRINT "GOOD";SPC(1);"GRIEF"
   ```

   will always cause the same output as the statement

   ```
   60 PRINT "GOOD GRIEF"
   ```
   T F
10. The PRINT USING statement allows you to include in a program an "image" of how you wish an output line to be formatted.   T F
11. The statement PRINT USING "CLASS###";5 will cause the output CLASS5.   T F
12. IF A = 1234.567, the statement

    ```
    70 PRINT USING "VALUE###.##" ;A
    ```

    will produce the display

    ```
    VALUE 234.56
    ```
    T F
13. If A$ = "ABC" the statement

    ```
    80 PRINT USING "! \\ &";A$;A$;A$
    ```

    will produce the display

    ```
    A  AB  ABC
    ```
    T F
14. The statements PRINT USING F$;A;B;C; and PRINT USING F$;A,B,C, are equivalent.   T F
15. PRINT USING "A#";1;2;3 will produce the display A1A2A3.   T F

8 The Computer as a Decision Maker

All of the programs shown in the preceding chapters share a common characteristic. In each program, the computations performed on data do not depend on the particular data values but are the same whatever these values are. For instance, to calculate the weekly gross salary W of a person who works H hours at an hourly rate of R dollars, we used the statement

LET W=H*R

(See Example 3 of Chapter 6.) In practice, however, you would take overtime into consideration, and a different formula would be necessary should the overtime rate apply. If time and a half is paid for hours over 32, an appropriate LET statement for hours over 32 would be

LET W=32*R+(H-32)*(1.5*R)

It is in this sense that a computer makes *decisions*. You code the program so that the computer tests a condition (in this case, $H <= 32$) and selects one of two alternative actions depending on whether the condition is true or false.

In BASIC, the principal decision-making tool is the IF statement. Sections 8.1 and 8.2 describe the various forms of the IF statement allowed in BASIC and illustrate how they are used to transform the computer into a decision maker. In Section 8.4, we illustrate how IF statements can be used in menu-driven programs. Section 8.4 also describes the ON GOTO statement that can be helpful in coding menu-driven programs.

The rest of the chapter concerns the design and structure of algorithms and programs. Section 8.6 shows how a flowchart (pictorial representation of an algorithm) can clarify the logic of a program and how flowcharting can help you design algorithms. Section 8.8 reviews the loop structure and its application to the repetitive process of summing. In Section 8.10 we consider the general structure of algorithms, discuss what is meant by a structured program, and discuss some of the benefits derived from writing structured programs.

■ 8.1 IF as a Selection Statement

In Chapter 6 we used the form

IF *condition* THEN **ln**

to code loops. We now show how this and other forms of the IF statement are used to execute BASIC statements or groups of BASIC statements selectively.

EXAMPLE 1 Here is a program to display 6% of any input value, but only if the input value is positive:

```
10 INPUT "AMOUNT";A
20 IF A>0 THEN PRINT "TAX IS";0.06*A
30 END
RUN

AMOUNT? 43
TAX IS 2.58
Ok
```

After a value for A is input, the condition A>0 in line 20 is tested. If it is true, the PRINT statement following the keyword THEN is executed. If it is false, the PRINT statement is not executed. In either case control passes to the next line, which in this example is an END statement.

■ REMARK Using only the form of the IF statement described in Chapter 6, we could code line 20 in the following equivalent way:

```
20 IF A<=0 THEN 30
25 PRINT "TAX: ";0.06*A
```

The single-line form is more desirable because it is more readable. It reads, "If A is greater than zero, print the tax." The two-line form reads, "If A is less than or equal to zero, skip the line that prints the tax."

□

Line 20 of Example 1 illustrates the following form of the IF statement:

IF *condition* THEN *statement*

If the statement that follows the keyword THEN is a GOTO statement, you can omit the keyword GOTO or the keyword THEN, but not both. Thus, the following are equivalent:

IF *condition* THEN GOTO **ln**
IF *condition* THEN **ln**
IF *condition* GOTO **ln**

The next example shows that the statement that follows the keyword THEN does not have to be a PRINT or GOTO statement. It can, in fact, be any BASIC statement.

EXAMPLE 2 Here is a program to count how many of three input values are greater than the average of all three.

```
100 REM **** A SIMPLE COUNTING PROGRAM ****
110 REM     X,Y, AND Z DENOTE THE INPUT VALUES.
120 REM     A DENOTES THEIR AVERAGE.
130 REM     C COUNTS INPUT VALUES THAT EXCEED A.
140 PRINT "ENTER THREE NUMBERS."
150 INPUT X,Y,Z
160 LET A=(X+Y+Z)/3
170 REM *** BEGIN COUNTING ***
180 LET C=0
190 IF X>A THEN LET C=C+1
200 IF Y>A THEN LET C=C+1
210 IF Z>A THEN LET C=C+1
220 PRINT "AVERAGE: ";A
230 PRINT "COUNT OF INPUT VALUES THAT EXCEED AVERAGE: ";C
240 END
RUN

ENTER THREE NUMBERS.
? 79,70,85
AVERAGE: 78
COUNT OF INPUT VALUES THAT EXCEED AVERAGE: 2
```

Lines 140–160 accept input values for X, Y, and Z and assign their average to A. For the input values shown, (79 + 70 + 85)/3 = 78 is assigned to A. Line 180 sets the counter C to zero. The condition X > A in the first IF statement is true, so the statement LET C = C + 1 is executed, and C becomes 1. The condition Y > A is false, so the statement LET C = C + 1 in line 200 is skipped. The condition Z > A is true, so the statement LET C = C + 1 in the third IF statement is executed to give C = 2. Finally, the PRINT statements cause the output shown.

■ REMARK 1   The first time the statement LET C = C + 1 is executed, it increases the value of C from 0 to 1; the second time from 1 to 2. Thus, the statement LET C = C + 1 actually does the counting. The use of such "counting" statements is widespread in computer programming.

■ REMARK 2   Since the keyword LET is optional, we could have written lines 190–210 as follows:

```
190 IF X>A THEN C=C+1
200 IF Y>A THEN C=C+1
210 IF Z>A THEN C=C+1
```

Thus far we have used two forms of the IF statement:

   IF *condition* THEN **ln**
   IF *condition* THEN *statement*

Microsoft® BASIC also allows the more general form:

   IF *condition* THEN *clause* [ELSE *clause*]

where *clause* denotes one or more statements separated by colons. The part in brackets is optional. If the *condition* is true, the statements immediately following the keyword THEN (the THEN *clause*) are executed. If the *condition* is false, the ELSE *clause*, if present, is executed.

EXAMPLE 3   In each part of this example, we are given an IF statement and are to explain its effect.

a. `30 IF A<B THEN BIG=B ELSE BIG=A`

This statement assigns the larger of the values of A and B to the variable BIG. (Recall that BIG=B and BIG=A are admissible abbreviations for LET BIG=B and LET BIG=A, respectively.)

b. `40 IF X>0 THEN PRINT X : GOTO 20`

If the condition X>0 is true, the value of X is displayed and control passes to line 20. If the condition is false, control passes immediately to the line following line 40.

c. `50 IF X>60 THEN S=S+X : M=M+1`
   `        ELSE T=T+X : N=N+1`

If the condition X>60 is true, X is added to S and M is increased by 1. If the condition is false, X is added to T and N is increased by 1.

d. `60 IF A<0 THEN NEG=NEG+1`
   `     ELSE IF A>0 THEN POS=POS+1 ELSE ZER=ZER+1`

If A<0, NEG is increased by 1. Otherwise, the ELSE clause

   `IF A>0 THEN POS=POS+1 ELSE ZER=ZER+1`

is executed. This statement increases POS by 1 if A>0, and ZER by 1 if A = 0.

e. `70 IF S<>0 THEN IF S<0 THEN PRINT "NEG" ELSE PRINT "POS"`

If the condition S<>0 is true, the THEN clause

   `IF S<0 THEN PRINT "NEG" ELSE PRINT "POS"`

is executed. (If an IF statement contains fewer ELSE clauses than THEN clauses, as does line 70, each ELSE is matched with the closest THEN.) You should now verify that line 70 displays NEG if S<0, displays POS if S>0, and displays nothing if S = 0.

Here is an equivalent alternative to line 70:

```
70 IF S<0 THEN PRINT "NEG"
      ELSE IF S>0 THEN PRINT "POS"
```

Note that this form has the same number of ELSE and THEN clauses.

■ **REMARK** Note that the IF statement in part (b)

```
40 IF X>0 THEN PRINT X : GOTO 20
```

is not a multiple-statement line as described in Section 3.8. Line 40 is not equivalent to

```
40 IF X>0 THEN PRINT X
41 GOTO 20
```

□ This two-line form transfers control to line 20 whatever the value of X, whereas the first form transfers control to line 20 only if X>0.

EXAMPLE 4 Let's write a program to count how many input values are positive and how many are negative, and also to find the sum of the positive numbers and the sum of the negatives. The input value 0 will mean that all numbers have been typed.

PROBLEM ANALYSIS

The input and output for this problem are as follows:

Input: A list of numbers terminated by 0.

Output: Two counts and two sums as specified in the problem statement.

Counting and summing problems are not new to us. The following algorithm describes one way to carry out the specified task. To keep the algorithm as short as possible, let's use variable names for the values of interest.

X = the value being input
CP = the number of positive values
SP = the sum of the positive values
CN = the number of negative values
SN = the sum of the negative values

THE ALGORITHM

a. Set CP, SP, CN, and SN to zero.
b. Input X.
c. While X≠0 do the following:
   c1. If X>0, add X to SP and 1 to CP. Otherwise, add X to SN and 1 to CN.
   c2. Input X.
d. Display the results and stop.

THE PROGRAM

```
100 REM----A counting and summing program----
110 LET CP=0         'count of positive values
120 LET CN=0         'count of negative values
130 LET SP=0         'sum of positive values
140 LET SN=0         'sum of negative values
150 PRINT "After each ? type a number. Type 0 when done."
160 INPUT X
170 WHILE X<>0
180     IF X>0 THEN CP=CP+1 : SP=SP+X
                ELSE CN=CN+1 : SN=SN+X
190     INPUT X
200 WEND
210 PRINT
```

```
220 PRINT "Positive count:";CP
230 PRINT "Positive sum:    ";SP
240 PRINT "Negative count:";CN
250 PRINT "Negative sum:    ";SN
260 END
RUN

After each ? type a number. Type 0 when done.
? 23
? -15
? -29
? 10
? 7
? 0

Positive count: 3
Positive sum:    40
Negative count: 2
Negative sum:    -44
```

8.2 Logical Expressions

A **logical expression** is an expression that is either *true* or *false*. The relational expressions encountered to this point are either true or false; hence they are logical expressions. BASIC allows you to write *compound* logical expressions by using the logical operators AND, OR, and NOT.* These are best illustrated by example.

EXAMPLE 5   **Here are illustrations of the logical operators AND, OR, and NOT.**

    a. The logical expression

```
C$="YES" OR C$="NO"
```

    is true if either of the relational expressions C$ = "YES" and C$ = "NO" is true. Thus, the given logical expression is true if C$ has the string value YES or the string value NO; otherwise it is false.

    b. The logical expression

```
A<B AND B<C
```

    is true if *both* of the relational expressions A < B and B < C are true; otherwise, it is false. Thus, if X has the value 3, the expression 2 < X AND X < 5 is true; if X has the value 6, the expression 2 < X AND X < 5 is false.

    c. The logical expression

```
A<B OR A<C
```

    is true if *either* or *both* of the relational expressions are true. Thus, the given expression is true if A is less than B, if A is less than C, or if A is less than both B and C. You should verify that this expression is true only if the expression

```
A>=B AND A>=C
```

    is false.

---

* Microsoft® BASIC also allows the logical operators XOR (exclusive OR), EQV (equivalent), and IMP (implies). These are described in Tables 8.4, 8.5, and 8.6, but are not otherwise illustrated in this book.

d. The logical expression

    NOT (A<B)

is true if the relational expression A < B is *not* true; otherwise it is false. Note that the given expression NOT (A < B) is equivalent to the relational expression A >= B. By "equivalent," we mean that for any values of A and B, the expressions are both true or both false.

In Tables 8.1–8.6 we give precise definitions of the Microsoft® BASIC logical operators. In each table le_1 and le_2 denote logical expressions.

Table 8.1 **The AND operator**

le_1	le_2	(le_1) AND (le_2)
True	True	True
True	False	False
False	True	False
False	False	False

Table 8.2 **The OR operator**

le_1	le_2	(le_1) OR (le_2)
True	True	True
True	False	True
False	True	True
False	False	False

Table 8.3 **The NOT operator**

le_1	NOT (le_1)
True	False
False	True

Table 8.4 **The XOR operator**

le_1	le_2	(le_1) XOR (le_2)
True	True	False
True	False	True
False	True	True
False	False	False

Table 8.5 **The EQV operator**

le_1	le_2	(le_1) EQV (le_2)
True	True	True
True	False	False
False	True	False
False	False	True

Table 8.6 **The IMP operator**

le_1	le_2	(le_1) IMP (le_2)
True	True	True
True	False	False
False	True	True
False	False	True

EXAMPLE 6 **The following statements illustrate typical uses of logical expressions containing the AND and OR operators.**

a. The statement

    IF A>0 AND B>0 THEN PRINT A;B

will print the values of A and B if both are positive. Otherwise, the PRINT statement is not executed.

b. The statement

    WHILE G>=80 AND G<=89

initiates a loop that will be repeated as long as the value of G is between 80 and 89, inclusive.

c. The statement

```
IF G<80 OR G>89 THEN 300
```

will cause a transfer to line 300 if G is not between 80 and 89, inclusive; otherwise control passes to the line following the IF statement.

A logical expression may contain more than one logical operator. For example, an expression such as

```
M=0 OR A<B AND A<C
```

is admissible. The order in which the OR and AND operators are carried out, however, matters. For instance, if M has the value 0, the expression

```
M=0 OR (M<5 AND M>1)
```

is true, whereas the expression

```
(M=0 OR M<5) AND M>1
```

is false. If parentheses are not included, BASIC uses the following priorities:

Logical operator	Priority
NOT	1
AND	2
OR	3
XOR	4
EQV	5
IMP	6

In any logical expression, the order in which the logical operators are performed is determined first by the indicated priority and then, in any priority class, from left to right. As with arithmetic expressions, parentheses may be used to override this order or simply to clarify what order is intended. Thus, the logical expression

```
M=0 OR A<B AND A<C
```

is equivalent to the expression

```
M=0 OR (A<B AND A<C)
```

If you want the OR to be performed first, you must use parentheses and write

```
(M=0 OR A<B) AND A<C
```

EXAMPLE 7

Here is a program to input four numbers and display IN ORDER if they are in increasing order, and NOT IN ORDER if they are not.

```
10 INPUT A,B,C,D
20 IF A<B AND B<C AND C<D THEN PRINT "IN ORDER"
   ELSE PRINT "NOT IN ORDER"
30 END
```

REMARK This short example illustrates the importance of being able to make more than one comparison in an IF statement. The program was easy to code and is quite easy to read. As an exercise, we suggest that you write a program for the specified task, but making only single comparisons in IF statements. However you do this, your program will be more complicated than the one shown, and probably much more difficult to read.

We conclude this section by giving rules governing the order in which the PC carries out the operations in any logical, numerical, or string expression. As always, parentheses can be used to override this order. In any expression, the operations are carried out from highest to lowest priority, and operations having the same priority are carried out from left to right. Note that the arithmetic operators come first, then the relational operators, and finally the logical operators.

BASIC operators		Priority
^		1
−	(negation)	2
* /		3
\	(integer division quotient)	4
MOD	(integer division remainder)	5
+ −	(subtraction)	6
> >= < <= <> =		7
NOT		8
AND		9
OR		10
XOR		11
EQV		12
IMP		13

8.3 Problems

1. If $A = 1$, $B = 2$, and $C = 3$, which of the following logical expressions are true?

   a. A<B OR A>C   **b.** A<C AND A+B=C
   c. (A>B OR B>C) AND C=3   **d.** A=B OR 2*B−1=C
   e. NOT (A>B OR C>A)   **f.** NOT (A>B) OR NOT (C>A)
   g. NOT (A>B) AND NOT (C>A)

2. Correct the following programs:

   a.
```
10 REM TELL WHETHER AN INPUT VALUE
20 REM IS POSITIVE OR NEGATIVE.
30 INPUT N
40 IF N>0 THEN PRINT "POSITIVE"
50 GOTO 70
60 IF N<0 THEN PRINT "NEGATIVE"
70 END
```

   b.
```
10 REM DISPLAY OK IF THE INPUT
20 REM VALUE IS EITHER 7 OR 11.
30 INPUT R
40 IF R=7 OR 11 THEN PRINT OK
50 END
```

   c.
```
10 REM DISPLAY BETWEEN IF THE INPUT VALUE
20 REM IS BETWEEN 2 AND 8, EXCLUSIVE.
30 INPUT Y
40 IF 2<Y<8 THEN PRINT "BETWEEN"
50 END
```

d. ```
10 REM DISPLAY OK IF THE INPUT VALUE
20 REM IS FROM 0 TO 100, BUT NOT 50.
30 INPUT X
40 IF X>=0 AND X<=100 OR X<>50 THEN PRINT "OK"
50 END
```

3. Show the output of each of the following programs:

**a.** ```
10 LET A=3
20 LET B=A
30 LET C=(A+B)/B
40 LET D=B/A-C
50 IF D>=0 THEN D=13
60 PRINT D
70 END
```

b. ```
10 LET A=5
20 LET B=-A
30 IF A+B<>0 THEN 60
40 LET A=-B
50 PRINT A
60 PRINT B
70 END
```

**c.** ```
10 LET A$="JONES"
20 LET B$="SMITH"
30 LET C$=B$
40 LET B$=A$
50 LET A$=C$
60 PRINT "THAT'S ALL"
70 IF B$=C$ THEN PRINT B$
80 IF C$=A$ THEN PRINT C$
90 END
```

d. ```
10 LET S=5
20 LET J=3
30 IF S<7 AND J>10 THEN PRINT J
40 LET J=S+J
50 IF S+J<15 THEN PRINT S ELSE PRINT J
60 PRINT "THAT'S ALL"
70 END
```

**e.** ```
10 LET L=22
20 WHILE L<40 OR L>60
30    IF L<40 THEN LET L=L+50
40    IF L>60 THEN LET L=L-10
50 WEND
60 PRINT L
70 END
```

In Problems 4–18, write a program to perform each task specified. Be sure to write each program so that the user can try any number of input values during a single program run.

4. Two numbers A and B are to be typed. If the first is larger, display LARGER; otherwise, display NOT LARGER.
5. Two numbers M and N are to be typed. If the sum equals 5, display 5; otherwise display NOT 5.
6. Two numbers X and Y are to be typed. If the product is less than or equal to the quotient, display PRODUCT; otherwise display QUOTIENT.
7. Three numbers are to be typed. If the second is less than the sum of the first and third, display LESS; otherwise display NOT LESS.
8. A person earns R dollars an hour with time and a half for all hours over 32. Determine the gross pay for a T-hour week.
9. The cost of sending a telegram is $1.35 for the first 10 words and 9¢ for each additional word. Find the cost if the number of words is input.
10. If the wholesale cost of an item is under $100, the markup is 20%. Otherwise the markup is 30%. Determine the retail price for an item whose wholesale cost is given.

11. A finance charge is added each month to the outstanding balance on all credit card accounts at Knox Department Store. If the outstanding balance is not greater than $33 the finance charge is 50¢; otherwise, it is 1.5% of the outstanding balance. Find the finance charge if the outstanding balance is input.
12. A number is to be typed. If it is between 7 and 35 inclusive, display BETWEEN. If it is less than 7, increase it by 5; if it is greater than 35, decrease it by 5. In either case, display the value obtained and check to see if this new value is between 7 and 35. Repeat the process until BETWEEN is displayed. Don't forget to allow the user to try several input values during a single program run.
13. For any two numbers M and N, display POSITIVE if both are positive and NEGATIVE if both are negative. Otherwise, display NEITHER.
14. For any three numbers input, display ALL NEGATIVE if all are negative, ALL POSITIVE if all are positive, and NEITHER in all other cases.
15. Using the information in the following table, find the tax due for a single taxpayer whose taxable income I is less than $89,560.

Taxable income I	Tax due
$0 < I \leq 17,850$	15% of I
$17,850 < I \leq 43,150$	2677.50 + 28% of (I − 17,850)
$43,150 < I \leq 89,560$	9761.50 + 33% of (I − 43,150)

16. Display the largest of the four input values N1, N2, N3, and N4.
17. Change Fahrenheit temperatures to Celsius and Celsius temperatures to Fahrenheit. Enter a letter (F or C to indicate the given scale) and a temperature, and then change this temperature to the other scale [F = (9/5)C + 32].
18. Determine the final checkbook balance given the beginning balance and a list of transactions, either deposits to the account or checks drawn on the account. Each transaction is to be entered by typing a letter and a number. The letter D indicates a deposit, C a check, and X that the final transaction has been entered; the number entered is the amount of the transaction. If the account becomes overdrawn, display an appropriate message and continue program execution. Typing X should be the only means of stopping program execution.

■ 8.4 Menu-Driven Programs

Many programming applications require a program that can carry out several tasks but that will perform only those specified by the user. In such situations, it is natural to write a **menu-driven program.** This means that the program displays a list of the options available to the user (this is the **menu**) and permits the user to select options from the list.

It is customary to include two special options in each menu-driven program: an option to end the program and one to display instructions to the user. The following algorithm can be used for many menu-driven programs:

Algorithm for menu-driven programs

    a. Display instructions to the user. (This step may be omitted if one of the options in the menu is to display instructions.)
    b. Repeat the following until the end option:
        b1. Display the menu. (This step is omitted if one of the options is to display the menu.)
        b2. Specify an option at the keyboard.
        b3. Carry out the specified task.

The following programming lines show how you might write a BASIC program for this menu:

```
MENU:

    1    Carry out Task A.
    2    Carry out Task B.
    3    End the program.

OPTION NUMBER? _
```

```
200 REM -------- DISPLAY THE MENU --------
210 PRINT
220 PRINT "MENU:"
230 PRINT
240 PRINT "    1    Carry out Task A."
250 PRINT "    2    Carry out Task B."
260 PRINT "    3    End the program."
270 PRINT
280 INPUT "OPTION NUMBER";OP
290 IF OP=1 THEN 1000
300 IF OP=2 THEN 2000
310 IF OP=3 THEN 3000
320 PRINT "??? Invalid option number ---"
330 IF OP<>3 THEN 200
340 END
1000 REM ----- CODE FOR TASK A ------
     .
     .
     .
1900 GOTO 330
2000 REM ----- CODE FOR TASK B ------
     .
     .
     .
2900 GOTO 330
3000 REM -- ANY CODE THAT MUST BE EXECUTED --
3010 REM --     BEFORE THE PROGRAM STOPS    --
     .
     .
     .
3900 GOTO 330
```

Notice that the program segment for each option ends with the statement GOTO 330. If OP is not 3, line 330 returns control to line 200 so that the menu is displayed again and the user can select another option. If OP is 3, the condition OP=3 in line 330 is false and control passes to line 340, which ends the program. Notice also that if the user types any option number other than 1, 2, or 3, line 330 returns control to the menu, but only after line 320 has displayed the message

```
??? Invalid option number ---
```

The program segment (lines 3000–3900) that is executed when the End option is specified might simply display a concluding message to the user. As you learn more about the BASIC language, you will find situations in which other, more significant tasks must be carried out just prior to halting a program. In any case, it is excellent programming practice to include such a program segment in every menu-driven program. By doing so, each option, including the End option, is handled in exactly the same way.

This makes the action of the program easier to follow and also makes the program easier to modify at a later date, should that be required.

With the given programming lines as a model, you can write a menu-driven program to carry out any tasks, provided only that you know how to write BASIC code for each task. We illustrate in Example 8 with a short menu-driven program designed to assist the user in carrying out simple and compound interest calculations.

EXAMPLE 8 Here is a menu-driven program to perform interest calculations.

```
100 REM       A MENU-DRIVEN PROGRAM
110 REM
120 REM *******************
130 REM * DISPLAY THE MENU *
140 REM *******************
150 REM
160 PRINT : PRINT
170 PRINT TAB(10); "TYPE AN OPTION AS FOLLOWS:"
180 PRINT
190 PRINT TAB(12); "1   FOR INSTRUCTIONS"
200 PRINT TAB(12); "2   FOR SIMPLE INTEREST"
210 PRINT TAB(12); "3   FOR COMPOUND INTEREST"
220 PRINT TAB(12); "4   TO END PROGRAM"
230 REM
240 REM *****************
250 REM * SELECT OPTIONS *
260 REM *****************
270 REM
280     PRINT : PRINT
290     INPUT "ENTER OPTION NUMBER";OP
300     IF OP=1 THEN 500
310     IF OP=2 THEN 600
320     IF OP=3 THEN 700
330     IF OP=4 THEN 800
340     PRINT "??? Invalid option number ---"
350 IF OP<>4 THEN 160
360 END
370 REM *********************************************
380 REM * PROGRAM SEGMENTS TO PERFORM THE OPTIONS *
390 REM *********************************************
400 REM
500 REM -------- CHOICE 1 : DISPLAY INSTRUCTIONS ---------
510 PRINT
520 PRINT "THIS PROGRAM COMPUTES EITHER THE SIMPLE OR THE"
530 PRINT "COMPOUND INTEREST ON A ONE-YEAR INVESTMENT. YOU"
540 PRINT "MUST CHOOSE THE METHOD OF CALCULATION AND ENTER"
550 PRINT "THE NECESSARY INFORMATION. MAKE YOUR CHOICE FROM"
560 PRINT "THE LIST OF OPTIONS."
570 GOTO 350
600 REM --------- CHOICE 2 : SIMPLE INTEREST -------------
610 PRINT
620 INPUT "AMOUNT OF INVESTMENT";P
630 INPUT "RATE OF INTEREST AS PERCENT";R
640 PRINT USING "SIMPLE INTEREST:  $$########.##";P*R/100
650 GOTO 350
700 REM --------- CHOICE 3 : COMPOUND INTEREST -----------
710 PRINT
720 INPUT "AMOUNT OF INVESTMENT";P
730 INPUT "RATE OF INTEREST AS PERCENT";R
740 INPUT "NUMBER OF TIMES COMPOUNDED PER YEAR";T
750 LET AMT=P*(1+R/100/T)^T
760 PRINT USING "COMPOUND INTEREST:  $$########.##";AMT-P
770 GOTO 350
800 REM --------- CHOICE 4 : END THE PROGRAM -------------
810 PRINT
820 PRINT "PROGRAM TERMINATED"
830 GOTO 350
```

This program consists of three parts, as described by the REM statements at lines 130, 250, and 380. The first displays the menu, the second allows the user to choose from four options by typing option numbers, and the third contains the four program segments that carry out the tasks corresponding to the option numbers.

The action of the program should not be difficult to follow. It begins (lines 160–220) by displaying the menu. The INPUT statement in line 290 prompts the user for an option number, and the IF statements in lines 300–330 transfer control to the program segment that carries out the specified task. Option 1 (lines 500–570) displays instructions to the user; Option 2 (lines 600–650) prompts the user for input data and displays the result of a simple interest calculation; Option 3 (lines 700–770) does the same for compound interest; and Option 4 (lines 800–830) displays the message PROGRAM TERMINATED. Each of these four program segments returns control to line 350, which causes the program to continue, but only if the End option (OP=4) was not selected.

In the event of a bad choice (a number other than 1, 2, 3, or 4) the IF statement at line 350 returns control to line 160 to display the menu and prompt the user for another option number.

BASIC contains the ON GOTO statement, which you may find helpful in coding menu-driven programs.* This statement is used to transfer control to a selected line number depending on the value of a certain expression. For example,

```
ON X GOTO 300,700,300
```

will transfer control to

line 300 if X = 1
line 700 if X = 2
line 300 if X = 3

Thus, you can see that lines 300–330 of the program in Example 8

```
300 IF OP=1 THEN 500
310 IF OP=2 THEN 600
320 IF OP=3 THEN 700
330 IF OP=4 THEN 800
```

can be replaced by the single line

```
300 ON OP GOTO 500,600,700,800
```

This ON GOTO statement is not exactly equivalent to the IF statements in lines 300–330. The four IF statements will transfer control to one of the lines 500, 600, 700, or 800 only if OP is exactly 1, 2, 3, or 4. For any other value of OP, no transfer is made, and control passes to the line that follows line 330. The ON GOTO statement, however, is handled differently as we now explain.

The general form of the ON GOTO statement is

ln ON **e** GOTO **ln**$_1$, **ln**$_2$, . . . , **ln**$_k$

where **e** denotes a numerical expression and **ln**$_1$, **ln**$_2$, . . . , **ln**$_k$ denote line numbers (they don't have to be different). On execution, **e** is evaluated and rounded, if necessary, to an integer E. E must be in the range 0 to 255 or an illegal function call error occurs. If E is 1, control transfers to line **ln**$_1$; if it is 2, control transfers to line **ln**$_2$; and so on. If E is 0 or greater than **k,** control passes to the line after the ON GOTO statement.

---

* BASIC also contains the ON GOSUB statement, which is often used in menu-driven programs. This statement is described in Chapter 12 after BASIC subroutines are introduced. The effect of the ON GOSUB statement is similar but not identical to that of the ON GOTO statement described in this section.

Thus, when the statement

```
300 ON OP GOTO 500,600,700,800
```

is encountered, the computer rounds OP if necessary to obtain an integer. If this integer is 1, 2, 3, or 4, control passes to line 500, 600, 700, or 800, respectively. To ensure that the integer is 1, 2, 3, or 4, you can include the statement

```
295 IF OP<1 OR OP>4 THEN 340
```

to skip over the ON GOTO statement should the user inadvertently enter an incorrect value for OP. Including such an IF statement just before each ON GOTO statement is an excellent programming practice.

It isn't necessary to use option numbers in menu-driven programs; you can use words. To use word options for the program of Example 8, for example, you could display this menu

```
TYPE AN OPTION AS FOLLOWS:

        INSTR     FOR INSTRUCTIONS
        SIMPLE    FOR SIMPLE INTEREST
        COMP      FOR COMPOUND INTEREST
        END       TO END PROGRAM

SELECT AN OPTION? _
```

and code the program segment for option selection as follows:

```
290 INPUT "SELECT AN OPTION";OP$
300 IF OP$="INSTR" THEN 500
310 IF OP$="SIMPLE" THEN 600
320 IF OP$="COMP" THEN 700
330 IF OP$="END" THEN 800
340 PRINT "??? Invalid option ---"
350 IF OP$<>"END" THEN 160
```

If you make these changes to the program of Example 8, the user will have to use only uppercase letters while typing menu selections. The program would be greatly improved if it did not have this restriction—for instance, if it were coded so that it recognized Instr and instr as the INSTR option. To accomplish this, you would change any lowercase letters in OP$ to uppercase before executing the IF statements in lines 300–330. How this is done is explained in Section 14.7.

8.5 Problems

1. While studying the current day's receipts, a bookkeeper must perform numerous calculations to answer certain questions. Write a menu-driven program to assist the bookkeeper in obtaining answers to these questions.
   a. What is the selling price of an item whose list price and discount percent are known?
   b. What is the discount percent for an item whose list and selling prices are known?
   c. What is the list price of an item whose selling price and discount percent are known?
2. An investor must carry out several calculations while assessing the performance of the family's current stock portfolio. These include finding the equity (paper value) given the number of shares and the current price, and finding the profit (or loss) for a holding given the total price paid for all shares, the number of shares owned, and the current selling price. Write a menu-driven program to assist the investor in carrying out these calculations.
3. First write a menu-driven program as described in Problem 2. Then modify it by including a new option: allow the investor to find the sum of any column of numbers typed at the keyboard.
4. A menu-driven program is desired that will allow students to practice addition, multiplication, or taking powers. If addition is chosen, have the computer prompt the student for two

numbers and then ask for their sum. If the correct answer is typed, have the computer say so. If the answer is not correct, display the correct answer. In either case, allow the student to try another addition or to return to the menu. Handle multiplication (of two numbers) the same way. If the student chooses to practice powers, have the computer ask for a number whose powers are to be found. If the student types 3, have the computer display, in order,

```
WHAT IS 3 TO THE POWER 2?
WHAT IS 3 TO THE POWER 3?
WHAT IS 3 TO THE POWER 4?
    .
    .
    .
WHAT IS 3 TO THE POWER 10?
```

Ask each question, however, only if the previous answer is correct. If an answer is incorrect, display the correct answer. Congratulate a student successful to high powers, perhaps in a way reflective of how high the power. In any case, allow the student to try powers of another number or to return to the menu.

5. First write a menu-driven program as described in Problem 4. Then modify it by changing the addition option so that the student practices summing three numbers instead of two.

■ 8.6 Flowcharts and Flowcharting

The following diagram is a pictorial representation of a simple algorithm to recognize whether an input value is 5.

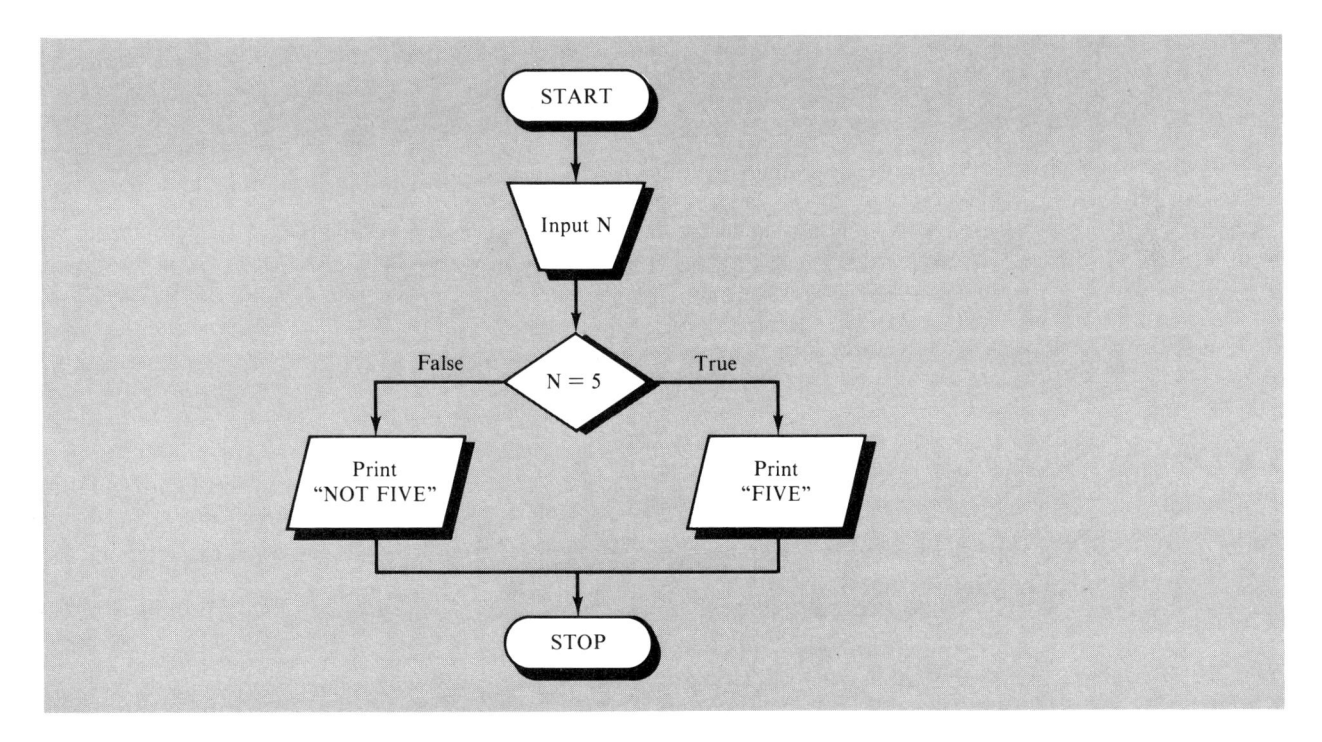

```
        START
          ↓
        Input N
          ↓
  False  ⟨N = 5⟩  True
    ↓              ↓
  Print          Print
 "NOT FIVE"      "FIVE"
    ↓              ↓
        STOP
```

Such a pictorial representation of the sequence of steps in an algorithm or a program is called a **programming flowchart,** or simply a **flowchart.** Flowcharts are useful for program documentation. In addition, it is often easier to prepare a pictorial description of a process to be followed than to attempt a detailed description in words. The flowchart is an excellent way to do this. Some of the components used to construct flowcharts can be seen in the following examples.

108   *Chapter 8   The Computer as a Decision Maker*

EXAMPLE 9   Here are two equivalent flowcharts for a program to display the numbers 100, 110, 120, . . . , 200.

```
        START                              START
          │                                  │
    ┌───────────┐                      ┌───────────┐
    │ Let N = 100│                     │ Let N = 100│
    └───────────┘                      └───────────┘
          │                                  │
          │◄──────┐                   ①─────►│
    ┌───────────┐ │                   ┌───────────┐
    │  Print N  │ │                   │  Print N  │
    └───────────┘ │                   └───────────┘
          │       │                          │
    ┌────────────┐│                   ┌────────────┐
    │Let N = N+10││                   │Let N = N+10│
    └────────────┘│                   └────────────┘
          │       │                          │
         ╱ ╲      │                         ╱ ╲
    True╱   ╲     │                        ╱   ╲  True
    ───╱N≤200╲────┘                  ─────╱N≤200╲──────►①
       ╲     ╱                            ╲     ╱
        ╲   ╱                              ╲   ╱
         ╲ ╱                                ╲ ╱
       False│                              False│
          │                                  │
        STOP                               STOP
```

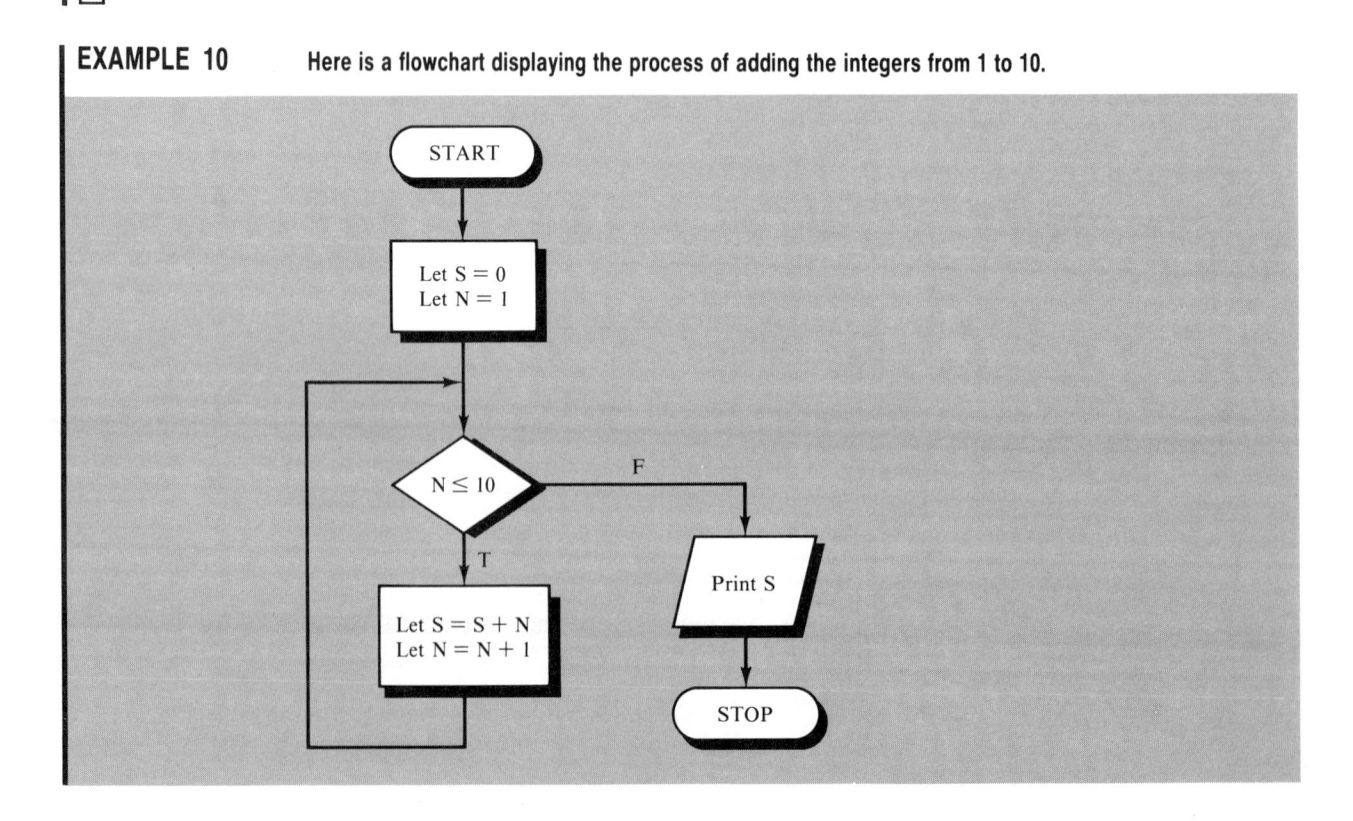

EXAMPLE 10   Here is a flowchart displaying the process of adding the integers from 1 to 10.

```
              START
                │
        ┌───────────────┐
        │  Let S = 0    │
        │  Let N = 1    │
        └───────────────┘
                │
                │◄──────────┐
               ╱ ╲           │
              ╱   ╲      F   │
         ───╱N ≤ 10╲─────────┼──────┐
             ╲     ╱         │      │
              ╲   ╱          │  ┌────────┐
               ╲ ╱           │  │ Print S│
              T │            │  └────────┘
        ┌───────────────┐    │      │
        │ Let S = S + N │    │    STOP
        │ Let N = N + 1 │    │
        └───────────────┘    │
                │            │
                └────────────┘
```

■ **REMARK 1** When two or more statements are included in a single box they are carried out from top to bottom.

■ **REMARK 2** Note that we have labeled the flow lines from the diamond-shaped decision symbol with the letters T and F for true and false, respectively.

In these examples, arrows connecting six different types of symbols are used to describe the sequence of steps in an algorithm. When possible, the flow should be directed from top to bottom or from left to right, as was done in the examples. Although there are many flowchart symbols in use,* the six shown here are adequate for displaying the flow of instructions for many BASIC programs. A brief description of how these symbols are used is given in Table 8.7.

Table 8.7 Flowchart symbols

The symbol	Its use
(rounded rectangle)	To designate the start and end of a program
(trapezoid)	To describe data to be INPUT during program execution
(parallelogram)	To describe the output
(rectangle)	To describe any processing of data
(diamond)	To designate a decision that is to be made
(circle)	A connector—used so that flow from one segment of a flowchart to another can be displayed and also to avoid drawing long lines

We conclude this section with two examples illustrating the process of flowcharting—that is, of designing flowcharts. Once a flowchart is prepared, the task of writing the program is reasonably routine; it consists of coding the steps indicated in the flowchart.

EXAMPLE 11 Construct a flowchart to find the largest number in a list of input values. The special value 9999 is to be typed to indicate that all numbers in the list have been entered.

PROBLEM ANALYSIS One way to determine the largest number in a list is to read the numbers one at a time, remembering only the largest of those already read. (This method was illustrated and discussed in Chapter 2, Example 2.) To help us give a precise description of this process, let's use the following variable names:

---

* Flowchart symbols as proposed by the American National Standards Institute (ANSI) are described in "Flowcharting with the ANSI Standard: A Tutorial," by Ned Chapin, *Computer Surveys*, Vol. 2, No. 2, June 1970.

L = largest of those numbers already read
N = the number currently being read

It is not difficult to construct a flowchart describing an algorithm for this task. First, we must input the first number and assign it to L. Thus, we can begin with the following flowchart segment:

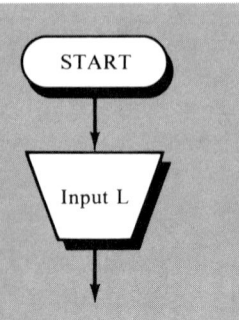

```
         START
           │
           ▼
        Input L
           │
           ▼
```

The next step is to input another value and compare it with 9999 to determine whether the end of the input list has been reached. To display this step, we can add the following to our partial flowchart:

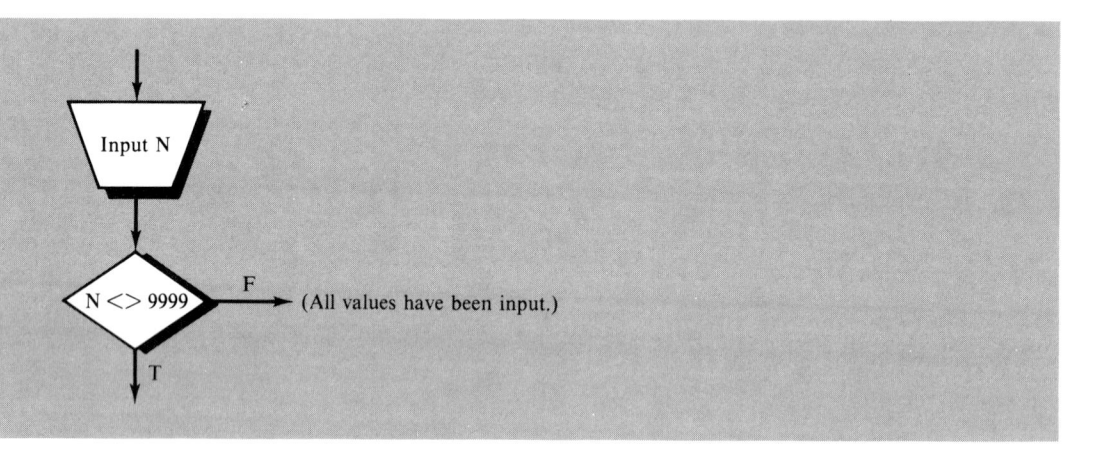

```
           │
           ▼
        Input N
           │
           ▼
        ╱     ╲      F
       ╱ N<>9999 ╲ ──────▶ (All values have been input.)
        ╲     ╱
           │ T
           ▼
```

If N = 9999, that is, if the condition N <> 9999 is false, we simply display L, the largest number, and stop. Thus, we can complete the F (*False*) branch by adding the following to our partial flowchart:

```
     F
     │
     ▼
   Print L
     │
     ▼
    STOP
```

Note that while constructing the flowchart (that is, while discovering an algorithm), we always have a partial flowchart in front of us to help us decide what the next step should be. As we continue this process of flowchart construction, a flowchart such as the following will emerge:

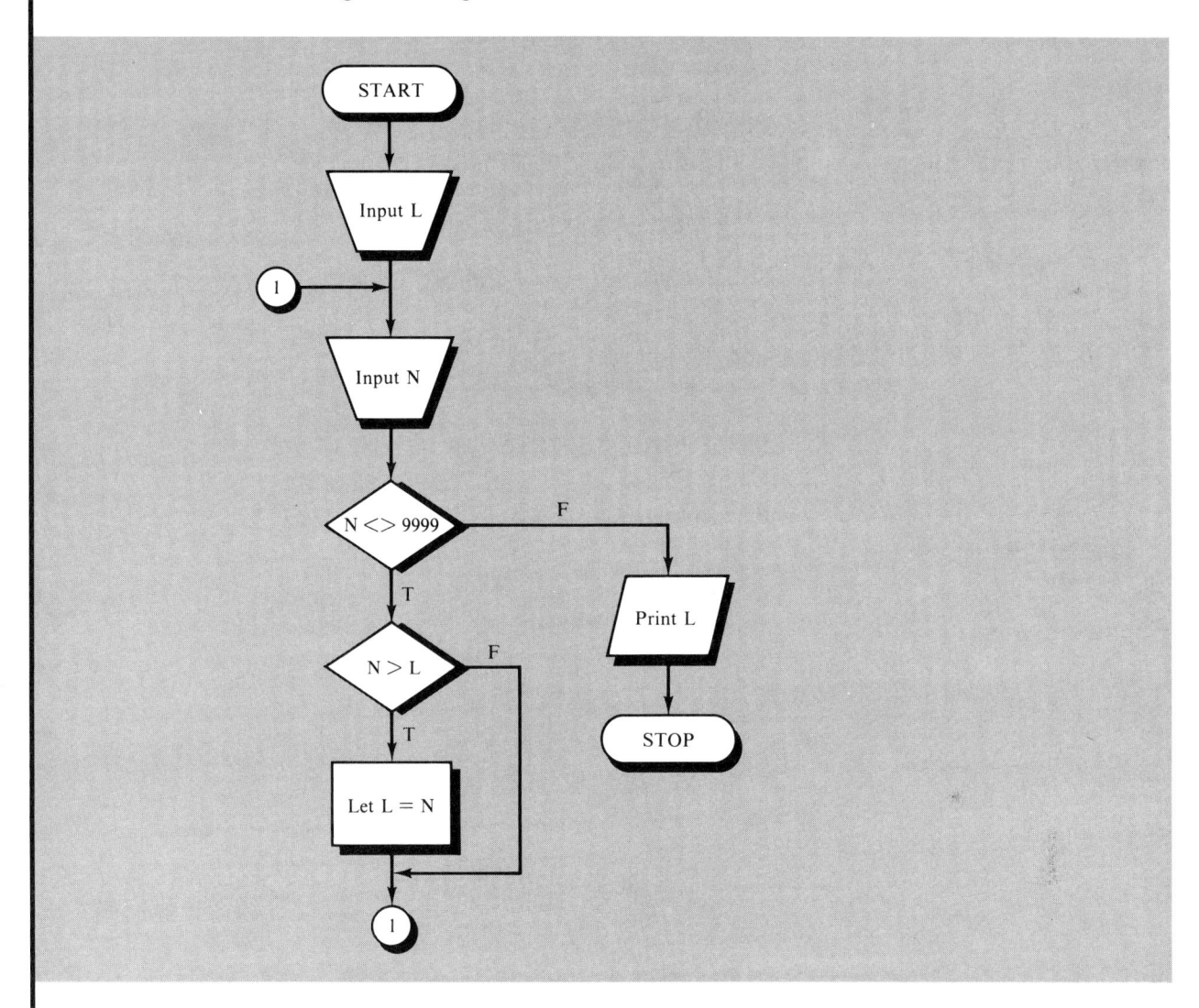

Here is one way to code this flowchart:

```
100 PRINT "AFTER EACH ? ENTER A NUMBER."
110 PRINT "WHEN FINISHED TYPE 9999."
120 INPUT L
130 INPUT N
140 WHILE N <> 9999
150     IF N>L THEN L=N
160     INPUT N
170 WEND
180 PRINT "LARGEST NUMBER ENTERED: "; L
190 END
```

The following table summarizes the values of the variables when this program is run with the input list

8, 3, 9, 2, 9999

Line number	N	L	Output
120	—	8	
130	3	8	
160	9	8	
150	9	9	
160	2	9	
160	9999	9	
180	9999	9	9

■ REMARK   The value 9999 used as a final input value to indicate that all numbers in the list have been entered is called an **EOD** (end-of-data) **tag.**

EXAMPLE 12   Construct a flowchart for a program to determine the number of years required for an investment of $1,000 earning 7.5% compounded annually to double in value.

PROBLEM ANALYSIS

The compound interest formula is

$$A = P(1 + R)^N$$

in which

P   denotes the principal (P = 1000)
R   denotes the rate per period (R = 0.075)
N   denotes the number of periods
A   denotes the value after N periods

We can begin our flowchart construction by assigning initial values to P, R, and N:

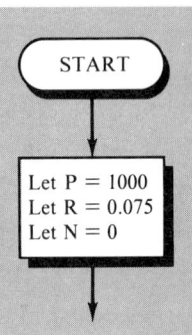

```
START
  │
  ▼
Let P = 1000
Let R = 0.075
Let N = 0
  │
  ▼
```

Next, we must compare the value of A after 1 year with 2P. Since N denotes the number of years that have passed, we can add the following to our partial flowchart:

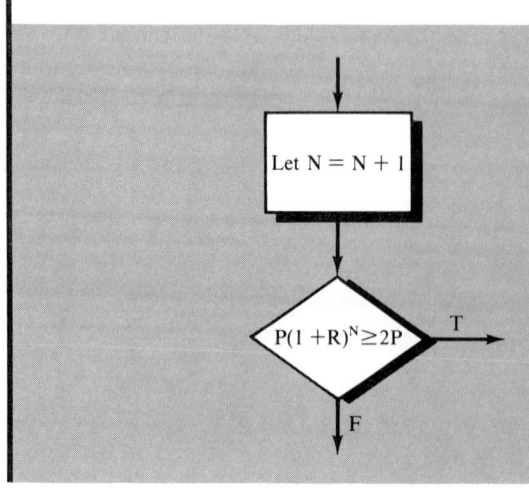

```
  │
  ▼
Let N = N + 1
  │
  ▼
  ◇ P(1+R)^N ≥ 2P ◇ ──T──►
  │
  F
```

If the condition is true, we simply display N and stop. If it is false, we increase N by 1 and repeat the comparison. Adding these two steps to the partial flowchart we obtain the following complete algorithm.

THE FLOWCHART

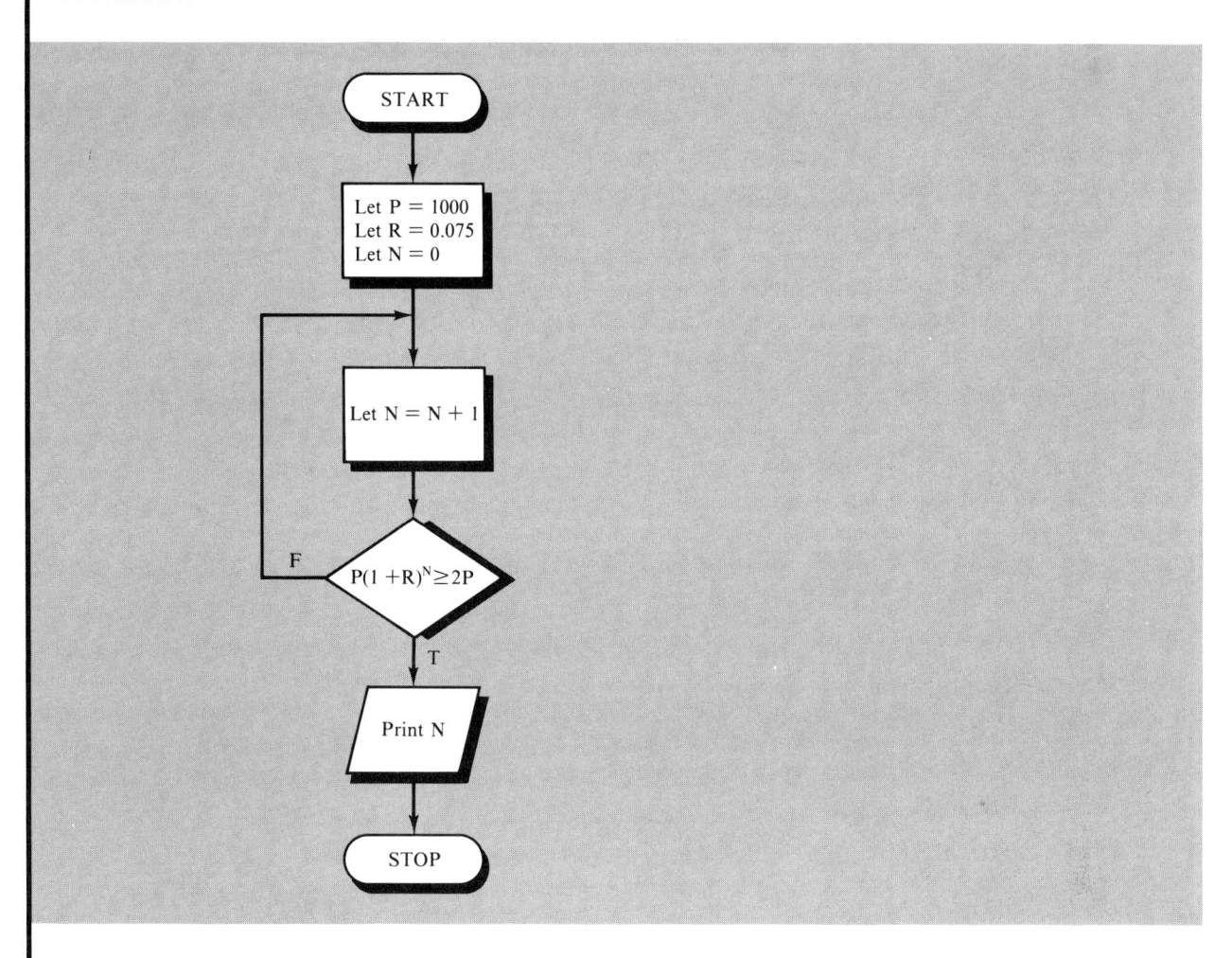

```
        START
          │
          ▼
   ┌─────────────┐
   │ Let P = 1000│
   │ Let R = 0.075│
   │ Let N = 0   │
   └─────────────┘
          │
   ┌──────▼──────┐
   │             │
   │  Let N = N+1│
   │             │
   └──────┬──────┘
          │
          ▼
        ╱   ╲
   F  ╱       ╲
  ◄──$P(1+R)^N \geq 2P$
       ╲       ╱
        ╲   ╱
          │ T
          ▼
      Print N
          │
          ▼
        STOP
```

If this flowchart is coded exactly as written, a GOTO statement will be needed following the IF statement. This can be avoided by using $<$ rather than $\geq$ in the decision box. The flowchart will have exactly the same structure, but the program will be easier to read.

THE PROGRAM

```
100 LET P=1000
110 LET R=0.075
120 LET N=0
130     LET N=N+1
140 IF P*(1+R)^N<2*P THEN 130
150 PRINT "NUMBER OF YEARS TO DOUBLE: ";N
160 END
RUN

NUMBER OF YEARS TO DOUBLE: 10
```

■ 8.7 Problems

In Problems 1–11, prepare a flowchart and then a program to accomplish each task specified. Try to avoid GOTO statements in your programs.

1. Input one number. If it is between 3 and 21, display BETWEEN. Otherwise, display NOT BETWEEN.
2. Input two numbers. If either one is positive, display EITHER. Otherwise, display NEITHER.
3. Input three distinct numbers. If the first is the largest, display LARGEST. Otherwise, display NOT LARGEST.
4. Input three distinct numbers. If the second is the largest, display LARGEST. If it is the smallest, display SMALLEST. Otherwise, display NEITHER.
5. Input two values A and B. Display the value 1 if A and B are both 0 or both 1. Display the value 0 in all other cases.
6. Input a list of numbers whose last value is 9999. Display the smallest and largest values in the list excluding the 9999.
7. Input a list of numbers whose last value is 9999. Display the largest number and a count of how many numbers are included in the list.
8. Several pairs (X, Y) of numbers are to be input. Any pair with X = Y serves as the EOD tag. Determine and display counts of how many pairs satisfy $X < Y$ and how many pairs satisfy $X > Y$.
9. Each salesperson earns a base weekly salary of $185. In addition, if a salesperson's total weekly sales exceed $1,000, a commission of 5.3% is earned on any amount up to $5,000 and 7.8% is earned on any amount in excess of $5,000. Determine the weekly pay, before deductions, for any salesperson whose total weekly sales amount is input. Use an EOD tag to terminate the program.
10. A company payroll clerk needs a computer program to assist in preparing the weekly payroll. For each employee the clerk is to enter the hours worked H, the hourly pay rate R, the federal tax rate F, the state tax rate S, and the Social Security rate T. The clerk needs to know the gross pay, the net pay, and the amount of each deduction. Employees receive time and a half for each hour worked over 40 hours. (The algorithm should not be too detailed. For example, after H, R, F, S, and T have been called for, a single line might read "Determine the gross pay, the three deductions, and the net pay." The details for doing this would then be worked out during the flowchart construction.)
11. A salesperson's monthly commission is determined according to the following schedule:

Net sales	Commission rate
Up to $10,000	6%
Next $4,000	7%
Next $6,000	8%
Additional amounts	10%

Determine the monthly commission given the total monthly sales.

8.8 Summing with the WHILE Statement

As a programmer you will often encounter problems whose solutions require you to find the sum of many numbers. Since summing is a repetitive process, it is most conveniently done in a loop that terminates only after the required sum has been obtained. The examples in this section illustrate two ways to exit from a loop:

1. Before the loop is initiated, specify the exact number of terms to be added (Example 13).
2. Cause an exit from the loop when some prescribed condition has been satisfied (Example 14).

EXAMPLE 13   Construct a flowchart and write a program to evaluate the sum

$$S = 1^2 + 2^2 + 3^2 + \cdots + N^2$$

where N is to be specified by the user. If the input value N is less than 1, display the sum S = 0.

PROBLEM ANALYSIS

A simple algorithm for this task is as follows.

a. Input N.
b. Calculate the sum $S = 1^2 + 2^2 + \cdots + N^2$.
c. Display S and stop.

To carry out Step (b), you can start with a sum S of 0 and add the squares of the numbers 1, 2, 3, ..., N to S, one at a time. The following flowchart describes this process:

THE FLOWCHART

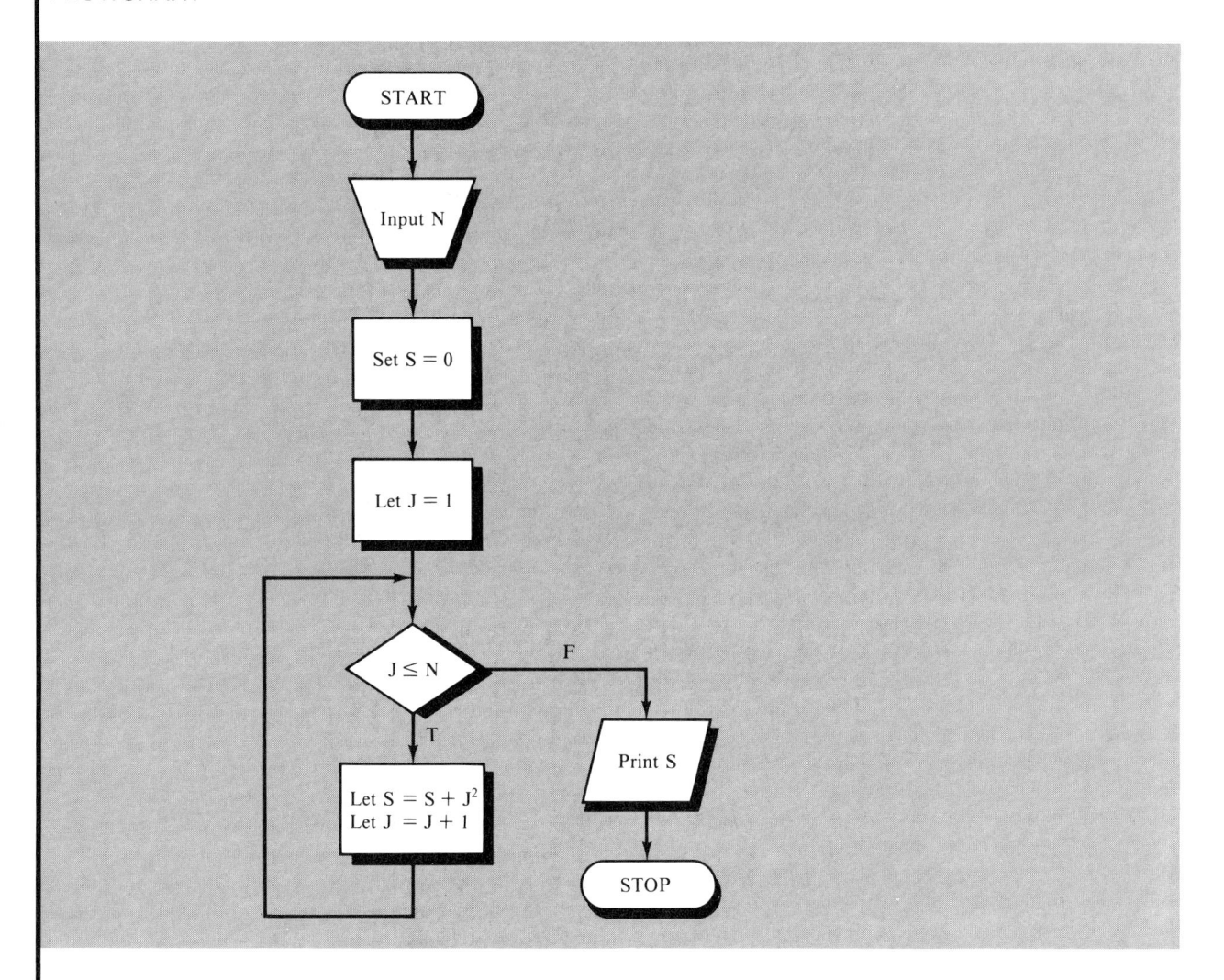

```
            START
              │
              ▼
          Input N
              │
              ▼
          Set S = 0
              │
              ▼
          Let J = 1
              │
              ▼
     ┌──►  ┌──────┐   F
     │     │ J≤N  ├──────►  Print S
     │     └──┬───┘              │
     │        │ T                ▼
     │        ▼                STOP
     │   Let S = S + J²
     │   Let J = J + 1
     └────────┘
```

THE PROGRAM

```
100 PRINT "HOW MANY SQUARES SHOULD BE ADDED?";
110 INPUT N
120 LET S=0
130 LET J=1
140 WHILE J<=N
150     LET S=S+J^2
160     LET J=J+1
170 WEND
180 PRINT "SUM: "; S
190 END
RUN

HOW MANY SQUARES SHOULD BE ADDED? 5
SUM:  55
```

The following table traces the values of N, S, and J as the program is executed with the input value of N = 5:

Line number	N	S	J	Output
110	5	—	—	
120	5	0	—	
130	5	0	1	
150	5	1	1	
160	5	1	2	
150	5	5	2	
160	5	5	3	
150	5	14	3	
160	5	14	4	
150	5	30	4	
160	5	30	5	
150	5	55	5	
160	5	55	6	
180	5	55	6	SUM: 55

EXAMPLE 14

A person wishes to borrow $1,000 but can afford to pay back only $40 per month. A loan officer at the bank states that such a loan is possible at an interest rate of 1.2% per month on the unpaid balance. Write a program to compute the total number of payments, the amount of the final payment, and the total amount the borrower must pay to the bank. (Assume that the first $40 payment is to be made 1 month after the date of the loan.)

PROBLEM ANALYSIS

So that the program will be applicable to any problem of this type, let's assign the variables as follows:

R = the monthly rate of interest (R = .012).
P = the monthly payment (P = 40 except for last payment).
B = the balance still owed to the bank at any time (initially 1000).
I = the interest due for the previous month (I = B * R).
N = the number of payments made to date (initially 0).
T = the total amount paid to date (initially 0).

At the end of each month, the bank calculates the new balance as follows. The interest I = B * R for the month is added to the old balance (LET B = B + I). If this balance B is at least as great as P, the monthly payment is the regular monthly payment P ($40). If B is less than P, however, the monthly payment—the final one—is B dollars. We'll use the statement

    IF B<P THEN P=B

so that the current payment is always denoted by P. In either case, the payment P is subtracted from B to give the new balance, 1 is added to N since 1 month has passed, and the current payment P is added to the total T of all payments. This process is repeated as long as the new balance B is greater than 0.

THE FLOWCHART

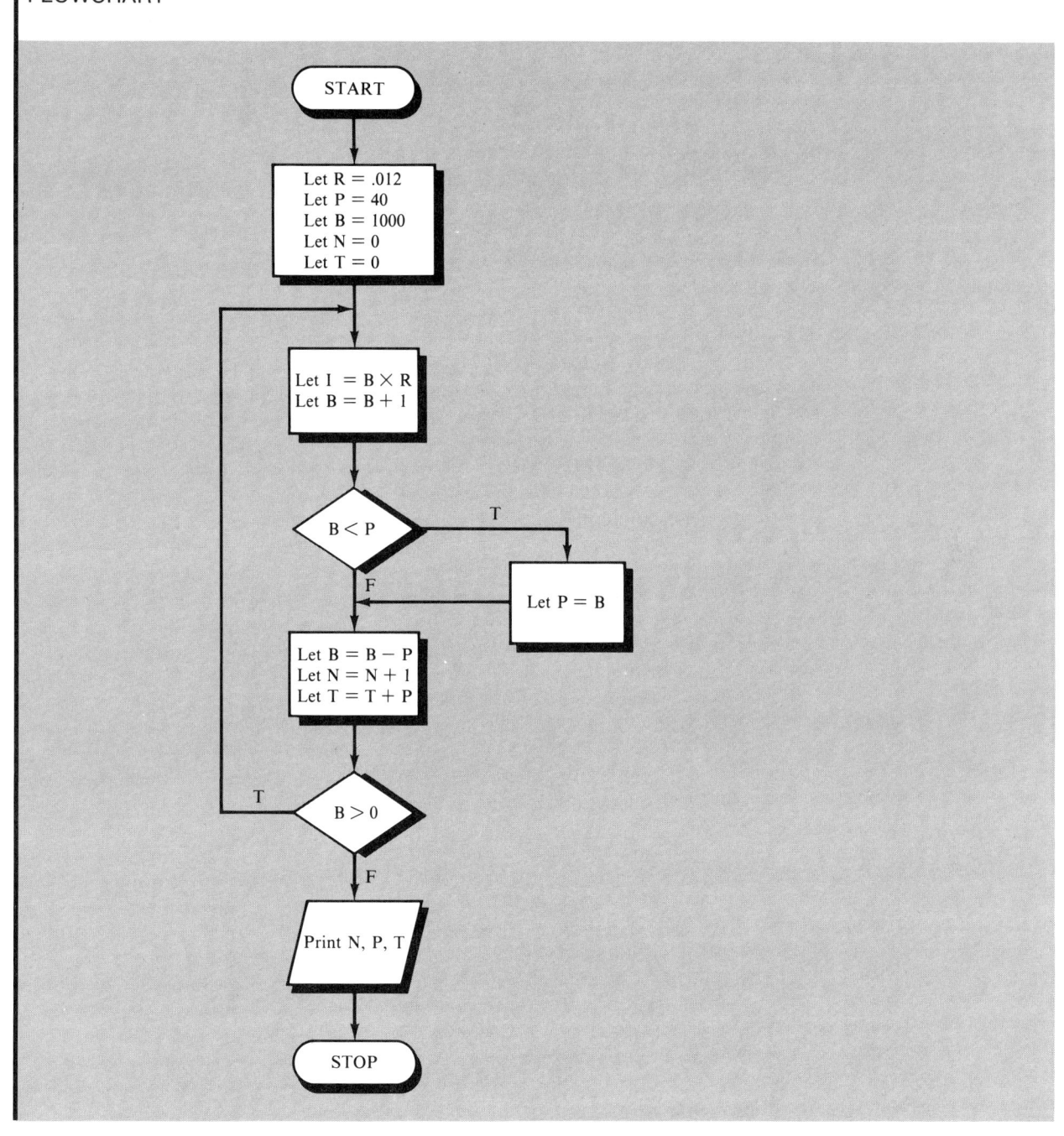

```
                    START
                      │
                      ▼
            ┌──────────────────┐
            │ Let R = .012     │
            │ Let P = 40       │
            │ Let B = 1000     │
            │ Let N = 0        │
            │ Let T = 0        │
            └──────────────────┘
                      │
         ┌────────────▼
         │  ┌──────────────────┐
         │  │ Let I = B × R    │
         │  │ Let B = B + 1    │
         │  └──────────────────┘
         │            │
         │            ▼
         │         ╱─────╲         T    ┌──────────┐
         │        ╱ B < P ╲─────────────▶│ Let P = B│
         │        ╲       ╱              └──────────┘
         │         ╲─────╱                    │
         │            │ F                     │
         │            ◀───────────────────────┘
         │            ▼
         │  ┌──────────────────┐
         │  │ Let B = B − P    │
         │  │ Let N = N + 1    │
         │  │ Let T = T + P    │
         │  └──────────────────┘
         │            │
         │            ▼
         │         ╱─────╲
         │  T     ╱ B > 0 ╲
         └───────╲        ╱
                  ╲─────╱
                     │ F
                     ▼
              ┌──────────────┐
              │ Print N, P, T│
              └──────────────┘
                     │
                     ▼
                   STOP
```

THE PROGRAM

```
100 REM INITIALIZE VARIABLES.
110 LET R=0.012
120 LET P=40
130 LET B=1000
140 LET T=0
150 LET N=0
160 WHILE B>.001
170     REM ADD INTEREST TO OLD BALANCE.
180     LET I=B*R
190     LET B=B+I
200     REM DETERMINE CURRENT PAYMENT P.
210     IF B<P THEN P=B
220     REM MAKE A PAYMENT OF P DOLLARS.
230     LET B=B-P
240     LET N=N+1
250     LET T=T+P
260 WEND
270 REM DISPLAY THE RESULTS.
280 PRINT "LOAN PAYMENT SUMMARY: "
290 PRINT "NO. OF PAYMENTS  ";N
300 PRINT "FINAL PAYMENT    ";P
310 PRINT "TOTAL REPAYMENT  ";T
320 END
RUN

LOAN PAYMENT SUMMARY:
NO. OF PAYMENTS   30
FINAL PAYMENT     36.0570632
TOTAL REPAYMENT   1196.05706
```

■ **REMARK 1** Note that the flowchart continues looping if $B > 0$, whereas the program continues looping if $B > .001$. Remember, the computer may store only close approximations for real numbers. Thus, if a value $B = .000023$ is reached instead of $B = 0$, the condition $B > 0$ would be true, causing an unwanted pass through the loop. By using the condition $B > .001$, we avoid this difficulty.

■ **REMARK 2** So that the program can be used for other loans, R, P, and B should be input and not assigned values in LET statements.

■ **8.9 Problems**

1. Write programs to compute the following sums S. If present, N is to be assigned with an INPUT statement.
   a. $S = 1 + 2 + 3 + \cdots + N$
   b. $S = 5 + 7 + 9 + \cdots + 91$
   c. $S = 3 + 8 + 13 + 18 + \cdots + 93$
   d. $S = 1 + \frac{1}{2} + \frac{1}{3} + \cdots + \frac{1}{99} + \frac{1}{100}$
   e. $S = 1 + \frac{1}{2} + \frac{1}{3} + \frac{1}{4} + \cdots + 1/N$
   f. $S = 1 - \frac{1}{2} + \frac{1}{3} - \frac{1}{4} + \cdots + \frac{1}{99} - \frac{1}{100}$

Write a program to perform each task specified in Problems 2–11.

2. Input a list of numbers whose last value is 999. Calculate the sum and average of all input values excluding 999.
3. Many numbers are to be input. The number 0 is used as the EOD tag. Determine the sum of all positive numbers and the sum of all negative numbers. Display both sums.
4. A list of numbers is to be input as in Problem 3. Determine and display the average of all positive numbers and the average of all negative numbers.

5. A young man agrees to begin working for a company at the very modest salary of a penny per week, with the stipulation that his salary will double each week. At the end of 6 months what is his weekly salary and how much has he earned?
6. Find the total amount credited to an account after 4 years if $25 is deposited each month at an annual interest rate of 5.5% compounded monthly.
7. Mary deposits $25 in a bank at the annual interest rate of 6% compounded monthly. After how many months will her account first exceed $27.50?
8. On the first of each month other than January, a person deposits $100 into an account earning 6% interest compounded monthly. The account is opened on February 1. How much will the account be worth in 5 years just before the February deposit?
9. Andrew's parents deposit $500 in a savings account on the day of his birth. The bank pays 6.5% compounded annually. Construct a table showing how this deposit grows in value from the date of deposit to his 21st birthday.
10. Sally receives a graduation present of $1,000 and invests it in a long-term certificate that pays 8% compounded annually. Construct a table showing how this investment grows to a value of $1,500.
11. Find the averages of several sets of numbers typed at the keyboard. The value 999, when typed, means that all entries for the set being typed have been made. The input value -999 means that all input sets have been processed.

8.10 Structured Programming

The importance of preparing an algorithm before beginning the coding process cannot be overemphasized. However, just as unreadable programs are often written by people who begin a programming task while seated at a computer keyboard, so too, unreadable algorithms can be written if certain guidelines are not followed. The algorithms we have presented in this book take one of two forms:

1. An English-like step-by-step process describing how to carry out a specific task. This mixture of the English language and programming statements is called **pseudocode.**
2. A flowchart displaying the steps to be followed.

In the pseudocode form, the individual steps often correspond to program segments rather than to single program statements. For instance, the following algorithm was written for the task given in Example 13:

a. Input N.
b. Calculate the sum $S = 1^2 + 2^2 + \cdots + N^2$.
c. Display S and stop.

If you can see how to code Step (b), there is no need to include more detail in this algorithm. However, if it is not obvious to you how to code Step (b), you can try to rewrite the step in more detail. Here is one way to do this:

b1. Let $S = 0$.
b2. For $J = 1, 2, 3, \ldots, N$, add J^2 to S.

This process of refining the steps in an algorithm is called the *method of stepwise refinement* and has been illustrated in several of the worked-out examples, beginning with those in Chapter 2.

120 Chapter 8 *The Computer as a Decision Maker*

With flowcharts, the same process of refinement can be used. For the example cited, you could have begun by writing the flowchart on the left:

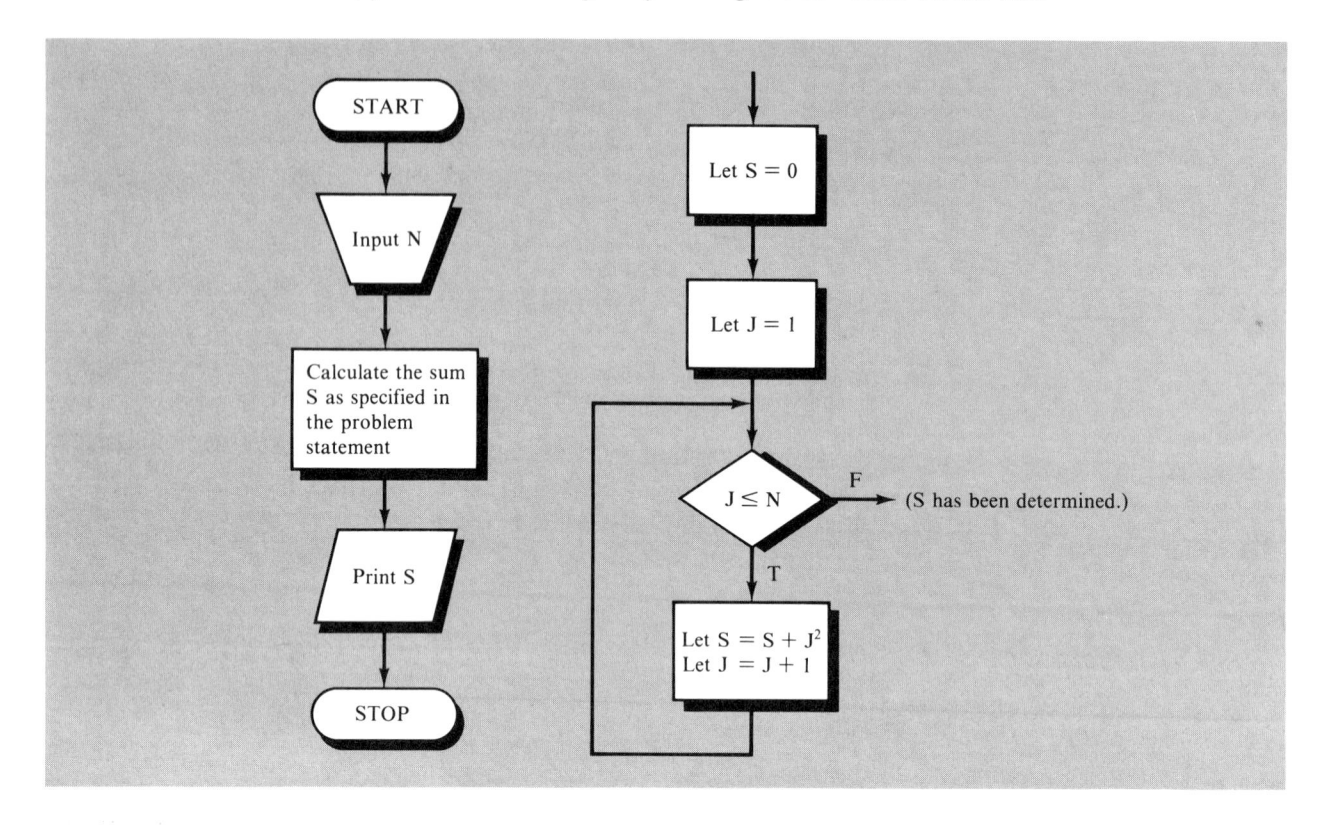

[Flowchart on left: START → Input N → Calculate the sum S as specified in the problem statement → Print S → STOP]

[Flowchart on right: Let S = 0 → Let J = 1 → (loop) J ≤ N ? F → (S has been determined.); T → Let S = S + J²; Let J = J + 1 → back to J ≤ N test]

As before, if coding this flowchart is easy for you, there is no need to include more detail. However, if it is not clear how to code the box that calculates S, you should try to rewrite this step by including more detail. In Example 13 we displayed this detail by using the flowchart segment on the right.

When writing an algorithm, whether in pseudocode or as a flowchart, or in BASIC, you will encounter the following situations:

1. Two or more tasks are to be carried out in sequence (Figure 8.1).

[Flowchart: Task 1 → Task 2]

Figure 8.1 Sequence.

2. One of two tasks is to be selected depending on a specified condition. It may be that one of the two tasks is to do nothing (Figure 8.2).
3. A task is to be carried out repeatedly (Figure 8.3).

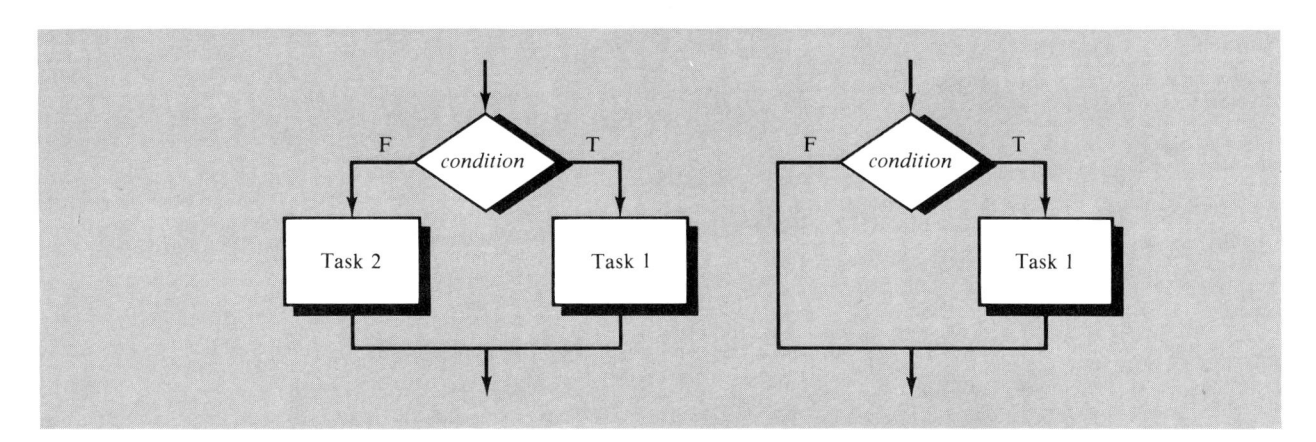

Figure 8.2 Selection.

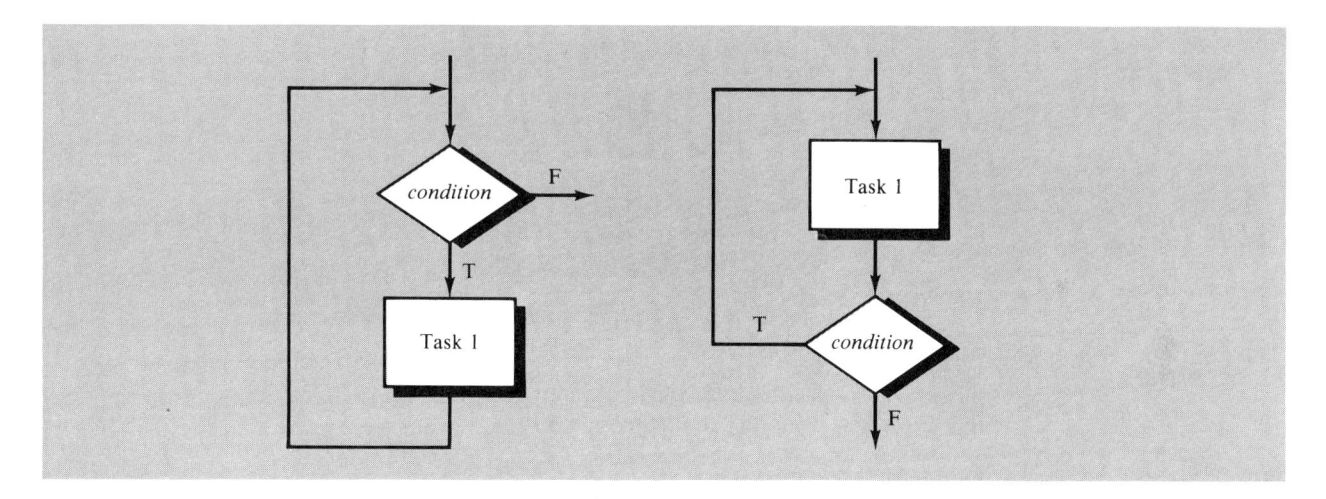

Figure 8.3 Repetition.

These three control structures are referred to as **structured programming constructs.** It has been shown that any algorithm can be written using only these constructs.* The following diagram shows how two of these constructs (*sequence* and *repetition*) are used in the algorithm, shown in Example 13, to calculate the sum

$$S = 1^2 + 2^2 + 3^2 + \cdots + N^2$$

---

* "Flow Diagrams, Turing Machines and Languages with only Two Formation Rules," by Corrado Bohm and Giuseppe Jacopini, *Commun. ACM,* 9 (May 1966), pp. 366–371.

122 Chapter 8 The Computer as a Decision Maker

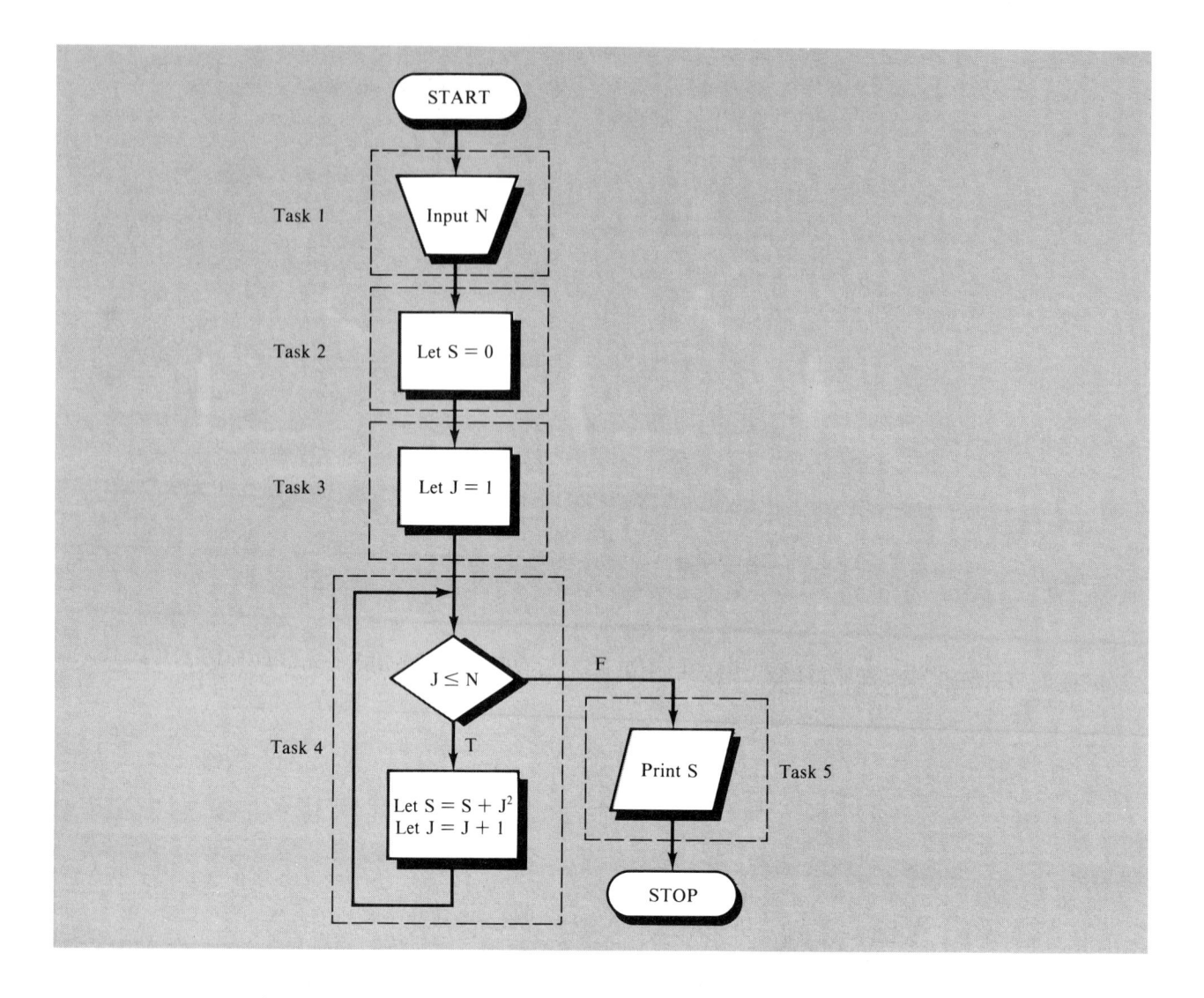

```
                    START
                      │
                      ▼
Task 1           ┌─────────┐
                 │ Input N │
                 └─────────┘
                      │
                      ▼
Task 2           ┌─────────┐
                 │ Let S = 0│
                 └─────────┘
                      │
                      ▼
Task 3           ┌─────────┐
                 │ Let J = 1│
                 └─────────┘
                      │
         ┌────────────▼
         │        ╱ J ≤ N ╲───F───┐
         │        ╲       ╱       ▼
Task 4   │           T         ┌────────┐
         │           │         │Print S │  Task 5
         │           ▼         └────────┘
         │      ┌──────────┐        │
         │      │Let S=S+J²│        ▼
         │      │Let J=J+1 │      STOP
         │      └──────────┘
         └───────────┘
```

Note that Task 4 is an instance of the construct *repetition*, whereas the entire program is simply the *sequence* of Tasks 1 through 5 in that order. Note also that the task being repeated within Task 4 is the *sequence* of two LET statements.

Algorithms written using only the constructs *sequence, selection,* and *repetition* are called **structured algorithms.** The process of writing such algorithms is called **structured programming,** and the resulting programs are called **structured programs.**

Because the BASIC language allows you to use GOTO and IF statements to transfer control to any line in a program, it is easy to write BASIC programs that are very difficult to understand. The time to avoid writing an unreadable program is during the process of discovering the algorithm. Specifically, each time you are tempted to write a step such as *Go to Step (b),* or *If N < 5, go to Step (b),* you should ask whether this transfer of control is part of a selection or repetition structure. If it is not, you should try something else.

By using only the programming constructs described in this section, your final product, the program, will have a simpler structure and hence will be easier to read, to debug, and to modify, should that be required. For instance, note that each of the suggested constructs has exactly one entry point and exactly one exit point. This means that an entire program can be broken down into blocks of code, each block having but one entry point and one exit point. Since each of these blocks will perform a known task, the individual blocks can be debugged separately, thus greatly simplifying the task of verifying the correctness of the entire program. As you write larger and larger programs, you will find this method of debugging not only useful but essential.

Once you have written an algorithm using the suggested constructs, the task of coding it as a BASIC program is routine, as we now show. (As you learn more about BASIC, you will discover other convenient ways to code these structured programming constructs.)

EXAMPLE 15   **To code the selection construct**

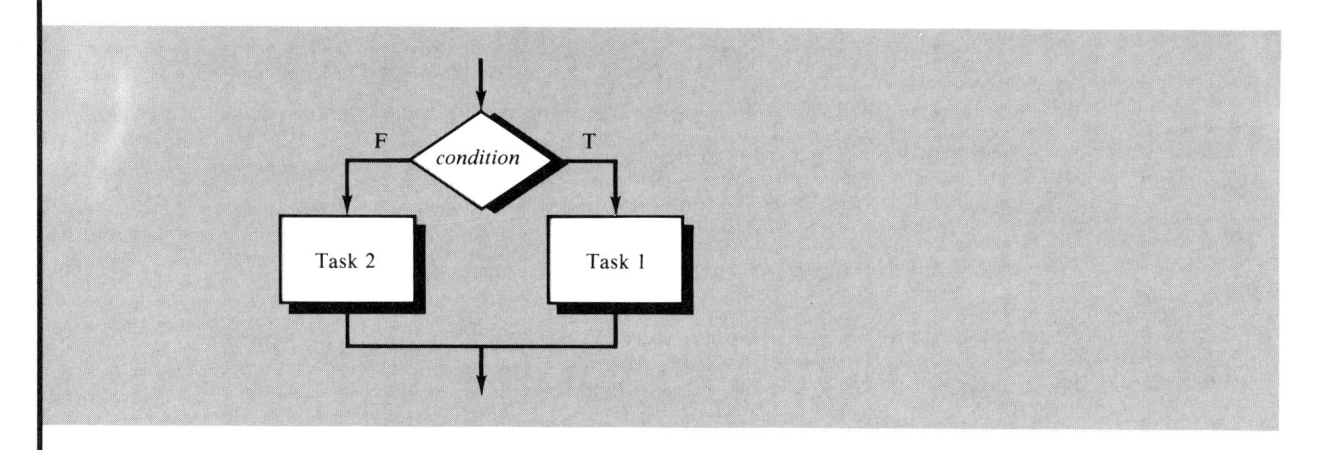

[Flowchart: condition diamond with F branch to Task 2 and T branch to Task 1, both merging below]

you can write (the line numbers are for illustration only):

    500 IF *condition* THEN 600

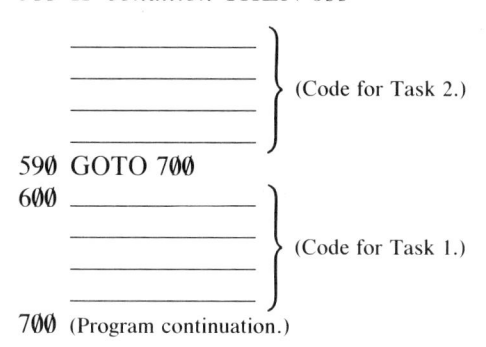

    ⎯⎯⎯⎯⎯⎯⎯⎯⎯
    ⎯⎯⎯⎯⎯⎯⎯⎯⎯ } (Code for Task 2.)
    ⎯⎯⎯⎯⎯⎯⎯⎯⎯

    590 GOTO 700
    600 ⎯⎯⎯⎯⎯⎯⎯⎯⎯
    ⎯⎯⎯⎯⎯⎯⎯⎯⎯ } (Code for Task 1.)
    ⎯⎯⎯⎯⎯⎯⎯⎯⎯

    700 (Program continuation.)

If the code for Task 1 and Task 2 is relatively short and contains no GOTO statements, you can use the form

    500 IF *condition* THEN Code for Task 1 ELSE Code for Task 2

EXAMPLE 16   **To code the selection construct**

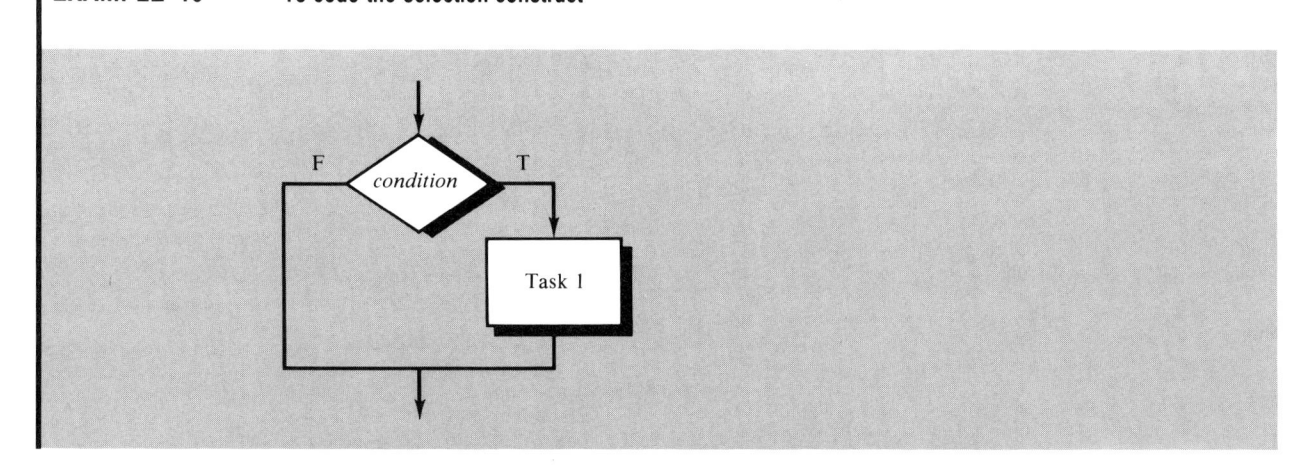

[Flowchart: condition diamond with F branch bypassing and T branch going to Task 1, both merging below]

you can write

500 IF NOT *(condition)* THEN 600

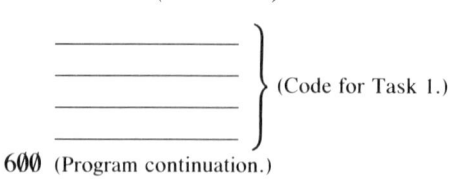

$\left.\begin{array}{l}\rule{3cm}{0.4pt}\\ \rule{3cm}{0.4pt}\\ \rule{3cm}{0.4pt}\\ \rule{3cm}{0.4pt}\end{array}\right\}$ (Code for Task 1.)

600 (Program continuation.)

If the code for Task 1 is short and contains no GOTO statements, you can write
500 IF *condition* THEN Code for Task 1

EXAMPLE 17   **To code the repetition construct**

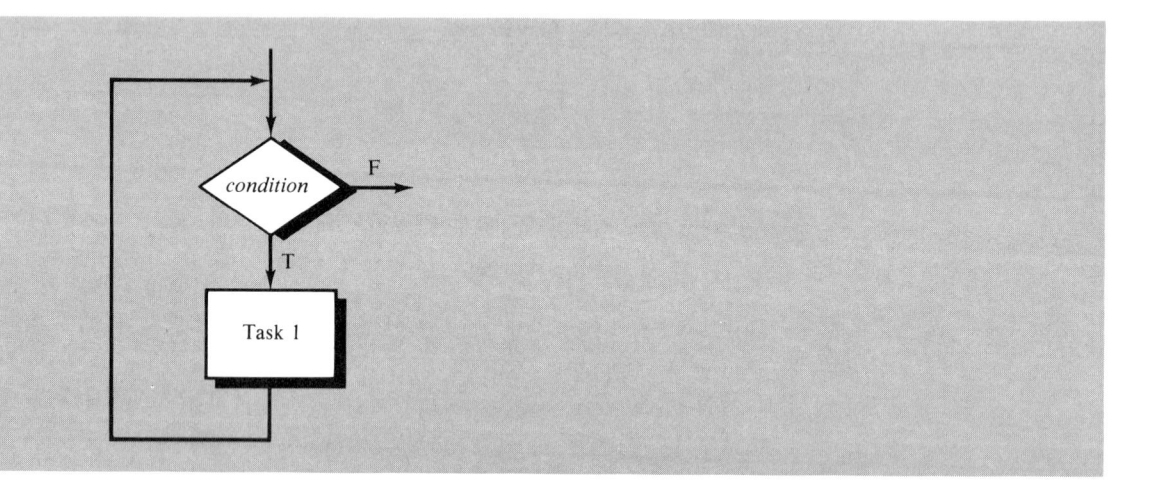

you can write

500 WHILE *condition*

$\left.\begin{array}{l}\rule{3cm}{0.4pt}\\ \rule{3cm}{0.4pt}\\ \rule{3cm}{0.4pt}\\ \rule{3cm}{0.4pt}\end{array}\right\}$ (Code for Task 1.)

590 WEND
600 (Program continuation.)

REMARK   Note that the code for Task 1 must contain a statement that changes some variable appearing in the *condition*. Indeed, the *condition* must eventually become *false;* otherwise you have an infinite loop.

EXAMPLE 18   **To code the repetition construct**

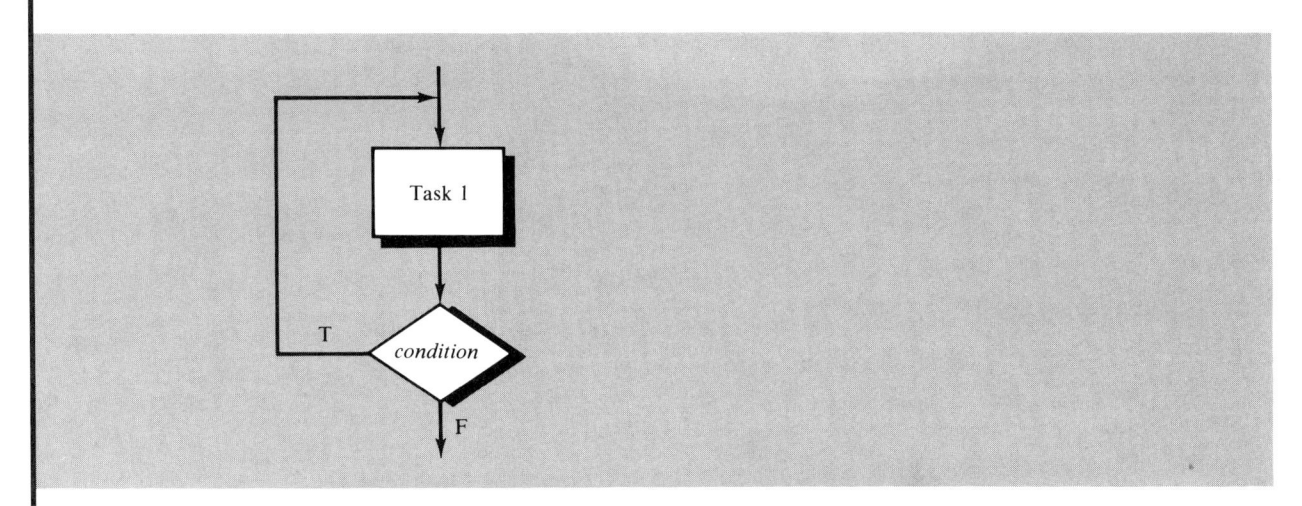

[Flowchart: arrow down into Task 1 box, then down to "condition" diamond; T branch loops back up to before Task 1; F branch exits downward.]

you can write

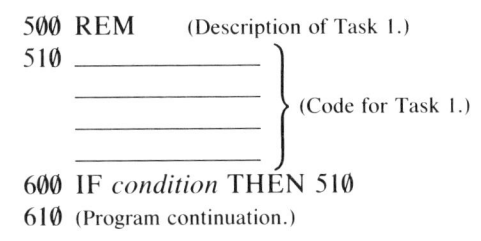

```
500 REM        (Description of Task 1.)
510 ──────────── ⎫
    ────────────  ⎬ (Code for Task 1.)
    ────────────  ⎪
    ──────────── ⎭
600 IF condition THEN 510
610 (Program continuation.)
```

You may or may not wish to code this loop as a WHILE loop. If you do, you must make sure that *condition* is true before entering the loop. Having done this, you can make these two changes:

```
505 WHILE condition
600 WEND
```

■ 8.11 Problems

Construct a flowchart for each algorithm shown in Problems 1–6. In each case use only the sequence, selection, and repetition constructs presented in Section 8.10.

1. **a.** Input values for N, R, and T.
   b. If $N \leq 40$, let $S = N \times R$. Otherwise, let $S = 40 \times R + (N - 40) \times (1.5) \times R$.
   c. Reduce S by the amount $S \times T$.
   d. Print S and stop.

2. a. Input a value for N.
   b. If N = 0, print the message GOODBYE and stop.
   c. If N > 0, print the integers from 1 up to N. Otherwise, print the integers from 0 down to N.
   d. Input another value for N and repeat Step (b).
3. a. Input values for A and B.
   b. If A and B have the same sign (the condition for this is A × B > 0), print POSITIVE or NEGATIVE according to whether A and B are positive or negative.
   c. If either A or B is 0, print FINI and stop. Otherwise, repeat Step (a).
4. a. Input an integer N.
   b. If N = 0, stop.
   c. Print BETWEEN if N is between 70 and 80, exclusive; otherwise print NOT BETWEEN.
   d. Go to Step (a).
5. a. Input values for X, Y, and Z.
   b. If X < Y, print Y − X and go to Step (d).
   c. Print Z − X only if X < Z.
   d. Print X, Y, and Z.
   e. Stop.
6. a. Input a value for N.
   b. If N is less than or equal to 0, go to Step (a).
   c. If N > 100, print VALUE IS TOO LARGE and go to Step (g).
   d. If N > 50, calculate SUM = 50 + 51 + 52 + ··· + N and go to Step (f).
   e. Calculate SUM = 1 + 2 + 3 + ··· + N.
   f. Print the value of SUM.
   g. Print the message GOODBYE and stop.

Reconstruct the flowcharts shown in Problems 7–10 by using only the sequence, selection, and repetition constructs shown in Figures 8.1, 8.2, and 8.3. In the given flowcharts, C1, C2, and C3 denote logical expressions, and S1, S2, and S3 denote single statements or groups of statements. To illustrate, the unstructured flowchart

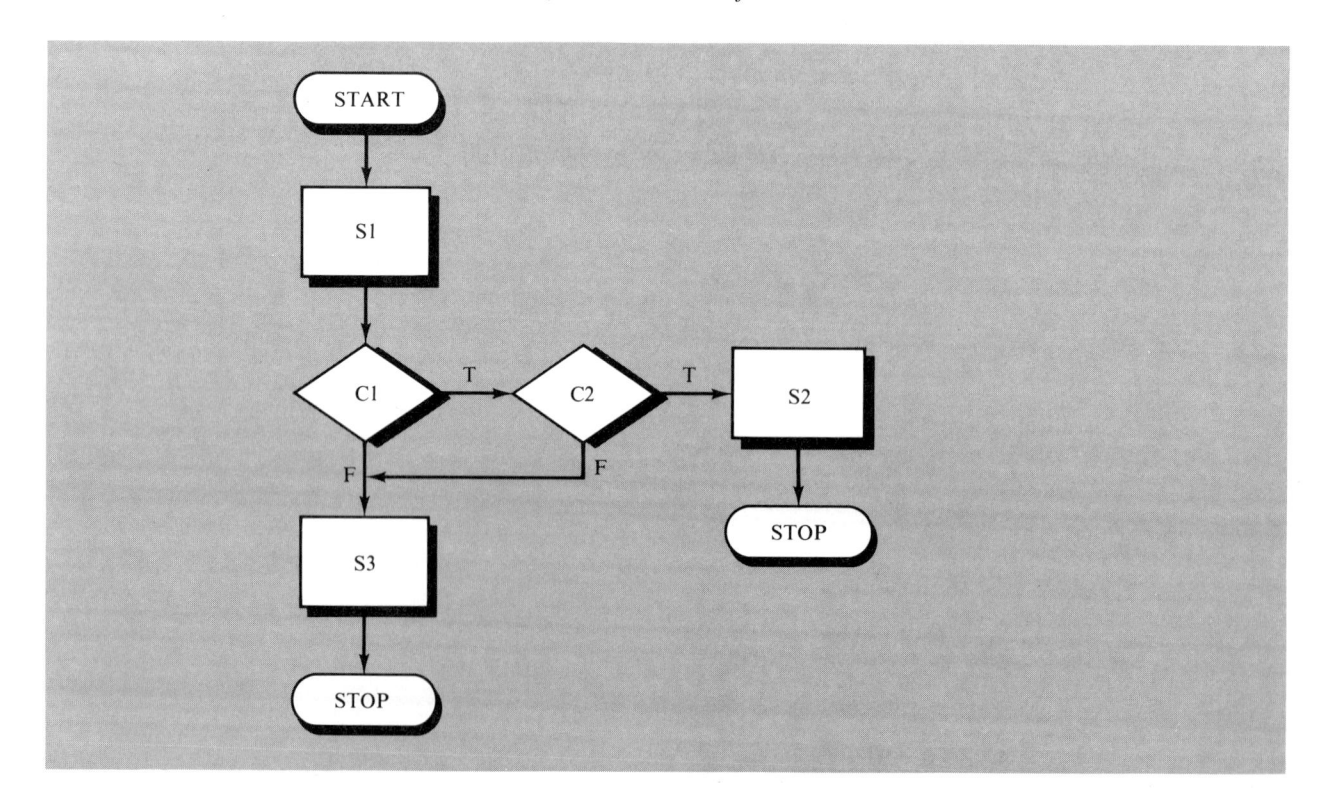

can be written in the equivalent structured form:

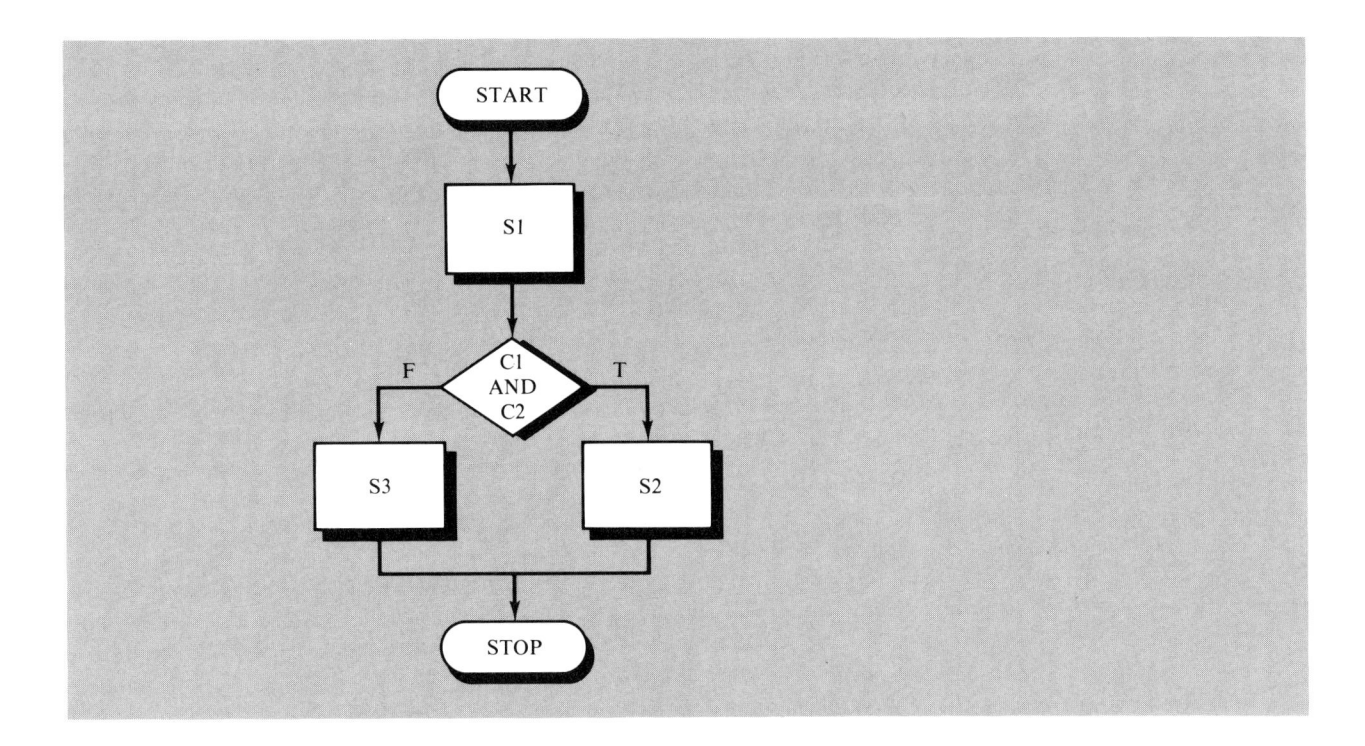

In this illustration, we had to combine two symbols. For the problems, you may also have to write a symbol more than once.

7.

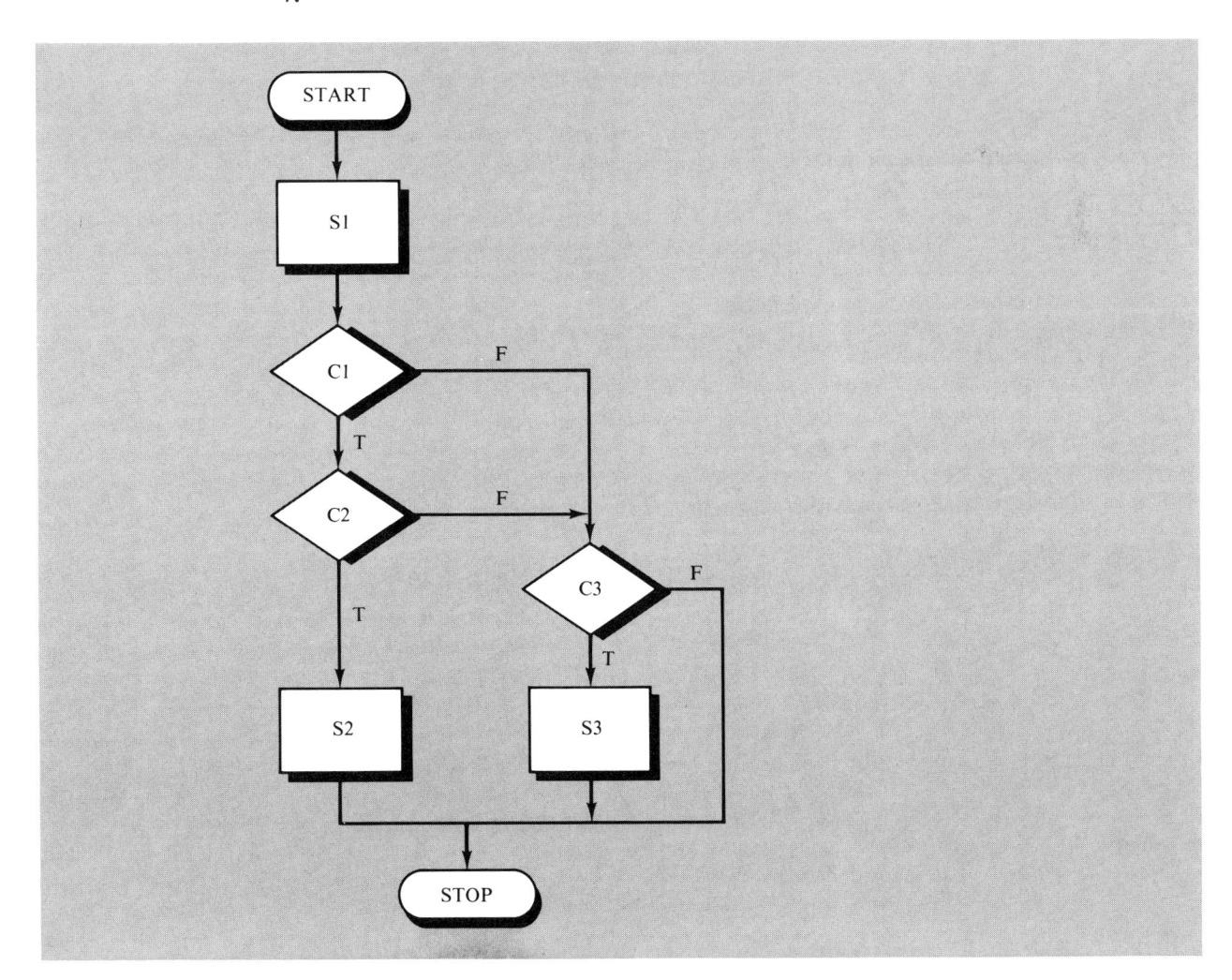

128 *Chapter 8 The Computer as a Decision Maker*

8.

[Flowchart: START → S1 → C1 (T → STOP; F → C2); C2 (F → loop back to before S1; T → S2 → loop back to before S1)]

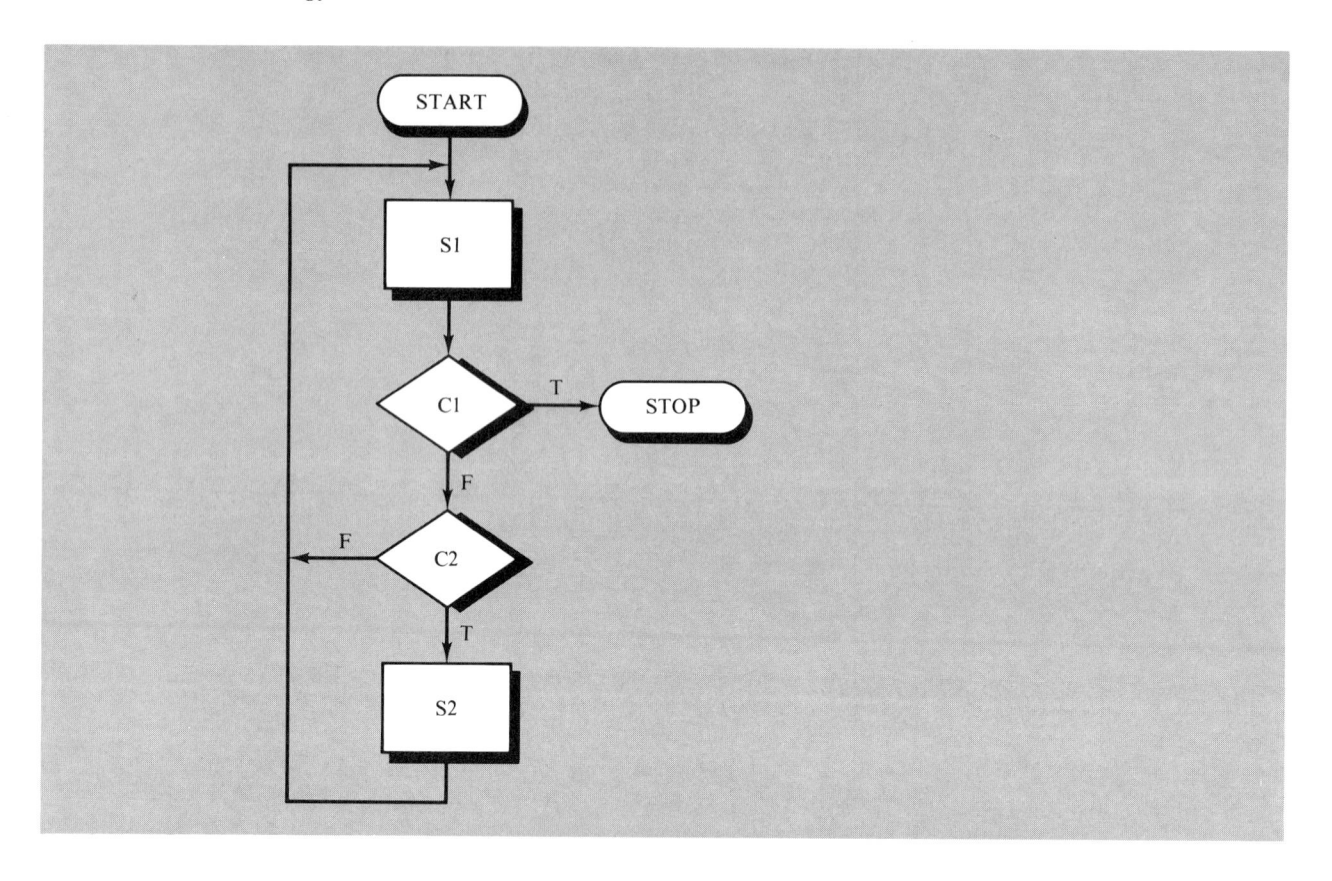

9.

[Flowchart: START → S1 → C1 (T → C2; F → S3 → STOP); C2 (T → C3; F → S3); C3 (T → S3; F → S2 → STOP path)]

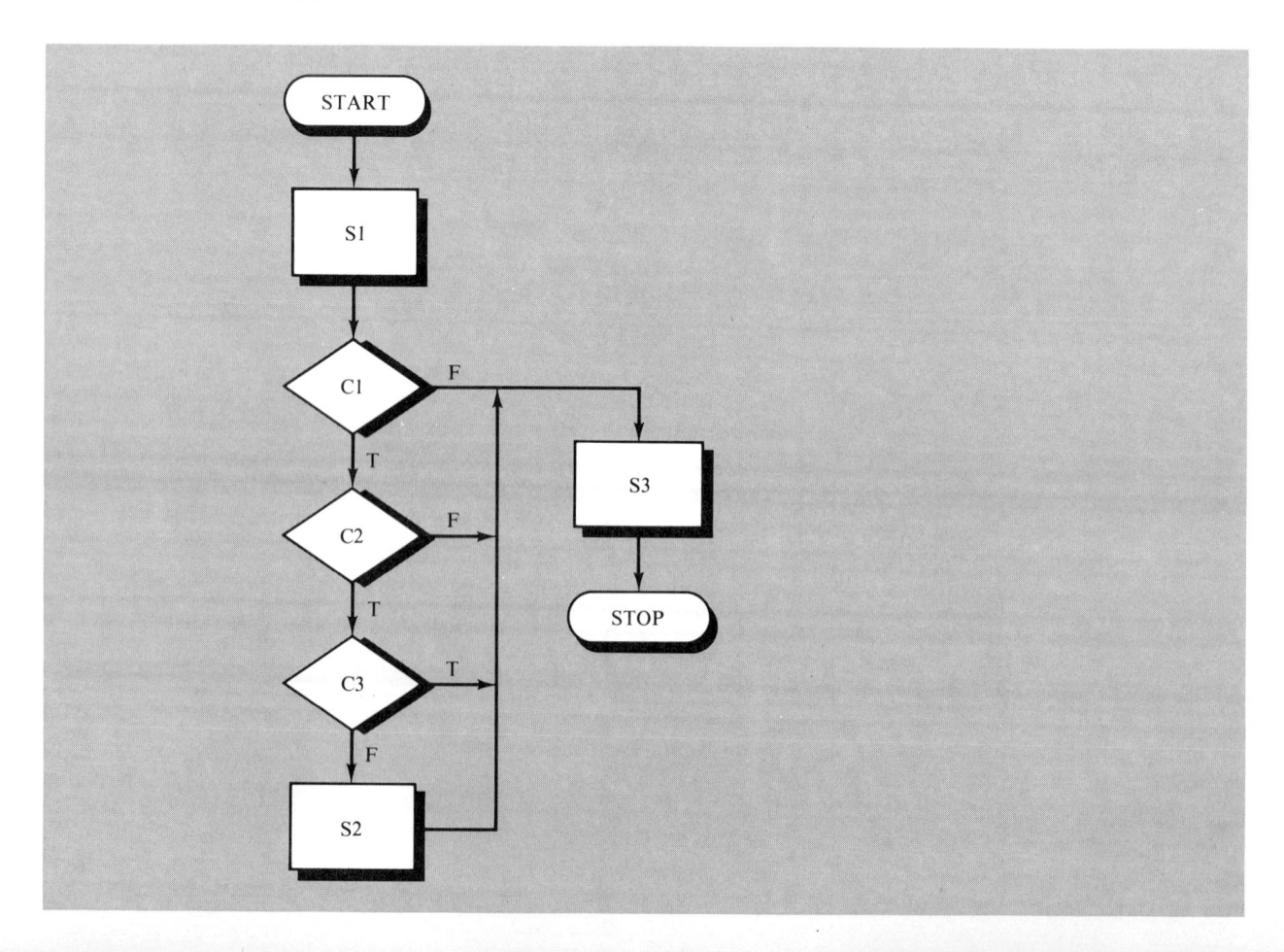

10.

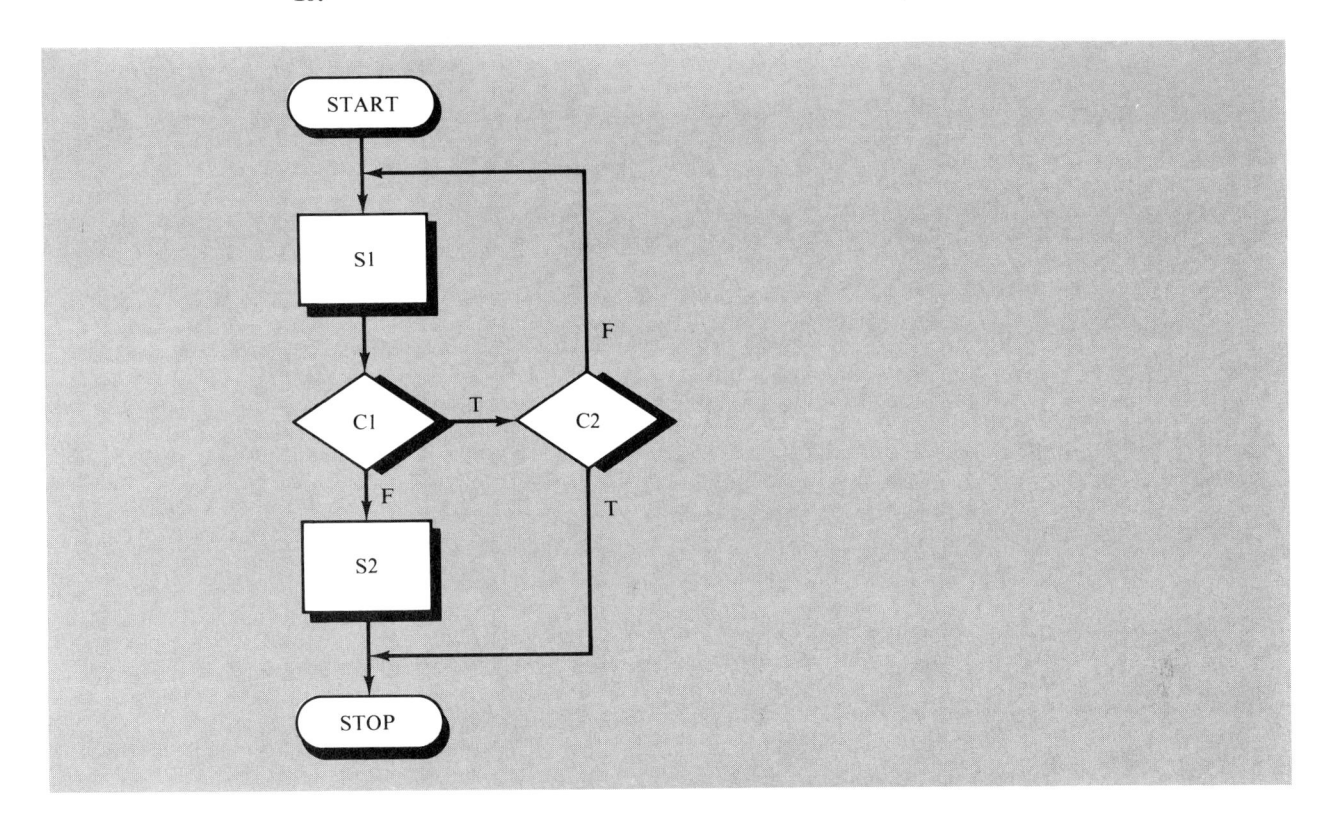

8.12 Review True-or-False Quiz

1. The statement

    50 IF X>0 THEN PRINT "GOOD" ELSE PRINT "BAD"

   is equivalent to the two statements

    50 IF X>0 THEN PRINT "GOOD"
    51 IF X<=0 THEN PRINT "BAD"   T F

2. The statement

    50 IF A=B THEN PRINT A : C=C+1

   is equivalent to the two statements

    50 IF A=B THEN PRINT A
    51 LET C=C+1   T F

3. If A=1 and B=2, this IF statement will print 3.

    IF B=1 AND A>B OR B<3 THEN PRINT A+B   T F

4. The statement

    IF A>5 THEN IF A<10 THEN PRINT A

   is equivalent to the statement

    IF A>5 AND A<10 THEN PRINT A   T F

5. These two logical expressions are equivalent:

    NOT (A=1 AND B=2)
    A<>1 OR B<>2   T F

6. Any program that performs several tasks is a menu-driven program.   T F

7. The following is an admissible ON GOTO statement:

    50 ON NUM GOTO 100,300,200,200,100   T F

8. If N=0, the statement

    50 ON N GOTO 200,300,400

   will transfer control to line 200.   T F

9. The single statement

    50 ON X THEN 200,300,400

   is exactly equivalent to the three statements

    50 IF X=1 THEN 200
    51 IF X=2 THEN 300
    52 IF X=3 THEN 400   T F

10. A flowchart is a pictorial representation of an algorithm.   T F
11. A written algorithm will usually contain more detail than the corresponding flowchart.   T F
12. A flowchart is an excellent way to display the logic of a program, but flowcharting is of little value while writing the program.   T F
13. A BASIC program containing only LET, PRINT, and INPUT statements, together with a proper END statement, is necessarily *structured*.   T F
14. A similar program that also contains IF statements of the form IF *condition* THEN *statement*, where *statement* denotes a LET, PRINT, or INPUT statement, may or may not be structured.   T F
15. A BASIC program that contains GOTO statements or statements of the form IF *condition* THEN *ln* is not structured.   T F

9 Loops Made Easier

So far we have coded each loop by using either an IF or a WHILE statement to specify a looping condition. BASIC also contains the FOR statement, which in many situations can be used to simplify writing loops and also to produce more readable programs. The FOR statement, like the WHILE statement, is used only to code loops. Loops constructed with the FOR statement are called FOR loops. In this chapter we describe how FOR loops are written and give guidelines to help you decide when loops should be coded as FOR loops and when they should not.

■ 9.1 FOR Loops

Here are two ways to display the integers from 1 to 5:

Program 1

```
100 LET N=1
110     PRINT N;
120     LET N=N+1
130 IF N<=5 THEN 110
140 END
RUN

 1  2  3  4  5
```

Program 2

```
100 LET N=1
110 WHILE N<=5
120     PRINT N;
130     LET N=N+1
140 WEND
150 END
RUN

 1  2  3  4  5
```

The same thing can be accomplished by the following program:

Program 3

```
100 FOR N=1 TO 5
110     PRINT N;
120 NEXT N
130 END
RUN

 1  2  3  4  5
```

This program instructs the computer to execute line 110 five times, once for each integer N from 1 to 5. In Microsoft® BASIC, Program 3 is equivalent to Program 2. Thus the action of Program 3 can be described as follows:

a. Line 100 (the FOR statement) assigns an initial value of 1 to N.
b. N is compared with the terminal value 5. If N > 5, control passes to the line

132   Chapter 9   Loops Made Easier

following the NEXT statement (line 130). The loop has been satisfied. If N ≤ 5, control passes to the line following the FOR statement (line 110).

   c. Line 110 displays the current value of N.

   d. When the NEXT statement, line 120, is encountered, N is incremented by 1, and the comparison in Step (b) is repeated.

The following examples further illustrate the use of the FOR and NEXT statements to construct loops. To clarify the meaning of the FOR loops, we have written each program in two equivalent ways—with and without the FOR and NEXT statements.

EXAMPLE 1

Here is a program to calculate and display the price of one, two, three, four, five, and six items selling at seven for $1.00.

```
100 REM U DENOTES THE            100 REM U DENOTES THE
110 REM UNIT PRICE.              110 REM UNIT PRICE.
120 LET U=1.00/7                 120 LET U=1.00/7
130 FOR K=1 TO 6                 130 LET K=1
140     LET P=U*K                140 WHILE K<=6
150     PRINT K,P                150     LET P=U*K
160 NEXT K                       160     PRINT K,P
170 END                          170     LET K=K+1
                                 180 WEND
                                 190 END
```

The FOR loop instructs the computer to execute the statements

```
LET P=U*K
PRINT K,P
```

six times, once for each integer K from 1 to 6. These two statements are called the **body** or **range** of the loop. It is an excellent programming practice to indent the body of each FOR loop to improve program readability.

EXAMPLE 2

Here is a loop to display the numbers −4, −2, 0, 2, 4, 6.

```
100 FOR J=-4 TO 6 STEP 2         100 LET J=-4
110     PRINT J;                 110 WHILE J<=6
120 NEXT J                       120     PRINT J;
130 END                          130     LET J=J+2
RUN                              140 WEND
                                 150 END
-4 -2  0  2  4  6                RUN

                                 -4 -2  0  2  4  6
```

The starting value for J is −4. Including STEP 2 in the statement

```
100 FOR J=-4 TO 6 STEP 2
```

specifies that J is to be increased by 2 each time NEXT J is encountered. Thus, the FOR loop instructs the computer to execute the statement

```
110 PRINT J;
```

for the successive J values −4, −2, 0, 2, 4, and 6.

EXAMPLE 3

Here is a loop to display the numbers 5, 4, 3, 2, 1.

```
100 FOR N=5 TO 1 STEP -1         100 LET N=5
110     PRINT N;                 110 WHILE N>=1
120 NEXT N                       120     PRINT N;
130 END                          130     LET N=N-1
RUN                              140 WEND
                                 150 END
 5  4  3  2  1                   RUN

                                  5  4  3  2  1
```

This example illustrates that negative increments are acceptable. The initial value of N is 5, and, after each pass through the loop, N is *decreased* by 1 (STEP −1). As soon as N attains a value *less* than 1 (as specified in the FOR statement), control passes out of the loop to the statement following the NEXT statement.

The general form of a FOR loop is

    FOR v = a TO b STEP c
          ·
          · (Body of the loop)
          ·
    NEXT v

where **v** denotes a *simple* numerical variable name* and **a**, **b**, and **c** denote arithmetic expressions. (IF STEP **c** is omitted, **c** is assumed to have the value 1.) **v** is called the **control variable**, and the values of **a**, **b**, and **c** are called the **initial, terminal,** and **step** values, respectively. The action of a FOR loop is described by the following flow diagrams.

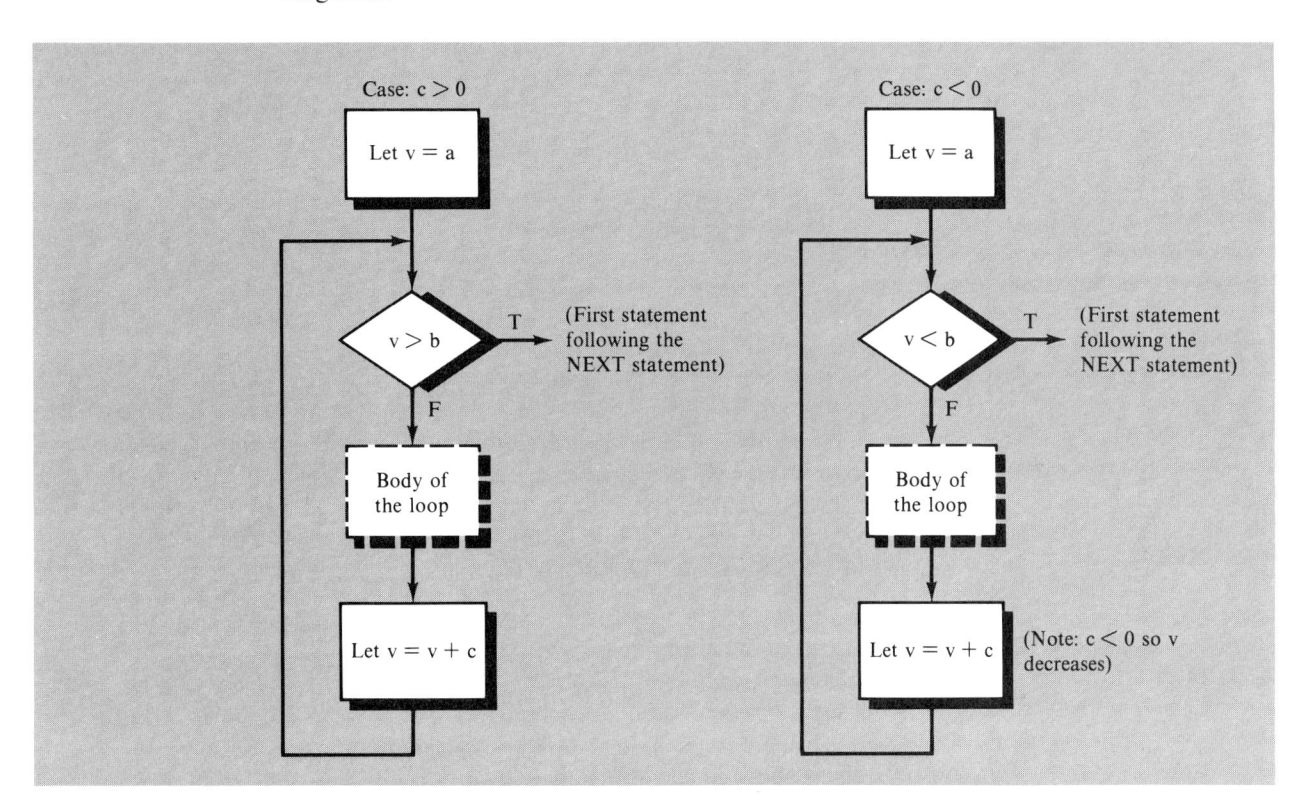

Case: c > 0

Let v = a

↓

v > b ──T──→ (First statement following the NEXT statement)

↓ F

Body of the loop

↓

Let v = v + c

(loops back to v > b test)

Case: c < 0

Let v = a

↓

v < b ──T──→ (First statement following the NEXT statement)

↓ F

Body of the loop

↓

Let v = v + c   (Note: c < 0 so v decreases)

(loops back to v < b test)

In each FOR loop shown in Examples 1–3, the control variable appears in a statement in the body of the loop. The next example shows that you are not required to do this. Indeed, in many cases, as in this one, the control variable serves only as a counter.

EXAMPLE 4   **Here is a loop to display a row of N dashes**

```
200 FOR I=1 TO N
210    PRINT "-";
220 NEXT I
```

---

* The numerical variables considered to this point are called *simple* to distinguish them from the *subscripted* variables considered in Chapter 15.

Of course, N must be assigned a value before line 200 is executed. If N is 15, a row of 15 dashes will be displayed.

■ **REMARK** If the terminal value N is 0, then the entire loop will be skipped, since the initial value, I = 1, will be greater than the terminal value, N = 0.

In the next example, we use a FOR loop to produce a table of values. This is a common application of FOR loops. The example also illustrates that the initial, terminal, and step values of a FOR loop do not have to be integers.

EXAMPLE 5 Here is a program to produce a table showing the 5.5%, 6%, 6.5%, . . . , 8% discount on any amount A typed at the keyboard. The maximum discount, however, is $50.

```
100 REM *** DISCOUNT CALCULATIONS ***
110 INPUT "AMOUNT";A
120 PRINT
130 PRINT "PERCENT RATE","DISCOUNT"
140 FOR R=5.5 TO 8 STEP 0.5
150     LET D=R/100*A
160     IF D>50 THEN LET D=50
170     PRINT R,D
180 NEXT R
190 END
RUN

AMOUNT? 700

PERCENT RATE   DISCOUNT
 5.5            38.5
 6              42
 6.5            45.5
 7              49
 7.5            50
 8              50
```

The FOR statement in line 140 specifies that the control variable R is to range from 5.5 to 8, with 0.5 as the increment. For R = 5.5, 6, 6.5, and 7, the discount values D determined by line 150 do not exceed 50; hence the statement LET D = 50 in line 160 is not executed. When R = 7.5 and 8, the D values determined by line 150 do exceed 50, so the statement LET D = 50 in line 160 is executed.

■ **REMARK** Special care must be taken when writing FOR loops with initial, terminal, or step values that are not integers. As we have mentioned previously, the computer stores only close approximations for most numbers that are not integers. The loop in this example causes no difficulty because 0.5 is one of the fractional numbers computers store exactly. If we had used STEP 0.1 instead of STEP 0.5, however, the control variable R would have taken on only close approximations to the values 5.6, 5.7, 5.8, . . . , 8. If your computer reaches R = 8.00010 instead of R = 8, the loop will not be executed for the final value R = 8. To avoid such awkward situations, many programmers use only integers for the initial, terminal, and step values in FOR loops. To write the program in this example so that the control variable R takes on only integer values, you can make these two changes:

```
140 FOR R=55 TO 80 STEP 5
150     LET D=R/1000*A
```

If increments of 0.1 instead of 0.5 are required, you can simply use STEP 1 rather than STEP 5.

In this section we have described and illustrated the syntax that must be used in writing FOR loops. Although the examples also illustrate certain situations in which loops are best coded as FOR loops, more needs to be said on this topic.

You may have noticed that all FOR loops share a common characteristic: the number of times the body of the loop must be executed to satisfy the loop (this is called the **iteration count** of the loop) can be determined before the loop is entered. For example, the statement

```
FOR N=1 TO 500
```

initiates a loop with iteration count 500, the statement

```
FOR N=1 TO 20 STEP 4
```

initiates a loop with iteration count 5 (the five N values are 1, 5, 9, 13, and 17), and if M has been assigned a positive integer value,

```
FOR K=1 TO M
```

initiates a loop with iteration count M.

There is a simple formula for determining the iteration count for any FOR loop. If **i**, **t**, and **s** denote the initial, terminal, and step values, respectively, the iteration count is the larger of the two values

$$\left[\frac{t - i + s}{s} \right] \text{ and } 0$$

where the expression in brackets is truncated, if necessary, to obtain an integer.

FOR statement	i, t, s	(t − i + s)/s	Iteration count
FOR N=1 TO 20 STEP 3	1, 20, 3	$(20 - 1 + 3)/3 = 7\frac{1}{3}$	7
FOR K=1 TO 1000	1, 1000, 1	$(1000 - 1 + 1)/1 = 1000$	1000
FOR L=2 TO 100 STEP 50	2, 100, 50	$(100 - 2 + 50)/50 = 2.96$	2
FOR M=20 TO 1 STEP -3	20, 1, −3	$(1 - 20 + (-3))/(-3) = 7\frac{1}{3}$	7
FOR P=10 TO 1	10, 1, 1	$(1 - 10 + 1)/1 = -8$	0
FOR R=5.5 TO 8 STEP 0.5	5.5, 8, 0.5	$(8 - 5.5 + 0.5)/0.5 = 6$	6

A common method used by computers to process FOR statements is first to calculate the iteration count, and then to use a counter to control looping. An exit from the loop occurs when the predetermined number of passes has been made.* Loops that are controlled by such counters are called **counter-controlled loops.** Thus, every FOR loop that does not contain an IF or GOTO statement to terminate the loop prematurely is a counter-controlled loop.

The worked-out examples in this section and the preceding discussion of counter-controlled loops suggest this guideline concerning the use of FOR loops:

Use a FOR loop only if both of the following conditions are met:

1. *The number of times the loop will be repeated can be determined before the loop is entered.* It isn't necessary that you determine this count, but it is necessary that you know it can be determined. For instance, to produce a report showing the equivalent annual salaries for people working at the hourly rates 4.00, 4.25, 4.50, . . . , 9.00, we could use a FOR loop beginning

```
FOR H=4 TO 9 STEP 0.25
```

We would not determine the iteration count, but it is obvious that it can be determined

---

* The flow diagrams shown after Example 3 explain the effect of a FOR loop, but they are not intended to describe exactly how the computer causes this effect. For instance, our description of the action caused by the statement FOR R=5.5 to 8 STEP 0.5 suggests that the computer first assigns 5.5 to R and then compares R with the terminal value 8. Although this helps us understand the effect of the FOR statement, it does not necessarily correspond to what actually happens.

simply by counting the H values. As an example of a loop that should not be coded as a FOR loop, suppose we must find the smallest of these hourly rates that gives an equivalent annual salary of $11,500. In this case, an iteration count cannot be determined without actually performing some calculations—that is, without entering the loop. Thus, we would code the loop by including the condition SALARY < 11500 in a WHILE statement.

2. *A meaningful control variable can be found for the loop.* If you determine the iteration count C for a loop, you can use a counter, say N, as the control variable and use a FOR loop beginning

```
FOR N=1 TO C
```

Such a counter, however, is not always meaningful. For instance, in Example 5 we used a FOR loop beginning

```
FOR R=5.5 TO 8 STEP 0.5
```

to display R percent discounts. The iteration count for the loop is

$$\frac{8 - 5.5 + 0.5}{0.5} = \frac{3}{0.5} = 6$$

But it would not be particularly meaningful to code the loop by using

```
FOR N=1 TO 6
```

The control variable R, however, is meaningful—it denotes the discount rate.

Following are some points concerning the use of FOR loops that were not raised explicitly in this section:

1. The initial, terminal, and step values are determined once, when the FOR statement is executed, and cannot be altered within the body of the loop.
2. Entry into a FOR loop should be made only by executing the FOR statement.
3. Although the control variable can be modified inside the FOR loop, don't do it. The resulting program may be very difficult to understand.
4. Never use an IF or GOTO statement to terminate a FOR loop. Doing so will give you a loop with two exit points and your program will not be structured (see Section 8.10).
5. When a FOR loop has been satisfied (that is, when an exit is made via the NEXT statement), the value of the control variable is the first value not used.
6. FOR loops can be nested. (This is the subject of Section 9.3.)

■ 9.2 Problems

1. Show the output of each program.

   a.
   ```
   10 FOR J=2 TO 4
   20     PRINT J+2
   30 NEXT J
   40 END
   ```

   b.
   ```
   10 FOR N=5 TO -3 STEP -4
   20     PRINT N
   30 NEXT N
   40 END
   ```

   c.
   ```
   10 LET C=0
   20 LET X=1
   30 FOR Q=1 TO 4.9 STEP 2
   40     LET C=C+1
   50     LET X=X*Q
   60 NEXT Q
   70 PRINT "TIMES THROUGH LOOP=";C
   80 PRINT X
   90 END
   ```

   d.
   ```
   10 FOR I=1 TO 3
   20     PRINT "+";
   30 NEXT I
   40 FOR J=5 TO 7
   50     PRINT "/";
   60 NEXT J
   70 END
   ```

e. ```
10 FOR J=2 TO 2
20   PRINT "LOOP"
30 NEXT J
40 END
```

f. ```
10 FOR J=5 TO 1
20     PRINT "LOOP"
30 NEXT J
40 END
```

g. ```
10 PRINT "123456789"
20 FOR V=1 TO 4
30   PRINT TAB(V);"V";TAB(10-V);"V"
40 NEXT V
50 PRINT TAB(5);"V"
60 END
```

h. ```
10 FOR R=1 TO 7
20     IF R=1 OR R=7 THEN 50
30     PRINT TAB(8-R);"Z"
40     GOTO 60
50     PRINT "ZZZZZZZ"
60 NEXT R
70 END
```

i. ```
10 FOR N=1 TO 4
20   PRINT USING "ITEM# ";N;
30 NEXT N
40 PRINT
50 FOR N=1 TO 4
60   PRINT USING "###   ";N;
70 NEXT N
80 END
```

2. Each of the following programs contains an error—either a syntax error that will cause an error message or a programming error that the computer will not recognize but will nevertheless cause incorrect results. In each case find the error and tell which of the two types it is.

a. ```
10 REM 6 PERCENT PROGRAM
20 FOR N=1 TO 6
30     INPUT X
40     PRINT X,.06*X
50 NEXT X
60 END
```

b. ```
10 REM COUNT THE POSITIVE
20 REM NUMBERS TYPED.
30 FOR I=1 TO 10
40   LET C=0
50   INPUT N
60   IF N>0 THEN C=C+1
70 NEXT I
80 PRINT C;"ARE POSITIVE."
90 END
```

c. ```
10 REM SUMMING PROGRAM
20 LET S=0
30 FOR X=1 TO 4
40     INPUT X
50     LET S=S+X
60 NEXT X
70 PRINT "SUM IS";S
80 END
```

d. ```
10 REM DISPLAY THE NUMBERS
20 REM 1 3 6 10 15
30 LET S=1
40 FOR N=1 TO 15 STEP S
50   PRINT N
60   LET S=S+1
70 NEXT N
80 END
```

*In Problems 3–12, write a program for each task specified.*

3. A positive integer N is to be entered, followed by N numbers. Determine the sum and average of the N numbers.

4. A positive integer N is to be entered, followed by N numbers. Determine how many of the N numbers are negative, how many are positive, and how many are 0.

5. Display the integers from 1 to 72, eight to the line.

6. Display the integers from 1 to 72, eight to the line, equally spaced.

7. A program is needed to assist grade school students with their multiplication tables. After an
```

initial greeting, the computer should ask the student to type a number from 2 to 12 so that products involving this number can be practiced. (Call this number N, but don't confuse the student with this information.) Next, the student should be asked to answer the questions $2 \times N = ?, 3 \times N = ?, \ldots, 12 \times N = ?$ Of course, the *value* of N should be displayed, not the letter N. If a question is answered correctly, the next question should be asked; if not, the question should be repeated. If the same question is answered incorrectly twice, the correct answer should be displayed and then the next question should be asked. After all questions pertaining to N have been answered, display the student's score and give the student the choice of trying another multiplication table or stopping.

8. Produce a two-column table with column headings showing P percent of the amounts $1, $2, $3, . . . , $20. P is to be input.

9. Prepare a report showing the effect of a flat across-the-board raise of F dollars in addition to a percentage increase of P percent on the salaries $20,000, $20,500, $21,000, . . . , $30,000. F and P are to be input. Include three columns labeled PRESENT SALARY, RAISE, and NEW SALARY.

10. Evaluate the following sums. If a value for N is required, it is to be input.

   a. $1 + 2 + 3 + \cdots + N$
   b. $1 + 3 + 5 + 7 + \cdots + 51$
   c. $1 + 3 + 5 + 7 + \cdots + (2N - 1)$
   d. $2 + 5 + 8 + 11 + \cdots + K$, where $N - 3 < K <= N$
   e. $(.06) + (.06)^2 + (.06)^3 + \cdots + (.06)^N$
   f. $1 + 1/2 + 1/3 + 1/4 + \cdots + 1/N$
   g. $1 + 1/4 + 1/9 + 1/16 + \cdots + 1/N^2$
   h. $1 + 1/2 + 1/4 + 1/8 + \cdots + 1/2^N$
   i. $1 - 1/2 + 1/3 - 1/4 + \cdots - 1/100$
   j. $4[1 - 1/3 + 1/5 - 1/7 + \cdots + (-1)^{N+1}/(2N - 1)]$

11. Produce a two-column table with the headings N and $1 + 2 + 3 + \cdots + N$. The first column is to show the N values 1,2,3, . . . , 20, and the second is to show the indicated sums. [*Hint:* The second column value for row N (N>1) is simply N plus the previous sum.]

12. For any positive integer N, the product $1 \times 2 \times 3 \times \cdots \times N$ is denoted by the symbol N! and is called N factorial. Also, zero factorial (0!) is defined to be 1. (Thus, 0! = 1! = 1.) Produce a two-column table with column headings showing the values of N and N! for N = 0, 1, 2, . . . , 10. [*Hint:* For N>0, N! = (N − 1)! × N.]

■ 9.3 Nested Loops

It is permissible, and often desirable, to have one FOR loop contained in another. When nesting loops in this manner, there is one rule that must be observed:

If the body of one FOR loop contains either the FOR or the NEXT statement of another loop, it must contain both of them. This is illustrated in Figure 9.1.

EXAMPLE 6   **Here is an illustration of nested FOR loops.**

```
10 FOR I=1 TO 3
20     FOR J=1 TO 5
30         PRINT I;
40     NEXT J
50     PRINT
60 NEXT I
70 END
RUN

1  1  1  1  1
2  2  2  2  2
3  3  3  3  3
```

The FOR and NEXT statements in lines 10 and 60 cause the four program lines between them to be executed three times. The first three of these lines (20, 30, 40) display the value of I five times on one line, leaving the cursor positioned at the end of that line. Line 50 causes a RETURN to be executed so that subsequent output will appear on a new line. Since lines 20 to 50 are executed for the successive I values 1, 2, and 3, the program produces three lines of output as shown.

■ REMARK   Since the J-loop (lines 20 to 40) is short and performs such a simple and well-defined task (displays a single digit five times), you may find it convenient to replace these three lines by the equivalent multiple-statement line

```
20 FOR J=1 TO 5 : PRINT I; : NEXT J
```

As shown in Section 9.1, the value of the control variable of a FOR loop can be used in the body of the loop in any way you wish. In the preceding example, the control variable I was used to supply output values; in the next example, we use the control variable of an outer loop to supply the terminal value for an inner loop.

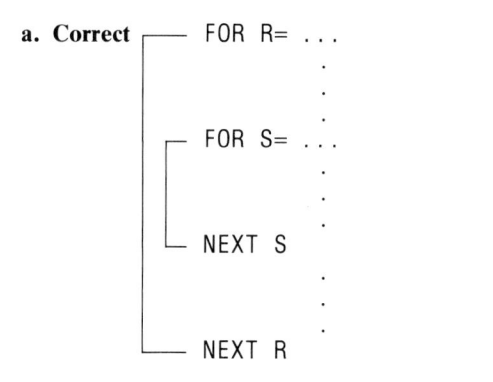

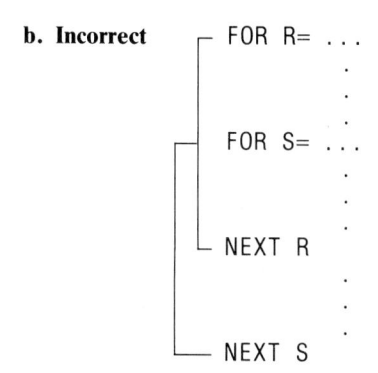

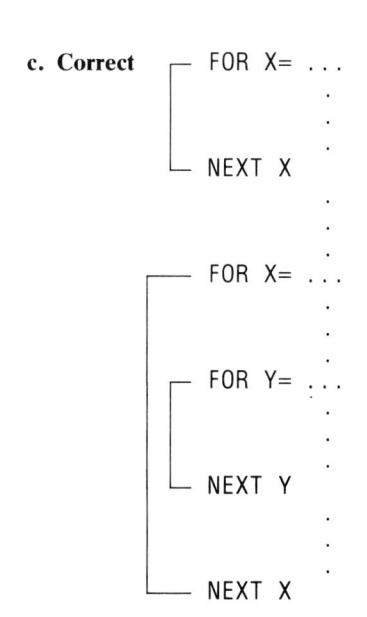

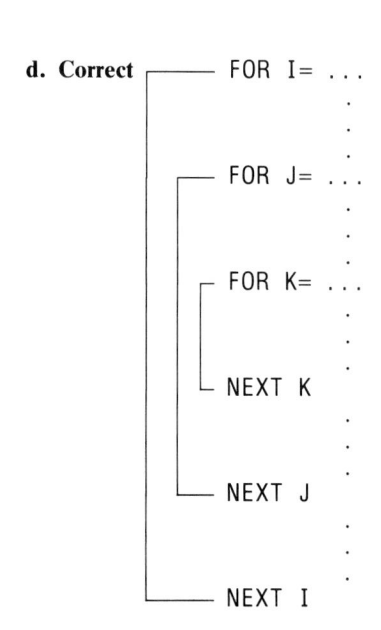

a. Correct
```
┌── FOR R= ...
│      .
│      .
│   ┌── FOR S= ...
│   │      .
│   │      .
│   └── NEXT S
│      .
│      .
└── NEXT R
```

b. Incorrect
```
┌── FOR R= ...
│      .
│      .
├── FOR S= ...
│      .
│      .
└── NEXT R
       .
       .
    NEXT S
```

c. Correct
```
┌── FOR X= ...
│      .
│      .
└── NEXT X
       .
       .
┌── FOR X= ...
│      .
│      .
│   ┌── FOR Y= ...
│   │      .
│   │      .
│   └── NEXT Y
│      .
│      .
└── NEXT X
```

d. Correct
```
┌── FOR I= ...
│      .
│      .
│   ┌── FOR J= ...
│   │      .
│   │      .
│   │   ┌── FOR K= ...
│   │   │      .
│   │   │      .
│   │   └── NEXT K
│   │      .
│   │      .
│   └── NEXT J
│      .
│      .
└── NEXT I
```

Figure 9.1 Correctly and incorrectly nested loops.

EXAMPLE 7   Here is a program to display five lines containing the word BASIC—once in the first row, twice in the second, and so on.

```
10 REM *** R COUNTS THE ROWS ***
20 FOR R=1 TO 5
30    REM *** C COUNTS THE NUMBER OF TIMES PER ROW ***
40    FOR C=1 TO R
50       PRINT "BASIC ";
60    NEXT C
70    PRINT
80 NEXT R
90 END
RUN

BASIC
BASIC BASIC
BASIC BASIC BASIC
BASIC BASIC BASIC BASIC
BASIC BASIC BASIC BASIC BASIC
```

To display the output nearer the center of the screen, you can use the TAB function. To cause the output of each row to begin in column position 20, for example, simply include the statement

```
35 PRINT TAB(20);
```

This statement causes the cursor to move to position 20 so that the loop in lines 40 to 60 will display BASIC R times beginning in position 20.

Nested FOR loops are especially useful when tables must be prepared in which the rows and columns each correspond to equally spaced data values. We conclude this chapter with an example illustrating one such application of nested loops.

EXAMPLE 8   Prepare a table showing the possible raises for salaried employees whose salaries are $10,000, $11,000, $12,000, . . . , $17,000. A raise is to consist of a flat across-the-board increase of F dollars and a percentage increase of either 2, 3, or 4%.

PROBLEM ANALYSIS

Let's agree on the following variable names.

    SALARY = present salary ($10,000, $11,000, . . . , $17,000)
      FLAT = flat across-the-board increase (to be input)
  PERCENT = percentage increase (2, 3, 4%)
     RAISE = amount of raise for a given SALARY, FLAT, and PERCENT

The formula governing this situation is

```
RAISE=(PERCENT/100)*SALARY+FLAT
```

For each salary SALARY, we must display three possible raises RAISE—one for each of the indicated percentages PERCENT. Thus a four-column table is appropriate, the first showing the present salary SALARY and the others showing the three possible raises. The following program segment can be used to display these values.

```
FOR SALARY=10000 TO 17000 STEP 1000
   PRINT SALARY,
   FOR PERCENT=2 TO 4
      LET RAISE=(PERCENT/100)*SALARY+FLAT
      PRINT RAISE,
   NEXT PERCENT
   PRINT
NEXT SALARY
```

All that remains is to include an INPUT statement, so that a value can be typed for FLAT, and to add the PRINT statements needed to display a title for the table and appropriate column headings. We will use PRINT USING rather than PRINT statements to align the columns by decimal point.

```
100 LET A$="          SALARY INCREASE SCHEDULE"
110 LET B$="        **** ADDITIONAL PERCENTAGE INCREASE ****"
120 LET C$="  SALARY      2 PERCENT    3 PERCENT    4 PERCENT"
130 LET D$="  #####.##"
140 LET E$="        ####.##"
150 PRINT A$ : PRINT
160 INPUT "ACROSS THE BOARD INCREASE $",FLAT
170 PRINT
180 PRINT B$
190 PRINT
200 PRINT C$
210 FOR SALARY=10000 TO 17000 STEP 1000
220    PRINT USING D$;SALARY;
230    FOR PERCENT=2 TO 4
240       LET RAISE=(PERCENT/100)*SALARY+FLAT
250       PRINT USING E$;RAISE;
260    NEXT PERCENT
270    PRINT
280 NEXT SALARY
290 END
RUN
          SALARY INCREASE SCHEDULE

ACROSS THE BOARD INCREASE $700

        **** ADDITIONAL PERCENTAGE INCREASE ****

  SALARY      2 PERCENT    3 PERCENT    4 PERCENT
 10000.00        900.00      1000.00      1100.00
 11000.00        920.00      1030.00      1140.00
 12000.00        940.00      1060.00      1180.00
 13000.00        960.00      1090.00      1220.00
 14000.00        980.00      1120.00      1260.00
 15000.00       1000.00      1150.00      1300.00
 16000.00       1020.00      1180.00      1340.00
 17000.00       1040.00      1210.00      1380.00
```

■ 9.4 Problems

1. Show the output for each program.

   a.
   ```
   10 FOR I=1 TO 3
   20    FOR J=2 TO 3
   30       PRINT J;
   40    NEXT J
   50 NEXT I
   60 END
   ```

   b.
   ```
   10 FOR J=9 TO 7 STEP -2
   20    FOR K=4 TO 9 STEP 3
   30       PRINT J+K;
   40    NEXT K
   50 NEXT J
   60 END
   ```

   c.
   ```
   10 FOR X=1 TO 4
   20    FOR Y=X+1 TO 5
   30       PRINT Y;
   40    NEXT Y
   50    PRINT
   60 NEXT X
   70 END
   ```

   d.
   ```
   10 LET X=0
   20 FOR P=1 TO 6
   30    FOR Q=2 TO 7
   40       FOR R=2 TO 4
   50          LET X=X+1
   60       NEXT R
   70    NEXT Q
   80 NEXT P
   90 PRINT X
   99 END
   ```

e.
```
10 LET F$="## "
20 FOR R=7 TO 13 STEP 2
30    FOR C=1 TO 3
40       PRINT USING F$; R;
50    NEXT C
60    PRINT
70 NEXT R
80 END
```

2. Each of the following programs contains an error—either a syntax error that will cause an error message to be displayed or a programming error that the computer will not recognize but will cause incorrect results. In each case, find the error and tell which of the two types it is.

a.
```
10 REM DISPLAY PRODUCTS.
20 FOR I=1 TO 3
30 FOR J=2 TO 4
40 PRINT I; "TIMES"; J; "="; I*J
50 NEXT I
60 NEXT J
70 END
```

b.
```
10 REM DISPLAY SUMS.
20 FOR A=3 TO 1
30 FOR B=4 TO 1
40 PRINT A; "PLUS"; B; "="; A+B
50 NEXT B
60 NEXT A
70 END
```

c. A program to display

```
1  2
1  3
1  4
2  3
2  4
3  4
```

```
10 FOR I=1 TO 4
20 FOR J=2 TO 4
30 IF I<>J THEN PRINT I; J
40 NEXT J
50 NEXT I
60 END
```

d. A program to display

```
XXXXX
XXXX
XXX
XX
X
```

```
10 FOR R=1 TO 5
20 FOR C=1 TO 5
30 IF R>=C THEN PRINT "X";
40 IF R<C THEN PRINT " ";
50 NEXT C
60 NEXT R
70 END
```

In Problems 3–14, write a program to perform each task specified.

3. Produce a tax rate schedule showing the 4, 5, 6, and 7% tax on the dollar amounts $1, $2, $3, . . . , $20.

4. Prepare a table showing the interest earned on a $100 deposit for the rates 0.05 to 0.08 in increments of 0.01 and for times 1, 2, . . . , 8 years. Interest is compounded annually ($I = P(1 + R)^N - P$).

5. Prepare the table for Problem 4 except that rates are to be in increments of 0.005 instead of 0.01.

6. Present the information required in Problem 5 by producing seven short tables, one for each interest rate specified. Label each of these tables and also the information contained in the tables.

7. For each of the tax rates 5, $5\frac{1}{8}$, $5\frac{1}{4}$, $5\frac{3}{8}$, and $5\frac{1}{2}$%, produce a table showing the tax on the dollar amounts $1, $2, $3, . . . , $20. Each of the five tables is to have an appropriate title and is to contain two labeled columns—the first showing the dollar amounts $1, $2, $3, . . . , $20 and the second showing the corresponding tax amounts.

8. Produce a listing of all three-digit numbers whose digits are 1, 2, or 3. Spaces are not to appear between the digits of the numbers. (*Hint:* Use triple-nested loops with control

variables I, J, and K ranging from 1 to 3. If I, J, and K are the digits, the number is $100 \times I + 10 \times J + K$.)

9. Produce a listing of all three-digit numbers as described in Problem 8. If no digit is repeated in a number, however, it is to be preceded by an asterisk. Thus a portion of your display should be as follows:

```
   .
   .
   .
 121
 122
*123
 131
*132
 133
   .
   .
   .
```

10. Let's define an operation whose symbol is & on the set A = {0, 1, 2, 3, 4, 5} as follows. The "product" of two integers **i** and **j** is given by

    $i \mathbin{\&} j = (i \times j) \bmod 6$

    Write a program to display a table showing all possible "products" of numbers in the set A. The table values should be labeled as follows:

    ```
    &   0   1   2   3   4   5
       --- --- --- --- --- ---
    0
    1
    2
    3
    4
    5
    ```

11. Determine the largest value the expression $XY^2 - X^2Y + X - Y$ can assume if X and Y can be any integers from 1 to 5, inclusive.

12. Find the maximum and minimum values of the expression $3X^2 - 2XY + Y^2$ if X and Y are subject to the following constraints.

    $X = -4, -3.5, -3, \ldots, 4$
    $Y = -3, -2.5, -2, \ldots, 5$

13. The expression $X^3 - 4XY + X^2 + 10X$ is to be examined for all integers X and Y between 1 and 5 to determine those pairs (X, Y) for which the expression is negative. All such pairs are to be displayed, together with the corresponding negative value of the expression.

14. Find all pairs of integers (X, Y) that satisfy the following system of inequalities.

    $2X - Y < 3$
    $X + 3Y \geq 1$
    $-6 \leq X \leq 6$
    $-10 \leq Y \leq 10$

    The solutions are to be displayed as individual ordered pairs (X, Y). (*Hint:* The last two conditions give the initial and terminal values of FOR loops.)

■ 9.5 Review True-or-False Quiz

1. If a group of statements is to be executed several times in a program, it is always a good practice to use a FOR loop.   T F
2. If a loop begins with the statement FOR K = 1 TO 35, the variable K must occur in some statement before the NEXT K statement is encountered.   T F

3. The statement FOR J = X TO 10 STEP 3 is valid even though X may have a value that is not an integer. T F
4. In the statement FOR N = 15 TO 200 STEP C, C must be a positive integer. T F
5. The initial, terminal, and step values in a FOR loop cannot be changed in the body of the loop. T F
6. The control variable in a FOR loop can be changed in the body of the loop; moreover, doing so represents a good programming practice. T F
7. The control variable of a loop containing a loop may be used as the initial, terminal, or step value of the inner loop. T F
8. Some loops must be coded by using the FOR and NEXT statements. T F
9. The statement FOR X = Y TO Z STEP W contains a syntax error. T F
10. The statement FOR X$ = ''A'' TO ''Z'' contains a syntax error. T F
11. All counter-controlled loops are best coded as FOR loops. T F

10 More on Screen Displays

Microsoft® BASIC allows much greater control of the display screen than shown in the preceding chapters. In this chapter, we describe how the LOCATE statement can be used to specify *any* screen position for your output without affecting the rest of the screen (Section 10.1). We also show how the COLOR statement can be used to create reverse image and blinking displays, and, if your screen allows color, to specify colors for all output values (Section 10.3). Finally, in Section 10.4 we show how certain nonstandard characters, such as

☺ ♥ ♦ ♣ ♠ → æ ½ Σ π ≤

and many others, can be included in your screen displays.

■ 10.1 The Cursor Moving Statement: LOCATE

The LOCATE statement allows you to move the cursor to any position on the PC's display screen without affecting the current screen display. (This is called a **pure cursor move.**) For example, the two statements

```
200 LOCATE 20,5
210 PRINT "A"
```

will display the letter A in the fifth character position of display line 20. The statement LOCATE 20,5 moves the cursor up or down, depending on the current display line, to line 20 and left or right to position 5. Since the two statements shown are so closely related, it is natural to write the equivalent multiple-statement line

```
200 LOCATE 20,5 : PRINT "A"
```

Any numerical expressions can be used to specify positions in the LOCATE statement. For example, if L=20 and P=5, line 200 can be changed to

```
200 LOCATE L,C : PRINT "A";
```

EXAMPLE 1   Here is a program to produce the following screen display beginning at position 30 of display line 10:

```
IBM PC
 IBM PC
  IBM PC
   IBM PC
```

145

146 *Chapter 10 More on Screen Displays*

THE PROGRAM

```
100 CLS                       'Clear screen
110 LET L=10                  'Starting line
120 LET C=30                  'Starting column
130 FOR N=0 TO 3
140     LOCATE L+N, C+N       'Pure cursor move
150     PRINT "IBM PC";       'Output
160 NEXT N
170 END
```

When N=0, the LOCATE statement causes a pure cursor move to screen position 10,30 (position 30 on line 10); when N=1, the move is to screen position 11,31; and so on.

■ **REMARK 1** Without line 100, you may end with a cluttered screen. The output will be displayed over whatever happens to be on the screen when the RUN command is entered.

■ **REMARK 2** Exactly the same screen display will be produced if the FOR statement is changed to

```
130 FOR N=3 TO 0 STEP -1
```

With this change, the output will be displayed from the bottom line up. The difference, however, will not be noticeable.

■ **REMARK 3** Notice that the PRINT statement ends with a semicolon. In this program the output would be the same without the semicolon. However, if we were to direct output to screen line 24, a PRINT statement without a final semicolon would cause a RETURN and everything on screen lines 1–24 would scroll up one line. Situations that can lead to unwanted scrolling are discussed following Example 3.

In Example 1, we used CLS to clear screen lines 1–24. To clear line 25, which displays information about the function keys, use

```
KEY OFF
```

either in immediate mode or as part of your program. This turns off the display on line 25 until it is turned on again with the statement

```
KEY ON
```

If you clear line 25 with the KEY OFF statement, you can use this line in your displays. For instance,

```
LOCATE 25,37 : PRINT "LINE25";
```

displays LINE25, centered on screen line 25. Without the terminating semicolon in the PRINT statement, lines 1–24 would scroll up one line. (As mentioned in Section 4.2, line 25 is never scrolled upward.) At this point, CLS will clear all 25 screen lines. Thus, CLS clears lines 1–24 if KEY ON is in effect, but clears lines 1–25 if KEY OFF is in effect.

EXAMPLE 2 Here is a program to display BASIC at the four corners and the center of an otherwise clear screen.

```
10 KEY OFF : CLS                   'Clear screen lines 1-25.
20 LET B$="BASIC"
30 LOCATE 25,1  : PRINT B$;        'Bottom left corner
40 LOCATE 25,76 : PRINT B$;        'Bottom right corner
50 LOCATE 1,1   : PRINT B$;        'Top left corner
60 LOCATE 1,76  : PRINT B$;        'Top right corner
70 LOCATE 13,38 : PRINT B$;        'Center of screen
80 END
```

■ **REMARK** The order of the PRINT statements in this program matters. The last PRINT statement (line 70) displays BASIC near the center of line 13 and when the program ends, the

BASIC prompt Ok is displayed at the beginning of the next line. If the last PRINT statement causes output to screen lines 24 or 25 the Ok prompt will appear on line 24, but only after lines 1–24 have been scrolled upward with the top line being scrolled off the screen. To avoid such scrolling when an END statement is encountered, you must make sure the cursor is on some line other than 24 or 25. A good way to do this is to cause a statement such as LOCATE L,P, with L a number from 1 to 23, to be executed just before the END statement.

The LOCATE statement will position the cursor at a location on the screen whether or not a character is already displayed at that location. Thus, the statements

```
100 LET A$="COMPUTER"
110 LET B$="IBM"
120 LOCATE 15,5 : PRINT A$
130 LOCATE 15,5 : PRINT B$
```

will display the string COMPUTER beginning at the fifth position on display line 15, and then will display the string IBM beginning at this same location. The effect is to display the characters IBMPUTER. If the intent is to replace one string by a second, you must make sure that blanks are displayed over positions in the first string that are not used by the second. Here are two ways to do this for the given example.

1. Include the line

```
125 LOCATE 15,5 : PRINT STRING$(8," ")
```

to "erase" COMPUTER by displaying enough blank characters over it.

2. Use PRINT USING rather than PRINT statements:

```
100 LET A$="COMPUTER"
110 LET B$="IBM"
115 LET F$="\      \"
120 LOCATE 15,5 : PRINT USING F$;A$
130 LOCATE 15,5 : PRINT USING F$;B$
```

Remember that string output values are displayed left justified with trailing blanks. Thus, the value IBM of B$ is displayed with five trailing blanks that "erase" PUTER.

There are many coding situations in which you should erase old screen displays before generating new ones. Most involve the use of the PRINT statement to display new information in specified screen positions, as just illustrated. Another situation concerns displays produced because of INPUT statements. Suppose, for example, that the programming line

```
350 LOCATE 20,1 : INPUT "AMOUNT";AMT
```

is included in a loop and the user enters 5239.46 for AMT. The display on screen line 20 will be

AMOUNT? 5239.46

If the amount 5239.46 is not erased before the INPUT statement is encountered a second time, the user will be confronted with the above display, and not with the desired prompt

AMOUNT?

If this time the user types 467, the display will be

AMOUNT? 4679.46

and not

AMOUNT? 467

To ensure that such confusing (and erroneous) information will not appear in the display, you might precede line 350 by

```
345 LOCATE 20,1 : PRINT STRING$(20," ")
```

to erase the old amount before prompting the user for a new one.

EXAMPLE 3 Here is a program segment that prompts the user for an input value from 50 to 80 and that rejects any other values.

```
400 LOCATE 10,1
410 INPUT "AMOUNT (50-80)";AMT
420 WHILE AMT<50 OR AMT>80
430     LOCATE 10,30                    'Position for message
440     PRINT "BAD INPUT - REENTER";    'The message
450     LOCATE 10,1
460     PRINT STRING$(29," ")           'Erase old input.
470     LOCATE 10,1
480     INPUT "AMOUNT (50-80)";AMT      'Ask again.
490 WEND
500 LOCATE 10,30                        'Position of message
510 PRINT STRING$(20," ");              'Make sure it's clear
520 (Program continuation)
```

Lines 400 and 410 display the prompt

AMOUNT (50-80)?

If the value typed for AMT is not in the range from 50 to 80 as specified, the WHILE loop is entered. Lines 430 and 440 display an appropriate error message, lines 450 and 460 erase the old input, and lines 470–480 again prompt the user. At this point, the display on line 10 is as follows:

AMOUNT (50-80) ?   BAD INPUT - REENTER

An exit will be made from the WHILE loop only after the user has typed a value in the specified range. If the user types 58.27, the WHILE condition will be false and control will pass to line 500. Lines 500 and 510 ensure that the message BAD INPUT—REENTER is erased. If no such message was displayed, lines 500–510 simply display blanks on screen positions that are already blank.

The general form of the LOCATE statement is

LOCATE **l,p**

where **l** and **p** are numerical expressions. The values of **l** and **p** are rounded, if necessary, to obtain integers (call them L and P). If L is in the range 1–24 (1–25 if KEY OFF is in effect), and P is in the range 1–80 (1–40 if WIDTH 40 is in effect), the cursor is moved to position P of display line L. If either L or P is outside the specified range, an error message

Illegal function call in **ln**

is displayed and program execution terminates.

Note: If output is directed to a printer, LOCATE has no effect whatever.

In Examples 1 and 2, we mentioned two ways in which unwanted scrolling can occur and explained how to avoid the scrolling. We now summarize these and other situations in which unwanted scrolling can be avoided.

1. (See Example 1.) If a PRINT statement with no terminating semicolon causes output to screen line 24 or 25, lines 1–24 will scroll upward with the top line being scrolled off the screen. Except as explained in Item (2), placing a semicolon at the end of each PRINT statement resolves this difficulty.

2. Whenever a character is displayed in the rightmost position of a line, the cursor is moved to the next line even if the PRINT statement ends with a semicolon. This causes no difficulty if the output is to lines 1–23. However, if you display a character in the rightmost position of line 24, everything on lines 1–24 will scroll upward. Thus, *if scrolling is to be avoided, you should never display output in the last position of line 24.*

3. (See Example 2.) If the cursor is positioned at screen line 24 or 25 when the END statement is encountered, the Ok prompt will be displayed on line 24, but only after lines 1–24 have been scrolled upward. To avoid this scrolling, make sure that the cursor is positioned on one of lines 1–23 when the END statement is encountered. For instance, place LOCATE L,M (with L from 1 to 23) just before the END statement.

4. Unwanted scrolling may occur if an INPUT statement is executed while the cursor is on screen line 23, 24, or 25. The scrolling occurs when you press the Enter key after typing the input. One way to avoid this scrolling is to use a LOCATE statement to position the cursor on one of screen lines 1–22 before each INPUT statement. Some, but not all, versions of Microsoft® BASIC provide another method: place a semicolon just after the keyword INPUT. For instance, the following programming line allows you to enter a value for AMT on line 24 with no scrolling:

```
300 LOCATE 24,1 : INPUT; "ENTER AMOUNT";AMT
```

In addition to the scrolling problems just cited, screen displays are sometimes adversely affected by the Microsoft® BASIC prompt Ok that is displayed whenever program execution terminates. One way to prevent Ok from being displayed is to keep the program from ending. You can do this conveniently with the **INKEY$ variable,** a string variable that is part of the Microsoft® BASIC language. It causes the program to read a single character from the keyboard for its value. If the statement

```
600 IF INKEY$="" THEN 600
```

is included in a program, a value will be read from the keyboard and assigned to INKEY$. If that value is the null string " " (that is, no character has been typed) the condition INKEY$ = " " is true and program control is transferred back to line 600 to test the condition again. This process will continue until some character is typed (it will not be displayed). INKEY$ will at that point take the typed character as its value, the condition INKEY$ = " " will be false, and control will pass to the next line allowing the program to continue. Thus, including a statement of the form

ln IF INKEY$ = " " THEN **ln**

in which both occurrences of **ln** denote the same line number, is an effective method of delaying further execution of a program for as long as desired. In the present instance, it can prevent the Ok from being displayed by delaying the execution of the END statement. In summary, the program

```
490 KEY OFF
500 CLS             'Clear the screen.
510 LOCATE 1,1  : PRINT "FIRST LINE"
520 LOCATE 24,1 : PRINT "LAST LINE";
600 IF INKEY$="" THEN 600
610 END
```

will display the strings FIRST LINE on line 1 and LAST LINE on line 24, without any other character appearing anywhere on the screen. This display will remain on the screen until a key is pressed.

BASIC statements that clear the screen and move the cursor can be used effectively in many programming applications. For example, while coding a menu-driven program you can use CLS and LOCATE to control the screen placement of the menu, of any user prompts, and of any output generated when the options are carried out. By using CLS and LOCATE statements in this way, you can improve your programs significantly by giving the user neat and uncluttered screen displays.

150 Chapter 10 More on Screen Displays

Another important application of the LOCATE statement is in programming tasks that require you to modify screen displays by displaying new information over old information without affecting the rest of the screen. We conclude this section with an example illustrating this use of LOCATE.

EXAMPLE 4   **Selective modification of a screen display.**

The program given in this example consists of three parts as indicated by the REM statements. The first part simply assigns constant string values to certain string variables. The second part displays this table:

```
---------------
 ITEM  PERCENT
   1    10.00
   2    10.00
   3    10.00
   4    10.00
   5    10.00
---------------
```

The third part allows a user to enter different percent figures for one or more of the five items numbered 1 through 5.

```
100 REM ***************************************************
110 REM * ASSIGN STRING CONSTANTS AND OUTPUT FORMAT *
115 REM ***************************************************
120 REM
130 LET DASHES$="---------------"
140 LET HEADER$=" ITEM   PERCENT "
150 LET FORMAT$="   #     ###.## "
160 LET BLANKS$=STRING$(79," ")
170 REM
180 REM ***************************
190 REM * DISPLAY A SHORT TABLE *
200 REM ***************************
210 REM
220 KEY OFF : CLS                                       'Clear the screen.
230 LOCATE 5,15 : PRINT DASHES$;
240 LOCATE 6,15 : PRINT HEADER$;                        'Column headers
250 FOR N=1 TO 5
260     LOCATE 6+N,15 : PRINT USING FORMAT$;N;10;       'Table values
270 NEXT N
280 LOCATE 6+N,15 : PRINT DASHES$;
290 REM
300 REM ***********************************************************
310 REM * PROMPT FOR NEW PERCENT FIGURES AND CHANGE TABLE *
320 REM ***********************************************************
330 REM
340 LOCATE 19,1 : PRINT "TO CHANGE A PERCENT, TYPE ITEM NUMBER. "
350 LOCATE 20,1 : PRINT "MUST BE 1 TO 5; ELSE PROGRAM HALTS. "
360 LOCATE 22,1 : INPUT "ENTER ITEM NUMBER: ",N%
370 REM
380 WHILE 1<=N% AND N%<=5
390     LOCATE 23,1 : INPUT "ENTER NEW PERCENT: ",P
400     LOCATE 6+N%,15 : PRINT USING FORMAT$;N%;P;      'Change percent.
410     LOCATE 22,1 : PRINT BLANKS$;                    'Erase previous
420     LOCATE 23,1 : PRINT BLANKS$;                    'input values.
430     LOCATE 22,1 : INPUT "ENTER ITEM NUMBER: ",N%
440 WEND
450 END
```

The action caused by the third part is as follows.

   1. Lines 340 and 350 display the instructions

```
TO CHANGE A PERCENT, TYPE ITEM NUMBER.
MUST BE 1 TO 5; ELSE PROGRAM HALTS.
```

on display lines 19 and 20. These instructions stay on the screen during the entire input session.

2. Line 360 displays the input prompt

ENTER ITEM NUMBER: _

on display line 22 and if the user types a number in the range 1 to 5, the following input prompt is displayed on line 23.

ENTER NEW PERCENT: _

3. Line 400 makes the specified change in the table and then lines 410 and 420 erase the old input values from the screen so that another change can be made.

■ REMARK   When the given program is run, the user will have to respond to the two input prompts

ENTER ITEM NUMBER: _
ENTER NEW PERCENT: _

The only thing that will draw the user's attention to either of these prompts is the blinking cursor. In Microsoft® BASIC there are several better ways to draw attention to a particular prompt. You can display it in reverse image (black on white rather than white on black), in blinking characters, or in color, if you have a color monitor. How all of this can be done is explained in Section 10.3.

■ 10.2 Problems

1. Describe the screen displays produced by each program.

```
a. 10 CLS
   20 LET B$="BASIC"
   30 LET M=2
   40 FOR N=0 TO 10 STEP 5
   50     LOCATE M,40-N : PRINT B$;
   60     LOCATE M,40+N : PRINT B$
   70     LET M=M+1
   80 NEXT N
   90 END

b. 10 CLS
   20 LET A$="IBM"
   30 FOR N=1 TO 5 STEP 2
   40     LOCATE N,20+N : PRINT A$
   50     LOCATE 10+N,20+N : PRINT A$
   60 NEXT N
   70 END

c. 10 CLS
   20 LET R=15 : C=8
   30 FOR N=0 TO 6
   40     LOCATE R+N,C : PRINT "H   H"
   50 NEXT N
   60 LOCATE R+3,C+1 : PRINT "HHH"
   70 END

d. 100 FOR TIME=0 TO 50
   110     CLS
   120     FOR N=10 TO 15
   130         LOCATE N,15 : PRINT "GOOD"
   140     NEXT N
```

```
150     CLS
160     FOR N=10 TO 15
170         LOCATE N,20 : PRINT "GRIEF"
180     NEXT N
190 NEXT TIME
200 CLS : END
```

Write a program to produce each screen display described in Problems 2–9. Use the LOCATE statement. (Be sure to avoid the rightmost position of line 24. Remember, displaying a character in this position causes everything on lines 1–24 to scroll upward.)

2. Display the word COMPUTER near the four corners and then at the approximate center of the screen. Be sure that the top line is not scrolled off the screen when the program halts.
3. Display X's along all four edges of the screen. Then display your name near the center of the screen. Be sure that the entire display remains when the program halts. (You may use line 23 as the bottom edge, or column WIDTH − 1 as the right edge.)
4. Display your name and address, centered on an otherwise clear screen. When the program halts, the prompt Ok should appear in line 23.
5. Display a square block containing 36 X's at the center of the screen. When the program halts, the prompt Ok should appear in line 2.
6. Successively display the digits 0 through 9 in the 36-character block described in Problem 5. Be sure to clear the screen after each 36-character block is displayed. After this process has been repeated 20 times, the program should halt with a clear screen.
7. Display the following table approximately centered on the screen.

```
RANGE COUNT WEIGHT
----- ----- ------
0 -10   0     1
11-20   0     1
21-30   0     1
31-40   0     1
41-50   0     1
```

8. Display the table shown in Problem 7 and then prompt the user to enter five counts in place of the five 0's and five weights in place of the five 1's.
9. Display the table in Problem 7 and then allow the user to make selective changes in the count and weight columns. (For instance, you could require the user to enter 31,COUNT to specify that the count in the fourth line is to be changed.) Whatever dialogue you set up between the user and the computer, be sure to program an orderly exit from the program when the user indicates that all desired changes have been made.

■ 10.3 The COLOR Statement

Your video display unit is connected to the PC through one of two types of connectors:

1. The Color/Graphics Monitor Adapter or
2. The Monochrome (black and white only) Display and Parallel Printer Adapter.

If your PC is equipped with the first of these adapters and your display unit is a color monitor, you will be able to use any of the 16 colors listed in Table 10.1 during your sessions at the computer. You can also create reverse image and blinking screen displays. If your PC is equipped with the second of these adapters, you will be limited to black and white displays, but you will still have the capability of reverse image and blinking screen displays. All of this is accomplished with the COLOR statement.

Table 10.1 Colors for screen displays

Number	Color	Number	Color
0	Black	8	Gray
1	Blue	9	Light blue
2	Green	10	Light green
3	Cyan (medium blue)	11	Light cyan
4	Red	12	Light red
5	Magenta (purple)	13	Light magenta
6	Brown	14	Yellow
7	White	15	High-intensity white

The COLOR statement can include three numbers: the first sets the foreground color (the color of the actual characters), the second sets the background color (the box that contains the character), and the third sets the color of the border screen:

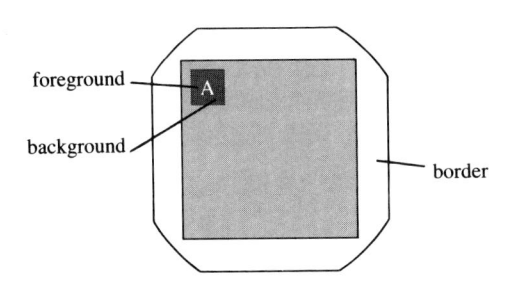

For example, type the statement COLOR 4,1,2. The border screen is set immediately to green (2). The statement just typed remains in white characters on a black background, but the prompt Ok appears in red (4) on a blue (1) background—the COLOR statement affects only those characters displayed subsequent to its execution. Now clear the screen with CLS. This colors the entire interior portion of the screen blue, the active background color.

When BASIC is first activated, the color is automatically set to 7,0,0, white foreground with a black background and a black border screen. Having the same background and border color makes these two regions indistinguishable. We will call this color combination the *normal* screen. To return to this normal screen, type

```
COLOR 7,0,0 : CLS
```

The CLS statement removes any previous display and leaves the entire screen black with the exception of the Ok prompt and the cursor in the upper left corner.

EXAMPLE 5 Here is a program to display the PC's 16 colors, one at a time.

```
100 CLS
110 PRINT "This program will display the PC's 16 colors-black first."
120 PRINT "To pass from one color to the next, press any key."
130 PRINT "Press any key to begin."
140 IF INKEY$="" THEN 140
150 KEY OFF
160 FOR N=0 TO 15
170     COLOR N,N,N
180     CLS
190     IF INKEY$="" THEN 190
200 NEXT N
210 KEY ON
220 COLOR 7,0,0
230 CLS
240 END
```

Line 170 specifies the same color (color code N) for the foreground, background, and border. The border is colored immediately. The CLS statement in line 180 clears the entire display area, coloring it the same color as the border. At this point, nothing is visible; everything is colored with the same color. Line 190 is executed repeatedly until a key is pressed. When this happens, the next color is selected. This process continues until all 16 colors have been displayed.

■ REMARK 1   It is important to note that once a color is set by a COLOR statement it remains so, until another COLOR statement changes it. Thus, line 220 returns the screen to normal, from the previous color specifications, 15,15,15, after the loop is completed.

■ REMARK 2   If you stop program execution by using the *Ctrl-Break* key combination, everything will be of one color—the last color displayed. Anything you type at the keyboard will be invisible. To return the screen to normal, carefully type COLOR 7,0,0 and press the Enter key.

Selected lines of text in a screen display can be highlighted by displaying them in reverse image—for instance, black characters on a white background (COLOR 0,7,0) instead of white on black (COLOR 7,0,0). In general, if the active color specification is

    COLOR A, B, C

change it to

    COLOR B, A, C

to display text in reverse image.

EXAMPLE 6   Here is a program to allow the user to specify which of five lines is to be displayed in reverse image.

```
100 REM --- Display five lines ---
110 COLOR 7,0,0 : CLS
120 FOR N=1 TO 5
130    LOCATE 4+N,10 : PRINT "Line number";N
140 NEXT N
150 REM --- Allow the user to select a line ---
160 LOCATE 1,1
170 INPUT "Enter 1, 2, 3, 4, or 5 : ",N
180 COLOR 0,7,0
190 LOCATE 4+N,10 : PRINT "Line number";N
200 COLOR 7,0,0
210 LOCATE 2,1
220 END
```

If the user enters 4 in response to line 170, the screen display will be as follows:

```
Enter 1, 2, 3, 4, or 5 : 4
Ok
_

              Line number 1
              Line number 2
              Line number 3
              Line number 4     ←reverse image
              Line number 5
```

Line 110 not only clears the screen, but ensures that the screen is set for normal displays. Lines 120–140 display the five lines.

After 4 is input for N, line 180 causes subsequent output to be displayed as black characters on a white background. Thus, line 190 displays the fourth line again, but this time in reverse image characters.

The preceding example shows how display lines can be changed from normal to reverse image, and back to normal. An excellent application of this technique is to highlight each prompt to the user of a program, but only at the time the prompt requires some action by the user. Another way to draw attention to a particular screen line is to display it in blinking characters.

Blinking characters are displayed in any color simply by adding 16 to the foreground color. Thus,

```
COLOR 23,0,0
```

will cause each subsequent character to be displayed in blinking white (7 + 16 = 23) on a black (0) background. Similarly,

```
COLOR 18,7,4
```

will cause subsequent characters to be displayed in blinking green (2 + 16 = 18) on white (7) with a red (4) border.

Microsoft® BASIC can operate in three modes: **text mode, medium-resolution graphics mode,** and **high-resolution graphics mode.** We have been operating in *text mode*. This means that only text—that is, sequences of characters such as letters, +, −, and so on—is displayed or printed. The form of the COLOR statement described in this section is for text mode only. COLOR as used in the two graphics modes is explained in Chapter 19.

The general form of the COLOR statement as used in *text mode* is

COLOR **fore,back,bord**

where **fore, back,** and **bord** denote numerical expressions that are rounded, if necessary, to integer values FORE, BACK, and BORD. These integers specify the foreground, background, and border colors, respectively. The following rules apply.

1. FORE should be in the range 0 to 31. The numbers 0 to 15 specify the foreground colors, and adding 16 causes displayed characters to blink on and off.
2. BACK should be in the range 0 to 7. Only these eight colors can be used for the background.
3. BORD should be in the range 0 to 15. The border color is changed as soon as the COLOR statement is executed.
4. Each of the color parameters **fore, back,** and **bord** is optional. Omitting a color parameter means it will not be changed.

EXAMPLE 7

In this table assume the current color specifications are 5,3,4.

COLOR statement	Equivalent COLOR statements		
COLOR 6,3,4	COLOR 6,3	COLOR 6,,4	COLOR 6
COLOR 5,3,7	COLOR 5,,7	COLOR,3,7	COLOR,,7
COLOR 7,3,6	COLOR 7,,6		

EXAMPLE 8

Here is a program to illustrate reverse image and blinking displays on any screen.

```
10 LET ND$="Normal display"
20 LET BD$="Blinking display"
30 LET RID$="Reverse image display"
40 LET BRID$="Blinking reverse image display"
50 COLOR 7,0,0
60 PRINT "*** "; : PRINT ND$; : PRINT " ***"
70 PRINT "*** "; : COLOR 23,0,0 : PRINT BD$; : COLOR 7,0,0 : PRINT " ***"
80 PRINT "*** "; : COLOR 0,7,0 : PRINT RID$; : COLOR 7,0,0 : PRINT " ***"
90 PRINT "*** "; : COLOR 16,7,0 : PRINT BRID$; : COLOR 7,0,0 : PRINT " ***"
99 END
```

10.4 The IBM PC Display Characters

Your PC is capable of displaying a wide variety of characters on its video screen. Some you have already seen; others will be introduced in this section. A table showing all of the IBM PC characters is given in Appendix F. Following is the portion of the table that shows the familiar characters used in BASIC.

Numeric code	Character	Numeric code	Character	Numeric code	Character	Numeric code	Character
032	(space)	056	8	080	P	104	h
033	!	057	9	081	Q	105	i
034	"	058	:	082	R	106	j
035	#	059	;	083	S	107	k
036	$	060	<	084	T	108	l
037	%	061	=	085	U	109	m
038	&	062	>	086	V	110	n
039	'	063	?	087	W	111	o
040	(	064	@	088	X	112	p
041	)	065	A	089	Y	113	q
042	*	066	B	090	Z	114	r
043	+	067	C	091	[	115	s
044	,	068	D	092	\	116	t
045	-	069	E	093	]	117	u
046	.	070	F	094	^	118	v
047	/	071	G	095	_	119	w
048	0	072	H	096	`	120	x
049	1	073	I	097	a	121	y
050	2	074	J	098	b	122	z
051	3	075	K	099	c	123	{
052	4	076	L	100	d	124		
053	5	077	M	101	e	125	}
054	6	078	N	102	f	126	~
055	7	079	O	103	g	127	△

You will note that each character is paired with a positive integer called its numeric code. For instance, "A" is associated with numeric code 65, "a" with 97, "5" with 53, and so on. These are, incidentally, the numeric codes of the *American Standard Code of Information Interchange* (ASCII).

In addition to these standard characters, Appendix F shows other characters that can be displayed on the IBM PC video screen. Following are some of these characters with their numeric codes.

Numeric code	Character	Numeric code	Character
001	☺	169	⌐
003	♥	170	¬
004	♦	171	½
005	♣	219	■
006	♠	220	▬
145	æ	221	▮
146	Æ	227	π
147	ô	228	Σ
148	ö	234	Ω

All of the characters shown in Appendix F are called **display characters** since they can be displayed on the video screen. (You will note that Appendix F shows the numeric codes 0–255, but that not all of these correspond to display characters. In particular, numeric codes 0, 7, 9–13, and 28–31 have special meanings as indicated in the table.)

There are no individual keys to press for many of the PC display characters. All, however, can be included in your screen displays. In what follows we show three ways to do this.

The Character Function CHR$

If **n** denotes an integer from 0 to 255, the value of the expression CHR$(**n**) is the character with numeric code **n**. Thus,

```
PRINT CHR$(3);CHR$(4);CHR$(5);CHR$(6)
```

will produce the screen display

♥ ♦ ♣ ♠

Similarly, the loop

```
FOR N=224 TO 235 : PRINT CHR$(N); : NEXT N
```

will display (see Appendix F):

αβΓπΣσμτΦθΩδ

EXAMPLE 9   Here is a program to display the English alphabet in upper- and lowercase letters.

```
10 FOR K=65 TO 90
20     PRINT CHR$(K);CHR$(K+32);
30 NEXT K
40 FOR L=1 TO 5
50     PRINT CHR$(7);
60 NEXT L
70 END
RUN

AaBbCcDdEeFfGgHhIiJjKkLlMmNnOoPpQqRrSsTtUuVvWwXxYyZz
```

The numeric code for each lowercase letter is 32 more than the code for the same letter in uppercase. Thus, when K is 65 line 20 displays Aa, when K is 66 line 20 displays Bb, and so on.

The argument **n** in CHR$(**n**) can be any of the numeric codes 0–255. As shown in Appendix F, numeric code 7 corresponds to a beep. Thus, lines 40–60 cause the PC's speaker to beep five times. [Early computer output devices had a bell rather than a speaker. For this reason, CHR$(7) is often called the *bell character*.]

The following short program illustrates how the special characters can be combined to create a screen display different from the usual line-by-line displays.

EXAMPLE 10   Here is a program to produce the screen display:

```
100 A$=CHR$(204)
110 B$=CHR$(185)
120 FOR N=1 TO 7
130     PRINT A$;B$
140 NEXT N
150 END
```

Numeric code 204 corresponds to the character

╠

and numeric code 185 corresponds to

╣

When displayed next to each other, you get

╠╣

Displaying seven of these pairs of characters, one under the other, gives the display shown.

The Alt Key

If you use CHR$ to include display characters in a BASIC program, the characters do not actually appear in the program. For instance, the representation CHR$(204) of the character

╠

appears in the program of Example 10, but not the character itself. A picture of most of the display characters can be included in programs by using the *Alt key* (just to the left of the space bar) and the *numeric keypad* (the rightmost portion of the PC keyboard). To enter a character, type its numeric code on the numeric keypad while holding down the Alt key. When you release the Alt key the character will appear on the screen.

Note: Some of the numeric codes, when entered on the numeric keypad, have special meaning to the BASIC program editor. For example, the program editor interprets Alt/3 as a carriage return and will not display the heart symbol. Most of the special characters, however, will be displayed as described.

The Alt key can be used to assign character strings to string variables. For example, you could assign the diamond symbol to the string variable DIAMOND$ by using either of the following equivalent statements:

```
20 LET DIAMOND$=CHR$(4)     ' ♦ symbol
20 LET DIAMOND$="♦"         ' Alt/4
```

Simply type the line as usual and when you get to the diamond symbol, use Alt/4. To assign the name of the fraternity ΣN to the variable CLUB$, use

```
200 LET CLUB$="ΣN"
```

To type Σ you must use Alt/228. Although you can use Alt/78 for N, it is easier simply to type N.

You can even respond to INPUT statements with any characters that can be entered with the Alt key. Thus, you can respond to the question mark caused by

```
20 INPUT CLUB$
```

with ΣN, or ΓΣ, or any other character string that can be entered at the keyboard.

EXAMPLE 11

Here is a program to produce the screen display:

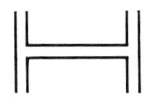

```
10 REM A$ IS A 5 CHARACTER STRING.
20 A$="|⊢|  "     'Alt/204,Alt/205,Alt/205,Alt/205,Alt/185
30 REM B$ IS ANOTHER 5 CHARACTER STRING.
40 B$="||   ||"     'Alt/186,space,space,space,Alt/186
50 PRINT TAB(10);B$
60 PRINT TAB(10);A$
70 PRINT TAB(10);B$
80 END
```

The String Function STRING$

If **n** and **c** denote integers in the range 0–255 and **S$** denotes a string expression then

STRING$(**n,c**) is the string that repeats **n** times the character whose numeric code is **c**.

STRING$(**n,S$**) is the string that repeats **n** times the first character of **S$**.

We have already illustrated the second of these two forms. For instance, we have used

    PRINT STRING$(N,"-")

to display a row of N dashes. Since we know how to enter special characters with the Alt key, we can write

    PRINT STRING$(N,"♦")

to display a row of N diamond symbols.

The first form STRING$(**n,c**) includes the numeric code **c** of the character to be repeated. Thus, STRING$(5,4) has the value

♦♦♦♦♦

since 4 is the numeric code of the diamond symbol. Similarly, the statement

    PRINT STRING$(N,4)

will display a row of N diamonds.

EXAMPLE 12

Use the block character ■ (numeric code 219) to display a rectangle W positions wide and R rows high:

PROBLEM ANALYSIS

To display the required figure all that is needed is to:

1. Draw the first row ■■■■■■■
2. Draw R − 2 rows ■   ■
3. Draw the last row ■■■■■■■

To draw the first and last rows, simply display ■ W times. Let BLOCK$="■" and print STRING$(W,BLOCK$).

To draw each of the other rows, display ■, then W − 2 blanks and ■ again. Let BLANK$=" " and print BLOCK$;STRING$(W−2,BLANK$);BLOCK$.

THE PROGRAM

```
100 CLS                                         'Clear screen.
110 INPUT "How many positions wide (3 to 79)";W
120 IF W<3 OR W>79 THEN 110
130 INPUT "How many rows high (3 to 18)";R
140 IF R<3 OR R>18 THEN 130
150 PRINT : PRINT
160 LET BLOCK$="■"                              'Code 219
170 LET BLANK$=" "
180 LET A$=STRING$(W,BLOCK$)
190 LET B$=STRING$(W-2,BLANK$)
200 PRINT A$                                    'First row
210 FOR N=1 TO R-2                              'Middle rows
230 NEXT N
240 PRINT A$                                    'Last row
250 END
RUN

How many positions wide (3 to 79)? 8
How many rows high (3 to 18)? 4
```

■ **REMARK** Lines 180 and 190 can be replaced by

```
180 LET A$=STRING$(W,219)
190 LET B$=STRING$(W-2,32)
```

☐ STRING$(W − 2,32) can also be written SPACE$(W − 2).

EXAMPLE 13 Here is a program to display 16 horizontal bars showing the 16 PC colors.

```
100 CLS                                         'Clear screen.
110 PRINT TAB(37);"COLORS"
120 PRINT
130 BAR$=STRING$(20,219)                        'Code 219 is ■.
140 FOR N=0 TO 15
150     COLOR 7,0,0 : PRINT TAB(25);N;          'Display number of bar.
160     COLOR N,0,0 : PRINT TAB(30);BAR$        'Display bar in color.
170 NEXT N
180 COLOR 7,0,0                                 'Normal screen
190 END
```

■ **REMARK** The first bar (color 0) cannot be seen because the background color is also black. Its
☐   number, however, is seen—all numbers are displayed in the normal white on black.

■ 10.5 Problems

1. Describe the screen display produced by each program.

   a. ```
       10 COLOR 7,0,0
       20 CLS
       30 FOR N=1 TO 5
       40   PRINT "NORMAL"
       50 NEXT N
       60 COLOR 0,7,0
       70 FOR N=1 TO 5
       80   PRINT TAB(7);"REVERSE"
       90 NEXT N
       95 COLOR 7,0,0
       99 END
       ```

   b.  ```
       10 COLOR 7,0,0
       20 CLS
       30 FOR T=1 TO 5
       40     LOCATE 10+T,38
       50     PRINT "BASIC"
       60 NEXT T
       70 COLOR 23
       80 LOCATE 13,38
       90 PRINT "BASIC"
       95 COLOR 7
       99 END
       ```

```
c. 10 COLOR 7,0,0              d. 10 COLOR 0,7,0
   20 CLS                         20 CLS
   30 COLOR 0,7                   30 ROW$=STRING$(80," ")
   40 FOR R=1 TO 10               40 FOR K=0 TO 15
   50   FOR C=1 TO 5              50   COLOR 0,K
   60     PRINT TAB(2*C);" ";     60   LOCATE K+1,1
   70   NEXT C                    70   PRINT ROW$
   80   PRINT                     80 NEXT K
   90 NEXT R                      90 COLOR 7,0,0
   95 COLOR 7,0                   99 END
   99 END
```

2. Describe the screen display produced by each program. (These displays involve the PC special characters.)

```
a. 10 COLOR 7,0,0              b. 10 COLOR 7,0,0
   20 CLS                         20 CLS
   30 FOR Y=1 TO 5                30 FOR N=1 TO 5
   40   PRINT STRING$(Y,219)      40   PRINT TAB(6-N);STRING$(N,219)
   50 NEXT Y                      50 NEXT N
   60 END                         60 END

c. 10 COLOR 0,7,0              d. 10 COLOR 0,7,0 : CLS
   20 CLS                         20 LET A$="■ ■ ■ ■"      'Alt/219
   30 LET L$=CHR$(169)            30 LET B$=" ■ ■ ■ "
   40 LET R$=CHR$(170)            40 COLOR 4,0,0
   50 PRINT                       50 FOR N=1 TO 2
   60 FOR N=1 TO 3                60   PRINT A$ : PRINT B$
   70   PRINT L$;R$;              70 NEXT N
   80 NEXT N                      80 PRINT A$
   90 COLOR 7,0,0                 90 COLOR 7,0,0
   99 END                         99 END
```

In Problems 3–7, write a program for each task specified. The PC special characters described in Section 10.4 are not required.

3. Color the entire display area white and then display your name and address in black characters centered on the screen.

4. Color the entire display area white and then display the following five lines (in black characters) centered on screen lines 6–10. The first line is to be displayed in reverse image characters.

```
This is line 1
This is line 2
This is line 3
This is line 4
This is line 5
```

5. First produce the display described in Problem 4. Then use the bottom portion of the screen to instruct the user to type an integer from 0 to 5. If the user types a number 1–5, the line currently in reverse image should be displayed in black characters on a white background, the line specified by the user should appear in reverse image, and the user should be instructed to type another number. This process should be repeated until the user types 0.

6. Display the five lines shown in Problem 4 in black characters on a white background, with the first line displayed in blinking characters. The user should then be able to cause the current blinking line to stop blinking and the next one to start blinking, simply by pressing any key other than 0. If line 5 is the blinking line, the next one is line 1. When the user presses the 0 key, the program is to halt.

7. A user should be allowed to type up to ten dollar amounts in the range −9999.99 to 9999.99 to

obtain their sum. The value 0, if typed, is to indicate that all numbers have been entered. The screen display is to be as follows.

   a. All interaction between user and computer is to take place in screen lines 20–23.
   b. As the user types input values (other than 0), they are to be displayed in a column in the top portion of the screen with negative amounts appearing in red (reverse image if your screen does not allow color).
   c. After all numbers have been entered, a row of dashes is to be displayed under the column of numbers.
   d. The sum is to be displayed under the row of dashes. All numbers in the column, including the sum, are to line up by decimal points. (Use a PRINT USING statement with the specification #####.## to display all numbers.)

In Problems 8–11 write a program for each task specified. You should use the PC special display characters.

8. Color the entire screen white and then use the block character (numeric code 219) to color in black a rectangular region 15 blocks high and 25 blocks wide, centered on the screen.
9. For integers L and H, with L in the range 1–80 and H in the range 1–22, use the block character (code 219) to color in black a rectangular region H blocks high and L blocks wide, centered on the screen. The user is to enter values for L and H during program execution.
10. Produce a table showing the numeric codes 128–255, each with its corresponding display character. Use eight double columns labeled CODE CHAR so that the entire table will fit on the screen. (You should find the PRINT USING statement helpful.)
11. Produce a table as in Problem 10 for the numeric codes 0–127. However, display the block character (CHR$(219)) for each of the numeric codes 0, 7, 9–13, and 28–31. As mentioned previously, these have special meanings as shown in Appendix F.

■ 10.6 Review True-or-False Quiz

1. The CLS statement sometimes clears screen line 25 and sometimes doesn't clear this line.   T F
2. The statement LOCATE 5,9 will cause the next output value to be displayed beginning in position 9 of display line 5.   T F
3. The programming line

    ```
    200 LOCATE 12,6 : PRINT "BASIC"
    ```

   will cause five blanks followed by the word BASIC to be displayed on screen line 12.   T F
4. The programming line

    ```
    200 LOCATE 24,1 : PRINT "DONE"
    ```

   will display DONE on screen line 24 and will not affect screen lines 1–23.   T F
5. If all output is produced by using LPRINT statements, the LOCATE statement can be used to specify print positions along a line.   T F
6. The programming line

    ```
    50 IF INKEY$<>"." THEN 50
    ```

   will cause the computer to loop until the period key is pressed.   T F
7. The statement COLOR 0,7,0 will cause subsequent output to be displayed in black characters on a white background.   T F
8. The statement COLOR 16,7,7 will cause subsequent output to be displayed in blinking black characters on a white background.   T F
9. Colors specified in a COLOR statement remain in effect until another COLOR statement is encountered or until program execution terminates, whichever comes first.   T F

10. The expression *reverse image* always means that characters are displayed in black letters on a white background.   T   F

11. The statement COLOR,,7 is admissible. When executed, the border screen is immediately colored in white.   T   F

12. The programming line

     10 CLS : COLOR 0, 7, 7

will cause the entire screen to be colored in white.   T   F

13. Any of the IBM PC display characters can be displayed by using the statement PRINT CHR$(N) where N denotes the numeric code of the character to be displayed.   T   F

14. Any of the IBM PC display characters can be displayed by using the Alt key together with the numeric keypad.   T   F

15. Any of the IBM PC display characters can be displayed by using the statement PRINT STRING$(1,N) where N denotes the numeric code of the character to be displayed.   T   F

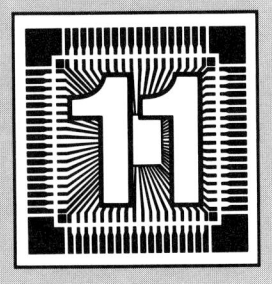

11 Data as Part of a Program

To this point, values have been assigned to variables by using only LET and INPUT statements. BASIC provides alternative ways of presenting data to the computer. In this chapter, we describe three statements: the DATA statement, which allows you to include data as part of your programs; the READ statement, which is used to assign these data to variables; and the RESTORE statement, which allows you to "read" these data more than once during a single program run.

As you work through the examples in this chapter, you will see that these statements often provide a convenient, and sometimes necessary, alternative to the LET and INPUT statements.

■ 11.1 The READ and DATA Statements

These two statements are best illustrated by example. The general forms that must be used for READ and DATA statements, together with rules governing their use, are given following Example 5.

EXAMPLE 1 Here is a program to "read" two numbers and display their sum.

```
100 READ A
110 READ B
120 PRINT "VALUES: ";A;B
130 PRINT "SUM: ";A+B
140 DATA 17,8
150 END
RUN

VALUES: 17  8
SUM: 25
```

Line 140 contains the numbers to be added. Line 100 assigns the first of these (17) to A, and line 110 assigns the second number (8) to B. When line 140, the DATA line, is encountered, it is ignored, and control passes to the next line, which in this program terminates the run.

■ REMARK Lines 100 and 110 can be replaced by the single READ statement

```
100 READ A,B
```

This statement obtains the first datum (17) for the first variable (A) and the second datum (8) for the second variable (B).

165

166 *Chapter 11 Data as Part of a Program*

EXAMPLE 2 Here are BASIC statements to "read" and display a list of numbers.

```
100 PRINT "DATA VALUES: "
110 READ X
120 PRINT X
130 GOTO 110
140 DATA 7,-123,40
RUN

DATA VALUES:
 7
-123
 40
Out of data in 110
```

Line 140 contains the list of numbers. When line 110 is first executed, the first datum (7) is assigned to X, and control passes to line 120, which displays the value of X. The GOTO statement transfers control back to line 110, which then assigns the next value (−123) to X. This process is repeated until the data list is exhausted. This will happen when the READ statement is executed a fourth time. Since only three values are supplied in the DATA line, the attempt to read a fourth value causes the error condition identified by the Out of data message, and execution terminates.

■ **REMARK** Out of data errors should be avoided. The examples in this chapter illustrate the most common ways to do this.

EXAMPLE 3 Here is a program to "read" and display three strings.

```
100 READ A$,B$,P$
110 PRINT B$;" ";A$;P$
120 DATA FLIES,TIME,.
130 END
RUN

TIME FLIES.
```

The READ statement assigns the first datum (FLIES) to A$, the second (TIME) to B$, and the third (a period) to P$. The PRINT statement then produces the output shown.

■ **REMARK** Both upper- and lowercase letters are allowed in DATA statements. Thus line 120 could be written

```
120 DATA flies,Time,.
```

to produce the output

```
Time flies.
```

Note that the strings in the DATA line of Example 3 are not in quotation marks. Strings must be quoted only if:

1. They contain significant leading or trailing blanks. (If not quoted, these blanks are ignored.)
2. A comma or colon appears in the string. (The comma is used to delimit the constants contained in the DATA lines and the colon to separate statements.)

It is always correct to enclose strings in quotation marks.

EXAMPLE 4 Here is a program to illustrate quoted and unquoted strings in DATA lines.

```
10 READ Z$
20 WHILE Z$<>"END-OF-DATA"
30    PRINT Z$
40    READ Z$
50 WEND
```

```
60 DATA 1234567,VI,"   AL",TO GO,"CLARK,JACK"
70 DATA END-OF-DATA
80 END
RUN

1234567
VI
   AL
TO GO
CLARK,JACK
```

Quotes are needed for "   AL" because of the leading blanks and for "CLARK, JACK" because of the comma. Quotes are not needed for the string TO GO because the blank is not a leading blank.

■ REMARK 1   Note that the string END-OF-DATA in line 70 is not displayed in the output. It serves only as an *end-of-data* (EOD) *tag*. The use of end-of-data tags in DATA statements represents a common method of avoiding Out-of-data errors.

■ REMARK 2   Note also that the string 1234567 is displayed without a leading blank. When the READ statement obtains the value 1234567 for the *string* variable Z$, the computer stores it as seven distinct characters. This would not be so if 1234567 were assigned to a *numerical* variable. The statement

```
LET Z=1234567
```

stores the numbers 1234567 in a special binary form the computer uses to store numerical values.

As illustrated in the next example, both string and numerical data can be included in a single DATA statement, and a single READ statement can be used to read values for both string and numerical variables.

EXAMPLE 5   Here is a program to produce a table summarizing the information contained in DATA statements.

```
100 REM ********* DISPLAY COLUMN HEADINGS *********
110 PRINT "NAME","SCORE1","SCORE2","AVERAGE"
120 PRINT
130 REM ******* READ THE NUMBER OF STUDENTS *******
140 READ N
150 REM **** READ THE DATA AND DISPLAY TABLE VALUES ****
160 LET COUNT=1
170 WHILE COUNT<=N
180     READ STUDENT$,SCORE1,SCORE2
190     LET AV=(SCORE1+SCORE2)/2
200     PRINT STUDENT$,SCORE1,SCORE2,AV
210     LET COUNT=COUNT+1
220 WEND
230 REM
300 REM *** FIRST DATA ITEM IS THE NUMBER OF STUDENTS ***
310 DATA 4
320 DATA CARL,71,79
330 DATA MARLENE,82,88
340 DATA SUZANNE,89,62
350 DATA WILLIAM,58,96
999 END
RUN

NAME            SCORE1          SCORE2          AVERAGE

CARL            71              79              75
MARLENE         82              88              85
SUZANNE         89              62              75.5
WILLIAM         58              96              77
```

The first READ statement (line 140) assigns the first datum (4) to the variable N. This N is then used to ensure that exactly four names with their corresponding scores are read and processed. This procedure illustrates another common method of avoiding Out of data errors. Include a count as the first datum, and then use this count to cause an exit from the loop when the prescribed number of data values has been read.

■ **REMARK** Note that the variable COUNT serves as a counter for the loop described by lines 160–220. Thus, the loop is a counter-controlled loop as described in Section 9.1 and is perhaps more conveniently coded as a FOR loop. To do this, delete lines 160 and 210 and make these changes:

```
170 FOR COUNT=1 TO N
220 NEXT COUNT
```

□

The general forms of the READ and DATA statements are as follows:

ln READ (List of variables separated by commas)
ln DATA (List of BASIC constants separated by commas)

The following rules govern the use of these two statements:

1. As many DATA lines as desired may be included in a program, and as many values as will fit may appear on each line. The values must be constants.

2. All values appearing in the DATA lines constitute a single list called the **data list.** The order in which data appear in this list is precisely the order in which they appear in the program—that is, from lowest to highest line numbers and, within a DATA line, from left to right.

3. When a READ statement is executed, the variables appearing are assigned successive values from the data list. You must write your READ and DATA statements so that only numerical values are assigned to numerical variables and only string values to string variables. The data appearing in DATA lines constitute a *single* data list; no special treatment is given to string constants. The execution of a READ statement will attempt to assign the next value in this list to the variable being assigned. If this next value is not of the same type as the variable, either an error message will be displayed or your program will simply produce incorrect results.

4. It is not necessary that all data values be read. However, an attempt to read more data than appear in DATA lines will result in an error condition that causes an Out of data message and program execution to stop. Errors that stop program execution are called **fatal errors.**

5. If a DATA statement is encountered during program execution, the statement is ignored and control passes to the next line. Thus, DATA lines may appear anywhere in the program, although you should position them to make your programs more readable. Placing them near the end of a program is a common practice, especially if different data will be processed each time the program is run. If DATA lines will never be changed, it is sometimes better to place them just after the READ statements that read the data.

In flowcharting, the symbol

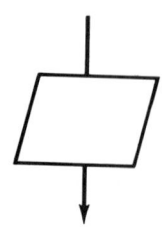

is used to designate any input or output that is carried out automatically with no user interaction. The PRINT and READ statements designate such actions; hence this symbol is used for both of these statements. You will recall that we have used the flowchart symbol

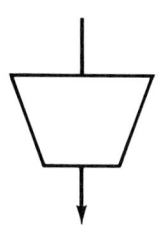

for all INPUT statements. In flowcharting, this symbol is used to designate any process that requires user interaction, thus causing a temporary halt in execution. The INPUT statement does precisely this—the program waits until you enter data at the keyboard.

There is no flowchart symbol for DATA statements. DATA statements simply provide a means of presenting data to the computer for processing. When encountered during program execution, they cause nothing to happen. Thus they have no place in a flowchart, whose purpose is to describe the flow of activity in a program.

We conclude this section with another example illustrating the use of an EOD tag. Using an EOD tag as the last datum, rather than a count as the first, relieves us of the burden of counting the values in a data list.

EXAMPLE 6

In this example, we are given the results of a golf tournament and must produce a two-column table showing the names and total scores of all golfers. We must also tell how many golfers are tied for the lead (lowest total score). If there is a single winner, however, the winner's name and total score are to be displayed instead of the count. The results of the tournament are given to us in DATA lines as follows:

```
DATA BROUHA, 70, 72, 68, 69
DATA HERMAN, 66, 68, 73, 76
DATA MITCHELL, 66, 75, 72, 74
DATA NICKLAUS, 73, 70, 70, 65
DATA SANDERS, 73, 73, 71, 72
DATA SMYTHE, 68, 72, 77, 68
DATA XXX
```

PROBLEM ANALYSIS

Producing a two-column table as specified in the problem statement is not new to us. After displaying a title and column headings, we can process the DATA lines one at a time to produce the table values.

In addition to producing the table, the problem statement says that we must find the lowest total score and count how many golfers have achieved this lowest score. Moreover, if there is a winner, we'll need that winner's name. This short analysis suggests that we use variable names for the following values:

N$	= player's name
S1, S2, S3, S4	= scores for player N$
TTL	= total score for N$
LOW	= lowest total score
WIN$	= winner's name
CNT	= count of players with lowest score

Each time we read N$ and the four scores S1, S2, S3, and S4, we will calculate TTL = S1 + S2 + S3 + S4 and display N$ and TTL. Then if TTL = LOW, we have another player with the best score LOW so we'll add 1 to CNT. If TTL < LOW we have a new lowest score, so we'll assign TTL to LOW, assign N$ to WIN$, and set CNT to 1. Since the first player's total TTL will be the lowest score to that point, we'll start with LOW = a large number to ensure that TTL < LOW will be true for the first player.

170 *Chapter 11 Data as Part of a Program*

THE ALGORITHM

  a. Display a title and column headings.
  b. Initialize: LOW = 9999.
  c. Read N$ (first player's name).
  d. Repeat the following as long as N$ <> "XXX":
    d1. Read S1, S2, S3, S4.
    d2. Calculate their sum TTL.
    d3. Display N$ and TTL.
    d4. If TTL = LOW, add 1 to CNT.
    d5. If TTL < LOW, assign TTL to LOW, N$ to WIN$, and set CNT to 1.
    d6. READ N$ (next player's name).
  e. Display the lowest score LOW.
  f. If CNT = 1, display winner's name WIN$; otherwise display CNT.
  g. Stop.

THE PROGRAM

```
100 REM GOLF TOURNAMENT PROGRAM
110 REM
120 REM      N$         PLAYER'S NAME
130 REM      S1-S4      SCORES FOR N$
140 REM      TTL        TOTAL SCORE FOR N$
150 REM      LOW        LOWEST SCORE
160 REM      WIN$       WINNER'S NAME
170 REM      CNT        NUMBER OF PLAYERS WITH LOW SCORE
180 REM
190 REM ********************************
200 REM DISPLAY TITLE AND COLUMN HEADINGS.
210 REM
220 PRINT "    GOLF TOURNAMENT"
230 PRINT "       (ROUNDS 1-4)"
240 PRINT
250 PRINT "PLAYER","TOTAL"
260 PRINT
270 REM ********************************
280 REM READ DATA TO PRODUCE TABLE VALUES
290 REM AND TO FIND LOW, CNT, AND WIN$.
300 REM
310 LET LOW=9999
320 READ N$
330 WHILE N$<>"XXX"
340     READ S1,S2,S3,S4
350     LET TTL=S1+S2+S3+S4
360     PRINT N$,TTL
370     IF TTL=LOW THEN CNT=CNT+1
380     IF TTL>=LOW THEN 420
390     LET LOW=TTL
400     LET WIN$=N$
410     LET CNT=1
420     READ N$
430 WEND
440 REM
450 REM *********************
460 REM DISPLAY FINAL RESULTS.
470 PRINT
480 PRINT "BEST FOUR-ROUND TOTAL: ";LOW
490 IF CNT=1 THEN PRINT "TOURNAMENT WINNER: ";WIN$
500 IF CNT<>1 THEN PRINT CNT;"PLAYERS ARE TIED FOR THE LEAD."
510 REM
800 REM *****************
810 REM TOURNAMENT RESULTS
820 REM
830 DATA BROUHA,70,72,68,69
840 DATA HERMAN,66,68,73,76
850 DATA MITCHELL,66,75,72,74
860 DATA NICKLAUS,73,70,70,65
870 DATA SANDERS,73,73,71,72
```

```
880 DATA SMYTHE,68,72,77,68
890 DATA XXX
900 END
RUN

        GOLF TOURNAMENT
         (ROUNDS 1-4)

PLAYER          TOTAL

BROUHA          279
HERMAN          283
MITCHELL        287
NICKLAUS        278
SANDERS         289
SMYTHE          285

BEST FOUR-ROUND TOTAL: 278
TOURNAMENT WINNER: NICKLAUS
```

11.2 Problems

1. Show the output of each program.

   a.
   ```
   10 READ X
   20 WHILE X>=0
   30     LET Y=X-5
   40     PRINT X;Y
   50     READ X
   60 WEND
   70 DATA 2,5,0,-1
   80 END
   ```

   b.
   ```
   10 READ A,B$,M$
   20 LET M$=B$
   30 PRINT M$;
   40 READ A,B$,M$
   50 LET M$=B$
   60 LET B$=M$
   70 PRINT B$
   80 DATA 6,CAT,MOUSE
   90 DATA 8,"WOMAN","MAN"
   99 END
   ```

   c.
   ```
   10 LET N=0
   20 READ X
   30 WHILE X<>9999
   40     LET N=N+1
   50     PRINT X
   60     READ X
   70 WEND
   80 PRINT N
   90 DATA 7,3,18,-5,9999
   99 END
   ```

   d.
   ```
   100 LET B=0
   110 READ V
   120 WHILE V<>0
   130     IF V>24 and V<76 THEN 160
   140     PRINT "BAD VALUE: ";V
   150     LET B=B+1
   160     READ V
   170 WEND
   180 IF B=0 THEN PRINT "DATA ARE OK."
   190 DATA 36,42,71,22,63,68,84,51,0
   200 END
   ```

2. Find and correct the errors in these programs.

a.
```
10 READ X, X$
20 PRINT X$; X
30 DATA "1"; A
40 END
```

b.
```
10 READ Y; Z$
20 PRINT Z$; " OF "; Y
30 DATA 42, SUMMER
40 END
```

c.
```
10 READ B$
20 IF B$=HELLO THEN 10
30 PRINT B$
40 DATA HELLO, GOODBYE
50 END
```

d.
```
10 READ N$
20 READ A, B, C
30 PRINT "NAME: "; N$
40 PRINT "AVERAGE: "; (A+B+C)/3
50 DATA TOM DOOLEY, JR
60 DATA 85, 81, 76
70 END
```

3. The following programs do not do what they claim. Find and correct all errors.

a.
```
10 REM DISPLAY SQUARES OF
20 REM 12, 37, 21, 96.
30 WHILE A<>999
40     READ A
50     LET A=A*A
60     PRINT A
70     READ A
80 WEND
90 DATA 12, 37, 21, 96
98 DATA 999
99 END
```

b.
```
10 REM AVERAGE N NUMBERS.
20 READ X
30 WHILE X<>1E-30
40     LET S=0
50     LET S=S+X
60 WEND
70 PRINT "AVERAGE IS"; S/N
80 DATA 18, 23, 17, 22
90 DATA 1E-30
99 END
```

c.
```
100 REM COUNT DATA VALUES,
110 REM BUT NOT 999.
120 LET C=0
130 WHILE V<999
140     READ V
150     LET C=C+1
160 WEND
170 PRINT "DATA COUNT: "; C
180 DATA 275, 863, 947, 1262
190 DATA 1344, 2765, 999
200 END
```

In Problems 4–11, write a program to perform each task specified.

4. Read values from DATA lines two at a time. Display each pair of values, their sum, and their average on one line. Run your program using the following DATA lines. The last two values (−1,−1) are to be used to detect the end of the data.

```
800 DATA 70, 80, 90, 65, 75, 85
810 DATA 50, 40, 65, 80, 78, 76
820 DATA 62, 60, 65, 50, 60, 85
830 DATA 35, 45, 60, 90, 96, 92
890 DATA -1, -1
```

5. Read values three at a time from DATA lines and display them only if the third is greater than the average of the first two. Run your program using the data in Problem 4. (Change only line 890.)

6. Read values three at a time from DATA lines and display them only if they are in ascending order. Use the data in Problem 4. (Change only line 890.)

7. Find how many of the numbers appearing in DATA lines lie between 40 and 60, inclusive, and determine the average of these numbers. Use the data in Problem 4.

8. A list of scores in the range 0 to 100 is to be examined to determine the following counts:

   C1 = number of scores less than 40
   C2 = number of scores between 40 and 60, inclusive
   C3 = number of scores greater than 60

   Determine these counts for any list appearing in DATA lines. Use the data in Problem 4.

9. A list of scores in the range 0 to 100 is to be examined to determine the following counts:

   C1 = number of scores less than 20
   C2 = number of scores less than 40 but at least 20
   C3 = number of scores less than 60 but at least 40
   C4 = number of scores less than 80 but at least 60
   C5 = number of scores not less than 80

   Determine these counts for any list appearing in DATA lines. Use the data in Problem 4.

10. A candidate for political office conducted a preelection poll. Each voter polled was assigned a number from 1 to 3 as follows:

    1 = will vote for candidate
    2 = leans toward candidate but still undecided
    3 = all other cases

    Tally the results of this poll. Use DATA lines to present the data to the computer.

11. Modify Problem 10 by assigning two values to each voter. The first is as stated; the second is to designate whether the voter is female (F) or male (M). There are now six counts to be determined. (Use READ A,S$ to read the two values assigned to a voter.)

For Problems 12–16, write programs to produce reports as specified. Make sure each report has a title and each column has an appropriate heading. All data are to be presented in DATA lines.

12. The following DATA lines show the salaries for all salaried employees in a small firm. [The first value (10) denotes how many salaries are listed.]

    ```
    800 DATA 10
    810 DATA 19923, 20240, 20275, 21390, 22560
    820 DATA 22997, 23423, 24620, 29240, 32730
    ```

    Prepare a report showing the effect of a flat across-the-board raise of R dollars in addition to a percentage increase of P percent. R and P are to be input. Include three columns labeled PRESENT SALARY, RAISE, and NEW SALARY.

13. The following DATA lines show the annual salaries for all salaried employees in a firm. Each salary amount is followed by a count of the number of employees earning that amount. This firm has a salary step schedule. [The first value (8) denotes the number of salary steps.]

    ```
    800 DATA 8
    810 DATA 19020, 4, 20250, 8, 22330, 16, 22940, 30
    820 DATA 23570, 21, 24840, 86, 25920, 28, 26520, 7
    ```

    Prepare a three-column report as in Problem 12. In addition, conclude the report by displaying the total cost to the owners of the old salary package, the total cost of the new salary package, the total dollar amount of all raises (the difference of the previous two figures), and the overall percent increase this amount represents.

14. Given the following information, produce a three-column report showing the employee number, monthly sales, and commission for each employee if the commission rate for each person is 6%.

Employee number	Monthly sales
018266234	$4,050
026196551	6,500
034257321	3,750
016187718	3,640
023298049	7,150

15. Given the following information, produce a four-column report showing the employee name, the monthly sales, the commission rate, and the total commission for each employee.

Employee name	Monthly sales	Commission rate
Hart	$28,400	2 %
Wilson	34,550	2.5 %
Brown	19,600	3 %
Ruiz	14,500	2 %
Jensen	22,300	3.25%
Grogan	31,350	1.5 %

16. (Electric bill problem) Given the following information, produce a report showing the customer number, total number of kilowatt-hours (kWh) used, and total monthly bill. The charges are computed according to the following schedule: $1.41 for the first 14 kWh, the next 85 kWh at $0.0389/kWh, the next 200 at $0.0214/kWh, the next 300 at $0.0134/kWh, and the excess at $0.0099/kWh. In addition, there is a fuel-adjustment charge of $0.0322/kWh for all kilowatt-hours used.

Customer number	Previous month's reading	Current reading
0516	25,346	25,973
2634	47,947	48,851
2917	21,342	21,652
2853	893,462	894,258
3576	347,643	348,748
3943	41,241	41,783
3465	887,531	888,165

■ 11.3 The RESTORE Statement

We have described a *data list* as the list of all data values appearing in all DATA lines in a program. Associated with a data list is a conceptual *pointer* indicating the value to be read by the next READ statement. The pointer is initially set to the first value in the list; then each time a value is read, the pointer moves to the next value. The BASIC statement

    ln RESTORE

positions this pointer back to the beginning of the data list (the first DATA line) so that the values can be read again. The statement

    ln RESTORE **ln$_1$**

positions the pointer to the first data value in line number **ln$_1$**.

EXAMPLE 7   This example illustrates the action caused by the two forms of the RESTORE statement.

The program segment

```
10 READ A, B
20 RESTORE
30 READ C
40 RESTORE
50 READ D, E, F
60 DATA 1, 2, 3, 4, 5, 6
```

assigns values to A, B, C, D, E, and F as follows:

Line 10 assigns the first two data values (1 and 2) to A and B, respectively.
Line 20 positions the pointer back to the first datum.
Line 30 assigns the first datum (1) to C.
Line 40 once again restores the pointer to the first datum.
Line 50 assigns the values 1, 2, and 3 to D, E, and F, respectively.

The program segment

```
10 READ A,B
20 RESTORE 80
30 READ C
40 RESTORE 70
50 READ D,E,F
60 DATA 1,2,3
70 DATA 4,5,6
80 DATA 7,8,9
```

assigns values to A, B, C, D, E, and F as follows:

Line 10 assigns the first two data values (1 and 2) to A and B, respectively.
Line 20 positions the pointer ahead to line 80.
Line 30 assigns the first datum (7) on line 80 to C.
Line 40 positions the pointer back to line 70.
Line 50 assigns the values 4, 5, and 6 to D, E, and F, respectively.

Following are two short examples that illustrate typical ways in which the RESTORE statement is used.

EXAMPLE 8 Here is a program to display two lists obtained from a single data list.

```
100 PRINT "SCORES 70 OR MORE: ";
110 FOR N=1 TO 10
120     READ X
130     IF X>=70 THEN PRINT X;
140 NEXT N
150 PRINT
160 RESTORE
170 PRINT "SCORES LESS THAN 70: ";
180 FOR N=1 TO 10
190     READ X
200     IF X<70 THEN PRINT X;
210 NEXT N
220 DATA 78,84,65,32,93,58,88,76,68,83
230 END
RUN

SCORES 70 OR MORE:  78  84  93  88  76  83
SCORES LESS THAN 70:  65  32  58  68
```

The PRINT statements in lines 100 and 170 describe what this program does. Since all numbers 70 or greater must be displayed before any number less than 70 is displayed, the data must be examined twice. The RESTORE statement in line 160 allows this to happen.

REMARK Without the RESTORE statement, 10 variables would be needed for the 10 numbers appearing in the DATA line. With the RESTORE statement, only one (X) is needed.

EXAMPLE 9 Here is a program to search a list for any value typed at the keyboard.

```
100 REM ***************** ON MIXING COLORS *****************
110 REM
120 REM    X$ = A COLOR INCLUDED IN DATA LINES
```

```
130 REM      Y$ = INFORMATION ABOUT COLOR X$
140 REM      C$ = A STRING INPUT VALUE
150 REM
160 PRINT "THIS PROGRAM GIVES INFORMATION ABOUT COLORS."
170 PRINT "ALL ENTRIES YOU MAKE MUST BE IN UPPERCASE."
180 PRINT
190 INPUT "COLOR (TYPE END TO STOP)";C$
200 WHILE C$<>"END"
210    REM ---------- SEARCH DATA LIST FOR COLOR C$ ----------
220    READ X$,Y$
230    WHILE X$<>C$ AND X$<>"XXX"
240       READ X$,Y$
250    WEND
260    REM ---------------- DISPLAY OUTPUT ----------------
270    IF X$="XXX" THEN PRINT C$;" IS NOT IN MY LIST OF COLORS."
280    IF X$<>"XXX" THEN PRINT Y$
290    REM ---------- PREPARE FOR NEXT INPUT VALUE ----------
300    RESTORE
310    PRINT
320    INPUT "COLOR (TYPE END TO STOP)";C$
330 WEND
500 DATA WHITE, USED FOR TINTING
510 DATA BLACK, USED FOR SHADING
520 DATA YELLOW, A PRIMARY COLOR
530 DATA RED, A PRIMARY COLOR
540 DATA BLUE, A PRIMARY COLOR
550 DATA ORANGE, MIX YELLOW AND RED.
560 DATA GREEN, MIX YELLOW AND BLUE.
570 DATA PURPLE, MIX RED AND BLUE.
580 DATA PINK, MIX RED AND WHITE.
590 DATA GRAY, MIX BLACK AND WHITE.
600 DATA MAGENTA, MIX RED WITH A SPECK OF BLACK.
610 DATA XXX, YYY
999 END
RUN

THIS PROGRAM GIVES INFORMATION ABOUT COLORS.
ALL ENTRIES YOU MAKE MUST BE IN UPPERCASE.

COLOR (TYPE END TO STOP)? BLUE
A PRIMARY COLOR

COLOR (TYPE END TO STOP)? MAGENTA
MIX RED WITH A SPECK OF BLACK.

COLOR (TYPE END TO STOP)? AQUA
AQUA IS NOT IN MY LIST OF COLORS.

COLOR (TYPE END TO STOP)? END
```

The list of colors being searched in lines 220–250 consists of every other datum—we use READ X$,Y$ to read the data and compare the input value C$ with X$, a color, and not with Y$ that contains information about the color.

When the value read for X$ is the input value C$ or the EOD tag XXX, the WHILE statement in line 230 causes an exit from the search loop to line 260. If X$ = "XXX", the input value C$ is not one of the colors included in the DATA lines, and line 270 displays a message that this is so. If X$ ≠ "XXX", then X$ = C$ is one of the included colors, and line 280 displays Y$, which contains information about this color.

After the output for the input value C$ is displayed, lines 300–330 restore the data pointer to the first datum, request another input value C$, and transfer control back to line 220. This process is repeated until the user types END.

11.3 The RESTORE Statement

■ REMARK

Note that the information in DATA lines does not represent input data in the usual sense. Rather, it represents more or less permanent data that the program uses while processing other information (values typed at the keyboard). This represents a common usage of DATA statements.

☐

Many applications require that the values given in DATA lines be used more than once. In Example 8, data included in DATA line had to be examined twice to produce two lists, and in Example 9, a table of colors and color-mixing instructions had to be examined from its beginning to search for each input value typed at the keyboard. We conclude this chapter with a detailed analysis of another programming task that requires examining input data more than once.

EXAMPLE 10

A clothing manufacturer has retail outlets in Miami, Orlando, Chicago, Austin, Seattle, and Montreal. Each month, the company compiles a report showing three amounts for each location: the month's sales, payroll, and building maintenance costs. Our task is to write a program that uses this information to help answer questions that management might ask concerning the company's financial operations. Following is a portion of last month's report:

Location	Sales	Payroll	Maintenance
Miami	$45,620	$15,600	$3,400
Orlando	27,000	16,000	2,540
Chicago	64,000	14,280	5,250
.	.	.	.
.	.	.	.
.	.	.	.

PROBLEM ANALYSIS

The problem statement is incomplete—in practice, many are. We need to know what questions the program should answer. Even without this knowledge, however, there is something that we can do. Whatever tasks the program will carry out, it should begin by displaying a list of these tasks. It should also tell the user how to specify which tasks are to be performed. We'll assign the option numbers 1, 2, 3, and so on, to these tasks and require the user to select a task by typing its option number. Thus, we will write a menu-driven program.

This brief discussion allows us to write the following simple but complete algorithm. As in all menu-driven programs, one of the options will be to end program execution. We will also include an option to display the menu.

THE ALGORITHM

    a. Display a menu showing the available options.
    b. Repeat until the end option is selected:
        b1. Input an option number OP.
        b2. Carry out the task specified by OP.

In addition to the end and menu options, we should allow the user to see the current monthly report. Thus, we can begin by writing a program with only these three options:

1. Display this menu.
2. End the program.
3. Display this month's report.

We will use an ON GOTO statement of the form

    ON OP GOTO ln_1, ln_2, ln_3

to transfer control to the program segment that carries out the specified option OP. The program, however, must be organized so that it's a simple matter to include new options as they are determined. Toward this end, we will designate line 1000 for the menu option (OP=1), 2000 for the End option (OP=2), 3000 for the option to display the monthly report (OP = 3), and we will use line numbers less than 1000 for the rest of the program—that is, for all but the program segments that carry out the options. For the options mentioned, this program segment will contain the statement

```
ON OP GOTO 1000,2000,3000
```

for option selection. For the reasons discussed in Section 8.4, each of the program segments at lines 1000, 2000, and 3000 will end by transferring control back to an IF statement of the form

```
IF OP<>2 THEN ln
```

to allow the program to continue at line **ln** if the End option (OP=2) was not selected. The END statement will follow this IF statement.

Even though we have not yet written a single line of code (other than indicating the above-mentioned ON GOTO, IF, and END statements), it isn't difficult to see how we will be able to include new options. For example, suppose we are told that management might ask for a report showing the sales/payroll ratio for each outlet. We could write the code for this new task at line 4000, being sure to end by transferring control back to the IF statement mentioned above. The only other changes needed would be to add the option

4. Display the sales/payroll ratios.

to the menu and change the ON GOTO statement to

```
ON OP GOTO 1000,2000,3000,4000
```

Let's write a program to allow the four options already mentioned:

1. Display this menu.
2. End the program.
3. Display this month's report.
4. Display the sales/payroll ratios.

Writing BASIC code to carry out these options is rather routine and requires no new programming technique. Thus, we can proceed directly to the coding stage. Since both Options 3 and 4—and any new options to be added later—will require examining the current month's sales, payroll, and maintenance report, we will include these data in DATA statements and use RESTORE to allow the data to be read as many times as is necessary. Also, since the DATA lines must be changed each month, we'll place them in a prominent position near the beginning of the program.

THE PROGRAM

```
100 PRINT "PROGRAM TO EXAMINE MONTHLY REPORT OF: "
110 PRINT
120 PRINT "          SALES"
130 PRINT "          PAYROLL"
140 PRINT "          MAINTENANCE"
150 PRINT
160 REM ********************
170 REM *      DATA        *
180 REM ********************
190 REM
200 REM LOCATIONS FOLLOWED BY:
210 REM SALES,PAYROLL,MAINTENANCE
220 REM
230 DATA MIAMI,45620,15600,3400
240 DATA ORLANDO,27000,16000,2540
250 DATA CHICAGO,64000,14280,5250
260 DATA AUSTIN,33500,10270,2600
270 DATA SEATTLE,59200,17200,4290
280 DATA MONTREAL,52000,15000,5100
```

```
399 DATA END,0,0,0
400 REM
410 REM ****************************
420 REM * OPTION SELECTION SECTION *
430 REM ****************************
440 REM
450 GOTO 1000                                'Display menu.
460 PRINT
470 INPUT "OPTION NUMBER: ";OP               'Select option.
480 IF OP<0 OR OP>255 THEN 500               'Avoid crash.
490 ON OP GOTO 1000,2000,3000,4000
500 PRINT "-----INVALID OPTION-----"
510 IF OP<>2 THEN 460                        'Was End picked?
520 END                                      'Yes. Stop.
530 REM
540 REM ***********************************************
550 REM * PROGRAM SEGMENTS TO CARRY OUT OPTIONS *
560 REM ***********************************************
570 REM
1000 REM ***********************************************
1010 REM          OPTION 1:   DISPLAY MENU
1020 PRINT
1030 PRINT "AVAILABLE OPTIONS:"
1040 PRINT
1050 PRINT "    1    DISPLAY THIS MENU."
1060 PRINT "    2    END THE PROGRAM."
1070 PRINT "    3    DISPLAY THIS MONTH'S REPORT."
1080 PRINT "    4    DISPLAY SALES/PAYROLL RATIOS."
1200 REM
1210 GOTO 510                                'Return
1220 REM
2000 REM ***********************************************
2010 REM          OPTION 2:   END OPTION
2020 PRINT
2030 PRINT "PROGRAM TERMINATED."
2040 GOTO 510                                'Return
2050 REM
3000 REM ***********************************************
3010 REM          OPTION 3:   MONTHLY REPORT
3020 PRINT
3030 PRINT "           CURRENT MONTHLY REPORT"
3040 PRINT
3050 PRINT " LOCATION    SALES     PAYROLL    MAINTENANCE"
3060 LET F$="  \         \  ######    ######      #####"
3070 PRINT
3080 READ L$,S,P,M
3090 WHILE L$<>"END"
3100    PRINT USING F$;L$,S,P,M
3110    READ L$,S,P,M
3120 WEND
3130 RESTORE
3140 GOTO 510                                'Return
3150 REM
4000 REM ***********************************************
4010 REM          OPTION 4:   SALES/PAYROLL REPORT
4020 PRINT
4030 PRINT "SALES/PAYROLL RATIOS"
4040 PRINT
4050 PRINT " LOCATION       RATIO"
4060 LET G$="  \         \   ##.##"
4070 PRINT
4080 READ L$,S,P,M
4090 WHILE L$<>"END"
4100    PRINT USING G$;L$,S/P
4110    READ L$,S,P,M
4120 WEND
4130 RESTORE
4140 GOTO 510                                'Return
```

We ran this program for the Options 3, 4, and 2, in that order, and obtained the following output:

```
PROGRAM TO EXAMINE MONTHLY REPORT OF:

    SALES
    PAYROLL
    MAINTENANCE

AVAILABLE OPTIONS:

    1    DISPLAY THIS MENU.
    2    END THE PROGRAM.
    3    DISPLAY THIS MONTH'S REPORT.
    4    DISPLAY SALES/PAYROLL RATIOS.

OPTION NUMBER ? 3

        CURRENT MONTHLY REPORT

    LOCATION    SALES     PAYROLL   MAINTENANCE

    MIAMI       45620     15600     3400
    ORLANDO     27000     16000     2540
    CHICAGO     64000     14280     5250
    AUSTIN      33500     10270     2600
    SEATTLE     59200     17200     4290
    MONTREAL    52000     15000     5100

OPTION NUMBER ? 4

SALES/PAYROLL RATIOS

    LOCATION      RATIO

    MIAMI         2.92
    ORLANDO       1.69
    CHICAGO       4.48
    AUSTIN        3.26
    SEATTLE       3.44
    MONTREAL      3.47

OPTION NUMBER ? 2

PROGRAM TERMINATED.
```

■ REMARK 1   Each time a new task is added to this program, the programmer must include a RESTORE statement that will be executed after the data have been read. If it is forgotten, the program will produce an Out of data error when carrying out the next task. To ensure that this doesn't happen, we can include the line

    485 RESTORE

which will be executed each time the user selects an option. No other RESTORE statement is needed.

■ REMARK 2   In addition to reserving line numbers for new tasks (lines 5000 on), we have reserved line numbers for possible new DATA statements (lines 290–390) and for future additions to the menu (lines 1090–1190).

11.4 Problems

1. Show the output of each program.

   a.
   ```
   10 LET I=2
   20 WHILE I<=6
   30    READ Y
   40    PRINT Y
   50    LET I=I+2
   60 WEND
   70 RESTORE
   80 DATA 9, 3, 5, 8, 12
   90 END
   ```

   b.
   ```
   100 FOR I=1 TO 4
   110    READ X
   120    IF X=5 THEN RESTORE
   130    PRINT X
   140 NEXT I
   150 DATA 3, 5, 8, 9, 6
   160 END
   ```

   c.
   ```
   10 READ A$, B$, C$
   20 RESTORE
   30 READ D$
   40 PRINT B$; C$; D$
   50 DATA HEAD, ROB, IN, HOOD
   60 END
   ```

   d.
   ```
   10 READ A1, A2, A3
   20 PRINT A1, A2, A3
   30 RESTORE
   40 READ A3, A2, A1
   50 PRINT A3, A2, A1
   60 DATA 10, 20, 30
   70 END
   ```

   e.
   ```
   100 FOR J=1 TO 4
   110    READ A$, S
   120    IF A$<>"BURNS"
             THEN PRINT A$; S
             ELSE RESTORE
   130 NEXT J
   140 DATA ALLEN, 40, BURNS, 36
   150 DATA CASH, 38, DOOR, 40
   160 END
   ```

   In Problems 2–8, write a program to carry out each task described.

2. Allow a user to input several words and determine whether they appear in the DATA lines. For each word input, display the message IS IN THE LIST or IS NOT IN THE LIST, whichever is appropriate. Let the user end the run by typing DONE. Try your program by using the following DATA statements and inform the user that conjunctions are to be typed. (You may wish to add to the data list.)

   ```
   500 REM SOME CONJUNCTIONS
   510 DATA ALTHOUGH, AS, BUT, HOWBEIT, HOWEVER
   520 DATA IF, OR, SINCE, THOUGH, YET
   599 DATA END-OF-DATA
   ```

3. Several pairs of values are included in DATA lines. The first value in each pair represents an item code, and the second represents the current selling price. Allow a user to type several item codes to obtain the current selling prices. If an incorrect code is typed, an appropriate message should be displayed. Allow the user to end the run by typing DONE. Use the following data lines:

   ```
   500 REM ITEMS WITH PRICES
   510 DATA X100, 12.39, X110, 17.97, X120, 23.55, X130, 20.50
   520 DATA Y100, 72.60, Y110, 85.00, Y120, 97.43
   530 DATA XXX, 0
   ```

4. A list of numbers appears in DATA lines in ascending order. Allow a user to type a number. If the number appears in the list, all numbers in the list up to but not including it should be displayed. If it doesn't appear, a message to that effect should be displayed. In either case let

the user enter another number. If 0 is typed, the run should terminate. Use the following DATA lines and inform the user that the numbers are in the range 1 to 50.

```
500 DATA 1, 3, 6, 9, 13, 18, 24, 31, 39, 48
510 DATA 0
```

5. A wholesale firm has two warehouses, designated A and B. During a recent inventory, the following data were compiled:

Item	Warehouse	Quantity on hand	Average cost/unit
6625	A	52,000	$ 1.954
6204	A	40,000	3.126
3300	B	8,500	19.532
5925	A	22,000	6.884
0220	B	6,200	88.724
2100	B	4,350	43.612
4800	A	21,500	2.741
0077	A	15,000	1.605
1752	B	200	193.800

Prepare a separate inventory report for each warehouse. Each report is to contain the given information and show the total cost represented by the inventory of each item.

6. Use the inventory data shown in Problem 5 to prepare an inventory report for the warehouse whose entire stock represents the greater cost to the company.

7. The O'Halloran Shoe Company wants to know the average monthly income for its retail store and the number of months in which the income exceeds this average. Carry out this task with the following DATA lines, which give the 12 monthly income amounts:

```
500 DATA 13200.57, 11402.48, 9248.23, 9200.94
510 DATA 11825.50, 12158.07, 11028.40, 22804.22
520 DATA 18009.40, 12607.25, 19423.36, 24922.50
```

8. I. M. Good, a candidate for political office, conducted a preelection poll. Each voter polled was assigned a number from 1 to 5 as follows:

1 = will vote for Good
2 = leaning toward Good but still undecided
3 = will vote for Shepherd, Good's only opponent
4 = leaning toward Shepherd but still undecided
5 = all other cases

The results of the poll are included in DATA lines as follows:

```
500 DATA 1, 1, 2, 5, 3, 5, 1, 2
510 DATA 5, 5, 2, . . .
        .
        .
        .
998 DATA 0
```

Write a program that displays two tables as follows:

```
                TABLE 1
                        FOR    LEANING
        GOOD             -        -
        SHEPHERD         -        -
                TABLE 2
                        FOR OR   PERCENTAGE OF TOTAL
                        LEANING  NUMBER OF PEOPLE POLLED
        GOOD             -              -
        SHEPHERD         -              -
        OTHERS           -              -
```

In Problems 9–12, write a menu-driven program to carry out the specified tasks. In your menu include an option to end the program and another to display the menu. Also write each program so that it is a simple matter to add new tasks at a later time.

9. Below are last year's monthly income figures for the Garruga Dating Service. Include these data in DATA lines for a program that allows the user to obtain one or more of the following:
   a. A two-column table showing precisely the given information.
   b. The total income for last year.
   c. A two-column table showing each month and the amount by which the income for the month exceeds the average monthly income. (Some of these amounts will be negative.)

January	18,000	July	20,000
February	13,500	August	22,650
March	11,200	September	18,500
April	16,900	October	12,500
May	20,500	November	9,250
June	22,200	December	11,300

10. First write a program as specified in Problem 9 and run it to make sure it works. Then modify the program so that the user also can obtain a list of the months for which the income amount exceeds a value that is entered by the user.

11. Below is a table containing information about employees of the Mendosa Publishing Company. Include this information in DATA lines for a program that will carry out, at the request of the user, any of the following tasks:
    a. Display precisely the given information.
    b. Display the names of all employees who have been with the company for at least Y years. (Have the program request a value for Y *after* this option has been selected.)

Name	Age	Years of service
Lia Brookes	22	1
Mary Crimmins	27	3
Lee Marston	46	18
Joe Nunes	58	9
Paul Reese	23	2
Jean Saulnier	34	12
Jesse Torres	68	21
Mara Walenda	32	7

12. First write a program as specified in Problem 11 and run it to make sure it works. Then modify the program so that it will also carry out, at the request of the user, the following additional tasks:
    a. Display the names of all employees.
    b. Display the average age and average years of service of all employees.

■ 11.5 Review True-or-False Quiz

1. The READ and DATA statements provide the means to present data to the computer without having to type them during program execution.   T   F
2. DATA statements must follow the READ statements that read the data values.   T   F
3. The line

   ```
   90 DATA 5, -3E2, 7+3, 12
   ```

   is a valid BASIC statement.   T   F

4. A *pointer* is a special value appearing in a data list. T F
5. It is not necessary to read an entire data list before the first value can be read for a second time. T F
6. At most one RESTORE statement may be used in a BASIC program. T F
7. The READ and DATA statements can be useful when no interaction between the computer and the user is required. T F
8. When we include a string in a DATA statement, quotation marks are sometimes necessary. T F
9. It is sometimes useful to assign values to both string variables and numerical variables using the same READ statement. T F

12 Subroutines

All but very simple programming applications involve carrying out several subtasks. As illustrated in many of the worked-out examples, these subtasks are coded as program segments, which are combined, as specified in an algorithm, to give the required program. BASIC subroutines, the topic of this chapter, provide a convenient way to include such program segments in your programs. By using subroutines as described in this chapter, you can write programs that are easy to read, to debug, and to modify, should that be required.

A BASIC **subroutine** is a program segment written in such a way that it can be referenced (that is, executed) from any part of the program, with program control returning to the BASIC statement following the one that caused the subroutine to be executed. Thus, if the same sequence of programming lines is needed in two or more places in a program you can code it once, as a subroutine, and reference it whenever it must be executed.

In Section 12.1 we describe the RETURN statement, which allows you to write subroutines, and the GOSUB statement, which allows you to execute these subroutines. In Section 12.3 we describe the ON GOSUB statement, which allows you to execute selectively any one of two or more subroutines.

■ 12.1 The GOSUB and RETURN Statements

The statement

GOSUB **ln**

transfers control to the subroutine at line **ln.** This subroutine can be any sequence of programming lines, but it must contain at least one RETURN statement. A RETURN statement will transfer control back to the statement that follows GOSUB **ln.**

Here is a subroutine to display a four-line output delimiter that can be used to highlight key portions of an output document. The first line of the delimiter is blank, the next two contain thirty dashes, and the fourth is blank.

```
500 REM ***** SUBROUTINE FOR OUTPUT DELIMITER *****
510 PRINT
520 PRINT STRING$(30,"-")
530 PRINT STRING$(30,"-")
540 PRINT
550 RETURN
```

Program control is transferred to this subroutine each time the statement GOSUB 500 is encountered during program execution. For example, in a program containing this subroutine, the lines

```
200 GOSUB 500
210 PRINT "TODAY'S STARTING LINEUP"
220 GOSUB 500
230 (Program continuation)
```

will cause the output

```
------------------------------
------------------------------

TODAY'S STARTING LINEUP

------------------------------
------------------------------
```

Line 200 transfers control to line 500 (the subroutine) and the delimiter is output. The RETURN statement in line 550 then transfers control back to line 210, the first line following the GOSUB statement just used. When line 220 is encountered, control again passes to the subroutine and the delimiter is output again. This time the RETURN statement transfers control back to the programming line following 220.

EXAMPLE 1   Here is a program to illustrate the GOSUB and RETURN statements.

```
100 PRINT "THIS PROGRAM DISPLAYS THE AVERAGE"
110 PRINT "OF ANY TWO NUMBERS YOU TYPE AND"
120 PRINT "ALSO THE AVERAGE OF THEIR SQUARES."
130 PRINT
140 INPUT "FIRST NUMBER"; A
150 INPUT "SECOND NUMBER"; B
160 GOSUB 300                    'Display their average.
170 PRINT
180 LET A=A*A
190 LET B=B*B
200 PRINT "FIRST SQUARE: "; A
210 PRINT "SECOND SQUARE: "; B
220 GOSUB 300                    'Display their average.
230 END
300 REM ************************
310 REM * SUBROUTINE TO DISPLAY *
320 REM *   AVERAGE OF A AND B. *
330 REM ************************
340 REM
350 LET M=(A+B)/2
360 PRINT "THEIR AVERAGE IS"; M
370 RETURN
RUN

THIS PROGRAM DISPLAYS THE AVERAGE
OF ANY TWO NUMBERS YOU TYPE AND
ALSO THE AVERAGE OF THEIR SQUARES.

FIRST NUMBER? 3
SECOND NUMBER? 4
THEIR AVERAGE IS 3.5

FIRST SQUARE: 9
SECOND SQUARE: 16
THEIR AVERAGE IS 12.5
```

For the run shown, lines 140 and 150 assign the input values 3 and 4 to A and B, respectively, and line 160 transfers control to the subroutine, which displays 3.5, the average of A and B. The RETURN statement then transfers control back to line 170, the line following the GOSUB statement just used. Lines 180–210 assign the squares (9 and 16) to A and B, and display these values. When line 220 is encountered, a second transfer is made to the subroutine, and 12.5, the average of 9 and 16, is displayed. This time the RETURN statement transfers control back to line 230, which in this program terminates execution.

■ **REMARK 1** The END statement (line 230) ensures that the subroutine is entered only under the control of a GOSUB statement.

■ **REMARK 2** When the GOSUB statement in line 160 or line 220 is executed, we say that the subroutine has been *called*.

■ **REMARK 3** The GOSUB statement differs from the GOTO statement in that it causes the computer to "remember" which statement to execute next when it encounters a RETURN statement. As described, this is the statement immediately following the GOSUB statement used to call the subroutine.

■ **REMARK 4** Note that we used M (for mean)—not A (for average)—in the subroutine. If line 350 is changed to

```
350 LET A=(A+B)/2
```

the original value of A will be lost during the first subroutine call, and incorrect results will be displayed. Thus, when writing subroutines make sure that the variable names you use do not conflict with variable names used in other parts of the program for different purposes.

The general forms of the GOSUB and RETURN statements are as follows:

ln₁ GOSUB ln₂   (ln₂ is the line number of the first statement of the subroutine.)
ln RETURN

Line **ln₁** transfers control to line **ln₂**, and program execution continues as usual. When the first RETURN statement is encountered, control transfers back to the line following line **ln₁**.

A subroutine may be called from within another subroutine. Following is a schematic representation of a program that does this. The action of the program is indicated by the arrows labeled a, b, c, and d.

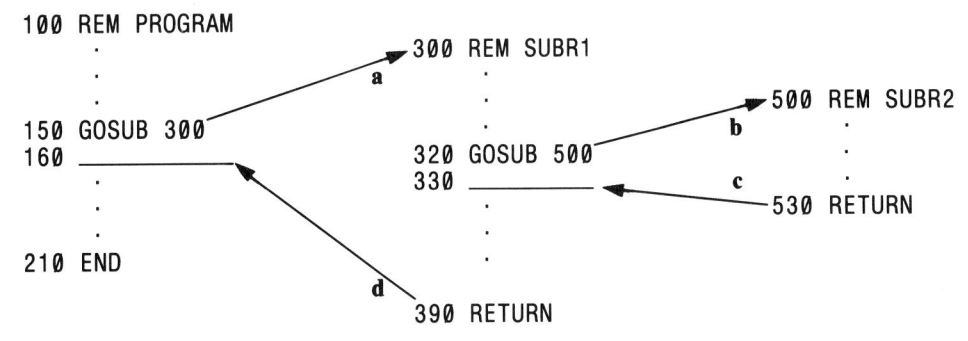

```
100 REM PROGRAM
    .                        ──► 300 REM SUBR1
    .                      a       .
    .                              .                        ──► 500 REM SUBR2
150 GOSUB 300 ──────────┘          .                      b       .
160 ─────────────────┐         320 GOSUB 500 ───────────┘         .
    .                │         330 ──────────────◄─────────c───── 530 RETURN
    .                │             .
210 END              │             .
                     └──────d──── 390 RETURN
```

Following are two examples that further illustrate the use of subroutines. The program in Example 2 uses a subroutine that calls another subroutine. Example 3 shows an application for an airline charter service.

EXAMPLE 2 Here is a program to display a short report for each employee whose name and annual salary are included in DATA lines. Two subroutines are used. The first displays the report for one employee. The second displays an output delimiter and is called by the first subroutine.

188 Chapter 12 Subroutines

THE PROGRAM

```
100 REM ----- SALARY REPORT PROGRAM ----
110 REM PRODUCE SALARY REPORTS FROM DATA
120 REM GIVEN IN DATA LINES 300 TO 398.
130 REM
140 REM N$ = EMPLOYEE'S NAME
150 REM A  = ANNUAL SALARY OF N$
160 REM
170 REM ****************************
180 REM READ DATA & DISPLAY REPORTS.
190 REM
200 READ N$,A
210 WHILE N$<>"END"
220    PRINT
230    GOSUB 400           'Report for N$
240    READ N$,A
250 WEND
260 END
300 REM ******************
310 REM      D A T A
320 REM
330 DATA S.J.BRYANT,18500
340 DATA T.S.ENDICOTT,25700
398 DATA END-OF-DATA,0
399 REM
```

FIRST SUBROUTINE

```
400 REM *******************************
410 REM SUBROUTINE TO DISPLAY ONE REPORT
420 REM
430 REM   WK=ROUNDED WEEKLY SALARY FOR N$
440 REM
450 GOSUB 600                  'Delimiter
460 LET WK=A/52                'Weekly salary
470 LET WK=INT(100*WK+.5)/100  'to nearest cent
480 PRINT "EMPLOYEE NAME:  ";N$
490 PRINT "ANNUAL SALARY: ";A
500 PRINT "WEEKLY SALARY: ";WK
510 GOSUB 600                  'Delimiter
520 RETURN
```

SECOND SUBROUTINE

```
600 REM ******************************
610 REM SUBROUTINE TO DISPLAY DELIMITER
620 REM
630 PRINT STRING$(30,"-")
640 PRINT STRING$(30,"-")
650 RETURN
```

For the given DATA lines 330–398, this program produces the following output:

```
------------------------------
------------------------------
EMPLOYEE NAME:  S.J. BRYANT
ANNUAL SALARY: 18500
WEEKLY SALARY: 355.77
------------------------------
------------------------------

------------------------------
------------------------------
EMPLOYEE NAME:  T.S. ENDICOTT
ANNUAL SALARY: 25700
WEEKLY SALARY: 494.23
------------------------------
------------------------------
```

■ **REMARK 1**   Line 470 uses the BASIC function INT to round the weekly salary WK to the nearest cent. The INT function is described in Section 13.1.

■ **REMARK 2**   Note that the first subroutine is called only from line 230. This means that we can delete the line

```
230 GOSUB 400    'Report for N$
```

and in its place insert the BASIC code included in lines 400–510 that displays a single salary report. The resulting program will be two lines shorter but not necessarily better. By using a subroutine, we do not force a person reading the program to read through the details of how a report is produced. The comment in line 230 tells the reader that a report will be produced but leaves out the details. A reader who needs more details would simply look down to line 400 and read the subroutine.

■ **REMARK 3**   Programming applications calling for lengthy reports are not uncommon. If confronted with such a programming task, examine the requirements carefully to see if the long report in fact consists of several short reports that are to be repeated several times. Program segments that produce such short reports are often ideal candidates for subroutines.

■ **REMARK 4**   An important advantage in using subroutines is that your programs can be modified more easily should a change be needed. For instance, if the program shown must be altered to display other information about each employee, only the subroutine in lines 400–520 needs to be changed. You may sometimes find that a method used to carry out a particular task is inefficient and needs to be improved. If the task is coded as a subroutine, the entire subroutine can be replaced with more efficient code with no need to modify, or even debug, the rest of the program.

EXAMPLE 3   **Charter service example—an illustration of subroutines.**

An airline charter service estimates that ticket sales of $1,000 are required to break even on a certain excursion. It thus makes the following offer to an interested organization. If 10 people sign up, the cost will be $100 per person. For each additional person, the cost per person will be reduced by $3. Produce a table showing the cost per customer and the profit to the airline for N = 10, 11, 12, . . . , 30 customers. In addition, display a message giving the maximum possible profit for the airline and the number of customers that gives this profit. Use column headings underlined by a row of dashes and highlight the final message.

PROBLEM ANALYSIS   The problem statement says to produce a three-column table showing the number of customers, the corresponding cost per customer, and the corresponding profit to the airline. Thus, for each value of N from 10 to 30 (the number of customers) we must calculate two values:

    C = cost per person (C = 130 − 3 × N)
    P = profit to the airline (P = N × C − 1000)

The problem statement also specifies that the three-column cost and profit table be followed by a message giving two values:

    NMAX = number of people yielding a maximum profit to the airline
    PMAX = the maximum profit

The following algorithm describes one way to produce the required output.

THE ALGORITHM
  a. Display column headings.
  b. Start with PMAX = 0
  c. For N = 10 to 30, do the following:
    c1. Determine C and P.
    c2. Display N, C, and P in the table.
    c3. Adjust NMAX and PMAX, if necessary.

d. Display a message showing NMAX and PMAX.
e. Stop.

Step (c3) is included to determine NMAX and PMAX. To carry out this step, we will compare the profit P for N customers with PMAX, the largest profit obtained to that point. If P is larger than PMAX, we will assign P to PMAX and N to NMAX. To keep the main part of the program as uncluttered as possible, we'll do this in a subroutine. To avoid writing the code for the specified highlighting delimiter twice, we use another subroutine for this purpose. Finally, it is not difficult to see that the output will not fit on a 24- or 25-line screen. Hence we will produce a printed report by using LPRINT and LPRINT USING statements.

THE PROGRAM

```
100 REM                     CHARTER SERVICE PROGRAM
110 REM
120 REM PRODUCE TABLE OF AIRLINE EXCURSION RATES AND FIND
130 REM THE MAXIMUM POSSIBLE PROFIT FOR THE AIRLINE.
140 REM
150 PRINT "This Charter Service Program produces a printed"
160 PRINT "report. Press any key after printer is turned on."
170 IF INKEY$="" THEN 170
180 REM
190 REM ***********************************************************
200 REM * DISPLAY COLUMN HEADINGS AND ASSIGN OUTPUT FORMAT. *
210 REM ***********************************************************
220 LPRINT
230 LPRINT "PASSENGERS         COST/PERSON         AIRLINE PROFIT"
240 LPRINT "-------------------------------------------------"
250 LET F$="      ##              ###.##              ####.##      "
260 REM
270 REM ***********************************************************
280 REM * DISPLAY TABLE VALUES AND FIND MAXIMUM POSSIBLE PROFIT. *
290 REM ***********************************************************
300 REM
310 LET PMAX=0
320 FOR N=10 TO 30              'Number of customers
330     LET C=130-3*N            'Cost per person
340     LET P=N*C-1000           'Profit to airline
350     LPRINT USING F$;N,C,P    'Print one line of table.
360     GOSUB 600                'Check max profit amount.
370 NEXT N
380 GOSUB 500                    'Display output delimiter.
390 REM
400 LET G$=" ## PASSENGERS YIELD A MAXIMUM PROFIT OF$$###"
410 LPRINT USING G$;NMAX,PMAX
420 REM
430 GOSUB 500                    'Display output delimiter.
440 END
450 REM ***********************************************************
460 REM *                      SUBROUTINES                        *
470 REM ***********************************************************
480 REM
490 REM ---------------------------
500 REM DISPLAY AN OUTPUT DELIMITER.
510 REM ---------------------------
520 REM
530 LPRINT STRING$(49,"-")
540 LPRINT STRING$(49,"-")
550 RETURN
560 REM ---------------------------
600 REM CHECK FOR NEW MAXIMUM PROFIT.
610 REM ---------------------------
620 REM
630 REM      PMAX = CURRENT MAXIMUM PROFIT AMOUNT
640 REM      NMAX = NUMBER OF CUSTOMERS FOR MAXIMUM PROFIT
650 REM
660 IF P>PMAX THEN PMAX=P : NMAX=N
670 RETURN
```

We ran this program and obtained the following printed report.

```
        PASSENGERS          COST/PERSON           AIRLINE PROFIT
        ------------------------------------------------------------
            10                100.00                  0.00
            11                 97.00                 67.00
            12                 94.00                128.00
            13                 91.00                183.00
            14                 88.00                232.00
            15                 85.00                275.00
            16                 82.00                312.00
            17                 79.00                343.00
            18                 76.00                368.00
            19                 73.00                387.00
            20                 70.00                400.00
            21                 67.00                407.00
            22                 64.00                408.00
            23                 61.00                403.00
            24                 58.00                392.00
            25                 55.00                375.00
            26                 52.00                352.00
            27                 49.00                323.00
            28                 46.00                288.00
            29                 43.00                247.00
            30                 40.00                200.00
        ------------------------------------------------------------
        ------------------------------------------------------------
        22 PASSENGERS YIELD A MAXIMUM PROFIT OF $408
        ------------------------------------------------------------
        ------------------------------------------------------------
```

REMARK If at a later date the airline decides to offer a different excursion package, you can simply change lines 330 and 340, which determine the cost per customer C and the profit to the airline P. If you suspect that the airline will be offering many different excursion packages, you should consider using a subroutine to determine C and P. If you do this, any method specified by the airline for determining C and P, even complex methods that may require many programming lines, can be handled simply by replacing the subroutine with a new one. No change would be required in the rest of the program.

The examples in this section illustrate several important points that should be summarized, since they must be understood if subroutines are to be used effectively. The following comments summarize the rules that govern the use of subroutines (comments 1–4), point out common practices used while coding subroutines (comments 5–7), and suggest situations in which subroutines can be used to advantage (comments 8–10).

1. A subroutine must contain one or more RETURN statements.
2. A subroutine must be entered only by using a GOSUB statement.
3. An exit from a subroutine must be made only by the execution of a RETURN statement. Do not use a GOTO statement to jump out of a subroutine.
4. A subroutine can contain a GOSUB statement transferring control to another subroutine.
5. The first line (or lines) of a subroutine should describe the task being performed. You should include these comments in addition to the comments used to explain the GOSUB that executes the subroutine.
6. It is a common, but not universal, practice to place all subroutines together near the end of a program. We did this in each of the example programs and will continue to do so in subsequent examples.
7. Do not write excessively long subroutines. Many professional programmers try to keep their subroutines to 50 or fewer lines. For beginners, a maximum of about 20 is suggested.
8. If the same sequence of programming lines is needed in two or more parts of a program, you should consider coding it as a subroutine.

9. A subroutine should be used if it will make your program easier to read and understand, even if it is referenced in only one programming line. This is a common practice. Indeed, the programs in Examples 2 and 3 contain such subroutines.
10. A subtask that you anticipate will need to be modified at a later date is an ideal candidate for a subroutine.

■ 12.2 Problems

1. Show the output of each program.

   a.
   ```
   100 READ X, Y
   110 WHILE X<>0
   120    GOSUB 180
   130    PRINT X; Y; Z
   140    READ X, Y
   150 WEND
   160 END
   170 DATA 4, 2, 3, -7, 0, 8
   180 LET Z=3*X+2*Y
   190 RETURN
   ```

   b.
   ```
   100 READ A, B
   110 WHILE A<>B
   120    IF A<B THEN GOSUB 200
   130    IF A>B THEN GOSUB 190
   140    READ A, B
   150 WEND
   160 DATA 2, 4, 8, 6, 5, 5
   170 PRINT A
   180 END
   190 PRINT A-B
   200 PRINT B-A
   210 RETURN
   ```

   c.
   ```
   100 FOR I=1 TO 4
   110    GOSUB 200
   120    PRINT I; S
   130 NEXT I
   140 END
   200 LET S=0
   210 FOR J=1 TO I
   220    LET S=S+J
   230 NEXT J
   240 RETURN
   ```

   d.
   ```
   110 LET M=1
   120 GOSUB 300
   130 PRINT M
   140 END
   300 LET M=M+1
   310 GOSUB 400
   320 RETURN
   400 LET M=(M+1)*(M+1)^2
   410 RETURN
   ```

*In problems 2–8, write a subroutine to carry out each task. In each case, test your subroutine by writing a short program that uses it. The lines you add to do this are called a **program stub.***

2. For any number N, assign OK to C$ if N is in the range 0–100 and assign BAD DATA to C$ in every other case.
3. Determine the sum S of the next N values appearing in DATA lines. (You may assume that only numbers appear in DATA lines.)
4. For any numbers A, B, and C, display the largest of the three values (A + B + C)/3, (A + B + 2*C)/4, and (B + C)/2.
5. For any string C$, assign a value to U as in the following table:

C$	U
ONE	1
TWO	2
THREE	3
FOUR	4
Anything else	0

6. N! (read "N factorial") is defined as the product

   $$N! = 1 \times 2 \times 3 \times \cdots \times N$$

if N is a positive integer and as 1 if N = 0. For any integer N ≥ 0, assign the value N! to the variable FACT. When you test your subroutine, run it for several input values to determine the largest for which the subroutine gives correct answers. Also find the largest input value that does not cause a fatal error.

7. Determine the greatest common divisor (GCD) of the two positive integers A and B. Use the following algorithm (and convince yourself that it works):

   a. Start with GCD = smaller of A and B.
   b. If GCD is a factor of both A and B, RETURN.
   c. Subtract 1 from GCD and repeat Step (b).

8. Use the following algorithm to find the GCD of two positive integers A and B:

   a. Let R = integer remainder when A is divided by B.
   b. If R = 0, let GCD = B and RETURN.
   c. Assign B to A and R to B.
   d. Repeat Step (a).

   The algorithm in Problem 7 can be slow for large numbers; this algorithm, the so-called Euclidean algorithm, is very fast.

In Problems 9–14, write a program for each task specified.

9. A data list contains many sets of scores S1, S2, and S3. The three values 0, 0, 0 are used to terminate the data list. Produce a four-column report: the three scores are to appear in the first three columns; the fourth is to contain the larger of the two values (S1 + S2 + S3)/3 and (S1 + S2 + 2∗S3)/4. Use a subroutine to find the two "averages" and to determine which is larger. The subroutine is to contain no PRINT statements.

10. The following DATA lines show the names and annual salaries of all employees in a small firm:

    ```
    1000 DATA SAUL JACOBS,23500,PAUL WINFIELD,29000
    1010 DATA MARIA KARAS,30000,SILVIA STORM,26400
    1020 DATA RAOUL PARENT,31400,RICHARD KELLY,28000
    1030 DATA PATTY SAULNIER,22000,MARTHA BRADLEY,31400
    1040 DATA XXX,0
    ```

    Calculate and display the total annual payroll of the firm, and then display a report showing the names and salaries of those whose salary exceeds the average annual salary for all employees. Use a subroutine to determine the total annual payroll—it is to have no PRINT statements. Use another subroutine to produce the specified report.

11. Include the data in Problem 10 in a program that displays a two-column table showing precisely the given information and displays after this table a message telling which employee (or employees) has the highest salary. Use a subroutine to display the two-column table—the subroutine is to do nothing else. Use another subroutine to find the highest salary amount—this subroutine also is to do nothing else. Use a third subroutine that displays the concluding message. This subroutine should search for employees with the highest salary.

12. An apple orchard occupying 1 acre of land now contains 25 apple trees, and each tree yields 450 apples per season. For each new tree planted, the yield per tree will be reduced by 10 apples per season. How many additional trees should be planted so that the total yield is as large as possible? Produce a table showing the yield per tree and the total yield if N = 1, 2, 3, . . . , 25 additional trees are planted. Use column headings underlined by a row of dashes. Separate the message telling how many additional trees to plant from the table by a row of dashes. Use a subroutine to keep track of the greatest total yield and the number of additional trees that give this greatest yield.

13. An organization can charter a ship for a harbor cruise for $9.75 a ticket provided that at least 200 people agree to go. However, the ship's owner agrees to reduce the cost per ticket by 25¢ for each additional 10 people signing up. Thus if 220 people sign up, the cost per person will be $9.25. Write a program to determine the maximum revenue the ship's owner can receive if

the ship's capacity is 400 people. Moreover, prepare a table showing the cost per person and the total amount paid for N = 200, 210, 220, . . ., 400 people. Use column headings underlined by a row of dashes. The maximum revenue the ship's owner can receive should be displayed following the table and separated from it by a row of dashes. Use a subroutine to keep track of the greatest revenue amount and the number of passengers that give this greatest revenue.

14. A merchant must pay the fixed price of $1 a yard for a certain fabric. From experience, the merchant knows that 1,000 yards will be sold each month if the material is sold at cost and also that each 10¢ increase in price means that 50 fewer yards will be sold each month. Write a program to produce a table showing the merchant's profit for each selling price from $1 to $3 in increments of 10¢. Also display a message giving the selling price that will maximize the profit. Use a subroutine to keep track of the greatest profit amount and the selling price that gives this greatest profit.

■ 12.3 The ON GOSUB Statement

The ON GOSUB statement is used to execute one of several subroutines selectively. It selects subroutines in exactly the same way that ON GOTO selects line numbers. For example, if a program contains subroutines at lines 500, 600, and 800, the statement

```
ON X GOSUB 500,800,600,800
```

will execute the subroutine at

line 500 if X = 1
line 800 if X = 2
line 600 if X = 3
line 800 if X = 4

The general form of the ON GOSUB statement is

ln ON e GOSUB ln$_1$,ln$_2$, . . . ,ln$_k$

where **e** denotes a BASIC numerical expression and **ln$_1$,ln$_2$, . . . ,ln$_k$** denote line numbers at which subroutines begin. On execution, **e** is evaluated and rounded to an integer E. If E is 1, the subroutine at line **ln$_1$** is executed, if it is 2 the subroutine at line **ln$_2$** is executed, and so on. If E is 0 or a number from **k** + 1 to 255, no subroutine is called and control passes to the statement following the ON GOSUB statement. If E is less than 0 or greater than 255, a fatal error occurs.

EXAMPLE 4 Here is a program that uses ON GOSUB to execute one or more of three subroutines.

```
100 PRINT "TYPE 1 WHEN DONE."
110     PRINT
120     INPUT "ENTER 1,2, OR 3 ";V
130     ON V GOSUB 200,300,400
140 IF V<>1 THEN 110
150 END
200 REM ------ SUBROUTINE 1 ------
210 PRINT
220 PRINT "THIS IS A CONCLUDING SUBROUTINE."
230 PRINT "THE PROGRAM IS ABOUT TO HALT."
240 RETURN
300 REM ------ SUBROUTINE 2 ------
310 PRINT
320 PRINT "THIS IS THE SECOND SUBROUTINE."
330 RETURN
400 REM ------ SUBROUTINE 3 ------
410 PRINT
420 PRINT "THIS IS THE THIRD SUBROUTINE."
430 RETURN
RUN
```

```
TYPE 1 WHEN DONE.

ENTER 1, 2, OR 3 ? 3

THIS IS THE THIRD SUBROUTINE.

ENTER 1, 2, OR 3 ? 1

THIS IS A CONCLUDING SUBROUTINE.
THE PROGRAM IS ABOUT TO HALT.
```

For the run shown, 3 and then 1 were entered in response to the INPUT statement. With V = 3, the ON GOSUB statement causes the subroutine at line 400, the third listed line number, to be executed. With V = 1, the ON GOSUB statement executes the subroutine at line 200, the first listed line number. In each case, control returns to the IF statement following the ON GOSUB statement (line 140). The second time this happens, the condition V <> 1 is false, so control passes to the next line (line 150), which terminates the program.

A common application of the ON GOSUB statement is in menu-driven programs. You code the various options the program can carry out as subroutines and use an ON GOSUB statement to select the subroutine corresponding to the option specified by the user. Thus, if a menu-driven program has three options carried out in subroutines at lines 500, 600, and 700, and if OP denotes the selected option number, you can transfer control to the correct subroutine by using the statement

```
ON OP GOSUB 500,600,700
```

By coding options as subroutines rather than program segments, you will avoid several GOTOs that can make the action of the program difficult to follow—the GOTOs that transfer control to the program segments and those that transfer control back from these program segments. The action caused by ON GOSUB, on the other hand, is easy to follow. An ON GOSUB statement says to execute the selected subroutine and then continue with the next line.

You should not interpret the preceding paragraph as a suggestion that you always use ON GOSUB in menu-driven programs. Sometimes, especially if there are few options, you can effectively use IF statements to execute subroutines. For example, you can use either

```
ON OP GOSUB 500,600,700
```

or the three lines

```
IF OP=1 THEN GOSUB 500
IF OP=2 THEN GOSUB 600
IF OP=3 THEN GOSUB 700
```

to execute the appropriate subroutine. Both methods represent good ways to do this. Their action is easy to follow because subroutines are used to carry out the options, rather than program segments that end with GOTOs.

The program in Example 4 illustrates how ON GOSUB can be used in menu-driven programs. Indeed, if we replace line 120

```
120 INPUT "ENTER 1, 2, OR 3 ";V
```

by lines that also display a menu—for instance, by

```
120 PRINT "SELECT OPTIONS FROM THIS MENU: "
121 PRINT
122 PRINT "    1    TO END THE PROGRAM"
123 PRINT "    2    TO CARRY OUT ....."
124 PRINT "    3    TO CARRY OUT ....."
125 PRINT
126 INPUT "YOUR CHOICE ";V
```

the program becomes menu-driven. Although the program will perform no useful task, it illustrates precisely how menu-driven programs can be coded by using ON GOSUB.

In every example of a menu-driven program considered to this point, we included option numbers in the menu and required the user to select options by typing option numbers. It isn't necessary to do this. You can use descriptive words, instead of numbers, to label the menu options and allow the user to choose options by typing these descriptive words. If you do this and also want to use the ON GOSUB statement, you will need BASIC code to determine the option numbers corresponding to words entered by the user. The option numbers are needed for the ON GOSUB statement. The following example illustrates a simple way to determine option numbers for word options typed by the user.

EXAMPLE 5 Here is a menu-driven program that allows the user to specify options by typing words instead of option numbers.

This program contains DATA statements (lines 9000 on) giving the name, weight in pounds, height in inches, and sex for each child born during the current month. The program allows the user to specify options by entering NAMES, LENGTH, or END as described in the menu displayed by lines 130–160. Program lines 200–230 determine the option numbers OP.

THE PROGRAM

```
100 PRINT "THIS PROGRAM ALLOWS YOU TO OBTAIN BIRTH"
110 PRINT "INFORMATION FOR THE CURRENT MONTH."
120     PRINT
130     PRINT "SELECT ONE OF THESE OPTIONS:"
140     PRINT "   NAMES     LIST OF NAMES"
150     PRINT "   LENGTH    AVG LENGTH BY SEX"
160     PRINT "   END       TO END THE PROGRAM"
170     INPUT "YOUR CHOICE ";C$
180     REM
190     REM ------ FIND OPTION NUMBER ------
200     LET OP=0
210     IF C$="END" THEN OP=1
220     IF C$="NAMES" THEN OP=2
230     IF C$="LENGTH" THEN OP=3
240     REM
250     REM -- CARRY OUT SPECIFIED OPTION --
260     REM
270     ON OP GOSUB 1000,2000,3000
280     IF OP=0 THEN PRINT "?BAD OPTION - TRY AGAIN."
290 IF C$<>"END" THEN 120
300 END
310 REM
1000 REM ****************************
1010 REM *      END SUBROUTINE      *
1020 REM ****************************
1030 RETURN
2000 REM ****************************
2010 REM *     NAMES SUBROUTINE     *
2020 REM ****************************
2030 PRINT
2040 PRINT "LIST OF NEWBORN NAMES:"
2050 READ N$,W,L,S$
2060 WHILE N$<>"EOD"
2070     PRINT N$
2080     READ N$,W,L,S$
2090 WEND
2100 RESTORE
2110 RETURN
```

```
3000 REM ****************************
3010 REM *     LENGTH SUBROUTINE    *
3020 REM ****************************
3030 REM
3040 REM FIND AND DISPLAY AVERAGE LENGTH BY SEX.
3050 REM
3060 LET MTOT=0         'Male total length
3070 LET FTOT=0         'Female total length
3080 LET MCOUNT=0       'Male count
3090 LET FCOUNT=0       'Female count
3100 READ N$,W,L,S$
3110 WHILE N$<>"EOD"
3120    IF S$="M"
            THEN MTOT=MTOT+L : MCOUNT=MCOUNT+1
            ELSE FTOT=FTOT+L : FCOUNT=FCOUNT+1
3130    READ N$,W,L,S$
3140 WEND
3150 PRINT
3160 PRINT "AVERAGE LENGTH (F):";FTOT/FCOUNT
3170 PRINT "AVERAGE LENGTH (M):";MTOT/MCOUNT
3180 RESTORE
3190 RETURN
9000 REM ****************************
9010 REM *     D   A   T   A        *
9020 REM ****************************
9030 REM (NAME,WEIGHT,LENGTH,SEX)
9040 DATA SUE COREY,6.9,19.5,F
9050 DATA LIA TSAO,7.2,18.8,F
9060 DATA JUAN MENDOSSA,8.9,23.0,M
9070 DATA CANDY FOBES,7.6,20.0,F
9080 DATA ADAM PROUST,8.0,22.0,M
9090 DATA MARCO SANTOS,7.4,20.3,M
9998 DATA EOD,0,0,X
```

The following output was produced when we specified the LENGTH option, the improper option LIST, and the END option.

```
THIS PROGRAM ALLOWS YOU TO OBTAIN BIRTH
INFORMATION FOR THE CURRENT MONTH.

SELECT ONE OF THESE OPTIONS:
   NAMES      LIST OF NAMES
   LENGTH     AVG LENGTH BY SEX
   END        TO END THE PROGRAM
YOUR CHOICE ? LENGTH

AVERAGE LENGTH (F): 19.43333
AVERAGE LENGTH (M): 21.76667

SELECT ONE OF THESE OPTIONS:
   NAMES      LIST OF NAMES
   LENGTH     AVG LENGTH BY SEX
   END        TO END THE PROGRAM
YOUR CHOICE ? LIST
?BAD OPTION - TRY AGAIN.

SELECT ONE OF THESE OPTIONS:
   NAMES      LIST OF NAMES
   LENGTH     AVG LENGTH BY SEX
   END        TO END THE PROGRAM
YOUR CHOICE ? END
```

■ **REMARK 1**   Lines 200–230 ensure that OP will be 0 or one of the valid option numbers, 1, 2, or 3. Thus the ON GOSUB statement (line 270) will either execute one of the subroutines or, if OP = 0, simply pass control to line 280. Each time OP is 0—that is, each time the user enters an invalid option name—line 280 displays ?BAD OPTION—TRY AGAIN. and control passes back to line 120 to display the menu and again prompt the user.

■ **REMARK 2** It is a simple matter to include a new option in this program. Suppose, for example, that you want an option SHOW that displays a four-column table showing precisely the information given in the DATA lines. To do this you could code the needed subroutine so that it begins in line 4000 and then make these three changes:

```
152     PRINT "   SHOW        DISPLAY EVERYTHING"
232     IF C$="SHOW" THEN OP=4
270 ON OP GOSUB 1000,2000,3000,4000
```

Line 152 displays SHOW in the menu, line 232 assigns 4 to OP when the user enters the new option SHOW, and line 270 allows the ON GOSUB statement to execute the new subroutine as well as the other three.

■ **REMARK 3** You may have noticed that the END subroutine (lines 1000–1030) does nothing. No harm is done, and it is there to use if needed in the future. Although this subroutine can be removed, we don't recommend it. Several changes will be needed to do so, and you will probably end with a program that is more difficult to read. If subroutines that do nothing seem confusing, you might add a line such as this one:

```
1025 REM RESERVED FOR POSSIBLE FUTURE USE.
```

In the preceding example we used the statements

```
200 LET OP=0
210 IF C$="END" THEN OP=1
220 IF C$="NAMES" THEN OP=2
230 IF C$="LENGTH" THEN OP=3
```

to assign to OP the option numbers of the menu options END, NAMES, and LENGTH, and to assign 0 to OP for any improper keyboard entry. For a longer menu, we could use the same method and include a similar IF statement for each menu item. Although this is a good way to determine option numbers, especially for small menus, there are other methods that you may find useful. For example, if your menu includes options labeled END, TOT, AVG, LIST, SHOW, PLOT, and INFO, you might want to include them in one or more DATA statements and use a loop to determine option numbers. If these DATA statements will be the only DATA statements in the program, you can use the following subroutine to assign option numbers:

```
1000 REM ----- OPTION SUBROUTINE -----
1010 REM FIND OPTION NUMBER OP FOR C$.
1020 REM RETURN OP=0 FOR INVALID C$.
1030 RESTORE
1040 READ X$ : OP=1
1050 WHILE X$<>C$ AND X$<>"EOD"
1060     READ X$ : OP=OP+1
1070 WEND
1080 IF X$="EOD" THEN OP=0
1090 DATA END, TOT, AVG, LIST, SHOW, PLOT, INFO
1100 DATA EOD
1110 RETURN
```

If C$ is a valid menu item, this subroutine assigns to OP the integer from 1 to 7 that gives the position of C$ in the data list. You will discover other ways to determine option numbers as you learn more about the BASIC language.

12.4 Problems

1. Show the output of each program.

   a.
   ```
   100 FOR I=1 TO 2
   110     ON I GOSUB 160,190
   120     PRINT S
   130 NEXT I
   140 DATA 5,3,7
   150 END
   160 READ A
   170 LET S=A/I
   180 RETURN
   190 READ A,B
   200 LET S=(A+B)/I
   210 RETURN
   ```

   b.
   ```
   10 READ A$,X
   20 ON X GOSUB 50,70
   30 IF X>0 THEN 10
   40 END
   50 PRINT A$;" IS A CONJUNCTION."
   60 RETURN
   70 PRINT A$;" IS AN ARTICLE."
   80 RETURN
   90 DATA A,2,AND,1,BUT,1,OR,1
   95 DATA THE,2,EOD,0
   ```

   In Problems 2–9, write a program for each task specified.

2. While studying the current day's receipts, a bookkeeper must often perform calculations to answer these questions:
   a. What is the selling price of an item whose list price and discount percent are known?
   b. What is the discount percent for an item whose list and selling prices are known?
   c. What is the list price of an item whose selling price and discount percent are known?
   Write a program to help the bookkeeper obtain answers to these questions.

3. An investor must carry out several different calculations while assessing the performance of the family's current stock portfolio. These include finding the equity (paper value) given the number of shares and the current price and finding the profit (or loss) for a holding given the total price paid for all shares, the number of shares owned, and the current selling price. In addition, the investor must often add lists of numbers. Write a program to help the investor carry out these calculations.

4. The table shown below describes an investor's stock portfolio. Include this information in DATA lines for a menu-driven program that allows the user to obtain one or more of these reports: a four-column report showing precisely the given information; a three-column report showing each stock name with its current value (numbers of shares × current price) and its value at the close of business last month; a short report showing the name and current value of the stock whose current value is greatest.

Name of stock	Number of shares	Last month's closing price	Current closing price
STERLING DRUG	800	16.50	16.125
DATA GENERAL	500	56.25	57.50
OWEN ILLINOIS	1,200	22.50	21.50
MATTEL INC	1,000	10.75	11.125
ABBOTT LAB	2,000	33.75	34.75
FED NATL MTG	2,500	17.75	17.25
IC GEN	250	43.125	43.625
ALO SYSTEMS	550	18.50	18.25

5. First write a menu-driven program as described in Problem 4. Then modify the program so that it will also display a simple list showing only the names of the companies in which stock is owned.

6. The table shown below contains information about employees of the Libel Insurance Company. Include this information in DATA lines for a menu-driven program that allows the user to obtain one or more of these reports: a five-column report showing precisely the given information; a two-column report showing the name and years of service of each person who has been with the company for at least Y years (the subroutine that produces this report should prompt the user for Y); and a short report showing the total payroll amount for men and that for women.

Name	Sex	Age	Years of service	Annual salary
J. R. Adamson	M	47	13	20,200.00
P. M. Martell	F	33	6	14,300.00
J. D. Carlson	F	41	15	23,900.00
S. T. Chang	M	22	2	21,400.00
R. T. Richardson	M	59	7	29,200.00
M. E. Thompson	F	25	3	13,000.00
C. B. Rado	M	33	13	21,500.00
O. L. Lawanda	F	28	4	33,400.00
C. Hartwick	M	68	30	25,500.00
C. Cleveland Barnes	M	35	6	14,300.00
M. L. Chou	F	21	3	19,200.00

7. First write a menu-driven program as described in Problem 6. Then modify the program so that it will display two additional options: one to display a list of employee names and another to display the average age of all employees.

8. A menu-driven program is desired that will allow students to practice addition, multiplication, or taking powers. The student should choose addition by typing the letter A, multiplication by typing M, and powers by typing P. If addition is chosen, have the computer prompt the student for two numbers and then ask for their sum. If the correct answer is typed, have the computer say so. If the answer is not correct, display the correct answer. In either case, allow the student to try another addition or to return to the menu. Handle multiplication (of two numbers) the same way. If the student chooses to practice powers, have the computer ask for a number whose powers are to be found. If the student types 3, have the computer display, in order,

```
WHAT IS 3 TO THE POWER 2?
WHAT IS 3 TO THE POWER 3?
WHAT IS 3 TO THE POWER 4?
    .
    .
    .
WHAT IS 3 TO THE POWER 10?
```

Ask each question, however, only if the previous answer is correct. If an answer is incorrect, display the correct answer. Congratulate a student successful to high powers, perhaps in a way reflective of how high the power. In any case, allow the student to try powers of another number or to return to the menu.

9. First write a menu-driven program as described in Problem 8. Then modify it by changing the addition option so that the student practices summing three numbers instead of two.

12.5 Review True-or-False Quiz

1. A program need not contain the same number of GOSUB statements as RETURN statements. T F
2. The GOSUB statement is really unnecessary, since the GOTO statement will accomplish the same thing. T F
3. An END statement must appear on the line that immediately precedes the first line of each subroutine. T F
4. If one subroutine calls a second subroutine, the first must appear in the program before the second. T F
5. Subroutines should be used only when a group of statements is to be performed more than once. T F
6. Subroutines can be useful even if their only purpose is to improve a program's readability. T F
7. The following statement contains a syntax error:

    200 ON A GOSUB 500,600,500,500,600   T F

8. Execution of the two lines

    200 LET S=2.3
    201 ON S GOSUB 300,400,500

    will necessarily result in an error. T F
9. If a program will selectively execute one or more of several subroutines, you will have to use an ON GOSUB statement. T F

13 Numerical Functions

BASIC is designed to assist you in manipulating both numerical and string data. For this reason, the language includes several functions, called **built-in functions,** to carry out automatically certain common calculations with numbers and operations with strings. In addition, BASIC allows you to define your own functions—functions that you may need but that are not part of the language. These are called **user-defined functions.**

In this chapter we consider only numerical functions. Section 13.1 describes and illustrates certain of the built-in functions and includes a table describing all of these functions available in Microsoft® BASIC. In Section 13.3 we show how you can write your own functions and illustrate common ways in which such user-defined functions are used.

The BASIC functions used with string data are described in Chapter 14. These two chapters on functions can be taken up in either order.

13.1 Built-in Numerical Functions

A list of Microsoft® BASIC numerical functions is provided in Table 13.1. These functions are an integral part of the BASIC language and can be used in any BASIC program. In this section we'll illustrate the square root function SQR, the absolute value function ABS, the integer conversion functions INT, CINT, and FIX, and the sine function SIN. The RND function (which is used somewhat differently from the other numerical functions) is considered in Chapter 18. The first sections of the RND chapter are written so that the material can be taken up at this time, should that be desired.

The Numerical Function SQR

SQR is called the **square root function.** Instead of writing N^0.5 to evaluate the square root of N, you can write SQR(N). The principal advantage in doing this is that your programs will be easier to read—SQR(N) is English-like, whereas N^0.5 is not. For instance, to evaluate the algebraic expression

$$\sqrt{\frac{S}{N-1}}$$

you can write

SQR(S/(N−1))

Table 13.1 Microsoft® BASIC numerical functions

Function	Purpose
ABS(x)	Gives the absolute value of x.
INT(x)	Gives the greatest integer less than or equal to x.
FIX(x)	Converts x to an integer by truncating.
CINT(x)	Converts x to an integer by rounding.
CDBL(x)	Converts x to a double precision value.
SGN(x)	Returns the value 1 if x is positive, -1 if x is negative, and 0 if x is zero.
SQR(x)	Calculates the principal square root of x if $x \geq 0$; results in an error if x is negative.
RND(x)	Returns a pseudorandom number between 0 and 1 (see Chapter 18).
SIN(x)	Calculates the sine of x, where x is in radian measure.
COS(x)	Calculates the cosine of x, where x is in radian measure.
TAN(x)	Calculates the tangent of x, where x is in radian measure.
ATN(x)	Calculates the arctangent of x; $-\pi/2 < $ ATN(x) $ < \pi/2$.
LOG(x)	Calculates the natural logarithm $\ln(x)$; x must be positive.
EXP(x)	Calculates the exponential e^x, where $e = 2.71828\ldots$ is the base of the natural logarithms.

instead of

(S/(N−1))^0.5

From left to right, the SQR form of the expression reads evaluate the square root of S/(N−1), whereas the exponential reads evaluate S/(N−1) to the one-half power. (See Problem 16 in Section 13.2 for an application of the expression $\sqrt{S/(N-1)}$.)

EXAMPLE 1

Here is an illustration of the SQR function.

```
10 PRINT "NUMBER","SQUARE ROOT"
20 PRINT "------","-----------"
30 FOR N=10 TO 20
40     PRINT N,SQR(N)
50 NEXT N
60 END
RUN

NUMBER          SQUARE ROOT
------          -----------
 10             3.162278
 11             3.316625
 12             3.464102
 13             3.605551
 14             3.741657
 15             3.872984
 16             4
 17             4.123106
 18             4.242641
 19             4.358899
 20             4.472136
```

The Numerical Function ABS

ABS is the **absolute value function:** for example, ABS(−3) = 3, ABS(7) = 7, and ABS(4 − 9) = 5. In general, if **e** denotes a BASIC numerical expression, then ABS(**e**) is the absolute value of the value of the expression **e**.

EXAMPLE 2   Here is an illustration of the ABS function.

```
100 REM PROGRAM TO FIND THE ABSOLUTE VALUE
110 REM OF THE SUM OF ANY TWO INPUT VALUES.
120 REM
130 PRINT "TYPE TWO NUMBERS PER LINE."
140 PRINT "TYPE 0,0 TO STOP."
150 PRINT
160 INPUT "FIRST PAIR ",X,Y
170 WHILE X<>0 OR Y<>0
180    LET Z=ABS(X+Y)
190    PRINT "ABSOLUTE VALUE OF SUM: ";Z
200    PRINT
210    INPUT "NEXT PAIR ",X,Y
220 WEND
230 END
RUN

TYPE TWO NUMBERS PER LINE.
TYPE 0,0 TO STOP.

FIRST PAIR 7,3
ABSOLUTE VALUE OF SUM: 10

NEXT PAIR 5,-9
ABSOLUTE VALUE OF SUM: 4

NEXT PAIR 0,-92.7
ABSOLUTE VALUE OF SUM: 92.7

NEXT PAIR 0,0
```

This program could have been written without using the ABS function. For example, if line 180 were replaced by the two lines

```
180 LET Z=X+Y
185 IF Z<0 THEN Z=-Z
```

the resulting program would work in the same way as the original. The first version is better—its logic is transparent, whereas the logic of the second version is somewhat obscure. As a general rule you should use the built-in functions supplied with your system. Not only will your programs be easier to code but they will also be easier to understand and hence simpler to debug or modify, should that be required.

A common application of the ABS function is in problems that require examining numerical data to determine how they deviate from a specified number. The following example illustrates this use of the ABS function.

EXAMPLE 3   A data list contains two items for each of 10 retail stores: the current week's sales figure preceded by the store's identification code. Let's write a program to identify those stores whose sales deviate from the average sales by more than 20% of the average sales amount.

PROBLEM ANALYSIS

The problem statement specifies the following input and output:

Input: Identification code and current sales for each store.

Output: A report identifying those stores whose sales deviate from the average sales by more than 20% of the average sales figure. Let's prepare a two-column report with title and column headings as follows:

```
STORES WITH SIGNIFICANTLY
HIGH OR LOW SALES FOR THE WEEK.

STORE CODE     WEEK'S SALES
----------     ------------
    •                •
    •                •
    •                •
```

To determine whether a store should be included in this report, we must compare the store's sales with the average sales of all stores. Thus, before attempting to prepare the report, we should first find the average sales figure. The following algorithm contains few details but shows precisely what must be done. In the algorithm, we use these variable names:

CODE$ = identification code of a store
SALES = current sales for store with code CODE$
AVG   = average sales of all stores
DEV   = 20% of AVG

THE ALGORITHM

  a. Determine AVG and DEV.
  b. Prepare a report showing CODE$ and SALES for each store whose current sales (SALES) differs from AVG by more than DEV.

To find the deviation of SALES from AVG, we could subtract SALES from AVG or AVG from SALES, depending on whether AVG is larger or smaller than SALES. Since we are interested only in how close SALES is to AVG, not which is larger, we will simply examine the absolute value of SALES − AVG (the two expressions SALES − AVG and AVG − SALES differ only in their signs). Thus, CODE$ and SALES for a particular store will be included in the report only if the logical expression

    `ABS(SALES-AVG)>DEV`

is true.

THE PROGRAM

```
100 REM PROGRAM TO PRODUCE REPORT SHOWING RETAIL
110 REM STORES WITH SIGNIFICANTLY HIGH OR LOW SALES.
120 REM
130 REM    CODE$      IDENTIFICATION CODE OF A STORE
140 REM    SALES      CURRENT SALES FOR STORE CODE$
150 REM    AVG        AVERAGE SALES OF ALL STORES
160 REM    DEV        20% OF AVG
170 REM
180 REM ******************************************
190 REM * READ DATA TO DETERMINE AVG AND DEV.    *
200 REM ******************************************
210 LET SUM=0
220 READ STORECOUNT
230 FOR N=1 TO STORECOUNT
240    READ CODE$,SALES
250    LET SUM=SUM+SALES
260 NEXT N
270 LET AVG=SUM/STORECOUNT
280 LET DEV=0.2*AVG
290 RESTORE
300 REM ******************************************
310 REM * PRODUCE THE SPECIFIED REPORT.          *
320 REM ******************************************
```

```
330 REM
340 PRINT "STORES WITH SIGNIFICANTLY"
350 PRINT "HIGH OR LOW SALES FOR THE WEEK."
360 PRINT
370 PRINT "STORE CODE","WEEK'S SALES"
380 PRINT "----------","------------"
390 FOR N=1 TO STORECOUNT
400    READ CODE$,SALES
410    IF ABS(SALES-AVG)>DEV THEN PRINT CODE$,SALES
420 NEXT N
430 REM ********************
440 REM *   D   A   T   A  *
450 REM ********************
460 DATA 10
470 DATA BX14,21000,AX17,16000,BX19,12500
480 DATA BY12,25740,AY33,14480,AX11,28700
490 DATA BX09,20400,AY04,14200,BX27,10200
500 DATA AY22,17850
510 END
RUN

STORES WITH SIGNIFICANTLY
HIGH OR LOW SALES FOR THE WEEK.

STORE CODE      WEEK'S SALES
----------      ------------
BX19            12500
BY12            25740
AY33            14480
AX11            28700
AY04            14200
BX27            10200
```

The Numerical Functions INT, FIX, and CINT

If **e** denotes a numerical expression, and E denotes its value, then:

1. The value of INT(**e**) is the greatest integer less than or equal to E. For example, INT(2.6) = 2, INT(7) = 7, INT(7 − 3.2) = 3, and INT(−4.35) = −5. For this reason INT is called the **greatest-integer function.**
2. The value of FIX(**e**) is obtained by truncating E. Thus, FIX(2.6) = 2, FIX(7) = 7, FIX(7 − 3.2) = 3, and FIX(−4.35) = −4. (For expressions **e** with positive values, INT and FIX are equivalent.)
3. The value of CINT(**e**) is obtained by rounding E to the nearest integer, provided this value is in the range −32768 to 32767. If E is not in this range, an Overflow error occurs. Thus, CINT(2.6) = 3, CINT(7) = 7, CINT(−4.35) = −4, and CINT(42345.6) results in an Overflow error.

If a program requires integer input, you can use INT to detect input values that are not integers. This common use of INT is illustrated in the following example.

EXAMPLE 4   Here is a program segment to reject numerical input values that are not integers.

```
300 INPUT "HOW MANY APPLES HAVE YOU";C
310 IF C<>INT(C) THEN 300
```

If the user types a number that is not an integer, the condition C<> INT(C) will be true, and control will pass back to line 300 so that another number can be entered.

REMARK 1   To inform the user why the prompt

    HOW MANY APPLES HAVE YOU?

is displayed a second time (the user may be thinking fruit instead of computers), and also to reject meaningless negative input values, you could use lines such as these:

```
300 INPUT "HOW MANY APPLES HAVE YOU";C
310 IF C<>INT(C) OR C<0 THEN
        INPUT "PLEASE ENTER A COUNT: ",C
        : GOTO 310
320    (Program continuation)
```

Should the user now enter an improper number, the message in line 310 will be displayed before the user is prompted a second time. Note that 0 as an input value is allowed and meaningful.

To round *any* number (not just those numbers in the range -32768 to 32767, which can be handled by CINT) you can use the INT function. For example, suppose X satisfies the inequalities

$$40136.5 \leq X < 40137.5$$

Then $X + 0.5$ satisfies the inequalities

$$40137 \leq X + 0.5 < 40138$$

and we see that

    INT(X+0.5) = 40137.

That is, to round a number X to the nearest integer, use the BASIC expression

    INT(X+0.5)

A slight modification of this method of rounding to the nearest integer can be used to round to any decimal position. We illustrate by rounding the number $X = 42567.382$ to the nearest tenth to obtain 42567.4.

Expression	Value	Comment
X	42567.382	(Number to be rounded.)
10*X	425673.82	(Move decimal point to the right.)
INT(10*X + 0.5)	425674	(Round to nearest integer.)
INT(10*X + 0.5)/10	42567.4	(Move decimal point back.)

Thus to round X to the nearest tenth, use the BASIC expression

    INT(10*X+0.5)/10

If you are sure that all numbers involved will be in the range -32768 to 32767, you can use CINT(10*X)/10. Note, however, that 10*X, not just X, must be in the restricted range. The safest policy is to use INT. If you change each 10 in the expression INT(10*X+0.5)/10 to 100, X will be rounded to two decimal positions, if you use 1000, it will be rounded to three, and so on. You are limited only because the PC keeps a fixed number of significant digits when numbers are stored in memory.

For more work with rounding numbers, see Problem 5 in Section 13.2.

EXAMPLE 5   Here is a program that uses INT to round the values 1/7, 2/7, 3/7, . . . , 6/7 to five decimal places.

```
10 PRINT " N"," N/7"
20 PRINT
30 FOR N=1 TO 6
40    PRINT N, INT(100000*N/7+0.5)/100000
50 NEXT N
60 END
RUN
```

N	N/7
1	.14286
2	.28571
3	.42857
4	.57143
5	.71429
6	.85714

In Example 4 we saw that the condition C = INT(C) is true if C is an integer and false if it is not. Thus, if N is any integer, the condition

N/2 = INT(N/2)

will be true precisely when N/2 is an integer—that is, when N is divisible by 2. Similarly, if N and D are any integers (with D not 0), the condition

N/D = INT(N/D)

is true precisely when N/D is an integer—that is, when N is divisible by D.

Relational expression	Truth value
63/7 = INT(63/7)	True
6/4 = INT(6/4)	False
INT(105/15) = 105/15	True
INT(100/8) <> 100/8	True

Here we must add a word of caution. In BASIC the condition

N/D=INT(N/D)

is used to determine whether N/D is an integer only if both N and D are integers. If either is not an integer, you may get unexpected results. For instance, in Microsoft® BASIC the condition

9/.3=INT(9/.3)

is false even though the fraction 9/.3 has the integer value 30. To see that this is so, type the immediate mode statement

PRINT 9/.3, INT(9/.3)

The PC will display 30 and 29. The reason for this discrepancy is that computers use an internal representation of numbers that does not allow all numbers to be stored exactly. As mentioned previously, .1 is one of these numbers. So is .3. Thus, calculations involving .3, as well as .1, may not be exact. The following short program with output produced by an IBM Personal Computer further illustrates this situation:

```
10 PRINT " X","X/.1","INT(X/.1)
20 PRINT
30 FOR X=2 TO 2.5 STEP .1
40    PRINT X,X/.1,INT(X/.1)
50 NEXT X
60 END
RUN
```

X	X/.1	INT(X/.1)
2	20	20
2.1	21	20
2.2	22	21
2.3	23	22
2.4	24	23
2.5	25	24

EXAMPLE 6

Here is a program to display the integers from 1 to 28, seven numbers per line.

```
10 FOR N=1 TO 28
20    PRINT USING "####";N;
30    IF N/7=INT(N/7) THEN PRINT
40 NEXT N
RUN
```

```
   1   2   3   4   5   6   7
   8   9  10  11  12  13  14
  15  16  17  18  19  20  21
  22  23  24  25  26  27  28
```

The only statement that moves the cursor to the next display line is the PRINT statement in line 30. This PRINT statement is executed only when the condition N/7 = INT(N/7) is true. As shown in the output, this happens when N is 7, 14, 21, and 28.

The INT function has many applications. We have shown that it can be used to validate user input (Example 4), to round numbers (discussion preceding Example 5), and to test for divisibility of one number by another (Example 6). As you work through the examples and problems in this and subsequent chapters, you will find that the INT function is a valuable programming tool that can be used to simplify many programming tasks.

In the example we give a detailed analysis for a prime number program. The example illustrates the use of the SQR and INT functions and also discusses simple ways to speed up program execution, should that be important.

EXAMPLE 7

PROBLEM ANALYSIS

Write a program to tell whether an integer typed at the keyboard is a prime number.

Let N denote the number to be tested. A number N is prime if it is an integer greater than 1 whose only factors are 1 and N. To determine whether a number N is prime, you can divide it successively by 2, 3, . . . , N − 1. If N is divisible by none of these, then N is a prime. It is not necessary to check all the way to N − 1, however, but only to the square root of N. Can you see why? We will use this fact.

Let's construct a flowchart to describe this process in detail. Since all primes are at least as large as 2, we will reject any input value that is less than 2. Thus we can begin our flowchart as follows:

```
                    START
                      │
      ┌──────────────▶│
      │               ▼
      │          ┌─────────┐
      │          │ Input N │
      │          └─────────┘
      │               │
      │               ▼
      │    T      ╱─────────╲
      └──────────<   N < 2   >
                  ╲─────────╱
                      │ F
                      ▼
```

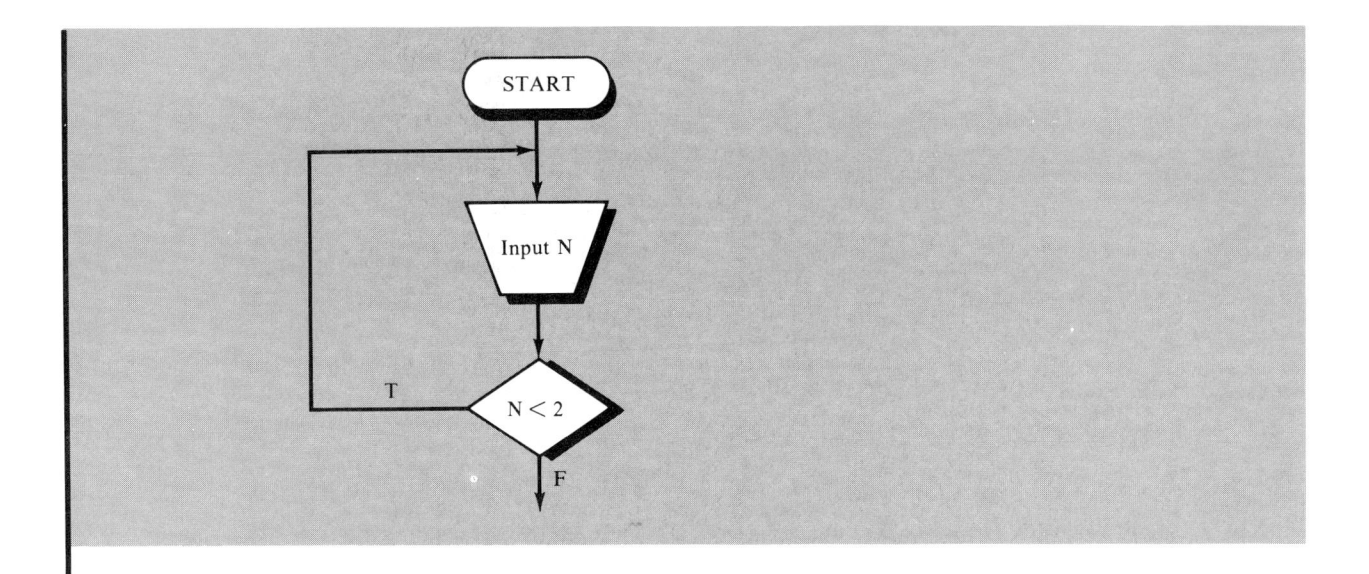

Next we test all integers from 2 to $\sqrt{N}$ as possible factors of N. If we test them in the order D = 2, 3, 4, and so on, we can stop testing when $D > \sqrt{N}$ or when D is a factor of N. Thus we can add the following segment to our partial flowchart:

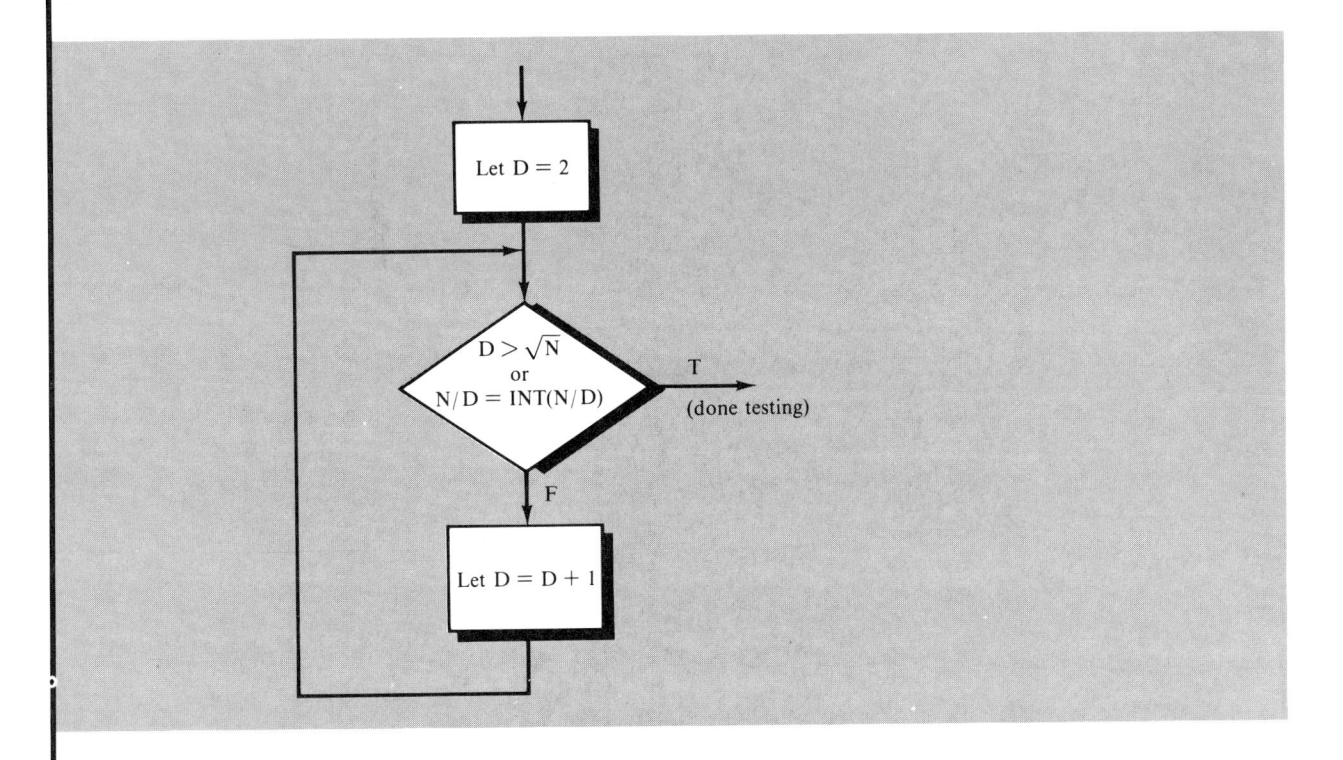

```
                      │
                      ▼
                ┌───────────┐
                │ Let D = 2 │
                └───────────┘
                      │
      ┌──────────────▶│
      │               ▼
      │         ╱──────────────╲
      │        ╱   D > √N        ╲      T
      │        ╲       or        ╱──────────────▶
      │         ╲ N/D = INT(N/D)╱      (done testing)
      │          ╲──────────────╱
      │               │ F
      │               ▼
      │       ┌─────────────┐
      │       │ Let D = D+1 │
      │       └─────────────┘
      │               │
      └───────────────┘
```

When we are done testing, we can be sure that N is prime if the last D value satisfies the condition $D > \sqrt{N}$, since this means that no factor less than or equal to $\sqrt{N}$ was found. On the other hand, if this last D value does not satisfy the condition $D > \sqrt{N}$, then it must satisfy the only other condition, N/D = INT(N/D), that can get us out of the loop. This means that D is a factor of N that lies between 2 and $\sqrt{N}$, inclusive; that is, N is not prime. Thus we can now complete the flowchart as follows.

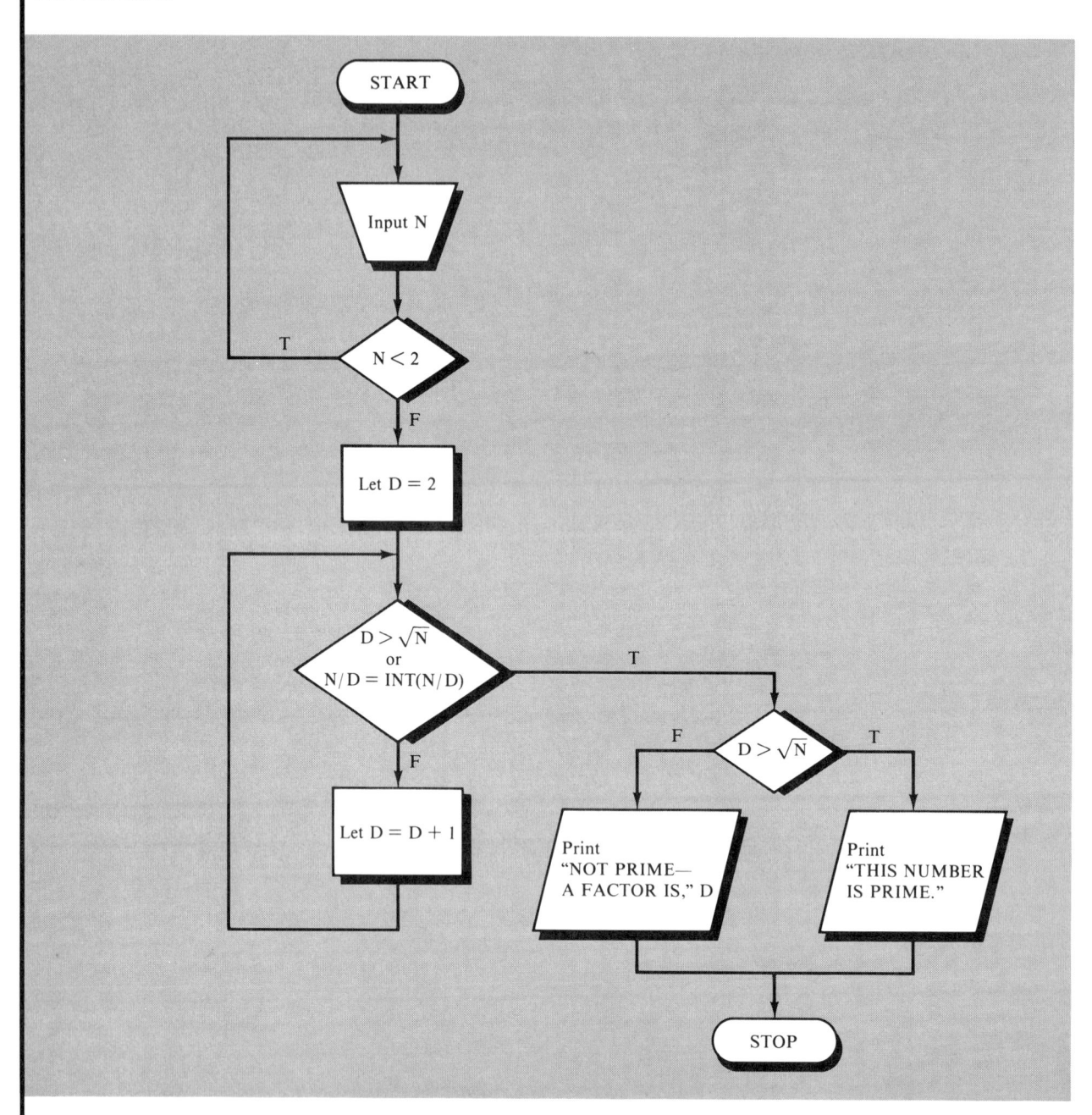

PRIME NUMBER FLOWCHART

```
START
  ↓
Input N
  ↓
N < 2 ? --T--> (back to Input N)
  |F
  ↓
Let D = 2
  ↓
D > √N  or  N/D = INT(N/D) ? --T--> D > √N ?
  |F                                  F↓        T↓
  ↓                              Print          Print
Let D = D + 1                    "NOT PRIME—    "THIS NUMBER
  |                              A FACTOR IS," D IS PRIME."
  (loop back up)                       ↓            ↓
                                        → STOP ←
```

REMARK   It is tempting to say that N is not a prime if the last value of D is a factor of N—that is, if N/D = INT(N/D) is true. If you use this condition (instead of the condition D > $\sqrt{N}$) to complete the flowchart, you will find that you have a bug. You should find it. (*Suggestion:* When debugging a program, test it for *extreme* values of any input variables. In this problem, the smallest value that the program will actually test is N = 2, so 2 is an extreme value here.)

THE PROGRAM

```
100 INPUT "TYPE AN INTEGER: ",N
110 IF N<2 THEN 100
120 LET D=2
130 WHILE D<=SQR(N) AND N/D<>INT(N/D)
140     LET D=D+1
150 WEND
160 IF D>SQR(N) THEN PRINT "THIS NUMBER IS PRIME."
170 IF D<=SQR(N) THEN PRINT "NOT PRIME - A FACTOR IS";D
180 END
RUN

TYPE AN INTEGER: 37769
NOT PRIME - A FACTOR IS 179

RUN

TYPE AN INTEGER: 765767
THIS NUMBER IS PRIME.
```

■ **REMARK 1** When we ran this program for the input value 37769, we had to wait approximately 4 seconds for the output to be displayed. For the input value 765767 we had to wait about 17 seconds. The PC spent essentially all of this time executing the loop in lines 130 to 150. It is often possible to reduce execution time significantly by making small changes in a loop.

Here are two ways to improve the prime number program:

1. Treat D = 2 as a special case before the loop is entered and use the loop to test only the odd numbers D = 3, 5, 7, . . . , SQR(N). This will cut execution time in half.
2. On each pass through the loop the PC must calculate SQR(N) anew. This is very time consuming. To avoid these calculations include the line

    115 LET ROOTN = SQR(N)

and change all the other occurrences of SQR(N) to ROOTN. The change in line 130 is the important one since line 130 is in the loop. By making this change we obtained execution times of approximately 3 seconds and 11 seconds instead of 4 seconds and 17 seconds. When we made this change in addition to the one suggested in (1), the execution times were further reduced to 1 second for the input value 37769 and 6 seconds for 765767.

■ **REMARK 2** If this program is run, there is no guarantee that the user will type an integer. Line 110 ensures that the prime number algorithm will not be carried out for N < 2, but if 256.73 is input the algorithm will produce a silly result. To avoid this, you can insert the line

    112 IF N<>INT(N) THEN 100

The Trigonometric Functions

If **e** denotes a BASIC numerical expression, then SIN(**e**), COS(**e**), TAN(**e**), and ATN(**e**) evaluate the sine, cosine, tangent, and arctangent of the value of **e**. If the value of **e** denotes an angle, this value must be in radian measure.

EXAMPLE 8 Here is a program to determine SIN(D) for D = 0, 5, 10, . . . , 45°.

Since D denotes an angle in degrees, it must be changed to radian measure. Recalling the correspondence

   1 degree = $\pi/180$ radians

we must multiply D by $\pi/180$ to convert to radian measure.

```
100 PRINT "DEGREES        SINE"
110 PRINT "-------        ----"
120 LET F$="   ##         #.####"
130 LET PI=3.14159
140 FOR DEGREE=0 TO 45 STEP 5
150    LET Y=SIN(PI/180*DEGREE)
160    PRINT USING F$;DEGREE,Y
170 NEXT DEGREE
180 END
RUN

DEGREES        SINE
-------        ----
   0           0.0000
   5           0.0872
  10           0.1736
  15           0.2588
  20           0.3420
  25           0.4226
  30           0.5000
  35           0.5736
  40           0.6428
  45           0.7071
```

EXAMPLE 9 Given side *a* and angles A and B in degrees, use the law of sines to determine side *b* of the following triangle:

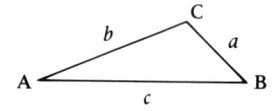

PROBLEM ANALYSIS

The law of sines states that

$$\frac{a}{\sin A} = \frac{b}{\sin B}$$

Solving for *b*, we obtain

$$b = \frac{a \sin B}{\sin A}$$

Since the angles A and B will be given in degrees, they must be changed to radian measure as required by the BASIC function SIN. In the following program, A1 and B1 denotes the sides *a* and *b*, respectively.

THE PROGRAM

```
100 REM APPLICATION OF LAW OF SINES
110 LET PI=3.14159
120 INPUT "ENTER ANGLES A,B IN DEGREES: ",A,B
130 INPUT "ENTER SIDE OPPOSITE ANGLE A: ",A1
140 REM CONVERT TO RADIANS AND COMPUTE SIDE B1.
150 LET A=PI/180*A
160 LET B=PI/180*B
170 LET B1=A1*SIN(B)/SIN(A)
180 PRINT
190 PRINT "THE SIDE OPPOSITE ANGLE B"
200 PRINT "HAS LENGTH";B1
210 END
RUN

ENTER ANGLES A,B IN DEGREES: 28,42
ENTER SIDE OPPOSITE ANGLE A: 2

THE SIDE OPPOSITE ANGLE B
HAS LENGTH 2.85057
```

13.2 Problems

1. Evaluate the following BASIC expressions.

   a. ABS(3*(2-5))
   b. ABS(-3*(-2))
   c. ABS(2-30/3*2)
   d. INT(26.1+0.5)
   e. INT(-43.2+0.5)
   f. 100*INT(1235.7/100+0.5)
   g. CINT(123.6)
   h. CINT(-123.6)
   i. FIX(123.6)
   j. FIX(-123.6)
   k. ABS(INT(-3.2))
   l. INT(ABS(-3.2))

2. Evaluate the following with A = −4.32, B = 5.93, and C = 2864.7144.

   a. INT(ABS(A))
   b. ABS(INT(A))
   c. INT(B+0.5)
   d. INT(A+0.5)
   e. INT(C+0.5)
   f. 10*INT(C/10+0.5)
   g. 100*INT(C/100+0.5)
   h. 1000*INT(C/1000+0.5)
   i. INT(1000*C+0.5)/1000
   j. CINT(ABS(A))
   k. FIX(ABS(A))
   l. CINT(10*B)

3. Show the output for each program.

   a.
   ```
   100 FOR N=0 TO 4
   110     LET X=N*(N-1)
   120     LET Y=ABS(X-8)
   130     PRINT N,Y
   140 NEXT N
   150 END
   ```

   b.
   ```
   100 LET X=1.1 : Y=X
   110 WHILE Y<=1.5
   120     LET Z=INT(Y)
   130     PRINT Y,Z
   140     LET Y=X*Y
   150 WEND
   160 END
   ```

   c.
   ```
   10 FOR X=3 TO 10
   20     PRINT "X";
   30     IF X/4=INT(X/4) THEN PRINT
   40 NEXT X
   50 END
   ```

   d.
   ```
   10 FOR X=3 TO 10
   20     PRINT "X";
   30     IF X\4=INT(X/4) THEN PRINT
   40 NEXT X
   50 END
   ```

   e.
   ```
   10 FOR X=3 TO 10
   20     PRINT X;
   30     IF X\4=CINT(X/4) THEN PRINT
   40 NEXT X
   50 END
   ```

   f.
   ```
   10 LET N=63 : D=1
   20 WHILE D<=N/2
   30     IF N/D=INT(N/D) THEN PRINT D;
   40     LET D=D+1
   50 WEND
   60 END
   ```

g. `10 LET M=24`
    `20 FOR D=2 TO 23 STEP 3`
    `30   PRINT "*";`
    `40   IF M/D=INT(M/D) THEN PRINT`
    `50 NEXT D`
    `60 END`

h. `100 LET S=13.99`
    `110 WHILE S<14`
    `120   LET R=INT(100*S+0.5)/100`
    `130   PRINT USING "##.### ##.##";S,R`
    `140   LET S=S+0.003`
    `150 WEND`
    `160 END`

4. Write a *single* BASIC statement for each task:

   a. For any two numbers A and B, display EQUAL if the absolute value of their sum is equal to the sum of their absolute values.
   b. For any two integers M and N, display DIVISIBLE if M is divisible by N.
   c. Transfer control to line 300 if X is a positive integer. (All you know about X is that it is a number.)
   d. Transfer control to line 400 if the integer K is divisible by either 7 or 11.
   e. Cause a RETURN to be executed if the integer L is even and also divisible by 25.
   f. For any integers A, B, and C, display OK if C is a factor of both A and B.

5. Using the INT function, write a single BASIC statement that will round the value of X:

   a. to the nearest hundredth.
   b. to the nearest thousandth.
   c. to the nearest hundred.
   d. to the nearest thousand.

In Problems 6–16, write a program for each task specified. For tasks that require keyboard input, a user should be able to try different input values without having to rerun the program.

6. Find the sum and the sum of the absolute values of any input list. Display the number of values in the list as well as the two sums.
7. The deviation of a number N from a number M is defined to be ABS(M − N). Find the sum of the deviations of the numbers 2, 5, 3, 7, 12, −8, 43, −16 from M = 6. (M and the list of numbers are to be input during program execution. Use an EOD tag to end each list.)
8. Find the sum of the deviations of numbers X from INT(X) where the X's are input.
9. For any input list, sums S1 and S2 are to be found. S1 is the sum of the numbers, and S2 is the sum of the numbers each rounded to the nearest integer. Display both sums and also the number of values in the list.
10. Determine all positive factors of a positive integer N input at the keyboard. (Include the factors 1 and N.)
11. A list of integers is to be input. Any integer less than 1 serves as the EOD tag. Display the sum and a count of the even input values and also the sum and count of the odd ones.
12. Include the following information in DATA lines for a program to determine the batting average and slugging percentage for each player. In the table, 1B indicates a single, 2B a double, 3B a triple, HR a homerun, and AB the number of times a player has been at bat.

$$\text{Batting average} = \frac{\text{number of hits}}{\text{AB}} \qquad \text{Slugging percentage} = \frac{\text{total bases}}{\text{AB}}$$

Player	1B	2B	3B	HR	AB
Gomez	100	22	1	14	444
Boyd	68	20	0	3	301
Jackson	83	15	8	7	395
O'Neil	68	22	1	8	365
Struik	65	11	3	6	310
McDuffy	54	11	4	0	256
Vertullo	78	18	1	15	418
Ryan	25	1	1	0	104
Torgeson	49	15	0	11	301
Johnson	54	5	2	0	246

Your program is to produce two tables: the first showing the players with their batting averages in adjacent columns, and the second showing the players with their slugging percentages. Each table is to have a title and each column a heading. The batting averages and slugging percentages are to be shown rounded to three decimal places.

13. Display the exact change received from a purchase of P dollars if an amount D is presented to the salesclerk. Assume that D is at most $100. The change should be given in the largest possible denominations of bills and coins, but $50 and $2 bills are not to be used. If P = 26.68 and D = 100, for example, the change D − P = 73.32 would be:

    3 $20 bills, 1 $10 bill, 3 $1 bills, 1 quarter, 1 nickel, and 2 pennies

    Suggestion: If C denotes the change in pennies, then N = INT(C/2000) gives the number of $20 bills. You would then subtract 2000*N from C and proceed to the next lower denomination. Because computers store some numbers only approximately, you must not use the statement LET C=100*(D−P) to get C. Rather, you must use the statement

    LET C=INT(100*(D-P)+0.1)

    and explain the reason for adding 0.1.

14. The Apex Gas Station is running a special on cut glassware regularly costing $3.29. The sale price of the glassware is determined by the number of gallons of gasoline purchased according to this table:

Number of gallons purchased	Sale price of glassware
Less than 10	Regular price
From 10 to 15	Twenty percent is deducted from regular price for each whole numbered gallon over the minimum of 10
More than 15	Free

Apex sells four grades of gasoline:

Grade	Code	Price per gallon
Regular leaded	R	80.9¢
Premium leaded	P	91.9¢
Regular unleaded	U	84.9¢
Premium unleaded	S	98.9¢

Write a program that prompts the user to enter the code for the grade of gasoline and the number of gallons purchased. Then have it display the sale price of the glassware and ask the user (Y or N) whether the glassware will be purchased. After the user enters a response, display the cost of the gasoline purchase and the total cost of the transaction.

15. Last year's sales report of the RJB Card Company reads as follows:

January	$32,350	July	$22,000
February	$16,440	August	$43,500
March	$18,624	September	$51,400
April	$26,100	October	$29,000
May	$30,500	November	$20,100
June	$28,600	December	$27,500

Display the average monthly sales and a short report showing the month and the monthly sales for those months for which the sales deviate from the average by more than P percent. Have the user enter a value for P.

16. Find the mean M and standard deviation D of a set of numbers contained in DATA lines. Use the following method to compute D. If the numbers are $x_1, x_2, x_3, \ldots, x_n$, then $D = \sqrt{S2/(n-1)}$, where

$$S2 = (x_1 - M)^2 + (x_2 - M)^2 + \cdots + (x_n - M)^2$$

In Problems 17–26, write a program for each task specified. (These are for the mathematically inclined reader.)

17. Determine all prime numbers that do not exceed N. N is to be input.
18. Determine all prime numbers between A and B. A and B are to be input and are to be rejected if either is not a positive integer.
19. Display the prime factorization of any positive integer greater than 1 typed at the keyboard. For example, if 35 is input, the output should be 35 = 5*7; if 41 is input, the output should be 41 IS PRIME; if 90 is input, the output should be 90 = 2*3*3*5.
20. Write a program to input a decimal constant containing fewer than five fractional digits, and display it as a quotient of two integers. For example, if 23.79 is input, the output should be 2379/100. (Remember, the computer may store only a close approximation of the input value. Be sure that your program works in all cases.)
21. Write a program to input a decimal constant as in Problem 20 and display it as a quotient of two integers that have no common factors. For example, if 4.40 is input, the output should be 22/5.
22. If a, b, and c are any three numbers with $a \neq 0$, the quadratic equation

$$ax^2 + bx + c = 0$$

can be solved for x by using the formula

$$x = \frac{-b \pm \sqrt{b^2 - 4ac}}{2a}$$

If $b^2 - 4ac > 0$, the formula gives two solutions: if $b^2 - 4ac = 0$, it gives one solution. If $b^2 - 4ac < 0$, however, there are no real solutions. Your program is to solve the quadratic equation for any input values a, b, and c, with $a \neq 0$.

23. The distance d of a point (x, y) in the xy-plane from the line $ax + by + c = 0$ is given by

$$d = \frac{|ax + by + c|}{\sqrt{a^2 + b^2}}$$

Write a program to input the coefficients a, b, and c, and compute the distance d for any number of points (x, y) typed at the keyboard. Be sure that all input requests and all output values are labeled. End the program when $a = 0$ and $b = 0$.

24. Produce a two-column table showing the value of X and the cotangent of X for all values of X from zero to $\pi/2$ in increments of 0.05. (The case X = 0 must get special treatment.)
25. Referring to the diagram in Example 9, write a program to determine side c if sides a and b and angle C are given. (Use the law of cosines: $c^2 = a^2 + b^2 - 2ab \cos(C)$.)

26. An object moves so that its distance d from a fixed point P at time t is

$$d = \frac{1}{1 - 0.999 \cos t}$$

Produce a table (with column headings) of the d values for t between zero and 2π in increments of 0.1.

13.3 User-Defined Functions: The DEF FN Statement

In addition to providing the built-in functions, BASIC allows you to define and name your own functions. These functions, called **user-defined functions,** can be referenced in any part of your program just as the built-in functions are referenced. We'll illustrate how functions are defined and used with a simple example. The statement

```
100 DEF FNR(X)=INT(100*X+0.5)/100
```

defines a function whose *name* is R (or FNR) and whose value for any number X is X rounded to the nearest hundredth (recall that the expression INT(100*X+0.5)/100 rounds X to two decimal places). The keyword DEF is an abbreviation for *define* and FN stands for *function*. The variable X is called a **formal parameter**—it serves only to define the function. To reference (or *call*) this function, you must use the form

    FNR(**argument**)

where **argument** denotes any numerical expression whose value is to be substituted for X in the function definition. Thus, if the expression FNR(943.828) appears in a program, its value will be 943.83. Similarly, if Y has the value 943.828, then FNR(Y) will again have the value 943.83. The following short program uses this user-defined function to round calculated values before they are displayed.

EXAMPLE 10 Here is a program to illustrate the DEF FN statement.

```
100 REM ******************************
110 REM     FUNCTION DEFINITION
120 REM
130 DEF FNR(X)=INT(100*X+0.5)/100
140 REM
150 REM ******************************
160 REM
170 INPUT "ENTER AN AMOUNT (0 TO STOP): ",AMT
180 WHILE AMT<>0
190    INPUT "ENTER A PERCENT: ",PCT
200    LET RESULT=(PCT/100)*AMT
210    PRINT PCT;"PERCENT OF";AMT;"IS";FNR(RESULT)
220    PRINT
230    INPUT "ENTER AN AMOUNT (0 TO STOP): ",AMT
240 WEND
250 END
RUN

ENTER AN AMOUNT (0 TO STOP): 100
ENTER A PERCENT: 12.625
 12.625 PERCENT OF 100 IS 12.63

ENTER AN AMOUNT (0 TO STOP): 154.49
ENTER A PERCENT: 6
 6 PERCENT OF 154.49 IS 9.270001

ENTER AN AMOUNT (0 TO STOP): 0
```

There are several advantages in defining your own functions:

1. A program containing a user-defined function is easily modified to treat different functions. For instance, if you change line 130 in the preceding program to

   ```
   130 DEF FNR(X)=INT(1000*X+0.5)/1000
   ```

   values will be rounded to three decimal places.
2. The expression defining a function is written only once even though it may be used several times in a program.
3. By assigning a name to an expression, you can often write programs so that they are easier to read and their logic is simpler to follow.

A program can contain any number of user-defined functions. In the next example we use two: a function to convert centimeters to inches and another to convert inches to feet.

EXAMPLE 11 Here is a program to produce a table showing conversions from centimeters to inches and to feet.

```
100 REM ****************************************
110 REM            FUNCTION DEFINITIONS
120 REM
130 DEF FNI(C)=C/2.54            'Centimeters to inches
140 DEF FNF(I)=I/12              'Inches to feet
150 REM
160 REM ****************************************
170 REM            DISPLAY CONVERSION TABLE.
180 REM
190 PRINT "CENTIMETERS     INCHES       FEET"
200 LET F$="     ###         ##.##       #.##"
210 PRINT
220 FOR CENT=10 TO 100 STEP 10
230     LET INCH=FNI(CENT)
240     LET FEET=FNF(INCH)
250     PRINT USING F$;CENT, INCH, FEET
260 NEXT CENT
270 END
RUN

CENTIMETERS      INCHES       FEET

     10           3.94        0.33
     20           7.87        0.66
     30          11.81        0.98
     40          15.75        1.31
     50          19.69        1.64
     60          23.62        1.97
     70          27.56        2.30
     80          31.50        2.62
     90          35.43        2.95
    100          39.37        3.28
```

REMARK The formal parameter C used in the definition in line 130 could have been any simple numerical variable name. It is called a **dummy variable** or **dummy argument** because it serves only to define the function; if used later in the program, it is treated the same as any other variable. For example, if the DEF statement in line 130 were changed to

```
130 DEF FNI(CENT)=CENT/2.54
```

the program would behave just as before. No conflict would arise because of the appearance of the variable CENT elsewhere in the program. In contrast, the variables CENT and INCH in the function references FNI(CENT) and FNF(INCH) in lines 230 and 240 do supply values to the function. For this reason they are called **actual arguments**.

Microsoft® BASIC allows you to use the DEF statement to define functions of more than one variable. For example, the statement

```
10 DEF FNI(P,R)=P*R/100
```

defines a function whose value for any numbers P and R is P∗R/100. If the expression FNI(2000,10) is used in the program, its value will be 2000×10/100 = 200. Similarly, if the variables A and B have the values 2000 and 10, respectively, then FNI(A,B) will again have the value 200.

EXAMPLE 12

Charges at a car rental agency are $14 a day plus 32¢ a mile. The following program calculates the total charge if the number of days D and the total mileage M are typed at the keyboard.

```
100 DEF FNC(D,M)=14*D+(.32)*M
110 INPUT "HOW MANY DAYS";D
120 INPUT "HOW MANY MILES";M
130 PRINT "CHARGE: ";FNC(D,M)
140 END
RUN

HOW MANY DAYS? 3
HOW MANY MILES? 523
CHARGE: 209.36
```

□

The general form of the DEF FN statement is

ln DEF FN**name(parameters)** = **e**

where **name** denotes any string allowed as a variable name, **parameters** denotes a list of simple variables separated by commas, and **e** denotes a BASIC expression defining a function of these simple variables. The expression **e** and the function name **name** must match in type: that is, both numerical or both string. (User-defined string functions are discussed in Section 14.8.) The function is referenced by using the form

FNname(arguments)

where **arguments** denotes a list of BASIC expressions separated by commas. These expressions supply values for the parameters in the function definition. Their number and types must agree with the number and types of the parameters.

The following rules govern the use of the DEF FN statement and user-defined functions.

1. A user-defined function may be referenced as an operand in any BASIC expression.
2. The DEF statement that defines a function must be executed before the function is referenced.
3. Microsoft® BASIC distinguishes between function names, as between variable names, by using their first 40 characters. As always, reserved words must be avoided when you are selecting function names.
4. The expression **e** used in a DEF statement may contain variables other than the dummy variables. When such a function is referenced, the current values of these variables are used in the evaluation. Thus if the function EVAL is defined by

```
100 DEF FNEVAL(S)=5*S+T
```

the programming line

```
200 LET T=1000 : PRINT FNEVAL(7)
```

will display the value 1035[FNEVAL(7) = 5 × 7 + 1000 = 1035].

5. The expression **e** used in a DEF statement may involve built-in functions and user-defined functions. Thus the two lines

```
100 DEF FNY(X)=X+3
110 DEF FNZ(S)=S*FNY(S)
```

are admissible. The reference FNZ(4) will have the value 28

[FNZ(4) = 4∗FNY(4) = 4 × (4 + 3) = 28]

6. The DEF statement can be used only in deferred execution mode.

■ 13.4 Problems

1. Each of these short programs contains an error—either a syntax error that will cause an error message or a programming error that the computer will not recognize but that will cause incorrect results. In each case, find the error and tell which of the two types it is.

   a.
   ```
   10 REM DISPLAY 6 PERCENT
   20 REM OF ANY NUMBER.
   30 DEF FNZ(U)=.06*U
   40 INPUT X
   50 LET V=FNZ(U)
   60 PRINT V
   70 END
   ```

   b.
   ```
   10 REM A TABLE OF SQUARES
   20 DEF FNS(I)=X^2
   30 FOR I=1 TO 9
   40    LET S=FNS(I)
   50    PRINT I,S
   60 NEXT I
   70 END
   ```

   c.
   ```
   10 REM BONUS CALCULATION
   20 DEF BONUS(S)=200+0.02*S
   30 INPUT "SALARY: ",S
   40 LET B=BONUS(S)
   50 PRINT "BONUS IS";B
   60 END
   ```

   d.
   ```
   10 REM DISPLAY RECIPROCALS
   20 REM OF 1,2,3,...,10
   30 DEF FNR(X)=X/N
   40 LET X=1
   50 FOR N=1 TO 10
   60    PRINT FNR(N)
   70 NEXT N
   80 END
   ```

2. Show the output of each program:

   a.
   ```
   10 DEF FNR(X)=100*INT(X/100+0.5)
   20 FOR I=1 TO 3
   30    READ S
   40    PRINT FNR(S)
   50 NEXT I
   60 DATA 227.376,1382.123,7.125
   70 END
   ```

   b.
   ```
   10 DEF FNY(X)=1+1/X
   20 LET X=2
   30 FOR I=1 TO 3
   40    LET X=FNY(X)-1
   50    PRINT X;
   60 NEXT I
   70 END
   ```

   c.
   ```
   10 DEF FNQ(A)=A+1
   20 DEF FNR(A)=A+2
   30 FOR X=0 TO 3
   40    LET A=FNR(FNQ(X))
   50    PRINT X;A
   60 NEXT X
   70 END
   ```

   d.
   ```
   10 DEF FNA(X,Y)=X/Y
   20 FOR I=1 TO 2
   30    FOR J=1 TO 4
   40       PRINT FNA(J,I);
   50    NEXT J
   60    PRINT
   70 NEXT I
   80 END
   ```

   e.
   ```
   10 DEF FNI(P,R,T)=P*R/100*T
   20 LET T=1/2
   30 LET P=1000
   40 FOR R=2 TO 5
   50    PRINT FNI(P,R,T)
   60 NEXT R
   70 END
   ```

3. Write a user-defined function that:
   a. gives the total cost of an article listed at L dollars if the sales tax is 5%.
   b. gives the simple interest earned in 3 months on $100 at an annual rate of R percent

c. gives the cost of covering a floor whose length and width (in feet) are L and W, respectively, if the covering costs $12.95 per square yard.
d. gives the excise tax on a car assessed at E dollars if the tax rate is $27/$1,000.
e. converts degrees Celsius to degrees Fahrenheit [F = (9/5)C + 32].
f. converts degrees Fahrenheit to degrees Celsius.
g. converts feet to miles.
h. converts kilometers to miles (1 mi = 1609.3 m).
i. converts miles to kilometers.
j. rounds X to the third decimal place.
k. gives the average speed in miles per hour for a trip of D miles that takes T hours.
l. gives the selling price if an article whose list price is X dollars is selling at a discount of Y percent.
m. gives the cost in dollars of a trip of X miles in a car that averages 15 mph if gasoline costs Y cents per gallon.
n. gives the area of a circle of radius R.
o. gives the volume of a sphere of radius R.
p. gives the sine of an angle of A degrees.

In Problems 4–14 write a program to perform each task specified.

4. Produce a three-column table showing the conversions from feet F to miles and then to kilometers for the values F = 1,000, 2,000, 3,000, . . . , 20,000. All output values are to be rounded to three decimal places. Write user-defined functions to perform the two conversions required and to do the rounding.

5. Produce a three-column table showing the conversions from grams G to ounces and then to pounds (1 oz = 28.3495 g) for G = 20, 40, 60, . . . , 400. All output values are to be rounded to three decimal places. Employ a user-defined function to do the rounding.

6. Produce a four-column table as follows. The first column is to contain the mileage figures 10 miles, 20 miles, . . . , 200 miles. The second, third, and fourth columns are to give the time in minutes required to travel these distances at the respective speeds 45 mph, 50 mph, and 55 mph. All output values are to be rounded to the nearest minute. Write user-defined functions to calculate the times and to do the rounding.

7. Following is the weekly inventory report of a sewing-supply wholesaler:

Item	Batches on hand Monday	Batches sold during week	Cost per batch	Sales price per batch
Bobbins	220	105	8.20	10.98
Buttons	550	320	5.50	6.95
Needles—1	450	295	2.74	3.55
Needles—2	200	102	7.25	9.49
Pins	720	375	4.29	5.89
Thimbles	178	82	6.22	7.59
Thread—A	980	525	4.71	5.99
Thread—B	1424	718	7.42	9.89

Produce a three-column report showing the item names, the number on hand at the end of the week, and the income per item. Denoting the markup by M and the quantity sold by Q, use a function FNP(M,Q) to calculate the income figures.

8. Using the inventory report shown in Problem 7, produce a five-column report showing the item names, the cost per batch, the sales price per batch, the dollar markup per batch, and the percent markup per batch. Denoting the markup by M and the cost by C, use a function FNA(M,C) to calculate the percent figures in the fifth column (M/C × 100 gives the required percentage). In addition, use a function to round the percentages to the nearest whole number.

9. Each salesperson for the Mod Dress Company is paid $140 a week plus 4.875% of all sales. Using the following sales figures, produce a five-column report showing the name, total sales, base pay, commission, and gross pay for each salesperson. All money amounts are to be rounded to the nearest cent.

	Total sales for the week	
Name	**Type-1 items**	**Type-2 items**
Barnes, James	$ 726.28	$1198.42
Colby, Irene	415.92	2092.50
Cole, Bruce	2606.95	700.40
Drew, Nancy	350.42	301.27
Hilton, Lynn	1300.23	1521.32
Moore, Warren	268.92	399.92
Rich, Steven	2094.50	227.03
Skinner, Kerry	1102.37	303.52

10. Assume that a salesperson for the Mod Dress Company is paid $230 a week plus a commission of 3.125% on all Type-1 sales and 5.875% on all Type-2 sales. However, a salesperson whose total sales do not exceed $700 receives only the base pay of $230. Using the sales figures given in Problem 9, produce a five-column report showing the name, base pay, Type-1 commission, Type-2 commission, and gross pay for each salesperson. All money amounts are to be rounded to the nearest cent.
11. Produce a three-column table showing the values of t, x, and y for $t = 0, 1, 2, \ldots, 10$, where $x = 5(1 + t)$ and $y = \sqrt{x^2 + 1}$. Determine x and y with user-defined functions.
12. Determine the area in square centimeters of any rectangle whose length and width in inches are typed by the user. Use a function to convert inches to centimeters.
13. Write a user-defined function AC to determine the area of a circle with circumference L. Also write a function AS to determine the area of a square with perimeter L. Use these two functions in a program to produce a three-column table showing L and the values of AC and AS for $L = 1, 2, 3, \ldots, 10$. The values of AC and AS are to be rounded to three decimal places.
14. A thin wire of length L is cut into two pieces of lengths L1 and L2. One piece is bent into the shape of a circle and the other into a square. Decide how the wire should be cut if the sum of the two enclosed areas is to be as small as possible. (Use the functions AC and AS described in Problem 13.) How should the wire be cut if the sum of the areas is to be as large as possible?

■ 13.5 Review True-or-False Quiz

1. If a BASIC function exists that performs a needed task, you should use it even if it is a simple matter to write your own programming lines to perform this task. T F
2. INT(5/2)<>5/2. T F
3. ABS(INT(−2.3)) = INT(ABS(−2.3)). T F
4. INT(X) = FIX(X). T F
5. CINT(42564.8) = 42565 T F
6. If A = ABS(INT(A)), then A is a positive integer. T F
7. If N and D are positive numbers but not necessarily integers, BASIC allows you to use the relational expression INT(N/D) = N/D to determine whether dividing N by D gives an integer. T F
8. The relational expression INT(N) = N is true if N is either 0 or a positive integer and is false in all other cases. T F

9. If the statement 1 DEF FNC(P) = 2*P + 2 appears in a program, then the function FNC may be referenced as often as desired and in exactly the same way as any built-in function is referenced.   T F
10. If the variable Y is used as the formal parameter in a DEF statement, then Y may be used elsewhere in the program for a different purpose.   T F
11. If FNF(X) is defined in a program, we may also define the function FNC(X) = 2 + FNF(X).   T F
12. The expression SIN(37*3.14159/180) may be used to find the sine of 37 degrees.   T F

14 More on Processing String Data

String processing is now a major application area for computers. For this reason, modern programming languages are designed to simplify tasks that require processing string data. In this chapter we describe the BASIC functions and operations used with string data.

In Sections 14.1–14.3 we show how programming tasks that require examining parts of strings or combining given strings to build new ones can be carried out by using the string functions LEFT$, RIGHT$, and MID$, the string-related functions LEN and INSTR, and the concatenation operator +. In Section 14.5 we discuss how computers store string data and explain how this knowledge allows you to give meaning to string comparisons involving the relational operators <, <=, >, and >=. To this point, strings have been compared only to determine whether they are equal (=) or not equal (<>). In Section 14.7 we describe the BASIC conversion functions CHR$, ASC, STR$, and VAL and show how they can be used effectively for many programming tasks that would otherwise be very difficult. In Section 14.8 we return to the topic of user-defined functions begun in Chapter 13 and show how you can use the DEF statement to write your own string and string-related functions.

■ 14.1 String and String-Related Functions

Four of the most useful functions included in Microsoft® BASIC are described in this section. The first determines the length of a string, and the other three are used to examine individual characters or groups of characters in a string.

The Length Function LEN

If **s** denotes a string, then LEN(**s**), read length of **s,** is the number of characters contained in **s.** Thus LEN("JOHN AND MARY") has the value 13. If Z$ = "JOHN AND MARY" then LEN(Z$) also has the value 13. As always, blanks are counted as characters. The **s** in LEN(**s**) is called the *argument* of the function and must be enclosed in parentheses as shown.

EXAMPLE 1   Here is a program to display only the strings that contain exactly three characters:

```
10 FOR I=1 TO 6
20    READ X$
30    IF LEN(X$)=3 THEN PRINT X$
40 NEXT I
50 DATA "THE","I DO","ONE","OLD ","THREE","127"
60 END
RUN

THE
ONE
127
```

Note that "I DO" has four characters—three letters and an embedded blank. Similarly, "OLD " has a trailing blank character.

EXAMPLE 2   Here is a program to display a column of words lined up on the right:

```
100 PRINT "12345678901234567890"
110 REM READ WORDS AND DISPLAY RIGHT JUSTIFIED.
120 READ A$
130 WHILE A$<>"XXX"
140    PRINT TAB(15-LEN(A$));A$
150    READ A$
160 WEND
170 DATA A,SHORT,LIST,OF,WORDS,XXX
180 END
RUN

12345678901234567890
              A
          SHORT
           LIST
             OF
          WORDS
```

The TAB function tabs to position 15−1 for the letter A, to position 15−5 for SHORT, and so on. This effectively displays the column of words with the last character of each word in column position 14.

The String Function LEFT$

If **s** denotes a string and **n** an integer from 0 to LEN(**s**), then LEFT$(**s,n**) is the string consisting of the first **n** characters of **s**. Thus, LEFT$("JOHN AND MARY",4) has the value JOHN. If A$="JOHN AND MARY" and N=4, then LEFT$(A$,N) also has the value JOHN. If N=0, LEFT$(A$,N) is the null string. (How Microsoft® BASIC handles LEFT$(**s,n**) when **n** is not an integer from 0 to LEN(**s**) is explained following Example 4.)

EXAMPLE 3   Here is a program that extracts strings with the LEFT$ function.

```
10 LET Y$="SEVEN"
20 FOR N=1 TO LEN(Y$)
30    PRINT LEFT$(Y$,N)
40 NEXT N
50 END
RUN

S
SE
SEV
SEVE
SEVEN
```

EXAMPLE 4   Here is a program that displays only words that begin with the prefix typed by the user:

```
100 INPUT "TYPE A PREFIX: ",P$
110 PRINT
120 PRINT "WORDS BEGINNING WITH THE PREFIX ";P$;":"
130 PRINT
140 FOR K=1 TO 13
150     READ A$
160     IF LEFT$(A$,LEN(P$))=P$ THEN PRINT TAB(6);A$
170 NEXT K
180 DATA ENABLE, ENACT, ENGAGE, ENSURE, ENDORSE
190 DATA HYPERACTIVE, HYPERMYSTICAL, HYPERNEUROTIC, HYPERPURE
200 DATA UNAFRAID, UNDO, UNEVEN, UNFOLD
210 END
RUN

TYPE A PREFIX: UN

WORDS BEGINNING WITH THE PREFIX UN:

      UNAFRAID
      UNDO
      UNEVEN
      UNFOLD
```

■ **REMARK 1**   If you enter the prefix HYPER for P$, the condition

LEFT$(A$,LEN(P$))=P$

in line 160 says to compare the first five characters of A$ with HYPER. But when the DATA value UNDO is read for A$, A$ will have only *four* characters. As we explain following this example, LEFT$("UNDO",5) is the four-character string UNDO. Thus, with P$ = "HYPER" and A$ = "UNDO", the condition in line 160 is false and UNDO is not displayed, as it shouldn't be. Thus, the program will work for any prefix you enter, not only for prefixes with fewer letters than the words in the DATA lines.

■ **REMARK 2**   On each pass through the loop, the computer determines the length LEN(P$) anew. Since P$ does not change in the loop, its length should be determined once, before the loop is entered. To do this, add the line

125 LET L=LEN(P$)

□   and change LEN(P$) in line 160 to L.

We have explained how the computer assigns to LEFT$(**s,n**) a substring of **s** in cases where **n** is an integer from 0 to LEN(**s**). If **n** is not an integer in this range, the PC rounds **n**, if necessary, to obtain an integer, say N. Then:

1. If N is greater than LEN(**s**) but no greater than 255, LEFT$(**s,n**) is **s**.
2. If N is not in the range 0–255, an Illegal function call error occurs.

The String Function RIGHT$

If **s** denotes a string and **n** an integer from 0 to LEN(**s**) then RIGHT$(**s,n**) is the string consisting of the last **n** characters in **s**. Thus RIGHT$("JOHN AND MARY",4) has the value MARY, and RIGHT$("JOHN AND MARY",0) is the null string.

If **n** is not an integer from 0 to LEN(**s**), it is rounded, if necessary, say to N. N must be in the range 0–255. If LEN(**s**) ≤ N ≤ 255, RIGHT$(**s,n**) is **s**.

EXAMPLE 5 Here is a program that extracts strings with the RIGHT$ function.

```
10 LET Y$="SEVEN"
20 FOR N=1 TO LEN(Y$)
30    PRINT RIGHT$(Y$,N)
40 NEXT N
50 END
RUN

N
EN
VEN
EVEN
SEVEN
```

The String Function MID$

There are two forms of the MID$ function: If **s** denotes a string and **m** and **n** denote integers, then

1. MID$(**s,m,n**) is the string of **n** characters from **s** beginning with the **m**th character of **s**.
2. MID$(**s,m**) is the string consisting of all characters in **s** from the **m**th character on.

In the following illustration, A$ = "JOHN AND MARY":

Expression	Its value	Length of its value
MID$(A$,6,3)	AND	3
MID$(A$,6)	AND MARY	8
MID$(A$,6,8)	AND MARY	8
MID$(A$,6,1)	A	1
MID$(A$,6,0)	null string	0

EXAMPLE 6 Here is a program to illustrate the two forms of the MID$ function.

```
10 LET Y$="ABCD"
20 FOR K=1 TO LEN(Y$)
30    PRINT MID$(Y$,K,1),MID$(Y$,K)
40 NEXT K
50 END
RUN

A          ABCD
B          BCD
C          CD
D          D
```

EXAMPLE 7 Here is a program to count the number of A's in a string A$ of any length.

```
100 LET C=0
110 INPUT "TYPE ANY STRING";A$
120 FOR K=1 TO LEN(A$)
130    IF MID$(A$,K,1)="A" THEN C=C+1
140 NEXT K
150 PRINT "NUMBER OF A'S IS";C
160 END
RUN

TYPE ANY STRING? ABRACADABRA
NUMBER OF A'S IS 5
```

The following special cases should be understood. When Microsoft® BASIC encounters MID$(**s,m,n**) or MID$(**s,m**) it rounds **m** and **n,** if necessary, to obtain integers—say M and N.

M must be in the range 1–255.
N must be in the range 0–255.

If M and N are in these ranges, then:

1. If M>LEN(**s**), both forms give the null string.
2. If there are fewer than N characters from the Mth character of **s** on, MID$(**s,m,n**) gives the same substring as MID$(**s,m**); that is, all characters of **s** from the Mth character on.

MID$ as a Statement

Microsoft® BASIC also allows you to use MID$ to replace characters in one string by characters from another. The *statement*

MID$(T$,M,N)=S$

replaces N characters in T$, beginning at position M, by the first N characters in S$. The argument N may be omitted if the intention is to replace a portion of T$ with all of S$. Thus,

MID$(T$,M)=S$

is equivalent to

MID$(T$,M,LEN(S$))=S$

Special cases are handled as follows:

1. If LEN(S$) is less than N, only LEN(S$) characters are replaced.
2. N can be in the range 0–255.
3. The length LEN(T$) is never changed.
4. M *must* be in the range 1 to LEN(T$).

EXAMPLE 8   This example illustrates MID$ as a statement.

```
100 LET T$="abcdefgh"      'String to be changed
110 LET S$="XYZ"           'Source of replacement characters
120 PRINT T$
130 MID$(T$,2,1)=S$        'Change T$ beginning in position 2.
140 PRINT T$
150 MID$(T$,8,2)=S$        'Change T$ beginning in position 8.
160 PRINT T$
170 MID$(T$,4)=S$          'Change T$ beginning in position 4.
180 PRINT T$
190 MID$(T$,9,1)=S$        'Change T$ beginning in position 9.
200 END
RUN

abcdefgh
aXcdefgh
aXcdefgX
aXcXYZgX
Illegal function call in 190
Ok
```

Line 130 changes T$ from abcdefgh to aXcdefgh.
Line 150 changes T$ from aXcdefgh to aXcdefgX.
Line 170 changes T$ from aXcdefgX to aXcXYZgX.
Line 190 causes the Illegal function call error because the position number 9 is not in the range 1 to LEN(T$).

14.2 Combining Strings (Concatenation)

The **concatenation operator +** allows you to combine two or more strings into a single string. Thus the statement

```
LET X$="PARA"+"MEDIC"
```

assigns the string PARAMEDIC to the variable X$. Similarly, if A$ = "PARA" and B$ = "MEDIC" the statement

```
LET X$=A$+B$
```

does exactly the same thing.

EXAMPLE 9 Here is a program to illustrate the concatenation operator:

```
10 LET X$="BIOLOGY"
20 LET Y$="ELECTRONICS"
30 LET Z$=LEFT$(X$,3)+RIGHT$(Y$,4)
40 PRINT Z$
50 END
RUN

BIONICS
```

Using only the functions LEFT$ and RIGHT$, we could have caused BIONICS to be displayed, but we could not have assigned the string BIONICS to the variable Z$.

EXAMPLE 10 Here is a program to assign the contents of A$ to B$, but in reverse order. For instance, if A$ = "AMNZ" then B$ will contain "ZNMA."

```
100 LET A$="RORRIM"
110 LET B$=""       'Start with the empty string.
120 REM
130 REM USING THE CONCATENATION OPERATOR,
140 REM APPEND EACH OF THE CHARACTERS OF A$ to B$.
150 REM
160 FOR K=LEN(A$) TO 1 STEP -1
170     LET B$=B$+MID$(A$,K,1)
180 NEXT K
190 PRINT A$;" IN REVERSE ORDER IS ";B$
200 END
RUN

RORRIM IN REVERSE ORDER IS MIRROR
```

Line 110 assigns a string containing no characters to B$. This step ensures that we will enter the FOR loop that appends letters to B$ with nothing in B$.

REMARK 1 The MID$ function allows you to display a string in reverse order. The concatenation operator is what allows you to assign the new string to B$.

REMARK 2 As mentioned previously, when you type RUN the PC sets all numerical variables to zero and all string variables to the empty string. We include line 110 for clarity just as we have consistently initialized numerical variables to zero when it is important that they have this initial value.

REMARK 3 The program shown in this example illustrates the principal reason why programming languages such as BASIC allow the empty string. When you wish to determine a numerical sum by adding a list of numbers, you begin with a sum of zero; when you wish to build a new string by concatenating a list of characters or strings, you begin with the empty string.

14.3 The Search Function INSTR

Searching a string for a specific character or sequence of characters is a common programming task. For this reason Microsoft® BASIC provides the INSTR function to search one string for another automatically. For example, you can use

```
LET P=INSTR(1,A$," ")
```

to determine the position P of the first blank in A$. The number 1 instructs the computer to begin the search with the first character in A$.

The general form of the INSTR function is

INSTR(**n,s,t**)

where **s** and **t** denote strings and **n** denotes a positive integer. The expression INSTR(**n,s,t**) has an integer value determined as follows. The string **s** is searched, beginning at position **n**, for the first occurrence of the string **t**. If **n** is omitted, the search begins at position 1.

1. If **t** is found, INSTR returns the first position in **s** at which the match occurs. Thus INSTR(1,"STOCKS AND BONDS","ND") has the value 9—the search for ND begins in position 1 and is successful at position 9. The expression INSTR(10,"STOCKS AND BONDS","ND") has the value 14—the search for ND begins in position 10 and is successful at position 14.
2. If **t** is not found, INSTR returns the value 0.
3. If **n** > LEN(**s**), INSTR returns the value 0.
4. **n** *must* be in the range 1 to 255. If **n** is not an integer, it is rounded and it is this rounded value that must be in the specified range.

EXAMPLE 11 Here is a program to search the words in DATA lines for any string input at the keyboard.

```
10 INPUT "FOR WHAT STRING ARE YOU LOOKING";S$
20 PRINT "THESE WORDS CONTAIN THE SPECIFIED STRING."
30 READ WORD$
40 WHILE WORD$<>"XXX"
50    IF INSTR(WORD$,S$)>0 THEN PRINT TAB(10);WORD$
60    READ WORD$
70 WEND
80 DATA THEORIZE,GUESS,HYPOTHESIZE,CONJECTURE
90 DATA XXX
99 END
RUN

FOR WHAT STRING ARE YOU LOOKING? THE
THESE WORDS CONTAIN THE SPECIFIED STRING.
         THEORIZE
         HYPOTHESIZE
```

EXAMPLE 12 Here is a program to interchange the first and last names given in the string EMILY DICKINSON:

```
100 LET A$="EMILY DICKINSON"
110 PRINT A$
120 REM FIND THE POSITION P OF THE BLANK IN A$.
130 LET P=INSTR(1,A$," ")
140 IF P=0 THEN 200
150 REM STORE THE FIRST NAME IN F$ AND THE LAST NAME IN L$.
160 LET F$=LEFT$(A$,P-1)
170 LET L$=MID$(A$,P+1)
180 LET A$=L$+", "+F$
190 PRINT A$
200 IF P=0 THEN PRINT A$;" CONTAINS NO BLANK."
210 END
RUN

EMILY DICKINSON
DICKINSON, EMILY
```

■ REMARK   The technique illustrated in this example has two immediate applications: it gives you additional control over the precise form of your output, and it allows you to alphabetize a list of names even if first names are given first. (Simply interchange first and last names and then use a standard sorting algorithm to alphabetize your list.) (See Chapter 16.)

EXAMPLE 13   This example shows how INSTR can be used to allow abbreviations for input values.

```
10 REM S$ CONTAINS A LIST OF ALLOWED WORDS.
20 LET S$=" APPLE   BANANA  LEMON   PEACH   PLUM   "
30 INPUT "ENTER AN ABBREVIATION: ", A$
40 LET P=INSTR(1,S$," "+A$)
50 IF P>0 THEN PRINT A$;" STANDS FOR ";MID$(S$,P,7)
60 END

RUN
ENTER AN ABBREVIATION: LE
LE STANDS FOR LEMON

RUN
ENTER AN ABBREVIATION: PLU
PLU STANDS FOR PLUM

RUN
ENTER AN ABBREVIATION: P
P STANDS FOR PEACH
```

Each word in S$ is preceded by a blank. Since line 40 searches S$ for the string " "+A$, this blank ensures that the abbreviation typed will be matched only with the beginnings of words included in S$. For instance, LE is matched with the LE in LEMON and not with the first occurrence of LE in APPLE.

Each word in S$ uses exactly 7 positions: the leading blank, the letters in the word, and trailing blanks if needed. This ensures that the string MID$(S$,P,7) displayed by line 50 will give the entire word corresponding to the abbreviation typed by the user.

Note that the input value P gives PEACH, the first word in S$ that begins with P. To ensure that abbreviations are unique, you can require abbreviations with more than one letter.

■ REMARK   You should check that the numerical expression 1 + (P − 1)/7 gives the values 1, 2, 3, 4, and 5 for the respective input values APPLE, BANANA, LEMON, PEACH, and PLUM. When using the ON GOSUB statement (Section 12.3), you may find that this method of assigning the integers 1, 2, 3, and so on, to different string input values can be very helpful.

■ 14.4 Problems

1. Show the output of each program.

   a. ```
   10 LET A$="CYBERNETIC"
   20 PRINT LEFT$(A$,LEN(A$)/2)
   30 END
   ```

   **b.** ```
   10 LET B$="A TO Z"
   20 PRINT RIGHT$(B$,1);" TO ";LEFT$(B$,1)
   30 END
   ```

   c. ```
   10 LET A$="CONSTRUCTION"
   20 LET B$="SULTAN OF SWAT"
   ```
   ```

```
     30 LET C$=LEFT$(A$,3)+LEFT$(B$,5)+RIGHT$(A$,4)
     40 PRINT C$
     50 END
```

d.
```
     10 LET A$="BIOLOGY"
     20 LET B$="PHYSICS"
     30 LET C$=LEFT$(A$,3)
     40 FOR I=1 TO LEN(B$)
     50     LET C$=C$+MID$(B$,I,1)
     60 NEXT I
     70 PRINT C$
     80 END
```

e.
```
     10 LET SP$=" "                    'Space
     20 READ X$
     30 LET A=1 : B=INSTR(A,X$,SP$)
     40 WHILE B>0
     50     PRINT MID$(X$,A,B-A)
     60     LET A=B+1 : B=INSTR(A,X$,SP$)
     70 WEND
     80 PRINT MID$(X$,A)
     90 DATA "Great Salt Lake Desert, Utah"
     99 END
```

f.
```
     10 LET S$="-ADD -LIST-STEP-STOP"
     20 FOR K=1 TO 7
     30     READ C$
     40     IF LEN(C$)<3 THEN 70
     50     LET P=INSTR(1,S$,"-"+C$)
     60     IF P>0 THEN PRINT MID$(S$,P+1,4)
     70 NEXT K
     80 DATA ADD,LIST,STOP,START,S,ST,STE
     90 END
```

g.
```
     10 LET S$="-ADD -LIST-STEP-STOP"
     20 FOR K=1 TO 4
     30     READ C$
     40     LET P=INSTR(1,S$,"-"+C$)
     50     LET N=1+(P-1)/5
     60     PRINT N;C$
     70 NEXT K
     80 DATA STEP,LIST,STOP,ADD
     90 END
```

2. Write a single program statement to perform each of the following tasks.

   a. Display the first character of A$.
   b. Display the second character of A$.
   c. Display the last character of A$.
   d. Display the first three characters of A$.
   e. Display the last three characters of A$.
   f. Display the first and last characters of A$.
   g. Increase N by 1 if A$ and B$ have the same number of characters.
   h. Display the first character in A$ only if it's the same as the last character in A$.
   i. Assign the string SAME to X$ if the first two characters in A$ are the same.
   j. Display the string COMMA if A$ contains a comma. (Use INSTR.)
   k. Display the string NO SPACES if A$ contains no spaces. (Use INSTR.)
   l. Assign the first N characters of A$ to B$.
   m. A$ is a two-letter string. Interchange these letters to obtain the string B$.

n. Interchange the first two characters in S$ to obtain T$.
o. Create a string F$ consisting of the first three characters of G$ and the last three characters of H$.
p. Display the string OK if the first character of A$, the second character of B$, and the third character of C$ spell "YES".
q. Replace the fourth character of A$ by the character Y.

In Problems 3–15, write a program for each task specified.

3. Display any five-character string typed at the keyboard in reverse order. If the string does not contain exactly five characters, display nothing. Allow the user to try many strings, and stop the program when the user types DONE.
4. Display any string typed at the keyboard in reverse order. Stop the program when the user types DONE.
5. Examine all strings appearing in DATA lines to determine and display those that begin with whatever letter is input. Allow the user to try different letters during a single run, and stop the program when * is typed.
6. The user types two five-letter words. Compare them letter by letter. If two corresponding letters are different, display a dollar sign. Otherwise display the letter. If CANDY and CHIDE are typed, for example, the output should be C$$D$.
7. The user types two words to obtain a listing of those letters in the second word that are also in the first. If the user types STRING and HARNESS, for example, the output should be RNSS, since these four letters in the second word HARNESS are also in the first word STRING.
8. The user types a string containing two words separated by a comma. Display the two words in reverse order without the comma. If the user types "GARVEY,STEVE", for example, the output should be STEVE GARVEY. Stop the program only when the user types DONE.
9. Include a list of names, with last names last, in DATA lines. Produce a listing of the names with last names first followed by a comma. Run your program with the given DATA lines. Note that

    ```
    BRICE, MARY ELLEN
    ```

    is how MARY ELLEN BRICE should be displayed. You may assume that *last* names contain no blanks.

    ```
    DATA MARY ELLEN BRICE,MARK BRONSON,MARIA MANDELA
    DATA LIZ WALKER,LI-JUAN WEI,SUE ANN TILTON
    DATA ART ROBELLO,RONALD MACDONALD
    DATA END-OF-DATA
    ```

10. Input a string and change all occurrences of the letter Y to the letter M.
11. Read a list of words from DATA lines to determine the average number of letters per word.
12. Read a list of words from DATA lines, and display only the words with exactly N letters. N is to be input by the user, who should be allowed to try several different values for N during a single program run.
13. Read a list of strings appearing in DATA lines to determine how many times a particular letter or other character appears in this list. The letter or character is to be input by the user, who should be allowed to try several different characters during the same run. Stop the program if the user types END.
14. Display the words appearing in an English sentence, one per line. You may assume that words are separated by exactly one space, that the sentence ends with a period, and that no other punctuation is used. The sentence is to be input into a string variable. Stop the program only when the user types DONE. If the input sentence does not contain a period, inform the user of this fact. Try your program with the sentences

    ```
    ALL GAUL IS DIVIDED INTO THREE PARTS.
    WHERE IS THE PERIOD?
    ```

15. Carry out the task described in Problem 14 with the following difference: words may be separated by more than one space and may be followed by a comma, semicolon, or colon, and sentences may end with a period or a question mark. Inform the user if a sentence does

not end with a period or question mark. Try your program with these sentences:

```
ALLOWED COMMANDS ARE ADD, LIST, STEP, AND STOP.
YOU MAY USE THE FOLLOWING: ADD, LIST, AND STOP.
IS ALL GAUL DIVIDED INTO THREE PARTS?
THERE IS NO PERIOD
```

■ 14.5 The BASIC Character Set

BASIC allows several operations with string data that we have yet to explain. For instance, although we have used relational expressions such as A$ = B$ and A$ <> B$ to determine if two strings are identical or not, we have not compared strings by using the other relational operators <, <=, >, and >=. As we explain shortly, there are many programming situations that require making such string comparisons. To understand these, and other operations with strings described in Section 14.7 you will need some knowledge of how a computer stores string data in memory.

Whenever a program requires the use of a string, each character of the string is assigned a numerical value called its **numeric code.** It is these numerical values that are compared. As we would expect, the numeric code for the letter A is smaller than that for B, the numeric code for B is smaller than that for C, and so on. But it is not only letters that can be compared; each BASIC character has its own unique numeric code so that any two characters may be compared. One BASIC character is less than a second character if the numeric code of the first is less than the numeric code of the second.

The **ordering sequence** (or **collating sequence**) of numeric codes for the IBM PC character set is given in Appendix F. As mentioned in Section 10.4, many of these characters are used only in screen displays. In this section we will use only characters that are the same whether displayed on the screen or printed by a printer. These are shown in Table 14.1 which is included here for easy reference.

Table 14.1 ASCII numeric codes 32–127

Numeric code	Character	Numeric code	Character	Numeric code	Character	Numeric code	Character
032	(space)	056	8	080	P	104	h
033	!	057	9	081	Q	105	i
034	"	058	:	082	R	106	j
035	#	059	;	083	S	107	k
036	$	060	<	084	T	108	l
037	%	061	=	085	U	109	m
038	&	062	>	086	V	110	n
039	'	063	?	087	W	111	o
040	(	064	@	088	X	112	p
041	)	065	A	089	Y	113	q
042	*	066	B	090	Z	114	r
043	+	067	C	091	[	115	s
044	,	068	D	092	\	116	t
045	-	069	E	093	]	117	u
046	.	070	F	094	^	118	v
047	/	071	G	095	—	119	w
048	0	072	H	096	`	120	x
049	1	073	I	097	a	121	y
050	2	074	J	098	b	122	z
051	3	075	K	099	c	123	{
052	4	076	L	100	d	124	|
053	5	077	M	101	e	125	}
054	6	078	N	102	f	126	~
055	7	079	O	103	g	127	⌴

Using this ASCII ordering sequence, we have:

"G" < "P" since 71 < 80
"4" < "Y" since 52 < 89
"$" < "^" since 36 < 94
"8" < "?" since 56 < 63
"M" < "m" since 77 < 109
"Z" < "a" since 90 < 97

If strings containing more than one character are to be compared, they are compared character by character beginning at the left. Strings consisting of uppercase letters of the alphabet are ordered just as they would appear in a dictionary, as are strings consisting only of lowercase letters. Here are some relational expressions and their truth values:

Relational expression	Truth value
"AMA" > "AM"	True
"Bat" <= "BAT"	False
"13N" < "14N"	True
"M24" < "M31"	True
"B2" < "A59"	False
"sect" > "Zen"	True
"BEAL TOM" < "BEALS TOM"	True

In the last expression, the fifth character in "BEAL TOM" is the blank character (ASCII code 32), whereas the fifth character in "BEALS TOM" is S (ASCII code 83). Since 32 < 83, the relational expression is true. Note that "sect" > "Zen" is true even though sect appears before Zen in the dictionary. The comparison of words that contain both upper- and lowercase letters is considered in Section 14.7.

EXAMPLE 14 Here is a program to read both upper- and lowercase words appearing in DATA lines and display those that begin with a letter D to M:

```
100 PRINT "WORDS WITH FIRST LETTER D TO M: "
110 PRINT
120 READ W$
130 WHILE W$<>"END OF LIST"
140     IF W$>="D" AND W$<"N" OR
           W$>="d" AND W$<"n" THEN PRINT TAB(5);W$
150     READ W$
160 WEND
170 DATA WHITE,BLACK,YELLOW,RED,BLUE,ORANGE,GREEN
180 DATA pink,gray,magenta,beige,brown,violet,lime
190 DATA END OF LIST
200 END
RUN

WORDS WITH FIRST LETTER D TO M:

    GREEN
    gray
    magenta
    lime
```

Each word from the data list is read into W$ and compared with the EOD tag END OF LIST. Line 140 displays words beginning with a letter from D to M or d to m.

EXAMPLE 15 Here is a program segment to display the value of WORD$ if it contains only letters of the alphabet and to display an informative message if it doesn't.

```
300 REM FLAG IS SET TO 1 IF A CHARACTER
310 REM OTHER THAN A LETTER IS FOUND IN WORD$.
320 LET FLAG=0
330 LET P=0                    'Current position in WORD$
340 LET L=LEN(WORD$)           'Length of WORD$
350 REM TEST EACH CHARACTER IN WORD$.
360 WHILE P<L AND FLAG=0
370     LET P=P+1
380     LET C$=MID$(WORD$,P,1)    'Character in position P
390     IF C$<"A" OR (C$>"Z" AND C$<"a") OR C$>"z" THEN FLAG=1
400 WEND
410 REM
420 IF FLAG=0 THEN PRINT WORD$
430 IF FLAG=1 AND C$=" " THEN PRINT WORD$;" CONTAINS A SPACE."
440 IF FLAG=1 AND C$<>" " THEN PRINT WORD$;" CONTAINS ";C$;"."
```

The WHILE loop (lines 360–400) ensures that looping continues until the characters in every position of WORD$ have been tested or a character that is not a letter is encountered. Line 380 assigns the Pth character in WORD$ to C$ and line 390 sets FLAG to 1 if this character is not a letter. (C$ is not a letter if it appears before A, between Z and a, or after z in the ordering sequence of Table 14.1.)

■ REMARK If it is important that all data processed by a program consist entirely of letters, lines 300–400 might be coded as a subroutine and used to test each data value.

EXAMPLE 16 Here is a program segment to interchange the word contents of W1$ and W2$ if they are not in alphabetical order.

```
200 REM INTERCHANGE THE CONTENTS OF W1$ and W2$
210 REM IF THEY ARE NOT IN ALPHABETICAL ORDER.
220 IF W1$>W2$ THEN SWAP W1$,W2$
230 REM   (Program continuation)
```

The contents of W1$ and W2$ are in alphabetical order if W1$≤W2$. Thus line 220 says to swap the contents of W1$ and W2$ if they are not in order. The Microsoft® statement

```
SWAP W1$,W2$
```

performs the same task as the three statements:

```
LET T$=W1$
LET W1$=W2$
LET W2$=T$
```

■ REMARK A program segment that interchanges two words when they are not in alphabetical order can be used in larger program segments (or subroutines) to alphabetize lists of any length. Before doing this you will need to understand how long lists can be stored conveniently. This topic is covered in Chapter 15.

■ 14.6 Problems

1. Show the output of each program:

a.
```
10 FOR I=1 TO 3
20    READ A$,B$
30    IF A$<=B$ THEN PRINT A$
40 NEXT I
50 DATA M,MO,A,AA,M,KANT
60 END
```

b.
```
10 FOR J=1 TO 3
20    READ C$,D$
30    IF C$>D$ THEN C$=D$
40    PRINT C$;D$
50 NEXT J
60 DATA CAT,DOG,7,10,MAN,BEAST
70 END
```

c.
```
10 LET M$="MIDDLE"
20 FOR N=1 TO 4
30    READ A$
40    IF A$>M$ AND A$<"ZZZ" THEN A$="LAST"
50    PRINT A$
60 NEXT N
70 DATA HARRY,ALICE,PAUL,ROSE
80 END
```

In Problems 2–6, write a program for each task specified.

2. Include a list of English words in DATA lines. First display those words beginning with a letter from A to M; then display the rest.
3. Write a program that contains the following DATA lines:

    ```
    800 DATA 9
    810 DATA MARIAN EVANS,JAMES PAYN,JOSEPH CONRAD
    820 DATA EMILY DICKINSON,HENRY THOREAU,JOHN PAYNE
    830 DATA JOHN FOX,MARY FREEMAN,GEORGE ELIOT
    ```

    Read the names twice. On the first pass, display only those names with a last name beginning with a letter from A to M. Display the remaining names on the second pass.
4. For any string typed at the keyboard, display THE FIRST CHARACTER IS A LETTER or THE FIRST CHARACTER IS NOT A LETTER, whichever message is correct. Allow the user to type many strings during a single program run, and stop the program when $ is typed.
5. Include a list of English words in DATA lines. Allow a user to type any two words to obtain a listing of all words alphabetically between them. Stop the program when both input words are the same. Do not use lowercase letters in the DATA lines, and instruct the user to use only uppercase letters.
6. Repeat Problem 5 but this time assume that the words are in alphabetical order and make use of this fact.

■ 14.7 BASIC Conversion Functions

A conversion function is a function that converts values from one data type to another.

The function CHR$ described in Section 10.4 is an example of a conversion function; it converts integer numeric codes to characters. In this section we describe three other conversion functions: the ASC function, which converts characters to their numeric codes, and the STR$ and VAL functions, which are used to convert between numbers and strings whose contents denote numbers. As illustrated in the examples, conversion functions provide a convenient way to code several string-related programming tasks.

The ASCII Function ASC

The ASC function converts the first character in a string to its numeric code. For example, ASC("BROOK") = 66, the numeric code for B, and ASC("brook") = 98, the code for b. When used with a one-character string, ASC converts the character to its numeric code. Thus ASC("A") = 65 and ASC("+") = 43.

You will recall that CHR$ converts each numeric code to its corresponding BASIC character. Moreover, if N denotes a valid numeric code and if A$ denotes a single BASIC character, then

ASC(CHR$(N)) = N   and   CHR$(ASC(A$)) = A$

Thus, ASC and CHR$ are inverses of each other, provided that only valid numeric codes and single-character strings are used.

EXAMPLE 17 This program illustrates the ASC function.

```
100 REM FIND THE POSITION OF A LETTER IN THE ALPHABET.
110 INPUT "TYPE A CAPITAL LETTER: ",L$
120 WHILE L$>="A" AND L$<="Z"
130    LET N=ASC(L$)-ASC("A")+1
140    PRINT "ITS POSITION IN ALPHABET IS";N
150    PRINT
160    INPUT "TYPE A CAPITAL LETTER: ",L$
170 WEND
180 PRINT "NOT A CAPITAL LETTER"
190 END
RUN

TYPE A CAPITAL LETTER: C
ITS POSITION IN ALPHABET IS 3

TYPE A CAPITAL LETTER: Z
ITS POSITION IN ALPHABET IS 26

TYPE A CAPITAL LETTER: +
NOT A CAPITAL LETTER
```

The numeric codes for the letters A, B, C, . . . , Z are 65, 66, 67, . . . , 90, respectively. Thus if L$ = "C" then ASC(L$) = 67, so that line 130 gives
N = 67 − 65 + 1 = 3.

REMARK 1 Since the numeric codes for A and Z are 65 and 90, respectively, it is correct to replace line 120 with

```
120 WHILE ASC(L$)>=65 AND ASC(L$)<=90
```

REMARK 2 To guard against a user's typing more than one character, simply change line 120 to

```
120 WHILE L$>="A" AND L$<="Z" AND LEN(L$)=1
```

It is sometimes important to convert lowercase letters to uppercase or uppercase letters to lowercase. Two such situations are as follows:

1. If a list of words containing only uppercase letters must be alphabetized, standard sorting algorithms such as those shown in Chapter 16 can be used. If the words contain both upper- and lowercase letters, the necessary comparisons can be very awkward. When sorting lists of strings, it is common practice to convert strings that must be compared to uppercase before making comparisons.

2. If an input string must be compared with other strings for equality, the comparisons are easily made if only uppercase letters are used. For example, if a program contains the lines

```
300 INPUT C$
310 IF C$="DONE" THEN 999
```

control will transfer to line 999 only if the user types *DONE*. Although it is unlikely that the user will type *doNE* or *DoNe,* it is quite likely that *Done* or *done* will be typed. By converting all lowercase letters in C$ to uppercase before the comparison C$ = "DONE" is made, the difficulty vanishes.

EXAMPLE 18 Here is a program segment to convert a single lowercase letter to uppercase.

```
200 INPUT "Type a letter: ",L$
210 IF L$>="a" AND L$<="z" AND LEN(L$)=1
      THEN L$=CHR$(ASC(L$)-32)
```

The ASCII code for each lowercase letter is 32 more than the code for the corresponding uppercase letter. Thus, if L$ is a lowercase letter, ASC(L$) − 32 gives the numeric code for the corresponding uppercase letter; hence, CHR$(ASC(L$) − 32) gives the uppercase letter itself.

The condition in line 210 ensures that L$ is changed only if its value is a single lowercase letter.

EXAMPLE 19 Here is a subroutine to change all lowercase letters in X$ to uppercase letters.

```
1000 REM SUBROUTINE: CONVERT LOWERCASE TO UPPERCASE.
1010 REM
1020 REM         X$ = STRING TO BE CONVERTED
1030 REM
1040 FOR N=1 TO LEN(X$)
1050     LET L$=MID$(X$,N,1)              'Nth letter in X$
1060     LET CODE=ASC(L$)                 'Numeric code of L$
1070     IF 97<=CODE AND CODE<=122 THEN
             MID$(X$,N,1)=CHR$(CODE-32)   'Convert to l.c.
1080 NEXT N
1090 RETURN
```

The numeric codes for the lowercase letters are 97–122. Thus line 1070 executes the statement

```
MID$(X$,N,1)=CHR$(CODE-32)
```

only if the Nth character in X$ is a lowercase letter. Since the code for each uppercase letter is 32 less than the code for the corresponding lowercase letter, the MID$ statement replaces the lowercase letter with the same letter in uppercase.

REMARK 1 If you require the user of a program to respond to the keyboard input statement

```
INPUT "NAME(type DONE when finished)";N$
```

you can use

```
LET X$=N$
GOSUB 1000
```

to transform N$ to X$ with only uppercase letters in X$. If you then compare X$ (instead of N$) with DONE, the user can respond in either lower- or uppercase letters. Although the user is not likely to type doNE, the responses Done and done are very likely and should be allowed.

REMARK 2 In many programming applications, you must include strings typed at the keyboard in your output. By using conversion subroutines such as the one in this example, you can control the exact form of the output, and you don't have to rely on the user to be consistent in how letters are typed.

The Value Function VAL

The VAL function converts a string whose contents represent a number to its numerical form. After ignoring leading blanks, it converts a string up to its first nonnumerical character into its numerical value. For example:

BASIC statement	Value assigned to A
LET A = VAL(" 29.04")	29.04
LET A = VAL("537.2 FEET")	537.2
LET A = VAL(" 1.234E2XYZ")	123.4
LET A = VAL("THREE")	0
LET A = VAL("-123")	−123
LET A = VAL("+123")	123

If no number occurs before the first nonnumerical character, VAL gives the value 0. Thus VAL("THREE") = 0 as shown.

EXAMPLE 20   This example illustrates the VAL function.

```
100 REM DETERMINE TOTAL NUMBER T OF TOOLS.
110 LET T=0
120 READ X$
130 WHILE X$<>"XXX"
140    LET C$=MID$(X$,9,3)
150    LET T=T+VAL(C$)
160    READ X$
170 WEND
180 PRINT "TOTAL NUMBER OF TOOLS: ";T
200 REM ******************
210 REM     D   A   T   A
220 REM   12345678901234567890
230 DATA HAMMERS 320 SHELF X
240 DATA PLIERS  100 SHELF L
250 DATA SAWS     57 SHELF B
260 DATA XXX
270 END
RUN

TOTAL NUMBER OF TOOLS: 477
```

Line 120 reads the first datum

HAMMERS 320 SHELF X

for X$, and line 140 assigns to C$ the string consisting of the characters in positions 9, 10, and 11 of X$. This gives C$ = "320". Line 150 converts this numeric string to the numerical value 320 and adds it to T. Line 160 reads the next datum, and the process is repeated until XXX is read.

The String Function STR$

The function STR$ reverses the process just described for VAL—it converts a numerical value to a string. If the number is positive, the string representation has a leading blank. For example, the statements

```
LET A$=STR$(-234.6)
LET B$=STR$(234.6)
```

assign the six-character string "−234.6" to A$ and the six-character string " 234.6" to B$. If you need to display a positive numerical value X without the leading blank, you can use

```
PRINT MID$(STR$(X),2)
```

For instance, the two lines

```
50 LET A=15.37 : B=10
60 PRINT MID$(STR$(A),2);"+";MID$(STR$(B),2);"=";MID$(STR$(A+B),2)
```

produce the output

```
15.37+10=25.37
```

with no blank spaces, as there would be if we had used

```
60 PRINT A;"+";B;"=";A+B
```

EXAMPLE 21   Here is a program to display the individual digits in any number, positive or negative.

```
10 INPUT "Type a number: ",X
20 LET X$=STR$(X)                            'Convert to string.
30 PRINT "The digits in ";X;"are: "
40 FOR K=2 TO LEN(X$)
50     LET D$=MID$(X$,K,1)                   'Kth position
60     IF D$<>"." THEN PRINT D$;" ";         'Display if not period.
70 NEXT K
80 END
RUN

Type a number: -102.9
The digits in -102.9 are: 1 0 2 9
```

■ 14.8 User-Defined Functions Involving String Data

Microsoft® BASIC allows you to use the DEF statement to define your own string and string-related functions. To illustrate, the statement

```
DEF FNNAME$(A$,B$)=A$+" "+B$
```

defines a function called NAME$ (also called FNNAME$) whose value for any two strings A$ and B$ is the concatenation of the strings with a separating blank. To reference (or *call*) this function, you must use the form

   FNNAME$(string1,string2)

where **string1** and **string2** denote string expressions whose values are to be substituted for A$ and B$ in the function definition. Thus, if FIRST$ = ''MAGIC'' and LAST$ = ''JOHNSON'', the statement

```
PRINT FNNAME$(FIRST$,LAST$)
```

will display

   MAGIC JOHNSON

An example of a user-defined string-related function is

```
DEF FNP(L$) = ASC(L$)-ASC("A")+1
```

This statement defines a numerical function that gives the position in the alphabet of any uppercase letter L$. (See Example 17, Section 14.7.)

The general form of user-defined functions given in Section 13.3 applies to both numerical and string functions. The following examples illustrate how some of the programming tasks considered previously might be coded by using user-defined functions.

EXAMPLE 22   Here is a program to display the names read from DATA lines in two ways, first name first and last name first.

```
100 REM ***** FUNCTION DEFINITIONS *****
110 DEF FNFIRSTLAST$(A$,B$)=B$+" "+A$
120 DEF FNLASTFIRST$(A$,B$)=A$+", "+B$
130 REM
140 PRINT "FIRST LAST",,"LAST FIRST"
150 PRINT "----------",,"----------"
160 READ C$,D$
170 WHILE C$<>"XXXX"
180     PRINT FNFIRSTLAST$(C$,D$),,FNLASTFIRST$(C$,D$)
190     READ C$,D$
200 WEND
```

```
210 DATA WORTHY,JAMES
220 DATA THOMPSON,MYCHAL
230 DATA ABDUL-JABBAR,KAREEM
240 DATA SCOTT,BYRON
250 DATA JOHNSON,MAGIC
260 DATA XXXX,ZZZZ
270 END
RUN

FIRST LAST                        LAST FIRST
----------                        ----------
JAMES WORTHY                      WORTHY, JAMES
MYCHAL THOMPSON                   THOMPSON, MYCHAL
KAREEM ABDUL-JABBAR               ABDUL-JABBAR, KAREEM
BYRON SCOTT                       SCOTT, BYRON
MAGIC JOHNSON                     JOHNSON, MAGIC
```

EXAMPLE 23   Here is a program to display the letters of the alphabet.

```
100 DEF FNLETTER$(N)=CHR$(N+ASC("A")-1)
110 REM
120 FOR P=1 TO 26
130   PRINT FNLETTER$(P)
140 NEXT P
150 END
RUN

ABCDEFGHIJKLMNOPQRSTUVWXYZ
```

To display the alphabet in lowercase letters, simply change ASC(''A'') in the function definition to ASC(''a'').

14.9 Problems

1. Show the output of each program.

   a.
   ```
   10 LET A$="31"
   20 LET B$="31"
   30 PRINT A$;"+";B$;"=";
   40 PRINT VAL(A$)+VAL(B$)
   50 END
   ```

   b.
   ```
   10 LET L$="E"
   20 LET N=ASC(L$)-ASC("A")+1
   30 PRINT L$;N
   40 END
   ```

   c.
   ```
   10 LET D$="7"
   20 LET N=ASC(D$)-ASC("0")
   30 PRINT D$;N
   40 END
   ```

   d.
   ```
   10 FOR K=48 to 58
   20   PRINT CHR$(K);
   30 NEXT K
   40 END
   ```

   e.
   ```
   10 REM W=NUMBER OF WINS
   20 REM G=NUMBER OF GAMES PLAYED
   30 LET W=42
   40 LET G=63
   50 LET B$=STR$(W)+" WINS AND "
   60 LET C$=STR$(G-W)+" LOSSES GIVES A PERCENTAGE OF "
   70 LET D$=STR$(INT(1000*W/G+0.5)/1000)
   80 PRINT B$;C$;D$
   90 END
   ```

f.
```
10 DEF FNXT$(D$)=CHR$(ASC(D$)+1)
20 FOR N=1 TO 7
30    READ X$
40    PRINT FNXT$(X$);
50 NEXT N
60 DATA B, N, Q, Q, D, B, S
70 END
```

g.
```
10 DEF FNPRE$(X$)=CHR$(ASC(X$)-1)
20 LET L$=":"
30 FOR N=1 TO 10
40    LET L$=FNPRE$(L$)
50    PRINT L$;
60 NEXT N
70 END
```

h.
```
100 DEF FNV(X$)=VAL(LEFT$(X$,2))
110 LET COUNT=0
120 FOR N=1 TO 3
130    READ A$
140    LET COUNT=COUNT+FNV(A$)
150 NEXT N
160 PRINT "COUNT: "; COUNT
200 DATA 12 DUCKS
210 DATA 15 GEESE
220 DATA 20 GULLS
230 END
```

In Problems 2–7, write a program for each task specified.

2. For any input string, display two columns. The first column is to contain the characters in the string and the second their numeric codes. Allow the user to try many strings during a single program run.

3. Input any decimal number and display its digits backward. For example, if 764.38 is typed, the output should be 83467; if −124.6 is typed, the output should be 6421.

4. Display any input string other than DONE but only after converting all lowercase letters to uppercase. Stop the program only when the user types DONE.

5. Display any word typed at the keyboard with its first letter uppercase and all other letters lowercase. However, if a character other than a letter is included, display nothing and allow the user to enter another word. Stop the program only when the user types DONE.

6. Each of the following DATA lines includes a person's name, the hours worked this week, and the hourly wage. (Line 800 is for reference only and line 899 contains the EOD tag.)

```
800 REM    123456789012345678901234567890
810 DATA   HARRY SMITHSON    36     8.25
820 DATA   SUSAN COREY       25     6.00
830 DATA   ABIGAIL ADAMS     32     6.85
840 DATA   BERT REGIS        32     7.00
850 DATA   EMERSON FOSDICK   40     9.50
860 DATA   BART BARTLETT     20     5.25
899 DATA   END-OF-DATA
```

Produce a four-column report showing the name, hours worked, hourly rate, and gross pay of each person. Time and a half is earned for all hours over 32.

7. Input two positive integers A and B for which A < B. The program should display the decimal expansion of A/B to N places where the positive integer N is also input during program execution. For example, if 1, 8, and 10 are input for A, B, and N, respectively, the output should be .1250000000.

14.10 Review True-or-False Quiz

1. If A is any number, LEN(A) will give the number of digits in A. T F
2. If LEN(X$) = LEN(Y$), then X$ = Y$. T F
3. LEN(X$ + Y$) = LEN(X$) + LEN(Y$). T F
4. B$ = LEFT$(B$,LEN(B$)). T F
5. Although it may be convenient to use the functions LEFT$ and RIGHT$, they are not necessary. The function MID$ can always be used in their place. T F
6. If X$ = "MADAM", then MID$(X$,3,3) has the value "D". T F
7. The BASIC statement

    ```
    IF A$>="A" AND A$<="Z" THEN PRINT "OK"
    ```

    will display OK whenever the first character in A$ is an uppercase letter of the alphabet. T F
8. The BASIC statement PRINT CHR$(1) will display the letter A. T F
9. ASC("Z") − ASC("A") = 25 T F
10. ASC("3") = ASC("2") + 1 T F
11. ASC(CHR$(32)) = 32 T F
12. VAL(STR$(55.23)) = 55.23 T F
13. CHR$(ASC("a") + 32) = "A" T F
14. The BASIC statement

    ```
    IF STR$(VAL(A$))=A$ THEN PRINT "OK"
    ```

    will display OK whatever the value of A$. T F
15. The BASIC statement

    ```
    IF VAL(STR$(N))=N THEN PRINT "OK"
    ```

    will display OK whatever the numerical value of N, even if N has a negative value. T F

15 Arrays

In this chapter you will encounter several programming situations for which the numerical and string variables we have been using are inadequate. To illustrate, suppose that many words are contained in a data list and you must determine counts of the number of A's, of B's, of C's, and so on, so that these counts can be used later in the program. If only the numerical variables considered to this point were available, you would need 26 different variable names, one for each of the 26 counts. If instead of words the data list contains integers in the range 1–100 and you must determine counts of the number of 1's, of 2's, of 3's, and so on, you would need 100 different variables, one for each of the 100 counts. Certainly, writing a program with 100 (or even 26) different variable names would be a long and tedious task and the program would be unwieldy.

To be useful, a programming language must provide the means for handling such problems efficiently. BASIC meets this requirement with the inclusion of the **array** data structure. As you work through the material in this chapter, you will learn how an array can be used to store an entire collection of values under a single name and how the values stored in an array are referenced simply by specifying their positions in the array. The array data structure not only provides the means to resolve the difficulties cited, but it also provides a way to simplify significantly many programming tasks involving both large and small quantities of data.

In Sections 15.1 and 15.2 we explain how data are placed into arrays and how these data are referenced, and we illustrate how arrays can be used in certain programming tasks that involve lists of numbers or lists of strings. The application of arrays in programming tasks that involve tables of values (other than lists) is taken up in Sections 15.3 and 15.5.

■ 15.1 One-Dimensional Arrays

A **one-dimensional array,** or list, is an ordered collection of items in the sense that there is a first item, a second item, and so on. For example, if you took five quizzes during a semester and received grades of 71, 83, 96, 77, and 92, you have a list in which the first grade is 71, the second grade is 83, and so forth. In mathematics we might use the following subscripted notation:

$g_1 = 71$
$g_2 = 83$
$g_3 = 96$
$g_4 = 77$
$g_5 = 92$

Since the BASIC character set does not include such subscripts, the notation is changed to the following:

G(1) = 71
G(2) = 83
G(3) = 96
G(4) = 77
G(5) = 92

We say that the *name* of the array is G, that G(1), G(2), G(3), G(4), and G(5) are **subscripted variables,** and that 1, 2, 3, 4, and 5 are the *subscripts* of G. G(1) is read **G sub 1,** and in general G(N) is read **G sub N**. G(1), G1, and G are all different variables and can be used in the same program; the computer has no problem distinguishing among them, even though we might.

The array G can be visualized as follows:

	1	2	3	4	5
G	71	83	96	77	92

The name of the array appears to the left, the subscripts are above each entry, and the entries are inside, just below their subscripts. Names that are acceptable for simple variables are also admissible array names.

To declare to the computer that your program will use the subscripted variables G(1) through G(5), you would include the DIM (for **dimension**) statement

```
DIM G(5)
```

so that it is encountered before any of the subscripted variables are referenced. If instead you include the statement

```
DIM G(100)
```

your program can reference any or all of the subscripted variables G(0) through G(100). The DIM statement is explained in greater detail in Section 15.2.

The value of a subscripted variable—that is, an entry in an array—is referenced in a program just as values of simple variables (variables with no subscripts) are referenced. For example, the two LET statements

```
LET G(1)=71
LET G(2)=G(1)+12
```

assign 71 to the subscripted variable G(1) and 83 to G(2); that is, 71 and 83 are assigned as the first and second entries of array G. To allow the user to enter a value for G(1) at the keyboard, you can use the statement

```
INPUT G(1)
```

The principal advantage in using subscripted variables is that the subscripts can be specified by using variables or other numerical expressions, rather than just integer constants. For instance, if N has the value 3, then G(N) refers to G(3), G(2 * N) refers to G(6), and G(2 * N − 1) refers to G(5). It is common practice to refer to *subscript expressions* such as N, 2 * N, and 2 * N − 1 as the subscripts, even though the actual subscripts are the integer values of these expressions.

EXAMPLE 1   Here is a program segment to assign values to G(1), G(2), G(3), G(4), and G(5).

```
100 DIM G(5)
110 FOR J=1 TO 5
120     READ G(J)
130 NEXT J
140 DATA 71,83,96,77,92
```

On each pass through the loop, the index J of the loop serves as the subscript. The first time through the loop, J has the value 1, so line 120 assigns the first data value 71 to G(1). Similarly, G(2) through G(5) are assigned their respective values during the remaining four passes through the loop.

■ **REMARK 1** To allow the user to enter the five array values at the keyboard, you can use

```
110 FOR J=1 TO 5
120     INPUT G(J)
130 NEXT J
```

■ **REMARK 2** Having assigned five values to array G—that is, to the subscripted variables G(1) through G(5)—you can process these values just as you process any other numerical variables. For instance, if you need to find and display the sum of the five entries in G, you can continue the program by writing

```
150 LET SUM=0
160 FOR J=1 TO 5
170     LET SUM=SUM+G(J)
180 NEXT J
190 PRINT "SUM OF THE 5 QUIZ SCORES: ";SUM
```

■ **REMARK 3** Note that we use the same control variable (J) for the FOR loops beginning at lines 110 and 160. Although we could have used different control variables, there is no good reason for doing so. There is reason, however, for using the same one. In each loop, J serves the *same* purpose—it provides subscripts for array G; hence the program will be easier to read if the *same* name is used.

□

Just as with simple variables, values assigned to subscripted variables are retained until they are changed in another programming line. Thus, individual entries in an array can be changed without affecting the rest of the array. For instance, if G has been assigned values as in Example 1

	1	2	3	4	5
G	71	83	96	77	92

the statement

```
200 LET G(1)=G(5)
```

will assign the value 92 of G(5) to G(1) but will not change G(5). The modified array will be as follows [note that the previous value 71 of G(1) is lost]:

	1	2	3	4	5
G	92	83	96	77	92

EXAMPLE 2 Here is a program segment that modifies each entry of the array G and then stores the resulting values in a second array M, but in the reverse order.

```
200 REM INCREASE ARRAY G ENTRIES BY 2.
210 FOR K=1 TO 5
220     LET G(K)=G(K)+2
230 NEXT K
240 REM CREATE ARRAY M.
250 DIM M(5)
260 FOR K=1 TO 5
270     LET M(K)=G(6-K)
280 NEXT K
```

Let's assume that before the execution of this program segment, values are read into array G as in Example 1. Pictorially,

	1	2	3	4	5
G	71	83	96	77	92

The first FOR loop adds 2 to each entry in G:

	1	2	3	4	5
G	73	85	98	79	94

The second FOR loop creates a new array M. For K = 1, the assignment statement is LET M(1) = G(5); for K = 2, LET M(2) = G(4); and so on. Thus, after execution of this second loop, M is as follows:

	1	2	3	4	5
M	94	79	98	85	73

■ REMARK 1 The two DIM statements

```
100 DIM G(5)
250 DIM M(5)
```

can be combined into the single statement

```
100 DIM G(5),M(5)
```

■ REMARK 2 Creating new arrays that are modifications of existing arrays is a common programming task. In this example, the entries in the array M are a rearrangement of the entries in array G. Note that the creation of array M by the second FOR loop in no way modifies the existing array G.

■ REMARK 3 Although it is common practice to refer to the symbols G(K), M(K), and G(6 − K) as variables, remember that the actual variable names are G(1), G(2), G(3), and so on. Each time the LET statements are executed, K has a particular value indicating which of these variables is being referenced.

The subscript expression that appears within the parentheses to indicate the position in an array (K and 6 − K in Example 2 and J in Example 1) can be any BASIC numerical expression. Thus the following are all admissible:

```
A(7)       X(I+1)
B(7+3/2)   Z(100-N)
```

When the computer encounters a subscript, the subscript is evaluated; if it is not an integer, it is rounded to the nearest integer. The *smallest* subscript allowed in Microsoft® BASIC is zero. A negative subscript causes a fatal error condition, producing the diagnostic

```
Illegal function call in ln
```

The *largest* subscript allowed is the subscript specified in the DIM statement. A subscript larger than that specified also causes a fatal error condition, this time producing the diagnostic

    Subscript out of range in **ln**

When storing a list of numbers in array A, it is common practice to store them beginning in A(1) and not A(∅). Programs are more easily understood if the first entry in a list is stored in A(1), the second in A(2), and the Nth in A(N). Moreover, if you do this then A(∅) can be used for some other purpose—for instance, in Remark 2 of Example 1, we could have used G(∅) rather than SUM to store the sum of the entries in positions 1, 2, 3, 4, and 5 of array G. If you do not use zero as a subscript, you can use the statement

    OPTION BASE 1

to specify 1 as the smallest subscript. If you do this, the OPTION BASE statement must be executed before any arrays are used.

BASIC allows string arrays for storing strings as well as numerical arrays for storing numbers. The only difference is that string array names must end with a $. The use of subscripts is the same as for numerical arrays.

EXAMPLE 3   **Here is a program segment to read string values into the string array DAY$.**

```
100 DIM DAY$(7)
110 FOR N=1 TO 7
120    READ DAY$(N)
130 NEXT N
140 DATA SUNDAY, MONDAY, TUESDAY, WEDNESDAY
150 DATA THURSDAY, FRIDAY, SATURDAY
```

When N is 1, the first datum SUNDAY is read into DAY$(1), when N is 2, MONDAY is read into DAY$(2), and so on. At this point we can use the string values stored in DAY$—that is, the values of the subscripted variables DAY$(1) through DAY$(7)—just as the values of any string variables can be used. For instance, if we follow line 150 with the statements

```
160 INPUT "ENTER DAY OF WEEK (1-7)";D
170 PRINT "YOU SELECTED ";DAY$(D);"."
```

and later enter 7 in response to the INPUT statement, the computer will display

```
ENTER DAY OF WEEK (1-7)? 7
YOU SELECTED SATURDAY.
```

■ **REMARK 1**   Since the variable D in lines 160 and 170 represents a day of the week (1–7), we could have used the more descriptive name DAY. Had we done this, line 170 would have been written

```
170 PRINT "YOU SELECTED ";DAY$(DAY);"."
```

The computer has no difficulty with the expression DAY$(DAY). It correctly interprets DAY as the name of a simple numerical variable whose value gives the position (subscript) of an entry in the string array DAY$. Thus, with DAY = 7, DAY$(DAY) refers to DAY$(7).

■ **REMARK 2**   The array DAY$ can be pictured as shown previously for array G:

	1	2	3	4	5	6	7
DAY$	SUNDAY	MONDAY	TUESDAY	WEDNESDAY	THURSDAY	FRIDAY	SATURDAY

There is no special significance in the placement of the array entries along a line. You may find it more convenient to think of the array as follows:

DAY$

1	SUNDAY
2	MONDAY
3	TUESDAY
4	WEDNESDAY
5	THURSDAY
6	FRIDAY
7	SATURDAY

The two diagrams contain the same information.

In each of Examples 1–3, we used a FOR loop to read values into an array. If you know exactly how many values are to be stored in an array, a FOR loop provides the most convenient way to do it. Thus, if a table of values to be read into one or more arrays appears in DATA statements and if the DATA are preceded by a data count, you would read the count into a simple numerical variable and use its value as the terminal value of a FOR loop that reads the data into the array or arrays.

The next example illustrates a common method used to store data in arrays when the data are given in DATA lines that end with an EOD tag rather than being preceded with a count.

EXAMPLE 4 Here is a program segment to read a table of flight numbers and arrival times into arrays. The data are presented in DATA lines terminated with the EOD tag XXX.

```
100 REM LOAD FLIGHT NUMBERS AND ARRIVAL TIMES.
110 REM
120 REM    COUNT     NUMBER OF FLIGHTS
130 REM    FLIGHT$   ARRAY OF FLIGHT NUMBERS
140 REM    ARR$      ARRAY OF ARRIVAL TIMES
150 REM
160 DIM FLIGHT$(50),ARR$(50)
170 LET COUNT=1
180 READ FLIGHT$(COUNT),ARR$(COUNT)
190 WHILE FLIGHT$(COUNT)<>"XXX" AND COUNT<50
200     LET COUNT=COUNT+1
210     READ FLIGHT$(COUNT),ARR$(COUNT)
220 WEND
230 REM
240 REM SUBTRACT ONE TO GET ACTUAL DATA COUNT.
250 LET COUNT=COUNT-1
260 REM
270 (Program continuation)
      .
      .
      .
```

```
5000 REM ********************
5010 REM * ARRIVAL TIME DATA *
5020 REM ********************
5030 REM
5040 REM FLIGHT, ARRIVAL TIME
5050 DATA 53,  "8:15 AM"
5060 DATA 172, "9:20 AM"
5070 DATA 122, "11:30 AM"
5080 DATA 62,  "2:20 PM"
5090 DATA 303, "4:45 PM"
5100 DATA 291, "6:15 PM"
5999 DATA XXX, XXX
```

The variable COUNT provides the successive subscripts 1, 2, 3, and so on, for the statement

```
READ FLIGHT$(COUNT), ARR$(COUNT)
```

Each time values are read into the arrays FLIGHT$ and ARR$ by this statement, the FLIGHT$ value is compared with the EOD tag XXX. If FLIGHT$(COUNT) is not XXX (and if 50 flight numbers have not yet been read), the WHILE loop is entered: line 200 increases COUNT by 1 and line 210 reads the next flight number and arrival time into the next array positions. When the EOD tag is read, we have FLIGHT$(COUNT) = "XXX" and the WHILE statement transfers control to the line following WEND. At this point, COUNT, FLIGHT$, and ARR$ are as follows (notice that the EOD tag XXX is in position COUNT of array FLIGHT$):

COUNT = 7   (One more than the number of flights)

	FLIGHT$	**ARR$**
1	53	8:15 AM
2	172	9:20 AM
3	122	11:30 AM
4	62	2:20 PM
5	303	4:45 PM
6	291	6:15 PM
7	XXX	XXX

Line 250 then decreases COUNT by 1 so that COUNT specifies the number of values read into each array, exclusive of the EOD tag XXX. In any subsequent processing of arrays FLIGHT$ and ARR$, we can use COUNT to denote their length. For example, to display a simple list of flight numbers, we could use the FOR loop

```
FOR F=1 TO COUNT
   PRINT FLIGHT$(F)
NEXT F
```

REMARK 1 Since line 160 specifies that the largest subscript allowed for FLIGHT$ and ARR$ is 50 and since XXX is stored in both FLIGHT$ and ARR$, the program can handle only up to 49 flights. If data for 50 or more flights are included in DATA lines, the program will read the data for the first 50 flights and simply ignore the others; it will never get to the EOD tag. Moreover, the user will not be aware that this has happened. If we change line 250 to

```
250 IF FLIGHT$(COUNT)="XXX"
       THEN COUNT=COUNT-1
       ELSE PRINT "TOO MUCH DATA!" : END
```

any attempt to include more data than the program is designed to handle will cause the computer (during a trial run) to halt after displaying the message

```
TOO MUCH DATA!
```

The user would understand this message or would seek help from a programmer.

■ **REMARK 2** The quotation marks used in the DATA statements are required since Microsoft® BASIC uses the colon (:) as a separator when two or more BASIC statements are included in a single programming line.

■ 15.2 The DIM Statement (Declaring Arrays)

As illustrated in the preceding examples, the DIM statement specifies the names and dimensions (sizes) of arrays. An array for which only one subscript is specified (variables with more than one subscript are considered in Section 15.5) is called a **one-dimensional** array. Thus, the statement

```
DIM G(5),DAY$(7)
```

specifies a one-dimensional numerical array G with 5 as the largest allowed subscript and a one-dimensional string array DAY$ with 7 as the largest subscript. It is common terminology to say that the arrays G and DAY$ have been **declared,** or that they have been **dimensioned.**

The general form of the DIM statement, as it applies to one-dimensional arrays (lists), is

ln DIM **a(e),b(f), . . . ,c(g)**

where **a,b,c** denote array names and **e,f,g** denote positive-integer constants or, as will be explained shortly, numerical expressions. The following points concerning the use of arrays should be understood:

1. BASIC requires that you use DIM statements to declare only those arrays whose subscripts exceed 10. If any of the subscripted variables A(1) through A(10) is referenced in a program that does not declare A in a DIM statement, BASIC, by default, will declare A as if the program included the statement

```
DIM A(10)
```

Thus, the DIM statements in Examples 1–3 are not actually required. It is an excellent programming practice, however, to use DIM statements to declare all arrays. Doing so will make your programs easier to read, since DIM statements explicitly establish which variable names represent arrays and indicate their sizes.

2. A DIM statement must be executed before any reference is made to the array (or arrays) being dimensioned. The customary practice is to place DIM statements near the beginning of a program unless they are used for dynamic storage allocation (see point 5, below).

3. When a numerical array is dimensioned, either explicitly with a DIM statement or implicitly by usage, all of its entries are assigned an initial value of zero. Similarly, all entries of a string array are assigned an initial value of the null string.

4. If an array has been dimensioned, either explicitly with a DIM statement or implicitly by usage, it cannot be dimensioned again without first erasing the original array from memory with an ERASE statement. For example, if the array A had been dimensioned early in a program by the statement

```
100 DIM A(300)
```

you could dimension A later in the program to have length 100 by using

```
500 ERASE A
510 DIM A(100)
```

Any attempt to redimension an array without first erasing it from memory will produce the diagnostic

Duplicate definition in **ln**

and program execution will terminate.

5. Microsoft® BASIC allows you to use numerical expressions other than constants to specify dimensions for arrays. This capability, called **dynamic storage allocation,** means that sizes for arrays can be determined during program execution. For example, if a list of words included in DATA lines is to be stored in an array WORDS$, you can precede the data list with a word count and use the statements

```
READ COUNT
DIM WORDS$(COUNT)
```

to declare the array WORDS$. You can then be sure that WORDS$ is just the right size, provided only that the word count is correct. Dynamic storage allocation can also be used if you end the data list with an EOD tag rather than precede it with a word count. Indeed, if the EOD tag is XXX, you can use a program segment such as the following, first to count the words and then to declare and read the words into the array WORDS$:

```
100 REM ********************
110 REM DETERMINE WORD COUNT.
120 REM
130 LET COUNT=0
140 READ W$
150 WHILE W$<>"XXX"
160     LET COUNT=COUNT+1
170     READ W$
180 WEND
190 RESTORE
200 REM **************************
210 REM READ DATA INTO ARRAY WORDS$.
220 REM
230 DIM WORDS$(COUNT)
240 FOR N=1 TO COUNT
250     READ WORDS$(N)
260 NEXT N
```

6. If you do not use dynamic storage allocation as explained in point 5, you must see to it that your DIM statements specify array sizes large enough to accommodate all the values to be stored in the arrays. Thus, if you know in advance that your program will never be required to read more than 1,000 values into an array A, the statement

```
DIM A(1000)
```

will suffice. This statement, however, actually reserves space in the computer's memory for the thousand variables A(1) to A(1000); that is, your program will tie up this memory space whether or not a particular run of the program uses it. This means that you should not only specify array sizes that are large enough, but should keep them as small as possible.

7. The numerical expressions **e, f,** and **g** shown in the general form are usually positive integer constants or simple variables whose values are positive integers. If a noninteger value is specified, it will be rounded to obtain an integer dimension.

At the outset of this chapter we mentioned that arrays can be used effectively in programming tasks that require us to determine many counts. The following example illustrates this use of arrays.

EXAMPLE 5

A list of integers, all between 1 and 100, is contained in DATA lines. Let's write a program to determine how many of each integer are included. We assume that 9999 terminates the list.

PROBLEM ANALYSIS

We must determine 100 counts: the number of 1s, the number of 2s, and so on. Let's use C(1), C(2), . . . , C(100) to store these counts. Each value appearing in the DATA lines must be read to determine which of the 100 integers it is. If it is 87, then C(87) must be increased by 1; if it is 24, then C(24) must be increased by 1. Using X to denote the value being read, we can write the following algorithm:

THE ALGORITHM

    a. Initialize: C(N) = 0 for N = 1 to 100.
    b. Read a value for X.
    c. Repeat the following until X = 9999.
        c1. Add 1 to C(X).
        c2. Read next value for X.
    d. Display the results and stop.

In the following program we display two columns showing N and the corresponding count C(N) but suppress the output if C(N) = 0—that is, if N is not in the given list.

THE PROGRAM

```
100 REM INITIALIZE COUNTERS.
110 DIM C(100)
120 FOR N=1 TO 100
130     LET C(N)=0
140 NEXT N
150 REM READ X AND ADD 1 TO C(X) UNTIL
160 REM THE EOD TAG 9999 IS ENCOUNTERED.
170 READ X
180 WHILE X<>9999
190     LET C(X)=C(X)+1
200     READ X
210 WEND
220 REM DISPLAY THE FREQUENCY TABLE.
230 PRINT "DATUM", "FREQUENCY"
240 PRINT "-----", "---------"
250 FOR N=1 TO 100
260     IF C(N)>0 THEN PRINT N,C(N)
270 NEXT N
500 DATA 80,80,80,80,80,60,60,50
510 DATA 50,50,45,45,50,50,50,32
998 DATA 9999
999 END
RUN
```

DATUM	FREQUENCY
32	1
45	2
50	6
60	2
80	5

15.3 Table Processing

Several of the examples considered in previous chapters involved processing data given in tabular form. In each case, we used READ statements to read the data into simple variables for processing and RESTORE statements to allow us to reuse the data. Although this method can be used for many programming tasks, there are times when the method is inadequate, or at least very inconvenient. The examples in this section illustrate how the array data structure sometimes can provide a useful and convenient alternative to this method of processing tabular data.

EXAMPLE 6

The hourly pay rate of each employee in a certain business is determined by the employee's job classification. We are to produce a report showing the week's gross pay for each employee.

PROBLEM ANALYSIS

We need more information. We need to know the name, job classification, and hours worked for each employee as well as the hourly pay rates for the job classifications.

Let's assume this information is given to us in two tables as shown and that time and a half is paid for all hours over 32.

Hours-Worked Table

Name	Job class	Hours
Jane Arcus	3	40
Jonathan Beard	6	45
Sandra Carlson	3	32
Susan Dahlberg	1	24
Thomas Farrell	5	29
Heidi Graves	1	40
.	.	.
.	.	.
.	.	.

Hourly Rate Table

Job class	Rate of pay
1	$ 4.00
2	4.75
3	5.75
4	7.00
5	8.50
6	10.75

To produce the required report, we must look up the job class and hours worked for each employee from the Hours-Worked Table and the corresponding rate of pay from the Hourly Rate Table. There is a difference in how these two tables should be used. In particular, the Hourly Rate Table is needed each time the week's pay for an employee is being calculated—that is, each time we process a line from the Hours-Worked Table. Thus, the data in the Hourly Rate Table must be accessed many times whereas the data in the Hours-Worked Table is needed only once. For this reason, we will read the Hourly Rate Table into an array. If we name this array PAYRATE and if JOB denotes a job class (1 through 6), the rate of pay corresponding to job class JOB will be PAYRATE(JOB).

The discussion in the preceding paragraph allows us to give a precise description of the input data and how they should be organized. (The output is simply a two-column report showing the name and gross pay for each employee.)

Input: Six hourly pay rates corresponding to job classes 1–6.
The name, job class, and hours worked for each employee.

All input data will be included in DATA statements. Since the Hourly Rate Table will be read into an array for use in determining the week's pay for each employee, the six hourly rate amounts should be first, before the data given in the Hours-Worked Table. To avoid having to count the employees, we will end this latter table with XXX,0,0, and use XXX to detect the end of the data. Since each employee's name, job class, and hours worked will be read and immediately processed, there is no need to read these data into arrays.

At this point, it should not be difficult to write an algorithm for the task specified in the problem statement. To keep our algorithm concise, we will use these descriptive variable names:

```
PAYRATE   = array of hourly rates for job classes 1–6
EMPNAME$  = an employee's name
JOB       = job classification for EMPNAME$
HOURS     = hours worked this week by EMPNAME$
GROSSPAY  = week's gross pay for EMPNAME$
```

THE ALGORITHM

    a. Read hourly rates for job classes 1–6 into array PAYRATE.
    b. Display report title and column headings.
    c. Read EMPNAME$, JOB, and HOURS.
    d. Repeat the following as long as (while) EMPNAME$ is not XXX:
        d1. Calculate GROSSPAY for EMPNAME$.

260 Chapter 15 Arrays

      d2. Display EMPNAME$ and GROSSPAY.
      d3. Read EMPNAME$, JOB, and HOURS.
   e. Stop

Note that Step (d1) does not explain how to calculate GROSSPAY. Recalling that time and a half is paid for all hours over 32, we can code this step as follows:

```
LET RATE=PAYRATE(JOB)
IF HOURS<=32
   THEN GROSSPAY=HOURS*RATE
   ELSE GROSSPAY=32*RATE+(HOURS-32)*1.5*RATE
```

THE PROGRAM

```
100 REM ********************************************
110 REM * LOAD HOURLY RATE TABLE INTO ARRAY PAYRATE *
120 REM ********************************************
130 REM
140 DIM PAYRATE(6)
150 FOR JOBCLASS=1 TO 6
160    READ PAYRATE(JOBCLASS)
170 NEXT JOBCLASS
180 REM
190 REM ********************************************
200 REM * DISPLAY REPORT TITLE AND COLUMN HEADERS.  *
210 REM ********************************************
220 REM
230 PRINT  "SALARIES FOR THE CURRENT WEEK"
240 PRINT
250 PRINT  "EMPLOYEE'S NAME        GROSS PAY"
255 LET F$="\              \        ####.##"
260 PRINT
270 REM ********************************************
280 REM * READ HOURS-WORKED DATA TO DETERMINE AND   *
290 REM * DISPLAY NAMES AND GROSS SALARY AMOUNTS.   *
300 REM ********************************************
310 REM
320 READ EMPNAME$,JOB,HOURS
330 WHILE EMPNAME$<>"XXX"
340    LET RATE=PAYRATE(JOB)
350    IF HOURS<=32
          THEN GROSSPAY=HOURS*RATE
          ELSE GROSSPAY=32*RATE+(HOURS-32)*1.5*RATE
360    PRINT USING F$;EMPNAME$,GROSSPAY
370    READ EMPNAME$,JOB,HOURS
380 WEND
390 REM
400 REM ------------------------------------
410 REM    DATA FROM HOURLY RATE TABLE
420 REM
430 DATA 4.00, 4.75, 5.75, 7.00, 8.50, 10.75
440 REM
450 REM ------------------------------------
460 REM    DATA FROM HOURS-WORKED TABLE
470 REM
480 REM NAME, JOB CLASS, HOURS WORKED
490 DATA JANE ARCUS,3,40
500 DATA JONATHAN BEARD,6,45
510 DATA SANDRA CARLSON,3,32
520 DATA SUSAN DAHLBERG,1,24
530 DATA THOMAS FARRELL,5,29
540 DATA HEIDI GRAVES,1,40
550 DATA XXX,0,0
560 END
RUN

SALARIES FOR THE CURRENT WEEK
```

```
            EMPLOYEE'S NAME        GROSS PAY

            JANE ARCUS              253.00
            JONATHAN BEARD          553.63
            SANDRA CARLSON          184.00
            SUSAN DAHLBERG           96.00
            THOMAS FARRELL          246.50
            HEIDI GRAVES            176.00
```

■ **REMARK** It is worth noting that we decided on the organization of the input data by considering how the data were to be used, not by the form in which the data were given. Specifically, we decided to store the Hourly Rate Table in an array because the information it contains must be used each time an employee's pay is to be calculated. Also, we decided not to store the Hours-Worked Table in arrays because the information it contains needs to be processed only once, in the order given. In other programming tasks involving exactly the same data, you may find it convenient to use a different organization of these data. To illustrate, suppose you must produce listings of employees whose job class numbers are typed at the keyboard. If you read the entire Hours-Worked Table into arrays EMP$, JOBCLASS, and HRS and use the simple variable CLASSNUM to store the job class number typed at the keyboard, it is a simple matter to produce the required listing. The following subroutine does this:

```
1000 REM SUBROUTINE TO LIST ALL EMPLOYEES
1010 REM WITH A SPECIFIED JOB CLASS NUMBER.
1020 REM
1030 REM    CLASSNUM = THE SPECIFIED JOB CLASS NUMBER
1040 REM    EMP$     = ARRAY OF THE EMPLOYEE NAMES
1050 REM    JOBCLASS = CORRESPONDING ARRAY OF JOB CLASSES
1060 REM    COUNT    = COUNT OF ALL EMPLOYEES
1070 PRINT
1080 PRINT "LIST OF EMPLOYEES IN JOB CLASS";CLASSNUM;":"
1090 FOR N=1 TO COUNT
1100    IF JOBCLASS(N)=CLASSNUM THEN PRINT EMP$(N)
1110 NEXT N
1120 RETURN
```

□

Each time the program in Example 6 references the array PAYRATE, it does so by specifying a position in the array. This happens because the integers 1 through 6 are used to specify both job class numbers and the positions of the corresponding pay rate in the array—PAYRATE(1) is the pay rate for job class 1, PAYRATE(2) is the pay rate for job class 2, and so on. Tabular data, however, are not often so conveniently stored in arrays. In most programming applications, two or more arrays are used to store a single table, and the positions of the table items that are needed must be determined by searching one or more of these arrays for a specified value or values (called **search arguments**). The remark following the program of Example 6 illustrates the use of multiple arrays to store a single table; we used three arrays—EMP$, JOBCLASS, and HRS—to store the Hourly Rate Table. Moreover, the table was searched for all employees with job class number CLASSNUM (the *search argument*) by comparing the value of CLASSNUM with each entry (or *table argument*) in the array JOBCLASS. The program in the next example further illustrates the use of multiple arrays to store a single table. The program also shows how a search argument can be used in a table look-up application.

EXAMPLE 7 Here is a program to display information about incoming flights whose flight numbers are entered at the keyboard. The REM statements in lines 130, 280, and 290 describe the purpose and action of the program.

```
100 REM ------ AIRLINE FLIGHT INFORMATION PROGRAM ------
110 REM
120 REM ********************************************************
130 REM *      LOAD INCOMING FLIGHT DATA INTO ARRAYS.          *
140 REM ********************************************************
```

```
150 REM
160 REM        COUNT         COUNT OF INCLUDED FLIGHTS
170 REM        FLIGHTNUM     ARRAY OF FLIGHT NUMBERS
180 REM        ORIGIN$       ARRAY SHOWING ORIGINATION POINTS
190 REM        ARRIVE$       ARRAY OF ARRIVAL TIMES
200 REM
210 DIM FLIGHTNUM(50),ORIGIN$(50),ARRIVE$(50)
220 READ COUNT
230 FOR F=1 TO COUNT
240    READ FLIGHTNUM(F),ORIGIN$(F),ARRIVE$(F)
250 NEXT F
260 REM
270 REM ********************************************
280 REM * DISPLAY AVAILABLE FLIGHT INFORMATION FOR *
290 REM * FLIGHT NUMBERS ENTERED AT THE KEYBOARD.  *
300 REM ********************************************
310 REM
320 INPUT "FLIGHT NUMBER (0 WHEN DONE)";FLIGHT
330 WHILE FLIGHT<>0
340    REM --- SEARCH ARRAY FLIGHTNUM FOR FLIGHT ---
350    LET F=1
360    WHILE FLIGHTNUM(F)<>FLIGHT AND F<COUNT
370       LET F=F+1
380    WEND
390    IF FLIGHTNUM(F)<>FLIGHT THEN
          PRINT FLIGHT;" IS NOT A LISTED FLIGHT NUMBER." :
          GOTO 430
400    PRINT "AVAILABLE INFORMATION ON FLIGHT";FLIGHT
410    PRINT "   ORIGINATION POINT:        ";ORIGIN$(F)
420    PRINT "   EXPECTED TIME OF ARRIVAL: ";ARRIVE$(F)
430    PRINT
440    INPUT "FLIGHT NUMBER (0 WHEN DONE)";FLIGHT
450 WEND
460 END
500 REM --------------------------------------------
510 REM              D   A   T   A
520 REM --------------------------------------------
530 REM        FLIGHT INFORMATION TABLE - INCOMING
540 REM
550 REM FLIGHT COUNT FOLLOWS - UP TO 50 ALLOWED.
560 DATA 6
570 REM FLIGHTNUMBER,POINT OF ORIGIN,ARRIVAL TIME
575 REM
580 DATA 53,MIAMI,"8:15 AM"
590 DATA 172,ATLANTA,"9:20 AM"
600 DATA 122,NEW YORK,"11:30 AM"
610 DATA 62,MONTREAL,"2:20 PM"
620 DATA 303,HOUSTON,"4:45 PM"
630 DATA 291,CHICAGO,"6:15 PM"
```

The following display was produced when we ran this program with the keyboard input values 62, 281 (an incorrect flight number), and 291:

```
FLIGHT NUMBER (0 WHEN DONE)? 62
AVAILABLE INFORMATION ON FLIGHT 62
   ORIGINATION POINT:        MONTREAL
   EXPECTED TIME OF ARRIVAL: 2:20 PM

FLIGHT NUMBER (0 WHEN DONE)? 281
 281  IS NOT A LISTED FLIGHT NUMBER.

FLIGHT NUMBER (0 WHEN DONE)? 291
AVAILABLE INFORMATION ON FLIGHT 291
   ORIGINATION POINT:        CHICAGO
   EXPECTED TIME OF ARRIVAL: 6:15 PM

FLIGHT NUMBER (0 WHEN DONE)? 0
```

- REMARK The loop in lines 360–380 compares the input value FLIGHT (the search argument) with the successive table arguments FLIGHTNUM(1), FLIGHTNUM(2), and so on, until a match is found or the last entry of array FLIGHTNUM is reached, whichever occurs first. Since FLIGHT is compared with the entries of array FLIGHTNUM *in order*, that is, *sequentially*, this method of searching an array for a specified value is called a **sequential search.** If long lists must be searched, a sequential search can be very time-consuming. In Section 16.2 we describe the significantly faster *binary search* that can be used to search lists whose entries are ordered as explained in Chapter 16.

■ 15.4 Problems

1. Show the output of each program.

   a.
   ```
   10 DIM X(4)
   20 LET I=2
   30 READ X(I),X(1)
   40 FOR I=1 TO 2
   50    PRINT X(I)
   60 NEXT I
   70 DATA 4,5,7,3
   80 END
   ```

   b.
   ```
   10 DIM X$(6)
   20 LET J=1
   30 READ X$(J)
   40 FOR I=1 TO 3
   50    READ X$(I+1)
   60    PRINT X$(I);" ";
   70 NEXT I
   80 DATA TO,BE,OR,NOT,TO BE
   90 END
   ```

   c.
   ```
   100 DIM M(7)
   110 READ J
   120 FOR J=5 TO 7
   130    READ M(J)
   140 NEXT J
   150 READ B,C
   160 FOR K=B TO C
   170    PRINT M(K);
   180 NEXT K
   190 DATA 2,9,8,4,6,6,3
   200 END
   ```

   d.
   ```
   100 DIM A$(4)
   110 FOR J=1 TO 4
   120    READ X$
   130    IF X$<>"HAT" THEN A$(J)=X$
   140 NEXT J
   150 FOR J=1 TO 4 STEP 2
   160    PRINT A$(J);
   170 NEXT J
   180 DATA IRAN,TOP,GATE,HAT
   190 END
   ```

   e.
   ```
   100 READ C
   110 DIM F$(C),L$(C)
   120 FOR K=1 TO C
   130    READ F$(K),L$(K)
   140 NEXT K
   150 FOR K=C TO 1 STEP -1
   160    PRINT L$(K);", ";F$(K)
   170 NEXT K
   180 DATA 4
   190 DATA JOHN,CASH,ELTON,JOHN
   200 DATA JOHN,DENVER
   210 DATA JOHN,PAYCHECK
   220 END
   ```

   f.
   ```
   100 DIM A$(5)
   110 FOR I=1 TO 5
   120    READ A$(I)
   130 NEXT I
   140 FOR I=1 TO 5
   150    LET N=LEN(A$(I))
   160    LET P=1
   ```

```
170     WHILE MID$(A$(K),P,1)<>"S" AND P<N :
            LET P=P+1 :
        WEND
180     IF MID$(A$(I),P,1)="S" THEN PRINT A$(I)
190 NEXT I
200 DATA SAM,HARRY,JESS,SANDI,OLIVER
210 END
```

2. Explain what is wrong with each of the following.

   a.
   ```
   10 FOR A=9 TO 12
   20     READ M(A)
   30     PRINT M(A);
   40 NEXT A
   50 DATA 7,3,5,2,9,1,-3,-2
   60 END
   ```

   b.
   ```
   10 READ A(1),A(2),A(3)
   20 PRINT A(3),A(2),A(1)
   30 DIM A(2)
   40 READ A(1),A(2)
   50 PRINT A(2),A(1)
   60 DATA 1,2,3,4,5
   70 END
   ```

   c.
   ```
   300 REM PROGRAM SEGMENT TO REVERSE THE
   310 REM ORDER IN AN ARRAY L$ OF LENGTH 10
   320 FOR K=1 TO 10
   330     LET L$(11-K)=L$(K)
   340 NEXT K
   ```

   d.
   ```
   400 REM PROGRAM SEGMENT TO FIND THE LARGEST
   410 REM NUMBER L IN AN ARRAY A OF LENGTH 10.
   420 FOR J=1 TO 10
   430     IF L<A(J) THEN A(J)=L
   440 NEXT J
   ```

In Problems 3–8, write a program for each task specified. In each program use a single numerical array or a single string array.

3. Input a list of numbers of undetermined length, and display the values in reverse order. Use an EOD tag to terminate the input list. (You may assume that the input list will contain fewer than 20 numbers.)
4. Input a list of words of undetermined length, and display them in reverse order. Use an EOD tag to terminate the input list. (You may assume that the input will contain fewer than 20 words.)
5. First read a list of words from DATA lines into a string array. Then allow the user to enter letters, one at a time, to obtain a list of those words that begin with the letter typed. The program should halt only when the user types DONE.
6. Input five numbers into an array B as follows: assign the first value to B(1) and B(10), the second to B(2) and B(9), and so on. Then display the array B and input five more values in the same way. Continue this process until the user types 0. When this happens, stop program execution with no further output.
7. Input a list of numbers of undetermined length into array A and display three columns as follows: Column 1 contains the input list in the order typed; Column 2 contains them in reverse order; and Column 3 contains the averages of the corresponding numbers in Columns 1 and 2. You may assume that the input list will contain fewer than 20 numbers.
8. Produce the following designs. Begin each program by reading the needed strings A, B, C, and so on, into an array from DATA lines. Use the arrays to produce the designs.

   a.
   ```
   A
   BB
   CCC
   DDDD
   EEEEE
   FFFFFF
   ```

   b.
   ```
   ABCDEFG
   BCDEFG
   CDEFG
   DEFG
   EFG
   FG
   G
   ```

   c.
   ```
   A A A A
    B B B
   C C C C
    D D
   E E E E
   ```

   d.
   ```
      A
     BBB
    CCCCC
   DDDDDDD
   EEEEEEEEE
   ```

In Problems 9–25, write a program for each task specified. Use one or more arrays in each program.

9. The following DATA lines show the annual salaries of all the employees in Division 72 of the Manley Corporation. The last value (72) is an EOD tag.

    ```
    500 DATA 14000, 16200, 10195, 28432, 13360
    510 DATA 19300, 16450, 12180, 25640, 18420
    520 DATA 18900, 12270, 13620, 12940, 31200
    530 DATA 72
    ```

    Read these data into an array S, and then create a new array T as follows. For each subscript K, obtain T(K) by subtracting the average of all the salaries from S(K). Then display arrays S and T as a two-column table with appropriate headings.

10. Use the salary data shown in Problem 9 to create two arrays as follows. Array A is to contain all salaries less than $14,000 and B is to contain the rest. Display arrays A and B in adjacent columns with appropriate headings.

11. Input an undetermined number of values into arrays P and N so that array P contains those that are positive and N contains those that are negative. Ignore zeros and let 999 serve as the EOD tag. When the EOD tag is encountered, display the two lists in adjacent columns with the headings POSITIVES and NEGATIVES.

12. Read a list of words from DATA lines into arrays A$ and B$. Have array A$ contain all words beginning with a letter from A to M. Put the other words into B$. Display the contents of the two arrays in adjacent columns with appropriate column headings.

13. The following DATA lines show a name and four scores for each student in a psychology class:

    ```
    700 DATA ARDEN MARK, 72, 79, 91, 70
    710 DATA AUDEN WINN, 95, 92, 86, 82
    720 DATA BRICE SALLY ANN, 90, 80, 70, 84
    730 DATA BRANT EMILY, 75, 62, 43, 65
    740 DATA RANDALL TONY, 52, 54, 50, 33
    750 DATA RANDOLPH KIM, 82, 72, 80, 79
                    .
                    .
                    .
    799 DATA XXX
    ```

    Create arrays S$ and A so that S$ contains the names and A contains the corresponding average scores. Then display two reports as follows. The first is to show the names and averages for students whose average is at least 60. The other students and their averages should be shown in the second report. Each report is to have an appropriate title and column headings.

14. Create arrays S$ and A exactly as described in Problem 13. Then allow the user to enter a string with one or more letters to obtain the names and averages of all students whose names begin with the letters typed.

15. Write a program as described in Problem 14. This time assume the names in DATA lines are in alphabetical order, and use this fact to reduce the number of string comparisons that must be made.

16. Letter grades for students in the psychology class mentioned in Problem 13 are determined by specifying four cutoff values for the four passing grades A, B, C, and D. Write a program to display the names and letter grades of all students. Include the four cutoff values, as well as the student names and scores shown in Problem 13, in DATA statements. (Determine how to organize the data by considering how they are to be used. For this, you may wish to reread Example 6.)

17. The names and precinct numbers of all residents of the town of Plymouth who voted in the last election are included in DATA lines in alphabetical order. Here are the first two DATA lines:

    ```
    1000 DATA ALDEN JOHN, 1, ALDEN PRISCILLA, 1
    1010 DATA BARTON JONATHAN, 4, BARTON MARY, 2
    ```

Plymouth has four precincts. You are to read the names into four arrays according to precinct, and then display the four lists as follows:

```
     PRECINCT 1              PRECINCT 2
     ---------------         ---------------
     ALDEN JOHN              BARTON MARY
     ALDEN PRISCILLA            .
          .                     .
          .                     .
          .

     PRECINCT 3              PRECINCT 4
     ---------------         ---------------
          .                  BARTON JONATHAN
          .                     .
          .                     .
                                .
```

The names in each precinct should be in alphabetical order, as are the names in the DATA lines.

18. A produce wholesaler uses the given price table while preparing invoices. A typical invoice is shown following the price table:

Current Price Table

Item	Item code	Price per crate
Artichokes	ART	8.50
Carrots	CAR	5.20
Cabbage	CAB	5.40
Collard greens	COL	5.90
Cucumbers	CUK	11.00
Lettuce—Iceberg	LET1	14.00
Lettuce—Romaine	LET3	12.75
Lettuce—Boston	LET7	10.50
Turnips	TUR	3.75

```
                NORTH END PRODUCE, INC.

     CUSTOMER: RAINBOW VEGETABLE STAND

     DESCRIPTION        QUANTITY     PRICE      AMOUNT
     ------------------------------------------------------
     CABBAGE                3         5.40       16.20
     ARTICHOKES            10         8.50       85.00
     LETTUCE-ICEBERG       10        14.00      140.00
     ------------------------------------------------------
     TOTALS                23                   241.20
```

Write a program to prepare an invoice for each produce order included in DATA statements. The order whose invoice is shown could be included by using the statement:

DATA CAB, 3, ART, 10, LET1, 10, XXX, 0

The pair XXX,0 would be used to indicate the end of the order. (If it is not obvious to you how the price information and order data should be organized, you may wish to reread Example 6.)

19. Write a program to produce invoices as in Problem 18 but with the produce orders typed at the keyboard rather than being included in DATA lines. A suitable display created while typing the order whose invoice is shown would be

```
CUSTOMER? RAINBOW VEGETABLE STAND

(ENTER X FOR ITEM WHEN ORDER IS COMPLETE)

ITEM? CAB
CRATES? 3
ITEM? ART
CRATES? 10
ITEM? LET1
CRATES? 10
ITEM? X
```

(A complete order must be entered before any part of the invoice is displayed. Thus, you will need either two arrays to store the order information as it is entered or one or more arrays to store the invoice as it is generated. Either method is appropriate.)

20. A number of scores, each lying in the range from 0 to 100, are given in DATA lines. Use these scores to create an array C so that

    $C(1)$ = a count of scores S satisfying $S \le 20$
    $C(2)$ = a count of scores S satisfying $20 < S \le 40$
    $C(3)$ = a count of scores S satisfying $40 < S \le 60$
    $C(4)$ = a count of scores S satisfying $60 < S \le 80$
    $C(5)$ = a count of scores S satisfying $80 < S \le 100$

    Display the results in tabular form as follows:

Interval	Frequency	
0–20	C(1)	[actually the value of C(1)]
20–40	C(2)	
40–60	C(3)	
60–80	C(4)	
80–100	C(5)	

21. Problem 20 asks for a count of the number of scores in each of five equal-length intervals. Instead of using five intervals, allow a user to type a positive integer N to produce a similar frequency table using N equal-length intervals.

22. A correspondence between x and y is given by the following table. (Each y entry corresponds to the x entry just above it.)

x	0	2	4	6	8	10	12	14	16	18	20
y	−5	3	27	67	123	195	283	387	507	643	795

    Your program is to allow a user to type two numbers: the first is to be 0, 1, or 2 and the second a value for x in the range 0 to 20. (Any other input values should be rejected and a new value requested.) The computer is to respond as follows:

    0: If the first number typed is zero, the y value corresponding to x is to be displayed. If the x value is not in the table, the message NOT FOUND should be displayed. The user should then be allowed to type two more numbers.

    1: If the first number typed is 1, the y value corresponding to x should be displayed. However, if x is not in the table, a linear interpolation should be performed to determine y. If x_1 and x_2 are successive values in the list with x lying between them, and if y_1 and y_2 are the corresponding y values, the value y to be displayed is given by

    $$y = y_1 + \frac{x - x_1}{x_2 - x_1}(y_2 - y_1)$$

    The user should again be allowed to type two more numbers.

    2: If the first number typed is 2, the program should terminate.

268 Chapter 15 Arrays

23. For any input string, display two columns. In the first show the letters appearing in the string; in the second display how many times these letters occur in the string. For example, if the string constant "BOB,ROB,OR BO" is typed (quotation marks are included because of the commas), the output should be

    B 4
    O 4
    R 2

    Use F(1) to store the count of A's, F(2) for the B's, and so on, up to F(26). The method used in Example 17 of Section 14.7 to find the position in the alphabet of any letter, can be used here to find the appropriate subscript for any letter in the input string. It isn't necessary to use a second array to hold the letters of the alphabet. You may check that the letter whose count is stored in F(K) is CHR$(ASC("A") + K − 1).

24. Each of many DATA lines contains a single string (it may be long). The last string is the EOD tag END-OF-DATA. Produce a two-column table as described in Problem 23 for all letters appearing in all DATA lines but the last. Label the columns LETTER and FREQUENCY. Run your program with the following DATA lines:

    ```
    800 DATA "BASIC IS FUN! ESPECIALLY WHEN I MUST CONVERT"
    810 DATA "STRINGS TO NUMBERS AND NUMBERS TO STRINGS, "
    820 DATA "AND SO ON, AND SO ON, AND SO ON,....."
    899 DATA END-OF-DATA
    ```

25. A list of words terminated with an EOD tag is contained in DATA lines. Determine how many of the words begin with the letter A, how many begin with B, and so on. Display these counts in a two-column frequency table as described in Problem 24.

■ 15.5 Higher-Dimensional Arrays

All arrays used to this point have been one-dimensional, a term indicating that the array entries are referenced by using a single subscript. As illustrated in Sections 15.1–15.3, programming tasks involving tables represent an important application of one-dimensional arrays. There are some table-processing applications, however, for which the one-dimensional array structure is inadequate. For example, consider the following table that summarizes the responses of 10 families to a product survey:

Product Survey Table

Key to table entries	
Rating	**Survey response**
0	POOR
1	FAIR
2	GOOD
3	VERY GOOD
4	EXCELLENT

Family number

Product number	1	2	3	4	5	6	7	8	9	10
1	0	1	1	2	1	2	2	1	0	1
2	2	3	3	0	3	2	2	3	4	1
3	1	3	4	4	4	1	4	2	3	2
4	3	4	2	4	3	1	3	4	2	4
5	0	1	3	2	2	2	1	3	0	1
6	4	4	4	3	2	1	4	4	1	1
7	1	3	1	3	2	4	1	4	3	4
8	2	2	3	4	2	2	3	4	2	3

To store these data in one-dimensional arrays, we could use a string array to store the responses (POOR, FAIR, and so on) corresponding to the rating keys 0 through 4, but it would not be convenient to use one-dimensional arrays to store the table of numerical ratings. Doing so would require eight numerical arrays if a separate array is used for each product or ten arrays if an array is used for each family. The program would be unnecessarily complicated (each array would have a different name) and very difficult to modify to handle other than eight products and ten families.

What is needed is a convenient way to store such tables. BASIC provides this capability by allowing you to declare arrays whose entries are referenced by using two subscripts. First, we will introduce some terminology to make it easier to refer to arrays used to store tables such as the Product Survey Table. To keep things as simple as possible, however, we will use the following smaller table for illustration. The data in this table summarize the responses of college students to a hypothetical opinion poll concerning the abolition of grades.

Class	In favor of abolishing grades	Not in favor of abolishing grades	No opinion
Freshmen	207	93	41
Sophomores	165	110	33
Juniors	93	87	15
Seniors	51	65	8

A **two-dimensional array** is a collection of items arranged in a rectangular fashion. That is, there is a first (horizontal) row, a second row, and so on, and a first (vertical) column, a second column, and so on. An array with *m* rows and *n* columns is called an ***m*-by-*n* array** (also written ***m* × *n* array**). Thus the opinion-poll data are presented as a 4-by-3 array.

An item in a two-dimensional array is specified by giving its row number and column number. For example, the item in the third row and second column of the opinion-poll table is 87. By convention, the row number is specified first. Thus, in the opinion-poll table, 33 is in the 2,3 position and 51 is in the 4,1 position. In mathematical notation we could write

$$P_{1,1} = 207, \quad P_{1,2} = 93, \quad P_{1,3} = 41$$

to indicate the values in the first row of our table. Since the BASIC character set does not include such subscripts, this notation is changed as it was for one-dimensional arrays. Thus, the values in the opinion-poll table would be written as follows:

P(1,1) = 207   P(1,2) = 93   P(1,3) = 41
P(2,1) = 165   P(2,2) = 110   P(2,3) = 33
P(3,1) = 93   P(3,2) = 87   P(3,3) = 15
P(4,1) = 51   P(4,2) = 65   P(4,3) = 8

We say that P is the **name** of the array, that P(1,1), P(1,2), . . ., are **doubly subscripted variables,** and that the numbers enclosed in parentheses are the *subscripts* of P. The symbol P(I,J) is read **P sub I comma J** or simply **P sub IJ**.

The 4-by-3 array P can be visualized as follows:

```
                (Column)
         P  |   1     2     3
         ---+------------------
         1  |  207    93    41
         2  |  165   110    33
(Row)    3  |   93    87    15
         4  |   51    65     8
```

This schematic displays the array name P, the row number for each item, and the column numbers.

To declare to the computer that your program will use the 4-by-3 array P, you would include the statement

```
DIM P(4,3)
```

so that it is encountered before any of the doubly subscripted variables P(1,1), P(1,2), and so on, are referenced. If instead you include the statement

```
DIM P(100,100)
```

your program can reference any or all of the subscripted variables P(R,C) with R and C integers in the range 0 to 100—there are 10,201 (101 × 101) such subscript assignments.

The value of a doubly subscripted variable—that is, an array entry—is referenced in a program just as values of singly subscripted variables are referenced. The subscripts can be integer constants, variables, or expressions. For example, the FOR loop

```
FOR C=1 TO 3
    LET P(1,C)=5*C
NEXT C
```

assigns the values 5, 10, and 15 to the first row, P(1,1), P(1,2), P(1,3), of P. Similarly,

```
LET C=1
FOR R=1 TO 4
    LET P(R,C)=P(R,C)+6
NEXT R
```

adds 6 to each entry in the first column, P(1,1), P(2,1), P(3,1), P(4,1), of P.

EXAMPLE 8

Here is a program segment to read the college students opinion-poll data into an array P.

```
100 REM READ VALUES FOR THE 4-BY-3 ARRAY P.
110 DIM P(4,3)
120 FOR R=1 TO 4
130     REM READ VALUES FOR THE RTH ROW OF P.
140     FOR C=1 TO 3
150         READ P(R,C)
160     NEXT C
170 NEXT R
500 DATA 207,93,41
510 DATA 165,110,33
520 DATA 93,87,15
530 DATA 51,65,8
```

When the first FOR statement (line 120) is executed, R is assigned the initial value 1. The C loop then reads the first three data values 207, 93, and 41 for the variables P(1,1), P(1,2), and P(1,3), respectively. That is, when R = 1, values are read into the first row of P. Similarly, when R = 2, values are read into the second row, P(2,1), P(2,2), P(2,3), of P, and so on, until all 12 values have been assigned to P.

REMARK

The data do not have to be given in four lines as shown here. The single line

```
500 DATA 207,93,41,165,110,33,93,87,15,51,65,8
```

could replace lines 500–530. The order in which they appear is all that matters.

EXAMPLE 9

Let's use the program segment of Example 8 in a program to count the number of students in each class who participated in the opinion-poll survey.

PROBLEM ANALYSIS

The following algorithm describes one way to carry out the specified task.

a. Read the opinion-poll data into array P (done in Example 8).
b. Determine and display how many students in each class participated in the survey.

Since all three entries in any one row of P correspond to students in one of the four classes, the task in Step (b) is to add the three entries in each row of P and display these four sums. Let's use S(1) to denote the sum of the entries in the first row and S(2), S(3), and S(4) for the other three row sums. These sums can be determined as follows:

```
LET S(1)=P(1,1)+P(1,2)+P(1,3)
LET S(2)=P(2,1)+P(2,2)+P(2,3)
LET S(3)=P(3,1)+P(3,2)+P(3,3)
LET S(4)=P(4,1)+P(4,2)+P(4,3)
```

However, note that S(R), for R = 1, 2, 3, and 4, is obtained by summing P(R,C) for C = 1, 2, and 3. This is exactly the order of subscripts determined by the nested FOR loops

```
FOR R=1 TO 4
    FOR C=1 TO 3
        .
        .
        .
    NEXT C
NEXT R
```

The following program can now be written. Lines 100–170, which carry out Step (a) of the algorithm, are the program segment shown in Example 8. To this we add lines 180–330, which represent one way to code Step (b) of the algorithm.

THE PROGRAM

```
100 REM READ VALUES FOR THE 4-BY-3 ARRAY P.
110 DIM P(4,3)
120 FOR R=1 TO 4
130     REM READ VALUES FOR THE RTH ROW OF P.
140     FOR C=1 TO 3
150         READ P(R,C)
160     NEXT C
170 NEXT R
180 REM DETERMINE AND DISPLAY THE ROW SUMS OF P.
190 PRINT "PARTICIPATION IN SURVEY BY CLASS."
200 PRINT "--------------------------------"
210 FOR R=1 TO 4
220     LET S(R)=0
230 NEXT R
240 FOR R=1 TO 4
250     FOR C=1 TO 3
260         LET S(R)=S(R)+P(R,C)
270     NEXT C
280     IF (R=1) THEN PRINT "FRESHMEN",
290     IF (R=2) THEN PRINT "SOPHOMORES",
300     IF (R=3) THEN PRINT "JUNIORS",
310     IF (R=4) THEN PRINT "SENIORS",
320     PRINT S(R)
330 NEXT R
500 DATA 207,93,41
510 DATA 165,110,33
520 DATA 93,87,15
530 DATA 51,65,8
999 END
RUN

PARTICIPATION IN SURVEY BY CLASS.
--------------------------------
FRESHMEN        341
SOPHOMORES      308
JUNIORS         195
SENIORS         124
```

REMARK This program could have been written with only one pair of nested FOR loops by inserting appropriate lines in the program segment

```
100 REM READ VALUES FOR THE 4-BY-3 ARRAY P.
110 DIM P(4,3)
120 FOR R=1 TO 4
130     REM READ VALUES FOR THE RTH ROW OF P.
140     FOR C=1 TO 3
150         READ P(R,C)
160     NEXT C
170 NEXT R
```

that was used to carry out Step (a) of the algorithm. Specifically, inserting the line

```
125 LET S(R)=0
```

serves to initialize the counters S(1), S(2), S(3), and S(4). Also, if the line

```
155 LET S(R)=S(R)+P(R,C)
```

is included, the required row sums S(1), S(2), S(3), and S(4) will be calculated. The lines that display the caption

```
PARTICIPATION IN SURVEY BY CLASS.
---------------------------------
```

can be placed anywhere before line 120 and, finally, the lines that display the counts S(R) with the identifying labels can be placed just after S(R) is determined—that is, between lines 160 and 170.

Although these changes result in a shorter program, it is not necessarily better. In the program as given, each of the two subtasks [Steps (a) and (b)] in the algorithm occupies its own part of the program. (The REM statements in lines 100 and 180 identify these program segments.) That the resulting program may not be the shortest possible is of little consequence. The longer program obtained by segmenting is easier to read and certainly easier to modify, should that be required. The axiom "the shorter the better" is not always valid in programming.

Many programming applications involve rearranging the entries in arrays. The next two examples illustrate the rearrangement of entries in two-dimensional arrays.

EXAMPLE 10 Here is a program segment to interchange rows K and L of an N × N array A:

```
200 FOR J=1 TO N
210     SWAP A(K,J),A(L,J)
220 NEXT J
```

When J = 1, the SWAP statement causes A(K,1) and A(L,1), the first entries in the Kth and Lth row of A, to be interchanged; when J = 2, the second entries A(K,2) and A(L,2) are interchanged; and so on.

EXAMPLE 11 Here is a self-explanatory program:

```
100 DIM A(4,4)
110 REM READ VALUES FOR ARRAY A, ROW BY ROW.
120 FOR I=1 TO 4
130     FOR J=1 TO 4
140         READ A(I,J)
150     NEXT J
160 NEXT I
170 REM FIND THE ROW NUMBER K OF THE ROW OF ARRAY A
180 REM WITH THE LARGEST FIRST VALUE A(K,1)
190 LET K=1
200 FOR I=2 TO 4
210     IF A(I,1)>A(K,1) THEN K=I
220 NEXT I
```

```
230 REM INTERCHANGE ROW K AND ROW 1.
240 FOR J=1 TO 4
250     SWAP A(K,J),A(1,J)
260 NEXT J
270 REM DISPLAY THE MODIFIED ARRAY A, ROW BY ROW.
280 FOR I=1 TO 4
290     FOR J=1 TO 4
300         PRINT A(I,J);
310     NEXT J
320     PRINT
330 NEXT I
500 DATA 22.25,21.75,28.63,29.84
510 DATA 61.23,55.47,59.55,62.33
520 DATA 33.35,42.78,39.25,48.62
530 DATA 44.45,43.25,27.62,39.04
999 END
RUN

 61.23   55.47   59.55   62.33
 22.25   21.75   28.63   29.84
 33.35   42.78   39.25   48.62
 44.45   43.25   27.62   39.04
```

Microsoft® BASIC does not restrict you to one or two subscripts. For example, the statement

```
DIM A(2,2,2)
```

specifies a three-dimensional array whose entries can be referenced by using A(I,J,K), where the subscripts I, J, and K can be any of the integers 0, 1, or 2. Similarly,

```
DIM B(3,3,3,3,3)
```

specifies a five-dimensional array whose entries can be referenced by B(I,J,K,L,M), where the five subscripts can be any of the values 0, 1, 2, or 3.

Arrays with more than two dimensions are sometimes used in technical engineering and mathematical applications, but they are rarely used in nontechnical programming tasks. For this reason, they are not illustrated here.

We conclude this section with three points concerning the use of higher-dimensional arrays that were not specifically mentioned or illustrated in this section:

1. Every higher-dimensional array should be declared in DIM statements. As with one-dimensional arrays, however, failure to do so will cause a fatal error only if you use a subscript that's not in the range 0 to 10.
2. Both one- and higher-dimensional arrays can be declared with the same DIM statement. The following DIM statement properly declares a one-dimensional numerical array A with largest subscript 5, a two-dimensional 5-by-2 array B, and a one-dimensional string array M$ with largest subscript 25:

```
100 DIM A(5),B(5,2),M$(25)
```

3. Higher-dimensional string arrays are permitted. At the beginning of this section we showed an 8-row-by-10-column Product Survey Table. Each entry in the table is a numerical rating whose meaning is as follows:

Key to table entries

Rating	Survey response
0	POOR
1	FAIR
2	GOOD
3	VERY GOOD
4	EXCELLENT

Thus, to store the given Product Survey Table in the two-dimensional array PRODUCT, we could declare PRODUCT as follows:

```
DIM PRODUCT(8,10)
```

If we wanted to store the actual responses (POOR, FAIR, and so on) rather than the corresponding rating numbers in a table, we would specify a string array as follows:

```
DIM PRODUCT$(8,10)
```

■ 15.6 Problems

1. Show the output of each program.

   a.
   ```
   100 DIM M(4,4)
   110 FOR R=1 TO 4
   120     FOR C=1 TO 4
   130         LET M(R,C)=R*C
   140     NEXT C
   150 NEXT R
   160 FOR K=1 TO 4
   170     PRINT M(K,K);
   180 NEXT K
   190 END
   ```

   b.
   ```
   100 DIM A(3,2),B(2,3)
   110 FOR R=1 TO 3
   120     FOR C=1 TO 2
   130         READ A(R,C)
   140         LET B(C,R)=A(R,C)
   150     NEXT C
   160 NEXT R
   170 PRINT B(2,1);B(2,2);B(2,3)
   180 DATA 1,2,3,4,5,6,7,8,9
   190 END
   ```

   c.
   ```
   100 DIM S(3,3)
   110 FOR K=1 TO 3
   120     FOR L=1 TO K
   130         READ S(K,L)
   140         LET S(L,K)=S(K,L)
   150     NEXT L
   160 NEXT K
   170 FOR N=1 TO 3
   180     PRINT S(N,2);
   190 NEXT N
   200 DATA 1,2,3,4,5,6
   ```

   d.
   ```
   100 DIM YESNO$(4,4)
   110 FOR R=1 TO 4
   120     FOR C=1 TO 4
   130         IF R>C THEN A$="N" ELSE A$="Y"
   140         LET YESNO$(R,C)=A$
   150     NEXT C
   160 NEXT R
   ```

```
        170 FOR R=1 TO 4
        180     FOR C=1 TO 4
        190         PRINT YESNO$(R,C);
        200     NEXT C
        210     PRINT
        220 NEXT R
        230 END
```

e.
```
    100 DIM T$(3),P$(3,4)
    110 FOR N=1 TO 3
    120     READ T$(N)
    130     FOR P=1 TO 4
    140         READ P$(N,P)
    150     NEXT P
    160 NEXT N
    170 FOR N=1 TO 3
    180     PRINT T$(N);":",
    190 NEXT N
    200 PRINT
    210 FOR P=1 TO 4
    220     FOR N=1 TO 3
    230         PRINT P$(N,P),
    240     NEXT N
    250     PRINT
    260 NEXT P
    270 DATA DEVILS,ED,JANE,JOHN,SUE
    280 DATA HOOFERS,ANN,JIM,RON,RUTH
    290 DATA SAINTS,DEB,DOT,RUSS,TIM
    300 END
```

2. Find and correct the errors in the following program segments. Assume that values have already been assigned to the 5-by-5 array A.

a.
```
    200 REM DISPLAY THE SUM S
    210 REM OF EACH ROW OF A.
    220 LET S=0
    230 FOR R=1 TO 5
    240     FOR C=1 TO 5
    250         LET S=S+A(R,C)
    260     NEXT C
    270     PRINT S
    280 NEXT R
```

b.
```
    200 REM INTERCHANGE ROWS R1 AND R2 OF ARRAY A.
    210 FOR C=1 TO 5
    220     LET A(R1,C)=A(R2,C)
    230     LET A(R2,C)=A(R1,C)
    240 NEXT C
```

In Problems 3–16, write a program to perform each task specified.

3. Read 16 values into the 4 × 4 array M. Then display the array. Further, display the four column sums below their respective columns.
4. Repeat Problem 3 for an N × N array M in which N can be any integer up to 6.
5. Read 16 values into the 4 × 4 array M. Then display the array. Have row sums appear to the right of their respective rows and column sums below their respective columns.
6. Repeat Problem 5 for an N × N array M in which N can be any number up to 6.

7. Read values into an N × N array A. Display the array and then display the sum of the entries in the upper-left to lower-right diagonal of A. This sum is called the *trace* of array A. (Input N before the array values are read. Assume that N will never exceed 6.)
8. The *transpose* of an N × N array A is the N × N array whose rows are the columns of A in the same order. Read the entries of A from DATA lines, and display A and the transpose of A. (Assume that N will be less than 6.)
9. The *sum* S of two N × N arrays A and B is the N × N array whose entries are the sums of the corresponding entries of A and B. Read A and B from DATA lines, and display arrays A, B, and S. (Assume that N will be less than 6.)
10. Create the following 5 × 5 array N

    ```
     0   1   1   1   1
    -1   0   1   1   1
    -1  -1   0   1   1
    -1  -1  -1   0   1
    -1  -1  -1  -1   0
    ```

    Determine the values N(I,J) during program execution without using READ or INPUT statements. Display array N. [*Hint:* The value to be assigned to N(I,J) can be determined by comparing I with J.]
11. A manufacturing company sends a package consisting of eight new products to each of ten families and asks each family to rate each product. Here are the survey results:

    Product Survey Table

Key to table entries	
Rating	Survey response
0	POOR
1	FAIR
2	GOOD
3	VERY GOOD
4	EXCELLENT

    Family number

	1	2	3	4	5	6	7	8	9	10
1	0	1	1	2	1	2	2	1	0	1
2	2	3	3	0	3	2	2	3	4	1
3	1	3	4	4	4	1	4	2	3	2
4	3	4	2	4	3	1	3	4	2	4
5	0	1	3	2	2	2	1	3	0	1
6	4	4	4	3	2	1	4	4	1	1
7	1	3	1	3	2	4	1	4	3	4
8	2	2	3	4	2	2	3	4	2	3

    Product number (row labels)

    Write a menu-driven program that will carry out any or all of the tasks listed. (Have your program read the given data into arrays. You may find it convenient to use a string array to store the possible responses POOR, FAIR, and so on, and a two-dimensional array to store the data given in the table of numerical ratings.)
    a. Display the entire Product Survey Table essentially as shown.
    b. Display a two-column report showing the average rating for each product.
    c. Display a two-column report as follows: the first column gives the product numbers receiving at least six ratings of 3 or better; the second gives the number of these ratings obtained.
    d. Display a two-column table showing how many times each of the five possible responses (POOR, FAIR, and so on) were made.

12. An N × N array of numbers is called a *magic square* if the sums of each row, each column, and each diagonal are all equal. Test any N × N array in which N will never exceed 10. Values for N and array values should be input. Be sure to display and identify all row, column, and diagonal sums, the array itself, and a message indicating whether or not the array is a magic square. Try your program on the following arrays:

a.						**b.**						**c.**					
1	1					11	10	4	23	17		4	139	161	26	174	147
1	1					18	12	6	5	24		85	166	107	188	93	12
						25	19	13	7	1		98	152	138	3	103	157
						2	21	20	14	8		179	17	84	165	184	22
						9	3	22	16	15		183	21	13	175	89	170
												102	156	148	94	8	143

13. Input five numbers to produce a five-column table as follows. The first column is to contain the five numbers in the order they are input. The second column is to contain the four differences of successive values in the first column. For example, if the first column contains 2, 4, 8, 9, 3, the second column will contain 2, 4, 1, −6. In the same way, each of columns 3–5 is to contain the differences of successive values in the column before it. If the values 1, 5, 9, 6, 12 are input, the output should be

1	4	0	−7	23
5	4	−7	16	
9	−3	9		
6	6			
12				

In the following suggested algorithm, M denotes a 5 × 5 array:

  a. Input the first column of M.
  b. Generate the remaining four columns of M as specified in the problem statement.
  c. Display the table as specified.

14. Input N numbers to produce a table of differences as described in Problem 13. Assume that N is an integer from 2 to 10.

15. Read values into a 5 × 3 array N. Then display the subscripts corresponding to the largest entry in N. If this largest value appears in N more than once, more than one pair of subscripts must be displayed. Use the following algorithm:

  a. Read values for array N.
  b. Determine M, the largest number in array N.
  c. Display all subscripts I, J for which N(I,J) = M.

16. Read values into a 5 × 3 array N. Display the row of N with the smallest first entry. If this smallest value is the first entry in more than one row, display only the first of these rows. Then interchange this row with the first row and display the modified array N. Use the following algorithm:

  a. Read values for array N.
  b. Find the first K such that row K has the smallest first entry.
  c. Display row K.
  d. Interchange rows 1 and K.
  e. Display the modified array N.

15.7 Review True-or-False Quiz

1. The two programming lines

    ```
    100 DIM A(25)
    110 LET A=0
    ```

    will assign the value 0 to all 25 positions in the array A. T F
2. Once array L is assigned values in a program, the statement PRINT L is sufficient to cause the entire array to be displayed. T F
3. If arrays A and B are declared by using DIM A(20),B(20), then the statement LET A = B will replace all entries of A by the corresponding entries of B. T F
4. The programming line

    ```
    50 LET A(I)=7
    ```

    can cause an error message to be displayed. T F
5. The statement LET A(7) = 25 can never cause an error message to be displayed. T F
6. If a noninteger subscript is encountered during program execution, an error message will be displayed and the program run will terminate. T F
7. Array values may be assigned by READ, INPUT, or LET statements. T F
8. The statement LET G = 5 may appear in a program that contains the statement DIM G(100). T F
9. If both one-dimensional and two-dimensional arrays are to be used in a program, two DIM statements must be used. T F
10. Two or more arrays are sometimes needed to store a single table of values. T F
11. If a program is needed to process data given in tabular form, it is always best to store the data by using one or more arrays. T F

16 Sorting

Many programming tasks require sorting (arranging) arrays according to some specified order. When lists of numbers are involved, this usually means arranging them according to size—from smallest to largest or from largest to smallest. For example, you may be required to produce a salary schedule in which salaries are displayed from largest to smallest. When lists of names are involved, you may wish to arrange them in alphabetical order. The principal reason we sort data is to allow needed items to be found in a timely manner. As we explain in this chapter, this applies not only to printed data used by people but also to data that must be searched by computers.

In Section 16.1 we'll describe the bubble sort algorithm and show how it can be used to sort either numerical or string data. In Section 16.2 we show two algorithms that can be used when speed is important: the Shellsort algorithm, for use when a faster sort than the bubble sort is needed, and the binary search algorithm, which can improve program speed significantly when long lists must be searched for specified values.

■ 16.1 The Bubble Sort

The bubble sort algorithm described in this section is very inefficient (slow) when used to sort large arrays, but for small arrays (up to about 30 entries) it will execute as rapidly as most sorting algorithms. Moreover, the bubble sort algorithm is easy to understand and easy to code. Thus it serves as an excellent introduction to the topic of sorting.

The idea behind the bubble sort is to compare adjacent array entries beginning with the first pair and ending with the last pair. If two values being compared are in the proper order, we leave them alone. If not, we interchange them. Thus to sort the short numerical array

	1	2	3	4
A	6	5	8	3

into ascending order, we begin the bubble sort by comparing the values in positions 1 and 2. Since these values (6 and 5) are not in order, they are swapped:

6 5 8 3   becomes   **5 6** 8 3

Next we compare the values in positions 2 and 3 in the same manner:

5 **6 8** 3   remains   5 **6 8** 3

Then we compare the values in positions 3 and 4:

5 6 **8 3** becomes 5 6 **3 8**

The effect of these three comparisons is to move the largest value to the last position. If we repeat exactly the same process for the modified array

1 2 3 4

A | 5 | 6 | 3 | 8 |

the array entries will be rearranged as follows:

5 6 3 8 remains **5 6** 3 8
5 **6 3** 8 becomes 5 **3 6** 8
5 3 **6 8** remains 5 3 **6 8**

The effect of these three comparisons is to move the next-to-largest value (6) to the next-to-last position. Repeating the process a third time will move the third-from-largest value (5) to the third-from-last position and the array will be in order:

5 3 6 8 becomes **3 5** 6 8
3 **5 6** 8 remains 3 **5 6** 8
3 5 **6 8** remains 3 5 **6 8**

You probably noticed that several of the comparisons shown are unnecessary. After the first three comparisons are made (we'll refer to these three comparisons as *a pass through the array*), we can be sure that the largest array value is in the last position. Hence, it isn't necessary to make further comparisons involving the last array entry. Similarly, after the second pass through the array, it isn't necessary to make further comparisons involving the next-to-last array entry. If we include these unnecessary comparisons, however, it is a simple matter to code the process described. Indeed, since the statement

```
SWAP A(I),A(I+1)
```

interchanges the values of the adjacent entries A(I) and A(I + 1), we can cause a single pass through the array A of size 4, swapping values that are not in order, with a FOR loop of the form

```
FOR I=1 TO 3
    IF A(I)>A(I+1) THEN SWAP A(I),A(I+1)
NEXT I
```

If the array A is of size N, we would simply change the FOR statement to

```
FOR I=1 TO N-1
```

The number of passes that must be made to sort an array depends on the array size and the array values. For an array of size N, at most $N - 1$ passes are required because on each pass another array value is moved to its proper position. But it isn't always necessary to make $N - 1$ passes through the array. For instance, to sort the four-element array

1 2 3 4

A | 5 | 3 | 8 | 6 |

we make one pass through the array to move the largest entry to the last position:

5 3 8 6 becomes **3 5** 8 6
3 **5 8** 6 remains 3 **5 8** 6
3 5 **8 6** becomes 3 5 **6 8**

```
500 REM BUBBLE SORT TO ARRANGE THE N TERMS
510 REM OF ARRAY A INTO ASCENDING ORDER.
520 REM
530 LET FLAG=1              'Force a pass through WHILE loop.
540 WHILE FLAG=1
550    LET FLAG=0
560    FOR I=1 TO N-1
570       IF A(I)>A(I+1) THEN
             SWAP A(I),A(I+1) :
             LET FLAG=1
580    NEXT I
590 WEND
599 REM ARRAY A IS NOW IN ASCENDING ORDER.
```

Figure 16.1 Program segment to perform a bubble sort.

Thus, for this array, one pass is enough. Rather than attempting to keep count of how many passes have been made, we'll simply repeat the process described until a pass is made in which no array entries are swapped—this will happen only if the array is in order. The program segment shown in Figure 16.1 accomplishes this by using the variable FLAG. Just before each pass through the array (that is, through the FOR loop), FLAG is set to 0. If a swap occurs in the loop, FLAG is set to 1. If the loop is completed with FLAG = 1, another pass is made; but if FLAG = 0 the array is sorted.

The bubble sort algorithm shown in Figure 16.1 can be used in any program to sort, in ascending order, any one-dimensional array A of size N. If you need to sort array A into descending rather than ascending order, simply change A(I) > A(I + 1) in line 570 to A(I) < A(I + 1).

As we explained in the preceding analysis, the bubble sort we have devised makes many unnecessary comparisons. Even so, it is only a bit slower than a bubble sort that includes extra statements to avoid these comparisons. If speed is essential, you would not try to improve the bubble sort. Rather, you would use a different and faster sorting algorithm, such as the one given in the next section.

Any sorting algorithm used to sort numerical arrays is easily modified to sort string arrays. To use the bubble sort in Figure 16.1 to sort strings, simply change the array name A to A$ or to any other string array name.

EXAMPLE 1 Here is a program to alphabetize lists of names typed at the keyboard.

```
100 REM       BUBBLE SORT AS APPLIED TO STRINGS
110 REM
120 REM ********************************************
130 REM          D A T A   E N T R Y
140 REM
150 DIM A$(51)
160 PRINT "ENTER UP TO 50 NAMES TO BE ALPHABETIZED."
170 PRINT "USE ONLY UPPERCASE. TYPE FINI WHEN DONE."
180 PRINT
190 LET N=1                        'Name count
200 PRINT "NAME";N;                'Prompt for name
210 INPUT A$(N)
220 WHILE A$(N)<>"FINI" AND N<51
230    LET N=N+1
240    PRINT "NAME";N;
250    INPUT A$(N)
260 WEND
270 LET N=N-1                      'Actual name count
280 REM
290 REM ********************************************
300 REM ALPHABETIZE THE N ENTRIES OF ARRAY A$.
310 REM
```

```
320 LET FLAG=1          'Force a pass through WHILE loop.
330 WHILE FLAG=1
340     LET FLAG=0
350     FOR I=1 TO N-1
360         IF A$(I)>A$(I+1) THEN
                SWAP A$(I),A$(I+1) :
                LET FLAG=1
370     NEXT I
380 WEND
390 REM ********************************
400 REM DISPLAY THE ALPHABETIZED ARRAY A$.
410 PRINT
420 PRINT "THE ALPHABETIZED LIST:"
430 PRINT
440 FOR I=1 TO N
450     PRINT A$(I)
460 NEXT I
470 END
RUN

ENTER UP TO 50 NAMES TO BE ALPHABETIZED.
USE ONLY UPPERCASE. TYPE FINI WHEN DONE.

NAME 1? LINCOLN
NAME 2? JOHNSON
NAME 3? GRANT
NAME 4? HAYES
NAME 5? GARFIELD
NAME 6? FINI

THE ALPHABETIZED LIST:

GARFIELD
GRANT
HAYES
JOHNSON
LINCOLN
```

■ **REMARK 1** A list of words to be alphabetized should contain all uppercase or all lowercase letters. Otherwise, as you can see by referring to Table 14.1,

"CRANSTON" < "Carlson"

even though Carlson should precede CRANSTON in an alphabetical listing.

■ **REMARK 2** If you must alphabetize an array A$ that contains both upper- and lowercase letters, you can use the lowercase-to-uppercase conversion subroutine given in Example 19 of Section 14.7. A common way to do this is to create a second array B$ containing the entries of A$ with each lowercase letter changed to uppercase. Then to sort A$ you would sort B$, being sure to swap entries in array A$ whenever the corresponding entries in B$ are swapped. If A$ contains N entries, the following loop will give you B$ (the conversion subroutine begins at line 1000 and converts lowercase letters in X$ to uppercase):

```
FOR K=1 TO N
    LET X$=A$(K)
    GOSUB 1000
    LET B$(K)=X$
NEXT K
```

You may have noticed that you don't have to create a new array B$ as described. One way to avoid B$ is to make the lowercase-to-uppercase conversions in array A$. You may not want to do this, however, if array A$ is needed for another purpose—for instance, to produce output containing both lower- and uppercase letters. Another way to avoid the use of a second array B$ would be to make conversions only as they are needed. For instance, to make a comparison involving A$(I), you could use the BASIC statements

```
LET X$=A$(I)
GOSUB 1000
LET Y$=X$
```

to assign A$(I) to Y$, but with lowercase letters converted to uppercase, and then make the comparison by using Y$ instead of A$(I). Although this method saves memory space by avoiding the use of the second array B$, it is not recommended. Each time a comparison involving A$(I) must be made—many comparisons may be needed for each A$(I)—Y$ must be determined anew. This is very time-consuming and can slow program execution significantly.

Many applications requiring arrays to be sorted involve more than one array. For example, suppose NAME$ and SAL denote one-dimensional arrays with each pair NAME$(I),SAL(I) giving a person's name and salary. If the contents of these two arrays must be displayed in a two-column report with the salaries appearing from largest to smallest, the list of pairs NAME$(I),SAL(I) must be sorted so that the entries in SAL are in descending order. This is easily accomplished by modifying a bubble sort that sorts array SAL. Simply insert a statement to interchange NAME$(I) and NAME$(I+1) whenever SAL(I) and SAL(I+1) are interchanged. If a second two-column report must be displayed with the names in alphabetical order, you would modify a bubble sort that alphabetizes NAME$ by inserting a statement to swap SAL(I) and SAL(I+1) whenever NAME$(I) and NAME$(I+1) are swapped. The next example demonstrates this procedure.

EXAMPLE 2

Several pairs of numbers are included in DATA lines. The first of each pair is a quality point average (QPA), and the second gives the number of students with this QPA. Write a program to produce a table with the column headings QPA and FREQUENCY. The frequency counts in the second column are to appear in descending order.

PROBLEM ANALYSIS

Two lists are given in the DATA lines. Let's use Q to denote QPAs and F to denote the frequency counts. The following algorithm shows the three subtasks that must be performed:

    a. Read arrays Q and F.
    b. Sort the two arrays so that the frequencies appear in descending order.
    c. Display the two arrays as a two-column table and stop.

To code Step (a), we must remember that the lists are presented in DATA lines as pairs of numbers. Thus, we will read values for Q(I) and F(I) for I = 1, 2, and so on, until all pairs have been read. We'll use the dummy pair 0, 0 as the EOD tag.

To code Step (b), we will use a bubble sort to sort array F in descending order. However, since a pair Q(I), F(I) must not be separated, we will interchange Q values whenever the corresponding F values are interchanged.

In the following program, note that the REM statements at lines 110, 210, and 320 correspond exactly to Steps (a), (b), and (c) of the algorithm.

THE PROGRAM

```
100 REM ********************************
110 REM      READ ARRAYS Q AND F.
120 REM
130 DIM Q(50),F(50)
140 LET N=1 : READ Q(N),F(N)
150 WHILE NOT (Q(N)=0 AND F(N)=0)
160     LET N=N+1 : READ Q(N),F(N)
```

```
170 WEND
180 LET N=N-1
190 REM
200 REM *******************************************
210 REM     SORT ARRAYS Q AND F SO THAT THE
220 REM FREQUENCIES APPEAR IN DESCENDING ORDER.
230 REM
240 LET FLAG=1      'Force a pass through WHILE loop.
250 WHILE FLAG=1
260     LET FLAG=0
270     FOR I=1 TO N-1
280         IF F(I)<F(I+1) THEN
                SWAP F(I),F(I+1) : SWAP Q(I),Q(I+1) :
                LET FLAG=1
290     NEXT I
300 WEND
310 REM *******************************************
320 REM     DISPLAY THE ARRAYS Q AND F.
330 REM
340 PRINT "QPA","FREQUENCY"
350 PRINT
360 FOR I=1 TO N
370     PRINT Q(I),F(I)
380 NEXT I
390 END
500 REM *******************************************
510 REM             D A T A
520 REM
530 DATA 4.00,2,3.75,16,3.40,41,3.20,38,3.00,92
540 DATA 2.75,162,2.30,352,2.00,280,1.70,81,1.50,27
599 DATA 0,0
RUN

QPA         FREQUENCY
 2.3         352
 2.          280
 2.75        162
 3.           92
 1.7          81
 3.4          41
 3.2          38
 1.5          27
 3.75         16
 4.            2
```

The statement SWAP Q(I),Q(I+1) is inserted in the bubble sort that sorts F so that Q values will be interchanged whenever the corresponding F values are interchanged.

■ 16.2 The Shellsort and Binary Search Algorithms

The bubble sort is one of the easiest sorting algorithms to understand, to remember, and to code. For this reason many beginners tend to use it exclusively. This is fine if the lists to be sorted are short and the program will see only limited use, but the bubble sort is very inefficient for long lists. For example, the PC, using the bubble sort shown in Figure 16.1, took 4 seconds to sort a list of 20 numbers—but it took about 3.5 minutes for a list of 200 numbers and more than an hour for a list of 800 numbers. These sorting times are unacceptably slow and clearly show the need for faster sorting algorithms.

Much attention has been given to the problem of sorting, and many fast sorting algorithms have been developed. The reasons for this activity go deeper than the need to produce well-formatted output documents with values printed in a certain order. A common task is that of searching an array A(1),A(2), . . . , A(N) for some specified

16.2 The Shellsort and Binary Search Algorithms

```
500 REM SHELLSORT TO SORT ARRAY A WITH
510 REM N TERMS INTO ASCENDING ORDER
520 S=INT(N/2)
530 WHILE S>=1
540    FOR K=1 TO S
550       FOR I=K TO N-S STEP S
560          LET J=I : T=A(I+S)
570          LET DONE=0
580          WHILE J>=K AND DONE=0
590             IF T>=A(J) THEN DONE=1
                ELSE A(J+S)=A(J) : J=J-S
600          WEND
610          LET A(J+S)=T
620       NEXT I
630    NEXT K
640    LET S=INT(S/2)
650 WEND
660 REM ARRAY A IS NOW SORTED.
```

Figure 16.2 Program segment to perform a Shellsort.

value V. If the array is not arranged in a known order, the best we can do is to compare V with A(1), then with A(2), and so on, until V is found or the entire list has been examined. This is called a **sequential search** and is easily coded:

```
500 LET I=1
510 WHILE A(I)<>V and I<N
520    LET I=I+1
530 WEND
540 IF A(I)=V
       THEN PRINT V; "HAS THE INDEX"; I
       ELSE PRINT V; "NOT FOUND."
```

If a long array A is to be searched for many different values V (the usual situation), and if you use a sequential search, you and others waiting to use the PC may have a long wait. However, if the array A is sorted (say, in ascending order), a much more efficient search can be made for V. (To turn to page 216 of this book, for instance, you would not start from page 1 and turn pages until you found page 216; you would use a more efficient method.) Principally, it is this need for a fast searching algorithm that prompted much of the attention given to sorting algorithms.

Although a detailed discussion of fast sorting and searching algorithms is beyond the scope of this introductory text, we do include two efficient algorithms you may wish to use. The first (Figure 16.2) is a fast sorting algorithm known as **Shellsort**,* and the second (Figure 16.3) is an efficient search algorithm called the **binary search.** They are presented here as alternatives to the bubble sort and the sequential search, should you have a need for them.† The following table shows comparative sorting times on an IBM PC for the bubble sort and the Shellsort:

Length of list	Bubble sort	Shellsort
50	14 seconds	11 seconds
100	55 seconds	25 seconds
150	2 minutes	45 seconds
200	3.5 minutes	1 minute
400	14 minutes	2.5 minutes
800	58 minutes	6 minutes
1,600	3.9 hours	12.6 minutes

---

* "A High-Speed Sorting Procedure," by Donald L. Shell, *Commun. ACM*, vol. 2, July 1959, pp. 30–32.
† A detailed explanation of how and why the two algorithms work may be found in our text *BASIC: An Introduction to Computer Programming,* 3rd ed. (Pacific Grove, Calif.: Brooks/Cole, 1986).

```
700 REM BINARY SEARCH TO SEARCH ARRAY A
710 REM OF LENGTH N FOR V.  M IS SET EQUAL
720 REM TO THE INDEX I FOR WHICH A(I)=V.
730 REM M=0 MEANS V WAS NOT FOUND.
740 LET L=1 : R=N
750 LET M=INT(L+R)/2
760 WHILE A(M)<>V AND L<=R
770    IF V<A(M) THEN R=M-1 ELSE L=M+1
780    LET M=INT((L+R)/2)
790 WEND
800 IF A(M)<>V THEN M=0
810 REM SEARCH IS COMPLETE.
```

Figure 16.3 Program segment to perform a binary search.

The Shellsort algorithm can be modified to sort two arrays A and B so that the pairs A(I), B(I) are not separated (see Example 2). Make these changes:

   Add : T1 = B(I + S) to line 560
   Add : B(J + S) = B(J) to the ELSE clause in line 590
   Add : B(J + S) = T1 to line 610

■ 16.3 Problems

In Problems 1–23, write a program to perform each task specified.

1. Display, in ascending order, any five input values L(1), L(2), L(3), L(4), and L(5). Have your program process many such sets of five numbers during a single run. Test your program with the following input data:

5	4	3	2	1
5	1	2	3	4
−1	−2	−3	−4	−5
2	1	4	3	5
15	19	14	18	10
1	2	3	4	5

2. Modify your program for Problem 1 so that each group of five integers is displayed in descending order. (Only one line needs to be changed.)
3. Display any list of numbers typed at the keyboard in ascending order. Use the value 9999 to indicate that the entire list has been entered.
4. Read a list of numbers to obtain a two-column table with the column headings ORIGINAL LIST and SORTED LIST. Have the first column contain the list values in the order in which they are read and the second column contain the same values displayed from largest to smallest. Use the following algorithm:

   a. Read the list values into identical arrays A and B.
   b. Sort array A into descending order.
   c. Display the two-column table as described.

   Try your program using the following DATA lines:

   ```
   500 DATA 80,70,40,90,95,38,85,42,60,70
   510 DATA 40,60,70,20,18,87,23,78,85,23
   998 DATA 9999
   ```

5. Read several numbers, ranging from 0 to 100, and store them in two arrays A and B. Let array A contain numbers less than 50 and array B the others. Then sort arrays A and B in descending order and display them side by side with the column headings LESS THAN 50 and 50 OR MORE. Test your program by using the data shown in Problem 4.

6. A study of Tidy Corporation's annual reports for 1980–1988 yielded the following statistics:

Year	Gross sales in thousands	Earnings per share
1980	18,000	−0.84
1981	18,900	0.65
1982	20,350	0.78
1983	24,850	1.05
1984	24,300	0.68
1985	27,250	0.88
1986	34,000	2.05
1987	51,000	1.07
1988	46,500	0.22

Include the first and third columns of this table in DATA lines for a program to produce a two-column report with the same headings as those shown. However, have the earnings-per-share figures appear in ascending order.

7. Include all three columns given for the Tidy Corporation (Problem 6) in DATA lines for a program to produce a three-column table with the same headings. However, have the gross sales figures appear in descending order.

8. Compute the semester averages for all students in a psychology class. A separate DATA line should be used for each student and should contain the student's name and five grades. A typical DATA line might read

```
700 DATA LINCOLN JOHN, 72, 79, 88, 97, 90
```

Produce the output in tabular form with the column headings STUDENT and SEMESTER AVERAGE. Have the names appear in alphabetical order.

9. Modify Problem 8 as follows: round averages to the nearest integer and give letter grades according to this table:

Average	Grade
90–100	A
80–89	B
70–79	C
60–69	D
Below 60	E

Read the five strings A, B, C, D, and E into an array. Produce the output in tabular form with the column headings STUDENT, SEMESTER AVERAGE, and LETTER GRADE. Have the names appear in alphabetical order.

10. Following is the weekly inventory report of a sewing-supply wholesaler:

Item	Batches on hand Monday	Batches sold during week	Cost per batch	Sales price per batch
Bobbins	220	105	$8.20	$10.98
Buttons	550	320	5.50	6.95
Needles—1	450	295	2.74	3.55
Needles—2	200	102	7.25	9.49
Pins	720	375	4.29	5.89
Thimbles	178	82	6.22	7.59
Thread—A	980	525	4.71	5.99
Thread—B	1424	718	7.42	9.89

Include all five columns in DATA lines by using one DATA statement for each item. Have your program produce a three-column report showing the item names and, for each item, the number of batches on hand at the end of the week and the income generated by that item. Have the income column appear in descending order.

11. Using the inventory report shown in Problem 10, produce a five-column report showing the item names, the cost per batch, the sales price per batch, the dollar markup per batch, and the percent markup per batch. Have the figures in the last column appear in descending order. [The percentages in the fifth column are given by (M/C)∗100, where M denotes the markup and C denotes the cost.]

12. A program is to contain the following DATA lines.

    ```
    800 DATA 9
    810 DATA MARIAN EVANS, JAMES PAYN, JOSEPH CONRAD
    820 DATA EMILY DICKINSON, HENRY THOREAU, JOHN PAYNE
    830 DATA JOHN FOX, MARY FREEMAN, GEORGE ELIOT
    ```

    Use the following algorithm to alphabetize the list of names:

    a. Read the names into an array A$.
    b. Create a new array B$ containing the names in A$ but with last names first.
    c. Sort B$ into alphabetical order. When a swap is made in B$, make the corresponding swap in A$.

13. A program is to contain the following DATA lines.

    ```
    800 DATA 9
    810 DATA MARIAN, EVANS, JAMES, PAYN, JOSEPH, CONRAD
    820 DATA EMILY, DICKINSON, HENRY, THOREAU, JOHN, PAYNE
    830 DATA JOHN, FOX, MARY, FREEMAN, GEORGE, ELIOT
    ```

    (Note that these are the names given in Problem 12 but with first names and last names included as separate strings.) Have your program produce an alphabetical listing with each name appearing in the form

    LAST, FIRST

    with a space after the comma as shown. (*Suggestion:* Use the concatenation operator + to place the names in a single string array with each name in the form specified for the output. Then simply sort and display this array. No other arrays are needed.)

14. A list of English words is presented in DATA lines. The last datum is the EOD tag XXX. The user should be allowed to issue any of the following commands: LIST, to display the list in the order given in the DATA lines; SORT, to display the list in alphabetical order; and DONE, to terminate the run. After any command other than DONE, the user should be allowed to issue another command. The command LIST must produce the list in the order given in DATA lines, even after SORT has been carried out. You should avoid lowercase letters in the DATA lines and instruct the user to use only uppercase when typing LIST, SORT, or DONE.

15. Display a list of words as described in Problem 14 in two adjacent columns with the column headings A–M and N–Z. Have the words in each column appear in alphabetical order.

16. Write a program as specified in Problem 14, but allow both lower- and uppercase letters in the DATA lines and in the keyboard input.

17. If a set of N scores is arranged in either increasing or decreasing order, the *median* score is the middle score when N is odd and the average of the two "middle" scores when N is even. Thus the sixth score is the median for a set of 11 scores, whereas the average of the fifth and sixth scores is the median for a set of 10 scores. Determine the median for an undetermined number of scores typed at the keyboard.

18. Read N pairs of numbers so that the first of each pair is in array A and the second is in array B. Sort the pairs A(I), B(I) so that $A(1) \leq A(2) \leq \cdots \leq A(N)$ and so that $B(I) \leq B(I + 1)$

whenever A(I) = A(I + 1). Display the modified arrays in two adjacent columns with the headings LIST A and LIST B. [*Hint:* If A(I) > A(I + 1), a swap is necessary; if A(I) < A(I + 1), no swap is necessary; otherwise—that is, if A(I) = A(I + 1)—swap only if B(I) > B(I + 1).]

19. English prose can be written in DATA lines by representing each line of text as a string occupying a single DATA line:

    ```
    500 DATA "WHEN IN THE COURSE OF HUMAN EVENTS, "
    501 DATA "IT BECOMES NECESSARY FOR ONE PEOPLE"
    502 DATA "TO DISSOLVE THE POLITICAL"
         .
         .
         .
    998 DATA "END-OF-TEXT"
    ```

    Write a program to determine some or all of the following statistics:
    a. A count of the number of words of text.
    b. A count of the number of N-letter words for N = 1,2,3, ...
    c. A two-column table giving each word used and its frequency. The column of words should be in alphabetical order.
    d. A two-column table showing the number of sentences with one word, the number with two words, and so on.
    e. A count of the number of words used from a list of words you include in DATA lines. For instance, to determine the number of times the author uses articles and conjunctions, your list might include A, AN, AND, BUT, HOWEVER, NOR, OR, THE, and others. If you were studying an author's use of color imagery, your list might be one of colors.

    Avoid lowercase letters in the DATA lines and instruct the user to use only uppercase at the keyboard.

20. Write a program as specified in Problem 19, but allow both lower- and uppercase letters in the DATA lines and in the keyboard input.

21. Read values into a 5 × 3 array A. Rearrange the rows of A so that their first entries are in ascending order. Display the modified array row by row. (Use a bubble sort to place the first-column entries A(1,1), A(2,1), A(3,1), A(4,1), A(5,1) in ascending order. Instead of swapping only A(I,1) and A(I + 1,1) whenever they are out of order, you must interchange all of row I with row I + 1.)

22. Modify your program for Problem 21 to handle M × N arrays rather than just 5 × 3 arrays.

23. Read N pairs of numbers into an N × 2 array A. Sort these pairs (that is, the rows of A) so that first-column entries are in ascending order and so that A(I,2) ≤ A(I + 1,2) whenever A(I,1) = A(I + 1,1). Use a bubble sort that will place the first-column entries A(1,1), A(2,1), . . . , A(N,1) in ascending order with the following modification. If A(I,1) > A(I + 1,1), swap rows I and I + 1; if A(I,1) < A(I + 1,1), no swap is necessary; otherwise—that is, if A(I,1) = A(I + 1,1)—swap only if A(I,2) > A(I + 1,2).

■ 16.4 Review True-or-False Quiz

1. The bubble sort can be used to arrange a list of numbers in either ascending or descending order. T F
2. The bubble sort can be used to arrange a list of words in alphabetical order but not in reverse alphabetical order. T F
3. The bubble sort is inefficient when it's used to sort arrays with fewer than 30 values. T F
4. The Shellsort can be used to arrange a list of numbers in ascending or descending order but cannot be used to sort string data. T F

5. If an array N$ of employee names and an array S containing the corresponding salaries of the employees are to be used to produce a two-column salary report with the names in alphabetical order, two loops will be needed, one to alphabetize the array N$ and another to make the corresponding changes to array S.   T   F
6. Sorting algorithms are useful in producing printed reports in which lists of numbers appear in ascending or descending order or in which names appear in alphabetical order. Such tasks represent the principal and only major application area of sorting.   T   F
7. An array must be sorted in ascending or descending order before a sequential search can be made.   T   F
8. A binary search can be made only on lists that are sorted.   T   F

17 Data Files

In the preceding chapters, all data to be processed by programs have been included in DATA lines or entered at the keyboard, and all output has been directed to the display screen or to a printer. Although these methods of handling I/O are adequate for many programming applications, situations do arise for which they are inadequate. For example, the output values of one program might be required as the input values of another program, or even of several other programs. Also, it might be necessary to store extensive output for printing at a later time when the computer isn't otherwise being used—long reports can be generated very quickly by computers, but comparatively, printers are very slow. To make all of this possible, BASIC allows for input data to come from a source external to the program (other than a keyboard), and for the output to be stored on secondary storage devices for later use. This is accomplished with data files.

A **data file** is a named collection of related data that can be referenced by a BASIC program.

In this chapter, we assume that you are using Diskette or Advanced Microsoft® BASIC. On the IBM PC, the disk unit is the principal storage device used for data files.

Microsoft® BASIC allows you to use two types of data files: **sequential access files** (or simply *sequential files*) and **random access files** (or simply *random files*). The contents of both types of files are ordered in sequence—there is a first entry, a second entry, a third, and so on. There are two main differences in the uses of sequential and random access files:

1. Data in a sequential file are accessed in order, beginning with the first datum, whereas data in a random file can be accessed in any order.

2. Data are added only at the end of a sequential file. This means that to change an entry in an existing file you would create a completely new file that contains this change. With random files, individual entries can be changed and there is no need to create a completely new file each time a file must be changed.

In this chapter we show how to create both sequential and random access files and explain how they are used in several programming applications. Sequential files are described first (Sections 17.1, 17.2, and 17.4) because they are somewhat easier to use and are adequate for applications encountered by beginning programmers. Random access files are considered in Section 17.6.

■ 17.1 Sequential Access Files

Associated with each data file you use in a program are a **name** and a **file number.** The statement

```
OPEN "SCORES" FOR OUTPUT AS #1
```

declares SCORES as the *name* and 1 as the *file number* of a sequential file to be used as an output file. If F$ = "SCORES" and N = 1, the statement

```
OPEN F$ FOR OUTPUT AS #N
```

does the same thing. The statement

```
OPEN "STUDENTS.DAT" FOR INPUT AS #3
```

declares STUDENTS.DAT as the *name* and 3 as the *file number* of a sequential file to be used as an input file.

File names have the form

name [.extension]

where **name** contains from 1 to 8 characters and **extension** contains up to 3 characters. DAT is often used as the extension for data files. As indicated by the brackets, the extension is optional.

If you load Microsoft® BASIC with either of the two DOS commands

```
A>BASIC
A>BASICA
```

the *file number* must be 1, 2, or 3. This means that up to three files can be processed simultaneously by a BASIC program. This number can be increased (up to 15) by loading BASIC with either of the commands

```
A>BASIC/F:n
A/BASICA/F:n
```

where *n* is an integer from 1 to 15.

Brief descriptions of the BASIC statements most often used to process sequential files are as follows.

- OPEN   Establishes a communication link between a program and a file. As shown in the two examples above, the name and number of the file, and its designation as an input or output file, are specified in the OPEN statement.
- INPUT#*n*   Specifies that input values are to be obtained from the file with file number *n*, rather than from the keyboard.
- PRINT#*n*   Specifies that output values are to be transmitted to file *n*. Exactly the same information is written on the file as would be displayed on the screen if PRINT were used. (You can also use PRINT#*n*,USING to specify an output format.)
- WRITE#*n*   Specifies that output values are to be transmitted to file #*n*. The significant differences between WRITE# and PRINT# are that WRITE# encloses strings in quotation marks and inserts commas between output values. As explained below, WRITE# is often preferred if the file being created is intended only for later use as an input file.
- CLOSE#*n*   Terminates the communication link established by the OPEN statement. We say that file #*n* has been closed. More than one file can be closed by a CLOSE statement: CLOSE #2,#3 (or more simply CLOSE 2,3) closes files 2 and 3; CLOSE with no file numbers closes all active files. Every file that has been opened with an OPEN statement should be closed. Failure to do so may result in a loss of data.

Let's assume that a file named SCORES contains the following six lines. (The use of the term "lines" as it applies to files will be explained shortly.)

```
NICKLAUS
206
MILLER
208
WATSON
205
```

In Example 1 we show how a BASIC program can access the data contained in this file, and in Example 2 we show how the file SCORES can be created.

EXAMPLE 1 Here is a program to read and display the information stored in file SCORES.

```
10 OPEN "SCORES" FOR INPUT AS #1
20 FOR N=1 TO 3
30    INPUT#1,A$
40    INPUT#1,S
50    PRINT A$,S
60 NEXT N
70 CLOSE 1
80 END
RUN

NICKLAUS      206
MILLER        208
WATSON        205
```

Line 10 specifies SCORES and 1 as the name and number of the input file. Whenever the file is used by the program, it is referenced by its number, not by its name. As shown in lines 30 and 40, this is accomplished by using INPUT#1 instead of INPUT. Each time the INPUT# statements at lines 30 and 40 are executed, values for A$ and S are obtained from the file SCORES. Line 50 displays these two values as shown in the output.

■ **REMARK** When an INPUT statement obtains a value from a file, we say that it *reads* the value, or that the value is *read*.

EXAMPLE 2 Here is a program that can be used to create the file SCORES.

```
100 OPEN "SCORES" FOR OUTPUT AS #1
110 REM
120 PRINT "Type X for NAME to stop."
130 PRINT
140 INPUT "NAME";N$
150 WHILE N$<>"X" AND N$<>"x"
160    PRINT#1,N$
170    INPUT "SCORE";S
180    PRINT#1,S
190    INPUT"NAME";N$
200 WEND
210 CLOSE 1
220 END
RUN

Type X for NAME to stop.

NAME? NICKLAUS
SCORE? 206
NAME? MILLER
SCORE? 208
NAME? WATSON
SCORE? 205
NAME? X
```

Line 100 specifies SCORES and 1 as the name and number of the output file. If SCORES is the name of an existing diskette file, its previous contents are lost. If SCORES does not already exist, the name SCORES is added to the diskette's directory of files.

Each time an INPUT statement is executed, we type a name or a score as shown in the display produced when the program was run. The PRINT# statements in lines 160 and 180 transmit these values to file 1 (that is, to the file SCORES), rather than to the screen or printer. When a PRINT# statement transmits a value to a file, we say that it *writes* the value or that the value is *written*.

In the preceding example, each time either of the statements PRINT#1,N$ or PRINT#1,S is executed, a single value followed by a *return* and *line feed* character [CHR$(13) and CHR$(10)] is written to the file SCORES. Following is a schematic representation of how information is organized in the file scores. (↵) denotes the *return* character and **lf** the *line feed* character.)

| NICKLAUS | ↵ | lf | 206 | ↵ | lf | MILLER | ↵ | lf | 208 | ↵ | lf | WATSON | ↵ | lf | 205 | ↵ | lf | . . . |

Because of the return and line feed characters, it is customary to visualize this file as containing six distinct lines. Indeed, if you issue the DOS command* TYPE SCORES, the screen will display:

```
NICKLAUS
 206
MILLER
 208
WATSON
 205
```

(Note the blank in front of each numerical value. Remember, PRINT# writes exactly the same information on a file as would be displayed if PRINT were used.)

If you replace lines 160 and 180 of the program in Example 2 by the single line

```
180 PRINT#1,N$;S
```

the program would create file SCORES with three lines:

```
NICKLAUS 206
MILLER 208
WATSON 205
```

If the intent is to save the file for later printing, you may want this form, but if the file is intended only as an input file, you should not use it. If SCORES has this form, the statement

```
INPUT#1,N$
```

will give

```
N$="NICKLAUS 206"
```

Unless a string appearing in a file is enclosed in quotation marks, the PC obtains a value for a string variable by using all characters on the current line up to the first comma. To obtain the intended values you could include a separating comma

```
180 PRINT#1,N$;",";S
```

---

* DOS commands cannot be issued from BASIC. You must return control of the system to DOS by using the BASIC command SYSTEM.

or you could enclose the string in quotation marks:

    180 PRINT#1, CHR$(34); A$; CHR$(34); S

(34 is the numeric code for the quotation mark.) A simpler way is to use WRITE# instead of PRINT#. *The WRITE# statement encloses all strings in quotation marks and inserts commas between output values.* If you replace lines 160 and 180 of the program in Example 2 with the single statement

    180 WRITE#1, N$, S

or equivalently,

    180 WRITE#1, N$; S

the program will create file SCORES as follows:

```
"NICKLAUS", 206
"MILLER", 208
"WATSON", 205
```

The statement

    INPUT#1, N$, S

will now give the intended values for N$ and S.

    If you consistently use WRITE# statements to create files that will be used as input files, you can think of the items as constituting a single list of input values (just as do the items appearing in DATA lines). Input# statements will access these items in order (just as items in DATA lines are accessed in order by READ statements). That the file may consist of lines as described above is of no consequence if all strings are quoted. Thus (in Microsoft® BASIC), the statement

    INPUT#1, N$, S

is equivalent to the two statements

    INPUT#1, N$
    INPUT#1, S

All that matters is the order in which the input variables N$ and S appear. Note that this means INPUT# does *not* obtain values from files in exactly the same way INPUT obtains values from the keyboard. With keyboard input, the statement

    INPUT N$, S

requires that you type two values with a separating comma. If you respond in any other way, the PC will display

    Redo from start

and you must retype the input. The topic of how INPUT# obtains values from a file is considered in greater detail following Example 3.

EXAMPLE 3   **Here is a program to create a short file and then read it.**

```
100 REM ****************************************
110 REM * CREATE FILE CITIES FROM DATA LINES. *
120 REM ****************************************
130 REM
140 OPEN "CITIES" FOR OUTPUT AS #1
150 READ COUNT
160 FOR C=1 TO COUNT
170    READ CITY$, STATE$, ZIP$
180    WRITE#1, CITY$, STATE$, ZIP$
190 NEXT C
```

```
200 REM
210 REM ***************************
220 REM * READ AND DISPLAY DATA   *
230 REM * STORED IN FILE CITIES.  *
240 REM ***************************
250 REM
260 CLOSE 1
270 OPEN "CITIES" FOR INPUT AS #1
280 FOR C=1 TO COUNT
290    INPUT#1,CITY$,STATE$,ZIP$
300    PRINT CITY$;", ";STATE$;" ";ZIP$
310 NEXT C
320 CLOSE 1
500 REM ******************
510 REM *  D   A   T   A *
520 REM ******************
530 DATA 4
540 DATA MONTEREY,CA,93940
550 DATA BRIDGEWATER,MA,02324
560 DATA AUSTIN,TX,78731
570 DATA JOHNSON CITY,TN,37601
999 END
RUN

MONTEREY, CA 93940
BRIDGEWATER, MA 02324
AUSTIN, TX 78731
JOHNSON CITY, TN 37601
```

The action of the first program segment (lines 140–190) is as follows. Line 140 assigns the number 1 to the file CITIES that is to be created. Then on each pass through the FOR loop, line 170 reads values from the DATA statements into the variables CITY$, STATE$, and ZIP$, and line 180 transmits these values with separating commas to the output file CITIES. After execution of this program segment, the contents of file CITIES will be as follows:

```
"MONTEREY","CA","93940"
"BRIDGEWATER","MA","02324"
"AUSTIN","TX","78731"
"JOHNSON CITY","TN","37601"
```

The action of the second program segment (lines 260–320) is a follows. Line 260 closes the output file CITIES and line 270 reopens CITIES but this time as an input file. Then on each pass through the FOR loop, line 290 reads values from the file CITIES into the variables CITY$, STATE$, and ZIP$, and line 300 displays them as shown in the output.

■ REMARK Line 260 is necessary. The file number of an active file cannot be used in an OPEN statement. Without the close statement in line 260, you would have to specify a different file number in line 270. Doing this, although allowed, makes little sense.

There may be times when you need to process files that were created with PRINT# statements instead of WRITE# statements. In such situations, you should know more about how INPUT# obtains values from files. As we have already mentioned, string values that are enclosed in quotation marks are obtained as expected, and if a string input value is not quoted the PC uses all characters up to the next comma or up to the end of the line. If the input variable is numerical, the PC uses all characters up to the next space or comma, or up to the end of the line. If these characters do not represent a numerical constant, the value 0 is assigned to the input variable and program execution continues. The following table illustrates how INPUT# obtains values from files that were created by using PRINT# statements.

Statement	Contents of file #1	Values obtained
INPUT#1, A$, S	NICKLAUS 206 MILLER 208	A$="NICKLAUS 206", S=0 (The character string MILLER gives the value 0 for S.)
INPUT#1, A$, S	NICKLAUS, 206	A$="NICKLAUS", S=206
INPUT#1, S, A$	206 NICKLAUS	S=206, A$="NICKLAUS"
INPUT#1, A$	NICKLAUS, JACK	A$="NICKLAUS"
INPUT#1, A$	"NICKLAUS, JACK"	A$="NICKLAUS, JACK"
INPUT#1, A, B, C	10 20 30	A=10, B=20, C=30
INPUT#1, A, B, C	10, , 30	A=10, B=0, C=30 (As with keyboard input, the empty string gives the value 0.)

■ 17.2 Detecting the End of a Sequential File

Each file used as an input file contains a special **end of file** mark following its last datum. In Microsoft® BASIC it is CHR$(26), which is called the **Ctrl-Z** character: it can be entered at the keyboard by typing Z while holding down the key labeled Ctrl. This end of file mark serves two purposes.

1. While reading data from a file, the end of file mark is sensed by the computer. Any attempt to read information beyond this end of file mark produces a fatal Input past end error.
2. Microsoft® BASIC includes the **end of file function EOF.** If *n* is the file number of an active sequential file, EOF(*n*) is true if the end of file *n* has been reached; otherwise, EOF(*n*) is false. In Example 4 we show how you can use the EOF function to write programs that do not attempt to read beyond the ends of files.

EXAMPLE 4 Here is an illustration of the EOF function. The program displays the contents of a file named BIRTHS that contains these three lines:

```
SUE COREY, 2, 4, 89
ADAM JONES, 2, 15, 89
CANDY FOBES, 2, 28, 89

100 OPEN "BIRTHS" FOR INPUT AS #1
110 LET N=0        'Name count
120 WHILE NOT EOF(1)
130    INPUT#1, N$, M, D, Y
140    PRINT N$, M; "/"; D; "/"; Y
150    LET N=N+1
160 WEND
170 PRINT
180 PRINT "THERE WERE"; N; "BIRTHS THIS MONTH."
190 CLOSE 1
200 END
RUN

SUE COREY      2 / 4 / 89
ADAM JONES     2 / 15 / 89
CANDY FOBES    2 / 28 / 89

THERE WERE 3 BIRTHS THIS MONTH.
```

Line 120 checks whether more data are available on file 1. If the end of file mark has not been reached, NOT EOF(1) is true and the WHILE loop is entered. On each pass through this loop, lines 130 and 140 read and display one line of the file and line 150 increases the name count N by 1. After the last line of file BIRTHS has been processed by lines 130–150, the WHILE condition NOT EOF(1) is false; that is, the end of file mark has been sensed. The WHILE statement then transfers control out of the loop to line 170 and program execution continues from that point.

Microsoft® BASIC contains the LINE INPUT# statement, which can be used with the EOF function to count the number of lines in any sequential file. The statement

```
LINE INPUT#1, A$
```

assigns to A$ all characters (including any commas) on the current line of file #1. It skips over the RETURN/line feed sequence that ends the line so that the next LINE INPUT# statement will read the next line of the file.

EXAMPLE 5 Here is a program to count the number of lines in any sequential file.

```
100 INPUT "Enter file name: ", F$
110 OPEN F$ FOR INPUT AS #1
120 LET N=0                'Line counter
130 WHILE NOT EOF(1)
140     LINE INPUT#1, A$
150     LET N=N+1
160 WEND
170 CLOSE 1
180 PRINT "File ";F$;" contains";N;"lines."
190 END
```

REMARK Notice that the program does not display what is read from the file. If you insert the line

```
145 PRINT A$
```

the modified program will display the exact contents of file F$.

17.3 Problems

1. Here is a program to create a file COMM.

```
100 OPEN "COMM" FOR OUTPUT AS #1
110 READ N$, S, Q
120 WHILE N$<>"XXX"
130     WRITE#1, N$, S, Q
140     READ N$, S, Q
150 WEND
160 CLOSE 1
170 END
300 DATA J. D. SLOANE, 13000, 10000
310 DATA R. M. PETERS, 5000, 5000
320 DATA A. B. CARTER, 7400, 5000
330 DATA I. O. ULSTER, 12000, 10000
340 DATA XXX, 0, 0
```

Show the output of each program in parts (a) and (b).

a.
```
10 OPEN "COMM" FOR INPUT AS #1
20 WHILE NOT EOF(1)
30     INPUT#1, N$, S, Q
40     IF S>Q THEN
           PRINT N$ : PRINT "EXCESS;";S-Q : PRINT
50 WEND
60 CLOSE 1
70 END
```

b.
```
10 OPEN "COMM" FOR INPUT AS #2
20 WHILE NOT EOF(2)
30     INPUT#2, A$, S, Q
40     IF S>Q
           THEN C=0.10*(S-Q)
           ELSE C=0
50     LET W=265+C
60     PRINT A$, W
70 WEND
80 CLOSE 2
90 END
```

2. Here is a program to create a file GRADES.

```
100 OPEN "GRADES" FOR OUTPUT AS FILE 1
110 READ A$, N1, N2
120 WHILE A$<>"X"
130     WRITE#1, A$, N1, N2
140     READ A$, N1, N2
150 WEND
160 CLOSE 1
170 END
300 DATA JOAN, 80, 90
310 DATA SAM, 100, 80
320 DATA GREG, 80, 40
330 DATA MARY, 70, 30
340 DATA MARK, 50, 90
350 DATA X, 0, 0
```

Show the output of each program in parts (a) and (b).

a.
```
10 OPEN "GRADES" FOR INPUT AS #1
20 WHILE NOT EOF(1)
30     INPUT#1, B$, A, B
40     IF A>B THEN PRINT B$
50 WEND
60 CLOSE 1
70 END
```

b.
```
10 OPEN "GRADES" FOR INPUT AS #2
20 LET P$="PASS"
30 LET F$="FAIL"
40 WHILE NOT EOF(2)
50     INPUT#2, N$, X, Y
60     LET A=(X+2*Y)/3
70     IF A>65
           THEN PRINT N$, P$
           ELSE PRINT N$, F$
80 WEND
90 CLOSE 2
99 END
```

In Problems 3–20, write a program for each task specified.

3. Create a file named WORDS containing whatever English words are typed at the keyboard. After WORDS has been created, display its contents, three words per line. The file is to be used as an input file for Problems 4 and 5.

4. Given the file WORDS described in Problem 3, display all words beginning with a letter A through M, and follow this list by two counts—a count of how many words are in the file and a count of how many words were displayed.

5. Given the file WORDS described in Problem 3, create two files—one containing all words beginning with a letter A through M and the other containing the remaining words. Use

appropriate names for the two files. After the two new files have been created, display their contents in adjacent columns with appropriate headings.

6. Create a file NAMES containing up to 50 names typed at the keyboard. If a name is typed a second time, display an appropriate message but do not store the name twice. If at any time LIST is typed, display all names entered to that point. If END is typed, halt program execution. (*Suggestion:* Input names into an array and create the file NAMES only after the user types END.)

7. Create two files named ALPHA and BETA. ALPHA is to contain all numbers from 1 to 200 that are multiples of either 2, 3, 5, or 7. The rest of the numbers from 1 to 200 go in file BETA. After the files have been created, display their contents with appropriate titles.

8. The following table describes an investor's stock portfolio. Create a file STOCKS that contains this information. After file STOCKS has been created, display its contents as a four-column table with headings similar to those shown. The file STOCKS is to be used as an input file in Problems 9 and 10.

Name of stock	Number of shares	Last week's closing price	Current week's closing price
STERLING DRUG	800	16.50	16.125
DATA GENERAL	500	56.25	57.50
OWEN ILLINOIS	1,200	22.50	21.50
MATTEL INC	1,000	10.75	11.125
ABBOTT LAB	2,000	33.75	34.75
FED NATL MTG	2,500	17.75	17.25
IC GEN	250	43.125	43.625
ALO SYSTEMS	550	18.50	18.25

9. Produce a five-column report with the first four columns as in Problem 8 and a fifth column showing the percentage increase or decrease for each security.

10. Produce a four-column report showing the stock name, the equity at the close of business last week, the equity this week, and the dollar change in equity. End the report with a message showing the total net gain or loss for the week.

11. Create a file named LIBEL containing the following information about employees of the Libel Insurance Company. After file LIBEL has been created, display its contents as a five-column table with headings similar to those shown. The file LIBEL is to be used as an input file in Problems 12–16.

ID	Sex	Age	Years of service	Annual salary
012-24-2735	M	47	13	25,200.00
024-18-2980	F	33	6	19,300.00
018-26-3865	F	41	15	28,900.00
035-14-4222	M	22	2	16,400.00
026-21-4740	M	59	7	24,200.00
024-25-5200	F	25	3	18,000.00
018-17-5803	M	33	13	26,500.00
016-24-7242	F	28	4	18,400.00
021-18-7341	M	68	30	30,500.00
021-25-8004	M	35	6	19,300.00
031-42-9327	F	21	3	14,200.00

12. Produce two reports showing the employee information contained in LIBEL by sex. Give each report a title and four appropriately labeled columns.

13. Produce a report showing the ID numbers, years of service, and salaries of all employees who have been with the firm for more than 5 years.

14. Produce a two-column report showing ID numbers and annual salaries of all employees

whose annual salary exceeds $15,000. In addition to column headings, be sure the report has an appropriate title.

15. Produce a two-column report as described in Problem 14 for all employees whose annual salaries exceed the average annual salary of all Libel employees. Following the report, display the total annual salary earned by these employees. The title of the report should include the average salary of all Libel employees. (Do not read the file contents into arrays. Rather, read through the file to determine the total annual salary and average annual salary figures; then read the file a second time to produce the report.)

16. Write a menu-driven program to perform some or all of the tasks specified in Problems 11–15.

17. Create a file INVTRY containing the following inventory data. After file INVTRY has been created, display its contents as a five-column table with headings similar to those shown. The file INVTRY is to be used as an input file in Problems 18–20.

Item code	Item type	Units on hand	Average cost per unit	Sales price per unit
ITEM 1	A	20,500	1.55	1.95
ITEM 2	A	54,000	0.59	0.74
ITEM 3	B	8,250	3.40	4.10
ITEM 4	B	4,000	5.23	6.75
ITEM 5	A	15,000	0.60	0.75
ITEM 6	A	10,500	1.05	1.35
ITEM 7	B	6,000	7.45	9.89
ITEM 8	B	7,500	5.10	5.43
ITEM 9	B	15,500	3.10	4.10

18. Produce two separate reports, the first displaying the given information for type-A items and the second for type-B items.

19. Produce a five-column report showing the item code, the number of units on hand, and the total cost, total sales price, and total income these units represent (income = sales − cost). Conclude the report with a message showing the total cost, total sales price, and total income represented by the entire inventory.

20. Write a menu-driven program to perform some or all of the tasks specified in Problems 17–20.

17.4 Maintaining Sequential Files

Updating existing data files is a common programming application. In this section we give two examples illustrating this practice. The first involves updating a short simplified inventory file and the second a short personnel file. It should be remarked, however, that data files usually are not short and require rather complicated programs to maintain them. Our objective is simply to show that file maintenance is possible. A complete discussion of the many techniques used in file maintenance programs is beyond the scope of this introductory book.

EXAMPLE 6 A file update example.

A file named INVTRY contains the following data:

```
A10010, 2000
A10011, 4450
C22960, 1060
D40240, 2300
X99220, 500
X99221, 650
Y88000, 1050
Y88001, 400
```

302 Chapter 17 Data Files

The first entry in each line denotes an item code, and the second entry gives the quantity on hand. Our task is to write a program to allow a user to update INVTRY to reflect all transactions since the last update.

PROBLEM ANALYSIS

Let's assume that the user must specify, for each item to be changed, the item code, the number of units shipped since the last update, and the number of units received since the last update. Thus the user might come to the computer armed with a list like this:

Item code	Shipped	Received
A10010	1,200	1,000
A10011	1,000	550
D40240	1,800	2,000
Y88000	300	0

A person carrying out this task by hand might proceed as follows:

a. Read an item code.
b. Search the file INVTRY for this code, and change the units-on-hand figure as required.
c. If more changes are to be made, go to Step (a).
d. Have the updated copy of INVTRY typed.

This algorithm is not suitable for a BASIC program. Step (b) says to change a *single* number appearing on the file INVTRY, and this is not done when using sequential files. We will first input the data from INVTRY into two arrays and make the necessary changes in these arrays. After this has been done for each item requiring a change, Step (d) will involve creating a new copy of INVTRY by using the PRINT# or WRITE# statement. Since INVTRY is used as an input data file, we'll use WRITE#. Before rewriting this algorithm in a form suitable for a BASIC program, let's choose variable names:

CODES$ = array of item codes from file INVTRY
UNITS = corresponding array of quantities from INVTRY
ITEM.COUNT = number of lines in the file INVTRY
X$ = item code to be typed
S = quantity shipped
R = quantity received

In the following algorithm we require the user to type END after all changes have been made.

THE ALGORITHM

a. Input arrays CODES$ and UNITS from the file INVTRY.
b. Enter an item code X$.
c. While X$ is not END do the following:
  c1. Search for subscript K with CODES$(K) = X$.
  c2. If X$ is not found display an appropriate message, otherwise input quantities S and R for X$ and change UNITS(K) to UNITS(K) + R − S.
  c3. Enter next item code X$.
d. Make a new copy of INVTRY.
e. Stop.

Step (a) is easily coded. We simply open INVTRY as an input file and use a loop to read its contents into arrays CODES$ and UNITS.

Step (c) is also easily coded. We will include the code for Steps (c1)–(c3) in a loop that terminates when the input value X$ is END. Writing code for Steps (c1)–(c3) is not new to us and is relatively straightforward.

Code for Step (d) is also straightforward. We simply close INVTRY, open it again as an output file, and then write the contents of arrays CODES$ and UNITS on the file.

THE PROGRAM

```
100 REM ---------- INVENTORY UPDATE PROGRAM ----------
110 REM
120 REM         CODES$ = ARRAY OF ITEM CODES
130 REM          UNITS = ARRAY OF QUANTITIES
140 REM     ITEM.COUNT = NUMBER OF ITEMS
150 REM
160 REM *******************************************
170 REM INPUT ARRAYS CODES$ AND UNITS FROM FILE INVTRY.
180 REM
190 OPEN "INVTRY" FOR INPUT AS #1
200 DIM CODES$(50),UNITS(50)
210 LET ITEM.COUNT=0
220 WHILE NOT EOF(1) AND ITEM.COUNT<50
230     LET ITEM.COUNT=ITEM.COUNT+1
240     INPUT #1, CODES$(ITEM.COUNT),UNITS(ITEM.COUNT)
250 WEND
260 IF NOT EOF(1) THEN
        PRINT "INADEQUATE ARRAY DIMENSIONS - SEE PROGRAMMER." :
        CLOSE 1 : END
270 CLOSE 1
280 REM
290 REM ***********************************************
300 REM GET KEYBOARD CHANGES AND UPDATE ARRAYS CODES$ AND UNITS.
310 REM
320 PRINT "ENTER UPDATE INFORMATION AS REQUESTED."
330 PRINT
340 INPUT "ITEM(END WHEN DONE)";X$            'Keyboard input
350 WHILE X$<>"END"
360     REM
370     LET K=1                               'Search array
380     WHILE CODES$(K)<>X$ AND K<ITEM.COUNT  'CODES$ for
390         LET K=K+1                         'item X$.
400     WEND
410     IF CODES$(K)<>X$ THEN
            PRINT X$;" IS NOT AN INVENTORY ITEM." : GOTO 460
420     REM
430     INPUT "UNITS SHIPPED";S               'Keyboard input
440     INPUT "UNITS RECEIVED";R              'Keyboard input
450     LET UNITS(K)=UNITS(K)+R-S             'Update array.
460     PRINT
470     INPUT "ITEM(XXX WHEN DONE)";X$
480 WEND
490 REM
500 REM *******************************
510 REM MAKE A NEW COPY OF FILE INVTRY.
520 REM
530 OPEN "INVTRY" FOR OUTPUT AS #1
540 FOR K=1 TO ITEM.COUNT
550     WRITE#1,C$(K),Q(K)
560 NEXT K
570 CLOSE 1
580 PRINT "INVTRY IS UPDATED."
590 END
```

We ran this program, with file INVTRY as shown in the problem statement, and obtained the following screen display:

```
ENTER UPDATE INFORMATION AS REQUESTED.

ITEM(END WHEN DONE)? A10010
UNITS SHIPPED? 1200
UNITS RECEIVED? 1000
```

```
             ITEM(END WHEN DONE)? A10011
             UNITS SHIPPED? 1000
             UNITS RECEIVED? 550

             ITEM(END WHEN DONE)? D40241
             D40241 IS NOT AN INVENTORY ITEM.

             ITEM(END WHEN DONE)? D40240
             UNITS SHIPPED? 1800
             UNITS RECEIVED? 2000

             ITEM(END WHEN DONE)? END
             INVTRY IS UPDATED.
```

■ REMARK This last output line INVTRY IS UPDATED is intended to reassure us that the file has been correctly updated. To see that this is so, we could use the DOS command TYPE INVTRY.

```
A>TYPE INVTRY

"A10010",1800
"A10011",4000
"C22960",1060
"D40240",2500
"X99220",500
"X99221",650
"Y88000",1050
"Y88001",400
```

In the next example we modify an existing sequential file by adding data to the end of it. Changing a sequential file in this way does not require making a completely new copy of the file. The Microsoft® BASIC statement

```
OPEN "DATA5" FOR APPEND AS #1
```

opens DATA5 as an output file, but positions the file at the end of any data already on the file. Subsequent output to this file will be written at the end of the file.

EXAMPLE 7 The ID numbers and names of all employees of the Land Foundry Company are stored on the personnel file EMPLOY.DAT. A typical line is

"23501","AHEARN JOHN F."

Let's write a program to allow a user to add new employees to this file.

PROBLEM ANALYSIS

Input: Data stored in the file EMPLOY.DAT
New names and ID numbers typed at keyboard

Output: File EMPLOY.DAT updated as specified in the problem statement

A person carrying out this task by hand might proceed as follows.

 a. Get the employee file.
 b. For each new employee:
  b1. Select an ID not yet used.
  b2. Add the employee to the file.
 c. Return the file to the file cabinet.

Since each ID for a new employee must not already be in use, the first task in Step (b) requires that each new ID be compared with all IDs that are currently being used. We should not search the actual file each time these comparisons must be made. Rather we will read all IDs into an array and use this array for each search. (Although information on a diskette can be accessed very quickly, accessing information that is already in memory is much faster.) Of course, each new ID must be added to the array of ID codes so that the same code will not be used for two new employees. The second task in Step (b) requires that we add information to the end of a file. To accomplish this we will close EMPLOY after reading the array of ID numbers and then reopen it as an APPEND file.

■ REMARK   In some versions of BASIC, you can open a file as an INPUT file, read all of its contents leaving the file positioned at the end of file mark (as we do to get the array of ID numbers), and then write new information at the end of the file. If you use this method in Microsoft® BASIC, you will not get an error message, but the new information will not properly be added to the file. Thus, in Microsoft® BASIC you should open a file as an APPEND file if the intent is to add information at the end of an existing file.

To allow us to write a concise algorithm with sufficient detail to be coded to a BASIC program, we will use the following variable names.

    ID$ = array of ID numbers
ID.COUNT = number of entries in array ID$
NEW.EMP$ = name of a new employee to be added to the file
 NEW.ID$ = ID code assigned to employee NEW.EMP$

In the following algorithm we require the user to type XXX after all new names have been entered.

THE ALGORITHM

a. Read the file EMPLOY.DAT to obtain the array ID$ of ID codes and the count ID.COUNT of how many codes are included.
b. Enter a name NEW.EMP$.
c. While NEW.EMP$ is not XXX do the following:
  c1. Enter NEW.ID$.
  c2. Search array ID$ for NEW.ID$.
  c3. If NEW.ID$ is found:
      Display an appropriate message.
      Repeat Step (c1).
    Otherwise:
      Append NEW.ID$ and NEW.EMP$ to the file.
      Add 1 to the ID.COUNT.
      Assign NEW.ID$ to ID$(ID.COUNT).
      Enter the next name NEW.EMP$.
d. Close EMPLOY.DAT and stop.

THE PROGRAM

```
100 REM     PROGRAM TO UPDATE THE FILE EMPLOY.DAT
110 REM
120 REM         ID$ = ARRAY OF ID CODES.
130 REM    ID.COUNT = NUMBER OF ENTRIES IN ARRAY ID$
140 REM    NEW.EMP$ = NAME OF A NEW EMPLOYEE
150 REM     NEW.ID$ = ID CODE ASSIGNED TO NEW.EMP$
160 REM
170 REM *******************************************
180 REM READ ID CODES FROM FILE EMPLOY.DAT INTO
190 REM IN ARRAY ID$.  STORE COUNT IN ID.COUNT.
200 REM
210 DIM ID$(300)
220 LET ID.COUNT=0
230 OPEN "EMPLOY.DAT" FOR INPUT AS #1
240 WHILE NOT EOF(1) AND ID.COUNT<300
250     LET ID.COUNT=ID.COUNT+1
260     INPUT#1, ID$(ID.COUNT),OLD.EMP$
270 WEND
280 CLOSE 1
290 REM *******************************************
300 REM GET NEW EMPLOYEE NAMES AND ID'S FROM
310 REM KEYBOARD AND APPEND TO FILE EMPLOY.DAT.
320 REM
```

```
330 OPEN "EMPLOY.DAT" FOR APPEND AS #1
340 REM
350 PRINT "Enter each new employee with last name first."
360 PRINT "Do NOT use commas. Thus, type"
370 PRINT "    DOE SUSAN B.  and not   DOE,SUSAN B."
380 PRINT
390 INPUT "NAME (XXX when done)";NEW.EMP$
400 REM
410 WHILE NEW.EMP$<>"XXX"
420    INPUT "IDENTIFICATION CODE";NEW.ID$
430    LET K=1
440    WHILE NEW.ID$<>ID$(K) AND K<ID.COUNT    'Search array
450       LET K=K+1                            ' ID$ for new
460    WEND                                    ' ID number.
470    IF NEW.ID$=ID$(K) THEN
          PRINT NEW.ID$;" is already being used." : GOTO 420
480    LET ID.COUNT=ID.COUNT+1
490    LET ID$(ID.COUNT)=NEW.ID$
500    WRITE #1,NEW.ID$,NEW.EMP$
510    IF ID.COUNT=300 THEN
          PRINT "EMPLOY.DAT is too large. See programmer." :
          CLOSE 1 : END
520    PRINT
530    INPUT "NAME (XXX when done)";NEW.EMP$
540 WEND
550 CLOSE 1
560 PRINT : PRINT "File EMPLOY.DAT has been updated."
570 END
RUN

Enter each new employee with last name first.
Do NOT use commas. Thus, type
    DOE SUSAN B.  and not   DOE,SUSAN B.

NAME (XXX when done)? MANN HEATHER A.
IDENTIFICATION CODE? 63334

NAME (XXX when done)? JACKSON SALLY J.
IDENTIFICATION CODE? 23501
23501 is already being used.
IDENTIFICATION CODE? 33501

NAME (XXX when done)? XXX

File EMPLOY.DAT has been updated.
```

We ran the program with a short file containing eight names. After the run shown, we used the DOS command TYPE EMPLOY.DAT to verify that the two new names were added to the file.

```
A>TYPE EMPLOY.DAT
"23501","AHEARN JOHN F."
"53241","ANDERSON ALBERT G."
"15653","SIMPSON DONALD C."
"37671","HENDRIX SAMUEL D."
"49313","POST EDWARD L."
"44446","MURRAY HAROLD N."
"23786","SILVA JOSE R."
"83817","CONNORS FRANK P."
"63334","MANN HEATHER A."
"33501","JACKSON SALLY J."
```

■ **REMARK** As it stands, the program in this example cannot be used to create the file EMPLOY.DAT. It can be used only to add new information to an existing file. If a file named EMPLOY.DAT does not exist (on the diskette in the disk unit) when the program is run, the OPEN statement in line 230 will cause a *fatal* File not found error. Only files that exist can be opened for INPUT. Microsoft® BASIC, however, contains two statements

ON ERROR GOTO ln$_1$
RESUME ln$_2$

that allow you to handle such errors. Once the ON ERROR statement is executed, any *fatal error*—that is, any error that would otherwise cause an error message and halt program execution—will cause an immediate transfer to line ln$_1$. The statements beginning at line ln$_1$ will be executed and when the RESUME statement is encountered, normal program execution will resume at line ln$_2$. For the program in this example, we can avoid the File not found error by including these two lines:

```
1 ON ERROR GOTO 1000
1000 RESUME 330
```

Now if we run the program to create the new file EMPLOY.DAT, the error condition caused by the attempt to open a nonexistent file for input will transfer control to line 1000, which simply resumes program execution at line 330. The File not found error has been avoided and the program can now be used to create a new file named EMPLOY.DAT.

■ 17.5 Problems

In Problems 1–17, write a program for each task specified.

1. The Hollis Investment Company maintains a file EMPLOY containing the name, age, years of service, and monthly salary of salaried employees. Include the following information in DATA lines for a program to create the file EMPLOY. The file will be used as an input file in Problems 2–5.

Name	Age	Years of service	Monthly salary
Murray George	53	21	2,100.00
Ritchie Albert	41	13	1,850.00
Galvin Fred	62	35	2,475.00
Cummings Barbara	37	16	1,675.00
Gieseler Norma	41	20	2,200.00
Hughes Bette	52	18	2,050.00
Meland Ralph	29	5	1,550.00
Tibeau Betty	30	7	1,340.00

2. A 5% across-the-board salary increase has been negotiated for all Hollis employees. Write a program to update the file EMPLOY to reflect this increase.

3. Write a program to remove employees from the file or to add new employees. Use your program to delete Fred Galvin and add the following:

   BING MELINDA 23 0 1200
   DEREK SUSAN 24 0 1800

   (*Suggestion:* If you use an array to store the names, do not actually delete Fred Galvin. Rather, store a special value such as DELETE in place of the name. Then when you make an updated copy of the file EMPLOY, simply omit employees stored as DELETE.)

4. Using the file EMPLOY as an input file, create a file EMPLOY1 that contains precisely the information in EMPLOY but with the names in alphabetical order. After EMPLOY1 has

been created, display its contents. (*Suggestion:* Read the file contents into four arrays, sort the arrays so that the names are in alphabetical order, and then create EMPLOY1.)

5. Create a file EMPLOY2 that contains the same information as EMPLOY, but with monthly salaries in descending order. After EMPLOY2 has been created, display its contents.

6. A manufacturing company sends a package consisting of eight new products to each of ten families and asks each family to rate each product on the following scale:

0 = poor   1 = fair   2 = good   3 = very good   4 = excellent

Here are the results in tabular form:

		\multicolumn{10}{c}{Family number}
		1	2	3	4	5	6	7	8	9	10
Product number	1	0	1	1	2	1	2	2	1	0	1
	2	2	3	3	0	3	2	2	3	4	1
	3	1	3	4	4	4	1	4	2	3	2
	4	3	4	2	4	3	1	3	4	2	4
	5	0	1	3	2	2	2	1	3	0	1
	6	4	4	4	3	2	1	4	4	1	1
	7	1	3	1	3	2	4	1	4	3	4
	8	2	2	3	4	2	2	3	4	2	3

Create a file RATE containing the information in this table. Then use this file to produce a two-column report showing the product numbers and the average rating for each product. (The file RATE will be used as an input file in Problems 7–9.)

7. Errors in the transcription of the numbers in the survey are discovered. The correct results for Families 1 and 7 are as follows:

Family 1	3	2	4	2	2	4	1	3
Family 7	2	3	4	4	2	4	3	2

Write a program to allow the user to change the eight ratings for any family. Use your program to correct the ratings for Family 1 and Family 7.

8. Use the file RATE to produce a report as in Problem 6. However, have the average ratings appear from smallest to largest.

9. Use the file RATE to produce a two-column report as follows: The first column is to give the product numbers receiving at least six ratings of 3 or better and the second column is to give the number of these ratings obtained.

10. The Sevard Company maintains files SST and WEEKLY. Create these two files so that they contain the following information. The files are to be used as input files in Problems 11–13.

File SST

Employee ID number	Year-to-date income	Hourly rate
024-25-5200	18240.00	12.00
018-26-2980	16800.00	10.50
021-18-7341	21150.50	14.25
031-42-9327	25600.00	16.00
035-14-4222	47250.00	25.00
026-21-1274	44980.00	23.00

File WEEKLY

Employee ID number	This week's hours
024-25-5200	42
018-26-2980	36
021-18-7341	32
031-42-9327	52
035-14-4222	50
026-21-1274	48

11. A Social Security tax deduction of 7.51% is taken on the first $45,000 earned by an employee. Once this amount is reached, no further deduction is made. Using the files SST and WEEKLY, produce a report giving the ID number, the current week's gross pay, and the current week's Social Security deduction for each employee. Employees are paid time and a half for all hours over 32.

12. Modify the program written for Problem 11 to update the year-to-date income in the file SST.

13. Using the files SST and WEEKLY, display a list of the ID numbers of all employees who have satisfied the Social Security tax requirement for the current year. With each ID number, give the year-to-date income figure.

14. Write a program to allow the user to create a mailing list file by typing its contents at the keyboard. Organize the file so that each entry occupies six lines as follows:

    Line 1   Last Name
    Line 2   First Name and Middle Initial
    Line 3   Street Address
    Line 4   City or Town
    Line 5   State
    Line 6   Zip Code

    After the file has been created, display its contents by using a standard three-line address format.

15. Write a menu-driven program to allow the user to create a mailing list file as described in Problem 14 and also to maintain the file by specifying changes at the keyboard. Since the user can modify the mailing list, you should store all mailing list entries in arrays (for instance, six string arrays) and make any changes in these arrays. This means that the file will be opened in only two situations: when any previously entered data must be read into the arrays (at the outset), and when the user specifies that the file should be updated (see UPDATE option below). Following is a suggested menu:

    ADD   To add new names and addresses.
    DEL   To delete names from the mailing list. (To delete a name, you can change the array entry that stores the last name to DELETE. Then, while updating the file, ignore any entries marked in this way.)
    LIST   To display the current mailing list entries with each entry occupying a single display line.
    UPDATE   To make a new copy of the mailing list file.
    END   To end the program. (In the subroutine that carries out this option, remind the user that UPDATE is required to save the latest version of the mailing list. Then give the user the chance to cancel this option selection.)

16. Write a menu-driven program as described in Problem 15. Then add the following options:

    SORT   To alphabetize the mailing list. (As explained in Problem 15, the array entries should be rearranged, not the file entries.)
    SLIST   To display all or part of the mailing list in a standard address format. (This option should be preceded by the SORT option. After SLIST is specified, the user

should be prompted for two words to obtain a listing of all entries with names alphabetically between the two words. Don't display entries that were deleted as described under the DEL option.)

17. Write a menu-driven program as described in Problem 15 or 16. Then add the following options:

ZSORT   To sort mailing list by zip codes. (As explained in Problem 15, the array entries should be rearranged, not the file entries.)

ZLIST   To display all or part of the mailing list in a standard address format. (This option should be preceded by the ZSORT option. After ZLIST is specified, the user should be prompted for a lowest and a highest zip code to obtain a listing of all entries with zip codes in this range. Don't display entries that were deleted as described under the DEL option.)

■ 17.6 Random Access Files

The following points concerning random files and how they differ from sequential files are significant.

1. Data in random files are organized in equal-length subdivisions called **records.** These records are numbered in sequence from 1 up to a maximum of 32767, but can be accessed randomly—that is, in any order. With sequential files data are accessed in order from the beginning of each file.

2. Any record or any part of a record can be changed without affecting other records in the file. With sequential files, changing a single item in a file involves making an entirely new copy of the file.

3. Only the contents of string variables are written to random files—numerical values are first converted to strings. This is not a disadvantage; the numerical values are stored in a compact binary form that not only saves space on diskettes, but also results in faster execution times for programs that process random files.

4. Most often, random files are created for use only as input files for programs. You will recall that sequential files are used for this purpose and also to store formatted output for later printing.

An OPEN statement that does not contain a mode specifier FOR INPUT, FOR OUTPUT, or FOR APPEND, opens the named file for random access. The statement

```
OPEN "DATA5" AS #1 LEN=40
```

specifies DATA5 as a random file with file number 1 and record length 40. This means that each record consists of exactly 40 *characters,* or *bytes.** If F$ = "DATA5", N = 1, and R = 40, the statement

```
OPEN F$ AS #N LEN=R
```

does the same thing. The record length R can be any integer from 1 to 32767. If the LEN = R specifier is omitted, the record length is 128. The CLOSE statement is used with random files just as it is used with sequential files.

Whenever a file is opened, a portion of main memory is reserved as the **file buffer.** If the OPEN statement specified LEN = R, the first R bytes in this buffer are used to store a record to be transmitted to the file or read from the file. If you load Microsoft®

---

* On the IBM PC, a *byte* is a sequence of eight bits (binary digits 0 and 1), and each character uses one byte for storage. Thus, *byte* and *character position* mean the same thing. It is also a common practice to refer to the characters themselves as bytes.

BASIC with either of the DOS commands

```
A>BASIC
A>BASICA
```

the buffer size will be 128 bytes, and 128 is the maximum record length you can specify in an OPEN statement. The buffer size can be increased by loading BASIC with either of the DOS commands

```
A>BASIC/S: n
A>BASICA/S: n
```

where *n* is an integer (from 1 to 32767) that specifies the buffer size.* You can then use any record length from 1 to *n*.

Brief descriptions of the BASIC statements, other than OPEN and CLOSE, most often used with random files are as follows.

FIELD   Associates string variable names with portions of the first *n* bytes in the file buffer when *n* denotes the record length. If file #1 has record length 17, the statement

```
FIELD#1, 15 AS C$, 2 AS S$
```

associates C$ with the first 15 bytes in the buffer and S$ with bytes 16 and 17. Since the first 17 bytes store the record to be transmitted to the file (see PUT statement) or read from the file (see GET statement), the FIELD statement effectively assigns string variable names to sequences of bytes in records. We say that the records have been **fielded:** bytes 1–15 constitute a field with the name C$ and bytes 16 and 17 constitute a field with name S$. As explained in what follows, records can be fielded simultaneously in more than one way.

LSET/RSET   These statements are used to move data into a file buffer for subsequent writing to the file with a PUT statement. If file #1 has been fielded as shown above, the statements

```
LSET C$="AUSTIN"
LSET S$="TX"
```

move AUSTIN to the 15 bytes in the buffer associated with C$ and TX to the two bytes associated with S$. Since AUSTIN requires only 6 of the available 15 bytes, it is left-justified with 9 trailing blanks. (RSET right-justifies with leading blanks.) If a string being moved to the file buffer is longer than the available space it is truncated from the right.

Note: You should never use LET, READ, or INPUT statements to assign values to fielded variables such as C$ and S$. Doing so terminates their association with the file buffer. In Microsoft® BASIC, LSET, RSET, and the GET statement described below provide the only means for moving data into a file buffer.

PUT#**n**[,**k**]   Writes a record from the file buffer for file #**n** as record **k** of the file. After executing the statements

```
OPEN "CITIES" AS #1 LEN=17
FIELD#1, 15 AS C$, 2 AS S$
LSET C$="AUSTIN"
LSET S$="TX"
```

---

* The PC always moves data to and from random files in blocks of 128 bytes. Thus, the common practice is to specify only multiples of 128 as buffer sizes.

the statement

    PUT#1, 3

writes the 17-byte record

    AUSTIN   TX

as record 3 of the file CITIES. If N = 1 and R = 3, the statement PUT#N,R does the same thing.

If the record number (,**k**) is omitted, sequential record numbers are used. A common practice is to use the abbreviated form PUT#**n** when creating a new file by writing its records in order from record 1.

GET#**n**[,**k**]   Reads record **k** from file #**n** into the file buffer for this file. If the file CITIES has been opened and fielded as above, and if the 17-byte string "JOHNSON CITY   TN" had previously been stored as record 4 of this file, the statement

    GET#1, 4

reads these 17 bytes into the file buffer. The field variables C$ and S$ will then have the values

    C$="JOHNSON CITY   "   (15 bytes)
    S$="TN"   (2 bytes)

If the record specifier (,**k**) is omitted, the records are accessed sequentially. It is common practice to use the abbreviated form GET#**n** if all records are to be read in order from the beginning of a random file.

EXAMPLE 8   Here is a program to create a random file containing data included in DATA lines.

```
100 OPEN "CITIES" AS #1 LEN=17
110 FIELD#1, 15 AS C$,2 AS S$
120 FOR N=1 TO 4
130     READ CITY$,STATE$
140     LSET C$=CITY$
150     LSET S$=STATE$
160     PUT#1,N
170 NEXT N
180 CLOSE 1
500 DATA MONTEREY,CA
510 DATA BRIDGEWATER,MA
520 DATA AUSTIN,TX
530 DATA JOHNSON CITY,TN
999 END
RUN
Ok
```

Line 100 opens CITIES as a random file with file number 1 and record length 17. If CITIES does not already exist, it is added to the diskette directory of files. If CITIES does exist, its contents are preserved but will be changed by the program.

On the first pass through the FOR loop, the read statement gives

    CITY$="MONTEREY"   (8 bytes)
    STATE$="CA"   (2 bytes)

Then the two LSET statements give

    C$="MONTEREY   "   (15 bytes)
    S$="CA"   (2 bytes)

That is, MONTEREY and CA are moved to the file buffer with MONTEREY left-justified in the 15-byte field associated with C$ by the FIELD statement. Since N = 1, line 160 writes the record that was assigned values by the LSET statements as record 1 of file CITIES. Similarly, the other three passes through the FOR loop write information into records 2, 3, and 4 of the file CITIES.

■ **REMARK**   It would not be correct to replace line 130 with

```
130 READ C$, S$
```

The FIELD statement associates C$ and S$ with portions of the file buffer. As mentioned previously, this association is terminated if C$ and S$ are assigned values by using READ, LET, or INPUT statements. Fielded variables, however, can be used in any other way. For instance, to cause the program to display information being written to the file, you can include

```
155 PRINT C$, S$
```

EXAMPLE 9   Here are two programs to read and display the contents of the file CITIES.

```
          Program A                    Program B

10 OPEN "CITIES" AS #1 LEN=17    10 OPEN "CITIES" AS #1 LEN=17
20 FIELD#1, 15 AS X$, 2 AS Y$    20 FIELD#1, 17 AS ALL$
30 FOR N=1 to 4                  30 FOR N=1 TO 4
40    GET#1, N                   40    GET#1, N
50    PRINT X$; Y$               50    PRINT ALL$
60 NEXT N                        60 NEXT N
70 CLOSE 1                       70 CLOSE 1
80 END                           80 END
RUN                              RUN

MONTEREY        CA               MONTEREY        CA
BRIDGEWATER     MA               BRIDGEWATER     MA
AUSTIN          TX               AUSTIN          TX
JOHNSON CITY    TN               JOHNSON CITY    TN
Ok                               Ok
```

Program A fields records in file CITIES exactly as in the program that created the file, except that field variables X$ and Y$ are used instead of C$ and S$. On each pass through the FOR loop, line 40 reads record N into the file buffer and line 50 displays the first 17 bytes of the file buffer.

In *Program B* the FIELD statement associates the variable ALL$ with the first 17 bytes in the file buffer—that is, with all 17 bytes in a single record. Hence, on each pass through the FOR loop, line 40 gets record N from the file and line 50 displays all 17 bytes of the record.

■ **REMARK 1**   If we change line 30 in either program to

```
30 FOR N=4 TO 1 STEP -2
```

the output will be

```
JOHNSON CITY    TN
BRIDGEWATER     MA
```

The records in a random file can be accessed or created in any order.

■ **REMARK 2**   A file can be fielded in more than one way in the same program. For instance, if we modify *Program A* by typing

```
25 FIELD#1, 2 AS A$
50 PRINT X$; "First two letters are "; A$; "."
```

the output will be

```
MONTEREY        First two letters are MO.
BRIDGEWATER     First two letters are BR.
AUSTIN          First two letters are AU.
JOHNSON CITY    First two letters are JO.
```

In the modified program, line 20 fields Y$ as a 2-byte string, but doesn't use it. Note also that line 25 associates A$ with the first two bytes in the file buffer but does not field bytes 3 to 17.

■ **REMARK 3** In *Program A,* X$ contains the name of a city or town followed by trailing blanks. If you need to display the name without the trailing blanks, you must first find the position P of the last letter in X$. The statement

```
LET CITY$=X$
```

does not get rid of these blanks—all 15 characters in X$ are assigned to CITY$. Nor can you use the statement

```
LET P=INSTR(X$," ")-1
```

This will give the position of the letter just before the first blank, but for "JOHNSON CITY" this is not the letter we need. Following is a good way to find P.

```
40 LET P=15
44 WHILE MID$(X$,P,1)=" "
46     LET P=P-1
48 WEND
```

If you insert these lines in *Program A* and change line 50 to

```
50 PRINT LEFT$(X$,P);", ";Y$
```

the output will be

```
MONTEREY, CA
BRIDGEWATER, MA
AUSTIN, TX
JOHNSON CITY, TN
```

□

As stated earlier, all variables appearing in FIELD statements must be string variables. This means that only strings can be moved to a file buffer for writing to a random file. Thus, to store numerical data on a random file, you must first convert the numbers to strings. Microsoft® BASIC provides three string-valued functions, called **Make functions,** that are used to convert numbers to a compact binary form for storage in random files.

MKI$(**n**)   converts an integer **n** in the range -32768 to 32767 to a 2-byte string.
MKS$(**n**)   converts a single-precision number **n** to a 4-byte string.
MKD$(**n**)   converts a double-precision number **n** to an 8-byte string.

When these strings are later accessed for processing, they are converted back to numerical values by using the following **Convert functions.**

CVI(A$)   converts the 2-byte string A$ to an integer.
CVS(A$)   converts the 4-byte string A$ to a single-precision numerical value.
CVD(A$)   converts the 8-byte string A$ to a double-precision numerical value.

EXAMPLE 10   Here is a program to create and then read a random file whose contents represent integer, single-precision, and double-precision numerical values.

```
100 OPEN "DATA.R14" AS #1 LEN=14
110 FIELD#1, 2 AS N1$, 4 AS N2$, 8 AS N3$
120 FOR RECNUM=1 TO 4
130     LET N=1000*RECNUM
```

```
140     LSET N1$=MKI$(N)
150     LSET N2$=MKS$(N/7000)
160     LSET N3$=MKD$(N/7000)
170     PUT#1,RECNUM
180 NEXT RECNUM
190 PRINT
200 PRINT "INTEGER","SINGLE PREC."," DOUBLE PREC."
210 PRINT " (NUM) ","  (NUM/7000) ","   (NUM/7000) "
220 PRINT
230 FOR RECNUM=1 TO 4
240     GET#1,RECNUM
250     PRINT CVI(N1$),CVS(N2$),CVD(N3$)
260 NEXT RECNUM
270 CLOSE 1
280 END
RUN

INTEGER         SINGLE PREC.        DOUBLE PREC.
 (NUM)           (NUM/7000)          (NUM/7000)

  1000           .1428571            .1428571343421936
  2000           .2857143            .2857142686843872
  3000           .4285715            .4285714328289032
  4000           .5714286            .5714285373687744
```

The OPEN statement specifies 14-byte records, and the FIELD statement associates variables with records as follows.

N1$ first two bytes
N2$ next four bytes
N3$ next eight bytes

On each pass through the first FOR loop, line 140 obtains a string value for N1$ by converting the integer value of N to a 2-byte string, line 150 converts N/7000 to a 4-byte string for N2$, and line 160 converts N/7000 to an 8-byte string for N3$. Line 170 writes these data as record RECNUM of the file DATA.R14.

On each pass through the second FOR loop, GET#1,RECNUM reads record RECNUM from file DATA.R14 into the file buffer, and line 250 displays the numbers obtained by converting N1$, N2$, and N3$ back to an integer, single-precision number, and double-precision number, respectively.

■ **REMARK 1** If you issue the DOS command TYPE DATA.R14, the screen display will not be readable. A string produced by a Make function may or may not consist of display characters; even if it does, the characters will not display the number being represented. (See Remark 2.)

■ **REMARK 2** Although BASIC allows you to use the string function STR$ to convert numbers to strings for random file storage and VAL to convert these strings back to numbers, there are many reasons you should not do this.

1. Most often, the Make functions give shorter strings than STR$. Following are some comparisons you can verify in immediate mode.

String expression	Number of bytes	
MKI$(12345)	2	
STR$(12345)	6	(Note leading blank.)
MKI$(7)	2	
STR$(7)	2	
MKS$(1.234567)	4	
STR$(1.234567)	10	

316 Chapter 17 Data Files

2. With the Make functions, you always know exactly how much space to allocate for numbers. With STR$, you may have to guess.
3. STR$ and VAL require more processing time than do the Make and Convert functions. Each string produced by a Make function is essentially an exact representation of how the number being converted appears in memory. If you know how to convert integers to binary form, you should try to explain why the immediate mode statement PRINT MKI$(1028) produces the display

◆◆

In each of the preceding programs to access data in a random file we used a FOR loop because we knew exactly how many records were in the file. If you don't know how many records are in a file you can find out, provided that you know the record length. To help explain how this is done, let's display the file CITIES created in Example 8.

```
A>TYPE CITIES
MONTEREY         CABRIDGEWATER    MAAUSTIN          TXJOHNSON CITY   TN

A>
```

The line immediately following the TYPE command displays the four 17-byte records that were written to the file. However, the file actually contains 128 bytes—the PC writes to random files in blocks of 128 bytes. All but the first 68 (4 × 17 = 68) of these 128 bytes contain *null* characters CHR$(0) which the PC displays as blank spaces. (That's why the display contains a blank line.) To count how many actual data records are in the file CITIES, we can simply compare the first character of each record, starting with the first, until a null (not blank) character is encountered. The program in the next example uses this method to count records in random files.

EXAMPLE 11   Here is a program to count the actual data records in any file.

```
100 INPUT "Name of file";F$
110 INPUT "Record length";R
120 OPEN F$ AS #1 LEN=R
130 FIELD#1,R AS ALL$
140 LET K=0                     'Count of actual data records.
150 GET#1                       'Get first record.
160 WHILE ASC(ALL$)<>0          'Loop while record not empty.
170     LET K=K+1               'Count the data record.
180     GET#1                   'Get the next record.
190 WEND
200 PRINT F$;" contains";K;"data records."
210 CLOSE 1
220 END
RUN

Name of file? CITIES
Record length? 17
CITIES contains 4 data records.

RUN

Name of file? CITIES
Record length? 1
CITIES contains 68 data records.

RUN

Name of file? NOFILE.TMP
Record length? 1
NOFILE.TMP contains 0 data records.
```

The first run shows that CITIES contains four 17-byte records. The second shows that it contains sixty-eight 1-byte records (one byte for each of the 68 characters written to the file). The third run shows that the program works for empty files—for instance, files that didn't exist before the program was run.

■ REMARK Since the program examines only the first character in each record—ASC(ALL$) gives the numeric code of the first character in ALL$—it would be correct to change line 130 to

```
130 FIELD#1,1 AS ALL$
```

The program would work exactly as before. (If you make this change you should of course use a name other than ALL$.)

Microsoft® BASIC contains two file-related functions that you might find helpful.

LOF(n) This is the **length of file function.** It gives the number of bytes in file **#n**. Bytes containing null characters are counted, but the end of file character Ctrl-Z is not.

LOC(n) this is the **record locator function.** It gives the number of the last record written to or read from file **#n**. When file **#n** is first opened, LOC(**n**) is 0.

The program in Example 11 can be improved slightly by using the LOC function. The variable K in the program counts records, but LOC does the same thing. Thus, lines 140 and 170 that initialize and increment K can be deleted if you replace the counter K in the PRINT statement with LOC(1).

Two common uses of the *length of file* function LOF are as follows:

1. LOF provides a simple way to ensure that you don't mistakenly write over data previously stored in files. The two lines

```
200 OPEN F$ AS #1 LEN=R
210 IF LOF(1)=0 THEN 300
```

will open F$ and immediately test the condition LOF(1) = 0. If this condition is false— that is, if F$ contains data—control passes to the line following line 210, where this situation is handled. For instance, lines 220–290 might allow the user to specify another file name F$, or they might determine the record number of the last data record so that new data can be appended to the file. If the condition LOF(1) = 0 is true, control will pass around the program segment that handles existing file names.

2. If file #1 has record length R, the statement

```
LET N=LOF(1)\R
```

gives the number N of records (both data records and records containing only null characters) in the file. Integer division (\) is used because the PC writes only complete records to random files. The record number of the last data record can then be found by examining the first character in record N, in record N − 1, and so on, until a character other than the null character is encountered. This alternative to the method shown in Example 11 should be used with very large data files. There will be only a few null records to test, whereas the method of Example 11 may require testing many hundreds of data records.

In this section, we have described the statements and functions used with random files:

Statements		
OPEN	LSET	PUT
CLOSE	RSET	GET
FIELD		

Functions		
MKI$	CVI	LOC
MKS$	CVS	LOF
MKD$	CVD	

318 Chapter 17 Data Files

The preceding examples illustrate how these statements are used to create random files and to access the information contained in existing files. We conclude this chapter by showing how they can be used in file maintenance programs.

EXAMPLE 12   Let's write a program to add new data typed at the keyboard to a student information file. The program must work for files that already exist and also to create new files.

The information for each student is to be stored in a record as follows.

Field 1	9-digit identification number	Bytes 1–9
Field 2	Student's name	Bytes 10–34
Field 3	Student's local address	Bytes 35–80

PROBLEM ANALYSIS

It is not difficult to write an algorithm for this task if we omit the details.

a. Open the student information file.
b. Use a FIELD statement to define fields for each record.
c. Find the record number of the last record in the file. If a new file is being created, set the record number to 0.
d. Obtain the input data from the keyboard and write this information to the file.
e. Close the file and stop.

So that the program can be used to create or modify more than one file, we will allow the user to specify the name of the file to be used. With this in mind, a quick reading of the algorithm might suggest the following variables.

```
    F$ = name of the file to be used
     N = record counter
    N$ = student's name
  SSN$ = ID number for N$
 ADDR$ = local address of N$
```

Since values must not be input for field names, we will use N.$, SSN.$, and ADDR.$ in the FIELD statement.

Writing BASIC code for Steps (a), (b), (c), and (e) is not new to us. For Step (a) we will input a value for F$ and open F$ as a random file with record length 80 (80 is specified in the problem statement). Step (b) is accomplished with a single FIELD statement (line 200 in the program). For Step (c) we will use the method that was used in Example 11.

When obtaining input for records that contain more than one field [as in Step (d)], the usual practice is to allow an end-of-data indicator as the value of the first field to be input. In the following refinement of Step (d), we use the N$ value XXX for this purpose.

d1. Input N$.
d2. While N$ is not XXX, do the following.
 d1. Input values for SSN$ and ADDR$.
 d2. Add 1 to the record count N.
 d3. Write a record containing N$, SSN$, and ADDR$ as record N.
 d4. Input the next N$.

THE PROGRAM

```
100 REM PROGRAM TO ADD NEW NAMES TO STUDENT INFORMATION FILES.
110 REM
120 REM        F$ = NAME OF FILE TO BE USED
130 REM         N = LARGEST RECORD NUMBER IN USE
140 REM        N$ = STUDENT'S NAME
150 REM      SSN$ = IDENTIFICATION NUMBER FOR N$
160 REM     ADDR$ = LOCAL ADDRESS FOR N$
```

```
170 PRINT
180 INPUT "FILE NAME";F$
190 OPEN F$ AS #1 LEN=80
200 FIELD#1,9 AS SSN.$,25 AS N.$,46 AS ADDR.$
210 REM
220 REM ------ DETERMINE LARGEST RECORD NUMBER N IN USE -----
230 LET N=0
240 IF LOF(1)=0 THEN 290    'Test if new file is being created.
250 GET#1
260 WHILE ASC(SSN.$)<>0
270     LET N=N+1 : GET#1
280 WEND
290 REM
300 REM --------------- DATA ENTRY SECTION -----------------
310 PRINT
320 PRINT "Be sure to enter last names first." : PRINT
330 LINE INPUT "NAME(type XXX when done): ";N$
340 WHILE N$<>"XXX"
350     LINE INPUT "IDENTIFICATION NUMBER:     ";SSN$
360     IF LEN(SSN$)<>9 THEN
            PRINT "Please retype using 9 digits." : GOTO 350
370     LINE INPUT "LOCAL ADDRESS:             ";ADDR$
380     INPUT "Is entry correct(Y or N) ";C$
390     IF C$<>"Y" AND C$<>"y" THEN
            PRINT "Entry ignored, retype it." : GOTO 440
400     LSET SSN.$=SSN$
410     LSET N.$=N$
420     LSET ADDR.$=ADDR$
430     LET N=N+1 : PUT#1,N
440     PRINT
450     LINE INPUT "NAME(type XXX when done): ";N$
460 WEND
470 CLOSE 1
480 END
RUN

FILE NAME? STUDENTS

Be sure to enter last names first.

NAME(type XXX when done): BYRON, SALLY ANN
IDENTIFICATION NUMBER:     123456789
LOCAL ADDRESS:             BIRCH 122, CAMPUS
Is entry correct(Y or N)? Y

NAME(type XXX when done): TREMONT, JOSEPH E.
IDENTIFICATION NUMBER:     987654321
LOCAL ADDRESS:             ASPEN 312, CAMPUS
Is entry correct(Y or N)? Y

NAME(type XXX when done): HAVERLY, BARRY A.
IDENTIFICATION NUMBER:     012333012
LOCAL ADDRESS:             123 SUMMER ST., DEVON CT
Is entry correct(Y or N)? Y

NAME(type XXX when done): PRICE, HARRY A.
IDENTIFICATION NUMBER:     412444321
LOCAL ADDRESS:
Is entry correct(Y or N)? N
Entry ignored, retype it.

NAME(type XXX when done): PRICE, HARRY O.
IDENTIFICATION NUMBER:     412444321
LOCAL ADDRESS:             ASPEN 226, CAMPUS
Is entry correct(Y or N)? Y

NAME(type XXX when done): XXX
Ok
```

We used LINE INPUT for keyboard entries to allow the user to include commas in names and addresses without having to enclose the input strings in quotation marks. Lines 380 and 390 are included so that the user can reject incorrect entries before they are written to the file. In the run shown, the incorrect entry PRICE, HARRY A. was noticed after the identification number was typed. We simply pressed the Enter key for the address, typed N as shown, and then retyped all three lines.

Line 360 rejects ID numbers that do not contain exactly 9 digits. Although the user can reject incorrect entries as described above, an incorrect 8- or 10-digit ID number could easily go unnoticed.

■ **REMARK 1** If the file STUDENTS did not exist before the run shown, it would now contain four records. If it did exist (on the diskette in the disk unit), it would now contain whatever was already on the file followed by these four records. (Since all data stored in the file STUDENTS represent string data, you can use the DOS command TYPE STUDENTS to see these records. We used a record length of 80 so that each record would occupy a single display line.)

■ **REMARK 2** This program provides a way to correct errors made while typing student information, but does nothing to assist the user in the selection of file names. For instance, if the intent is to create a new file, but an existing file name is typed, all new student information will be appended to the existing file—even if its contents have nothing to do with student information. Your programs should not let this happen. For the program in this example, we could include the line

```
290 IF N=0 THEN PRINT F$;" is a new file name."
    ELSE GET#1,1 : PRINT "First name in ";F$;" is ";N$
```

to tell the user something about the file name selected. To select another name, the user would type XXX for the first name N$. The program would halt, with no harm done, and it could be run again with another file name.

As mentioned at the outset of this section, any record or any part of a record can be changed without affecting other records in the file. This is possible because a file can be fielded in any way you wish and also because the PUT statement can write to any record in the file. Thus, programs used to maintain random files should allow for changes in individual records as well as for the addition of new records as illustrated in the preceding example. File maintenance programs should also allow for the deletion of records. As illustrated in the next example, deleting a record does not necessarily remove it from the file. Rather, a special character is written in a record (usually as the first byte) to indicate that the record is no longer in use.

EXAMPLE 13

Let's write a program to allow the user to modify records in a student information file. Specifically, the user should be allowed to change the name and address of any student or to delete a student from the file.

PROBLEM ANALYSIS

We will use the same variable names used in the preceding program to create and add to student information files. We will also open and field files exactly as before. If we omit details, we can write the following algorithm for the stated task.

  a. Open the student information file.
  b. Use a FIELD statement to define fields for each record.
  c. Input an ID number SSN$ (XXX when done).
  d. If SSN$ is not XXX, obtain changes from the keyboard, update the file, input the next ID number SSN$, and repeat Step (d).
  e. Close the file and stop.

We require the user to identify students by ID number rather than by name because two students might have the same name. If the record identified by SSN$ is to be modified, we will prompt the user for a new name and address and then write the new information to the file. If the record is to be deleted, we will write the character CHR$(255) as the first byte of the record by using the two statements

```
LSET SSN.$=CHR$(255)
PUT#1,R
```

This will leave the name and address fields as they were, but will erase the ID number and replace it with CHR$(255) followed by 8 spaces. In subsequent processing of the file, records with CHR$(255) as the first character will be ignored. We chose CHR$(255) as the *delete character* simply because it is rarely, if ever, used for another purpose. The following refinement of Step (d) of the algorithm carries out the process just described.

d. While SSN$ <> "XXX", do the following.
    d1. Specify whether the record is to be deleted or modified.
    d2. If the record is to be deleted, write CHR$(255) as the first character of the record.
    d3. If the record is to be modified, input a new name and/or address and write the new information to the file.
    d4. Input another value for SSN$.

THE PROGRAM

```
100 REM PROGRAM TO CHANGE ENTRIES IN STUDENT INFORMATION FILES.
110 REM
120 INPUT "NAME OF FILE TO BE MODIFIED";F$
130 OPEN F$ AS #1 LEN=80
140 FIELD#1, 9 AS SSN.$, 25 AS N.$, 46 AS ADDR.$
150 REM
160 REM -------------- DATA ENTRY SECTION --------------
170 PRINT
180 PRINT "This program allows you to change information for "
190 PRINT "any student.  After typing the identification number "
200 PRINT "of a student, enter changes requested.  To leave an"
210 PRINT "entry as it was, simply press the Enter key."
220 PRINT
230 INPUT "ID NUMBER(type XXX when done)";SSN$
240 WHILE SSN$<>"XXX"
250    REM -------- FIND RECORD NUMBER R FOR SSN$ --------
260    LET R=1 : GET#1,R
270    WHILE SSN.$<>SSN$ AND ASC(SSN.$)<>0
280       LET R=R+1 : GET#1,R
290    WEND
300    IF SSN.$<>SSN$ THEN
           PRINT "The ID number ";SSN$; " is not in use.":GOTO 420
310    PRINT "STUDENT'S NAME:      ";N.$
320    PRINT "STUDENT'S ADDRESS:   ";ADDR.$
330    REM
340    REM ---------- GET CHANGES FROM KEYBOARD ------------
350    INPUT "IS STUDENT TO BE REMOVED(Y OR N)";C$
360    IF C$="Y" OR C$="y" THEN LSET SSN.$=CHR$(255) : PUT#1,R:
           PRINT "Student has been deleted." : GOTO 420
370    LINE INPUT "ENTER NEW NAME: ",N$
380    LINE INPUT "ENTER NEW ADDRESS: ",ADDR$
390       IF N$<>"" THEN LSET N.$=N$
400       IF ADDR$<>"" THEN LSET ADDR.$=ADDR$
410       PUT#1,R : PRINT "New information has been recorded."
420    PRINT
430    INPUT "ID NUMBER (type XXX when done)";SSN$
440 WEND
450 CLOSE 1
460 PRINT "The file ";F$;" has been updated."
470 END
RUN

NAME OF FILE TO BE MODIFIED? STUDENTS
```

```
          This program allows you to change information for
          any student.  After typing the identification number
          of a student, enter changes requested.  To leave an
          entry as it was, simply press the Enter key.

          ID NUMBER(type XXX when done)? 987654321
          STUDENT'S NAME:     TREMONT, JOSEPH E.
          STUDENT'S ADDRESS:  ASPEN 312, CAMPUS
          IS STUDENT TO BE REMOVED(Y OR N)? Y
          Student has been deleted.

          ID NUMBER(type XXX when done)? 412444321
          STUDENT'S NAME:     PRICE, HARRY O.
          STUDENT'S ADDRESS:  ASPEN 226, CAMPUS
          IS STUDENT TO BE REMOVED(Y OR N)? N
          ENTER NEW NAME:
          ENTER NEW ADDRESS:  226 GROVE AVE, DEVON CT
          New information has been recorded.

          ID NUMBER(type XXX when done)? XXX
          The file STUDENTS has been updated.
          Ok
```

Before the run shown, we used the DOS command TYPE STUDENTS to obtain:

```
A>TYPE STUDENTS
123456789BYRON, SALLY ANN         BIRCH 122, CAMPUS
987654321TREMONT, JOSEPH E.       ASPEN 312, CAMPUS
012333012HAVERLY, BARRY A.        123 SUMMER ST., DEVON CT
412444321PRICE, HARRY O.          ASPEN 226, CAMPUS
```

After the run, we obtained the following screen display.

```
A>TYPE STUDENTS
123456789BYRON, SALLY ANN         BIRCH 122, CAMPUS
         TREMONT, JOSEPH E.       ASPEN 312, CAMPUS
012333012HAVERLY, BARRY A.        123 SUMMER ST., DEVON CT
412444321PRICE, HARRY O.          226 GROVE AVE, DEVON CT
```

(On the display screen, CHR$(255) appears as a blank space.)

Each new record added to a file causes the file to get longer, but deleting records by writing CHR$(255) as the first byte does not decrease the size of the file. Thus, after a file has been in use for some time, you may have to remove the "deleted" records. The following short program can be used for this purpose.

EXAMPLE 14 Here is a program to remove each record whose first character is CHR$(255) from any file.

```
100 INPUT "NAME OF FILE TO BE PROCESSED";F$
110 INPUT "RECORD LENGTH FOR FILE";L
120 OPEN F$ AS #1 LEN=L
130 OPEN "FILE2.TMP" AS #2 LEN=L
140 FIELD#1, L AS ALL1$
150 FIELD#2, L AS ALL2$
160 GET#1
170 WHILE ASC(ALL1$)<>0
180     IF ASC(ALL1$)<>255 THEN LSET ALL2$=ALL1$ : PUT #2
190     GET#1
200 WEND
210 CLOSE
220 KILL F$
230 NAME "FILE2.TMP" AS F$
RUN

NAME OF FILE TO BE PROCESSED? STUDENTS
RECORD LENGTH FOR FILE? 80
Ok
```

After the run shown, the file STUDENTS will contain only three records. The student TREMONT (see preceding example) has actually been removed.

Line 120 opens F$ with record length L as specified by the user. Line 130 opens FILE2.TMP to have the same record length. Line 140 associates ALL1$ with all L bytes in each record of F$ and line 150 associates ALL2$ with all L bytes of records for FILE2.TMP. The loop in lines 160–200 reads each record from file F$ and writes it to FILE2.TMP if it does not begin with the delete character CHR$(255).

After all records to be kept have been written to FILE2.TMP, line 210 closes both files, line 220 deletes F$ from the diskette file directory, and line 230 assigns the name F$ to the file FILE2.TMP.

■ 17.7 Problems

1. Write a program to create a random access file INVTRY containing the following information.

Item code	Units on hand	Warehouse number
A2000	7	39
A3500	25	39
C2255	0	39
D4296	100	46
E7250	19	46
P2243	5	39

   The information in this table is to be stored in records 1–6.

2. Write a menu-driven program to allow a user to modify the file INVTRY created in Problem 1. The user should be able to issue the following commands:

   ADD   to add new items to the file
   LIST   to display the current contents of the file INVTRY
   END   to stop the program

3. Write a program to allow a person to use the file INVTRY in the following ways.

   a. If the user types S (for search) the computer is to request a single-item code. The user would then type an item code to obtain the units on hand amount and the warehouse number for the item.

   b. If the user types C (for change) the computer should request an item code and a number. The units on hand figure for the specified item is to be decreased by this number.

   c. If the user types E (for end) the program is to stop.

4. Write a program to allow the user to create a mailing list file MAIL.LST by typing its contents at the keyboard. Each record is to contain six fields as follows:

   Field 1   Byte 1   Contains CHR$(255) for "deleted" records.
   Field 2   Bytes 2–26   Name
   Field 3   Bytes 27–58   Street address
   Field 4   Bytes 59–73   City or town
   Field 5   Bytes 74–75   State (two-letter code)
   Field 6   Bytes 76–80   Zip code

   After the file has been created, its contents are to be displayed by using one 80-character display line for each record.

5. Write a program to allow the user to add new entries or delete existing entries in the file MAIL.LST created in Problem 4.

6. Write a program to display the contents of the file MAIL.LST by using a standard address format. Ignore entries that are designated for deletion.
7. Write a program to allow the user to change any part of any existing record in the file MAIL.LST.

■ 17.8 Review True-or-False Quiz

1. At most two files can be referenced in a program—one for input data and one for output data.   T   F
2. If a program uses a file as an input file, then the program cannot also use this file as an output file.   T   F
3. Input data to a program cannot be read from a file and also from DATA lines. These two methods of supplying input data are incompatible.   T   F
4. Any attempt to read data from a file after the end of file mark has been detected by the computer will result in a fatal error.   T   F
5. The contents of a sequential file can be displayed in a readable form by using the DOS command TYPE.   T   F
6. The only difference between sequential files and random files is that data in sequential files must be read in order, whereas data in random files can be read in any order.   T   F
7. If a file named F1 does not exist, the statement

    `OPEN "F1" FOR INPUT AS #1`

places the name F1 in the diskette directory of files.   T   F
8. If a file named F2 does not exist, the statement

    `OPEN "F2" AS #1 LEN=50`

will cause a File not found error.   T   F

18 Random Numbers and Their Application

If you toss a coin several times, you'll obtain a sequence such as HTTHTHHHTTH, where H denotes a head and T a tail. We call this a **randomly generated sequence** because each letter is the result of an experiment (tossing a coin) and could not have been determined without actually performing the experiment. Similarly, if you roll a die (a cube with faces numbered 1 through 6) several times, you'll obtain a randomly generated sequence such as 5315264342. The numbers in such a sequence are called **random numbers.**

BASIC contains a built-in function called **RND** used to generate sequences of numbers that have the appearance of being randomly generated. Although these numbers are called random numbers, they are more accurately referred to as **pseudorandom numbers** because the RND function does not perform an experiment such as tossing a coin to produce a number; rather, it uses an algorithm carefully designed to generate sequences of numbers that emulate random sequences. This ability to generate such sequences makes it possible for us to use the computer in many new and interesting ways. Using "random number generators," people have written computer programs to simulate the growth of a forest, to determine the best location for elevators in a proposed skyscraper, to assist social scientists in their statistical studies, to simulate game playing, and to perform many other tasks.

In this chapter we describe the RND function and illustrate its use in several areas.

■ 18.1 The RND Function

The RND function is used somewhat differently from the other BASIC functions. For any number X, RND(X) has a value between 0 and 1.

$$0 < RND(X) < 1$$

If $X > 0$, the value assumed by RND(X) is unpredictable—it will appear to have been selected randomly from the numbers between 0 and 1. In this section we illustrate the use of RND(X) for the case $X > 0$. The use of RND(X) with $X \leq 0$ is considered in Section 18.2.

EXAMPLE 1   Here is a program to generate six random numbers lying between 0 and 1:

```
10 FOR N=1 TO 6
20     PRINT RND(1)
30 NEXT N
40 END
RUN
```

```
.7151002
.683111
.4821425
.9992938
.6465093
.1322918
```

Observe that each time line 20 is executed a different number is displayed, even though the same expression RND(1) is used.

If you run this program a second time, the same list of six numbers will be displayed. How you obtain different lists on each run is explained in Example 5.

When X > 0 in RND(X), Microsoft® BASIC allows the use of the abbreviated form RND. The expressions RND, RND(1), RND(2), and RND(any positive number) are equivalent. For instance, in Example 1 you can replace RND(1) by RND(2), or even by RND(.125) and get exactly the same result. In what follows we'll use the shortened form RND; nothing is gained by using RND(X) with X > 0.

EXAMPLE 2

Here is a program to generate 1,000 random numbers between 0 and 1 and determine how many are in the interval from 0.3 to 0.4:

```
10 LET C=0          'C does the counting.
20 FOR K=1 TO 1000
30     LET R=RND
40     IF R>0.3 AND R<0.4 THEN C=C+1
50 NEXT K
60 PRINT
70 PRINT "OF 1000 NUMBERS GENERATED,"
80 PRINT C;"WERE BETWEEN 0.3 AND 0.4."
90 END
RUN

OF 1000 NUMBERS GENERATED,
 90 WERE BETWEEN 0.3 AND 0.4.
```

Each time line 30 is executed, RND takes on a different value, which is then assigned to R. The IF statement at line 40 determines whether R lies in the specified interval. In this example it was necessary to assign the value of RND to a variable R so that the comparisons could be made. If we had written

```
40 IF (RND>0.3) AND(RND<0.4) THEN C=C+1
```

the two occurrences of RND would have different values—which is not what we wanted in this situation.

The numbers generated by the RND function are nearly uniformly distributed between 0 and 1. If many numbers are generated, approximately as many will be less than 0.5 as are greater than 0.5, approximately twice as many will be between 0 and 2/3 as are between 2/3 and 1, approximately one-hundredth of the numbers will be between 0.37 and 0.38, and so on. The examples throughout the rest of this chapter illustrate how this property of random number sequences can be put to use by a programmer.

EXAMPLE 3

Let's write a program to simulate tossing a coin 20 times. An H is to be displayed each time a head occurs and a T each time a tail occurs.

PROBLEM ANALYSIS

Since RND will be less than 0.5 approximately half the time, let's say that a head is tossed whenever RND is less than 0.5. The following program is then immediate:

```
10 FOR N=1 to 20
20     IF RND<0.5 THEN PRINT "H"; ELSE PRINT "T";
30 NEXT N
40 END
```

```
RUN

TTHTTHHTHTHHHTTHHTHH
```

REMARK   If you wish to simulate tossing a bent coin that produces a head twice as often as a tail, you could say that a head is the result whenever RND < 0.66667. Thus one change in line 20 allows the same program to work in this case.

The next example shows how the RND function can be used to simulate a real-life situation.

EXAMPLE 4   **A professional softball player has a lifetime batting average of .365. Assuming that the player will have four official times at bat (walks are not official at bats) in each of the next 100 games, estimate the number of games in which 0, 1, 2, 3, and 4 hits are made.**

PROBLEM ANALYSIS

To simulate one time at bat, we will generate a number RND and concede a hit if RND < .365. For any one game we will compare four such numbers with .365. If in a particular game H hits are made (0 ≤ H ≤ 4), we will record this by adding 1 to the counter C(H). Thus, C(0) counts the number of hitless games, C(1) the games in which one hit is made, and so on. This problem analysis suggests how to code Step (b) of the following algorithm. Steps (a) and (c) are routine.

THE ALGORITHM

a. Set counters C(0), C(1), . . . , C(4) to zero.
b. Repeat the following 100 times:
  b1. Simulate one game to obtain the number H of hits.
  b2. Add 1 to C(H).
c. Display the results C(0), C(1), . . . , C(4) and stop.

THE PROGRAM

```
100 REM         SOFTBALL SIMULATION - 100 GAMES
110 REM
130 REM  B = AT BAT NUMBER (1-4) FOR EACH GAME
140 REM  C = COUNTING ARRAY.  C(H) COUNTS NUMBER
150 REM      OF GAMES IN WHICH H HITS ARE MADE.
160 REM
170 REM *******************************************
180 REM         INITIALIZE COUNTERS TO ZERO.
190 DIM C(4)
200 FOR H=0 TO 4
210     LET C(H)=0
220 NEXT H
230 REM *******************************************
240 REM              SIMULATE 100 GAMES.
250 REM
260 FOR GAME=1 TO 100
270     LET H=0          'Number of hits for this game
280     FOR B=1 TO 4
290         IF RND<0.365 THEN H=H+1
300     NEXT B
310     LET C(H)=C(H)+1
320 NEXT GAME
330 REM *******************************************
340 REM              DISPLAY THE RESULTS.
350 REM
360 PRINT "HITS PER GAME   FREQUENCY"
370 LET F$="      #              ##"
380 FOR H=0 TO 4
390     PRINT USING F$;H;C(H)
400 NEXT H
410 END
RUN
```

```
HITS PER GAME    FREQUENCY
      0              23
      1              32
      2              28
      3              15
      4               2
```

■ **REMARK 1** This program is easily modified to handle different batting averages. Simply make these two changes:

```
255 INPUT "BATTING AVERAGE";AV
290 IF RND<AV THEN H=H+1
```

■ **REMARK 2** In this example, we concede a hit if the condition RND < .365 in line 290 is true. If we change this condition to RND <= .365, essentially the same results will occur; it is extremely unlikely that RND will ever take on the exact value .365. In fact, if AV denotes any constant, it is extremely unlikely that RND will take on the exact value AV. But even if it does, it will happen so rarely that no significant change in the simulation being carried out will occur.

☐

As mentioned at the outset of this chapter, the random sequences generated are actually the result of a carefully defined mathematical algorithm. This algorithm requires an initial value to start the process. This initial value is called a **random number seed.** Each time the same seed is supplied to the algorithm, the same sequence results. For every run of a program that uses RND (or equivalently RND(X) with X > 0), BASIC supplies its own default seed. Thus two runs will generate exactly the same sequence of random numbers. Although this result can be useful during the debugging process, it does not reflect what actually happens in real-life situations. Microsoft® BASIC provides the RANDOMIZE statement to cause different and unpredictable sequences to be generated each time a program is run. Its general form is

  ln RANDOMIZE

or

  ln RANDOMIZE **e**

where **e** is a numerical expression. If used in the first form, the PC will respond with

```
Random number seed (-32768 to 32767)?
```

and you must supply a numerical value between the limits shown. When the second form is used, **e** must be an expression that evaluates to a number between −32768 and 32767. In either case the sequence of random numbers generated subsequent to the RANDOMIZE statement will depend on the value of the seed. How you can cause the PC to assign different seeds for different runs automatically is explained in Example 5.

EXAMPLE 5 Here are two runs of a program that uses RANDOMIZE.

```
10 RANDOMIZE
20 FOR N=1 TO 5
30    PRINT RND
40 NEXT N
50 END
RUN

Random number seed (-32768 to 32767)? 2
 .6638697
 .5281477
 .861278
 7.227527E-02
 .8667126

RUN
```

```
Random number seed (-32768 to 32767)? 14.3
 .1030176
 .2224226
 .7901721
 .2621557
 .3087903
```

■ **REMARK 1** If line 10 were changed to RANDOMIZE 2, a run would result in the same five numbers appearing in the first output, but there would be no request for a random number seed.

■ **REMARK 2** To obtain different random number sequences each time a program is run, you *must* use different seeds. If Diskette or Advanced BASIC is used, you can have your program obtain the seed for you by using the PC's internal clock. The string function TIME$ given an 8-character string in the form

hh:*mm*:*ss*

where *hh* gives the hour, *mm* the minute, and *ss* the second. To use *ss* to obtain a seed you can write

ln RANDOMIZE VAL(RIGHT$(TIME$,2))

If TIME$ = 00:01:49, you will get the numerical seed 49. If your program is intended for use by others, they should not be required to specify a seed. The method just described makes this possible.

■ 18.2 Repeating a Random Process

In this section we show how zero and negative arguments for RND can be used to repeat previously generated random numbers.

A zero argument always produces the last random number generated by your PC. If you type

```
PRINT RND : LET B=RND(0)
```

the value generated for RND will be displayed and then assigned to B. Similarly, the following line will display a single random number three times*:

```
PRINT RND,RND(0),RND(0)
```

Since you can always use a variable to "remember" the most recent random number, you will have little need to use RND(0). Instead of using RND(0), assign RND to R and then use R. As we now show, negative arguments for RND can be useful.

Each negative argument of RND has associated with it a fixed number between 0 and 1. If you type

```
PRINT RND(-1);RND(-2);RND(-3.2)
```

you will always obtain the same (predictable) numbers. We did this and got the numbers

 .8188288   .8188288   .6120051

---

* The three values displayed may differ in the last decimal position. Because of the approximate way computers store fractional numbers, RND(0) and the last random number generated are approximately, but not exactly, equal. To see that they are not exactly the same, run the following:

```
10 IF RND=RND(0) THEN PRINT "EQUAL" : END
20 GOTO 10
```

The PC will not display EQUAL—you will have to halt execution by using Ctrl-Break. (This should serve as a reminder that it is risky business to test numbers that are not integers for equality.)

These particular values are of no significance, however. What is important is that using RND with a negative argument will cause subsequent random numbers generated with positive arguments to follow a sequence associated with this negative argument. For example, note that the two FOR loops in the following program produce exactly the same output.

```
100 PRINT RND(-1)
110 FOR N=1 TO 5
120     PRINT RND;
130 NEXT N
140 PRINT
150 PRINT RND(-1)
160 FOR N=1 TO 5
170     PRINT RND;
180 NEXT N
RUN

 .8188288
 .2677991    8.733116E-02   7.081251E-02   .8175731   .5208339
 .8188288
 .2677991    8.733116E-02   7.081251E-02   .8175731   .5208339
```

It is not necessary that RND(−1) be output; it simply must be used. For instance, if line 150 is changed to

```
150 LET Q=RND(-1)
```

the two FOR loops will again produce exactly the same random numbers.

This short program illustrates the major difference in using RND with a negative argument to select a random number sequence instead of using a RANDOMIZE statement. The program uses RND(−1) to produce the same random sequence twice in a single program. RANDOMIZE is not used for this purpose. Indeed, if you change lines 100 and 150 to

```
100 RANDOMIZE 2
150 RANDOMIZE 2
```

the two FOR loops will not produce the same random numbers. RANDOMIZE is included in BASIC for one reason—to allow you to generate different sequences of random numbers each time a program is run. If you need or want to generate the same sequence twice in a program, use RND with a negative argument. That is the purpose of negative arguments.

EXAMPLE 6 Here is a program to display 10 random numbers in the order generated and also in ascending order.

```
100 REM PROGRAM TO ILLUSTRATE USE OF RND WITH NEGATIVE ARGUMENT
110 REM
120 REM -------- STORE N RANDOM NUMBERS IN ARRAY A ------------
130 LET N=10 : DIM A(N)
140 LET Q=RND(-1)                          'Select random sequence
150 FOR K=1 TO N
160     LET A(K)=RND
170 NEXT K
180 REM --------- SORT ARRAY A INTO ASCENDING ORDER -----------
190 GOSUB 500
200 REM
210 REM ----- DISPLAY UNSORTED AND SORTED RANDOM NUMBERS ------
220 REM
230 PRINT  "10 RANDOM NUMBERS      SAME 10 - IN ORDER"
240 LET F$="     .#######           .#######      "
250 LET Q=RND(-1)                          'Select same rand. seq.
260 FOR K=1 TO N
270     PRINT USING F$; RND, A(K)
280 NEXT K
290 END
500 REM SUBROUTINE -----------BUBBLE SORT --------------------
```

```
510 LET FLAG=1
520 WHILE FLAG=1
530    LET FLAG=0
540    FOR I=1 TO N-1
550       IF A(I)>A(I+1) THEN SWAP A(I),A(I+1) : FLAG=1
560    NEXT I
570 WEND
580 RETURN
RUN

10 RANDOM NUMBERS         SAME 10 - IN ORDER
   .2677991                  .0708125
   .0873312                  .0873312
   .0708125                  .2677991
   .8175731                  .2680091
   .5208339                  .5208339
   .5921427                  .5921427
   .8115049                  .7090380
   .8301151                  .8115049
   .7090380                  .8175731
   .2680091                  .8301151
```

■ **REMARK**   We could have stored the random numbers in two arrays and sorted one of them before producing the output. By using RND(−1) as in lines 140 and 250, we avoided the need for a separate array to preserve the original order. We simply generated the random numbers a second time when needed for the output.

□

■ 18.3 Problems

1. Approximately how many asterisks are displayed by each program segment?

   a.
   ```
   10 FOR I=1 TO 100
   20    IF RND<0.8 THEN PRINT "*";
   30 NEXT I
   ```

   b.
   ```
   10 FOR K=1 TO 100
   20    LET X=RND
   30    IF X<0.4 OR X>0.7 THEN PRINT "*";
   40 NEXT K
   ```

   c.
   ```
   10 FOR K=1 TO 100
   20    IF RND>0.4 AND RND(0)<0.7
            THEN PRINT "*";
   30 NEXT K
   ```

   d.
   ```
   10 FOR J=1 TO 10
   20    IF RND=RND THEN PRINT "*";
   30 NEXT J
   ```

   e.
   ```
   10 FOR L=1 TO 100
   20    IF RND<>0.5 THEN PRINT "*";
   30 NEXT L
   ```

   f.
   ```
   10 LET X=RND(-4)
   20 FOR L=1 TO 10
   30    LET A(L)=RND
   40 NEXT L
   50 LET Y=RND(-4)
   60 FOR N=1 TO 10
   70    LET Z=RND
   80    IF Z=A(N) THEN PRINT "*";
   90 NEXT N
   ```

2. Which of these logical expressions are always true? Which are always false? Which may be true or false?

   a. RND>0
   b. 4*RND<4
   c. RND<RND
   d. RND+RND<3*RND
   e. RND+1>RND
   f. INT(RND)=0

In Problems 3–12, write a program to perform each task specified.

3. Display approximately one-fourth of all values appearing in DATA lines. Make a decision to display or not to display as the number is read.
4. Display approximately 1% of all integers from 1000 to 9999, inclusive. Select the integers randomly.
5. Simulate tossing two coins 100 times. The output should be a count of the number of times each of the possible outcomes HH, HT, TH, and TT occurs.
6. Simulate tossing three coins 10 times. The output should be a list of 10 terms such as HHH, HTH, HHT, and so on.
7. Simulate tossing K coins N times. The output should be a list of N terms in which each term is a sequence of K H's and T's. N and K are to be input.
8. A game between players A and B is played as follows. A coin is tossed three times or until a head comes up, whichever occurs first. As soon as a head comes up, player A collects $1 from player B. If no head comes up on any of the three tosses, player B collects $6 from player A. In either case, the game is over. Have your program simulate this game 1,000 times to help decide whether A or B has the advantage (or if it is a fair game).
9. Generate an array L of 500 random numbers between 0 and 1. Using L, determine an array C as follows. C(1) is a count of how many entries of L are between 0 and 0.1, C(2) a count of those between 0.1 and 0.2, and so on. Display a two-column table showing the intervals and the corresponding counts stored in array C.
10. The first three hitters in the Bears' batting order have lifetime batting averages of .257, .289, and .324, respectively. Simulate their first trip to the plate for the next 100 games, and tabulate the number of games in which they produce zero, one, two, and three hits. Allow the user to specify the three batting averages during program execution.
11. Jones and Kelley are to have a duel at 20 paces. At this distance Jones will hit the target on the average of two shots in every five, and Kelley will hit one in every three. Kelley shoots first. Who has the best chance of surviving? Use a FOR loop to run the program 20 times and display the results.
12. (Drunkard's walk.) A poor soul, considerably intoxicated, stands in the middle of a 10-foot-long bridge that spans a river. The inebriate staggers along, either toward the left bank or toward the right bank, but fortunately cannot fall off the bridge. Assuming that each step taken is exactly 1 foot long, how many steps will the drunkard take before a bank is reached? Assume that it is just as likely that a step will be toward the left bank as toward the right.

    You must do three things:

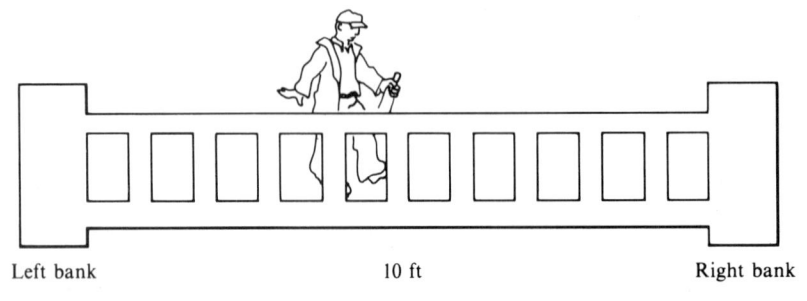

    a. Find how many steps are taken in getting off the bridge.
    b. Tell which bank is reached.
    c. Let the drunkard go out for several nights and arrive at the same point (the center) on the bridge. Find, on the average, how many steps it takes to get off the bridge.

18.4 Random Integers

Many computer applications require generating **random integers** rather than just random numbers between 0 and 1. For example, suppose a manufacturer estimates that a proposed new product will sell at the rate of 10 to 20 units each week and wants a program to simulate sales figures over an extended period of time. To write such a program, you must be able to generate random integers from 10 to 20 to represent the estimated weekly sales. To do this, you can multiply RND, which is between 0 and 1, by 11 (the number of integers from 10 to 20) to obtain

$$0 < 11 * RND < 11$$

If many numbers are obtained using 11*RND, they will be nearly uniformly distributed between 0 and 11. This means that the value of INT(11*RND) will be one of the integers 0, 1, 2, . . . , 10. Thus, if you add 10 to this expression, you will get an integer from 10 to 20:

$$10 \leq INT(11*RND) + 10 \leq 20$$

The important thing here is that integers generated in this way will appear to have been chosen randomly from the set of integers {10, 11, 12, . . . , 20}.

In general, if A and B are integers with A < B,

$$INT((B-A+1)*RND)$$

will generate an integer from 0 to B − A. (Note that B − A + 1 gives the number of integers between A and B, inclusive.) Thus, adding A to this expression, we obtain

$$INT((B-A+1)*RND) + A$$

whose value is an integer chosen randomly from the set {A, A + 1, A + 2, . . . , B}. The following table illustrates how to obtain random integers within specified bounds:

Expression	Value of the expression
INT(10*RND)	A random integer from 0 to 9
INT(N*RND)	A random integer from 0 to N − 1
INT(N*RND)+1	A random integer from 1 to N
INT(51*RND)+100	A random integer from 100 to 150
INT(11*RND)−5	A random integer from −5 to 5

EXAMPLE 7

Let's write a program to generate 15 numbers randomly selected from the set {1, 2, 3, 4, 5}.

PROBLEM ANALYSIS

From the preceding discussion we know that the expression INT(5*RND) will be an integer from 0 to 4. Thus, INT(5*RND)+1 will be an integer from 1 to 5, as required.

```
10 FOR I=1 TO 15
20    PRINT INT(5*RND)+1;
30 NEXT I
40 END
RUN

 1  2  5  1  5  5  4  3  5  3  3  4  2  4  2
```

EXAMPLE 8

Let's write a program to generate 15 numbers randomly selected from the set {100, 101, 102, . . . , 199}.

PROBLEM ANALYSIS

The technique used in Example 7 is also applicable here. Since INT(100*RND) is an integer from 0 to 99, we add 100 to obtain an integer from the specified set. Thus, the program required is that of Example 7 with line 20 changed to

```
20    PRINT INT(100*RND)+100;
```

18.5 Simulation

Example 4 of Section 18.1 shows how the RND function can be used to simulate a ballplayer's future performance based on past performance. The example illustrates a major category of simulation problems encountered in computer programming—namely, the simulation of future events based on data obtained by observing the results of similar or related previous events. In this section we show how such a simulation can be used to advantage in a business setting.

EXAMPLE 9 A retail store will soon handle a new product. A preliminary market survey indicates that between 500 and 1,000 units will be sold each month. (The survey is no more specific than this.) Write a program to simulate sales for the first 6 months. The retail store management is to be allowed to experiment by specifying two values: the number of units to be purchased initially and the number to be purchased on the first of each subsequent month.

PROBLEM ANALYSIS

The input values are:

IPUR = initial inventory purchase
PUR = inventory purchase for subsequent months

The problem statement does not specify the nature of the output. Let's agree to produce a four-column report showing the following items:

MONTH = month (1, 2, . . . , 6)
SALES = estimated sales (500–1,000) for 1 month
FIRST = quantity on hand at beginning of month (initially, IPUR)
LAST = quantity on hand at end of month

For each month we must generate a random integer SALES from 500 to 1000. There are 501 integers to choose from (501 = 1000 − 500 + 1). Thus, we can use the following expression to select an integer randomly from 500 to 1000:

```
INT(501*RND)+500
```

After the initial and periodic purchase quantities (IPUR and PUR) are input, we will display column headings and then assign the input value IPUR to FIRST so that the simulation can begin. The actual simulation of sales for each of the 6 months (MONTH = 1 to 6) can be carried out as follows:

1. Estimate sales for 1 month (SALES = INT(501*RND)+500).
2. Determine the quantity on hand at the end of the month (LAST=FIRST−SALES).
3. Display MONTH, SALES, FIRST, LAST.
4. Determine the quantity on hand at the start of the next month (FIRST=LAST+PUR).

Since the problem statement specifies that the store management is to be allowed to experiment, we should have the program generate different sequences of random numbers each time it is run. Rather than require management to choose a random number seed each time the program is run, we'll use the TIME$ function as explained in Remark 2 of Example 5.

THE PROGRAM

```
100 REM              NEW PRODUCT SIMULATION
110 REM
130 REM        PUR = MONTHLY INVENTORY PURCHASE
140 REM      MONTH = MONTH (1,2,...,6)
150 REM      FIRST = ON HAND - BEGINNING OF MONTH
160 REM      SALES = SALES FOR ONE MONTH (500-1000)
170 REM       LAST = ON HAND - END OF MONTH
180 REM
190 REM ********************************************
200 REM              KEYBOARD INPUT
210 REM
```

```
220 INPUT "INITIAL INVENTORY PURCHASE"; IPUR
230 INPUT "SUBSEQUENT MONTHLY PURCHASE"; PUR
240 PRINT
250 REM ********************************************
260 REM DISPLAY HEADINGS AND ASSIGN OUTPUT FORMAT F$.
270 REM
280 PRINT  "                        INVENTORY"
290 PRINT  "                        -------------------"
300 PRINT  "MONTH     ESTIMATED    START OF     END OF"
310 PRINT  "NUMBER      SALES       MONTH       MONTH"
320 LET F$=" ##         ####        #####       #####"
330 PRINT
340 REM
350 REM ********************************************
360 REM    SIMULATE AND DISPLAY SALES FOR SIX MONTHS.
370 REM
380 RANDOMIZE VAL(RIGHT$(TIME$,2))    'Random seed
390 LET FIRST=IPUR                    'On hand first month
400 FOR MONTH=1 TO 6
410     LET SALES=INT(501*RND)+500    'Sales for the month
420     LET LAST=FIRST-SALES          'On hand end of month
430     PRINT USING F$; MONTH, SALES, FIRST, LAST
440     LET FIRST=LAST+PUR            'On hand start of month
450 NEXT MONTH
460 END
RUN

INITIAL INVENTORY PURCHASE? 1000
SUBSEQUENT MONTHLY PURCHASE? 900

                        INVENTORY
                        -------------------
MONTH     ESTIMATED    START OF     END OF
NUMBER      SALES       MONTH       MONTH

  1          865         1000         135
  2          672         1035         363
  3          712         1263         551
  4          690         1451         761
  5          965         1661         696
  6          990         1596         606
```

■ REMARK A user would run this program several times and use the results as a guide to determining a reasonable purchasing strategy. The increasingly larger values in the last two columns suggest that a monthly purchase of 900 units is excessive.

We wrote the new-product simulation program so that sales of 500 to 1,000 units would be selected with equal likelihood. We did this not because it is realistic, but because the preliminary market analysis gave no further information. A more careful market analysis would probably show that the number of units would range from 500 to 1,000—with sales near 750 more likely than sales near the extremes 500 and 1,000. We'll now show how random numbers that cluster about a specific number can be generated.

The subroutine

```
500 LET R=0
510 FOR K=1 TO 5
520     LET R=R+RND
530 NEXT K
540 LET R=R/5
550 RETURN
```

generates a random number R from 0 to 1 by averaging five random numbers RND. If many numbers R are generated by this subroutine, they will tend to cluster about the midpoint 0.5 of the interval 0 to 1, with fewer occurring toward the endpoints 0 and 1. If a number larger than 5 is used in the subroutine, the numbers generated will cluster more closely around the midpoint 0.5.

With R obtained from this subroutine, the statement

```
LET SALES=INT(501*R)+500
```

will generate random integers SALES from 500 to 1000. Since the R values will cluster about the midpoint 0.5 of the interval 0 to 1, the corresponding SALES values will cluster about the midpoint 750 of the interval 500 to 1000. The new-product simulation program given in Example 9 is easily modified to generate sales by this method. Simply insert the given subroutine and make these changes:

```
410 GOSUB 500
415 LET SALES=INT(501*R)+500
```

Here is a run of the program after the changes were made:

```
INITIAL INVENTORY PURCHASE? 1000
SUBSEQUENT MONTHLY PURCHASE? 900
```

		INVENTORY	
MONTH NUMBER	ESTIMATED SALES	START OF MONTH	END OF MONTH
1	658	1000	342
2	757	1242	485
3	773	1385	612
4	720	1512	792
5	761	1692	931
6	778	1831	1053

Note that the estimated sales figures are nearer 750 than before. Note also that the figures in the last column give more evidence that purchasing 900 units per month is excessive.

■ 18.6 Problems

1. Write a single BASIC statement to display each of the following:
   a. A nonnegative random number (not necessarily an integer) less than 4
   b. A random number less than 11 but greater than 5
   c. A random number less than 3 but greater than -5
   d. A random integer between 6 and 12, inclusive
   e. A random number from the set $\{0, 2, 4, 6, 8\}$
   f. A random number from the set $\{1, 3, 5, 7, 9\}$

2. What values can be assumed by each of the following expressions? For each expression, tell whether the possible values are all equally likely to occur.

   a. INT(2*RND+1)
   b. 3*INT(RND)
   c. INT(5*RND)-2
   d. INT(2*RND+1)+INT(2*RND+1)
   e. INT(6*RND+1)+INT(6*RND+1)
   f. INT(3*RND+1)*(INT(3*RND)+1)

3. If two coins are tossed, two heads, two tails, or one of each may result. The following program was written to simulate tossing two coins a total of 20 times. If it is run, the output will not reflect what would happen if the coins were actually tossed. Explain why, and then write a correct program.

```
100 FOR I=1 TO 20
110     LET R=INT(3*RND)
120     IF R=0 THEN PRINT "TWO HEADS"
130     IF R=1 THEN PRINT "TWO TAILS"
140     IF R=2 THEN PRINT "ONE OF EACH"
150 NEXT I
160 END
```

In Problems 4–18, write a program to perform each task specified.

4. Display a sequence of 20 letters that are selected randomly from the word RANDOM.
5. Randomly select and display an integer from 1 to 100 and then another integer from the remaining 99.
6. Create an array B of exactly 20 different integers from 1 to 100. Choose the integers randomly. Display the array, but only after it is completely determined.
7. Read 20 different English words into an array A$. Then create another array B$ containing exactly 10 different words randomly selected from those in array A$.
8. Starting with D(1) = 1, D(2) = 2, D(3) = 3, . . . , D(52) = 52, rearrange the entries of array D as follows: select an integer K from 1 to 52 and swap D(K) with D(52), select K from 1 to 51 and swap D(K) with D(51), select K from 1 to 50 and swap D(K) with D(50), and so on. The last step in this process is to select K from 1 to 2 and swap D(K) with D(2). Then display the entries of D in four adjacent columns, each containing 13 numbers. Explain in what sense your program shuffles a standard bridge deck and deals one hand in bridge.
9. A retail store will soon carry a new product. A preliminary market analysis indicates that between 300 and 500 units will be sold each week. (The survey is no more specific than this.) Assuming that each unit costs the store $1.89, write a program to simulate sales for the next 16 weeks. Allow the store management to specify the selling price to obtain output showing the week, the estimated sales in number of units, the total revenue, the income (revenue − cost), and the cumulative income. Allow the user to try many different selling prices during a single program run.
10. Carry out the task specified in Problem 9, but this time assume that the market analysis says the number of units sold per week (300–500) will cluster about the midpoint (400), as described in Section 18.5.
11. Juanita Fernandes is offered the opportunity to transfer to another sales territory. She is informed that, for each month of the past year, sales in the territory were between $18,000 and $30,000, with sales of $25,000 or more being twice as likely as sales under $25,000. A 4% commission is paid on all sales up to $25,000 and 8% on all sales above that figure. Simulate the next 6 months' sales, and print the monthly sales and commission to give Juanita some information on which to base her decision to accept or reject the transfer.
12. The IDA Production Company will employ 185 people to work on the production of a new product. It is estimated that each person can complete between 85 and 95 units each working day. Experience shows that the absentee rate is between 0 and 15% on Mondays and Fridays and between 0 and 7% on the other days. Simulate the production for 1 week. Display the results of this simulation in four columns showing the day of the week, the number of workers present, the number of units produced, and the average number produced per worker.
13. Two knights begin at diagonally opposite corners of a chessboard and travel randomly about the board but always making legitimate knight moves. (The knight moves either one step forward or backward and then two steps to the right or left or else two steps forward or backward and one step to the right or left.) Calculate the number of moves before one knight captures the other. However you number the squares, each knight's move should be displayed as it is taken.
14. A single trip for a knight is defined as follows. The knight starts in one corner of the chessboard and randomly makes N knight moves to arrive at one of the 64 squares of the chessboard. (See Problem 13 for a description of an admissible knight move.) Write a program to simulate 1,000 such trips for a knight to determine how many times each square was reached at the end of a trip. These counts should be presented as an 8 × 8 table displaying the counts for the 64 squares. Allow the user to obtain a frequency table for many values of N during a single program run.
15. SIM is a game in which two players take turns drawing lines between any two of the six dots numbered 1 through 6 in the following diagram:

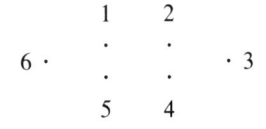

```
           1   2
              .
   6 ·     .   .    · 3
              .
           5   4
```

The first player's lines are colored red; the second player's are colored blue. The loser is the first player to complete a triangle with three of these six dots as vertices. For example, if the second player draws a line (blue) between dots 2 and 4, 6 and 4, and 2 and 6, this player has completed a blue triangle and hence loses. Write a program in which the computer is the second player. The computer is to record all moves and announce the end of each game with a message stating who won. [*Hint:* Use a 6 × 6 array H(I,J) to record the moves. If the first player types 3,5 to indicate that a red line is drawn between these two dots, set H(3,5) and H(5,3) to 1. If the computer picks 2,6 (to be done randomly), then set H(2,6) and H(6,2) to 2. Note that a triangle of one color has been completed when there are three different numbers I, J, K for which H(I,J) H(J,K), and H(K,I) are all 1 or all 2.]

16. Write a program for the game of SIM described in Problem 15, but this time the second player is a person, not the computer.
17. Write a subroutine to generate random numbers between 0 and 1 by averaging N random numbers rather than 5 as in Section 18.5. Include this subroutine in a program that allows the user to specify a positive integer N to obtain a frequency table showing counts of how many of 500 random numbers generated by the subroutine are in each of the 10 intervals 0–0.1, 0.1–0.2, . . . , 0.9–1. The user should be allowed to obtain tables for many positive integers N during a single program run. The program should halt when the user types zero. (Be sure to try the cases N = 1, 10, and 20.)
18. Display 20 sets of three integers D, L, and F with $0 \leq D < 360$, $5 \leq L \leq 15$, and $1 \leq F \leq 4$. (*Note:* If you interpret D as a direction and L as a length, you can create a design using these numbers. Starting at a point on a piece of paper, draw a line of length L in the direction given by D. At the end of this line segment draw one of four figures as specified by F—for example, different colored circles the sizes of a dime, nickel, quarter, and half dollar. Using the end of this first line segment as a new starting point, repeat the process by using the second of the 20 triples D, L, F. This process illustrates, in a very elementary way, what some people refer to as random art.)

■ 18.7 A Statistical Application

Programmers are often confronted with tasks that simply cannot be programmed to run within a specified time limit. When this happens, it is not always necessary to abandon the task. Sometimes satisfactory results can be obtained by doing only part of the job. The following example, which illustrates one such situation, makes use of the statistical fact that the average of a large collection of numbers can be estimated by taking the average of only a fraction of the numbers, provided that the numbers are chosen randomly.

EXAMPLE 10 A researcher has compiled three lists A, B, and C of 500 measurements each and wishes to determine the average of all possible sums obtained by adding three measurements, one from each of the three lists. We are to write a program to assist the researcher in this task.

PROBLEM ANALYSIS

On the surface this appears to be a simple programming task. For each set A(I), B(J), C(K) of measurements, we can add A(I) + B(J) + C(K) to a summation accumulator SUM and then divide SUM by the number of sets A(I), B(J), C(K) used. The following program segment will do this:

```
300 LET SUM=0
310 FOR I=1 TO 500
320    FOR J=1 TO 500
330       FOR K=1 TO 500
340          LET SUM=SUM+A(I)+B(J)+C(K)
350       NEXT K
360    NEXT J
370 NEXT I
380 PRINT "REQUIRED AVERAGE IS";SUM/500^3
```

If you use this program segment to find the required average, however, you'll have a long wait. To see that this is so, precede the program segment shown with the line

```
290 DIM A(500),B(500),C(500)
```

and type RUN. (The PC takes just as long to add zeros—which is what will happen here—as other numbers.) We did this and after one minute used Ctrl-Break to stop program execution. The immediate mode command

```
PRINT I,J,K
```

gave the values I = 1, J = 12, and K = 472. This means that J × 500 + K = 6,472 passes through the triply nested loops were made in one minute. Since 500^3 = 125,000,000 passes must be made in all, the estimated execution time is 125,000,000 ÷ 6,472 = 19,313.97 minutes—which is approximately 322 hours, or thirteen 24-hour days.

About the only way out of this dilemma is to treat only a fraction of the 125 million sets A(I), B(J), C(K) and use the average of *their* sums as an estimate of the average desired. Using 1 in 10,000 of these sets will take approximately 1.9 minutes (19,313.97 ÷ 10,000). To ensure that the average obtained will be a reliable estimate of the average desired, the sets A(I), B(J), C(K) must be chosen randomly. In the following program segment we use the expression INT(500 * RND) + 1 to select subscripts from 1 to 500 randomly. The statement FOR N = 1 TO 12500 is appropriate since using 1 in 10,000 of the sets A(I), B(J), C(K) means that a total of 125,000,000 ÷ 10,000 = 12,500 sets will be used.

```
300 LET SUM=0
310 FOR N=1 TO 12500
320     LET I=INT(500*RND)+1
330     LET J=INT(500*RND)+1
340     LET K=INT(500*RND)+1
350     LET SUM=SUM+A(I)+B(J)+C(K)
360 NEXT N
370 PRINT "ESTIMATE OF AVERAGE";SUM/12500
```

■ **REMARK 1** When this program segment is executed, the same subscripts I, J, K may be selected more than once. Since each set A(I), B(J), C(K) has an equal chance of being selected, however, the effect on the final average will be statistically insignificant.

■ **REMARK 2** It is not necessary to use 12,500 of the sets A(I), B(J), C(K) to obtain a reliable estimate of the average desired. Indeed, random number generators used with BASIC will eventually repeat the sequence of random numbers being produced. If you use only 2,500 of the sets (1 in 50,000), you will probably get just as accurate an estimate of the average as you would with 12,500 sets.

■ 18.8 Monte Carlo

The speed of modern computing machines, together with their ability to generate good random sequences, allows us to approach many problems in ways not previously possible. The following example illustrates one such method, called the **Monte Carlo method.** When you complete the example, you should have little difficulty explaining why this name is applied to the technique involved.

EXAMPLE 11 Consider the following figure of a circle inscribed in a square:

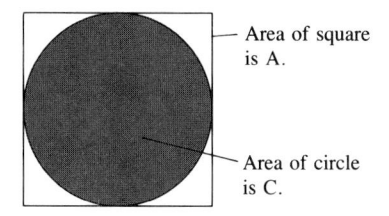

Area of square is A.

Area of circle is C.

340 Chapter 18 Random Numbers and Their Application

If darts are randomly tossed at this figure and tosses landing outside the square are ignored, we can expect the number of darts falling within the circle to be related to the number falling on the entire square as the area C of the circle is related to the area A of the square. We will use this observation to approximate the area C of a unit circle (circle of radius 1).

PROBLEM ANALYSIS

Let's suppose that N darts have landed on the square and that M of these are in the circle. Then, as noted in the problem statement, we will have the approximation

$$\frac{M}{N} \approx \frac{C}{A}$$

or, solving for C,

$$C \approx M \times \frac{A}{N}$$

The more darts thrown (randomly), the better we can expect this approximation to be. The problem, then, is to simulate this activity and keep an accurate count of M and N. To simplify this task, let's place our figure on a coordinate system with its origin at the center of the circle:

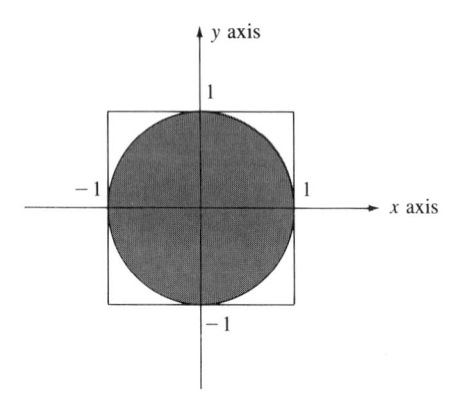

A point (x, y) will lie in the square if both x and y lie between -1 and $+1$. Such a point will lie within the circle if

$$x^2 + y^2 < 1$$

To simulate tossing a single dart, we randomly generate two numbers x and y between -1 and $+1$. The following algorithm describes this process for N = 10,000 tosses. The approximate area of the circle M × A/N is displayed for the values N = 1000, 2000, 3,000, . . . , 10,000.

    a. Let M = 0. (M counts the darts falling within the circle.)
    b. For N = 1 to 10,000, do the following:
        b1. Generate x and y between -1 and 1.
        b2. If $x^2 + y^2 < 1$, add 1 to M.
        b3. If N is a multiple of 1,000, display N and M × A/N.
    c. Stop.

Since 2*RND − 1 gives a random number between −1 and +1, and since the area A of the square is 4, the above algorithm translates rather easily into the following program:

THE PROGRAM

```
100 REM      A MONTE CARLO SIMULATION
110 REM
130 REM DISPLAY HEADINGS AND ASSIGN OUTPUT FORMAT F$.
140 REM
150 PRINT   " NUMBER OF     ESTIMATED AREA"
160 PRINT   "DARTS THROWN   OF UNIT CIRCLE"
```

```
170 PRINT     "------------     --------------"
180 LET F$="     #####         #.#####"
190 REM
200 REM ********************************************
210 REM         SIMULATE TOSSING 10000 DARTS.
220 REM
230 LET M=0                    'Darts falling in circle
240 LET A=4                    'Area of rectangle
250 FOR N=1 TO 10000
260     LET X=2*RND-1
270     LET Y=2*RND-1
280     IF X^2+Y^2<1 THEN M=M+1
290     IF N/1000=INT(N/1000) THEN PRINT USING F$;N;M*A/N
300 NEXT N
310 END
RUN

    NUMBER OF         ESTIMATED AREA
    DARTS THROWN      OF UNIT CIRCLE
    ------------      --------------
       1000             3.23200
       2000             3.15000
       3000             3.12667
       4000             3.14300
       5000             3.13920
       6000             3.14133
       7000             3.13886
       8000             3.13750
       9000             3.14711
      10000             3.14560
```

REMARK Since we know that the area of a circle of radius 1 is π (approximately 3.1416), we see that the final estimate is accurate to two decimal places. To obtain greater accuracy, you might be tempted to use more than 10,000 points. Indeed, if RND were a true random number generator—that is, if it actually performed a random experiment such as tossing coins to generate numbers—you could expect to obtain any degree of accuracy desired by taking N large enough. The fact that RND is not a true random number generator places a limit on the accuracy obtainable.

18.9 Problems

In Problems 1–3, write a program for each task specified.

1. A principle of statistics tells us that the mean (average) of a large collection of numbers can be approximated by taking the mean of only some of the numbers, provided that the numbers are chosen randomly. Generate a one-dimensional array L containing 500 numbers (any numbers will do), and display the mean M of these 500 numbers. To test the stated principle of statistics, randomly select approximately 30 numbers from L and display their mean. Use a loop to repeat this process 20 times. The 20 means obtained should cluster about M.

2. Let L be an array of N numbers between 0 and 1. Using array L, determine an array C as follows: C(1) is a count of how many entries of L are between 0 and 0.1, C(2) a count of those between 0.1 and 0.2, and so on. If L emulates a random sequence, we can expect each C(J) to be approximately E = N/10. In statistics, the value

$$X = \frac{(C(1) - E)^2}{E} + \frac{(C(2) - E)^2}{E} + \cdots + \frac{(C(10) - E)^2}{E}$$

is called the *chi-square statistic* for C. If it is small, it means that the C(J) do not differ drastically from the expected value E. For the present situation, statistics tells us that if $X \geq 16.92$, we can be 95 percent confident that L does not emulate a random sequence. Thus, unless $X < 16.92$, we should reject L as a potential random sequence.

a. Assuming that N and the list C are known, write a subroutine to compute and display the chi-square statistic X.

b. Use the subroutine of part (a) in a program to test RND as a random number generator. For any positive integer $N \geq 200$, the program is to determine the counts C(1), C(2), . . . , C(10) for N numbers generated by RND and then determine and display the chi-square statistic. The program should halt if a value of N less than 200 is typed.

[*Note:* If C gives a count of numbers in intervals other than (0, 0.1), (0.1, 0.2), and so on, a critical value other than 16.92 must be used. The test described here is called a *chi-square goodness-of-fit test* and is described in most introductory statistics books.]

3. Let a function $y = f(x)$ have positive values for all x between A and B as in the following diagram:

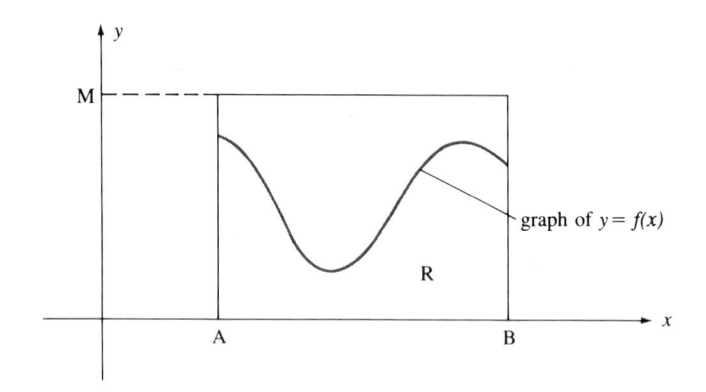

A point (x, y) with $A < x < B$ will lie in the region R if $0 < y < f(x)$. If M is a number such that $f(x) \leq M$ for all such x, the area of the rectangle of height M shown in the diagram is $M*(B - A)$. Use the Monte Carlo method to approximate the area R. Try your program for the following cases:

a. $y = 1 - x^3$, $A = 0$, $B = 1$
b. $y = \sin(x)$, $A = 0$, $B = \pi/2$
c. $y = \sin(x)/x$, $A = 0$, $B = 1$

■ 18.10 Review True-or-False Quiz

1. The RND function generates sequences of numbers by using a well-defined algorithm. T F
2. If 100 numbers are generated by the statement LET R = RND, then approximately half these numbers will be less than 50. T F
3. With equal likelihood, the expression INT(2*RND) will have the value 0 or 1. T F
4. With equal likelihood, the expression INT(3*RND) + INT(2*RND) will have one of the values 1, 2, 3, 4, or 5. T F
5. Let L$ be an array of 100 different names. If we wish to select exactly 20 of these names randomly, we can generate 100 random numbers between 0 and 1 and select the Ith name in array L$ if the Ith number generated is less than 0.2. T F
6. A certain experiment has two possible outcomes: Outcome 1 and Outcome 2. To simulate this experiment on the computer, you can generate a number R = RND and specify that Outcome 1 occurs if R is less than 0.5 and Outcome 2 occurs otherwise. T F
7. RND/RND = 1. T F
8. The value of the expression INT(17*RND)+1 is an integer from 1 to 17. T F
9. The value of the expression INT(5*RND)+5 is an integer from 5 to 10. T F

10. The loop

```
500 LET S=0
510 FOR K=1 TO 100
520     LET S=S+RND
530 NEXT K
```

will generate random numbers S between 0 and 100. Moreover, the S values will cluster about the midpoint 50 of this interval. T F

19 Graphics

All screen displays thus far have been produced by displaying up to 25 horizontal lines each with up to 80 characters chosen from the PC character set. This is referred to as operating in **text mode**—only *text* (that is, letters, digits, and other character symbols) is displayed. In Microsoft® BASIC, text mode is called *Mode 0*. If your PC system contains the Color/Graphics Monitor Adapter, you can also operate in the PC's two graphics modes:

Medium-resolution graphics (Mode 1) allows you to produce graphic images in color on a screen of 200 lines with each line containing up to 320 points.

High-resolution graphics (Mode 2) allows you to produce black and white graphic images on a screen of 200 lines with each line containing up to 640 points.

In this chapter we assume that your PC system contains the Color/Graphics Monitor Adapter. With it you can use the following Microsoft® BASIC statements to produce graphic displays.

SCREEN	The statement SCREEN 0 selects text mode, SCREEN 1 selects medium-resolution graphics mode, and SCREEN 2 selects high-resolution graphics mode.
PSET	Used to plot individual points.
COLOR	Used to specify colors to be used in medium-resolution graphics. The COLOR statement is not allowed in high-resolution graphics mode.
LINE	Used to draw lines and boxes.
CIRCLE	Used to draw circles and elipses.
PAINT	Used to color selected areas of the screen.
GET/PUT	Used to move graphic images from one part of the screen to another.

The use of these statements to produce medium-resolution graphics displays is described in Sections 19.1 through 19.8. Each of these statements, other than COLOR, can also be used in high-resolution graphics mode. The same forms are used in both graphics modes, but there are differences in the displays produced. In medium-resolution graphics mode colors can be displayed, text will appear in the WIDTH 40 size, and points will be spaced so that a horizontal line across the entire screen contains 320 points. In high-resolution graphics mode all displays will be in black and white, text will appear in the smaller WIDTH 80 size, and points will be spaced so that a horizontal line across the entire screen contains 640 points. These differences are described in greater detail in Section 19.10.

Note: You should use Advanced BASIC while working through the material in this chapter. Of the graphics statements shown, only PSET and LINE can be used to produce displays when using Diskette or Cassette BASIC.

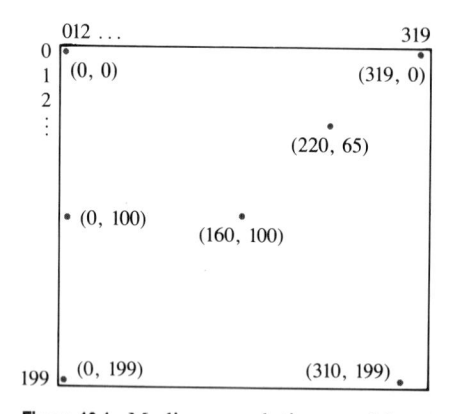

■ 19.1 Medium-Resolution Graphics: Getting Started

In **medium-resolution graphics mode** the screen is divided into a 320-column by 200-row grid of points, sometimes called **picture elements** (or **pixels**). The columns in the grid are numbered 0 to 319 from left to right; the rows are numbered 0 to 199 from top to bottom (Figure 19.1).

An individual point is specified by giving its column number followed by its row number. As shown in Figure 19.1, (0, 0) identifies the point in the upper-left corner, the point (0, 100) is located 100 point positions below this corner point, (220, 65) is the point in column 220 and row 65 (since positions are numbered from zero, this is the two hundred twenty-first column and sixty-sixth row), and (160, 100) is located at about the center of the screen.

The two numbers used to specify a point in the grid are called its *coordinates*. The first is the *x-* or *horizontal* coordinate; the second is the *y-* or *vertical* coordinate. This terminology is borrowed from mathematics. We can also refer to the top row as the *x*-axis (labeled 0 to 319 from left to right), the left-hand column as the *y*- axis (labeled 0 to 199 from top to bottom), and the point (0, 0) in the upper-left corner as the origin.

To enter the PC's medium-resolution graphics mode of operation, use the statement SCREEN 1; to return to text mode, use SCREEN 0. (All graphics statements can be issued in either immediate mode or deferred mode.)

SCREEN 1   Sets the PC to its medium-resolution graphics mode. In this operating mode you can use all previously introduced BASIC statements as well as the graphics statements to be introduced in this chapter. Text will still be displayed on the screen but in the larger WIDTH 40 characters. Each character uses the same space as an 8-by-8 block of points.* While in medium-resolution mode, you will notice that the cursor is a solid block rather than the blinking underscore character in text mode.

SCREEN 0   Sets the PC to its normal text mode. If the PC was previously in medium-resolution graphics mode, you will return to text mode with a screen width of 40. To return to text mode with the usual line width of 80, use

```
SCREEN 0 : WIDTH 80
```

```
         012...                          319
       0 •--------------------------------•
       1 | (0, 0)                  (319, 0)
       2 |
       : |
         |                    •
         |                  (220, 65)
         |
         | • (0, 100)       •
         |              (160, 100)
         |
         |
         |
         | • (0, 199)         (310, 199)
     199 •--------------------------------•
```

Figure 19.1   Medium-resolution graphics screen.

The SCREEN statement also clears the screen (except for the function-key display), but only if it specifies a *new* screen mode. Thus, if a program begins with the statement SCREEN 1 and you type RUN while in medium-resolution graphics mode (a

---

* The width of the screen is 320 points or 40 characters, and the height is 200 points or 25 characters. Since 320/40 = 8 and 200/25 = 8, each character is 8 points wide and 8 points high. Since the IBM PC screen (and most other video screens) display more points per inch in the horizontal direction than the vertical direction, this 8 × 8 block of points will be slightly higher than it is wide.

previous program run may have left the screen in this mode), the statement SCREEN 1 will not clear the screen. To ensure that you always enter graphics mode with a clear screen use

```
SCREEN 1 : CLS
```

To turn off the function-key display, you would use KEY OFF as usual. If you don't do this, you will not be allowed to use LOCATE to specify line 25 for text output.

Once in medium-resolution graphics mode (SCREEN 1) you can use the statement

```
PSET (X, Y)
```

to illuminate any one of the 64,000 (320 × 200) points (X, Y) on the screen. Illuminating a specific point is called **plotting the point** (another term borrowed from mathematics). For example,

```
PSET (319, 0)
```

plots the point with coordinates (319, 0). As shown in Figure 19.1 this point is in the upper-right corner of the screen.

EXAMPLE 1 Here is a program to plot the four corner points and the center point of the screen.

```
100 SCREEN 1              'Medium resolution graphics
110 CLS : KEY OFF         'Clear screen.
120 REM
130 REM ---- PLOT FIVE POINTS AND A MESSAGE ----
140 REM
150 PSET (0,0)            'Upper left corner
160 PSET (319,0)          'Upper right corner
170 PSET (319,199)        'Lower right corner
180 PSET (0,199)          'Lower left corner
190 PSET (160,100)        'Center of screen
200 LOCATE 25,5
210 PRINT "(Press any key to clear screen.)";
220 IF INKEY$="" THEN 220 'Wait for key.
230 SCREEN 0 : WIDTH 80   'Normal text screen
240 END
```

Lines 100 and 110 get you into graphics mode with a clear screen; lines 150 to 190 plot the five points; lines 200 and 210 display the "Press any key" message along the bottom of the screen; and line 220 preserves the display until a key is pressed. When a key is pressed, control passes to line 230 which gets you back to text mode with a line width of 80. Since line 230 selects a new screen mode, text mode is entered with a clear screen.

REMARK You can use LOCATE and PRINT statements in graphics mode exactly the way they are used in text mode. The output, however, will be in the larger WIDTH 40 characters. If you want the smaller WIDTH 80 characters in graphic displays, you must use the high-resolution graphics mode as explained in Section 19.10.

You can also specify the coordinates of a point to be plotted by indicating the number of units by which the *x*- and *y*-coordinates of the most recently plotted point must be changed to arrive at this new point. If (X, Y) has just been plotted, the statement

```
PSET STEP(A, B)
```

will plot the point (X + A, Y + B). For example, the statements

```
PSET (50,70) : PSET STEP(10,-30)
```

will plot the point (50, 70) and then the point (50 + 10, 70 − 30) or (60, 40). The numbers 10 and −30 are called the *X-offset* and *Y-offset* values, respectively. The coordinates in the first PSET statement are said to be in **absolute form** (the actual coordinates 50 and

70 are specified) whereas the second PSET statement gives coordinates in **relative form** [STEP(10, −30) specifies coordinates *relative* to the most recently plotted point].

If the PC encounters the statement

```
PSET STEP(A,B)
```

before any point has been plotted, it uses the screen's center (160, 100) as the starting point and plots (160 + A, 100 + B) as the first point. The usual practice, however, is to plot at least one point before using STEP(A, B) to specify coordinates in relative form. In Example 2 we use

```
PSET (90,Y)
```

to plot the point (90,Y) and then execute the loop

```
FOR DOT=1 TO 46
    PSET STEP(3,0)
NEXT DOT
```

to plot 46 more points along the line specified by Y, with each point three pixels to the right [STEP(3, 0)] of the previous one.

EXAMPLE 2   Here is a program to display a rectangle by plotting every third point in a rectangular region of the screen.

```
100 SCREEN 1              'Medium resolution graphics
110 CLS : KEY OFF         'Clear screen.
120 REM
130 REM *********************************************
140 REM          DISPLAY FIGURE CAPTION
150 REM
160 LOCATE 18,13 : PRINT "A RECTANGLE WITH";
170 LOCATE 20,9  : PRINT "EVERY THIRD POINT PLOTTED"
180 REM
190 REM *********************************************
200 REM       DISPLAY RECTANGULAR ARRAY OF POINTS
210 REM
220 FOR Y=45 TO 115 STEP 3    'Every third line
230     PSET (90,Y)           'First point on line
240     FOR DOT=1 TO 46
250         PSET STEP(3,0)    '3 pixels to the right
260     NEXT DOT
270 NEXT Y
280 IF INKEY$="" THEN 280     'Wait for key.
290 SCREEN 0 : WIDTH 80       'Normal text screen
300 END
RUN
```

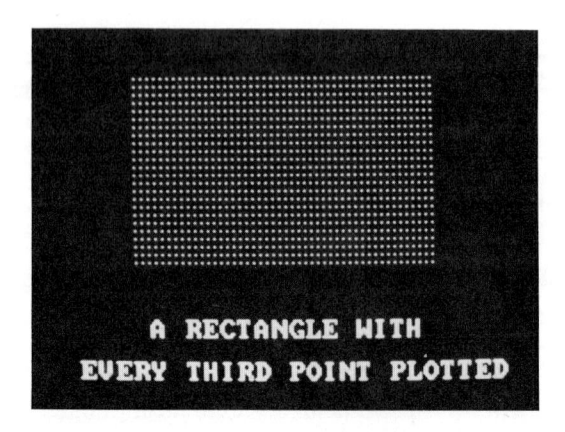

For each of the Y values

    45, 48, 51, 54, . . . , 111, 114

lines 230 to 260 plot the 46 points

    (90,Y), (93,Y), (96,Y), . . . , (225,Y), (228,Y)

that are three pixels apart and lie on the horizontal line specified by Y.

■ REMARK   The figure caption displayed by lines 160 and 170 begins on text line 18. Points along the top edge of this line have y-coordinate 136—each text line has a height of 8 pixels, so text lines 1–17 use $8 \times 17 = 136$ pixels numbered 0 to 135. Since points along the bottom edge of the rectangle have y-coordinate 115 (see lines 220–270), the figure caption begins 21 (136–115) pixels below the rectangle.

If you run the programs shown in Examples 1 and 2, you will obtain white output on a black background. To display images in color you will need to understand how the COLOR statement is used in medium-resolution graphics mode. (It is not used as in text mode.) The form used for medium-resolution graphics is

    COLOR **back, palette**

where **back** is an integer from 0 to 15 and **palette** is 0 or 1:

back   This first parameter specifies one of 16 colors (numbered 0–15 in Table 19.1) as the background color. The entire background, but not points or text already on the screen, is colored as soon as the color statement is executed. If **back** is omitted, the background color is not changed—this color is black when SCREEN 1 is executed.

palette   This second parameter specifies one of two palettes (numbered 0 and 1 in Table 19.2) from which the colors of images to be displayed will be chosen. If **palette** = 0 you can create images using four colors: the background color, and the three palette colors green (1), red (2), and brown (3). If **palette** = 1 you can use the background color and the palette colors cyan (1), magenta (2), and white (3). If **palette** is omitted, the palette is not changed—SCREEN 1 selects palette 1.

Table 19.1 **Medium-resolution background colors**

Number	Color	Number	Color
0	Black	8	Gray
1	Blue	9	Light blue
2	Green	10	Light green
3	Cyan (medium blue)	11	Light cyan
4	Red	12	Light red
5	Magenta (purple)	13	Light magenta
6	Brown	14	Yellow
7	White	15	High-intensity white

Table 19.2 **Medium-resolution palettes**

Color	Palette 0	Palette 1
1	Green	Cyan
2	Red	Magenta
3	Brown	White
(Color 3 is used for text and is called the foreground color.)		

We now explain how points and text are colored.

Color for Text

All text output (output produced by PRINT statements) will appear in color 3 of the palette (0 or 1) selected. As indicated in Table 19.2, this color is called the **foreground color.** For example, the statements

```
COLOR 1,0
LOCATE 12,1 : PRINT "BROWN ON BLUE"
```

display the string BROWN ON BLUE in brown (color 3 of palette 0) on a blue (1) background. If you now issue the statement

```
COLOR 4,1
```

to specify palette 1 with red (4) as the background, the text BROWN ON BLUE will immediately change to white (color 3 of palette 1) and the background to red. To see that everything is as explained, run the following short program. You will have to press a key twice: once to change colors, and again to halt program execution. When the program halts, the screen will return to its usual white-on-black text mode—COLOR statements executed while SCREEN 1 is in effect are cancelled when you return to text mode.

```
100 SCREEN 1
110 CLS : KEY OFF
120 COLOR 1,0
130 LOCATE 12,1 : PRINT "BROWN ON BLUE"
140 IF INKEY$="" THEN 140
150 COLOR 4,1
160 IF INKEY$="" THEN 160
170 SCREEN 0 : WIDTH 80
180 END
```

Color for Points

A color for a point displayed by a PSET statement can be specified by using the forms

```
PSET (X,Y), color
PSET STEP(A,B), color
```

where **color** denotes an integer from 0 to 3. The value 0 specifies the background color—to *erase* a point, plot it in the background color. The values 1, 2, and 3 specify colors from the current palette. For example,

```
COLOR 2,1
PSET (0,100),1
```

will plot the point (0, 100) in cyan (color 1 of palette 1) on a green (2) background. Similarly,

```
COLOR 2,1
PSET (0,100),1
FOR N=1 TO 159 : PSET STEP(2,0),1 : NEXT N
```

will plot every other point on the horizontal line with *y*-coordinate 100 in cyan on a green background. If you now issue the statement

```
COLOR 4,0
```

the dotted line will immediately change to green (color 1 of palette 0) and the background to red (4). To see that everything is as explained, run the following short program.

```
100 SCREEN 1
110 CLS : KEY OFF
120 COLOR 2,1
130 PSET (0,100), 1
```

```
140 FOR N=1 TO 159 : PSET STEP(2,0),1 : NEXT N
150 IF INKEY$="" THEN 150
160 COLOR 4,0
170 IF INKEY$="" THEN 170
180 SCREEN 0 : WIDTH 80
190 END
```

If the color parameter is omitted in a PSET statement, the point is displayed in color 3 of the current palette—called the foreground color in Table 19.2.

COMMENT   When producing color displays in medium-resolution graphics mode, the usual practice is to include a COLOR statement to select a background color and either palette 0 or palette 1. As mentioned previously, a background of black and palette 1 are used if these are not specified in a COLOR statement. Thus, even without the COLOR statement you can produce displays in the palette 1 colors cyan, magenta, and white, on a black background. All text will appear in white (the foreground color) and points will appear in the color specified in PSET statements. If the color parameter is omitted in a PSET statement, the point will also appear in the foreground color white. This explains why the programs in Examples 1 and 2 produce white output on a black background.

We conclude this section with the general forms of the COLOR and PSET statements. The general form of the COLOR statement as used in *medium-resolution graphics mode* is

COLOR back, palette

where **back** and **palette** denote numerical expressions that are rounded if necessary to integer values BACK and PALETTE. These integers specify the background color and palette of colors, respectively, to be used in color displays. The following rules apply.

1. BACK and PALETTE must be in the range 0–255. Any value outside this range results in an Illegal function call error.
2. If BACK is greater than 15 then BACK MOD 16 is used.
3. Any even value of PALETTE selects palette 0 and any odd value selects palette 1.
4. Each of the color parameters **back** and **palette** is optional. Omitting a color parameter means it will not be changed.

The general forms of the PSET statement are

PSET (x,y), c

or

PSET STEP(a,b), c

where **x, y, a, b,** and **c** are numerical expressions that are rounded, if necessary, to obtain integer values X, Y, A, B, and C. The integers X and Y specify the coordinates of a point to be plotted; the integers A and B are the offset values—if the previous point plotted has coordinates (X, Y), the point (X + A, Y + B) will be plotted. The integer C selects a color from the current palette; if C = 0 the background color is selected. The following rules apply:

1. If **c** is omitted, the foreground color (color 3 of the current palette) is used.
2. The rounded value C should be an integer from 0 to 3. If C > 3, the foreground color (color 3 of the current palette) is used. If C < 0 or C > 255 an Illegal function call error occurs.
3. The rounded coordinates X and Y must be in the range −32768 to 32767. Any values outside this range result in an Overflow error.
4. X should be in the range 0–319 and Y in the range 0–199. An attempt to plot (X,Y) with other X or Y values can lead to unexpected and unwanted results. For instance, PSET(320,100) plots the point (0,101) which is the first point on the next line. Similarly, PSET(639,100) plots (319,101). But, PSET(640,100) plots nothing at all.

19.2 Drawing Lines and Rectangles: The LINE Statement

In this section we describe the LINE statement and show how a single LINE statement can be used to plot an entire line segment, an entire rectangle, or an entire rectangular area. We first describe how lines are drawn.

The simplest form of the LINE statement is

```
LINE (X,Y)-(Z,W)
```

This statement plots a line segment joining the points (X, Y) and (Z, W) in the default color (color 3 of the current palette). To specify a different color, simply add a color parameter as was done with the PSET statement. If C is 0, 1, 2, or 3, the statement

```
LINE (X,Y)-(Z,W),C
```

plots the same line in color C of the current palette or in the background color if C = 0.

EXAMPLE 3 Here is a program to plot the triangle with vertices (160, 10), (260, 90), and (60, 90).

```
100 SCREEN 1                    'Med. res. graphics
110 CLS : KEY OFF               'Clear the screen.
120 COLOR 1,0                   'Blue bkgrd. - Palette 0
130 REM --------- DRAW A GREEN TRIANGLE ----------
140 LINE (160,10)-(260,90),1
150 LINE (260,90)-(60,90),1
160 LINE (60,90)-(160,10),1
170 REM ------- DISPLAY A FIGURE CAPTION --------
180 LOCATE 14,13
190 PRINT "A GREEN TRIANGLE"
200 IF INKEY$="" THEN 200
210 SCREEN 0 : WIDTH 80
220 END
RUN
```

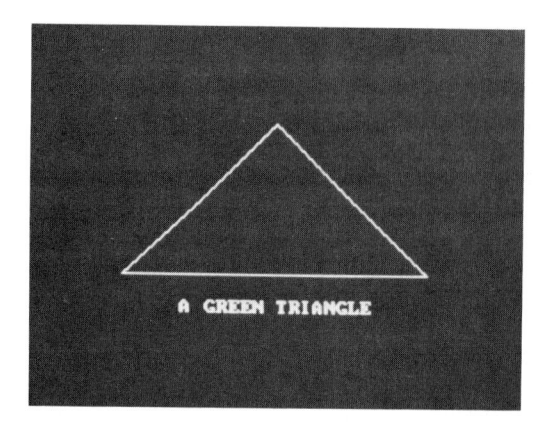

Line 120 specifies a blue background (color 1) and palette 0. Since each LINE statement specifies the color parameter 1, the three lines are drawn in green (color 1 of palette 0) on a blue background. Line 190 displays a figure caption in the foreground color brown (color 3 of palette 0).

■ **REMARK 1** Line 180 specifies screen line 14 for the caption A GREEN TRIANGLE. Since each text line of the screen is 8 points high, displaying the caption below the 13th text line means that it will not be above the line with y-coordinate 13 × 8 = 104. This is below the triangle; the y-coordinate for each point on the bottom edge of the triangle is 90.

■ **REMARK 2** Notice that the two upper edges of the triangle are not straight. You will find that only horizontal, vertical, and 45-degree lines (STEP(1,1)) consist of points that actually lie on a straight line. All other lines will have a more or less jagged appearance. The reason for this discrepancy is that the number of different points that can be plotted on the PC's video screen is inadequate for displaying most line segments. Consider, for example, the statement

```
LINE (0,0)-(50,1)
```

As the PC plots the segment from (0, 0) to (50, 1), the only *y*-coordinates available are 0 and 1. Since these two *y*-coordinates designate adjacent horizontal lines on the screen, each point displayed will lie on one of these lines. If you execute this LINE statement, the PC will display a broken line as follows.

If the first point in a LINE statement is the last point referenced in the program, it can be omitted. For example, the line plotted by the statement

```
LINE (243,50)-(84,148)
```

can also be plotted by using

```
PSET (243,50)
LINE -(84,148)
```

The second of these statements plots a line from the last point referenced—in this case, (243, 50)—to the point (84, 148). With this new form of the LINE statement, lines 140, 150, and 160 of the preceding program (which plot a triangle) can be replaced by

```
140 PSET (160,10)
150 LINE -(260,90)
160 LINE -(60,90)
165 LINE -(160,10)
```

thus simplifying somewhat the job of typing the program.

The form

```
LINE (X,Y)-(Z,W)
```

is most often used when isolated line segments are to be plotted. The form

```
LINE -(Z,W)
```

is intended for applications requiring a sequence of connecting line segments for which the coordinates of the endpoints must be determined during program execution.

The expression **last point referenced,** used in the preceding discussion, needs clarification—it does not necessarily refer to the last point plotted. After execution of each graphics statement (PSET, LINE, and others described later in this chapter), the PC stores the coordinates of a point called the *last point referenced*. After the statement

```
PSET (X,Y)
```

is executed, the *last point referenced* is (X, Y)—in this case, the last point plotted. After the statement

```
LINE (X,Y)-(Z,W)
```

is executed, the *last point referenced* is (Z, W), which may or may not be the last point plotted. If you execute the statement

```
LINE (319,100)-(0,0)
```

and look carefully, you may be able to detect that the line is plotted from (0, 0) to (319, 100) and not from (319, 100) to (0, 0). There are more compelling reasons than this for using the expression *last point referenced* rather than *last point plotted*. Indeed, as shown in Section 19.4 the *last point referenced* can be a point you specify in a graphics statement that is not plotted at all. With each graphics statement described in this chapter we will indicate what point is stored as the *last point referenced*.

The coordinates of either or both points in a LINE statement can be specified in relative form by using STEP just as it was used in the PSET statement. For example, the statement

```
LINE (50,75)-STEP(100,0)
```

plots a horizontal line segment connecting (50, 75) to (50 + 100, 75 + 0) or (150, 75). If the next statement is

```
LINE STEP(0,2)-(50,77)
```

STEP (0, 2) specifies coordinates relative to (150, 75), the point specified by STEP(100, 0) in the first LINE statement. Thus, STEP(0, 2) gives the point (150 + 0, 75 + 2) or (150, 77) and the line segment connecting (150, 77) to (50, 77) is plotted. Note that this second line segment is also horizontal (both endpoints have y-coordinate 77) and lies two points below the first line segment (its points have y-coordinate 75). The next example uses coordinates in relative form to display a design centered at the point (160, 100).

EXAMPLE 4

Here is a program to create a graphics display consisting of several lines emanating from the screen's center.

```
100 SCREEN 1                'Med. res. graphics
110 CLS : KEY OFF           'Clear the screen.
120 COLOR 3,1               'Cyan bkgrd. - Palette 1
130 REM
140 REM DRAW MAGENTA (PURPLE) LINES EMANATING
150 REM FROM CENTER (160,100) OF THE SCREEN.
160 LET S=-90
170 WHILE S<=90
180     LINE (160,100)-STEP (90,S),2
190     LINE (160,100)-STEP (-90,S),2
200     LET S=S+10
210 WEND
220 IF INKEY$="" THEN 220
230 SCREEN 0 : WIDTH 80
240 END
RUN
```

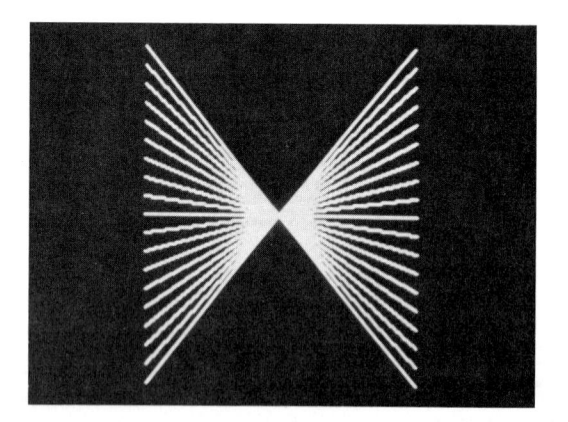

Each time through the loop, line 180 displays one of a sequence of line segments from the point (160, 100) directed toward the right. The second point determining each line segment always has an x-coordinate of 160 + 90 = 250, but the y-coordinates range from 100 + (−90) = 10 to 100 + 90 = 190 in increments of 10. Similarly, line 190 displays the line segments directed to the left.

At the outset of this section we mentioned that a single LINE statement can be used to plot an entire rectangle or an entire rectangular area. This is accomplished by including a final parameter B (for box) or BF (for filled box). The statement

    LINE (X,Y)-(Z,W),C,B

plots the rectangle whose diagonally opposite corners are at (X, Y) and (Z, W) in color C of the current palette. The statement

    LINE (X,Y)-(Z,W),C,BF

plots the same rectangle and its interior in color C of the current palette. Thus, the statements

    COLOR 8,1
    LINE (20,30)-(100-80),2,B

color the background in gray (color 8) and plot the four edges of the following rectangle in magenta (color 2 of palette 1).

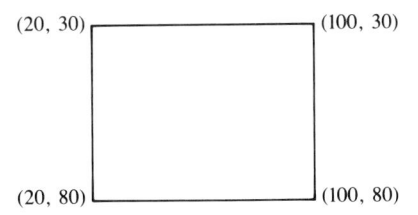

```
(20, 30) ┌─────────────┐ (100, 30)
         │             │
         │             │
         │             │
         │             │
(20, 80) └─────────────┘ (100, 80)
```

The statement

    LINE (20,30)-(100,80),2,BF

colors not only the edges of this rectangle in magenta, but its interior as well. Since the second point (100, 80) is 80 points to the right and 50 points below the first point (20, 30), this LINE statement may be written as

    LINE (20,30)-STEP(80,50),2,BF

This equivalent form shows explicitly that the rectangle has width 80 and height 50.

The next two examples illustrate the B and BF options in LINE statements.

EXAMPLE 5

Let's write a program to display

    ┌───────┐
    │CAPTION│
    └───────┘

PROBLEM ANALYSIS

Since CAPTION contains 7 letters and since each letter uses the same space as an 8-by-8 block of points, the required box must be at least $7 \times 8 = 56$ points across and 8 points high. So that the box will not touch the letters, we'll use a width of 58 and a height of 10. Thus, once we have determined the upper-left corner (X, Y) for the box, we'll draw it with the statement

    LINE (X,Y)-STEP(58,10),C,B

Before selecting the upper-left corner (X, Y), we must know where on the screen CAPTION will be displayed. Let's center it on screen line 5 by using

    LOCATE 5,16 : PRINT "CAPTION"

The bottom edge of the fourth text line has y-coordinate 31 ($4 \times 8 - 1$; minus 1 because point positions are numbered beginning with 0). Similarly, the right edge of the 15th character position on a line has x-coordinate 119 ($15 \times 8 - 1$). Thus, (119, 31) is the point just above and to the left of the caption. So that the box doesn't touch the letters we'll use (X, Y) = (118, 30). (We allowed for this by using a box size of 58 by 10 rather than 56 by 8.)

THE PROGRAM

```
10 SCREEN 1                      'Med. res. graphics
20 CLS : KEY OFF                 'Clear the screen.
30 COLOR 1,0                     'Blue bkgrd. - palette 0
40 REM
50 LOCATE 5,16 : PRINT "CAPTION" 'Display caption.
60 LINE (118,30)-STEP(58,10),1,B 'Box it in.
70 REM
80 IF INKEY$="" THEN 80
90 SCREEN 0 : WIDTH 80
99 END
```

☐ CAPTION is displayed in the foreground color brown (color 3 of palette 0) on a blue background. The LINE statement then draws the box in green (color 1 of palette 0).

EXAMPLE 6

Here is a program to display a rectangle centered in the graphics area. Colors for the rectangle and the background are specified by the user. The action of this program is described by the REM statements in lines 180, 280, 340, and 390.

```
100 CLS : KEY OFF
110 REM      B  = NUMBER FOR BACKGROUND COLOR
120 REM      B$ = BACKGROUND COLOR
130 REM      P  = PALETTE NUMBER (0 OR 1)
140 REM      S  = COLOR NUMBER FROM PALETTE P
150 REM      S$ = COLOR FOR BOX TO BE DISPLAYED
160 REM
170 REM ************************************************
180 REM     KEYBOARD INPUT : GET COLORS FOR THE DESIGN.
190 REM
200 INPUT "BACKGROUND COLOR (0-15)";B
210 IF B<0 OR B>15 THEN PRINT "Please reenter." : GOTO 200
220 INPUT "PALETTE (0 OR 1)";P
230 IF P<0 OR P>1  THEN PRINT "Please reenter." : GOTO 220
240 INPUT "COLOR OF THE RECTANGLE (1-3)";S
250 IF S<1 OR S>3  THEN PRINT "Please reenter." : GOTO 240
260 REM
270 REM ************************************************
280 REM   SELECT GRAPHICS MODE AND COLOR THE BACKGROUND.
290 REM
300 SCREEN 1                         'Med. res. graphics
310 COLOR B,P                        'Bkgrd B - Palette P
320 REM
330 REM ************************************************
340 REM            COLOR THE RECTANGLE.
350 REM
360 LINE (100,50)-(220,150),S,BF     'Color entire box.
370 REM
380 REM ************************************************
390 REM          SELECT AND DISPLAY A TITLE.
400 REM
410 FOR C=0 TO B
420    READ B$
430 NEXT C
440 IF P=0 THEN RESTORE 640          'Palette 0 selected
450 IF P=1 THEN RESTORE 680          'Palette 1 selected
460 FOR C=1 TO S
470    READ S$
480 NEXT C
490 LET COL=(37-LEN(S$)-LEN(B$))/2   'To center title
500 LOCATE 22,COL                    'Title position
510 PRINT S$;" ON ";B$
520 IF INKEY$="" THEN 520            'Wait for key.
530 SCREEN 0 : WIDTH 80              'Normal text screen
540 END                              'End program.
550 REM ------------------------------------------------
560 REM                BACKGROUND COLORS
```

```
570 REM
580 DATA BLACK, BLUE, GREEN, CYAN, RED, MAGENTA, BROWN, WHITE
590 DATA GRAY, LIGHT BLUE, LIGHT GREEN, LIGHT CYAN, LIGHT RED
600 DATA LIGHT MAGENTA, YELLOW, HIGH-INTENSITY WHITE
610 REM ---------------------------------------------------
620 REM                   PALETTE 0 COLORS
630 REM
640 DATA GREEN, RED, BROWN
650 REM ---------------------------------------------------
660 REM                   PALETTE 1 COLORS
670 REM
680 DATA CYAN, MAGENTA, WHITE
RUN

BACKGROUND COLOR (0-15)? 1
PALETTE (0 OR 1)? 0
COLOR OF THE RECTANGLE (1-3)? 2
```

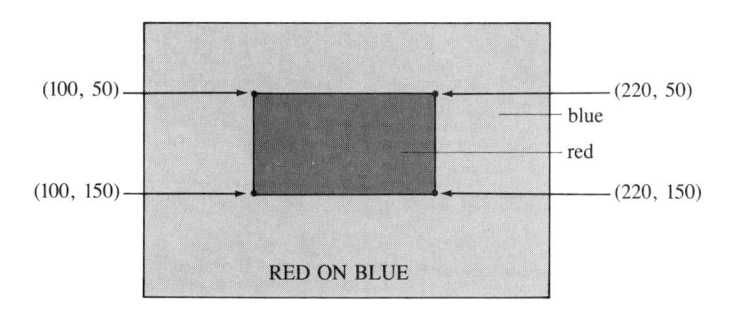

```
(100, 50)                           (220, 50)
                                    blue
                                    red
(100, 150)                          (220, 150)

             RED ON BLUE
```

The general form of the LINE statement is

LINE Point1–Point2,c,s

where **Point1** and **Point2** specify points in the absolute form **(x, y)** or in the relative form STEP **(a,b)**, **c** denotes the color parameter, and **s** is either B (for box) or BF (for filled box). **Point1, c,** and **s** may be omitted. The symbols **x, y, a, b,** and **c** denote numerical expressions that are rounded if necessary to obtain integer values X, Y, A, B, and C, respectively. The following rules govern the use of LINE statements:

1. The coordinates specified by **Point1** and **Point2** must be valid screen coordinates as described in Section 19.1.
2. If **Point1** is omitted, the *last point referenced* is used.
3. If **s** is omitted, a line segment connecting **Point1** and **Point2** is plotted. If **s** = B, a rectangle with **Point1** and **Point2** as opposite vertices is plotted. If **s** = BF, the same rectangle and its interior are plotted.
4. If **c** is omitted, the line, rectangle, or rectangular area is plotted in the default color 3 of the current palette. If **c** is included, its integer value C must be a valid color parameter as described in Section 19.1. C specifies a color from the current palette or the background color.
5. Since the IBM PC screen (and most other video screens) displays more points per inch in the horizontal direction than in the vertical direction, a "square" plotted by the statement

    LINE (X,Y)-STEP(R,R),,B

    will appear slightly longer from top to bottom than from left to right.
6. After execution of the LINE statement, the *last point referenced* is set to **Point2**.

We conclude this section with two examples further illustrating the use of the LINE statement. The first concerns plotting a bar chart showing grade distributions of students; the second uses the RND function to generate changing kaleidoscopic designs.

EXAMPLE 7 The number of students receiving the grades of A, B, C, D, and E at Easy University are given below. Write a program to display a bar chart showing the relative sizes of the five groups.

Number of students	Grade
432	A
567	B
673	C
123	D
53	E

PROBLEM ANALYSIS

To keep things as simple as possible, we'll include the five input values (432, 567, 673, 123, and 53) in a DATA statement. Since no specific details of the output are given in the problem statement, let's agree to produce a chart like the one shown here. (The column numbers 100, 140, 180, 220, and 260, and the row number 160 are for reference only.) Let's also agree to leave 10 positions between each of the vertical bars, thus making each bar 30 positions wide.

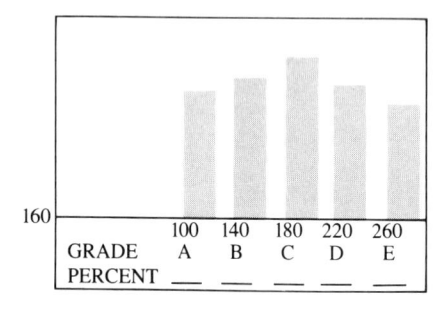

A simple two-step algorithm to produce this output is as follows.

   a. Display the vertical bars using lines 0–160 of the graphics screen.
   b. Display labels below the vertical bars as shown.

To display the bars we need to know the height of each rectangle. The height should represent the fraction F of students receiving a particular grade. If we use $160 \times F$ vertical points, we can be sure that each rectangle will fit in the graphics area above line y = 160. (F is between 0 and 1 so $160 \times F$ is between 0 and 160.)

Step (b) of the two-step algorithm is not difficult. It requires only that data be output in specified rows and columns. We will use LOCATE and PRINT USING statements to display the two lines. Step (a) requires more detail. To this end let's choose variable names:

   NUM = number of students receiving a certain grade
   TTL = total number of grades given
   F = fraction of TTL receiving a certain grade (F = NUM/TTL)
   COL = column position of the left side of a vertical bar
   HGT = height of vertical bar to be constructed

THE ALGORITHM (REFINED)

   a1. Add the five counts NUM to obtain TTL.
   a2. For each of the five counts NUM:
      a2.1. Calculate F = NUM/TTL.
      a2.2. Calculate HGT = $160 \times F$
      a2.3. Display a vertical bar HGT points high.
   b. Display the two lines of text below the bar chart and stop.

19.2 *Drawing Lines and Rectangles: The LINE Statement* 359

From the diagram we see that the bars begin at positions COL = 100, 140, 180, 220, and 260. To display them 30 columns wide we'll use the LINE statement

```
LINE (COL,160)-(COL+30,160-HGT),1,BF
```

at each of these column positions.

THE
PROGRAM

```
100 REM ********** GRADE REPORT BAR CHART **************
110 REM
120 REM **** DETERMINE THE TOTAL NUMBER TTL OF GRADES *****
130 LET TTL=0
140 FOR K=1 TO 5
150     READ NUM : TTL=TTL+NUM
160 NEXT K
170 RESTORE
180 REM ********** DISPLAY A BAR FOR EACH GRADE **********
190 SCREEN 1                        'Med. res. graphics
200 CLS : KEY OFF                   'Clear the screen.
210 COLOR 8,0                       'Gray bkgrd. - Palette 0
220 LET COL=100                     'Position of first bar
230 FOR K=1 TO 5
240     READ NUM
250     LET F=NUM/TTL
260     LET HGT=160*F
270     LINE (COL,160)-(COL+30,160-HGT),1,BF
280     LET COL=COL+40              'Position of next bar
290 NEXT K
300 RESTORE
310 REM ****** DISPLAY IDENTIFYING TEXT FOR BAR CHART *****
320 LOCATE 22,1
330 PRINT "GRADE         A    B    C    D    E"
340 LOCATE 24,1
350 PRINT "PERCENT     ";
360 FOR K=1 TO 5
370     READ NUM
380     PRINT USING "  ###";INT(100*NUM/TTL+0.5);
390 NEXT K
400 REM **************** DATA LINES ********************
410 DATA 432,567,673,123,53
420 REM *************************************************
430 IF INKEY$="" THEN 430
440 SCREEN 0 : WIDTH 80
450 END
RUN
```

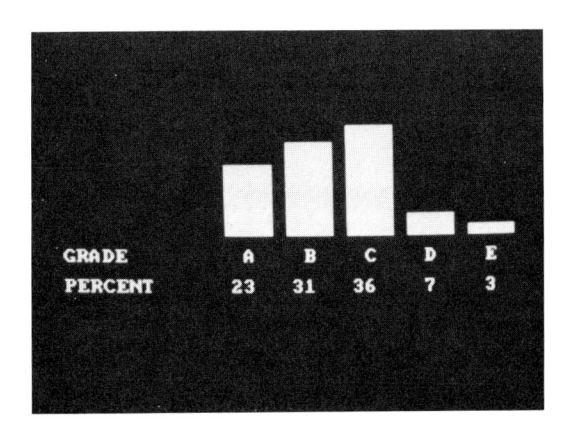

EXAMPLE 8   **Kaleidoscope designs.**

Kaleidoscopic designs make use of reflections to produce symmetrical sets of images. In this example we obtain the required symmetry as follows. First we divide the graphics area into four quadrants by means of imaginary horizontal and vertical lines that meet in the center:

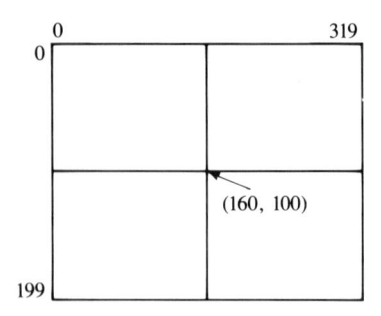

Next we select a point (X, Y) in the upper-left quadrant and plot the following four symmetrical points:

$$(X, Y) = \text{point selected}$$
$$(319 - X, Y) = \text{reflection of } (X, Y) \text{ in the vertical line}$$
$$(X, 199 - Y) = \text{reflection of } (X, Y) \text{ in the horizontal line}$$
$$(319 - X, 199 - Y) = \text{reflection of } (319 - X, Y) \text{ in the horizontal line}$$

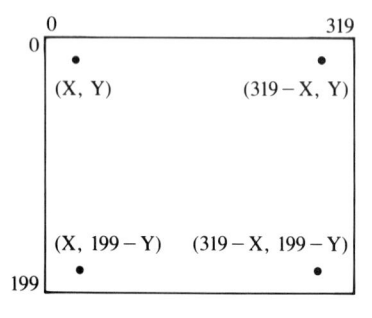

The following steps show one way to produce changing kaleidoscopic designs with the symmetries just described:

a. Randomly select a point (X, Y) in the upper-left quadrant.
b. Randomly select a color (0–3) from current palette or background.
c. Plot the four symmetrical points associated with (X, Y).
d. Go to Step (a).

The design that results from a program written from these four steps is slow to develop because of the very small size of the individual points plotted. To speed the development and also enhance the appeal of the design, we will plot 8-by-8 blocks rather than individual points. To do this we modify Step (a) so that the only points chosen in the upper-left quadrant are those with coordinates that are multiples of 8.

X = 0, 8, 16, . . . , 152
Y = 0, 8, 16, . . . , 96

Note that the statements

```
LET X=8*INT(20*RND)
LET Y=8*INT(13*RND)
```

will randomly select X and Y values from these sets.

Step (c) must also be modified to display 4 symmetrical 8-by-8 blocks as the following diagram illustrates.

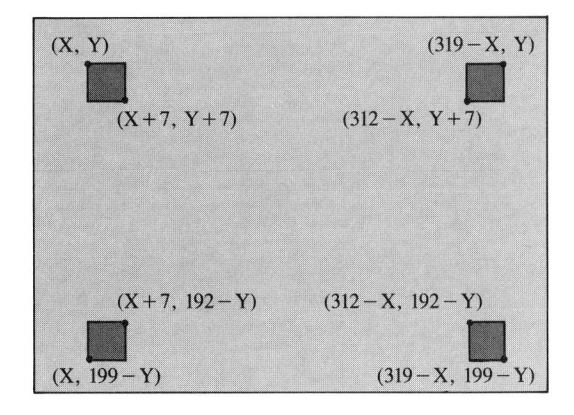

19.2 Drawing Lines and Rectangles: The LINE Statement

```
         (X, Y)                        (319 − X, Y)

              (X + 7, Y + 7)      (312 − X, Y + 7)




              (X + 7, 192 − Y)    (312 − X, 192 − Y)

         (X, 199 − Y)                  (319 − X, 199 − Y)
```

Such blocks are easily plotted by using LINE statements with the BF option. In the following program, which incorporates these two changes, we specify the coordinates of the inner vertex of each rectangle in relative form.

```
100 REM ************ KALEIDOSCOPE PROGRAM *************
110 REM
120 RANDOMIZE VAL(RIGHT$(TIME$,2))
130 SCREEN 1                      'Med. res. graphics
140 CLS : KEY OFF                 'Clear the screen.
150 COLOR 0,0                     'Black bkgrd. - palette 0
160 REM
170 WHILE INKEY$=""               'Loop until key is pressed.
180    REM
190    REM RANDOMLY SELECT A POINT IN TOP-LEFT QUADRANT
200    REM     AND A COLOR PARAMETER FROM 0 TO 3.
210    REM
220    LET X=8*INT(20*RND)        'Random X coordinate
230    LET Y=8*INT(13*RND)        'Random Y coordinate
240    LET C=INT(4*RND)           'Random color
250    REM
260    REM      DISPLAY FOUR   SYMMETRIC BLOCKS.
270    REM
280    LINE (X,Y)-STEP(7,7),C,BF              'Upper-left
290    LINE (319-X,Y)-STEP(-7,7),C,BF         'Upper-right
300    LINE (X,199-Y)-STEP(7,-7),C,BF         'Lower-left
310    LINE (319-X,199-Y)-STEP(-7,-7),C,BF    'Lower-right
320    REM
330 WEND
340 SCREEN 0 : WIDTH 80           'Normal text screen
350 END
RUN
```

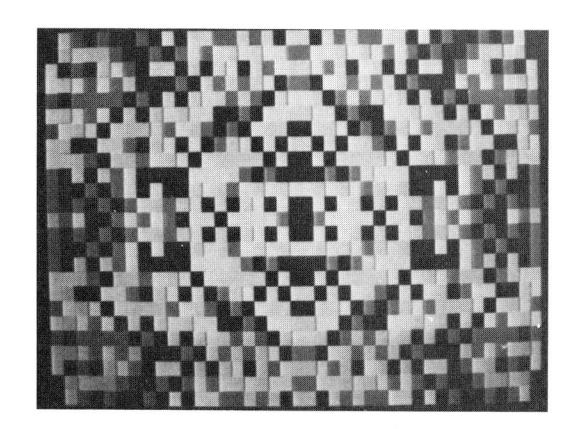

19.3 Problems

1. What graphics display results from each program?

   a.
   ```
   10 SCREEN 1 : CLS : KEY OFF
   20 FOR N=0 TO 90 STEP 10
   30     LINE (N,0)-STEP(5,5),,BF
   40 NEXT N
   50 IF INKEY$="" THEN 50
   60 SCREEN 0 : WIDTH 80
   70 END
   ```

   b.
   ```
   10 SCREEN 1 : CLS : KEY OFF
   20 LET X=30 : Y=50
   30 LINE (X,Y)-(X+20,Y+40),,BF
   40 LINE (X+5,Y)-(X+20,Y+35),0,BF
   50 IF INKEY$="" THEN 50
   60 SCREEN 0 : WIDTH 80
   70 END
   ```

   c.
   ```
   10 SCREEN 1 : CLS : KEY OFF
   20 LET X=30: Y=90
   30 LINE (X,Y)-STEP(5,-40),,BF
   40 LINE (X,Y)-STEP(20,-5),,BF
   50 IF INKEY$="" THEN 50
   60 SCREEN 0 : WIDTH 80
   70 END
   ```

   d.
   ```
   10 SCREEN 1 : CLS : KEY OFF
   20 FOR N=0 TO 99
   30     LINE (0,99-N)-(N,0)
   40     LINE (100+N,0)-(199,N)
   50 NEXT N
   60 IF INKEY$="" THEN 60
   70 SCREEN 0 : WIDTH 80
   80 END
   ```

In Problems 2–10, write a program to produce each display described.

2. On a white background, color the left half of the graphics area cyan and the right half magenta.
3. Divide the graphics area into four quadrants. Color the upper-left quadrant black, the upper-right green, the lower-left red, and the lower-right brown. Do this on a black background.
4. Divide the graphics area into 10 equal rows, each 20 points thick. On a background of yellow, color every other row green, beginning with the first. Color the remaining rows red.
5. Divide the graphics area into 20 equal columns, each 16 points wide. On a background of green, color every other column magenta, beginning with the first. Color the remaining columns white.
6. Display a sequence of twenty 8-by-8 squares: the upper-left corner of successive squares should be at the points (0, 0),(8, 8),(16, 16), and so on. Choose any background color and palette; let the rectangles be plotted in the foreground color.
7. Display the word HALT in large red block-letters centered in the graphics area on a yellow background.
8. Fill the graphics area with an 8 × 8 checkerboard pattern of 40-point × 20-point rectangles. A background color and two colors from palette 1 for the checkerboard should be specified by the user during program execution.
9. Fill the graphics area with a 40 × 40 checkerboard pattern of 8-point × 5-point rectangles. A background color and two colors from palette 0 for the checkerboard should be chosen by the user during program execution.

10. Produce a design consisting of three squares whose sides are 150, 100, and 50 points. All three squares have the common center (160, 100). You may use any background color, and the three squares should be in the three colors of whatever palette is chosen. (The smallest square is "on top" and the largest is on the "bottom.")

In Problems 11–13 write a program for each task specified.

11. Produce a bar chart to display the following sales figures graphically. The years and the sales amounts should be displayed below the chart. (Assume that a bar 160 points high represents the sales amount $1500 million.) Include the given data in DATA lines so that the program can be used for five other years and five different sales figures.

Year	Sales in millions
1984	$1,235
1985	1,421
1986	1,251
1987	1,025
1988	843

12. Produce a design consisting of filled squares of various sizes in one of three colors by the following method. For each square to be plotted choose four random numbers: the first (from 1 to 50) represents the size of the square, the second (from 1 to 3) gives the color, and the last two (from 0 to 319 and 0 to 199) are coordinates for the upper-left corner of the square. If the position specified for the square is not entirely in the graphics area, reject the corner coordinates and randomly select others. Each square is to remain on the screen unless it happens to be covered by subsequent squares. The display should end only when a key is pressed.

13. Produce changing kaleidoscopic designs by modifying the program of Example 8 in one or more of the following ways:
    a. If a randomly selected point (X, Y) satisfies the condition X + Y < 160, reject it and select another. (The designs will no longer occupy the full graphics area.)
    b. If a randomly selected point (X, Y) satisfies the condition

    $$(X - 160)^2 + (Y - 100)^2 > 75^2$$

    reject it and select another. (The designs will appear in a circle centered on the screen. If you change > to <, the designs will appear outside this circle.)
    c. Rather than 8-by-8 squares, use 4-by-4 squares and *x*- and *y*-coordinates that are multiples of 4.

■ 19.4 Drawing Circles and Ellipses: The CIRCLE Statement

In this section we describe the CIRCLE statement and show how a single CIRCLE statement can be used to plot an entire circle or ellipse, or an arc of a circle or ellipse. We first describe how circles are drawn.

The simplest form of the CIRCLE statement is

```
CIRCLE (X,Y),R
```

This statement plots the circumference of the circle with center (X, Y) and radius R in the foreground color (color 3 of the current palette). After this statement is executed, the *last point referenced* is the center (X, Y)—which is *not* plotted. To specify a different color, simply add a color parameter as was done with the PSET and LINE statements. If C is 0, 1, 2, or 3, the statement

```
CIRCLE (X,Y),R,C
```

plots the same circle in color C of the current palette or in the background color if C = 0.

EXAMPLE 9

Here is a program to display the Olympic symbol.

```
100 SCREEN 1              'Med. res. graphics
110 CLS : KEY OFF         'Clear the screen.
120 COLOR 1,0             'Blue bkgrd.-palette 0
130 CIRCLE (100,80),25,2
140 CIRCLE (160,80),25,2
150 CIRCLE (220,80),25,2
160 CIRCLE (130,100),25,2
170 CIRCLE (190,100),25,2
180 LOCATE 20,14
190 PRINT "OLYMPIC SYMBOL"
200 IF INKEY$="" THEN 200
210 SCREEN 0 : WIDTH 80
220 END
RUN
```

The five circles are colored red (color 2 of palette 0), the figure caption is brown (the foreground color), and the background is blue (color 1 is specified in the COLOR statement).

The radius R in the statement

CIRCLE (X,Y),R,C

specifies the radius in points in the horizontal *x*-direction. In Microsoft® BASIC, a radius in the vertical *y*-direction will contain (5/6) × R points. To see that this is so, run the following program, which displays a circle of radius 50 and a box with the same center with width 100 and height (5/6) × 100.

```
10 SCREEN 1                                    'Med. res. graphics
20 CLS : KEY OFF                               'Clear the screen.
30 LET R1=50                                   'Radius for circle
40 LET R2=5/6*R1                               '5/6th of radius
50 CIRCLE (160,100),R1                         'The circle
60 LINE (160-R1,100-R2)-STEP(2*R1,2*R2),,B     'Box-same center
70 IF INKEY$="" THEN 70
90 SCREEN 0 : WIDTH 80
99 END
RUN
```

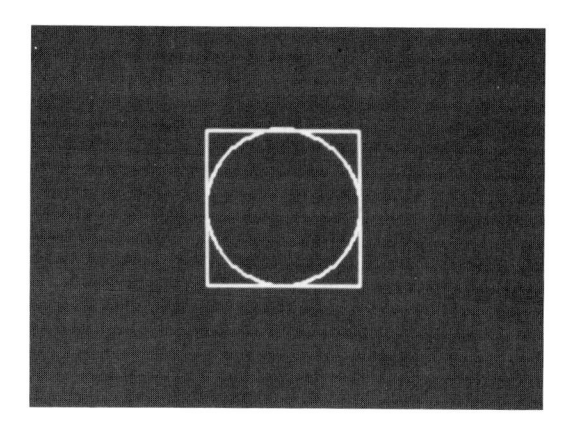

Microsoft® BASIC uses a vertical radius of (5/6) × R to accommodate screens on which 6 adjacent points in the horizontal direction have the same length as 5 adjacent points in the vertical direction. On such screens, circles will actually appear as circles. If your IBM PC screen does not faithfully display circles, you can adjust the Vertical Size control on the back of the display unit so that it does.

The coordinates of the center of a circle can be specified in relative form by using STEP just as with PSET and LINE statements. For example, the statements

```
CIRCLE (160,100),20
CIRCLE STEP(15,5),20
```

plot two circles of radius 20. The first plots the circle with center (160, 100) of radius 20 and sets (160, 100) as the last point referenced. Thus, the center of the second circle is at (160 + 15, 100 + 5) or (175, 105). In the next example we use STEP (8, 0) to specify centers along a horizontal line for 10 circles.

EXAMPLE 10

Here is a program to display 10 circles with centers (8, 100), (16, 100), (24, 100), . . . , (80, 100). The respective radii are 8, 16, 24, . . . , 80.

```
100 SCREEN 1                    'Med. res. graphics
110 CLS : KEY OFF               'Clear the screen.
120 COLOR 1,0                   'Blue bkgrd.-Pallette 0
130 PSET(0,100),2               'Set last point referenced.
140 FOR N=1 TO 10
150     CIRCLE STEP(8,0),8*N,2  'Next circle
160 NEXT N
200 IF INKEY$="" THEN 200
210 SCREEN 0 : WIDTH 80
220 END
RUN
```

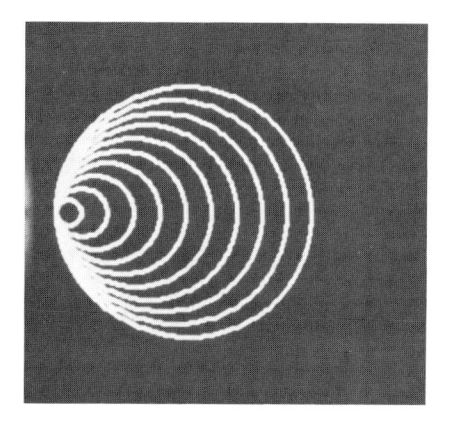

On the Nth pass through the FOR loop, the circle with center (8*N, 100) and radius 8*N is plotted. Since the radius is measured in points in the horizontal *x*-direction, the point (0, 100) lies on each circle as shown.

An arc of a circle can be plotted with the CIRCLE statement by adding a *start* and an *end* parameter to specify the angles at which the arc is to begin and end. The angles are positioned according to standard mathematical usage (see Figure 19.2) beginning at the right with 0° and increasing counterclockwise to 360°. The angles in the CIRCLE statement must be in radian measure. Since

a) Degree measure   b) Radian measure

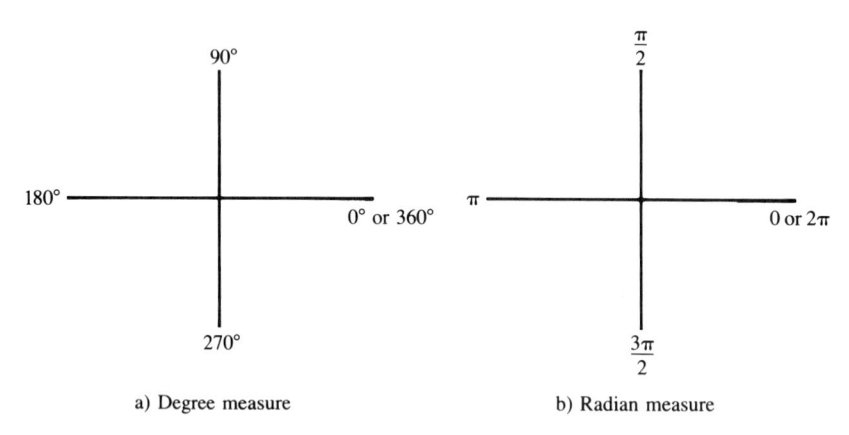

Figure 19.2 Angles used in CIRCLE statements.

$$1° = \frac{\pi}{180} \text{ radians}$$

the number of radians in D° is given by the formula

$$D° = \frac{\pi}{180} \times D \text{ radians}$$

Those more comfortable thinking in terms of degrees can continue to do so, if you remember to convert to radians in the program before using the CIRCLE statement. For example, if PI = 3.141593 the statement

```
CIRCLE (X,Y),R,C,0,(PI/180)*45
```

will plot the 45° arc (0–45°) of the circle with center (X, Y) and radius R. Since (PI/180)*45 = PI/4 it is easier to write (type)

```
CIRCLE (X,Y),R,C,0,PI/4
```

Either form plots the same arc

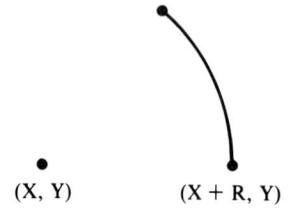

(X, Y)   (X + R, Y)

The arc produced by

```
CIRCLE (X,Y),R,C,PI/4,0
```

is different. The PC always plots the arc obtained by moving in the counterclockwise direction beginning at the first angle (the *start* parameter) and ending at the second (the *end* parameter). Thus, with *start* = PI/4 and *end* = 0, you will get the following 315° arc.

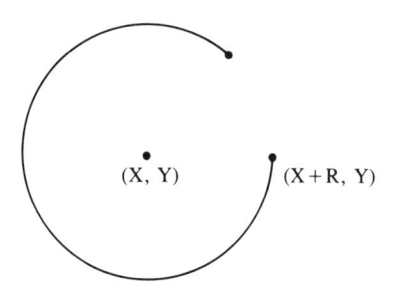

(X, Y)   (X+R, Y)

EXAMPLE 11   Here is a program to display six labeled arcs.

```
100 SCREEN 1                            'Med. res. graphics
110 CLS : KEY OFF                       'Clear the screen.
120 LET PI=3.141593                     'Approximation for pi
130 COLOR 0,1                           'Black bkgrd.-palette 1
140 LOCATE 8,1 : PRINT "0 to PI"
150 CIRCLE(30,30),20,3,0,PI             '180 deg arc (0-180)
160 LOCATE 8,16 : PRINT "PI to 0"
170 CIRCLE(150,30),20,3,PI,0            '180 deg arc (180-360)
180 LOCATE 8,31 : PRINT "0 to PI/2"
190 CIRCLE(270,30),20,3,0,PI/2          '90 deg arc (0-90)
200 LOCATE 17,1 : PRINT "PI/2 to 2PI"
210 CIRCLE(30,100),20,3,PI/2,2*PI       '270 deg arc (90-360)
220 LOCATE 17,16 : PRINT "3PI/2 to 0"
230 CIRCLE(150,100),20,3,3*PI/2,0       '90 deg arc (270-360)
240 LOCATE 17,31 : PRINT "PI to PI/2"
250 CIRCLE(270,100),20,3,PI,PI/2        '270 deg arc (180-90)
260 IF INKEY$="" THEN 260
270 SCREEN 0 : WIDTH 80
280 END
RUN
```

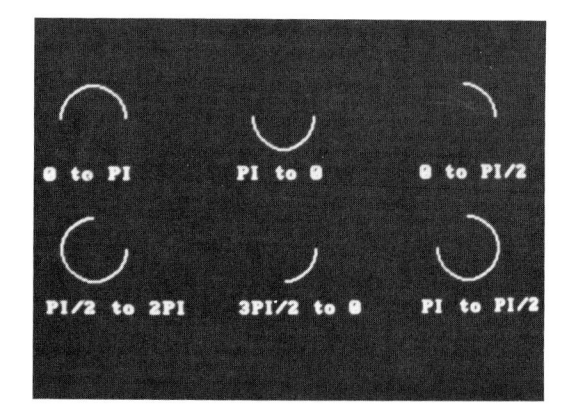

■ **REMARK**   The COLOR statement is not needed. It specifies the default background (0) and default palette (1). The color parameter 3 in each CIRCLE statement is also not needed since the default color is color 3 of the current palette.

EXAMPLE 12   Here is a program to display a "Horn of Plenty" design by drawing arcs of concentric circles.

```
100 SCREEN 1                            'Med. res. graphics
110 CLS : KEY OFF                       'Clear the screen.
120 LET PI=3.141593                     'Approximation for pi
```

```
130 LET R=0                          'R gives radius of arcs.
140 COLOR 1,0                        'Blue bkgrd.-palette 0
150 FOR A=0 TO PI STEP 0.1
160     LET R=R+3
170     CIRCLE (160,100),R,2,PI,PI+A
180 NEXT A
190 IF INKEY$="" THEN 190
200 SCREEN 0 : WIDTH 80
210 END
RUN
```

For angle A between 0 and PI (180°), line 170 plots the arc from PI to PI + A of the circle with center (160, 100) and radius R.

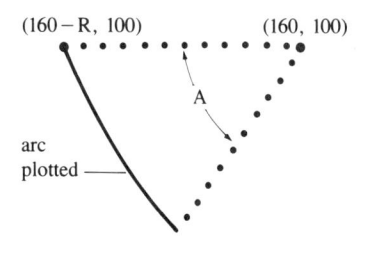

On each pass through the FOR loop the radius R and angle A are increased (R by 3 and A by 0.1) so the arcs are plotted from shortest to longest to produce the design.

■ **REMARK 1** If you display the arcs farther apart you will be able to distinguish between them more easily. If you increase successive radii by 6 instead of 3 and use STEP 0.2 instead of STEP 0.1 in the FOR statement, you will obtain a design of the same size and shape but with twice the distance between adjacent arcs.

■ **REMARK 2** If you change lines 150 and 160 to

```
150 FOR A=0 TO PI STEP (0.1)/3
160     LET R=R+1
```

the design will again have the same size and shape but the arcs will be so close that the entire design will be colored except for scattered points. The missing points occur because the number of points that can be plotted on the screen in medium-resolution graphics is insufficient for displaying circles (just as for displaying most lines).

The *start* and *end* parameters for arcs can be any numbers in the range -2π to 2π. Negative values, however, do not specify negative angles. Rather, a negative parameter $-A(0 < A \leq 2\pi)$ specifies that the arc is to be connected to the center of the circle by a radial line segment at the angle A.

EXAMPLE 13   This example illustrates the effect of negative *start* and *end* parameters in CIRCLE statements.

Starting value	Ending value	Output
$-\dfrac{\pi}{2}$	$-\pi$	
$-\dfrac{\pi}{2}$	-2π	
0	$-\pi$	
$-\dfrac{3\pi}{2}$	π	

■ **REMARK**   The angle specifier -0 is the same as 0. To connect an arc at angle 0 to the center, you must use -2π as in the second illustration.

EXAMPLE 14   Let's write a program to display a circle partitioned into 12 equal sectors.

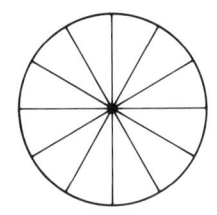

PROBLEM ANALYSIS

Since a circle contains 360° (2π radians), the arc for each sector must be a 30° arc ($\pi/6$ radian arc). If we start at 0° and move in the counterclockwise direction, the first arc will be from 0° to 30°, the second from 30° to 60°, and so on. To plot the first sector, we can use

```
CIRCLE (X,Y),R,C,0,-PI/180*30
```

This statement displays the required 30° arc and connects it to the center at the angle 30°.

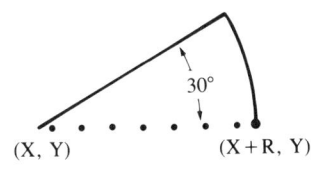

The next sector can be plotted by using the same CIRCLE statement with different *start* and *end* values.

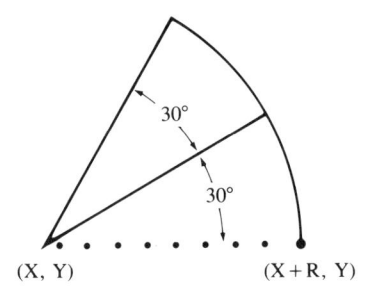

```
CIRCLE (X,Y),R,C,PI/180*30,-PI/180*60
```

Although it would be correct to use the start value −PI/180∗30, it is not necessary to do this, since the radial line segment at 30° was plotted when the first sector was plotted.

If we plot the 12 sectors in counterclockwise order, the starting angle for each sector other than the first will be the ending angle of the preceding sector. In the following program we use S to specify the starting angle and E for the ending angle. However, −E is used in the CIRCLE statement to plot the radial line segment at angle E. After a sector is plotted, we set S to E and increase E by PI/6 (that is 30°) to obtain starting and ending angles for the next sector.

THE PROGRAM

```
100 REM    S = STARTING ANGLE (RADIANS) FOR ARCS
110 REM    E = ENDING ANGLE (RADIANS) FOR ARCS
120 SCREEN 1                  'Med. res. graphics
130 CLS : KEY OFF             'Clear the screen.
140 LET PI=3.141593           'Approximation for pi
150 COLOR 1,1                 'Blue bkgrd.-palette 1
160 LET S=0
170 FOR DEGREES=30 TO 360 STEP 30
180     LET E=PI/180*DEGREES          'Convert to radians.
190     CIRCLE (160,100),50,1,S,-E    'Plot a sector.
200     LET S=E                       'Next starting angle
210 NEXT DEGREES
220 IF INKEY$="" THEN 220
230 SCREEN 0 : WIDTH 80
240 END
```

REMARK 1 By using (X, Y) to specify the center instead of (160, 100), the diagram can be displayed elsewhere on the screen. By using R instead of 50 to specify the radius, diagrams of different sizes can be displayed. Nothing else in the program needs to be changed except that values must somehow be assigned to X, Y, and R.

REMARK 2 The method illustrated in this example can be used to display "pie charts" with sectors of different sizes. For example, suppose A(1), A(2), A(3), A(4), and A(5) have been assigned values and their sum has been assigned to the variable SUM. The following modification of lines 160–210 of the above program will display a pie chart with 5 sectors whose sizes show the relative sizes of the numbers A(1), A(2), . . . , A(5).

```
160 LET S=0
170 FOR N=1 TO 5
180     LET E=A(N)/SUM*2*PI+S
190     CIRCLE (160,100),50,1,S,-E    'Plot a sector
200     LET S=E                       'Next starting angle
210 NEXT N
```

The numerical expression A(N)/SUM∗2∗PI gives the angular size of the sector; it does not give the sector's ending angle. Thus, in line 180 we add this value to S to obtain the angle E that ends the sector.

Following Example 9 of this section we mentioned that circles actually appear on the IBM PC screen as circles. (What you see is called the **visual circle.**) This is because Microsoft® BASIC makes adjustments to compensate for the way points are displayed on the screen. You will recall that 6 adjacent points in the horizontal direction have the same length as 5 adjacent points in the vertical direction. The ratio 5/6 is called the **aspect value.**

The CIRCLE statement allows one final parameter to allow you to specify different aspect values. The statement

CIRCLE (X, Y),R,*color,start,end,*V

specifies the numerical value of V as the aspect value. The center (X, Y) and the radius R are required. To specify an aspect value V, but accept the default values 3, 0, and 2π for *color, start,* and *end,* simply omit these parameters and write

```
CIRCLE (X,Y),R,,,,V
```

The PC uses the default aspect value 5/6 if you omit this final parameter as we have done to this point.

If you specify an aspect value V other than V = 5/6, the visual circles will be ellipses. For aspect values less than 5/6, each ellipse will have a longer *x*-radius than *y*-radius. For aspect values greater than 5/6 each ellipse will have a longer *y*-radius.

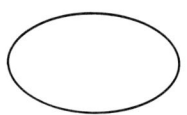

Aspect value < 5/6

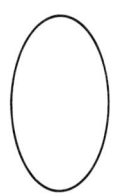

Aspect value > 5/6

The actual *x*- and *y*-radii (in screen points) of a visual circle depend on both the radius R and the aspect value V specified in the CIRCLE statement:

V ≤ 1   The *x*-radius is R points long and the *y*-radius is V∗R points long.

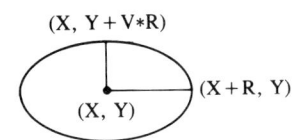

As explained previously, these screen lengths are the same only if V = 5/6. (The case V = 1 is of interest: the vertical and horizontal radii are both R points long, but the vertical radius is actually longer because points in the vertical direction are farther apart than points in the horizontal direction.)

V > 1   The *y*-radius is R points long and the *x*-radius is R/V points long.

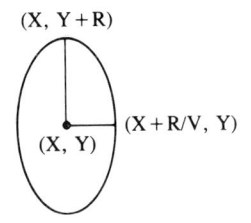

The following table illustrates how changing the aspect value results in variously shaped ellipses.

Radius	Aspect value	Ellipse (visual circle)
R = 40	V = 1/4	(X, Y+10), (X, Y), (X+40, Y)
R = 40	V = 1/2	(X, Y+20), (X, Y), (X+40, Y)
R = 40	V = 5/6	(X, Y + (5/6)*40), (X, Y), (X+40, Y)
R = 40	V = 1	(X, Y+40), (X, Y), (X+40, Y)
R = 40	V = 2	(X, Y+40), (X, Y), (X+20, Y)

The general forms of the CIRCLE statement are

CIRCLE (x,y),r,c,start,end,aspect
CIRCLE STEP(a,b),r,c,start,end,aspect

The symbols **x**, **y**, **a**, **b**, **r**, and **c** denote numerical expressions that are rounded if necessary to obtain integer values X, Y, A, B, R, and C, respectively. (X, Y) and STEP(A, B) specify coordinates of the center of a circle, R the radius of this circle, and C a color from the current palette or the background color. The last three parameters **start**, **end**, and **aspect** are also numerical expressions, but these values are not converted to integers. The parameters **start** and **end** give the starting and ending positions (in radian measure) for an arc of the specified circle. The last parameter **aspect** specifies the aspect value to be used by the PC while plotting the circle.

The following rules apply:

1. The parameters **c**, **start**, **end**, and **aspect** are optional. Their respective default values are 3, 0, 2π, and 5/6. A CIRCLE statement must not end with a comma. (If it does, a fatal Missing operand error results.) To omit a parameter, you would omit the comma preceding the parameter only if it violates this rule.

2. Points whose coordinates are not screen coordinates are not plotted by CIRCLE statements; that is, there is no wraparound.

3. The center coordinates X and Y, the offset values A and B, and the radius R must be in the range −32768 to 32767; otherwise a fatal Overflow error results. Because of Rule 2, it makes little sense to use most of these values. (*Caution:* If by accident you specify a large radius, such as R = 32767, you will have a long wait. The PC calculates coordinates for all points on specified circles, whether or not it plots them.)

4. The **start** and **end** parameters that specify angles in radian measure for circular arcs must be in the range -2π to 2π. A negative value −A does not indicate a negative angle; rather it specifies that a radius is to be plotted at the angle A. If either **start** or **end** is not in the range -2π to 2π, a fatal Illegal function call error results.

5. The aspect value parameter **aspect** should be positive. If you adjusted the Vertical Size control on the back of the display unit as described following Example 9 of this section, the aspect value 5/6 (.8333333) gives visual circles that look like circles. Other aspect values give ellipses as explained previously. (Because of the limited number of points that can be displayed on screens, positive aspect values that are close to zero will give horizontal line segments and large aspect values will give vertical line segments.)

6. After a CIRCLE statement is executed, the *last point referenced* is the center specified by (X, Y) or STEP(A, B).

■ 19.5 Coloring Areas of the Screen: The PAINT Statement

The PAINT statement fills in a region of the screen with a color you select from the current palette and background colors. To "paint" a region, you must know two things: the color B of the boundary of the region, and a point (X, Y) within the region whose color differs from the boundary color B.

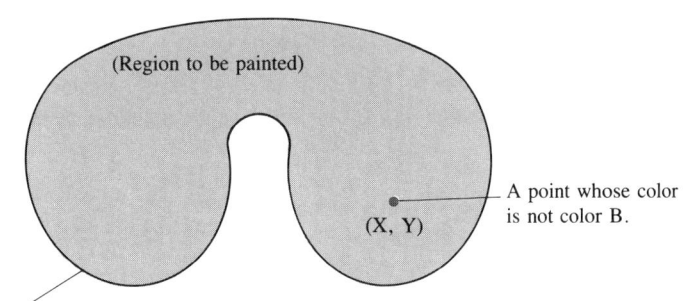

With color B and point (X, Y) as described, the statement

```
PAINT (X,Y),P,B
```

colors the entire region in color P. P can specify any of the four available colors.

Consider, for example, the program segment

```
100 SCREEN 1                    'Med. res. graphics
110 CLS : KEY OFF               'Clear the screen.
120 COLOR 8,0                   'Gray bkgrd.-palette 0
130 CIRCLE (160,100),50,2       'Draw a red circle.
140 PAINT (160,100),1,2         'Paint its interior green.
```

Since the point (160, 100) specified in the PAINT statement is inside the red circle, and since its color is not red (it is gray), the PAINT statement colors the interior of the circle green (color 1 of palette 0). The color (red) of the circle is not changed—only interior points are painted. To color both the circle and its interior green, use

```
120 CIRCLE (160,100),50,1
130 PAINT (160,100),1,1
```

As mentioned above, the painting color can be any of the four available colors, including B. The only requirement for painting is that the color of the point (X, Y) specified in the PAINT statement differ from the boundary color B.

A more precise description of the effect of the statement

```
PAINT (X, Y), P, B
```

is as follows (you will notice that the description does not use the word *boundary*): If the current color of the point (X, Y) is different from the color B, the PC begins painting in color P at the point (X, Y) and continues painting until all points in the graphics area that can be reached from (X, Y) without passing through a point of color B have been painted. If the current color of (X, Y) is color B, nothing is painted.

Either or both of the color parameters P and B can be omitted. The default for P is the foreground color (color 3 of the current palette). You will recall that this is the default value for color parameters omitted in PSET, LINE, and CIRCLE statements. If you omit B, however, the PC uses the painting color P for B.* Thus, the statements

```
120 CIRCLE (160, 100), 50, 2
130 PAINT (160, 100), 2
```

plot a red circle and paint its interior red as well. Line 130 is equivalent to the statement

```
130 PAINT (160, 100), 2, 2
```

If both P and B are omitted, P defaults to the foreground color (as already mentioned), and B defaults to P. Thus the statements

```
120 CIRCLE (160, 100), R
130 PAINT (160, 100)
```

plot a circle and its interior in the foreground color. Line 130 is equivalent to

```
130 PAINT (160, 100), 3, 3
```

EXAMPLE 15 This example further illustrates the use of the PAINT statement to color regions of the screen. In each of parts (a)–(c), we assume that the given program lines are preceded by these three lines:

```
100 SCREEN 1           'Med. res. graphics
110 CLS : KEY OFF      'Clear the screen.
120 COLOR 0, 1         'Black bkgrd.-palette 1
```

This will allow us to refer to the following colors:

Black	The background
Cyan	Color parameter 1
Magenta	Color parameter 2
White	Color parameter 3 (foreground color)

a.
```
130 LINE (160, 0)-(160, 199), 1    'Partition the screen.
140 LOCATE 1, 1
150 INPUT "X, Y"; X, Y              'Input a point.
160 PAINT (X, Y), 1, 1              'Paint part with point.
```

Line 130 draws (in cyan) a vertical line that completely divides the graphics area into a left half and a right half. If the input values specify a point (X, Y) in the left half the paint statement will color the entire left half (also in cyan). Similarly, the right half is colored if (X, Y) lies to the right of the vertical line. Nothing happens if (X, Y) lies on the vertical line.

---

* The boundary parameter in PAINT statements and the two parameters in COLOR statements are the only color parameters in graphics statements that do not default to color 3 of the current palette.

19.5 Coloring Areas of the Screen: The PAINT Statement

REMARK 1 If the vertical line were shortened by only one point—for instance if line 130 were changed to

```
130 LINE (160,1)-(160,199),1
```

this would no longer be a boundary and the entire screen except for this line would be painted.

REMARK 2 Since the boundary color defaults to the painting color, line 160 can be written in the equivalent form

```
160 PAINT (X,Y),1
```

REMARK 3 If each color parameter is changed to 3, the display will be in white on black instead of cyan on black. But then the color parameters wouldn't be needed: the default color for the LINE statement is 3, the default for the painting color is 3, and the default for the border is the painting color, which happens to be 3. When producing black and white displays, color parameters in PSET, LINE, CIRCLE, and PAINT statements are needed only if black points are to be plotted. As mentioned previously, points are plotted in black to erase them or to create black images on a white background.

```
b. 130 PSET (160,10),2      'Draw
   140 LINE - (260,90),2    'a magenta
   150 LINE - (60,90),2     'triangle.
   160 LINE - (160,10),2
   170 PAINT (160,11),2     'Color its interior.
```

The point (160, 11) specified in the PAINT statement lies inside the triangle (one point below the top vertex). Hence, the interior of the triangle is painted in magenta.

REMARK 4 To color the region outside of the triangle, simply change the point (160, 11) in the PAINT statement to (160, 9) or to any other point outside the triangle.

```
c. 130 REM ****** COLOR REGIONS INSIDE OF A RECTANGLE ******
   140 LINE (0,0)-STEP(120,120),1,B  'Cyan rectangular border
   150 CIRCLE(60,60),40,1            'Inner cyan circle
   160 PAINT (101,60),1              'Paint outside of circle.
   170 PAINT (60,60),3,1             'Paint inside of circle.
   180 LOCATE 8,6 : PRINT "White"
   190 LOCATE 14,6 : PRINT "Cyan"
   200 LOCATE 17,1 : PRINT "(Black background)"
```

The point (101, 60) in line 160 is inside the rectangle and outside the circle, so this region is colored in cyan. The point (60, 60) in the second PAINT is at the center of the circle, so this PAINT statement colors the circle's interior in white (3). The three captions displayed by lines 180–200 are in white (the foreground color) on a black background. The black background for each letter is what allows you to see the word "white" displayed in white letters within a white circular region.

REMARK 5 Essentially the same display will be produced more quickly if you replace the four lines 140–170 with the three lines

```
140 LINE (0,0)-STEP(120,120),1,BF
150 CIRCLE (60,60),40
170 PAINT (60,60)
```

You should verify that the only difference will be in the color of the circumference of the circle that separates the inner region from the cyan region. By using the BF option in LINE statements, you can often eliminate PAINT statements (which are slow to execute) and thus both simplify the coding process and speed up program execution.

The next example illustrates how a display can be altered by systematically changing the colors.

EXAMPLE 16 Here is a program to alternately color the upper and lower halves of a circle.

```
100 SCREEN 1                              'Med. res. graphics
110 CLS : KEY OFF                         'Clear the screen.
120 COLOR 1,1                             'Blue bkgrd.-palette 1
130 REM * DRAW BOUNDARIES FOR UPPER AND LOWER SEMICIRCLES *
140 CIRCLE (160,100),50,3
150 LINE (110,100)-(210,100),3
160 REM ***** ASSIGN POINTS IN UPPER AND LOWER HALVES *****
170 LET X=160                             'X for both points
180 LET Y=99                              'Y for upper half
190 LET Y1=101                            'Y1 for lower half
200 REM ** ALTERNATELY COLOR UPPER AND LOWER SEMICIRCLES **
210 REM ** USING COLORS 0,1,2,0,1,2, AND SO ON.           **
220 LET P=0                               'Starting color
230 WHILE INKEY$=""
240     PAINT (X,Y),P,3
250     LET P=(P+1) MOD 3                 'Next color
260     SWAP Y,Y1                         'Get Y for other half.
270 WEND
280 SCREEN 0 : WIDTH 80
290 END
```

Line 140 draws a circle in the center of the screen and line 150 draws a horizontal diameter to divide the circle into a top and bottom half. The circle and the line are colored white (color 3 of palette 1).

Lines 170–190 specify coordinates for two points, one in the top and the other in the bottom half of the circle.

Lines 230–270 form a loop to change the colors in the two halves of the circle. On each pass through this loop, line 250 increases P (the *paint* parameter) by 1 and resets it to 0 each time 3 is reached. Thus, the successive painting colors are 0, 1, 2, 0, 1, 2, and so on. The SWAP statement in line 260 interchanges Y and Y1, thereby alternating the point (X, Y) used in the PAINT statement between (160, 99) and (160, 101). This effectively alternates the top and bottom as the region being painted.

■ **REMARK** Since the boundaries of the half circles were colored white and remain white, we avoided white as a painting color. Had we not done so, a half circle that was painted white would stay that way—the interior point specified in the PAINT statement would be white, the same color as the boundary, so the PAINT statement would do nothing.

☐

The general forms of the PAINT statement are

PAINT (**x**, **y**),**paint**,**border**
PAINT STEP(**a**,**b**),**paint**,**border**

where **x**, **y**, **a**, **b**, **paint**, and **border** are numerical expressions that are rounded to integer values X, Y, A, B, P, and BORD, respectively. (X, Y) and STEP(A, B) specify the coordinates of a point within the region to be painted. P and BORD specify colors from the current palette or the background color. P specifies the color with which to paint, and BORD gives the color of the boundary of the region to be painted. The following rules apply:

1. If the point specified by (X, Y) or STEP(A, B) has the same color as the border (color BORD), nothing is painted. Otherwise, the PC paints in color P all points in the graphics area that can be reached from the specified point without passing through a point with color BORD.
2. If **paint** is omitted, the foreground color (color 3 of the current palette) is used.
3. If **border** is omitted, the painting color **paint** is used.
4. After a PAINT statement is executed the *last point referenced* is the point whose coordinates are given by (X, Y) or STEP(A, B).

19.6 Problems

In Problems 1–11, write a program to produce the display described. The PAINT statement is not needed.

1. Plot 10 circles in a row across the display screen. They should be equally spaced, have the same radius, and should not touch each other.
2. Plot 10 circles as in Problem 1, but in a vertical column rather than a row.
3. Plot 10 circles as in Problem 1, but have their centers lie along the line joining the points (0, 0) and (199, 199).
4. Display a smiling face, centered on the screen; the eyes and mouth should be arcs of ellipses.
5. For R in the range 1 to 115, display a circle with center (160, 100) and radius R. Also display a rectangle that encloses the circle and touches it at four points. R is to be input and is to be rejected if not in the specified range. (Do not specify an aspect value in the CIRCLE statement.)
6. For V in the range 0.7 to 1.1, use a CIRCLE statement with aspect value V to display an ellipse with center (160, 100) that fits on the screen. At the bottom-left corner of the screen, inform the user what radius was used. V is to be input and is to be rejected if not in the specified range.
7. Display an ellipse as in Problem 6 and also a rectangle that encloses the ellipse and touches it at four points.
8. Divide the screen into four parts by drawing horizontal and vertical lines through the center (160, 100). In each part, display a "Horn of Plenty" design as described in Example 12. Use the four points (80, 50), (240, 50), (80, 150), and (240, 150) as centers for the four designs.
9. Display four "Horn of Plenty" designs one after the other. The user will press a key to see the next design. All four designs are to be centered at (160, 100) but they are not to be identical. The first should be as in Example 12, and each successive design is to be the preceding one rotated 90°.
10. Divide the screen into four parts by drawing horizontal and vertical lines through the center (160,100). Display the four "Horn of Plenty" designs described in Problem 9, one in each of the four parts. Use the four points (80,50), (240,50), (80,150), and (240,150) as centers for the four designs.
11. Display a circle partitioned into N equal sections. The integer N is to be input and is to be from 1 to 360 (input values that are not integers in this range are to be rejected). The method used in Example 14 can be used for this problem as well.

In Problems 12–16, write a program to produce the display described. The PAINT statement should be used.

12. Plot a square, circle, and triangle as shown in the diagram.

    The numbers indicate the colors from the palette to be used to color the four regions of the display. (Use the BF option to plot the square.)
13. Display interlocking ellipses as shown in the diagram. The numbers indicate colors from the current palette to be used to color the regions.

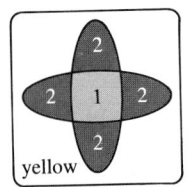

14. Display three interlocking circles as shown in the diagram.

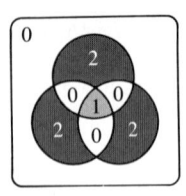

The numbers indicate colors from the current palette to be used to color the eight regions of the display. The circles themselves should be plotted in color 3.

15. Display a pie with a piece removed but placed just next to it as shown in the diagram.

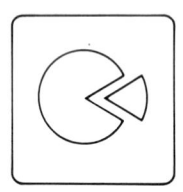

Choose one color for the background and one for both parts of the pie.

16. Divide the graphics area into eight parts by drawing four lines through the center as shown. The numbers indicate colors from the current palette to be used. Use color 3 for the four lines.

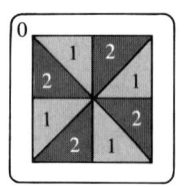

■ 19.7 Moving Objects: The GET and PUT Statements

While in graphics mode, the GET and PUT statements are used to move objects (rectangular screen images) from one part of the screen to another. This is accomplished by first using GET to store a numerical representation of the object to be moved in an array, and then using a PUT statement to specify a new position for the image represented by the array.* We will first describe the GET statement.

If (X1, Y1) and (X2, Y2) give valid screen coordinates, and if the numerical array A has been dimensioned (as will be explained shortly), the statement

```
GET (X1,Y1)-(X2,Y2),A
```

stores a numerical representation of the rectangular region with (X1, Y1) and (X2, Y2) as opposite corners in the array A. We will say, more simply, that the screen image is stored in array A. (The rectangular region is the same region that is colored by the statement LINE (X1, Y1)–(X2, Y2),C,BF.) The numerical representation stored in A consists of the dimensions of the rectangular region and the color numbers of all points in this region.

---

* As described in Section 17.6 on random access files, while in text mode GET moves a record from a diskette file to a file buffer (rather than a screen image to an array), and PUT writes the contents of a file buffer to the file (rather than the contents of an array to the screen).

19.7 *Moving Objects: The GET and PUT Statements* **379**

Consider, for example, the following program segment:

```
100 SCREEN 1              'Med. res. graphics
110 CLS : KEY OFF         'Clear the screen.
120 COLOR 1,0             'Blue bkgrd.-palette 0
130 LINE (0,0)-(8,8),1,BF 'Green rectangular area
140 LINE (2,2)-(6,6),2,BF 'Smaller red rectangular area
150 DIM A(7)
160 GET (0,0)-(8,8),A     'Store image in array A.
```

Lines 100–120 get you into medium-resolution graphics mode with a clear blue screen. Lines 130 and 140 produce the display shown below, and line 150 stores this 9-by-9 rectangular image in array A.

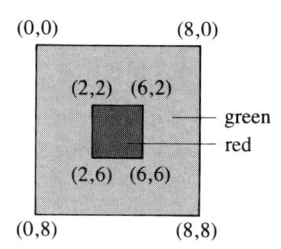

```
(0,0)           (8,0)
    ┌───────────────┐
    │   (2,2) (6,2) │
    │     ┌───┐     │─── green
    │     │   │     │─── red
    │     └───┘     │
    │   (2,6) (6,6) │
    └───────────────┘
(0,8)           (8,8)
```

Line 150 is necessary even though 7 does not exceed 10. An array specified in a GET statement must be dimensioned before the GET statement is executed. That the dimension 7 is adequate to store the 9-by-9 screen image is explained following the next example.

Having stored this rectangular screen image in array A you can use the PUT statement to display it elsewhere on the screen. The statement

```
PUT (20,0),A
```

will display it with its upper-left corner at the point (20, 0). If you execute the same PUT statement again, however, the image will disappear. The statement

```
PUT (X,Y),A
```

plots a point in the color specified by array A only if the point currently has the background color. If the current color of the point is the same as the color specified by array A, you get the background color. (What happens when the current color is some other color is explained later in this section.)

EXAMPLE 17   Here is a program that uses GET and PUT to display the following line drawing at several screen positions.

```
100 SCREEN 1                                         'Med. res. graphics
110 CLS : KEY OFF                                    'Clear the screen.
120 COLOR 1,1                                        'Blue bkgrd.-palette 1
130 REM ************* PRODUCE LINE DRAWING *******************
140 LINE (160,115)-STEP(0,-17),3                     'Body
150 LINE (140,100)-STEP(40,0),3                      'Arms
160 LINE (160,115)-STEP(-20,20),3                    'Left leg
170 LINE (160,115)-STEP(20,20),3                     'Right leg
180 CIRCLE (160,92),6,3                              'Head
190 REM *** STORE LINE DRAWING IN ARRAY F AND THEN ERASE IT ***
```

380   Chapter 19   Graphics

```
200 DIM F(135)
210 GET (140,87)-(180,135),F          'Store image in F.
220 PUT (140,87),F                    'Erase image.
230 REM ***** DISPLAY SEVERAL DRAWINGS NEXT TO EACH OTHER ******
240 FOR X=0 TO 250 STEP 41
250     PUT (X,0),F                   'Display image at (X,0).
260 NEXT X
270 IF INKEY$="" THEN 270             'Wait for key.
280 REM ********* ERASE THE DRAWINGS, ONE AT A TIME ***********
290 FOR X=0 TO 250 STEP 41
300     PUT (X,0),F                   'Display image at (X,0).
310 NEXT X
320 IF INKEY$="" THEN 320             'Wait for key.
330 SCREEN 0 : WIDTH 80
340 END
```

Lines 100 to 120 get you into medium-resolution graphics mode with a clear blue screen. The rest of the program is divided into four parts as indicated by the REM statements in lines 130, 190, 230, and 280.

Lines 130 to 180 display the specified figure in a 41-by-49 rectangular region as follows. (The dotted lines are for reference only.)

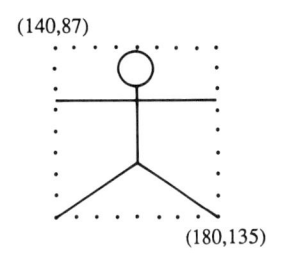

Note that line 180 plots the head with center (160, 92) and radius 6, but that the top point of this circle has y-coordinate $87 = 92 - 5$, and not $86 = 92 - 6$. Remember that the y-radius of a visual circle is 5/6 times the specified radius if the aspect value parameter is omitted. Since $5/6 \times 6 = 5$, the y-radius of the head is 5.

Lines 190 to 220 are self explanatory. The choice of 135 as the dimension of F is explained just after the example. Line 220 erases the figure because it was already in the rectangular region specified in the PUT statement.

Lines 230 to 260 display the figure seven times in rectangular regions with upper-left corners (0, 0), (41, 0), (82, 0), (123, 0), (164, 0), (205, 0), and (246, 0). Since each rectangle is 41 points wide, the figures touch. Following is the display produced by lines 230 to 260. (Line 270 causes this display to stay on the screen until you press a key.)

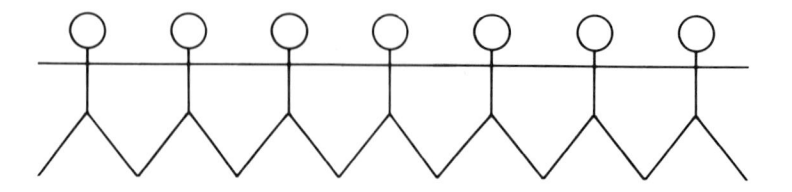

Lines 280 to 310 erase these seven figures, one at a time beginning at the left. This leaves you, once again, with a clear blue screen. (Note that this FOR loop that erases the figures is identical to the FOR loop that displays them.)

■ REMARK 1   If you include the line

```
245 IF INKEY$="" THEN 245
```

a single figure will be displayed each time you press a key. Similarly, if you include

```
295 IF INKEY$="" THEN 295
```

a single figure will be erased each time you press a key.

■ **REMARK 2** The point specified in a PUT statement must be chosen so that the entire rectangular image to be displayed lies on the screen. If it does not, a fatal Illegal function call error occurs. For example, if you replace line 240 by

```
240 FOR X=0 TO 319 STEP 41
```

the statement PUT (X, 0),F will be executed an eighth time with X = 287. Since the image to be displayed is 41 points wide, the x-coordinates 287–327 would be needed. But points with x-coordinates greater than 319 lie off the screen so an Illegal function call error will occur.

□

The following formulas can be used to obtain the array dimension N needed to store a rectangular screen region of size x-by-y (x points in the horizontal direction and y in the vertical direction). First calculate

$$B = 4 + y \times \text{INT}((2x + 7)/8)$$

and then use

$$N = \text{INT}(B/4) \quad \text{(for single-precision arrays—such as A)}$$

You needn't carry out these calculations by hand. Simply precede the statement

```
GET (X1,Y1)-(X2,Y2),A
```

by the statements

```
LET X=X2-X1+1 : Y=Y2-Y1+1
LET B=4+Y*INT((2*X+7)/8)
DIM A(INT(B/4))
```

For an integer array A%, use

```
DIM A%(INT(B/2))
```

COMMENT The number B is precisely the number of bytes the PC needs to store the information contained in an x-by-y rectangular screen region that is produced while in medium-resolution graphics mode. (You will recall that a byte is the memory space needed to store a single character.) To store a 9-by-9 rectangular screen image in an array A, you will get

$$B = 4 + 9 \times \text{INT}((2 \times 9 + 7)/8) = 31$$

But you don't have to dimension A to be of size 31. Each entry in a single-precision numerical array consists of four bytes. This means that array A must have at least B/4 entries. Since B/4 = 31/4 = 7.75, you could use DIM A(7) to give the eight entries A(0), A(1), . . . , A(7). The value N = 7 is precisely what the formula N = INT(B/4) gives for N when B is 31. To store a 41-by-49 image in an array F (as was done in Example 17), you would get

$$B = 4 + 49 \times \text{INT}((2 \times 41 + 7)/8) = 543$$

In this case, N = INT(543/4) = INT(135.75) = 135, so you could use DIM F(135) as was done in the example. If B happens to be a multiple of 4, the formula N = INT(B/4) gives a dimension N one larger than needed. This causes no difficulty; dimensions larger than needed to store a screen image are admissible. The second formula shown above for N is used if integer arrays are specified in GET statements. Each entry in an integer array consists of two bytes, so the dimension must be at least as large as B/2. Thus, just as the dimension N = INT(B/4) is adequate for single-precision arrays, the dimension N = INT(B/2) suffices for integer arrays.

We now describe precisely how PUT statements create displays. As we have already mentioned, the statement

   PUT (X,Y),A

plots a point in the color specified in array A if the point currently has the background color; if the current color is the same as the color specified in A, you get the background color. The following table shows how this statement colors any point, whatever its current color.

		\multicolumn{4}{c}{Color specified in array}
		0	1	2	3
Current screen color	0	0	1	2	3
	1	1	0	3	2
	2	2	3	0	1
	3	3	2	1	0

The first row (current color 0) says that the color specified in the array is used when the current color is the background color. By using this table you can verify that executing the same PUT statement twice restores any point (not just points with the background

Table 19.3 Colors produced by using action parameters in PUT statements

PSET

		\multicolumn{4}{c}{Color specified in array}
		0	1	2	3
Current screen color	0	0	1	2	3
	1	0	1	2	3
	2	0	1	2	3
	3	0	1	2	3

PRESET

		\multicolumn{4}{c}{Color specified in array}
		0	1	2	3
Current screen color	0	3	2	1	0
	1	3	2	1	0
	2	3	2	1	0
	3	3	2	1	0

AND

		\multicolumn{4}{c}{Color specified in array}
		0	1	2	3
Current screen color	0	0	0	0	0
	1	0	1	0	1
	2	0	0	2	2
	3	0	1	2	3

OR

		\multicolumn{4}{c}{Color specified in array}
		0	1	2	3
Current screen color	0	0	1	2	3
	1	1	1	3	3
	2	2	3	2	3
	3	3	3	3	3

color) to its original color. For instance, if the array specifies color 3 for a point with color 2, the table shows that you get color 1 the first time and then color 2 back again.

The PUT statement allows one additional parameter called the *action parameter.*

PUT (X, Y),A,**action**

For **action** you can use XOR, PSET, PRESET, AND, and OR. The parameter XOR gives screen displays as just described. That is, the statements

PUT (X,Y),A and PUT(X,Y),A,XOR

are equivalent. (XOR stands for *exclusive OR.*) The colors displayed when the other action parameters are used are given in Table 19.3. Note that PSET causes the colors specified in the array to be used regardless of what colors are currently on the screen. Thus, in Example 17 we could have used the PSET parameter in the PUT statements that create the display, but not in those that erase it. PRESET also gives colors that depend only on the array colors. Images produced by using PRESET are called *negative images.* The AND parameter is used to produce images only where images exist—this is called *masking.* The OR parameter is used to superimpose an image onto an existing image.

■ 19.8 Simulated Motion

By repeatedly displaying an image with a PUT statement, erasing it with the same PUT statement, and displaying it again in a nearby position, you can use the display screen for animation. The following algorithm describes how computers can simulate a moving object.

Motion Algorithm

- **a.** Select a starting position P.
- **b.** Display the object at position P.
- **c.** Delay (leave object on screen).
- **d.** Erase the object.
- **e.** Change P slightly.
- **f.** Go to Step (b) until done.

This is precisely how film projectors simulate motion. By using this algorithm, you will display "snapshots" of the object at different positions so quickly that the object will appear to be moving.

The delay in Step (c) can be caused by a loop that does nothing but loop:

FOR D=1 TO 10 : NEXT D

If a moving image flickers excessively, you can sometimes include a delay to reduce the flicker. Delays can also be used to help control the speed of a moving image.

EXAMPLE 18 Here is a program to move a small 2-by-2 block across the top edge of the screen.

```
100 SCREEN 1                    'Med. res. graphics
110 CLS : KEY OFF               'Clear the screen.
120 DIM A(1)
130 LINE (0,0)-(1,1),3,BF       'Display a 2-by-2 block.
140 GET (0,0)-(1,1),A           'Store this block in A.
150 PUT (0,0),A                 'Erase the block.
160 FOR X=0 TO 318 STEP 2
170     PUT (X,0),A             'Display the block at (X,0).
180     PUT (X,0),A             'Erase it.
190 NEXT X
200 SCREEN 0 : WIDTH 80
210 END
```

On the first pass through the FOR loop, the 2-by-2 image stored in array A is plotted at (0, 0) and immediately erased. On the successive passes through the loop, the same thing happens two points to the right (STEP 2).

■ **REMARK 1** If you run this program, you will see that the 2-by-2 image moves across the screen in about 2½ seconds, with little flickering. A good way to change this speed is to plot fewer points for greater speed, and more points for less. If you change the STEP value in the FOR statement from 2 to 4, you will approximately double the speed. If you change STEP 2 to STEP 1 you will approximately halve the speed.

■ **REMARK 2** The speed can also be reduced by including a delay. If you add the statement

```
175 FOR D=1 TO 10 : NEXT D
```

the image will take about five seconds to cross the screen. Delays should be executed while the image is on the screen. If you insert the delay as line 185 instead of 175, the image will not be on the screen during the delay. This will increase the flicker.

■ **REMARK 3** If you change lines 170 and 180 to

```
170 PUT (X,X),A
180 PUT (X,X),A
```

the motion will be along the line sloping down to the right that contains the points (0, 0) and (199, 199). If you make this change, you must also change the terminal value 318 in the FOR statement to a number 198 or less. Otherwise, the attempt to use PUT to display the image off the screen will result in an Illegal function call error.

■ **REMARK 4** Motion can be simulated without using GET and PUT. For instance, you could replace lines 170 and 180 with

```
170 LINE (X,0)-STEP(1,1),3,BF     'Display the block at (X,0).
180 LINE (X,0)-STEP(1,1),0,BF     'Erase it.
```

There are at least two good reasons for using GET and PUT. Most often, images are displayed more quickly with PUT statements than with PSET, LINE, CIRCLE, and PAINT statements. Also, the coding process can be simplified considerably by using GET and PUT. For instance, a complex image can be displayed once, stored in an array by using GET, and then displayed anywhere on the screen and as often as needed simply by specifying a single point and the array name in a PUT statement. To do this by using PSET, LINE, CIRCLE, and PAINT statements can be a formidable coding task.

□

In the rest of this section, we show how the PUT statement can be used to simulate the motion of a ball that moves along straight lines in an area enclosed by four walls and that rebounds whenever a wall is reached. The ball will be represented by a filled circle. In addition, we'll place a stationary target (also a filled circle) on the screen and detect a collision, should the ball strike the target.

Let's begin by displaying the filled circle that will represent the ball and storing it in an array for later use in PUT statements. Rather than using the default aspect value 5/6, we will specify the aspect value 1 in all circle statements. This will give us a visual circle whose horizontal and vertical radii have the same number of points. As you will see, this will somewhat simplify the task of detecting when the ball reaches a wall, and will greatly simplify the task of detecting when the target is hit. By using the aspect value 1, the ball and target will appear as ellipses that are taller than they are wide. To make them look like circles, simply adjust the Vertical Size control on the back of the display unit.

In what follows we will use R to denote the radius of the circle that represents the ball and BALL% as the name of the array that stores an image of the ball. Here is a program segment to store a representation of the ball in the array BALL%.

```
100 SCREEN 1                           'Med. res. graphics
110 CLS : KEY OFF                      'Clear the screen.
120 COLOR 10,1                         'Green bkgrd.-palette 1
130 REM ** DISPLAY BALL AND STORE IT IN ARRAY BALL% **
140 LET R=4                            'Radius for ball
150 CIRCLE (4,4),R,3,,,1
160 PAINT (4,4),3,3
170 LET B=4+9*INT((2*9+7)/8)           'Bytes needed in Ball%
180 DIM BALL%(INT(B/2))
190 GET (0,0)-(8,8),BALL%              'Store ball in BALL%.
```

Lines 150 and 160 display a white-filled circle of radius 4 on a green background. Line 190 stores in array BALL% the 9-by-9 region with (0, 0) and (8, 8) as opposite vertices. Because the CIRCLE statement specifies the aspect value 1, this region is as follows. (The dotted lines enclosing the circle and the labels are for reference only.)

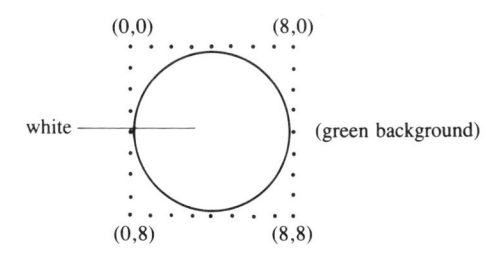

```
         (0,0)        (8,0)
          . . . . . . . . .
         .    _____  .
        .    /           \  .
       .    /             \  .
white ─────┤               ├  (green background)
       .    \             /  .
        .    _____/  .
         .                 .
          . . . . . . . . .
         (0,8)        (8,8)
```

The following program segment uses the motion algorithm that precedes Example 18 to move the ball across the screen from left to right. (To execute this program segment, simply add it to lines 100–190 above.)

```
200 LET X=0 : Y=100                    'Starting point
210 WHILE X<=311
220     PUT (X,Y),BALL%                'Display the ball.
230     FOR D=1 TO 5 : NEXT D          'Delay
240     PUT (X,Y),BALL%                'Erase the ball.
250     LET X=X+4                      'Select next position.
260 WEND
```

The programmed delay in line 230 helps reduce flicker. Note that the ball is on the screen during the delay. If you find the motion too slow, plot fewer images. For instance, if you use LET $X = X + 8$ in line 250, half as many images will be displayed, so the speed will be doubled. To cut the speed in half, use LET $X = X + 2$.

Lines 200 to 260 simulate a ball moving from left to right along the horizontal line $Y = 100$ (actually the upper-left corner of the rectangle stored in BALL% moves along the line $Y = 100$.) If you keep X fixed and vary Y, the ball will move along a vertical line. By changing both X and Y, the ball can be made to move in directions other than the horizontal and vertical. For example, the program segment

```
200 LET X=30 : Y=180                   'Starting point
210 WHILE X<=311 AND Y>=0
220     PUT (X,Y),BALL%                'Display the ball.
230     FOR D=1 TO 5 : NEXT D          'Delay
240     PUT (X,Y),BALL%                'Erase the ball.
250     LET X=X+4 : Y=Y-3              'Select next position.
260 WEND
```

simulates a ball moving from the lower-left screen position (30, 180), along the line containing the successive points (30, 180), (34, 177), (38, 174), (42, 171), and so on.

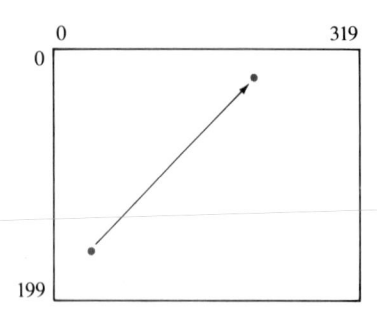

The WHILE condition ensures that the PUT statements will be executed only if the ball fits in the graphics area. As with horizontal and vertical motion, the speed can be increased by plotting fewer points and decreased by plotting more. Thus, if line 250 is changed to

    250 LET X=X+8 : Y=Y-6

the speed will double but the direction will remain the same. If you use

    250 LET X=X+2 : Y=Y-3/2

the speed will be cut in half.

Many video games involve a moving ball capable of rebounding off a wall. The following program segment shows one way to build a wall surrounding the graphics screen.

    300 FOR W=0 TO 4
    310   LINE (W,W)-(319-W,199-W),1,B
    320 NEXT W

These five rectangles, drawn one inside the other, give us four walls along the four edges of the graphics area. The inside boundaries of the left and right walls occur at X = 4 and X = 315, respectively. The inside boundaries of the top and bottom walls occur at Y = 4 and Y = 195, respectively.

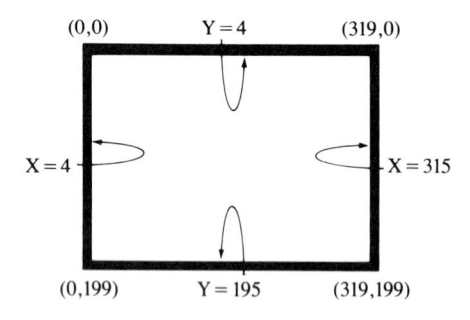

Assume now that a ball approaches one of these walls. To simulate a rebounding ball, two things must be done: we must detect when a wall has been encountered, and then we must start the ball off in a new direction just as if it were a real ball meeting a barrier.

To determine when a wall is encountered, remember that the statement

    PUT (X,Y),BALL%

displays the following 9-by-9 region:

```
                (X, Y)       (X + 8, Y)




              (X, Y + 8)    (X + 8, Y + 8)
```

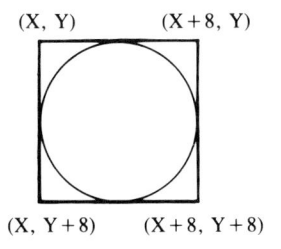

The circle touches all four edges of the region because we specified the aspect value 1 while drawing the filled circle stored in BALL%. Because of this, the ball will hit the left wall when the left side of the rectangle (X) encounters the left wall (4)—that is, when $X \leq 4$. Similarly the top wall is hit when $Y \leq 4$. The ball will hit the right wall when the right side of the rectangle (X + 8) encounters the right wall (315)—that is, when $X + 8 \geq 315$. Similarly, the bottom wall will be hit when $Y + 8 \geq 195$. These last two conditions can be written more simply as $X \geq 307$ and $Y \geq 187$, respectively.

In summary, a wall is encountered when the next position (X, Y) of the upper-left corner of the rectangle satisfies one of the following conditions:

$X \geq 307$ right wall is encountered
$X \leq 4$ left wall is encountered
$Y \geq 187$ bottom wall is encountered
$Y \leq 4$ top wall is encountered

To describe a method for selecting a new direction for a rebounding ball, let's assume that the ball moves by changing its coordinates X and Y by the respective amounts XCHANGE and YCHANGE. Having just plotted the ball in position (X, Y), we give the next position by the statements

```
LET X=X+XCHANGE : Y=Y+YCHANGE
```

Let's assume that $X \geq 307$—that is, the ball has reached the right vertical wall. To start it in the opposite direction, we'll let $X = 306$ and continue it in the new direction by letting XCHANGE = -XCHANGE. Similar remarks apply as the ball approaches the other three boundaries. The following program segment ensures that a moving ball will rebound when it reaches any of the four boundaries.

```
500 REM ************ REBOUND - INFINITE LOOP **************
510     PUT (X,Y),BALL%                              'Display ball.
520     FOR DELAY=1 TO 10 : NEXT DELAY
530     PUT (X,Y),BALL%                              'Erase the ball.
540     LET X=X+XCHANGE : Y=Y+YCHANGE                'Next position
550     REM -------- TEST FOR REBOUND ---------
560     IF X>=307 THEN X=306 : XCHANGE=-XCHANGE      'Right wall
570     IF X<=4   THEN X=5   : XCHANGE=-XCHANGE      'Left wall
580     IF Y>=187 THEN Y=186 : YCHANGE=-YCHANGE      'Bottom wall
590     IF Y<=4   THEN Y=5   : YCHANGE=-YCHANGE      'Top wall
600 GOTO 510
```

This program segment does not simulate the motion of a bouncing ball exactly. The method presented here gives an approximation of this motion that is adequate for beginning programming tasks. To improve significantly on this method would require a detailed mathematical analysis that is beyond the scope of this book.

EXAMPLE 19 **A simple video game.**

The program in this example makes use of the rebounding ball simulation and introduces one other element. There is a target on the graphics screen in the shape of a circle whose center (X1, Y1) and radius R1 are chosen randomly by the computer. The ball is given an initial position and a direction and then allowed to rebound off the four walls until it hits the target or until a predetermined number of rebounds has occurred. The following algorithm was used to write the program. You will note that code for much of the algorithm has already been described.

THE ALGORITHM

a. Display instructions for the user.
b. Display a ball image and store it in array BALL%.
c. Select the center (X1, Y1) and the radius R1 of the target.
d. Select a starting position (X, Y) for the ball.
e. Select a starting direction (XCHANGE and YCHANGE) for the ball.
f. Simulate the motion of the ball until the target is hit or until 20 rebounds have occurred.
g. Display the results of the simulation and stop.

We discuss these seven steps in order:

Step (a): This is routine. The necessary code, however, can be written only after the interaction that will take place between the user and the computer has been decided.

Step (b): Code for this step has already been described.

Step (c): As already stated, the position and radius of the target will be chosen randomly by the computer. The following code is used in the program.

```
500 RANDOMIZE VAL(RIGHT$(TIME$,2))
510 LET X1=INT(200*RND)+60          '60 to 259
520 LET Y1=INT(120*RND)+40          '40 to 159
530 LET R1=INT(16*RND)+10           '10 to 25
```

You may check that this will give the center (X1, Y1) and radius R1 of a circle (the target) that lies within the screen area bounded by the vertical lines X = 4 and X = 315 and the horizontal lines Y = 4 and Y = 195. (The walls drawn previously are also used in this video game program.)

Step (d): The starting position of the ball (the 9-by-9 rectangular region with its upper-left corner at (X, Y)) will be along the left wall; hence X = 5. The user will select the *y*-coordinate by typing a value from 25 to 180. This will ensure that the ball lies in the region surrounded by the four walls. The lower limit 25 is used to avoid cluttering user prompts that will be displayed near the top of the screen.

Step (e): A starting direction for the ball is determined by giving values to XCHANGE and YCHANGE. Since the ball starts at the left wall, XCHANGE should be positive: 0 gives the vertical direction, which makes no sense in this simulation, and negative XCHANGE values will start the ball off to the left directly into the wall. YCHANGE, however, can be negative, positive, or 0. A negative value starts the ball off with a positive inclination (upward and to the right), 0 gives the horizontal direction, and positive values give negative inclinations (downward to the right). The user will select the starting direction by typing a value for YCHANGE in the range −8 to 8. The computer will then determine XCHANGE by using the statement

```
LET XCHANGE = 9-ABS(YCHANGE)
```

This ensures that the starting XCHANGE value will be positive. Note that the second ball plotted will be XCHANGE points to the right and YCHANGE points above or below the first ball—above if YCHANGE is negative and below if it is positive. For instance, if the user types 6 for YCHANGE, XCHANGE will be 3 so the second ball will be 3 points to the right and 6 points below the first ball. The numbers 3 and 6 not only determine the direction, but also influence the speed of the moving image. If instead of using XCHANGE and YCHANGE, we had used 2*XCHANGE and

2∗YCHANGE, we would get 6 and 12 instead of 3 and 6; the direction would be the same, but the speed would be doubled since only half as many points would be plotted. In general, if you assign a positive value to the variable SPEED and use SPEED∗XCHANGE and SPEED∗YCHANGE, instead of XCHANGE and YCHANGE, you will get the same directions, but the speed will be changed by a factor of SPEED. The motion will be faster if SPEED is greater than 1, and slower if SPEED is less than 1.

Step (f): Everything needed to code the actual simulation has been explained except for how to detect when the ball hits the target. Recall that PUT (X, Y),BALL% displays the ball with its center at (X + 4, Y + 4). The center of the target is always at (X1, Y1). If the ball and target do not touch, the distance between their centers will be greater than the sum R + R1 of their radii.

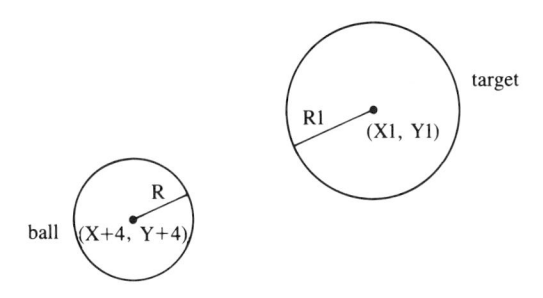

This condition, written as

$$(X+4-X1)^2+(Y+4-Y1)^2>(R+R1)^2$$

is used as a condition in a WHILE statement (line 860 of the program) to exit the loop that simulates motion should the ball meet the target. A second condition (C = 20) is used in the same WHILE statement to end the simulation should the number C of rebounds reach 20.

Step (g): The results of the simulation will be a message telling whether or not the target was hit and a count of how many rebounds occurred. Also, since the simulation is a visual simulation (you are "seeing" the motion of the ball rather than being told what happens), a visual effect should be produced if the ball hits the target. The program does this by displaying an array of lines through the center of the target when the target is hit.

REMARK The method described in Step (f) to detect when that ball hits the target can be used only if the aspect value 1 is specified in CIRCLE statements. With the default aspect value 5/6, the horizontal radii of the ball and target will be R and R1 as before, but the vertical radii will be 5/6 × R and 5/6 × R1. Thus, if you don't specify the aspect value 1, you will need a method to detect when two ellipses, rather than two circles, meet. This is more difficult.

In the following program the seven REM statements in lines 150, 400, 490, 590, 650, 840, and 990 correspond to the seven steps (a) to (g) of the algorithm.

```
100 REM ***************** A VIDEO GAME *********************
110 SCREEN 1                            'Med. res. graphics
120 CLS : KEY OFF                       'Clear the screen.
130 COLOR 10,1                          'Green bkgrd.-palette 1
140 REM
150 REM ********** DISPLAY INSTRUCTIONS TO THE USER ***********
160 PRINT "In this game a ball bounces off the"
170 PRINT "boundaries of an enclosed region until"
180 PRINT "it hits a target whose size and"
190 PRINT "location are chosen randomly by the"
200 PRINT "computer."
```

```
210 PRINT
220 PRINT "The object of the game is to select"
230 PRINT "a starting position and a direction"
240 PRINT "for the ball so that it hits the"
250 PRINT "target after the smallest number of"
260 PRINT "rebounds. At most 20 rebounds will"
270 PRINT "be made."
280 PRINT
290 PRINT "You will select a starting position"
300 PRINT "along the left wall by typing a"
310 PRINT "number from 25 to 180 (25 is highest)."
320 PRINT
330 PRINT "You will select a starting direction"
340 PRINT "by typing a number from -8 to 8. (8"
350 PRINT "gives the greatest declination.)"
360 PRINT
370 PRINT "Press any key to continue."
380 IF INKEY$="" THEN 380                       .'Wait for key.
390 REM
400 REM **** DISPLAY A BALL IMAGE AND STORE IN ARRAY BALL% ****
410 CLS                                         'Clear the screen.
420 LET R=4                                     'Radius of ball
430 CIRCLE(4,4),R,3,,,1 : PAINT (4,4),3,3       'Display filled ball.
440 LET B=4+9*INT((2*9+7)/8)                    'Bytes needed in BALL%
450 DIM BALL%(INT(B/2))
460 GET (0,0)-(8,8),BALL%                       'Store ball in BALL%.
470 PUT(0,0),BALL%                              'Erase ball.
480 REM
490 REM **** SELECT CENTER (X1,Y1) AND RADIUS R1 OF TARGET *****
500 RANDOMIZE VAL(RIGHT$(TIME$,2))
510 LET X1=INT(200*RND)+60                      '60 to 259
520 LET Y1=INT(120*RND)+40                      '40 to 159
530 LET R1=INT(16*RND)+10                       '10 to 25
540 REM
550 REM ********* DRAW THE BOUNDARIES AND THE TARGET **********
560 GOSUB 1140                                  'Boundaries
570 GOSUB 1200                                  'Target
580 REM
590 REM ****** SELECT STARTING POSITION ALONG LEFT WALL ********
600 LET X=5                                     'Left wall
610 LOCATE 2,2
620 INPUT "SELECT STARTING POSITION (25-180) ",Y
630 IF Y<25 OR Y>180 THEN
        LOCATE 2,2 : PRINT SPACE$(38) : GOTO 610
640 REM
650 REM ************ SELECT STARTING DIRECTION ***************
660 LOCATE 3,2
670 INPUT "SELECT STARTING DIRECTION (-8 TO 8) ",YCHANGE
680 IF YCHANGE<-8 OR YCHANGE>8 THEN
        LOCATE 3,2 : PRINT SPACE$(38) : GOTO 660
690 LET XCHANGE=9-ABS(YCHANGE)                  '1 to 9
700 REM **** DISPLAY STARTING POSITION AND DIRECTION OF BALL ***
710 LOCATE 23,5
720 PRINT "STARTING POSITION AND DIRECTION"
730 PUT (X,Y),BALL%                             'Ball
740 LINE (X+R,Y+R)-STEP(5*XCHANGE,5*YCHANGE)    'Direction line
750 LOCATE 24,5
760 PRINT "PRESS ANY KEY TO CONTINUE.";
770 IF INKEY$="" THEN 770                       'Wait for key.
780 REM
790 REM *********** PREPARE SCREEN FOR SIMULATION *************
800 CLS
810 GOSUB 1140                                  'Redraw the boundaries.
820 GOSUB 1200                                  'Redraw the target.
830 REM
840 REM ************ START THE BALL IN MOTION ***************
850 LET C=0                                     'C counts rebounds.
```

```
860 WHILE (X+R-X1)^2+(Y+R-Y1)^2>(R+R1)^2 AND C<20
870     PUT (X,Y),BALL%                              'Display the ball.
880     FOR DELAY=1 TO 10 : NEXT DELAY
890     PUT (X,Y),BALL%                              'Erase the ball.
900     LET X=X+XCHANGE : Y=Y+YCHANGE                'Next position
910     REM
920     REM ------ TEST IF WALL IS MET. IF SO, ADD 1 TO C -------
930     IF X>=307 THEN C=C+1 : PRINT CHR$(7)
                 : X=306  : XCHANGE=-XCHANGE         'Right wall
940     IF X<=4   THEN C=C+1 : PRINT CHR$(7)
                 : X=5    : XCHANGE=-XCHANGE         'Left wall
950     IF Y>=187 THEN C=C+1 : PRINT CHR$(7)
                 : Y=186  : YCHANGE=-YCHANGE         'Bottom wall
960     IF Y<=4   THEN C=C+1 : PRINT CHR$(7)
                 : Y=5    : YCHANGE=-YCHANGE         'Top wall
970 WEND
980 REM
990 REM ***** MOTION HAS STOPPED.  CHECK IF TARGET WAS HIT *****
1000 IF C=20 THEN LOCATE 23,8 :
         PRINT "20 REBOUNDS WITH NO HIT." : GOTO 1090
1010 REM ------------- TARGET WAS HIT -------------
1020 LINE (X1-30,Y1)-(X1+30,Y1),1
1030 LINE (X1-20,Y1+20)-(X1+20,Y1-20),1
1040 LINE (X1-20,Y1-20)-(X1+20,Y1+20),1
1050 LINE (X1,Y1-30)-(X1,Y1+30),1
1060 LOCATE 23,8
1070 PRINT "A HIT AFTER";C;"REBOUNDS.";
1080 FOR I=1 TO 10 : PRINT CHR$(7); : NEXT I
1090 IF INKEY$="" THEN 1090                          'Wait for key
1100 SCREEN 0 : WIDTH 80                             'Exit to text mode.
1110 END                                             'End the program.
1120 REM ****************** SUBROUTINES ********************
1130 REM
1140 REM ------------ SUBROUTINE TO DRAW BOUNDARIES ------------
1150 FOR W=0 TO 4
1160     LINE (W,W)-(319-W,199-W),2,B
1170 NEXT W
1180 RETURN
1190 REM
1200 REM ------------ SUBROUTINE TO DRAW THE TARGET ------------
1210 CIRCLE (X1,Y1),R1,1,,,1 : PAINT(X1,Y1),3,1
1220 CIRCLE (X1,Y1),2*R1/3,1,,,1
1230 CIRCLE (X1,Y1),R1/3,1,,,1
1240 CIRCLE (X1,Y1),0,1
1250 RETURN
```

■ 19.9 Problems

In Problems 1–11, write a program to produce each display described.

1. Store a representation of this arrow in an array. The arrow is to be 30 points long.

    $\longrightarrow$

    Then display 15 rows of arrows as follows. The odd-numbered rows are each to contain 8 arrows with adjacent arrows 30 points apart. The even-numbered rows are each to contain 7 arrows also 30 points apart. The first arrow in each odd-numbered row is to begin in the column position at which the first arrow in the row above it ends.

2. Produce the display described in Problem 1, but with the arrows in the even-numbered rows pointing to the left. (You should use a second array to store the left-pointing arrow.)

3. In this problem you are to display an image of a star-filled sky, and then simulate motion for shooting stars. Begin by displaying 1,000 stars at randomly generated screen positions.

Approximately 99% of the stars should be single points and the others should consist of the two diagonals of a 3-by-3 square. After all 1,000 stars have been displayed, the program is to select randomly a position in the upper half of the screen for a larger star (four line segments inside a 5-by-5 square and passing through its center will do). This larger star is to move downward to the right if its starting x-coordinate is less than 160; otherwise it is to move downward to the left. Many such shooting stars should be simulated, one at a time. The simulation should stop when the user presses a key.

4. Write a program for the simulation described in Problem 3, but with one additional feature incorporated into the program. Each time a new shooting star is created, generate a random number R in the range 5–15 and use this number to determine the speed of the star. (If the current position of the star is (X, Y) use (X + R, Y + R) as the next position if the star is to move downward to the right. If it is to move downward to the left, change the sign of R before starting the motion.)

5. In this problem you are to simulate simple horizontal motion for the arrow shown in Problem 1. The arrow is to begin at the left margin of the screen and move toward a target you will display at the right (a rectangle plotted with the B or BF option is good enough). As soon as the arrowhead has embedded itself in the target, the motion is to stop, but the arrow is to remain in its final position until a key is pressed to halt the program. Be sure that the target is thick enough to hold the entire arrowhead.

6. Simulate horizontal motion for an arrow that can change speeds while in flight. Do this as follows. With XC = 3, plot the first arrow at its starting position (X, Y) and then change X to X + XC so that (X, Y) now specifies the next position for the arrow. Before plotting the next arrow, change XC by generating a random number R in the range −1/4 to 1/4 and adding R to XC. If R is positive, the speed is increased slightly (not abruptly); if R is negative, the speed is decreased slightly. (Note that if R were always positive, the arrow would move faster and faster. Thus, R can be thought of as the acceleration. Negative R would give deceleration.) If XC should become negative, the arrow will move backward. Make sure that this doesn't happen. The program should halt as described in Problem 5.

7. Simulate the simultaneous motion of three arrows, one under another, that start off together at the left edge of the screen and head toward a vertical line drawn near the right edge. The speed of each arrow should vary as described in Problem 6. When one of the arrows reaches the vertical line, motion is to stop with the arrows in their final positions, and a message should be displayed telling which arrow reached the line first. The program should halt when the user presses a key.

8. In this problem (and the next two as well) you are to simulate motion by using the following three images.

Start by storing representations of the three images in three arrays—we'll call them P1, P2, and P3. Simulate a mouth that opens and closes by repeatedly displaying and erasing P1, P2, and P3, always with their centers at the point (160, 100). Allow the user to specify a common radius R for P1, P2, and P3 during program execution. R is to be rejected if it is less than 5 and also if it specifies positions for the three images that are not on the screen. Use a delay if you find that it gives a better simulation.

9. In this problem you are to simulate horizontal motion to the right by repeatedly displaying P1, P2, and P3 along the horizontal line with y-coordinate 100 beginning at the left edge of the screen. (P1, P2, and P3 are described in Problem 8.) As the image moves across the screen, its mouth should open and close. The program should halt when the right edge is reached.

10. Write a program for the simulation described in Problem 9, but with one additional feature incorporated into the program. Along the horizontal line on which the centers of P1, P2, and P3 are displayed, there is to be a row of dots (these can be placed as far apart as you wish, but they must appear as dots and not as a solid line). As the image created by P1, P2, and P3

moves through the points, they are to disappear. [*Suggestion:* Use the form PUT (X, Y),A,PSET to display images, and the form PUT (X, Y),A to erase them.]

11. Simulate the motion of two rebounding balls in search of a target (see Example 19). The game ends when one of the balls hits the target (a winner) or when the two balls strike each other (a draw). The user should specify starting positions and directions for the two balls during program execution. One ball (L) is to start along the left wall and the other (R) along the right. The program should announce at the end whether the game is a draw or which ball is the winner. (If the two balls are in the shape of circles with centers (x, y) and (z, w) and radii $r1$ and $r2$, respectively, there is a collision when $(x - z)^2 + (y - w)^2 \leq (r1 + r2)^2$, provided you specify the aspect value 1 in CIRCLE statements.)

■ 19.10 High-Resolution Graphics

In this section we'll assume that you are familiar with the PC's medium-resolution graphics mode. As mentioned at the outset of this chapter, all graphics statements except for the COLOR statement are allowed in either medium-resolution or high-resolution graphics mode. We also mentioned that although the same forms of these statements can be used in both modes, there are differences in the displays produced. These differences are summarized in Table 19.4. If you understand how graphics statements are used in medium-resolution graphics mode, you will find that this table contains the only additional information needed to produce high-resolution graphics displays. The table describes only differences. Items not mentioned in the table are the same in both modes.

Table 19.4 Medium-resolution and high-resolution differences

Topic	Medium-resolution	High-resolution
Mode selection	SCREEN 1	SCREEN 2
Points	A horizontal line contains 320 points numbered 0–319.	A horizontal line contains 640 points numbered 0–639.
Text	All characters are displayed in the WIDTH 40 form.	All characters are displayed in the smaller WIDTH 80 form.
COLOR statement	Used to specify a background color and a palette number.	Not used. The background color is black (0) and the foreground color is white (1).
Color parameter	Specifies a color from current palette, but 0 specifies the background color. The default is color 3 of the current palette except in PAINT, where the default for the boundary color is the painting color.	0 and 2 specify black; 1 and 3 specify white. The default is white except in PAINT, where the default boundary color is the painting color.
Color of text	Color 3 of the current palette.	White (1).
Aspect value	Default is 5/6.	Default is 5/12. (This gives visual circles that look like circles, just as 5/6 does in medium-resolution mode.)
Dimension needed to store an X-by-Y screen image by using a GET statement.	With B given by B=4+Y*INT((2*X+7)/8) use INT(B/2) for integer arrays, and INT(B/4) for single-precision arrays.	With B given by B=4+Y*INT((X+7)/8) use INT(B/2) and INT(B/4) just as in medium-resolution graphics mode.

In high-resolution graphics, the 640 columns are numbered 0 to 639 from left to right and the 200 rows are numbered 0 to 199 from top to bottom (see Figure 19.3). As in medium-resolution graphics a point is specified by giving its column number followed by its row number. Several labeled points are shown in Figure 19.3. Note that (320, 100) is approximately at the center of the graphics screen.

All displays produced while in high-resolution graphics mode (SCREEN 2) will be black and white displays. An attempt to execute a COLOR statement will give a fatal Illegal function call error. You can, however, include color parameters in PSET, LINE, CIRCLE, and PAINT statements just as in medium-resolution mode. These specify not colors from a palette, but rather black or white as shown in Table 19.4.

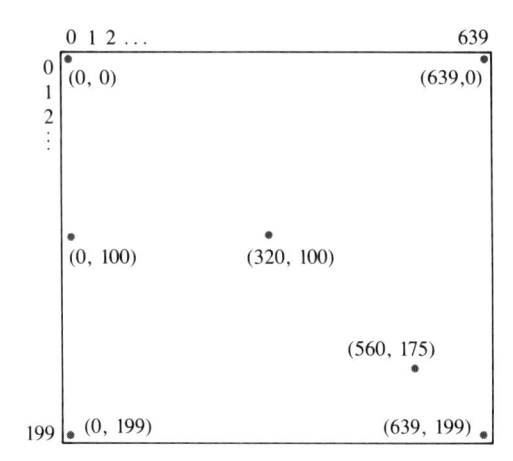

Figure 19.3 High-resolution graphics screen.

We conclude this chapter with three short programs that illustrate the use of graphics statements in high-resolution graphics mode. After reading through these examples, you may find it informative to modify some of the medium-resolution graphics programs from the preceding sections so that they will produce high-resolution displays. To do this, simply change SCREEN 1 to SCREEN 2 and delete all COLOR statements. You will get black and white displays that fit in the left half of the screen. (Some circles may be partially off the screen if CIRCLE statements specify aspect values: as shown in Table 19.4, high-resolution graphics mode uses the aspect value 5/12.) All text will be white. Points will be white if color 1 or 3 is specified and black for color 0 or 2.

EXAMPLE 20   Here is a program to display an underlined title.

```
100 SCREEN 2                            'High res. graphics
110 CLS : KEY OFF                       'Clear screen to black.
120 REM ---------- DISPLAY A TITLE ON LINE 2 ----------
130 LOCATE 2,20
140 PRINT "MICROSOFT"
150 REM ---------- UNDERLINE THE TITLE ----------------
160 LINE (152,16)-(223,16),1
170 IF INKEY$="" THEN 170
180 SCREEN 0
190 END
RUN
```

                            MICROSOFT

Line 100 gets you into high-resolution graphics mode and line 110 clears the screen and leaves it in the background color black.

Lines 130 and 140 display MICROSOFT beginning in character position 20 of line 2. With SCREEN 2 in effect, the WIDTH 80 size is used for display characters.

Line 160 underlines the title by drawing a line segment between the points (152, 16) and (223, 16) that lie just below the ends of the title. The coordinates of these two points are determined exactly as in medium-resolution graphics—each text character is 8 points high (200/25 = 8) and 8 points wide (640/80 = 8). Since the title appears on line 2, the y-coordinate of the bottom edge of the title is $2 \times 8 - 1 = 15$ (minus 1 because point positions are numbered beginning with 0 just as before). We used 16 as the y-coordinate of the underscore so that it would be below the title and not on its bottom edge. By using a similar analysis, you can verify 152 as the x-coordinate for the left edge of the title and 223 as the x-coordinate for the right edge.

■ REMARK The title is displayed in white (1), as is all text in high-resolution graphics. The color parameter 1 in the LINE statement specifies white for the underscore as well. This parameter, however, is not needed since the default color is also white. In high-resolution graphics, color parameters are needed in only two situations: to erase images previously plotted in white, or to display black points on a white background. (Displaying black images on a white background is not unusual. It's what you do when writing on white paper with black ink.)

EXAMPLE 21 Here is a program to display four concentric circles on a white background.

```
100 SCREEN 2                    'High res. graphics
110 LINE (0,0)-(639,199),,BF    'Color screen white.
120 PSET (320,100),0            'Color center point black.
130 FOR R=50 TO 200 STEP 50
140     CIRCLE (320,100),R,0    'Black circle, radius R
150 NEXT R
160 IF INKEY$="" THEN 160
170 SCREEN 0 : END
```

Line 100 selects high-resolution graphics and line 110 colors the entire screen white. (Because of line 110, CLS and KEY OFF are not needed. Remember, graphics points can be plotted anywhere on the screen; it is text that cannot be displayed in line 25 unless KEY OFF is in effect.)

The last circle drawn by the FOR loop has center (320, 100) and radius $R = 200$. Since an aspect value is not specified in the CIRCLE statement, the PC used the default aspect value 5/12. Thus, the horizontal radius contains 200 points, but the vertical radius contains only 83 ($5/12 \times 200 = 83.3333$ is rounded to 83). This means that the x-coordinates of points on this circle lie in the range 120 to 300 and the y-coordinates are from 17 (100 − 83) to 183 (100 + 83), so the circle fits on the screen.

■ REMARK 1 It would not be correct to omit the color parameter 0 in the PSET and CIRCLE statements. Remember, the default value is 1 (white) and not 0 (black).

■ REMARK 2 If the aspect value 1 were specified

```
140 CIRCLE (320,100),R,0,,,1
```

both the horizontal and vertical radii of the circle would be R. In this case, only the first circle (R = 50) would fit entirely on the screen. If you specify the aspect value 1 while SCREEN 2 is in effect, visual circles will be considerably elongated—in high-resolution graphics 5 points in the vertical direction have the same length as 12 points in the horizontal direction. Adjusting the Vertical Size control on the back of the display unit, we were unable to make these ellipses look like circles.

EXAMPLE 22 Here is a program to plot concentric circles and alternately color the ringed regions formed by the circles in black and white.

```
100 REM ---- CONCENTRIC CIRCLES - FILLED IN BLACK AND WHITE ----
110 SCREEN 2                    'High resolution graphics
120 CLS : KEY OFF               'Clear screen to black.
```

```
130 LET C=1                          'C MOD 2=1,0 for white, black.
140 FOR R=200 to 0 STEP -20
150    CIRCLE (320,100),R,C MOD 2    'Draw a circle of radius R.
160    PAINT (320,100),C MOD 2       'Paint the circle.
170    LET C=C+1                     'Increment C to change color.
180 NEXT R
190 IF INKEY$="" THEN 190
200 SCREEN 0
210 END
```

In this program C takes on the values 1, 2, 3, 4, and so on; hence C MOD 2 assumes the values 1, 0, 1, 0, ... The first time through the loop, line 150 draws a circle in white and line 160 colors its interior white. (Remember, the default boundary color in a PAINT statement is the painting color—in this case, C MOD 2.) The next time through the loop a smaller circle is drawn in black and colored black. This process continues until, on the last pass when R = 0, the circle is plotted as a single point.

19.11 Problems

Write a program to perform each task.

1. Draw a white boundary, 10 points wide, around the graphics area.
2. Color the region of the graphics area below the upper-left to lower-right diagonal white.
3. Color the upper-left and lower-right quadrants of the graphics area white.
4. Color the triangular region bounded by the three line segments connecting (320, 0), (0, 199), and (639, 199) white.
5. Divide the graphics area into five regions by drawing four rectangles that have the point (0, 0) as a common corner point. The sizes of the rectangles should be 40-by-128, 80-by-256, 120-by-384, and 160-by-512.
6. Assuming the graphics area to be divided into five regions as in Problem 5, color these adjacent regions in alternating colors with the smallest region white.
7. Divide the graphics area into quadrants by coloring the upper-left and lower-right quadrants white and leaving the other two black. A star is to move clockwise through the four quadrants. When it appears in a white quadrant it should be black (and vice versa). Make sure the star is centered in each quadrant. Include a delay so that the star is easily seen. After this delay, erase the star before going on to the next quadrant.
8. Allow the user to use the following method to create line drawings in the upper three-fourths of the graphics area. The lower portion of the screen is to be used to display any dialogue between the user and the computer. After entering a starting point, the user should be allowed to enter L, R, U, or D (for left, right, up, or down) and a number for the length of a line segment. A segment of the chosen length and direction should be drawn from the starting point. The user should then be allowed to specify a direction and length for another line segment that should be drawn from the end point of the previous segment. If instead of entering L, R, U, or D the user types A, the graphics area should be cleared and the user allowed to create another line drawing. If the user types S, program execution should terminate. Any entry other than L, R, U, D, A, or S should be ignored and a new entry requested. If the direction and length specify a line segment that will extend out of the viewing area, they should be rejected and a new entry requested.
9. Transform the 640-column by 200-row high-resolution graphics area into a Cartesian coordinate system whose origin is at the point (320, 100) in the graphics area. Draw horizontal and vertical axes through this point. Display the graphs of each of the following functions. (Any point (X, Y) in the Cartesian coordinate system will have coordinates (320 + X, 100 − Y) in the graphics area.)

   a. $Y = 10*SGN(X)$ $-200 \leq X \leq 200$
   b. $Y = ABS(X)$ $-75 \leq X \leq 75$
   c. $Y = 10*INT(X/10)$ $-75 \leq X \leq 75$
   d. $Y = 75/X$ $-75 \leq X \leq 75, \; X \neq 0$
   e. $Y = 5\sqrt{X + 30}$ $-30 \leq X \leq 200$
   f. $Y = 10X^2/(100 - X^2)$ $-200 \leq X \leq 200, \; X \neq -10, X \neq 10$
   g. $Y = X(X - 50)(X + 50)/1000$ $-60 \leq X \leq 60$

19.12 Review True-or-False Quiz

1. The two programming lines

    ```
    10 SCREEN 1 : COLOR 4,0
    ```

    and

    ```
    10 COLOR 4,0 : SCREEN 1
    ```

    are equivalent. T F
2. In high-resolution graphics, the COLOR statement determines whether points are plotted in black or in white. T F
3. The immediate mode command SCREEN 0 will return you from medium-resolution graphics to text mode with 40-character lines. T F
4. In medium-resolution graphics, the statements COLOR 1,0 : PSET(20,20) will always result in a white point at position (20, 20). T F
5. The statements

    ```
    50 LINE(23,130)-(85,35)
    ```

    and

    ```
    50 LINE(85,35)-(23,130)
    ```

    result in the same display. Subsequent output, however, may depend on which of these forms is used. T F
6. The statements PSET(X1,Y1) : LINE − (X2,Y2) are equivalent to the single statement LINE(X1,Y1) − (X2,Y2). T F
7. In graphics mode, the statement

    ```
    600 LOCATE 1,1 : PRINT "FIRST LINE"
    ```

    will display FIRST LINE at the top of the graphics area. T F
8. In graphics mode, the statements

    ```
    LOCATE 25,1 : PRINT "HELLO"
    ```

    will always display HELLO at the left margin of line 25. T F
9. In high-resolution graphics you are limited to white images on a black background. T F
10. In medium-resolution graphics mode, the default for any color parameter omitted from a PSET, LINE, CIRCLE, or PAINT statement is color 3 of the current palette. T F
11. The statement PAINT (X,Y),P,B will color only points that can be joined to (X, Y) by a straight line segment that contains no point of color B. T F

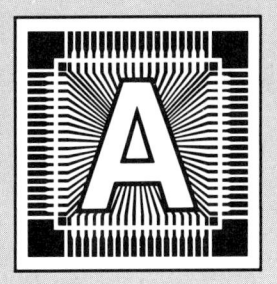

Getting Microsoft® BASIC Up and Running

The IBM personal computer comes with three versions of the BASIC programming language: **Cassette, Disk,** and **Advanced BASIC.** The three versions are upward compatible; that is, programs written in Cassette BASIC will also run in Disk BASIC, and programs written in Disk BASIC will run in Advanced BASIC.

The core of BASIC is the Cassette version; it is stored in the PC's read only memory (ROM). Most of this book can be studied using only Cassette BASIC—the principal exceptions are the file statements described in Chapter 17, the DEF statement described in Chapter 13, and certain graphics statements described in Chapter 19. If you use this version of BASIC, however, you will not be able to use the disk unit; in Cassette BASIC, the only available external storage device is a cassette tape recorder.

Disk BASIC is Cassette BASIC with some additional features, the most important of which is the ability to use disk units as external storage devices. With this version of BASIC you can store BASIC programs on diskettes for later use (see Appendix C). You can also store program output on diskettes and use information previously stored on diskettes as input to programs. (The use of a disk unit as an input/output device is described in Chapter 17.) Disk BASIC itself is a program on the DOS diskette and must be read into memory before it can be used.

Advanced BASIC is Disk BASIC with further enhancements. The CIRCLE, PUT, GET and PAINT statements, for example, simplify considerably the writing of graphics programs. Like Disk BASIC, the advanced version is a program on the DOS diskette that must be read into the PC's memory.

We now show how you can get each of these versions of BASIC up and running.

A.1 Cassette BASIC

Simply turn on the PC with no diskette in the disk unit. After some whirring of the disk unit a display similar to the following will appear at the top of the screen.

```
The IBM Personal Computer Basic
Version C1.10 Copyright IBM Corp 1981
62940 Bytes free
Ok
 _
```

The C in C1.10 stands for Cassette and the 62940 Bytes free indicates that this much storage is available for your programs and data. Ok is the BASIC prompt; it indicates that Cassette BASIC is ready for you to enter a BASIC statement or command.

A.2 Disk BASIC

To load Disk BASIC requires two steps:

1. Load the disk operating system (DOS) as explained in Appendix B.1.
2. With the DOS diskette inserted in drive A, type BASIC in response to the DOS prompt A> and press the Enter key. After some whirring by the disk unit as it reads the program BASIC into memory, a display similar to the following appears at the top of the screen.

```
The IBM Personal Computer Basic
Version D3.10 Copyright IBM Corp. 1981, 1985
61746 Bytes free
Ok
_
```

The D in D3.10 stands for Disk. The third line shows how much memory is available for your programs and data. The prompt Ok indicates that the procedure is complete and Disk BASIC is ready for you to enter a BASIC statement or command.

A.3 Advanced BASIC

Carry out Steps 1 and 2 shown in A.2, but type BASICA instead of BASIC. You will get a display similar to the following:

```
The IBM Personal Computer Basic
Version A3.10 Copyright IBM Corp. 1981, 1985
61318 Bytes free
Ok
_
```

The A in A3.10 stands for Advanced. You can now enter any statement or command allowed in Advanced BASIC.

To return to DOS from Disk or Advanced BASIC, type SYSTEM and press the Enter key. The DOS prompt A> will be displayed and you can then issue any of the DOS commands described in Appendix B.

B　The Disk Operating System (DOS)

The IBM Personal Computer's disk operating system (DOS) includes programs that allow you to use the disk unit as an external storage device. This appendix shows how to load DOS and explains how you can use it to perform certain tasks necessary for efficient use of the disk unit. (Many of these disk operations can also be carried out while Disk or Advanced BASIC is operational. The BASIC forms of disk commands are given in Appendix C.)

B.1　Starting DOS

The process of loading the disk operating system is called *starting* or *booting* DOS. To start DOS, insert the DOS diskette into the disk unit. (If your system has two disk units, they are designated drive A and drive B. Insert the DOS diskette into drive A.) As shown in Figure 1.7 (page 5), the label should be up and the edge nearest the oval cutout in the diskette's cover should enter the disk unit first. Diskettes should be handled gently; they must not be bent. And be sure to touch only the cover. The portion seen through the oval cutout contains densely packed information and touching it may render the diskette useless.

Next, close the door on the disk unit and proceed as follows:

1. If the video display unit has a separate power switch, turn it on.
2. If you will be using a printer, turn its power switch on.
3. If the PC's power switch is in the off position, turn it on. If it was already on, do one of the following (the effect is the same):
   a. Turn the PC off and then on again.
   b. Press the Del key while holding down the Ctrl and Alt keys. This process is called a **system reset.**

At this point, the PC's fan will start (it will run as long as the computer is on), the PC will automatically carry out a memory test (the test ends with a beep), and then the disk unit will begin to whir and continue to do so until DOS is read into memory. The *in use* light on the disk unit will glow while DOS is being read. The entire process takes from 3 to 45 seconds, depending on the amount of memory installed.

The PC will now display a message similar to

```
Current date is Tue  1-01-1985
Enter new date (mm-dd-yy):
```

At this point you can simply press the Enter key to leave the date as given, or you can enter a new date in the form *mm-dd-yy* where *mm* is the month (1 to 12), *dd* is the day (1 to 31), and *yy* is the year (for 1989 you can use either 1989 or 89). The PC will then display a message similar to

```
Current time is  0:01:41.39
Enter new time:
```

The three numbers separated by colons in 0:01:41.39 give the elapsed time since DOS was loaded into memory. As with date, you can simply press Enter, or you can enter a new time in the form *hh:mm:ss.xx,* which specifies time on a 24-hour clock: *hh* for the hour (0 to 23), *mm* for the minute (0 to 59), and *ss.xx* for the second (0 to 59.99).

Next, the PC will display a message similar to

```
The IBM Personal Computer  DOS
Version 3.10  (C)Copyright International Business Machines Corp 1981,1985
              (C)Copyright Microsoft Corp 1981, 1985
A>
```

indicating that DOS is operational. The DOS prompt A> is the signal that the system is waiting for you to enter a DOS command. For example, you can type BASIC to load Disk BASIC, or BASICA to load Advanced BASIC. DOS provides several other commands for specifying disk operations. In this book we describe seven of the DOS commands: BASIC and BASICA are described in Appendix A, and TYPE is described in Chapter 17, which deals with data files. In Section B.2 of this appendix we describe FORMAT and DISKCOPY, which you may need. In Section B.3 we describe DEL (to delete files) and DIR (to display a directory of files).* Section B.4 gives a summary of these DOS commands.

The letter A in the DOS prompt A> indicates that drive A is the default drive. This means that a disk command will be carried out on the diskette in drive A unless the command specifies a different drive. To specify drive B in a DOS command, you would include B: in the command. For instance, if a file named *fname* is to be specified in a DOS command, but the file is stored on the diskette in drive B, you would use *B:fname* in the DOS command. How B: is included in the DOS commands FORMAT, DISKCOPY, and DIR, which do not require a file name, is explained with the descriptions of these commands in Sections B.2 and B.3.

DOS allows you to change the default drive. To change it to drive B, simply type B: after the prompt A> and press the Enter key. Thus,

```
A>B:   (You type B:)
B>     (Displayed by the PC.)
```

gives B as the default drive, as indicated by the new DOS prompt B>. If you are a beginning programmer, we recommend that you not change the default drive. In what follows, we assume the default drive to be drive A.

B.2 Formatting and Copying Diskettes: The FORMAT and DISKCOPY Commands

Before a new diskette can be used to store information it must be **formatted** by using either the FORMAT or the DISKCOPY command. FORMAT writes information on a diskette that initializes it to a recording format acceptable to DOS. Formatting a diskette destroys any information that may previously have been stored on the diskette. DISKCOPY is used to make new copies of existing diskettes. The diskette being created is formatted before any files are copied; hence any information previously stored on the diskette is destroyed. To issue either of these commands, DOS must be operational and a DOS diskette must be in the default drive, which we assume is drive A.

---

* The DOS commands DEL and DIR have counterparts (KILL and FILES) in Disk and Advanced BASIC as described in Appendix C. As you work through the material in this book you will find it convenient to be able to issue these disk commands from either DOS or BASIC.

To format a diskette, type FORMAT (or format) and press the Enter key. The screen display will be:

```
A>FORMAT
Insert new diskette for drive A:
and strike any key when ready
```

When the drive A *in use* light is off, remove the DOS diskette, insert the diskette to be formatted, and press the Enter key. The PC will display

```
Formatting...
```

and after some further whirring of the disk unit, the message will be completed somewhat as follows:

```
Formatting...Format complete

    362496 bytes total disk space
    362496 bytes available on disk

Format another (Y/N)?
```

To format another diskette type Y (or y). If only one diskette is to be formatted, type N (or n) to get back the DOS prompt A>.

A diskette formatted by using FORMAT can be used to store programs (see Appendix C) and also to store the output of programs as described in Chapter 17. The newly formatted diskette, however, contains no programs. To format a diskette so that it includes the programs needed to run DOS, BASIC, and BASICA, you can use DISKCOPY to make an entirely new copy of a diskette that contains these programs. You may also get other programs that are not needed, but these can be deleted as described in the next section.

To issue the DISKCOPY command, make sure that the DOS prompt A> is displayed and place a DOS diskette into drive A (the default drive). Then enter one of the following two commands

```
DISKCOPY           (if only drive A is available)
DISKCOPY A: B:     (if drives A and B are available)
```

and follow the instructions displayed by the PC. The diskette you are copying is called the *source* diskette and the diskette being created is called the *target* diskette. The source diskette does not have to be the DOS diskette; any diskette can be copied. The following display was produced when we used DISKCOPY on a system with one disk drive to make a new copy of the system DOS diskette. You will notice that the source and target diskettes must be inserted and removed several times. This is not required if two drives are available.

```
A>diskcopy
Insert source diskette in drive A:
Strike any key when ready
Copying 9 sectors per track, 1 side(s)
Insert target diskette in drive A:
Strike any key when ready
Formatting while copying
Insert source diskette in drive A:
Strike any key when ready
Insert target diskette in drive A:
Strike any key when ready
Copy complete
Copy another (Y/N)?n
A>
```

B.3 The Directory and Delete Commands: DIR and DEL

If you use DISKCOPY to copy a diskette, all files will be copied even though some may not be needed. To obtain a directory of all files on a diskette, insert the diskette in the default drive (we assume it is drive A), type DIR, and press the Enter key. (Use Dir B: for a diskette in drive B.) The PC will display the names of all files currently on the diskette. The display will also show for each file the file size (in bytes) and the date and time the file was created. To obtain a listing of only the file names, use the form

    DIR/W

W stands for *wide*—you get a wide display that shows five file names per line. With this directory on the screen, you can decide which files to delete. To delete a file named *fname.ext* from the diskette in the default drive A, type

    DEL *fname.ext*

If the diskette containing *fname.ext* is in drive B, use

    DEL B:*fname.ext*

Files with the extensions SYS, COM, and EXE should not be deleted unless you know exactly what they are. If you have just made a new copy of a diskette that contains the programs needed to run DOS, BASIC, and BASICA, you can delete all files that do not have one of these three extensions and still be able to use the diskette to run DOS, BASIC, and BASICA. Having done this, the diskette will have room for files you will be saving.

Many files can be deleted with a single DEL command by using either of the following forms:

    DEL *.ext*
    DEL *fname*.*

The form *.ext* specifies all file names with the extension *ext*, and the form *fname*.* specifies all file names whose name without the extension is *fname*. Thus, the single command

    DEL *.BAS

will delete all BASIC programs that were not given an extension other than the default extension BAS. Similarly, the single command

    DEL TEMP.*

will delete all files named TEMP.*ext*, whatever the extension *ext*.

    The forms of the DOS commands given in this book are not the general forms of these commands. For a complete description of all DOS commands, consult the DOS manual.

B.4 Summary of DOS Commands Used in This Book

Command	Purpose	Text reference
BASIC	To get Disk BASIC up and running.	Appendix A.2
BASICA	To get Advanced BASIC up and running.	Appendix A.3
DEL	To delete files from a diskette.	Appendix B.3
DIR	To display all or part of a diskette's directory of files.	Appendix B.3
DISKCOPY	To make a new copy of a diskette.	Appendix B.2
FORMAT	To format a diskette.	Appendix B.2
TYPE	To list the contents of a file.	Section 17.1

(To use any of these commands, the system must be under the control of DOS. From Disk or Advanced BASIC, use the command SYSTEM to get the necessary prompt A>.)

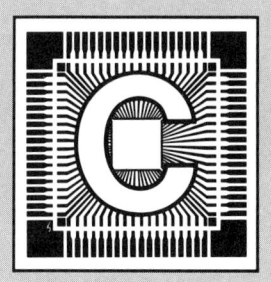

A Typical Session with Disk or Advanced BASIC

As mentioned in Appendix A, you enter Disk or Advanced BASIC by issuing the DOS command BASIC or BASICA. While in BASIC mode, you should be able to perform certain elementary tasks such as typing and running new programs, saving programs for later use, modifying programs that were previously saved, and deleting programs you no longer need. The following BASIC statements are used to carry out these tasks:

| FILES | KILL | LIST | LOAD |
| NAME | NEW | RUN | SAVE |

These statements can be executed in either deferred or immediate mode. Most often, however, each is executed in immediate mode to cause an action to take place at the time the statement is typed. For this reason we will refer to them as commands. The LIST, NEW, and RUN commands are described in Chapter 4. To understand the action caused by the other five commands, you should know that information stored on a diskette is organized into units called **files.** A file can contain a program or data other than a program (as described in Chapter 17). BASIC always references files by name.

A **file name** has the form

name [.extension]

where *name* contains from 1 to 8 characters and *extension* contains up to 3 characters. As indicated by the brackets the extension is optional. If you include more than 8 characters in *name,* the PC uses only the first 8. Similarly, only the first 3 characters after a period are used as the extension. The characters in *name* and *extension* can be letters (A–Z), digits (0–9), and certain other characters (but not all) from the PC character set. To help avoid using inadmissible file names, we suggest you use only letters and digits in *name* and *extension*. The following table shows some *file names,* both admissible and inadmissible.

File name	Comment
PROGRAM5	Admissible
PROGRAM25.DAT	Admissible, but PROGRAM2.DAT is used
S.S.N.	Inadmissible (only one period is allowed)
TEMP.TEMP	Admissible, but TEMP.TEM is used
PROG.TM5	Admissible
SCORE.BAS	Admissible

We now describe the BASIC commands FILES, KILL, LOAD, NAME, and SAVE, and show how they are used to carry out file operations. Throughout this appendix we assume that disk drive A is the default drive. We also assume that you are using a diskette that has been formatted as described in Appendix B, and that it is not "write protected." Diskettes that are not write-protected have a small square cutout along the edge opposite the label: if there is no such cutout, or if the cutout has been covered with some kind of tape, any attempt to write to the diskette will result in the message

```
Disk write protected
```

C.1 Saving Your Programs

To preserve a program for later use, place your diskette in the default drive and enter the command

    SAVE "*fn*"

where *fn* denotes an admissible file name.* This command copies the program currently in the PC's memory onto the diskette and gives it the name *fn*. However, if *fn* does not contain a period, BASIC automatically adds the extension .BAS to *fn*. Thus if you specify the name PROG23 in the SAVE command, BASIC will use the name PROG23.BAS; but if you specify PROG23.TM1 (or even PROG23.) BASIC will not add an extension. To copy a program onto a diskette in drive B rather than the default drive, use the command†

    SAVE "B:*fn*"

A program that is copied onto a diskette will continue to exist there even after the PC is turned off.

The following shows how you can type two programs and save a copy of each on your diskette:

```
NEW              (Clears memory so that a new program can be typed.)
Ok
 .
 .               (Type your first program.)
 .
SAVE "PROG1"     (Saves program on diskette under the name PROG1.BAS.)
Ok
NEW              (Clears memory so that a new program can be typed.)
Ok
 .
 .               (Type your second program.)
 .
SAVE "PROG2"     (Saves PROG2.BAS on diskette.)
Ok               (PROG2.BAS also exists in the PC's memory.)
```

Caution: If a program has been previously saved on your diskette under the name *fn* and you enter the command SAVE"*fn*", the copy of *fn* on your diskette will be lost and the program currently in PC's memory will be stored on your diskette under the name *fn*. Thus, by mistakenly choosing a program name already used on your diskette, you may erase a program—one that you want to keep.

To produce a listing of all file names stored on a diskette (its **directory**), use the BASIC command

```
FILES
```

---

* Pressing Function key 4 gives SAVE" so that you don't have to remember to include the quotes. (The closing quotation mark is always optional in BASIC.)
† If your system has only one disk drive, you should never specify drive B. Doing so can cause difficulties that will require you to reboot DOS (as described in Appendix B) and start anew.

This command displays the names with extensions of all files on the diskette in the default drive A. To obtain a directory listing for a diskette in drive B, use the command

```
FILES "B:"
```

The command FILES (or FILES "B:") produces a listing of *all* file names on a diskette. BASIC allows modified forms of the FILES command to allow you to obtain partial listings. You should find the following two forms helpful.

FILES "*.*ext*"
FILES "*fn*.*"

The first produces a listing of all files with the extension *ext* and the second lists all file names whose name without the extension is *fn*. For example,

```
FILES "*.BAS"
```

lists the names of all BASIC programs that were not given an extension other than the default extension BAS. If the two programs saved in the foregoing illustration of the SAVE command are the only .BAS programs on the diskette in drive A, the command FILES "*.BAS" will produce a display similar to the following:

```
FILES "*.BAS"
A:
PROG1    .BAS      PROG2     .BAS
 60416 Bytes free
```

C.2 Retrieving Programs from a Diskette

Let's assume that the programs PROG1.BAS and PROG2.BAS have been stored on your diskette by the SAVE command. If at a later session with Disk or Advanced BASIC you wish to run these programs, place the diskette in the default drive and proceed as follows (use Function key 3 for LOAD and key 2 for RUN).

```
LOAD "PROG1"    (PROG1.BAS is read into memory.)
Ok
RUN
 .
 .              (PROG1.BAS is executed.)
 .
Ok
LOAD "PROG2"    (PROG2.BAS is read into memory.)
Ok
RUN
 .
 .              (PROG2.BAS is executed.)
 .
Ok
```

It would be correct to use LOAD "PROG1.BAS", but the extension BAS is not necessary. BASIC assumes the default extension BAS in LOAD commands just as in SAVE commands.

If you specify an incorrect file name in a LOAD command you may or may not generate an error. Following are the three most common errors made with the LOAD command.

1. If *fn* (or *fn*.BAS) is not the name of a diskette file, a File not found error occurs. Any program currently in the PC's memory will remain intact.
2. If you mistakenly specify a file *fn* that is not a BASIC program, one of the following errors will occur, depending on the contents of the file:

```
Direct statement in file
Syntax error
```

(The first error indicates that the file contains a "line" that does not begin with a proper BASIC line number.)

3. If you include an extension other than BAS in *fn* when you SAVE a file, you must also include the extension when you LOAD it. If you don't, BASIC will assume the default extension BAS, which means the intended file will not be read into memory. If by coincidence there is a file with the specified name and the extension BAS, it will be read into memory rather than the intended file. If there is no such file, a more likely event, a File not found error occurs.

C.3 Modifying Diskette Programs

Often a program is saved before it is completely debugged. Let's assume that you saved such a program with the name POWER2.BAS. To modify POWER2.BAS, you can first use the LOAD command to read it into the PC's memory. Having done this you can modify the program just as you could when you created it. After making the necessary modifications, you may replace the old copy on the diskette with the modified version by typing

```
SAVE "POWER2"
```

The modified version is now stored on your diskette under the same name POWER2.BAS and can be retrieved at any subsequent session. (The original version of the program will be lost.) The following illustrates what has just been described.

```
LOAD "POWER2"     (Copy of POWER2.BAS is read into memory.)
Ok
LIST
100 LET A=5       (Contents of POWER2.BAS)
110 LET B=A^2
120 PRINT B
130 END
Ok
100 LET A=6       (Change line 100.)
LIST              (List the updated version.)
100 LET A=6
110 LET B=A^2
120 PRINT B
130 END
Ok
SAVE "POWER2"     (Updated version is saved as POWER2.BAS.)
Ok
RUN               (Updated version of POWER2.BAS is executed.)
 36
Ok
```

There will be times when you want to preserve both the original and the updated version of a program. To do this, use the SAVE command but with a different file name. Both versions will be preserved.

C.4 Renaming and Deleting Diskette Files

BASIC provides the NAME command to allow you to rename files already stored on a diskette and the KILL command (an unfortunate name) to delete files that are no longer needed. You should find both of these commands useful: the first to give files more appropriate names than those used when the files were first saved, and the second to delete files to make room for others. The storage capacity of a diskette, though rather large, is limited. Moreover, the disk operating system (DOS) places a limit on how many files can appear in a diskette directory, regardless of how much storage space is actually being used.

The command

> KILL "*fn*"

removes the name *fn* from the directory of the diskette in the default drive (which we continue to assume is drive A) and frees the storage space previously used to store the contents of *fn*. If the name of a file to be deleted has an extension, the extension must be included in *fn*; BASIC does not assume a default extension with the KILL command. Thus to delete POWER2.BAS you would use KILL "POWER2.BAS" and not KILL "POWER2". To delete file *fn* from a diskette in drive B you would use

> KILL "B:*fn*"

If *fn* is an admissible file name, but is not found in the diskette's directory, a File not found error occurs. If *fn* is not an admissible file name (for instance, S.S.N. is not a valid file name), a Bad file name error occurs.

The command

> NAME "*fn1*" AS "*fn2*"

changes the name of the existing file *fn1* to *fn2*. After this command has been carried out, the file must be referenced by using *fn2*; *fn1* is no longer in the diskette's directory. As with the KILL command, BASIC does not use default extensions for files named in NAME commands. Thus to change the name of an existing file PROG3.BAS to CHART3.BAS you would use

```
NAME "PROG3.BAS" AS "CHART3.BAS"
```

If instead you write

```
NAME "PROG3" AS "CHART3"
```

you will generate a File not found error unless PROG3 happens to be the name of another file stored on the diskette. If there is such a file, its name will be changed to CHART3 and not to CHART3.BAS. If either *fn1* or *fn2* is an inadmissible file name, a Bad file name error occurs.

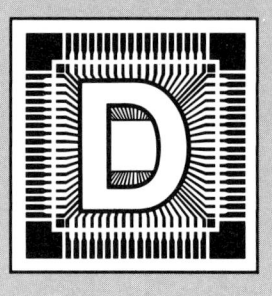

Microsoft® BASIC Reserved Words

ABS	EOF	LPRINT	RIGHT$
AND	EQV	LSET	RND
ASC	ERASE	MERGE	RSET
ATN	ERL	MID$	RUN
AUTO	ERR	MKD$	SAVE
BEEP	ERROR	MKI$	SCREEN
BLOAD	EXP	MKS$	SGN
BSAVE	FIELD	MOD	SIN
CALL	FILES	MOTOR	SOUND
CDBL	FIX	NAME	SPACE$
CHAIN	FN*xxxxxxxx*	NEW	SPC(
CHR$	FOR	NEXT	SQR
CINT	FRE	NOT	STEP
CIRCLE	GET	OCT$	STICK
CLEAR	GOSUB	OFF	STOP
CLOSE	GOTO	ON	STR$
CLS	HEX$	OPEN	STRIG
COLOR	IF	OPTION	STRING$
COM	IMP	OR	SWAP
COMMON	INKEY$	OUT	SYSTEM
CONT	INP	PAINT	TAB(
COS	INPUT	PEEK	TAN
CSNG	INPUT#	PEN	THEN
CSRLIN	INPUT$	PLAY	TIME$
CVD	INSTR	POINT	TO
CVI	INT	POKE	TROFF
CVS	KEY	POS	TRON
DATA	KILL	PRESET	USING
DATE$	LEFT$	PRINT	USR
DEF	LEN	PRINT#	VAL
DEFDBL	LET	PSET	VARPTR
DEFINT	LINE	PUT	VARPTR$
DEFSNG	LIST	RANDOMIZE	WAIT
DEFSTR	LLIST	READ	WEND
DELETE	LOAD	REM	WHILE
DIM	LOC	RENUM	WIDTH
DRAW	LOCATE	RESET	WRITE
EDIT	LOF	RESTORE	WRITE#
ELSE	LOG	RESUME	XOR
END	LPOS	RETURN	

E Editing Features

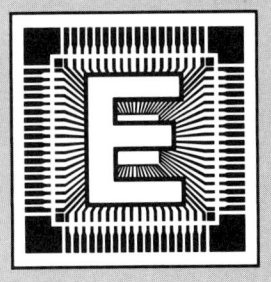

E.1 Typing BASIC Keywords by Pressing a Single Key

Use the Alt key in conjunction with an alphabetic (A–Z) character to type BASIC keywords according to the correspondence shown below. For example, hold down the Alt key and press P to type the keyword PRINT.

A	AUTO	J	(no word)	S	SCREEN
B	BSAVE	K	KEY	T	THEN
C	COLOR	L	LOCATE	U	USING
D	DELETE	M	MOTOR	V	VAL
E	ELSE	N	NEXT	W	WIDTH
F	FOR	O	OPEN	X	XOR
G	GOTO	P	PRINT	Y	(no word)
H	HEX$	Q	(no word)	Z	(no word)
I	INPUT	R	RUN		

E.2 Line Numbers Typed Automatically: The AUTO Command

The command

    AUTO **number, increment**

will generate line numbers beginning at **number** in increments of **increment.** The default value for each is 10. For example, AUTO 100,100 generates line numbers 100, 200, 300, . . . , whereas AUTO yields 10, 20, 30, ... This command saves you from typing line numbers when you enter a program. Exit from AUTO mode by Ctrl-Break.

E.3 Renumbering the Lines of a Program

The command

    RENUM **newnum, oldnum, increment**

will renumber the lines of your program beginning at line **oldnum** of your program. This line will now have **newnum** as its line number and each subsequent line will be incremented by **increment.** The default value for each is 10. For example, if a program starts with line number 10,

    RENUM 100,,100

will renumber the entire program using 100, 200, 300, ...

E.4 Deleting Lines from a Program

Use the DELETE command to delete a single line or a sequence of lines from a program. For example, DELETE 50 will delete line 50, and DELETE 200-400 will delete all lines numbered from 200 to 400. (Make sure that the line numbers used in the DELETE command are line numbers used in the program.)

E.5 Listing a Program

Use Ctrl-NumLock to interrupt the listing of a program; press any key (other than Shift, Break, or Ins) to continue the listing. This feature is useful while making corrections to a long program.

E.6 Clearing the Screen

Use the CLS command or Ctrl-Home to clear the screen and move the cursor to the beginning of the first line.

E.7 Cursor Movement

Use the keys

[7 Home] [8 ↑] [4 ←] [6 →] [2 ↓] [1 END]

on the numeric keypad for easy cursor movement. The NumLock key acts as a toggle switch controlling the number keypad: press it once to type the numerical characters, press it again to return to lowercase (in this instance, the special cursor moving functions). Pressing these keys causes cursor movement only; no character on the screen or in memory is changed or deleted. The keys have the following effects:

→	moves the cursor 1 position to the right.
↑	moves the cursor 1 position up.
←	moves the cursor 1 position to the left.
↓	moves the cursor 1 position down.
END	moves the cursor to the end of the current line.
HOME	moves the cursor to the beginning of the first screen line.

Once the cursor is in the proper position, you can proceed to make any correction needed (see Section E.8).

E.8 Correcting a Program Line

The most common corrections made to lines in a BASIC program involve changing, deleting, or inserting characters. To use the PC's editing features to make such changes you will need the cursor-moving keys described in Section E.7 and also the following three keys.

[←] Erases the character just before the cursor. (This key is located just above the Enter key.)

[Del] Erases the character at the current cursor position. If pressing this key gives you a period, press the NumLock key: see Section E.7. (The Del key is the bottom right key of the numeric keypad.)

[Ins key] Controls whether a typed character is written over the character at the current cursor position (overwrite mode), or inserted just before the cursor (insert mode). When you first enter BASIC, the PC is in overwrite mode. To change to insert mode, press this Ins key once. (You should notice that in overwrite mode the cursor is the usual underscore, but in insert mode it is a half-block character.) To get back to overwrite mode, press it again. Pressing the Enter key or any of the cursor-moving keys described in Section E.7 will also get you back to overwrite mode. If at any time you get 0 when you press the Ins key, press the NumLock key: see Section E.7. (The Ins key is on the numeric keypad just to the left of the Del key.)

To correct a BASIC program line, the line must appear on the display screen (use the LIST command if it doesn't—if the program is long, you could use LIST *ln* or LIST *ln1–ln2*). Move the cursor (see Section E.7) to the position where the mistake occurs and make the correction. If there are other mistakes on this line, correct them also.

When all corrections to this line have been made—with the cursor still positioned somewhere on the line (not necessarily at the end)—press the Enter key. Failure to *enter* the corrections this way results in the modified line appearing on the screen but not being stored in memory as part of your program. (If the program is stored as a diskette file, don't forget to use SAVE to save the corrected version.)

E.9 The KEY Statement

You have already seen (Section 4.8) how the statement KEY OFF erases the function key display on screen line 25 and how KEY ON turns it back on. Two other features of the KEY statement are of interest. The statement KEY LIST produces the listing

```
F1 LIST
F2 RUN ←
F3 LOAD"
F4 SAVE"
F5 CONT ←
F6 ,"LPT1:" ←
F7 TRON ←
F8 TROFF ←
F9 KEY
F10 SCREEN 0,0,0 ←
```

that displays the *complete* string values associated with each of the 10 keys, whereas the display on line 25 shows only the first *six* characters. A back arrow (←) as a last character means that the Enter key character, CHR$(13), is part of the string; hence the command given by the string will be executed as soon as the corresponding function key is pressed.

The above listing shows the 10 string values that the system assigns to the 10 function keys each time BASIC is brought up. But you can change any or all of these values by using another form of the KEY statement. The new values can be any strings with 1 to 15 characters (longer strings will be truncated at the fifteenth character). To change the string associated with function key N(1–10) to the string X$ (1–15 characters), use the statement

```
KEY N, X$
```

For example, to assign KEY OFF to F9 (in place of KEY), use

```
KEY 9, "KEY OFF"
```

To include the Enter key character as part of the string, use

```
KEY 9, "KEY OFF"+CHR$(13)
```

The only limitation for the string you assign to a function key is the maximum of 15 characters it can contain. For instance, you can use

```
KEY 5,"FILES"+CHR$(34)+"*.BAS"+CHR$(13)
```

to assign the 12-character string FILES"*.BAS ⏎ to function key 5 [CHR$(34) gives the quotation mark]. Once this KEY statement is executed, you can simply press F5 to obtain a listing of all files that have the extension BAS.

Each KEY statement that changes the strings associated with the function keys must be executed each time you enter BASIC. But you don't have to type them each time. The following shows a program that can be run at any time to change F5 and F9 as shown above.

```
10 KEY 9,"KEY OFF"+CHR$(13)
20 KEY 5,"FILES"+CHR$(34)+"*.BAS"+CHR$(13)
30 END
Ok
SAVE"START"
Ok
```

If you LOAD and RUN this program each time you enter BASIC (press F3, type START, and press F2), you can press F9 to erase screen line 25, and press F5 each time you want a listing of BASIC programs that have the default extension BAS.

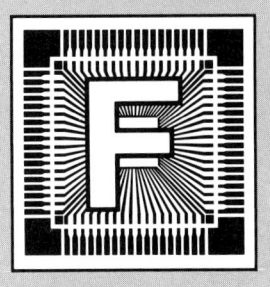

IBM PC Numeric Codes

Numeric code	Character	Numeric code	Character
000	(null)	038	&
001	☺	039	'
002	☻	040	(
003	♥	041	)
004	♦	042	*
005	♣	043	+
006	♠	044	,
007	(beep)	045	-
008	■	046	.
009	(tab)	047	/
010	(line feed)	048	0
011	(home)	049	1
012	(form feed)	050	2
013	(carriage return)	051	3
014	♪	052	4
015	☼	053	5
016	►	054	6
017	◄	055	7
018	↕	056	8
019	‼	057	9
020	¶	058	:
021	§	059	;
022	▬	060	<
023	↨	061	=
024	↑	062	>
025	↓	063	?
026	→	064	@
027	←	065	A
028	(cursor right)	066	B
029	(cursor left)	067	C
030	(cursor up)	068	D
031	(cursor down)	069	E
032	(space)	070	F
033	!	071	G
034	"	072	H
035	#	073	I
036	$	074	J
037	%	075	K

Appendix F IBM PC Numeric Codes

Numeric code	Character	Numeric code	Character
076	L	134	å
077	M	135	ç
078	N	136	ê
079	O	137	ë
080	P	138	è
081	Q	139	ï
082	R	140	î
083	S	141	ì
084	T	142	Ä
085	U	143	Å
086	V	144	É
087	W	145	æ
088	X	146	Æ
089	Y	147	ô
090	Z	148	ö
091	[	149	ò
092	\	150	û
093	]	151	ù
094	∧	152	ÿ
095	—	153	Ö
096	`	154	Ü
097	a	155	¢
098	b	156	£
099	c	157	¥
100	d	158	Pt
101	e	159	ƒ
102	f	160	á
103	g	161	í
104	h	162	ó
105	i	163	ú
106	j	164	ñ
107	k	165	Ñ
108	l	166	ª
109	m	167	º
110	n	168	¿
111	o	169	⌐
112	p	170	¬
113	q	171	½
114	r	172	¼
115	s	173	¡
116	t	174	«
117	u	175	»
118	v	176	░
119	w	177	▒
120	x	178	▓
121	y	179	│
122	z	180	┤
123	{	181	╡
124	|	182	╢
125	}	183	╖
126	~	184	╕
127	⌂	185	╣
128	Ç	186	║
129	ü	187	╗
130	é	188	╝
131	â	189	╜
132	ä	190	╛
133	à	191	┐

Numeric code	Character	Numeric code	Character
192	└	224	α
193	┴	225	β
194	┬	226	Γ
195	├	227	π
196	─	228	Σ
197	┼	229	σ
198	╞	230	μ
199	╟	231	τ
200	╚	232	Φ
201	╔	233	Θ
202	╩	234	Ω
203	╦	235	δ
204	╠	236	∞
205	═	237	ϕ
206	╬	238	ε
207	╧	239	$\cap$
208	╨	240	$\equiv$
209	╤	241	$\pm$
210	╥	242	$\geq$
211	╙	243	$\leq$
212	╘	244	⌠
213	╒	245	⌡
214	╓	246	$\div$
215	╫	247	$\approx$
216	╪	248	°
217	┘	249	●
218	┌	250	·
219	■	251	$\sqrt{}$
220	▬	252	n
221	▮	253	2
222	▮	254	■
223	▬	255	(blank 'FF')

Microsoft® BASIC Statements

(Also see Appendix H.)

Statement	Purpose	Text reference
CIRCLE	To plot a circle in graphics mode	Section 19.4
CLOSE	To terminate communication between a program and a file	Section 17.1
CLS	To clear the display screen	Section 4.2
COLOR (graphics mode)	To select a background color and palette for graphic displays	Section 19.1
COLOR (text mode)	To select colors for screen displays	Section 10.3
DATA	To include input data as part of a program	Section 11.1
DEF FN	To define a function	Sections 13.3, 14.8
DIM	To specify dimensions for arrays	Sections 15.1, 15.2, 15.5
END	To terminate execution of a program	Section 3.5
ERASE	To erase arrays from a program and thus to free memory space	Section 15.2
FIELD	To allocate space for variables in a random file buffer	Section 17.6
FOR	To initiate a FOR loop	Sections 9.1, 9.3
GET (files)	To read a record from a random file into the file buffer	Section 17.6
GET (graphics mode)	To store an image from the graphics screen in an array	Section 19.7
GOSUB	To transfer control to a subroutine	Section 12.1
GOTO	To transfer control to a specified line	Section 6.1
IF (as a transfer statement)	To transfer control to a specified line only if a specified condition is satisfied	Section 6.1
IF (as a statement selector)	To execute a specified sequence of statements only if a specified condition is satisfied	Section 8.1
INPUT	To obtain input data from the keyboard	Section 5.1

421

Statement	Purpose	Text reference
INPUT#	To obtain input data from a sequential file	Section 17.1
KEY	To turn the function key display (line 25) on or off; to change the value of a function key	Section 4.8 Appendix E.9
LET	To evaluate an expression and assign its value to a variable	Section 3.5
LINE	To plot line segments and rectangles in graphics mode	Section 19.2
LINE INPUT	To read an entire line from the keyboard	Section 17.2
LOCATE	To position the cursor at a specified row and column on the screen	Section 10.1
LPRINT	To transfer output to printer	Section 4.8, Chapter 7
LPRINT USING	To transfer output to printer according to a specified format	Section 7.6
LSET	To transfer data to a random file buffer (left-justified if necessary)	Section 17.6
MID$	To replace part of one string with another string	Section 14.1
NEXT	To terminate a FOR loop	Section 9.1
ON ERROR GOTO	To transfer to a specified line when a fatal error occurs	Section 17.4
ON GOSUB	To select one of several subroutines determined by the value of an expression	Section 12.3
ON GOTO	To select one of several line numbers determined by the value of an expression	Section 8.4
OPEN	To establish communication between a program and a file	Sections 17.1, 17.6
OPTION BASE	To select 0 or 1 as the smallest allowable subscript in a program	Section 15.1
PAINT	To color a region of the graphics screen	Section 19.5
PRINT	To transfer output to the video screen	Sections 3.6, 6.1, Chapter 7
PRINT USING	To transfer output to the video screen according to a specified format	Section 7.6
PRINT#	To transfer output to a sequential file	Section 17.1
PSET	To plot a point in graphics mode	Section 19.1
PUT (files)	To write a record from a file buffer to the random file	Section 17.6
PUT (graphics)	To display on the graphics screen an image stored by a GET statement	Section 19.7
RANDOMIZE	To reseed the random number generator	Section 18.1

Statement	Purpose	Text reference
READ	To obtain input data from DATA lines	Section 11.1
REM	To include comments in a program and to improve its readability	Section 3.7
RESTORE	To restore the data pointer to the first or to a specified DATA line	Section 11.3
RESUME	To continue program execution after an error recovery procedure	Section 17.4
RETURN	To return control from a subroutine	Section 12.1
RSET	To transfer data to a random file buffer (right-justified if necessary)	Section 17.6
SCREEN	To select text, medium-resolution graphics, or high-resolution graphics mode of operation	Sections 19.1, 19.10
SWAP	To interchange the values of two variables	Section 14.5
WEND	To terminate a WHILE loop	Section 6.2
WHILE	To initiate a WHILE loop	Section 6.2
WIDTH	To specify the number of characters in an output line	Section 7.1
WRITE#	To transfer output to a sequential file	Section 17.1

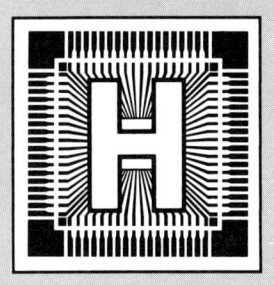

Microsoft® BASIC Commands

(These are BASIC statements that are most often used in immediate mode.)

Command	Purpose	Text reference
AUTO	To generate line numbers automatically	Appendix E.2
DELETE	To delete a sequence of lines from a program	Appendix E.4
FILES	To display the directory of files on a diskette	Appendix C.1
KILL	To delete a file from a diskette	Appendix C.4
LIST	To display an entire program or a sequence of lines from a program on the video screen	Section 4.4
LLIST	To print an entire program or a sequence of lines from a program on a printer	Section 4.8
LOAD	To retrieve a file from a diskette	Appendix C.2
NAME . . . AS	To rename a file stored on a diskette	Appendix C.4
NEW	To clear the current program from memory	Section 4.2
RENUM	To renumber the lines in a program	Appendix E.3
RUN	To execute a program from the beginning or from the specified line number	Section 4.4
SAVE	To save a program on a diskette	Appendix C.1
SYSTEM	To end BASIC and return to DOS control	Section 17.1, Appendix B.4

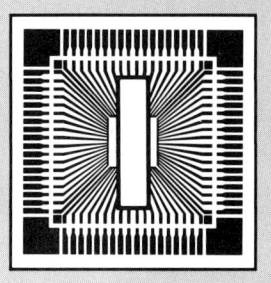

BASIC Functions

Function	Purpose	Text reference
ABS(x)	Returns the absolute value of x	Section 13.1
ASC($x\$$)	Returns the ASCII code of the first character in $x\$$	Section 14.7
ATN(x)	Returns the arctangent of x	Section 13.1
CDBL(x)	Converts x to a double-precision value	Section 13.1
CHR$($n$)	Returns the character whose ASCII code is n	Section 10.4
CINT(x)	Converts x to an integer by rounding	Section 13.1
COS(x)	Returns the cosine of x	Section 13.1
CVD($x\$$)	Converts $x\$$ to a double-precision numerical value	Section 17.6
CVI($x\$$)	Converts $x\$$ to an integer	Section 17.6
CVS($x\$$)	Converts $x\$$ to a single-precision numerical value	Section 17.6
EOF(f)	Indicates the end of file condition on file f	Section 17.2
EXP(x)	Raises e to the power x	Section 13.1
FIX(x)	Truncates x to an integer value	Section 13.1
INKEY *variable*	To read a single character from the keyboard	Section 10.1
INSTR($n,x\$,y\$$)	Returns the position of the first occurrence of $y\$$ in $x\$$ starting at position n	Section 14.3
INT(x)	Returns the greatest integer less than or equal to x	Section 13.1
LEFT$($x\$,n$)	Returns the first n characters of $x\$$	Section 14.1
LEN($x\$$)	Returns the number of characters in $x\$$	Section 14.1
LOC(f)	Returns the record number of last record accessed in file f	Section 17.6
LOF(f)	Returns the length of file f	Section 17.6
LOG(x)	Returns the natural logarithm of x	Section 13.1
MID$($x\$,n,m$)	Returns m characters from $x\$$ beginning at position n	Section 14.1
MKD$($x$)	Converts the double-precision value x to a string	Section 17.6
MKI$($x$)	Converts the integer x to a string	Section 17.6
MKS$($x$)	Converts the single-precision value x to a string	Section 17.6
RIGHT$($x\$,n$)	Returns the last n characters from $x\$$	Section 14.1
RND	Returns a random number between 0 and 1	Chapter 18
SGN(x)	Returns +1, 0, or −1 depending whether x is positive, zero, or negative	Section 13.1
SIN(x)	Returns the sine of x	Section 13.1
SPACE$($n$)	Returns a string of n spaces	Section 10.4

Function	Purpose	Text reference
SPC(*n*)	Skips *n* spaces	Section 7.4
SQR(*x*)	Returns the principal square root of *x*	Section 13.1
STR$(*x*)	Converts *x* to a string	Section 14.7
STRING$(*n,m*)	Returns the character whose ASCII code is *m*, repeated *n* times	Section 10.4
STRING$(*n,x$*)	Returns the first character of *x$*, repeated *n* times	Sections 10.1, 10.4
TAB(*n*)	Tabs to position *n*	Section 7.4
TAN(*x*)	Returns the tangent of *x*	Section 13.1
VAL(*x$*)	Returns the numerical value of *x$*	Section 14.7

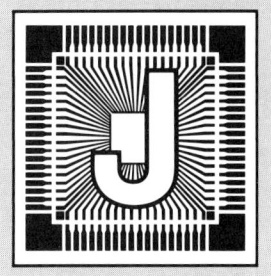

Answers to Selected Problems

■ Section 1.3

1. F **2.** F **3.** T **4.** F **5.** F **6.** T
7. T **8.** F **9.** F **10.** F **11.** F **12.** F

■ Section 2.3

1. 5% discount
2. Decide whether the discount is applicable.
3. 693.50
4. 250.00
5. 80.00 and 0, 128.00 and 0, 176.00 and 48.00, 206.00 and 78.00
6. $4
7. $6 per hour
8. Step (c) is used to determine whether there is any overtime. G denotes gross pay. B denotes pay for overtime hours.
9. 21
10. 1   1
    2   2
    3   6
    4   24
    5   120
    6   720
11. 55
12. 2, 4, 7, 8, 14, 28, 64
13. Process will *never* stop, since N is always less than 10.
14. Step (c) is ambiguous.
15. Variable names:

    NAME   = name of an item
    COST   = cost for the item NAME
    PRICE   = sale price for the item NAME
    QTY   = number of units of NAME sold
    GROSS   = gross sales for the item NAME
    INCOME = income from the item NAME

Algorithm

    a. Print column headings as specified.
    b. Read NAME and values for COST, PRICE, and QTY, for one item.
    c. Assign the value of the product QTY × PRICE to GROSS.
    d. Multiply QTY times (PRICE − COST) to obtain a value for INCOME.
    e. Enter NAME and the values GROSS and INCOME under the appropriate column headings.
    f. Return to Step (b) until the report is complete.

17. Variable names:

CORP	=	corporation name
SHARES	=	number of shares
PRICE	=	current price for one share
EARN	=	earnings for one share
EQTY	=	equity represented by all shares of corporation CORP
PE	=	price/earnings ratio for one share

Algorithm

    a. Print column headings as specified.
    b. Read CORP and values for SHARES, PRICE, and EARN.
    c. Assign the value of the product SHARES × PRICE to EQTY.
    d. Divide PRICE by EARN to obtain a value for PE.
    e. Enter CORP and the values SHARES, PRICE, EARN, EQTY, and PE under the appropriate column headings.
    f. Return to Step (b) until the report is complete.

19. Algorithm

    a. Start with SUM = 0 and COUNT = 0
    b. Add the number on the top card to SUM, and add 1 to COUNT.
    c. Remove the top card and return to Step (b) until all cards have been processed.
    d. Divide SUM by COUNT to obtain the average AV, and proceed to Step (e) with the original stack of cards in hand.
    e. If the number on the top card exceeds AV, write the letter G on the card; otherwise write the letter L.
    f. Remove the top card and return to Step (e) until all cards have been examined.

20. Algorithm

    a. Press the CLEAR key.
    b. Insert your ID card into reader as shown.
    c. Enter your four-digit code and press ENTER.
    d. Enter amount of check and press ENTER.
    e. Place check in punch unit, blank side toward you.
    f. Remove check and ID card when these items are released by the machine.

■ Section 2.4

1. F   2. T   3. F   4. F   5. F   6. T   7. T   8. T   9. F   10. T

Section 3.4

1. **a.** 17 **b.** 33 **c.** −2 **d.** −6 **e.** −15 **f.** −9 **g.** 17 **h.** 9 **i.** 0.25 **j.** −9 **k.** 64 **l.** −12.3 **m.** −12 **n.** 12300000 **o.** 0.00075 **p.** 4.5 **q.** 3 **r.** 3 **s.** 2 **t.** 0 **u.** 5
2. **a.** 3.5 **b.** 5 **c.** 0.75 **d.** 0.75 **e.** 10 **f.** 25 **g.** 4.5 **h.** 1.666667 **i.** 10 **j.** 3 **k.** −8 **l.** −8 **m.** 1 **n.** 2 **o.** 2
3. **a.** * missing between (Y + Z) and X.
   c. 7B is not admissible as an expression or variable name.
   e. KEY is a reserved word.
   f. 2B is not admissible as an expression or variable name.
   g. 2X is not admissible as an expression or variable name.
4. **a.** 0.06*P **b.** 5*X+5*Y **c.** A^2+B^2 **d.** 6/(5*A)
   e. A/B+C/D **f.** (A+B)/(C+D) **g.** A*X^2+B*X+C
   h. (B^2−4*A*C)^0.5 **i.** (X^2+4*X*Y)/(X+2*Y)
5. **a.** X+1+Y **b.** A^2−B^2 **c.** A^3+A^2*B+A **d.** A*B/C
   e. A/B/C **f.** X^4+X^3*D+X^2*C+X*B+A **g.** P^Q^R
   h. 1/A/B/C/D

Section 3.9

1. **a.** 110 LET M=7 **b.** 120 LET B=B+7
   c. 130 LET H=2*H **d.** 140 LET C2=(A−B)/2
   e. 150 LET A=(1+R)^10 **f.** 160 LET X=X−2*Y
   g. 170 LET C$="COST" **h.** 180 LET A$="DOE, JANE"
   i. 190 LET Q$=P$ **j.** 200 LET S$="*****"

2. **a.** 10 LET X=(A+B)*C
   b. admissible
   c. 20 LET S=A+B
   d. 25 LET DEPT5=17
   e. admissible
   f. 35 LET M5=2+7*X
   g. admissible
   h. admissible
   i. 50 LET Z=4*10^2.5
   j. 55 LET AREA=LENGTH*WDTH
   k. 60 LET SUM=SUM+NXT
   l. admissible
   m. 70 LET A$="SAMMY"
   n. 75 LET NME$="JANE DOE"
   o. admissible
   p. 85 LET D$="DEPT#7"
   q. 90 LET M$="MONTHLY RENT"
   r. admissible

3. **a.** 10 PRINT "SO-AND-SO"
   b. admissible
   c. admissible
   d. 25 PRINT SPC$; X
   e. admissible
   f. admissible
   g. 40 PRINT WDTH
   h. admissible

4. **a.** RESULT 12 **b.** AMOUNT= 108 **c.** RESULT−2
   d. RESULT 5 **e.** VOLUME 200
   　　　　　　　　　VOLUME 200
   f. LIST PRICE 45 **g.** BOBBY LOVES **h.** 1
   　　DISCOUNT 4.5 　　　MARY. 　　　　　 3
   　　SELLING PRICE 40.5

432   Appendix J   Answers to Selected Problems

5. a.

	A	B	C
10	1	2	1
20	1	2	3
30	4	2	3
40	4	5	3
50	4	20	2
60	2	20	11
70	2	20	11

b.

	N	Output
10	1	1
20	2	2
30	6	6
40	42	42
50	42	

c.

	X	Y	Z	Output
100	0	0	0	
110	0	7	0	
120	0	7	7	
130	0	7	7	7
140	7	7	7	
150	7	343	7	
160	7	343	7	343
170	7	343	7	

6. a.

	S	A	Output
10	0	25	
20	25	25	25
30	50	25	50
40	25	25	25
50	25	25	

b.

	X	Y	Output
100	1.5	0	
110	1.5	0.6	
120	1.5	0.6	.6
130	−1.5	0.6	
140	−1.5	0.6	−1.5
150	−1.5	0.6	.6
160	−1.5	0.6	

c.

	N	C	S	G	P	Output
10	130	0	0	0	0	
20	130	3	0	0	0	
30	130	3	3.6	0	0	
40	130	3	3.6	468	0	SALES 468
50	130	3	3.6	468	78	PROFIT 78
60	130	3	3.6	468	78	

d.

	A	P	Output
100	0	0	NTH POWERS OF 10
110	10	10	
120	10	10	FOR N=1 10
130	10	100	
140	10	100	FOR N=2 100
150	10	1000	
160	10	1000	FOR N=3 1000
170	10	10000	
180	10	10000	FOR N=4 10000
190	10	10000	
200	10	10000	

■ Section 3.10

1. F   **2.** T   **3.** F   **4.** F   **5.** T   **6.** F   **7.** T   **8.** F
9. F   **10.** T   **11.** F   **12.** F   **13.** F   **14.** F   **15.** T   **16.** T

Section 4.10

1.
```
100 LET A=14
110 LET B=30
120 LET S=A+B
130 PRINT "SUM IS";S
140 END
```
Output: SUM IS 44

2.
```
100 LET X=5
120 LET Y=20
125 LET S=X+Y
130 PRINT "X+Y=";S
140 END
```
Output: X+Y= 25

3.
```
110 LET P=120
120 LET D=0.1*P
130 LET C=P-D
140 PRINT "DISCOUNT";D
150 PRINT "COST";C
160 END
```
Output: DISCOUNT 12
COST 108

4.
```
100 LET L$="AVERAGE"
110 LET A=9
120 LET B=7
130 LET M=(A+B)/2
140 PRINT L$;M
150 END
```
Output: AVERAGE 8

5. Syntax: 30 LET D=23000
Programming: 40 LET R=0.06
Syntax: 50 LET A=R*D

Output: ANSWER IS 1380

6. Programming: 50 LET A=(N1+N2)/2
Syntax: 60 PRINT "AVERAGE IS";A

Output: AVERAGE IS 19.5

7. Programming:
```
20 T=5 : REM T=TAX RATE
30 P=120 : REM P=PRICE
```
Output: TOTAL COST: 126

8. Syntax and programming:
60 LET X=-B/A

Output:
SOLUTION IS -6.28571

9. Programming: 155 LET T$=A$
170 LET B$=T$

Output: A$=STOCK
B$=BOND
A$=BOND
B$=STOCK

10. Syntax: quotes missing in lines 150 and 170
Syntax: insert a semicolon before T in lines 150 and 170.
Programming: 165 LET T=V*R

Output: TAX ON FIRST CAR IS 297
TAX ON SECOND CAR IS 376.2

Section 4.11

1. T **2.** T **3.** T **4.** T **5.** F **6.** F **7.** T **8.** F
9. T **10.** F **11.** F **12.** F **13.** F **14.** F **15.** T **16.** T

Section 5.2

1. 120 LET A=100*(1.06)^X
5. 120 LET A=X/19.2
9. 120 LET A=198+.15*(X-1800)
14. 120 LET A=X/1.8045
18. 120 LET A=(4*X/3.14159)^0.5

3. 120 LET A=X+0.045*X
7. 120 LET A=X/(52*40)
12. 120 LET A=X/133.84
16. 120 LET A=(1.8045/133.84)*X
20. 120 LET A=X/2.54

Section 5.3

1. T **2.** F **3.** F **4.** F **5.** F **6.** T **7.** F **8.** F **9.** F

Section 6.3

1.
a.			b.	
1	1		1	1
2	3		2	2
4	7		3	6
8	15		4	24
16	31		5	120
			6	720

c.			d.	
1	50		1	
2	25		1	
3	12		2	
4	6		3	
5	3		5	
6	1		8	
7	0			

e.			f.	
A	B	C	10	
B	A	C	2	
C	A	B	0	
A	C	B		
B	C	A		
C	B	A		

2. a, b, d, and f are true.

3. **a.** If A < B, control is transferred to line 10. Infinite loop.
  b. Line 21 will be executed next whether or not X < X − B.
  c. Delete the comma. Syntax error.
  d. OK must be quoted. Syntax error.
  e. "NOT DONE" is not a proper condition. Syntax error.
  f. Change WHILE to IF. Syntax error.

4. **a.** Interchange the statements in lines 30 and 40.
  b. Change line 140 to 140 WHILE A <> B.
    Insert line 165 INPUT A,B.
  c. Change the line number of line 50 to 25.
    Interchange the statements in lines 60 and 70.

Section 6.4

1. F **2.** T **3.** F **4.** F **5.** T **6.** T **7.** T **8.** F **9.** F **10.** F

Section 7.3

1. a. BASEBALL'S HALL OF FAME **b.** PASCAGOULA RIVER
   COOPERSTOWN, NY 13326   BAYOU COUNTRY, U.S.A.
   c. 5 TIMES 8 = 40   **d.** HAPPY
                               HAPPY
                                 HOLIDAY

   e. 0   5   10   15   20   **f.** IF A= 5 A+2= 7
          25   30   35   FINI   IF A= 10 A+2= 12
                                              IF A= 15 A+2= 17

2. a. 10 PRINT X;"/";Y;"=";X/Y
   c. 30 PRINT "X -";Y;"= ";-X
   e. 50 PRINT "DEPT. NO. ";Y+Y+X
3. a. Prints TEAFORTWO
   b. 30 PRINT "Sleeping ";
        40 PRINT "Bear ";
   c. 50 PRINT "7A";
   d. 175 PRINT

Section 7.5

1. a.
```
SALES        COMMISSION
-----        ----------
2000         200
2500         250
3000         300
3500         350
4000         400
4500         450
5000         500
```

b. BASIC BASIC BASIC   BASIC

c. 1234567890   **d.** 7777777
       0   7
        -1   7
         -2   7
          -3   7
           -4   7
       THAT'S ENOUGH   7

e. 1234567890   **f.** X   X^2
       *
        *   1   1
         *   2   4
          *   3   9
                            4   16

2. a. 10 PRINT TAB(6);"B";TAB(9);3
   b. 20 PRINT X;SPC(13);2*X;SPC(13);3*X;SPC(13);4*X
   c. 30 PRINT TAB((80-N)/2);"...name..." where N = number of characters in *name*.
   d. 40 PRINT 0;SPC(10);0;SPC(10);0;SPC(10);
           0;SPC(10);0;SPC(10);0;SPC(10);" 0"
   e. 50 PRINT "0 ";SPC(10);0;SPC(10);
           0;SPC(10);0;SPC(10);0;SPC(10);0;SPC(10);0

Section 7.7

1. a. 9.00
4.50
2.25
1.13

b. RIVERBOAT
      BOATSWAIN

c. 1/8=12.5 CENTS
3/8=37.5 CENTS
5/8=62.5 CENTS
7/8=87.5 CENTS

d. TIME 1 A= 0.00
TIME 2 A= 0.01
TIME 3 A= 0.01

e. 123456789
23.60
23.6

f. POPEYE

g. BOBBY LOVES JUDITH
JUDI LOVES BOB

h. TAX-RATE 15   TAX-RATE 25   TAX-RATE 35

Section 7.8

1. F   **2.** F   **3.** F   **4.** T   **5.** T   **6.** F   **7.** T
8. F   **9.** T   **10.** T   **11.** F   **12.** F   **13.** T   **14.** T   **15.** T

Section 8.3

1. a, b, d, and f are true.

2. a. Insert line 35: 35 IF N = 0 THEN 30
Delete line 50.
  b. Change line 40 to 40 IF (R = 7) OR (R = 11) THEN PRINT "OK".
  c. Change line 40 to 40 IF (2 < Y) AND (Y < 8) THEN PRINT "BETWEEN".
  d. Change line 40 to 40 IF X>=0 AND X <=100 AND X <> 50 THEN PRINT "OK".

3. a. −1   **b.** 5   **c.** SMITH   **d.** 5   **e.** 52
            −5   THAT'S ALL

Section 8.12

1. T   **2.** F   **3.** T   **4.** T   **5.** T   **6.** F   **7.** T   **8.** F
9. F   **10.** T   **11.** F   **12.** F   **13.** T   **14.** F   **15.** F

Section 9.2

1. a. 4   b. 5   c. TIMES THROUGH LOOP= 2
      5   1
      6   −3
   d. +++///   e. LOOP   f. No output
   g. 123456789   h. ZZZZZZZ   i. ITEM1 ITEM2 ITEM3 ITEM4
      V   V   Z   1   2   3   4
       V   V   Z
        V   V   Z
         V V   Z
          V   Z
                     ZZZZZZZ

2. a. Syntax error: 50 NEXT N
   b. Programming error: 25 LET C=0
      Delete line 40.
   c. Programming error:
      40 INPUT Y
      50 LET S=S+Y
   d. Programming error: STEP S is admissible but the step value cannot be changed within the loop.
      30 LET S=0
      40 FOR N=1 TO 5
      50 LET S=S+N
      60 PRINT S

Section 9.4

1. a. 2 3 2 3 2 3   b. 13 16 11 14
   c. 2 3 4 5   d. 108   e. 7 7 7
      3 4 5   9 9 9
      4 5   11 11 11
      5   13 13 13

2. a. Syntax error: interchange lines 50 and 60.
   b. Programming error: include STEP −1 in lines 20 and 30.
   c. Programming error: 30 IF I<J THEN PRINT I; J
   d. Programming error: 30 IF R<=C THEN PRINT "X";
                         40 IF R>C THEN PRINT " ";

Section 9.5

1. F   2. F   3. T   4. F   5. T   6. F   7. T
8. F   9. F   10. T   11. F

Appendix J Answers to Selected Problems

■ Section 10.2

1. a.   BASIC   (The first B displayed is in row 2, column 40.)
            BASIC   BASIC
    BASIC   BASIC

b. IBM   (The first I displayed is in row 1, column 21.)

     IBM

      IBM

     IBM

    IBM

c. H   H   (The first H displayed is in row 15, column 8.)
    H   H
    H   H
    HHHHH
    H   H
    H   H
    H   H

d. The word GOOD is displayed successively 6 times on lines 10 through 15, each beginning in column 15. After all 6 GOOD's are displayed, the screen is cleared. A similar block of GRIEF's is then displayed on the same line but beginning in column 20 and the screen is cleared again. This same sequence is repeated 50 times.

■ Section 10.5

1. a.   NORMAL   **b.** BASIC
        NORMAL ← (normal)   BASIC
        NORMAL   ⎢BASIC⎥ ← (blinking)
        NORMAL   BASIC
        NORMAL   BASIC
             REVERSE
             REVERSE   (The first B is displayed in row 11, column 38.)
    (reverse → REVERSE
     image)   REVERSE
             REVERSE

c. The 10-row by 10-column block in the upper left corner of the display area is white and the rest of the screen is black.

d. The first 16 rows are colored by using color codes 0–15. The rest of the display area is white.

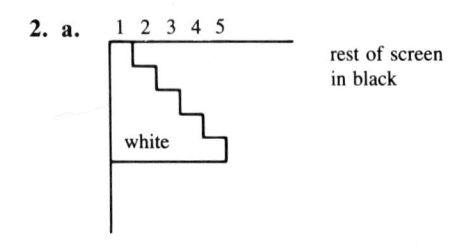

2. a.   1 2 3 4 5
                          rest of screen
                          in black

         white

b.

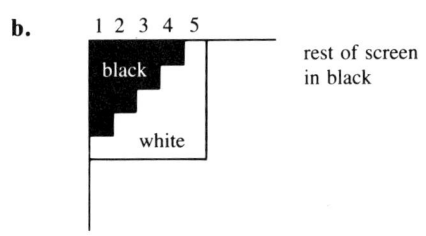

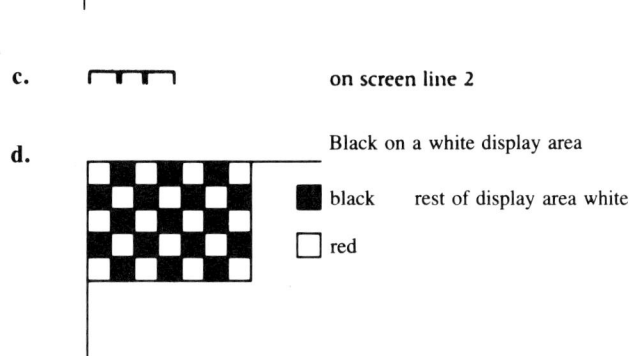

```
  1 2 3 4 5
 ┌─────┐
 │black│      rest of screen
 │     │      in black
 │white│
 └─────┘
```

c. ⌐⌐⌐   on screen line 2

d.   Black on a white display area

■ black   rest of display area white
□ red

■ Section 10.6

1. T **2.** T **3.** F **4.** F **5.** F **6.** T **7.** T **8.** T
9. F **10.** F **11.** T **12.** F **13.** T **14.** F **15.** T

■ Section 11.2

1. **a.** 2 −3   **b.** CATWOMAN   **c.** 7   **d.** BAD VALUE: 22
       5   0   3   BAD VALUE: 84
       0 −5   18
                                         −5
                                          4

2. **a.** Change line 30 to
       `30 DATA 1,A`
   b. Replace ; in line 10 by ,
   c. Replace HELLO in line 20 by "HELLO"
   d. Change line 50 to
       `50 DATA "TOM DOOLEY, JR"`

3. **a.** Interchange the statements in lines 30 and 40.
   b. `15 LET S=0`
       `16 LET N=0`
       `40 LET N=N+1`
       `55 READ X`
   c. `130 READ V`
       `140 WHILE V<>999`
       `155 READ V`

Section 11.4

1. a. 9 b. 3 c. ROBINHEAD d. 10 20 30 e. ALLEN 40
      3   5   10 20 30   ALLEN 40
      5   3
            5

Section 11.5

1. T   2. F   3. F   4. F   5. T   6. F   7. T   8. T   9. T

Section 12.2

1. a. 4 2 16   b. 2   c. 1 1   d. 8
      3 -7 -5   2   2 3
                   -2   3 6
                    5   4 10

Section 12.4

1. a. 5   b. A IS AN ARTICLE.
      5   AND IS A CONJUNCTION.
             BUT IS A CONJUNCTION.
             OR IS A CONJUNCTION.
             THE IS AN ARTICLE.

Section 12.5

1. T   2. F   3. F   4. F   5. F   6. T   7. F   8. F   9. F

Section 13.2

1. a. 9   b. 6   c. 18   d. 26   e. −43   f. 1200   g. 124   h. −124
   i. 123   j. −123   k. 4   l. 3

2. a. 4   b. 5   c. 6   d. −4   e. 2865   f. 2860   g. 2900   h. 3000
   i. 2864.714   j. 4   k. 4   l. 59

3. a. 0   8   b. 1.1   1
      1   8   1.21   1
      2   6   1.331   1
      3   2   1.4641   1
      4   4
   c. XX
      XXXX
      XX

```
        d. X          e. XX              f. 1   3   7   9   21
           X             X
           X             XXX
           X             X
           X             X
           X
           X
           X
        g. *          h. 13.990  13.99
           * *           13.993  13.99
           * * * * *     13.996  14.00
                         13.999  14.00
```

4. **a.** `10 IF ABS(A+B)=ABS(A)+ABS(B) THEN PRINT "EQUAL"`
   c. `30 IF (INT(X)=X) AND (X>0) THEN 300`
   e. `50 IF (INT(L/2)=L/2) AND (INT(L/25)=L/25) THEN PRINT`
5. **b.** `20 LET X=INT(1000*X+0.5)/1000`
   d. `40 LET X=1000*INT(X/1000+0.5)`

■ Section 13.4

1. **a.** Programming error: `50 LET V=FNZ(X)`
   b. Programming error: `20 DEF FNS(X)=X^2`
   c. Syntax error: `20 DEF FNB(S)=200+0.02*S` and `40 LET B=FNB(S)`
   d. Programming error:
   `30 DEF FNR(N)=X/N`

2. **a.** 200   **b.** .5 2 .5   **c.** 0 3   **d.** 1 2   3 4   **e.** 10
      1400   1 4   .5 1 1.5 2   15
      0   2 5   20
                                        3 6   25

3. **a.** `125 DEF FNT(L)=L+0.05*L`
   b. `130 DEF FNI(R)=100*(R/100)*(1/4)`
   c. `135 DEF FNC(L,W)=(L*W/9)*12.95`
   d. `140 DEF FNT(E)=E*(27/1000)`
   e. `145 DEF FNF(C)=9/5*C+32`
   f. `150 DEF FNC(F)=5/9*(F-32)`
   g. `155 DEF FNM(F)=F/5280`
   h. `160 DEF FNM(K)=K/1.6093`
   i. `165 DEF FNK(M)=1.6093*M`
   j. `170 DEF FNR(X)=INT(1000*X+0.5)/1000`
   k. `175 DEF FNS(D,T)=D/T`
   l. `180 DEF FNS(X,Y)=X-(X*Y/100)`
   m. `185 DEF FNC(X,Y)=X/15*Y`
   n. `190 DEF FNA(R)=3.14159*R^2`
   o. `195 DEF FNV(R)=4/3*3.14159*R^3`
   p. `200 DEF FNS(A)=SIN(3.14159/180*A)`

■ Section 13.5

1. T   2. T   3. F   4. F   5. F   6. F   7. F
8. F   9. T   10. T   11. T   12. T

Section 14.4

1. a. CYBER b. Z TO A c. CONSULTATION d. BIOPHYSICS
   e. Great f. ADD   g. 3 STEP
      Salt   LIST   2 LIST
      Lake   STOP   4 STOP
      Desert,   STEP   1 ADD
      Utah

2. a. 10 PRINT LEFT$(A$,1)
   b. 15 PRINT MID$(A$,2,1)
   c. 20 PRINT RIGHT$(A$,1)
   d. 25 PRINT LEFT$(A$,3)
   e. 30 PRINT RIGHT$(A$,3)
   f. 35 PRINT LEFT$(A$,1);RIGHT$(A$,1)
   g. 40 IF LEN(A$)=LEN(B$) THEN N=N+1
   h. 45 IF LEFT$(A$,1)=RIGHT$(A$,1) THEN PRINT LEFT$(A$,1)
   i. 50 IF LEFT$(A$,1)=MID$(A$,2,1) THEN X$="SAME"
   j. 55 IF INSTR(A$,",")>0 THEN PRINT "COMMA"
   k. 60 IF INSTR(A$," ")=0 THEN PRINT "NO SPACES"
   l. 65 LET B$=LEFT$(A$,N)
   m. 70 LET B$=RIGHT$(A$,1)+LEFT$(A$,1)
   n. 75 LET T$=MID$(S$,2,1)+LEFT$(S$,1)+RIGHT$(S$,LEN(S$)−2)
   o. 80 LET F$=LEFT$(G$,3)+RIGHT$(H$,3)
   p. 85 IF LEFT$(A$,1)+MID$(B$,2,1)+MID$(C$,3,1)="YES" THEN PRINT "OK"
   q. 90 MID$(A$,4,1)="Y"

Section 14.6

1. a. M   b. CATDOG   c. HARRY
      A   1010   ALICE
             BEASTBEAST   LAST
                             LAST

Section 14.9

1. a. 31+31= 62   b. E 5   c. 7 7   d. 0123456789:
   e. 42 WINS AND 21 LOSSES GIVES A PERCENTAGE OF .667
   f. CORRECT   g. 9876543210   h. COUNT: 47

Section 14.10

1. F 2. F 3. T 4. T 5. T 6. F 7. F 8. F
9. T 10. T 11. T 12. T 13. F 14. F 15. T

Section 15.4

1. **a.** 5 **b.** TO BE OR **c.** 8 **d.** IRANGATE
      4
   e. PAYCHECK, JOHN **f.** SAM
      DENVER, JOHN   JESS
      JOHN, ELTON   SANDI
      CASH, JOHN

2. **a.** DIM statement needed.
   b. Array A is redimensioned at line 30 after being implicitly dimensioned by line 10.
   c. Values of L$(6) through L$(10) are lost.
   d. 415 LET L=A(1)
      420 FOR J=2 TO 10
      430 IF L<A(J) THEN LET L=A(J)

Section 15.6

1. **a.** 1 4 9 16 **b.** 2 4 6 **c.** 2 3 5 **d.** YYYY
                                                     NYYY
                                                     NNYY
                                                     NNNY

   e. DEVILS: HOOFERS: SAINTS:
      ED   ANN   DEB
      JANE   JIM   DOT
      JOHN   RON   RUSS
      SUE   RUTH   TIM

2. **a.** Interchange lines 220 and 230.
   b. Insert:
      215 LET T=A(R1,C)
      Change line 230 to
      230 LET A(R2,C)=T

Section 15.7

1. F   2. F   3. F   4. T   5. F   6. F
7. T   8. T   9. F   10. T   11. F

Section 16.4

1. T   2. F   3. F   4. F   5. F   6. F   7. F   8. T

Section 17.3

1. a. J. D. SLOANE
    EXCESS: 3000

    A. B. CARTER
    EXCESS: 2400

    I. O. ULSTER
    EXCESS: 2000

b. J. D. SLOANE   565
    R. M. PETERS   265
    A. B. CARTER   505
    I. O. ULSTER   465

2. a. SAM
    GREG
    MARY

b. JOAN   PASS
    SAM   PASS
    GREG   FAIL
    MARY   FAIL
    MARK   PASS

Section 17.8

1. F   **2.** F   **3.** F   **4.** T   **5.** T   **6.** F   **7.** F   **8.** F

Section 18.3

1. a. 80   **b.** 70   **c.** 30   **d.** 0   **e.** 100   **f.** 10
2. a. T   **b.** T   **c.** either   **d.** either   **e.** T   **f.** T

Section 18.6

1. a. 10 PRINT 4*RND
  b. 20 PRINT 6*RND+5
  c. 30 PRINT 8*RND-5
  d. 40 PRINT INT(7*RND)+6
  e. 50 PRINT 2*INT(5*RND)
  f. 60 PRINT 2*INT(5*RND)+1
2. a. 1, 2 (equally likely)
  b. 0
  c. −2, −1, 0, 1, 2 (equally likely)
  d. 2, 3, 4 (3 about half the time; 2 and 4 each about one-fourth the time)
  e. 2, 3, 4, . . . , 12 (not equally likely—simulates rolling a pair of dice)
  f. 1, 2, 3, 4, 6, 9 (not equally likely)
3. ONE OF EACH, TWO HEADS, and TWO TAILS will be displayed about the same number of times. In practice, ONE OF EACH will occur about half the time.

Section 18.10

1. T   **2.** F   **3.** T   **4.** F   **5.** F   **6.** F   **7.** F   **8.** T   **9.** F   **10.** T

Section 19.3

1. a. A row of 10 white 6 × 6 blocks, five points apart.
  b. A block letter L with upper-left corner at (30, 70).

c. Same as part (b).
   d. A white arch created by drawing 200 line segments. Line 30 draws the left half and line 40 the right.

■ Section 19.12

    1. F   **2.** F   **3.** T   **4.** F   **5.** T   **6.** T
    7. T   **8.** F   **9.** F   **10.** F   **11.** F

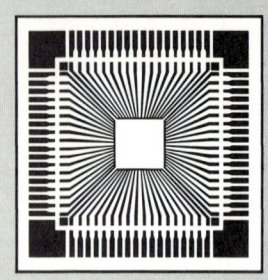

Index

Absolute value function **(ABS)**, 205
Action parameters (graphics), 382
Actual argument, 220
Addition:
　numbers, 24
　strings, 232
Advanced BASIC, 37, 400
Airline-flight-information examples, 254, 261
Algorithm, 9
Alphabetizing, 281
Alt key, 158, 413
Ampersand symbol (&), 86
AND operator, 97
ANSI (American National Standards Institute), 109
Apostrophe symbol ('), 30
Append file, 304
APPEND modifier, 304
Applications program, 7
Approximate representation of numbers, 64, 118, 134, 209
Arctangent function **(ATN)**, 204
Area under curve problems, 342
Argument of a function, 219, 227
Arithmetic and logic unit (ALU), 4
Arithmetic operations, 24
Arithmetic progression problem, 72
Arithmetic tutorial problems, 106, 137, 200
Array:
　higher dimensional, 273
　one-dimensional, 249, 253
　two-dimensional, 269
Array entry, 250
Array size for **GET** statement, 381
ASC function, 240
ASCII (American Standard Code for Information Interchange), 156, 237
Aspect value, 370
Assignment statement. See **LET** statement
AUTO command, 413

Backslash symbol (\):
　in format specifications, 86
　integer division, 25
Backspace key, 38, 41
Bank loan example, 116
Bar chart example (graphics), 358
Baseball-statistics problems, 49, 216
BASIC, 6
BASIC character set, 237
BASIC command, 292, 311, 400
BASIC commands (table), 425
BASIC compiler, 6
BASIC constants, 22, 23
BASIC expression, 24
BASIC file, 291
BASIC functions. See Functions
BASIC functions (table), 427
BASIC interpreter, 6
BASIC language, 6
BASIC program, 27
BASIC prompt (Ok), 37
BASIC reserved words (table), 411
BASIC statement, 27
BASIC statements (table), 421
BASIC subroutine, 185
BASIC syntax, 21
BASICA command, 292, 311, 400
Batting-average problems, 49, 216, 332
Bell character, 157
Binary search, 286
Birth-statistics example, 297
Bit, 310
Blinking characters, 155
Body of loop, 132
Bohm, Corrado, 121
Booting DOS, 401
Break key, 44
Breakeven volume, 80
Bubble sort, 249, 279, 281
Buffer, 310
Buffer size, 311
Bug, 28
Built-in functions. See Functions
Byte, 310

Calculator, 4, 60
Calling a subroutine, 187
Caps Lock key, 37
Car-loan repayment problem, 90
Car-rental examples, 52, 221
Card shuffling problem, 337
Carriage return. See **RETURN**
Cartesian coordinates problems (graphics), 396
Cassette BASIC, 37, 399
Cassette tape recorder, 4
CDBL function, 204
Central Processing Unit (CPU), 4
Chapin, Ned, 109
Charter-service example, 189
Charter-service problem, 193
Checkbook-balance problem, 102
Chi-square goodness-of-fit test, 341
CHR$ function, 157, 240
CINT function, 207
CIRCLE statement:
　aspect value, 370
　drawing arcs, 366
　drawing ellipses, 371
　a first example, 364
　general form, 372
　last point referenced, 373
　radial line segments, 368
　rules governing, 372
CLOSE statement, 293
CLS statement, 39, 146, 414
Coding a program, 46
Coin tossing example, 326
Coin tossing problems, 332
Collating sequence, 237
Collating sequence example, 241
Colon (:), 32
Color-mixing example, 175
Color/Graphics Monitor Adapter, 152
COLOR statement (graphics):
　colors, 349
　a first example, 349
　general form, 351
　rules governing, 351
COLOR statement (text mode):

COLOR statement (text mode): (*continued*)
　blinking displays, 155
　a first example, 153
　general form, 155
　reverse image displays, 154
　table of colors, 153
Combining strings, 232
Comma:
　on a file, 294
　in format specification, 86
　in **INPUT** statement, 52, 54
　in **PRINT** statement, 63, 76
　in **READ** statement, 165
Comments, 30, 32
Comments. See **REM** statement
Commission-on-sales problems, 49, 55, 71, 114, 173, 224
Comparing numerical expressions, 62
Comparing string expressions, 63, 238
Comparison of sorting times, 285
Compiler, 6
Compound-interest example, 68, 112
Compound-interest problems, 50, 55, 72, 119, 142
Compound-logical expressions, 97
Computer, 1
Computer hardware, 5
Computer peripherals, 5
Computer program, 5, 9, 27
Computer software, 7
Computer system:
　definition of, 1
　hardware, 5
　peripherals, 5
　schematic, 6
　software, 7
Concatenation, 232
Conditional transfer, 61, 93, 105, 194
Constants, 22, 23
Continuation line, 40
Control statements:
　FOR, 131
　GOSUB, 185
　GOTO, 59
　IF, 61, 95

446

Index **447**

Control statements:
 (*continued*)
 IF-THEN-ELSE, 95
 NEXT, 131
 ON GOSUB, 194
 ON GOTO, 102
 RETURN, 185
 WEND, 66
 WHILE, 66
Control variable, 133
Conversion functions, 240
Convert functions **(CVI, CVS, CVD),** 314
Coordinates (graphics):
 last point referenced, 353
 relative form, 348
 STEP function, 347
Copying a diskette, 402
Correcting a typing error, 41, 414
Cosine function **(COS),** 204
Counter-controlled loop, 135
Counting examples, 94, 96, 140, 167, 257, 270, 327
Counting problems, 19, 72, 173, 267
Credit card balance problem, 102
Ctrl Break, 44, 60
Ctrl PrtSc, 45
Ctrl-Num Lock, 60, 414
Ctrl-Z character, 297
Currency conversion problems, 56, 71
Cursor, 29, 37
Cursor move, 145
Cursor-moving keys, 414

Data file (random):
 file statements, 310, 312
 first examples, 312, 313
Data file (sequential):
 append file, 304
 file maintenance, 307
 file statements, 292
 first examples, 293
 input file, 293
 output file, 293
Data line. *See* **DATA** statement
Data list, 168
DATA statement:
 a first example, 165
 general form, 168
 quotation marks, 166
 rules governing, 168
 string data, 166
Dataproducts' B-series band printer, 5
Debug, 28
Decimal constant, 22
Decimal expansion problems, 246
Decimal point alignment, 87
DEF FN statement:
 dummy argument, 220
 a first example, 219
 general form, 221
 rules governing, 221
 string functions, 244
Deferred execution mode, 43
DEL command, 404
Delete character, 321
DELETE command, 414

Deleting a program line, 41, 414
Delimiter:
 colon, 32
 comma, 52, 63
 semicolon, 30, 73
Depreciation example, 16
Deutsche conversion problems, 56
Deviation, 205
Dictionary ordering, 238
Difference-table problem, 277
Digits-of-a-number example, 244
DIM statement:
 for one-dimensional arrays, 250, 256
 for two-dimensional arrays, 270
 rules governing, 256
DIR command, 403
Directory of files, 403, 406
Discount-table examples, 134
Disk BASIC, 37, 400
Disk operating system (DOS), 7, 401
Disk storage unit, 1, 4, 291
DISKCOPY command, 402
Diskette, 4
Display characters, 156
Display line, 39, 76
Display screen, 1, 4
Distance to horizon problem, 56
Distance to a line problem, 218
Divisibility, 209
Divisibility problems, 218
Division, 24
Dollar sign symbol ($):
 in format specification, 86
 in string variable, 23
DOS commands (table), 404
Double precision variable, 23
Doubly subscripted variable, 269
Drive-in-teller example, 9
Driving-expense-statistics problem, 57
Drunkard's walk problem, 332
Dummy argument, 220
Dynamic storage allocation, 257

E format, 22
Earnings report problem, 287
Eckert, J. Presper Jr., 3
Electric-bill problem, 174
Electronic computer, 4
Ellipses, 372
ELSE clause, 95
Employee information problems, 183, 200
Employee-file-update example, 304
Empty string, 28, 78
End of data (EOD) tag, 112, 167
End of file **(EOF)** function, 297
End of file mark, 297
END statement, 28
Enter key, 37
Entering a program, 38

EQV operator, 98
ERASE statement, 256
Error:
 correction of, 41, 414
 fatal, 168
 run time, 43
 syntax, 42
Error messages, 42
Error trapping, 307
Exact change problem, 217
Exclamation symbol (!), 86
Executing a program, 41
Exponential form **(nEm),** 22
Exponential function **(EXP),** 204
Exponentiation operator, 24
Expression:
 arithmetic, 24
 BASIC, 24
 logical, 97
 relational, 62, 63, 238
External (secondary) storage device, 4, 291, 401

Factorial problem, 138, 192
Fatal error, 168
Federal tax problems, 55, 102
FIELD statement, 311
File. *See* Data file
File buffer, 310
File buffer size, 311
File maintenance, 301
File names, 292, 405
File number, 292
File statements:
 CLOSE, 293
 FIELD, 311
 GET#, 312
 IF EOF(n), 297
 INPUT#, 293
 LINE INPUT#, 298
 LSET, 311
 OPEN, 293, 304, 310
 PRINT#, 293
 PUT#, 311
 RSET, 311
 WRITE#, 292, 295
File update examples, 301, 304, 320
FILES command, 402, 406
Financial report examples, 177
FIX function, 207
Floating-point constant, 22
Floppy disk unit. *See* Diskette
Flowchart, 107
Flowchart symbols:
 ANSI standard, 109
 READ statement, 168
 table of, 109
Flowcharting, 109
FOR loop:
 body of a loop, 132
 control variable, 133
 counter controlled, 135
 a first example, 131
 flow diagram, 133
 general form, 133
 guidelines, 135
 initial value, 133
 iteration count, 135
 nested, 138
 range of a loop, 132
 step value, 133
 terminal value, 133

Formal parameter, 219
FORMAT command, 402
Format specification, 85
Formatting characters, 85, 86
Formatting a diskette, 402
Frequency-table examples, 257, 283, 327
Frequency-table problems, 173, 267, 289
Function keys, 38, 41
 table, 415
Functions:
 argument of, 219, 227
 built-in, 204, 227, 240
 conversion, 240
 formal parameter, 219
 numerical, 203
 string, 227, 244
 string related, 227, 244
 trigonometric, 204, 213
 user-defined, 219, 244

Gas station promotion example, 217
Geometric-progression problem, 72
GET statement (graphics), 378
GET# statement (files), 312
Glassware promotion problem, 217
Golf-tournament-results example, 169
Goodness-of-fit test, 341
GOSUB statement, 185
GOTO statement, 59
Grade report problems, 265
Graphics:
 high-resolution, 393
 medium-resolution, 346
Graphics examples:
 bar chart, 358
 colored rectangle, 356
 concentric circles, 395
 concurrent lines, 354
 horn of plenty, 367
 kaleidoscope, 359
 moving ball, 385
 Olympic symbol, 364
 rebounding ball, 386
 sectors of a circle, 369
 tangent circles, 365
 triangle, 352
 video game, 387
Greatest common divisor problem, 193
Greatest-integer function **(INT),** 207

Hardcopy output, 45
Hardware, 5
Heron's formula, 50
Heuristic process, 15
High-resolution graphics (Mode 2), 345, 393
Higher-dimensional arrays, 268, 273
Home-mortgage problem, 57
Horn of plenty example (graphics), 367

I/O (input/output) devices, 4
IBM PC keyboard, 38
IBM personal computer, 1

Index

IF statement:
 to compare strings, 63, 238
 to describe loops, 61
 first examples, 61, 94
 flowchart symbol, 109
 general forms, 94, 95
 selection, 93
IF-THEN-ELSE statement, 95
Immediate execution mode, 43
IMP operator, 98
Income tax problems, 55, 102
Indenting a program, 61, 132
Initial values of a variable, 28
INKEY$ variable, 149
Input device, 4
Input file, 293
Input list, 55
Input prompt (?), 51
INPUT statement:
 for files, 293
 a first example, 51
 flowchart symbol, 109, 169
 general form, 55
 for string variables, 53
INPUT# statement, 293
Input/output specification, 11, 14, 45
Input-process-output diagram:
 for a computer system, 6
 a first example, 2
Ins key, 415
INSTR function, 233
INT function, 207
Integer constant, 22
Integer division, 25
Integer variable, 23
Integrated circuit (IC), 4
Interest-calculation examples:
 compound interest, 68, 104, 112
 simple interest, 46, 55, 104
Interpreter, 6
Inventory problems:
 using files, 301, 323
 report generation, 182, 223, 287
Inventory-file-update example, 301
Investment problems, 72, 119
Invoice problem, 266
IRS value, 60
Iteration count, 135

Jacopini, Guiseppe, 121

Kaleidoscope example (graphics), 359
Kemeny, John G., 6
KEY statements, 45
Keyboard, 1, 4, 38
Keyword, 21
KILL command, 402, 409
Knights'-move-simulation problems, 337
Kurtz, Thomas E., 6

Largest/smallest number examples, 14, 109, 169
Last point referenced, 353
Law of cosines problem, 218
Law of sines example, 214
LEFT$ function, 228
LEN function, 227
LEN specifier, 310

Length of file (LOF) function, 317
Length of program line, 40
Length of a string, 23
LET statement, 27
Level of refinement, 12
Line feed character, 294
LINE INPUT# statement, 298
Line number (ln), 21, 27
Line printer, 4
LINE statement:
 a first example, 352
 general form, 357
 plotting rectangles, 354
 rules governing, 357
 STEP function, 354
Line width, 75
Linear interpolation problem, 267
List. See Array
LIST command, 40, 408
LLIST command, 45
LOAD command, 407
Loan-repayment example, 116
Loan-repayment problems, 57, 90
LOC function, 317
LOCATE statement:
 a first example, 145
 general form, 148
Logarithm function (LOG), 204
Logical expression, 97
Logical operators, 98
Loops:
 body of, 132
 counter-controlled, 135
 a first example, 59
 iteration count, 135
 nested, 138
 range of, 132
 using FOR statement, 131
 using IF statement, 61
 using WHILE statement, 66
Lower- to upper-case conversion examples, 241, 242, 282
Lower- to upper-case subroutine, 242
LPRINT, 45
LPT1:, 75
LSET statement, 311

M-by-N array, 269
Machine infinity, 43
Machine language, 6
Magic-square problem, 276
Magnetic disk, 4
Magnetic tape unit, 4
Mailing list problems, 309, 323
Maintaining a file, 301
Make functions (MKI$, MKS$, MKD$), 314
Mauchly, John W., 3
Max/min examples, 14, 109, 169
Max/min problems, 143
Maximum length of a string, 23
Maximum-profit example, 189
Maximum-profit problems, 193
Median, 288
Medium-resolution background colors, 349

Medium-resolution graphics (Mode 1), 346
Medium-resolution palettes, 349
Memory unit, 4
Menu-driven program:
 algorithm for, 102
 definition of, 102
 examples, 104, 177, 196
 problems, 106, 183, 199, 301, 309, 323
 using ON GOSUB, 195
 using ON GOTO, 105, 177
Messages (strings), 29
Method of stepwise refinement, 12, 45, 119
Microcomputer, 4
Microprocessor, 4
Microsoft® BASIC, 6
MID$ function, 230
MID$ statement, 231
MOD operator, 25
Modular arithmetic problem, 143
Modularization, 11, 45
Module, 11
Monochrome Display and Parallel Printer Adapter, 152
Monte Carlo method, 339
Monthly payment formula, 57
Monthly-sales-report problem, 218
Mortgage problem, 57
Motion (graphics):
 direction, 385
 a first example, 383
 motion algorithm, 383
 rebound, 387
 speed, 383, 385, 386
Multiple-statement lines, 32
Multiplication, 24
Multiplication table problem, 137

NAME command, 408
Negation, 24
Nested FOR loops, 138
Nested WHILE loops, 69
NEW command, 38
New-product-simulation example, 334
New-product-survey problems, 308
Newborn-birth-statistics example, 297
NEXT statement, 131
Normal screen, 153
NOT operator, 97
Null string, 28, 78
Num Lock key, 60
Numeric code example, 241
Numeric codes, 156, 237
 table, 417
Numeric keypad, 38, 158
Numerical constant, 22
Numerical functions, 203
Numerical variable. See Variables

Olympic symbol example (graphics), 364
ON ERROR GOTO statement, 307

ON GOSUB statement, 194
ON GOTO statement, 102
One-dimensional array, 249, 253
OPEN statement, 293, 304, 310
Operating system, 7, 401
Operational symbols:
 arithmetic, 24
 logical, 98
 priorities, 24, 26, 99, 100
 relational, 62, 238
 string, 232
Opinion-poll example, 270
OPTION BASE statement, 253
OR operator, 63, 97
Ordering sequence, 237
Ordering sequence example, 241
Output device, 4
Output file, 293
Output format, 85

PAINT statement:
 boundary, 373
 a first example, 373
 general form, 376
 last point referenced, 376
 rules governing, 376
Paint-calculation example, 65
Palettes, 349
Parameter, 219
Parentheses, 25, 98, 99
PC keyboard, 1, 4, 38
Percent symbol (%), 23, 86
Peripherals, 5
Personal computer (PC), 1
Personnel file example, 304
Personnel information problems, 183, 200, 307
Picture elements, 346
Pie charts, 370
Pixel, 346
Pocket calculator, 4
Political survey problems, 173, 182, 265
Pound symbol (#):
 in format specification, 85
 to specify double precision, 23
Power supply, 2
Precedence. See Priority of operations
Prime number example, 210
Prime number problems, 218
Print positions, 76
Print screen (PrtSc) key, 38, 45
PRINT statement:
 comma as delimiter, 63, 76
 files, 293
 a first example, 29
 flowchart symbol, 109
 to produce a RETURN, 52
 semicolon as delimiter, 30, 77
 strings (messages), 29
 TAB and SPC, 80
PRINT USING statement:
 a first example, 85
 general form, 85
 numerical format specification, 85

Index   449

PRINT USING statement:
  (*continued*)
  repeated format, 89
  string format specification, 86
Print zones, 76
PRINT# statement, 293
Printer output, 45
Printers, 4
Priority of operations, 24, 26, 99, 100
Problem analysis, 11
Problem segmentation, 11, 46
Problem solving principles, 11
Problem solving process, 10
Product-survey problems, 276, 308
Profit-simulation example, 189
Program:
  applications, 7
  BASIC, 27
  computer, 5, 9
  systems, 7
Program statement, 27
Programmer, 5
Programming constructs, 120, 121
Programming error, 43
Programming flowchart, 107
Programming line, 27
Programming process, 45, 46
Property-tax example, 88
Property-tax problem, 49
PSET statement:
  absolute form, 347
  a first example, 347
  general form, 351
  last point referenced, 353
  relative form, 348
  rules governing, 351
  STEP function, 347
Pseudocode, 119
Pseudorandom numbers, 325
Pure cursor move, 145
PUT statement (graphics), 379
PUT statement parameters, 383
PUT# statement (files), 311

Quadratic equation problem, 218
Quality-point-average example, 283
Question mark character (?), 51
Quotation marks for strings:
  DATA statement, 166
  IF statement, 63
  INPUT statement, 53
  LET statement, 28

Radian measure, 56, 204, 213, 366
Random access device, 4
Random access file:
  file statements, 310, 312
  first examples, 312, 313
Random access memory (RAM), 4
Random integers, 333
Random number seed, 328
Random numbers, 325
RANDOMIZE statement, 328
Range of a loop, 132
Rate-of-return example, 30

Read only memory (ROM), 4
READ statement:
  a first example, 165
  flowchart symbol, 168
  general form, 168
  rules governing, 168
  for string variables, 166
Reading from a file, 293
Real variable, 23
Record, 310
Record length, 310
Record locator (LOC) function, 317
Redimension arrays, 256
Relational expression:
  for numerical data, 62
  for string data, 63, 238
Relational symbols, 62, 238
REM statement, 30
Remainder, 25
RENUM command, 413
Repeating a random process, 329
Repetition construct, 121, 124
Reserved words, 22, 411
Reset. *See* System reset
RESTORE statement, 174
RESUME statement, 307
Retrieving a file, 407
RETURN, 29, 52, 78
Return character, 294
Return key. *See* Enter key
RETURN statement, 185
Reverse image, 154
RIGHT$ function, 229
RND function, 325
Roots of numbers, 25, 203
Rounding of numbers, 207, 208
RSET statement, 311
RUN command, 41
Run-time error, 43

Salary examples:
  salary-increase schedule, 140
  salary-report, 63, 173, 187, 258
Salary problems:
  using files, 300, 307
  salary increase, 90, 119, 138
  salary reports, 138, 173, 193
  weekly-pay calculation, 49, 55, 101, 114, 246
Sales-promotion problem, 217
Sales report examples, 177, 205
Sales-report problems, 19, 218, 287
Sales-tax example, 30
SAVE command, 41, 406
Screen display modification example, 150
Screen displays (graphics mode):
  high-resolution, 393
  medium-resolution, 346
Screen displays (text mode):
  CLS statement, 39, 146
  COLOR statement, 153
  INKEY$ statement, 149
  KEY statement, 45, 146
  LOCATE statement, 145
  pure cursor move, 145

SCREEN statement, 346, 394
Scrolling, 39, 148, 149
Search:
  binary, 286
  sequential, 263, 285
Search argument, 261
Search function (INSTR), 233
Search problems, 181, 236, 264, 267, 299
Secondary storage device, 4, 291
Sectors of a circle example (graphics), 369
Seed. *See* Random number seed
Segmentation, 11, 45
Selection construct, 121, 123
Semicolon:
  as delimiter, 30, 77
  to suppress a RETURN, 54, 78, 89
Sequence construct, 120
Sequential access device, 4
Sequential access file:
  append file, 304
  file maintenance, 307
  file statements, 292
  first examples, 293
  input file, 293
  output file, 293
Sequential search, 263, 285
Shell, Donald E., 285
Shellsort, 285
Shift key, 37
Shooting stars problems (graphics), 391
Sign Function (SGN), 204
Silicon, 4
SIM, game of, 337
Simple variable, 133, 250
Simple-interest example, 46
Simple-interest problems, 49, 55, 71
Simulation examples:
  area-by-dart throwing, 339
  coin tossing, 326
  new product, 334
  softball, 327
Simulation problems:
  baseball, 332
  card dealing, 337
  coin tossing, 332
  drunkard's walk, 332
  duel, 332
  fair game, 332
  game of SIM, 337
  knight's tour, 337
  new product, 337
  sales, 337
Sine function (SIN), 213
Single precision variable, 23
Slugging-percentage problems, 49, 216
Social-security-tax problem (files), 308
Softball-simulation example, 327
Software, 7
Sorting algorithms:
  bubble sort, 281
  comparison of, 285
  paired lists, 283
  Shellsort, 285
Sorting string arrays, 281

SPACE$ function, 160
Spacing, 39
SPC function, 80
Specification, 85
Square root function (SQR), 203
Standard deviation, 218
Starting DOS, 401
Statistical application, 338
STEP. *See* FOR loop
STEP function, 347, 354
Stepwise refinement, 14, 46
Stock-investment problems, 19, 199, 300
Stopping a program, 60
Storage devices, 4
STR$ function, 243
String concatenation, 232
String constant, 23
String conversion, 240
String functions. *See* Functions
String search function (INSTR), 233
String variables. *See* Variables
STRING$ function, 78, 147, 159
String(s):
  allowed length, 23
  comparison of, 63, 238
  concatenation of, 232
  definition of, 23
  empty (null), 28, 78
  in relational expressions, 63, 238
Structured algorithm, 122
Structured program, 122
Structured programming, 119
Structured programming constructs, 120, 121
Student information file examples, 318, 320
Subprogram. *See* Subroutine
Subroutine:
  call, 187
  a first example, 185
  general form, 187
  guidelines, 191
Subscripted variable:
  for strings, 253
  one subscript, 250
  two subscripts, 269
Subtraction, 24
Summation examples, 62, 69, 96, 108, 114–118
Summation problems, 19, 72, 118, 138, 216
Suppressing a RETURN, 54, 78
SWAP statement, 239
Symbols:
  arithmetic, 24
  flowchart, 109
  logical, 98
  relational, 62, 238
Syntax error, 42
System board, 1
SYSTEM command, 294, 404
System commands, 38, 404, 425
System reset, 401
Systems program, 7

TAB function, 80
Table argument, 261
Table processing, 258
Table processing examples, 258, 261
Table processing problems, 266, 276
Tangent function **(TAN)**, 204
Tape unit, 4
Tax-rate-schedule problems, 90, 102, 142
Text mode, 155, 345
THEN clause, 95
TIME$ function, 329
Top-down design, 12
Town-meeting-voter-list problem, 265
Trace of an array, 276
Trace of a program, 28
Transfer statements. *See* Control statements
Translator, 6
Transpose of an array, 276
Trapping errors, 307
Trigonometric functions, 204, 213
Two-dimensional arrays, 269
TYPE command, 304
Typematic keyboard, 38
Typing a program, 38

Unconditional transfer statement, 59
Underscore symbol (_), 37
Univac I, 3
Updating a file, 301
User-defined functions. *See* Functions

VAL function, 242
Validating numerical input example, 148
Variables:
 control, 133
 definition of, 14
 double precision, 23
 doubly subscripted, 269
 integer, 23
 numerical, 22
 real, 23
 simple, 133, 250
 single precision, 23
 singly subscripted, 250
 string, 23
Vertical spacing, 52, 78
Video display screen, 1, 4
Video game example (graphics), 387

Visual circle, 370
Volatile memory, 4

WEND statement, 66
WHILE loops:
 a first example, 66
 general form, 66
 summing with, 114
Wholesaler invoice problem, 266
WIDTH statement, 75
Write protect, 406
WRITE# statement, 292, 295
Writing to a file, 294

XOR operator, 98

Year-end-bonus example, 10
Yearly savings example, 54
Yen conversion problems, 56, 71